LAW AND DEVELOPMENT PERSPECTIVE ON INTERNATIONAL TRADE LAW

Economic development is the most important agenda in the international trading system today, as demonstrated by the Doha Development Agenda adopted in the current multilateral trade negotiations of the World Trade Organization (WTO; the Doha Round). This book provides a relevant discussion of major issues in international trade law from the perspective of development in the following areas: general issues on international trade law and economic development and specific law and development issues in WTO, Free Trade Agreement, and regional initiatives.

Although there are publications on trade and development issues, mostly discussing developing countries, few deal comprehensively with law and development issues of international trade law in its key areas. This book offers an unparalleled coverage of the topic with its diversity of authorship, with seventeen scholars contributing chapters from nine major countries, including the United States, Canada, Japan, China (including Hong Kong), South Korea, Australia, Singapore, and Israel.

The Law and Development Institute (LDI) is a nonprofit, academic network with the objective of promoting law and development studies and projects. Currently, more than twenty leading scholars from various countries, including the United States, Canada, Australia, Singapore, Japan, Korea, and Israel, participate in the LDI. Further details about the LDI and its projects are presented on its Web site, http://www.lawanddevelopment.net.

Yong-Shik Lee is the founding Director and Professorial Fellow of the Law and Development Institute and the founding Editor-in-Chief of the *Law and Development Review*. He has developed the concept of microtrade and authored high-profile publications on international trade, including *Safeguard Measures in World Trade: The Legal Analysis* (2007) and *Reclaiming Development in the World Trading System* (Cambridge University Press 2009).

Gary N. Horlick is a highly ranked international trade lawyer by Chambers, Euromoney Institutional Investor, and *Who's Who Legal*. He has represented leading U.S. and global companies and more than twenty countries in international trade negotiations and disputes, and has chaired WTO and MERCOSUR dispute panels.

Won-Mog Choi is Professor of International Trade Law and Director at the WTO Law Center of the Ewha Law School in Seoul. His recent publications include *Defragmenting Fragmented Rules of Origin of RTAs: A Building Block to Global Free Trade*.

Tomer Broude is Senior Lecturer at the Hebrew University of Jerusalem in the Faculty of Law and Department of International Relations and the Academic Director of the Minerva Center for Human Rights in Jerusalem. His most recent publications include *The Politics of International Economic Law* (editor, with Marc L. Busch and Amy Porges; Cambridge University Press 2011).

Law and Development Perspective on International Trade Law

THE LAW AND DEVELOPMENT INSTITUTE

Edited by

YONG-SHIK LEE

GARY N. HORLICK

WON-MOG CHOI

TOMER BROUDE

The Law and Development Institute

CAMBRIDGE
UNIVERSITY PRESS

CAMBRIDGE UNIVERSITY PRESS
Cambridge, New York, Melbourne, Madrid, Cape Town,
Singapore, São Paulo, Delhi, Tokyo, Mexico City

Cambridge University Press
32 Avenue of the Americas, New York, NY 10013-2473, USA

www.cambridge.org
Information on this title: www.cambridge.org/9781107011618

First published 2011

Printed in the United States of America

A catalog record for this publication is available from the British Library.

Library of Congress Cataloging in Publication data

Law and development perspective on international trade law / [edited by]
Yong-Shik Lee . . . [et al.].
p. cm.
Includes bibliographical references and index.
ISBN 978-1-107-01161-8 (hardback)
1. Foreign trade regulation. 2. World Trade Organization. 3. Doha Development
Agenda (2001–) 4. International trade. I. Lee, Yong-Shik, 1968–
K3943.L38 2011
343′.087 – dc22 2011002168

ISBN 978-1-107-01161-8 Hardback

Contents

About the Editors and Authors

Yong-Shik Lee, the lead editor, currently directs the Law and Development Institute (LDI). He has taught at law schools and business schools throughout the United States, Asia, and Australia and has practiced law internationally with government and leading law firms. He graduated with an AB in economics, with academic distinction, from the University of California at Berkeley and studied law at the University of Cambridge, where he received his BA, MA, and PhD degrees. Author of *Reclaiming Development in the World Trading System* (Cambridge University Press 2009), *Safeguard Measures in World Trade: The Legal Analysis* (2007), and *Economic Development through World Trade: A Developing World Perspective* (2008), Lee has published widely in the areas of international trade law and economic development with leading publishers in the United States, Europe, and Asia. His recent work has focused on the impact that domestic and international legal systems, particularly the legal framework for international trade, has on economic development. He is currently Associate Editor of the *Journal of World Trade* and founding Editor-in-Chief of the *Law and Development Review*.

Gary N. Horlick is ranked at the very top among the world's international trade lawyers by Chambers, Euromoney Institutional Investor, and *Who's Who Legal*. He has represented leading U.S. and global companies and more than twenty countries in international trade negotiations and disputes, and he has chaired WTO and MERCOSUR dispute panels. He served as International Trade Counsel of the U.S. Senate Finance Committee and as head of the Import Administration of the U.S. Department of Commerce (where he was responsible for all U.S. antidumping and countervailing duty cases, Foreign Trade Zones, and Statutory Import Programs). He teaches at Yale Law School, Georgetown Law Center, and the University of Bern's World Trade Institute. He graduated from Dartmouth College, Cambridge University, and Yale Law School.

Won-Mog Choi is Professor of International Trade Law and Director of the WTO Law Center, Ewha Womans University School of Law in Seoul. He is also an editorial board member of leading academic journals, including the *Journal of International Economic Law* (Oxford), *Law and Development Review*, and *Indian Journal of International Economic Law*, and is a member of the New York bar. Professor Choi received his legal education in the United States (Georgetown Law, SJD and LLM) and Korea (Seoul National University, MPA and LLB). Before joining the faculty of Ewha, he worked for the Ministry of Foreign Affairs and Trade of Korea for eleven years as a diplomat and legal officer in charge of numerous trade issues, including WTO dispute settlements, trade remedy issues, and free trade agreements. Currently advising the Korean government on trade law and policy issues and working as columnist of major newspapers in Seoul, Professor Choi has actively published books and articles.

Tomer Broude is Senior Lecturer at the Hebrew University of Jerusalem in the Faculty of Law and Department of International Relations and the Academic Director of the Minerva Center for Human Rights in Jerusalem. He has taught international law at various law schools in Israel and abroad, including the University of Toronto, Georgetown University Law Center, and Johns Hopkins University School of Advanced International Studies. His fields of research are international public law, with focus on international economic law and the WTO, and its interaction with other fields of law. His publications include *International Governance in the WTO: Judicial Boundaries and Political Capitulation* (2004), *The Shifting Allocation of Authority in International Law: Considering Sovereignty, Supremacy and Subsidiarity* (editor, with Yuval Shany, 2008), and *The Politics of International Economic Law* (editor, with Marc L. Busch and Amy Porges, Cambridge University Press 2011). In 2007–2009, he served as Co-Chair of the International Economic Law Interest Group of the American Society of International Law. He is a founder of the Society of International Economic Law and a member of its Executive Council, and is a member of the International Law Association Committee on the International Law of Sustainable Development.

Anthony E. Cassimatis is Senior Lecturer at the TC Beirne School of Law and a Fellow of the Centre for Public, International and Comparative Law of the University of Queensland. He holds BA, LLB (Hons) (Qld), LLM (Cantab), and PhD (Qld) degrees.

Caf Dowlah is Professor of Economics at the City University of New York.

Katherine Fennell is JD Candidate at the Georgetown University Law Center and MA Candidate at the Johns Hopkins School of Advanced International Studies.

Moshe Hirsch is Maria Von Hofmannsthal Chair in International Law in the Faculty of Law and Department of International Relations of the Hebrew University of

Jerusalem. He is Director of the International Law Forum of the Hebrew University of Jerusalem and Principal Research Fellow of the Centre for Energy, Petroleum, Mineral Law and Policy in the Faculty of Law of the University of Dundee.

Maureen Irish is Professor of Law in the Faculty of Law of the University of Windsor, Canada.

Faizel Ismail is Ambassador Permanent Representative of South Africa to the WTO. He has published two books on the WTO and is Associate Editor of the *Journal of World Trade*.

Young-Ok Kim is Visiting Scholar at the Washington University School of Law.

Xiaojie Lu is Associate Professor at the Tsinghua University Law School, Beijing, China.

Mitsuo Matsushita is Emeritus Professor of Law at the University of Tokyo and a former member of the WTO Appellate Body.

Bryan Mercurio is Professor of Law at the Chinese University of Hong Kong Law School.

Andrew D. Mitchell is Associate Professor at the Melbourne Law School of the University of Melbourne; a barrister and solicitor of the Supreme Court of Victoria and High Court of Australia; and Fellow of the Tim Fischer Centre for Global Trade and Finance, Bond University. He is a former consultant to the International Monetary Fund, Geneva. He holds PhD (Cantab), LLM (Harv), Grad Dip (Int Law) (Melb), LLB (Hons) (Melb), and BCom (Hons) (Melb) degrees.

Hye Seong Mun is a Fellow of the Law and Development Institute and former faculty member in the School of Medicine of Chiba University, Japan.

Colin B. Picker is Associate Professor of Law in the Faculty of Law of the University of New South Wales. He holds an AB degree from Bowdoin College and a JD from Yale Law School.

Joanne Wallis is barrister and solicitor of the Supreme Court of Victoria and High Court of Australia. She is a PhD Candidate at the Department of Politics and International Studies of the University of Cambridge and Honorary Fellow of the School of Social and Political Sciences of the University of Melbourne. She holds MA (Melb), MPIL (Melb), LLB (Hons) (Melb), and BA (Hons) (Melb) degrees.

ABOUT THE LAW AND DEVELOPMENT INSTITUTE

The Law and Development Institute (LDI, www.lawanddevelopment.net) was founded in 2009 as a nonprofit, academic network with an objective of promoting law and development studies and projects. With the participation of over twenty leading scholars from several countries, including the United States, Canada, Australia, Singapore, Japan, Korea, and Israel, the LDI has initiated and supported major academic publications, such as this book and the *Law and Development Review* (www.bepress.com/ldr), organized international conferences, and has undertaken law and development projects to assist developing countries.

Law and development studies concern the impact of international and domestic legal orders on economic and social development. Development issues have become a subject of considerable attention in the recent Doha Round negotiations of the World Trade Organization (WTO) in relation to international trade law. The Doha Round was suspended because of the large gaps between the developed and developing countries in their positions on some of the key international trade law and development issues. The LDI has supported and promoted this book in an effort to bridge these gaps and promote regulatory reform to facilitate development in the world trading system.

Acknowledgments

This book would not have been possible without the valuable assistance of many individuals. The editors are grateful to all the authors, who contributed excellent chapters to this book, patiently waited during the lengthy review and editorial process, and cooperated with us on our various requests. We also appreciate comments made by several anonymous reviewers that have helped to improve this book significantly. We are also thankful to our editorial assistants, including Flora Ho, Sarah Choe, Hyunwoo Kim, Semi Kim, Hyuntae Choi, and Jesse Fishman, for their assistance. Last but not least, we are grateful to Cambridge University Press for its decision to publish this book and to its staff members for all their hard work. Our heart also goes out to many other individuals who have provided valuable assistance but could not all be listed in this limited space. We remember them with much gratitude and appreciation.

The Editors

LAW AND DEVELOPMENT PERSPECTIVE ON INTERNATIONAL TRADE LAW

Introduction

There is no doubt that economic and social development has become one of the most important agenda items for the global trading system. The importance of development has been well demonstrated by the adoption of the Doha Development Agenda (DDA) in the current round of multilateral trade negotiations in the World Trade Organization (WTO), the "Doha Round." The progress of the round has been interrupted and delayed on several occasions because of the considerable gap between developed- and developing-country members' positions on trade and development issues. A key issue of the debate is whether the current regulatory framework for international trade, as represented by the legal disciplines of the WTO, serves the development and trade interests of less developed economies.

This book attempts to address this issue from the perspective of law and development, that is, by evaluating the impact of law on economic and social development. From this perspective, an assessment of the current regulatory framework for international trade can be made to examine whether relevant rules of international trade and the world trading system as a whole meet the development interest of developing countries. In this book, seventeen leading scholars and professionals from several countries, including the United States, Canada, Australia, Japan, Korea, Israel, China, and United Kingdom, discuss relevant international trade law issues from the law and development perspective.

This book does not attempt to review theoretical aspects of law and development studies or evaluate their applicability to the current discussions of trade and development. Those who are interested in such an exploration may refer to other books, such as the excellent recent volume, *The New Law and Economic Development*, edited by David Trubek and Alvaro Santos (New York: Cambridge University Press, 2006). The orientation of the present book is more practical, in a research-based sense. It attempts, without relying on any particular theoretical stance or applying an ideological preference, to assess whether relevant rules of international trade in some key areas have served the development interest of developing countries and, if not, what reforms can be suggested for improvement.

We have selected four key topics for discussion and set out sixteen chapters in four parts: Part I covers general issues on international trade and developing countries, Part II discusses law and development issues in the World Trade Organization, Part III moves on to law and development issues in regional trade agreements, and Part IV engages with law and development issues concerning other regional initiatives. These four parts encompass much of the international trade and development debates today, and the assigned chapters in each part address specific issues as follows.

Part I of the book begins with the topic of economic development and international trade in general. Chapter 1 by Yong-Shik Lee points out that least developed countries (LDCs) have not benefited significantly from international trade, and proposes a new trade scheme ("microtrade") with the aim of reducing or eliminating extreme poverty prevalent in LDCs. Chapter 2 by Tomer Broude turns to the settlement of international disputes in which development policy issues arise. Chapter 3 by Bryan Mercurio brings out another important issue in international trade – namely, intellectual property rights – and discusses its implication on development. Following that, reflecting on the recent emphasis on security in international trade since 9/11, Chapter 4 by Maureen Irish presents security issues in international trade and discusses their impact on the trade of developing countries.

Part II focuses on law and development issues in the WTO system. Chapter 5 by Yong-Shik Lee reviews the legal framework of the WTO system from the perspective of developing countries and proposes extensive reform. Chapter 6 by Faizel Ismail discusses the role of developing countries in shaping issues in the WTO. Chapter 7 by Gary Horlick and Katherine Fennell explores the treatment of developing countries in the WTO dispute settlement system and examines difficulties that developing countries are facing in the current system. Chapter 8 by Andrew Mitchell and Joanne Wallis analyzes, based on case studies, legal problems of WTO accession process faced by developing countries.

Part III covers the proliferation of regional trade agreements, one of the most significant issues in the international trading system today. Chapter 9 by Moshe Hirsch opens this discussion by addressing the broader development interest in the context of regional integration. Chapter 10 by Mitsuo Matsushita and Yong-Shik Lee provides a more specific account of relevant rules regulating free trade agreements (FTAs) from the development perspective and proposes a global FTA network as a means to coordinate different and often conflicting rules among FTAs and to promote common interests of developing countries. Chapter 11 by Anthony Cassimatis explores the impact that human rights conditionalities of FTAs and Generalized System of Preferences (GSP) have on the trade of developing countries. Chapter 12 by Yong-Shik Lee concludes this part with the fundamental question of whether FTAs and foreign direct investment will be a viable answer for economic development and whether the recent proliferation of FTAs will benefit developing countries.

Part IV discusses the law and development aspects of regional trade initiatives intended to promote economic development. Chapter 13 by Colin Picker explores complexities arising from regional differences within countries with aspects of both developed and developing worlds. Chapter 14 by Caf Dowlah introduces the U.S. GSP program and discusses critical issues with the program. Chapter 15 by Yong-Shik Lee, Young-Ok Kim, and Hye Seong Mun provides a rare account of the development initiatives of North Korea and suggests possible law and policy reforms. Chapter 16 by Xiaojie Lu addresses China's development policy in the context of relevant subsidy regulations.

In the concluding chapter, Gary Horlick offers insight into the key political issues concerning trade and development, as well as some of the WTO attempts to address development issues.

We hope that this book will benefit all those who are interested in the enigmatic interaction between the areas of trade, law, and economic development and will, at least to a modest extent, contribute to finding legal solution for the significant disagreements surrounding trade and development issues. Ultimately, we subscribe to the saying that all things are uncertain the moment society departs from law, but in these areas, the law still remains to be explored, established, and elaborated.

The Editors
Sydney, Washington, D.C.,
Seoul, and Jerusalem.
March 2011

PART I

Developing Countries and International Trade

1

Law and Development for Least Developed Countries

Theoretical Basis and Regulatory Framework for Microtrade

Yong-Shik Lee

I. INTRODUCTION: POVERTY, TRADE, AND REGULATORY ISSUES

The world has witnessed unprecedented technological and economic advances in recent times, yet much of the world's population does not share this prosperity. Poverty remains one of the most serious global problems. Despite considerable efforts by international organizations, governments, and nongovernmental organizations (NGOs), the situation has not improved significantly, and nearly half of the world population lives below the poverty line.[1] This calls for new approaches that could lead to solutions for poverty problems around the world. This chapter proposes a theoretical and regulatory framework for a new type of international trade to improve the economic status of populations in least developed countries (LDCs).[2] This new

[1] For poverty lines, the World Bank uses references set at consumption levels of USD 1.25 per day (the mean of the national poverty lines for the fifteen poorest countries of the world) and USD 2 per day (the median poverty line for the developing world) at 2005 prices. It has been estimated that in 2005, 1.4 billion people had consumption levels below USD 1.25 a day and 2.6 billion (48% of the world population) under USD 2 per day. The "poverty line" refers to the latter in this chapter. See World Bank, *Poverty: At a Glance*, available at: http://web.worldbank.org. See also Y. S. Lee, *Reclaiming Development in the World Trading System* (New York: Cambridge University Press, 2009), chap. 1.

[2] LDCs are the poorest countries in the world. Although poverty is found among the populations in both developed and developing countries, it is most prevalent in LDCs. The United Nations currently designates forty-eight countries as LDCs. The list is reviewed every three years by the Economic and Social Council. The following three criteria are used to identify LDCs in its latest 2009 triennial review:

1. A low-income criterion, based on a three-year average estimate of the gross national income (GNI) per capita (under $905 for inclusion, above $1,086 for graduation)
2. A human capital status criterion, involving a composite Human Assets Index based on indicators of (a) nutrition – percentage of population undernourished; (b) health – mortality rate for children

An earlier version of this chapter was published in the *Law and Development Review*, Vol. 2, No. 1 (2009), 367–99. The author thanks Professors Jai Sheen Mah and Won-Mog Choi for providing comments on this chapter.

type of trade is called "microtrade." In this chapter, I use the term microtrade to describe international trade on a small scale, based primarily on manually produced products using small amounts of capital and low levels of technology available at a local level in LDCs.[3] Microtrade is conceived as a means to raise income to reduce or eliminate poverty when no other conventional means of economic development[4] is either available or sufficient to accomplish this.

Poverty is most serious in LDCs but exists in other, more advanced developing countries and even in developed countries. The poverty issue in developed countries is a problem of income distribution; it is not within the purview of this chapter, which focuses on poverty issues in LDCs and addresses ways in which poverty can be reduced or eliminated by improving the income of populations in LDCs through microtrade. The mechanism of microtrade and its legal framework are discussed in the next two sections.

The solution to the prevalent poverty problems in LDCs should come from economic development that will provide the majority of LDC populations with the economic capacities to meet the material requirements of daily life above the poverty level. Although aid and donations from other countries, international bodies, NGOs, and private individuals are important sources of temporary relief for impoverished populations in LDCs,[5] they are not a lasting solution to poverty in countries without viable economies. The countries that have escaped from poverty in the past fifty years (e.g., some East Asian economies, including South Korea, Taiwan, Hong Kong, Singapore, and, more recently, China) did so through successful economic development and not through aid and donations.

In all of the successful development cases, world trade has been a crucial element in success, as a number of leading scholars, such as Rodrik, Amsden, and Wade, have studied extensively.[6] LDCs do not typically have sufficient domestic markets

aged five years or under; (c) education – the gross secondary school enrolment ratio; and (d) adult literacy rate

3. An economic vulnerability criterion, involving a composite Economic Vulnerability Index based on indicators of: (a) population size; (b) remoteness; (c) merchandise export concentration; (d) share of agriculture, forestry and fisheries in gross domestic product; (e) homelessness owing to natural disasters; (f) instability of agricultural production; and (g) instability of exports of goods and services.

Source: http://www.unohrlls.org/en/ldc/related/59.

[3] A prominent futurist, Alvin Toffler, used the term "micro-trade" in his interview with *USA Today* and discussed briefly some of the microtrade elements explained in this chapter. "Can We End World Poverty?" *USA Today*, January 28, 2000, available at: http://www.usatoday.com/news/opinion/columnists/toffler/toff04.htm.

[4] These means include economic opportunities, such as employment or business opportunities arising from domestic sale of goods and services, as well as from conventional international trade of mass-produced manufactured products or primary products utilizing economies of scale.

[5] Official Development Assistance (ODA) to LDCs totaled more than USD 23.4 billion in 2008. OECD, *ODA by Recipients*, available at: http://stats.oecd.org.

[6] See infra notes 19, 20, 21, and 22.

for goods and services to support economic development because of the local population's low purchasing power. World trade opens up affluent foreign markets for the goods and services produced in developing countries, and economic development has been achieved by taking advantage of those foreign markets through export. This development strategy, called "export-oriented development policy," has been employed successfully by formerly developing economies in East Asia, such as South Korea, Taiwan, Singapore, and Hong Kong, from the 1960s through the 1990s, with remarkable success.[7]

This success has not been replicated in most LDCs.[8] Various political, social, and economic problems deter LDCs from undertaking the large-scale development initiatives that have been successfully completed in the East Asian countries. Microtrade is proposed as an alternative to overcome the typical supply constraints of LDCs, such as insufficient capital and low levels of production technology. This allows residents in LDCs to export local products to affluent foreign markets – albeit on a much smaller scale than that achieved by newly industrializing countries[9] – with the objective of generating income that will be beyond the poverty level. In facilitating exports from LDCs, some of the regulatory issues in international trade law also need to be addressed. Part IV of the General Agreement on Tariffs and Trade (GATT), which has long been considered to be a set of rules that are declaratory but not effective with binding force, along with some other reform proposals in international trade law, can be used as a regulatory basis to facilitate microtrade.

This chapter introduces the concept of microtrade and offers preliminary discussions on its mechanism and regulatory framework. Section II discusses the concept of microtrade and its mechanisms. Section III addresses relevant regulatory issues. The legal framework for international trade, as represented by the disciplines of the World Trade Organization (WTO), is relevant because it regulates the measures of government in international trade and can also be applied to microtrade. Consideration is given to possible reforms of the regulatory framework to facilitate

[7] These four economies have undergone rapid industrialization since the 1960s and have been called "newly industrializing countries" (NICs). All of them have passed the threshold for high-income country status as classified by the World Bank (GNI per capita of USD 11,906 or more based on 2008 data). Four decades ago, these countries were poor, with economies dependent on the production of cheap primary products. Between 1961 and 1996, South Korea increased its GDP by an average of 9.80% per annum, Hong Kong by 9.58%, Taiwan by 10.21%, and Singapore by 9.95%. Alan Heston, Robert Summers, and Bettina Aten, *Penn World Table Version 6.2* (Philadelphia: Center for International Comparisons of Production, Income and Prices, September 2006). In the same period, the export growth rate of these four economies ranged from around 15% to nearly 30%. Export was an "engine" for the high economic growth in all of these countries.

[8] From 1980 to 1990, the average annual economic growth rate for LDCs was –0.4%. From 1990 to 2000, it was a mere 1.3%. In the same period, the average growth rate for other developing countries was 1.8% and 3.4%, respectively. United Nations Commission on Trade and Development (UNCTAD), *The Least Developed Countries Report 2008*, p. 139, Statistical Index: Data on Least Developed Countries, Table 1, GDP per capita and population: levels and growth.

[9] Supra note 7.

microtrade. Section IV draws conclusions and offers suggestions to promote microtrade.

II. MICROTRADE: A NEW TYPE OF INTERNATIONAL TRADE

A. *Microtrade – Linking the World Market with Local Production*

According to United Nations' statistics, more developing countries were poorer by the beginning of the millennium than they were fifty years earlier, and few countries have escaped poverty.[10] This clearly shows that economic development has not been successfully facilitated in most developing countries, particularly in LDCs. The economic and human welfare situation in LDCs is, in fact, dire. Average GNP per capita of the LDCs was a mere USD 454 in 2006,[11] and the average proportion of the population living on under USD 1 a day among 22 LDCs was 43.6%.[12] Life expectancy was 51.6 years[13] compared with 79.3 years in developed countries.[14] The infant mortality rate was 9%[15] compared with 0.51% in developed countries.[16] Diseases kill millions of people in LDCs every year. As of 2005, 11.7 million people in LDCs – nearly 3% of the population – were estimated to have been infected by the HIV virus.[17] Armed conflicts have added to the suffering in LDCs, and millions of people have been killed or become refugees. Attaining political stability and economic development will be necessary to stop such human tragedy.

Promoting economic development in LDCs presents a number of difficulties. The following factors have been cited as reasons for sluggish economic progress and prevalent poverty in LDCs: poor social and industrial infrastructure, insufficient capital and low levels of technology, low literacy and education levels, lack of entrepreneurship and management expertise, insufficient political leadership for economic development coupled with political instability, corruption and weak government institutions with absence of effective administrative support, and even some

10 According to the UN Human Development Report 2003, fifty-four countries had become poorer by the beginning of the new millennium than they were in 1990, as measured by GDP per capita. United Nations Development Program, *U.N. Human Development Report 2003* (New York: Oxford University Press, 2003).

11 Supra note 8.

12 The covered period is 1990–2003. UN Office of the High Representative for the Least Developed Countries, *Selected Economic and Social Indicators for LDCs (2005)*, available at: http://www.un.org/special-rep/ohrlls/ldc/2005%20socio-econ%20indicators.pdf.

13 UNCTAD (2008), supra note 8, p. 146, Statistical Index: Data on Least Developed Countries, Table 8, Indicators on Demography.

14 OECD, *Health Data 2009* (the cited statistics are for 2006), available at: http://www.oecd.org.

15 UNCTAD (2008), supra note 8, p. 146, Statistical Index: Data on Least Developed Countries, Table 8, Indicators on Demography.

16 OECD (2009), supra note 14.

17 UNCTAD (2008), supra note 8, p. 147, Statistical Index: Data on Least Developed Countries, Table 9, Indicators on Health.

cultural issues that are deterrents to economic development.[18] Most of these problems will be difficult to solve in the short term. Large-scale development initiatives and the subsequent economic development in East Asia were possible because these countries, despite initial capital and supply constraints, did not suffer from some of the cited problems and were strong in certain key elements for development, such as a high literacy rate, strong political leadership, and effective administrative support from government.[19]

The East Asian countries moved beyond poverty by successfully undertaking a series of export-oriented economic development initiatives, which included promoting large-scale export industries.[20] The contribution of international trade to economic development and the role of government in successful cases have been widely studied and well documented.[21] Leading scholars such as Amsden and Wade have studied the industrial policies adopted by the East Asian countries and concluded that their governments had directed investments to certain key industries and intervened in international trade in various ways (i.e., by using subsidies and limiting foreign imports) while engaging in trade and promoting exports.[22] Although

[18] See A. F. Petrone (ed.), *Causes and Alleviation of Poverty* (Hauppauge, NY: Nova Science Publications, 2002). For the effect of culture on development, see Amartya Sen, *Culture and Development*, World Bank Paper (December 13, 2000), available at: http://info.worldbank.org/etools/docs/voddocs/354/688/sen_tokyo.pdf.

[19] Kwang-Suk Kim and Joon-Kyung Park, *Sources of Economic Growth in Korea: 1963–1981* (Seoul: Korea Development Institute, 1985), p. 6. Factors such as political and social stabilities, effective technocratic bureaucracies and organized government support, strong political leadership, educated workforce, strict work ethics, and higher ratio of savings are cited as important factors for the successful economic development of South Korea and the other NICs. Dani Rodrik has also suggested that an ideal institutional arrangement between the public and private sectors should be in place to facilitate development. Dani Rodrik, *Industrial Policy for the Twenty-First Century*, paper prepared for UNIDO (September 2004). According to Rodrik, the working institutional arrangement is dependent on the existence of effective cooperation and communications between the public and private sectors. Nonetheless, Rodrik also stresses that some measures of transparency and accountability should be imposed to prevent the moral hazards associated with government support. Ibid., pp. 20–21.

[20] For an evolution of industrial policies of the NICs, see Mari Pangestu, "Industrial Policy and Developing Countries," in Bernard Hoekman, Aaditya Mattoo, and Philip English (eds.), *Development, Trade, and the WTO: A Handbook* (Washington, DC: World Bank, 2002), p. 153, Table 17.1.

[21] See A. O. Krueger, "Trade Policies in Developing Countries," in R. W. Jones and P. B. Kenen (eds.), *Handbook of International Economics*, Vol. 1 (New York: North-Holland, 1984), pp. 519–69; R. Findlay, "Growth and Development in Trade Models," in R. W. Jones and P. B. Kenen (eds.), *Handbook of International Economics*, Vol. 1 (New York: North-Holland, 1984), pp. 185–236; T. N. Srinivasan, "Trade, Development, and Growth," *Princeton Essays in International Economics*, No. 225 (December 2001); G. K. Helleiner (ed.), *Trade Policy, Industrialization, and Development* (Oxford: Oxford University Press, 1992); World Bank, *The East Asian Miracle* (New York: Oxford University Press, 1993).

[22] See Alice H. Amsden, *Escape from Empire: The Developing World's Journey through Heaven and Hell* (Cambridge, MA: MIT Press, 2007); Alice H. Amsden, *Asia's Next Giant: South Korea and Late Industrialization* (New York: Oxford University Press, 1989); Robert Wade, *Governing the Market: Economic Theory and the Role of Government in East Asian Industrialization* (Princeton, NJ: Princeton University Press, 2003).

the question is whether such government interventions have always been successful in promoting economic development, there is little doubt that the development initiatives made by governments and followed by the private sector have led to the economic growth that drove the East Asian countries out of poverty.[23] Given the constraints and the problems discussed earlier, however, it will not be feasible for many LDCs to undertake large-scale development initiatives, by either the private sector or the government. The working institutional arrangement between the private and public sectors as described by Dani Rodrik[24] is not found in many LDCs, and it is not likely to occur in theforeseeable future.[25]

Microtrade will be an alternative approach to reduce or eliminate poverty when an LDC economy is not supported by a well-functioning government and effective administrative assistance, and when the private sector as a whole does not function to make economic progress. Microtrade will essentially be a local initiative that uses the mechanism of international trade but will not require the large-scale industrial initiatives promoted by East Asian countries during their rapid development periods. The essence of this new approach is to enable LDC residents to export locally produced products (LPPs) to the more affluent markets of developed countries to generate income that is beyond the poverty level. The distinction between microtrade and conventional trade lies in the use of the price difference, as described subsequently, rather than the economies of scale, which require mass production capacities that many LDCs lack and cannot obtain in the near future. Examples of possible LPPs for microtrade include portable items of everyday use, for ease of shipping and distribution, that can be produced without high-level technology or costly production facilities; such items include cups and dishes, utensils, small furniture, musical instruments, art objects, ornaments, and toys.[26]

The price difference between LDCs and developed countries, coupled with the higher purchasing power of consumers in developed countries,[27] can generate higher levels of income for LPP producers in LDCs engaged in microtrade, compared with what can be generated from local transactions. A monthly income of USD 75 per

[23] Supra notes 7, 22.

[24] Supra note 19.

[25] Peter Leeson and Claudia Williamson have taken this idea one step further, arguing that the absence of a government, rather than the presence of a repressive LDC government, has offered a better condition for economic development. Peter Leeson and Claudia Williamson, "Anarchy and Development: An Application of the Theory of Second Best" (2009) 2(1) *The Law and Development Review* 77–96.

[26] For ease of transportation, storage, and distribution, manufactured products, rather than agricultural products, which tend to be less value-added per unit than manufactured products and thus attract lower profits, will be more likely candidates for microtrade. The stringent Sanitary and Phytosanitary (SPS) requirements of developed countries may also create difficulties in the importation of agricultural products from LDCs, which is another reason to choose manufactured products for microtrade.

[27] The average price level of consumption for forty-seven LDCs was measured at 39.2 in 2007 (USA = 100.6), compared with 118.3 for OECD countries in the same year, showing a difference of nearly three times between LDCs and developed countries. Data compiled from "Price Level of Consumption" (Purchasing Power Parity over GDP/Exchange Rate in Current Prices), Alan Heston, Robert Summers, and Bettina Aten, *Penn World Table Version 6.3* (Philadelphia: Center for International Comparisons of Production, Income and Prices at the University of Pennsylvania, August 2009).

capita is required to graduate from the current LDC category and, presumably, to eliminate the most extreme levels of poverty. USD 75 is less than the price of a well-made, wooden dinner-table chair in many developed countries. The large differences in labor costs between developed countries and LDCs will render the cost of producing labor-intensive products to be only a small fraction of the production cost in developed countries, which will then be reflected in the price. Because production of labor-intensive LPPs on a small scale does not require large industrial initiatives that may not be possible in LDCs, microtrade is a new approach to link the world market with local production in LDCs toward the elimination of poverty – an alternative to the export-oriented economic development policies on large scales. The next subsection discusses the economic mechanism of microtrade.

B. *Economic Mechanism of Microtrade*

A simple economic model can be constructed to explain the mechanism of microtrade and assess possible earnings generated from it. Earnings for an LDC producer from microtrade (E_m) can be expressed as the total revenue generated in the foreign market ($P_f \times Q_f$), minus costs of microtrade to be borne by the producer, including production cost (C_p); distribution cost, including the cost of locating the distributors and customers in developed countries; and the revenue shares taken by distributors (C_d), shipping cost (C_s), and regulatory cost including customs (C_r). (P_f denotes the price in the foreign market, and Q_f denotes the quantities sold in the foreign market. All of these costs are portions of those to be borne by the producers in accordance with the terms to be set between the producer and the other parties to the transaction.)

$$E_m = (P_f \times Q_f) - C_{p,d,s,r}$$ [28]

Certain qualifications must be made for microtrade to be economically viable. First, the earnings retained by microtrade should be at least equal to or greater than the earnings that can be retained by the LDC producer from the domestic sales of the LPP (E_d). Otherwise, there will be no point in engaging in microtrade. The earnings from domestic sale can be illustrated as the following:

$$E_d = (P_d \times Q_d) - C_{p,d',s',r'}$$ [29]

[28] I previously considered that the earning for the LDC producer from microtrade (E_m) can be expressed as the share of the total revenue generated in the foreign market and retained by the LDC producer, S_m ($P_f \times Q_f$), minus costs of microtrade to be borne by the producer. Y. S. Lee, "Theoretical Basis and Regulatory Framework for Microtrade: Combining Volunteerism with International Trade towards Poverty Elimination" 2(1) *The Law and Development Review* (2009), 373–74. However, the revenue share taken by the distributors can be considered as being included in the distribution cost (C_d), and the microtrade equation is adjusted to $E_m = (P_f \times Q_f) - C_{p,d,s,r}$ for simplicity.

[29] The costs associated with domestic sale will comprise production cost (C_p), costs of domestic distribution ($C_{d'}$), shipping ($C_{s'}$) and regulatory costs ($C_{r'}$). Although production costs are expected to be identical, the other costs are expected to be higher in the case of microtrade.

Another point of consideration is any foregone earnings from economic opportunities other than engaging in microtrade (E_o), such as getting a job at a local company for wages or becoming a migrant worker in another country. Where this earning is greater than the earning to be generated from microtrade ($E_o > E_m$), microtrade will not be economically viable for the LDC producer. Thus, the final conditions for microtrade will be as follows:

$$E_m = (P_f \times Q_f) - C_{p,d,s,r} \quad \text{where } E_m \geq E_d \text{ and } E_m \geq E_o$$ [30]

Microtrade can be profitably engaged in only if the extra revenue generated from the price difference between the domestic and foreign markets ($P_f - P_d$) and from the possible difference in the sale quantities between the two markets, which is to be retained by the LDC producer, exceeds the amount of the extra costs associated with microtrade ($C_{p,d,s,r} - C_{p,d',s',r'}$), which will be borne by the producer. Given the significant difference in labor costs that exist between LDCs and developed countries, substantial differences in prices are expected to exist for most labor-intensive LPPs.[31] The higher purchasing power of developed-country consumers[32] may also lead to higher quantities being sold in the markets of developed countries, provided that LPPs can be admitted into developed-country markets and the shipping can be managed.[33]

The costs associated with microtrade, such as shipping costs, can be substantial, and the success of microtrade depends on the minimization of such costs. In addition, there are potentially complex logistical issues associated with microtrade,

[30] Professor Jai Sheen Mah has commented that microtrade may also take place even if E_m is not necessarily equal or greater than E_d because the producers can sell products in both domestic and foreign markets at the profit maximizing point. However, it will be difficult for LDC producers with limited information to decide how much LPPs should be sold in each of the domestic and foreign markets to maximize profit. Thus, the equation represents the LDC producer's decision on the basis of the expected revenue and the costs per given unit of LPP. Mah also pointed out that the accurate analysis of the E_m and E_o may not be made without consideration of a time sequence (i.e., a long-term and short-term analysis might be different). Again, the equation represents the decision of the LDC producers at a given point in time as to whether they should engage in microtrade or pursue another economic activity, and these individuals may not discern long-term from short-term effects. In fact, yet another commentator, Rajesh Chadha, has emphasized the highly limited information that LDC producers have and suggested that the equation should be further simplified to include only price terms. The cited microtrade equation represents a middle position between these two.

[31] See also supra note 27.

[32] Although the average GNP per capita of LDCs was USD 454 in 2006 (supra note 8), the minimal threshold per capita income of high-income countries set by the World Bank is USD 11,906, which is over 26 times higher in income per capita.

[33] Another view has been raised by Professor Won-Mog Choi: given the (likely) low quality of products that can be produced in LDCs, developing countries, rather than developed countries with sophisticated consumer taste and high consumer standards, will be more likely destinations for LPPs. Given the weaker purchasing power and the lower price level of developing countries, compared with those of developed countries, microtrade with other developing countries will be likely to generate less income for LDC producers than microtrade with developed countries. NGOs such as Oxfam have successfully marketed products from LDCs in developed countries.

such as market access issues, including identifying market demand and relaying the information to the appropriate local producers in LDCs, locating retailers and consumers in developed-country markets, and shipping products to foreign destinations. LPP producers in LDCs with limited financial resources may not be in a position to bear these costs and meet potentially complex logistical requirements. The relatively small profits that can be generated from microtrade may deter major international trading companies from assisting LDC producers to export LPPs to developed-country markets. Thus, the proposed microtrade scheme introduces certain elements of voluntary assistance to minimize costs and address logistical issues.

Elements of microtrade are already observed in developed countries where local shops acquire small quantities of goods directly from communities in developing countries.[34] These shops may have business relations with developing-country communities and receive goods from them, or the shop owner may have traveled overseas and located suitable products in a developing country, as the following anecdote suggests. On an autumn day in 2004, I was shopping at a local carpet and tapestry store in Minneapolis, Minnesota, and found a small piece of handmade tapestry. It was beautifully woven, and the marked price was only USD 7. It turned out that the shop owner had traveled to a developing country in South Asia on vacation and came across a town where a group of women were weaving tapestries. He liked the tapestries, negotiated the price with the townspeople, and ended up paying 50 cents (USD .50) for the piece that I purchased, and a bit more for larger pieces. He then carried the purchased tapestries with him to his store in Minneapolis and sold them at prices several times higher than what he had originally paid.

This anecdote validates at least one important element of the microtrade scheme: substantial price differences exist based primarily on the differences in labor costs, and these can generate extra income for those engaged in microtrade. With respect to cost elements, the shop owner assumed the costs of shipping, customs, and marketing and sales. However, this is not always a typical pattern of microtrade: retailers in developed countries cannot always be expected to take the trouble of visiting LDCs, locating suitable LPPs, and shipping them at their own expense, where all such costs and the risk of traveling to LDCs may exceed the expected profit.

34 A score of individual stores in developed countries, such as those of Oxfam, sell handmade goods from developing countries and return profits to the developing-country producers. The microtrade scheme would organize and systemize these efforts on a global scale with the assistance of an open, online database and financial devices, such as microfinance, as explained later in the chapter. The microtrade proposal also addresses regulatory issues on a global scale. Also, a point was made by a reviewer that the "fair-trade movement" should be considered in the context of microtrade. A distinction should be made between microtrade and the fair-trade movement. The former focuses on finding small quantities of tradable, locally produced products in LDC communities and raising income for LDC populations to escape from the extreme levels of poverty by selling LPPs in developed-country markets; the latter focuses on increasing profit margins for developing-country producers with existing trade of mostly agricultural products rather than manufactured products, which is often done on a much larger scale than is envisioned for microtrade.

As mentioned, it will also be difficult for major trading companies to help LPP producers in LDCs by engaging in trade for them when LPPs produced on a small scale may not be profitable enough. Thus, the cost and logistical issues need to be approached in another way, and this is where voluntary assistance can play an essential role.

The minimization of the costs of microtrade through voluntary engagement with transactional logistics by third parties, which is explained in each of the cost areas described subsequently, will enable LDC producers to capture more of the profit generated from microtrade. The remainder of this subsection attempts to address some of the logistics issues associated with microtrade and to explain how these issues can be resolved by voluntary engagement.[35] As shown in what follows, the use of information technology will be particularly essential for the success of microtrade.

a. Matching Supply and Demand

All trade, including microtrade, can take place only when there is a demand for goods to be supplied in trade. In the preceding episode, the tapestry shop owner knew when he saw the beautiful tapestries that there would be a demand for them in Minneapolis and a profit to be made. However, it is generally difficult for retailers in developed countries to visit LPP producers in LDCs, purchase LPPs, and then ship them for sale in a developed-country market, as happened in the preceding episode. A mechanism that links the market information in developed countries and LPP suppliers in LDCs is necessary. For microtrade to be feasible, relevant market information must be conveyed to LPP producers in LDCs.

One would think that problems with communication and transportation resulting from long distances between LDCs and developed countries[36] would make this information transmission difficult, if not impossible. However, the recent developments of Internet technology may enable volunteers to transmit market information at relatively low cost. The following is a possible scenario.

Numerous NGOs, religious groups, and individuals from developed countries are currently working in LDCs, and they travel back to their home countries on a

[35] Many of the problems facing microtrade, such as lack of market information and difficulties with shipping and transportation, may indeed be found in trade from developing countries in general. Some of the proposed solutions may be applicable to developing-country trade more generally, but the voluntary and charitable nature of the suggested solutions may reduce their applicability to general trade where the need for trade is not as intense from the perspective of poverty elimination. More general solutions, such as building a better, commercial-market information network and better infrastructure for transportation, require considerable resources and time, and thus alternative solutions with charitable elements have been proposed to address immediate problems associated with microtrade.

[36] The physical distance is amplified by the fact that most LDCs are located in the Southern Hemisphere, whereas most developed countries are located in the Northern Hemisphere. In this respect, the role of a few developed countries in the Southern Hemisphere, such as Australia and New Zealand, will be important for microtrade.

regular basis. Some of them may be organized to identify LPPs that can be produced in the towns and communities where they work and can be sold in the markets of the developed countries where they are based. For instance, certain boutiques in a city of a developed country may have an appetite for types of ornaments made in a particular place in an LDC. This information can be transmitted to the local ornament producers in the LDCs by those from the developed-country city who work in the relevant LDC area where such ornaments are produced. It will be more effective if this type of market information is uploaded and stored on an open, online database that is accessible to anyone, including interested retailers, and that is also interactive. The information on the open database could be viewed by either local producers who have Internet access or anyone else who can relay the information to the local LPP producers. The governments of LDCs and developed countries, as well as international organizations and NGOs, may also help organize and run this online information database.[37]

Internet access will be an important component of the microtrade scheme. It would be ideal for each town or community in LDCs to have at least one computer station or terminal that has Internet connectivity, including mobile devices, such as a laptop or mobile phone with Internet capability (and, of course, at least one person who can access the database and relay the necessary information to the locals) so that the local producers can access relevant market information for the identification of LPPs to be produced and microtraded. This means that the facilitation of microtrade will require establishment of Internet access throughout LDCs around the world. The feasibility of this undertaking is an issue. The Internet usage rate and the availability of personal computers are low in LDCs. As of 2006, there were, on average, only 19 personal computers per 1,000 inhabitants and an average of 91 Internet users per 1,000 inhabitants in LDCs.[38] Twenty-six LDCs had fewer than 10 personal computers per 1,000 inhabitants, and 21 LDCs had fewer than 10 Internet users per 1,000 inhabitants.[39]

However, the low Internet-usage rate and the small per capita number of personal computers in LDCs do not necessarily mean that setting up at least one personal computer with Internet capability in each town and community would be impossible. The recent development of wireless communication technology suggests that it is possible for more LDCs, perhaps with the help of other countries and international

[37] A question has been raised as to what incentives exist for commercial operators (or even NGOs) to publicize sensitive commercial information about market opportunities overseas, thereby potentially undermining the activities of existing market players. Such assistance will require a charitable motive with a recognition that trade is better than handing out aid to those living in poverty. Perhaps this is why an international organization devoted to microtrade may be necessary to help collect and process market information. For a further discussion of the possible microtrade organization, see Lee (2009), supra note 28, pp. 380–84.

[38] Compiled from UNCTAD (2008), supra note 8, p. 150, Statistical Index: Data on Least Developed Countries, Table 12, Indicators on Communication and Media.

[39] Ibid.

organizations, to build the necessary Internet infrastructure at a much lower cost than was possible in the past.[40] As for the availability of computers, it is possible that personal computers and laptops with Internet capability could be made available for as low as USD 100 per unit.[41] Low-cost laptops were initially contemplated for education purposes in developing countries, but they could also facilitate microtrade. The possibility of low-cost Internet access based on wireless technology and the availability of inexpensive computers will enable more LDCs to build the necessary communication infrastructure for microtrade.

b. Shipping and Distribution

Another important issue with microtrade is shipping and distribution of LPPs to the retail stores and consumers in developed countries. In many LDCs where road networks and transportation systems are poor, shipping can be a significant problem. International shipping is more difficult for landlocked LDC countries with no direct access to the sea.[42] For many localities in LDCs, international shipping service is either unavailable or prohibitively expensive for the local producers. Another issue is locating distributors and retail services in developed countries that are willing to sell LPPs from LDCs. The difficulties with communication are a considerable challenge to locating adequate distributors and retail services in developed countries.

As for the shipping and distribution problem, there are two possible solutions. One is creating an association of local producers with common resources and collective bargaining powers to negotiate with international commercial shippers and distributors in developed countries and set terms for shipping and distribution.[43] This solution may work for local producers who can collectively produce large quantities of products for which there is strong demand in developed-country markets. However, it will not work for many LDC local producers that operate on a smaller scale, have little bargaining power, and are unable to amass sufficient common resources

[40] Internet connection can be provided wirelessly through reception towers built at regular distances, without setting up costly infrastructures for wired connections. Nonprofit organizations such as Geekcorps have helped developing countries acquire wireless Internet access. For more information, see the Geekcorps Web site at http://www.geekcorps.org. Satellite-based, commercial wireless Internet providers are also available in Africa. See relevant information available at: http://www.satsig.net/ivsat-africa.htm.

[41] See Gregory M. Lamb, "A Closer Look at What '$100 Laptop' Will Be," *The Christian Science Monitor*, January 29, 2007, available at: http://www.csmonitor.com/2007/0129/p13s01-stct.html.

[42] It has been reported that export is generally hampered for a landlocked African LDC with a poor road network compared with an adjacent country with seaports. Francis Mangeni, "How Far Can LDCs Benefit from Duty-Free and Quota-Free Market Access? The Case of Uganda with Respect to the EU Market," in Y. S. Lee (ed.), *Economic Development through World Trade: A Developing Country Perspective* (The Hague: Kluwer Law International, 2008), p. 428.

[43] Some examples of producers associations in developing countries are Bangladesh Knitwear Manufacturers & Exporters Association (http://www.bkmea.com), the Christmas Décor Producers and Exporters Association of the Philippines, Fresh Produce Exporters Association of Kenya, and Ethiopian Horticulture Producers and Exporters Association.

to use international commercial shippers or to negotiate with commercial retailers in developed countries.

The other possible solution, which is more feasible for the smaller LPP producers in LDCs, requires voluntary assistance from third parties, such as aid workers and religious missionaries[44] from developed countries who work in LDCs. On a voluntary basis, they can deliver LPPs produced in the LDCs where they are working to places in developed countries when they travel back home. Relevant international organizations, governments, NGOs, and private corporations can help organize this "voluntary shipping network" for microtrade by using the open online database described earlier.[45] "Voluntary shippers" can register online and upload information on their availability. LPP producers in LDCs, as well as retailers and distributors in developed countries, can register online as to their need for shippers. International shipping and trading companies can make contributions by entering this shipping network and providing free or reduced-fee services.

c. Financing and Production

Those in LDCs who are interested in producing LPPs for microtrade may not be able to do so because they do not have even the small amount of resources necessary to produce LPPs or sufficient credit or assets to borrow from commercial lenders. Microcredit, devised by the 2006 Nobel Laureate Muhammad Yunus, has attained considerable success in providing small capital to those in developing countries who cannot otherwise borrow from commercial lenders.[46] Alternative credit devices such as microcredit can provide financial assistance for the production of LPPs and perhaps for the other steps of microtrade as well. Governments that have available

[44] It has been estimated that there are well over 200,000 aid workers and 40,000 missionaries, many of whom are working in LDCs. See Adele Harmer, Katherine Haver, and Abby Stoddard, *Providing Aid in Insecure Environments: Trends in Policy and Operations*, Humanitarian Policy Group Report, Overseas Development Institute (London, September 2006), available at: http://www.cic.nyu.edu/internationalsecurity/docs/hpgreport23.pdf. See also, Werner Ustorf, "Response to Wilhelm Dupre" (1998) 1(1) *Implicit Religion* 41–46.

[45] A reviewer pointed out that most NGO organizers use commercial providers for shipping and distribution. The voluntary shipping network is necessary for those NGOs and individuals who do not have the resources to use commercial providers. Commercial shippers can join the shipping network by providing free or reduced-fee services.

[46] A large body of literature on microfinance is available. See Beatriz Armendáriz De Aghion and Jonathan Morduch, *The Economics of Microfinance* (Cambridge, MA: MIT Press, 2005); Brigit Helms, *Access for All: Building Inclusive Financial Systems* (Washington, DC: Consultative Group to Assist the Poor, 2006); Madeline Hirschland (ed.), *Savings Services for the Poor: An Operational Guide* (Bloomfield, CT: Kumarian Press, 2005); Shahidur R. Khandker, *Fighting Poverty with Microcredit* (Bangladesh edition, Dhaka: The University Press, 1999); Joanna Ledgerwood and Victoria White, *Transforming Microfinance Institutions: Providing Full Financial Services to the Poor* (Washington, DC: World Bank, 2006); Graham A. N. Wright, *Microfinance Systems: Designing Quality Financial Services for the Poor* (Dhaka: The University Press, 2000); Muhammad Yunus, *Creating a World without Poverty: Social Business and the Future of Capitalism* (New York: Public Affairs, 2008).

capital can also provide financial support for microtrade in the form of grants and other subsidies. Lenders can help LPP producers by advancing money to the local LDC producer on the credit of the buyer, who places an order and agrees to pay the lender, and then collecting money from the buyer.

Because LPPs are likely to be labor-intensive rather than capital-intensive, microtrade will be an ideal venture for small capital lending available by financial devices such as microfinance. The aim of this lending is to enable those in LDCs with limited capital resources to gain maximum benefit from microtrade. As mentioned earlier, small, portable products that can be produced with simple tools and relatively brief training are ideal for financing.[47] Products that require considerable skills and production techniques, such as sophisticated tapestries and art pieces, are also good LPP candidates when local residents have the necessary skills to produce them. When possible, governments, NGOs, and international organizations can help train local residents in LDCs to produce LPPs that can attract consumers in the markets of developed countries.[48]

III. SETTING REGULATORY FRAMEWORK TO SUPPORT MICROTRADE

For microtrade to be a successful device to help populations in LDCs and to eliminate poverty, LPPs must be freely admitted to the markets of developed countries.[49] Rules of international trade control this issue and thus must be considered. Currently, WTO disciplines regulate the conduct of 153 sovereign member states on international trade. This section examines rules of international trade that are relevant to the facilitation of microtrade.

An ideal regulatory environment for microtrade is the adoption of policies of no tariffs and no quotas on products imported from LDCs. This treatment, however, is an exception to a core provision of the WTO rules, which requires the most-favored-nation (MFN) principle, prohibiting discrimination in accordance with the origin of product. Article 1.1 of the GATT, which constitutes the integral part of the current WTO disciplines, provides in relevant part:

> With respect to customs duties and charges of any kind imposed on or in connection with importation or exportation or imposed on the international transfer of payments for imports or exports, and with respect to the method of levying such duties and charges, and with respect to all rules and formalities in connection with importation and exportation, and with respect to all matters referred to in paragraphs 2 and 4 of

[47] Agricultural products may not be suitable for microtrade. See supra note 26.

[48] Arts and crafts, which are good LPPs for microtrade, have been included in priority products recommended by the Uganda Export Promotion Board for export. See Mangeni (2008), supra note 42, p. 436.

[49] Also, the rampant corruption and inefficiency of customs in many LDCs should be addressed. Perhaps international assistance can be directed toward correcting customs problems in LDCs with education of customs officials, proper supervision, and effective sanction, so that LPPs may be processed for exportation without undue delays and unnecessary hindrances at customs.

> Article III, any advantage, favour, privilege or immunity granted by any contracting party to any product originating in or destined for any other country shall be accorded immediately and unconditionally to the like product originating in or destined for the territories of all other contracting parties.[50]

This provision sets out the general principle of nondiscrimination for international trade. The notable exception to this rule is the authorization of free trade agreements (FTAs) and customs unions under GATT XXIV, which offer preferential treatments to member states of FTAs and customs unions. Another important MFN exception that is relevant to microtrade is the General System of Preference (GSPs) that provide lower tariff rates for imports from developing countries under certain criteria prescribed by the offering state.[51] Various GSP schemes, including the "Everything-but-Arms" (EBA) scheme[52] by the European Union that offers quota-free and tariff-free treatment for imports from LDCs, have been implemented. The preferential, quota-free, and tariff-free treatment for microtrade may also qualify as a GSP scheme approved under the current WTO rules.

It should be noted, however, that the preferential treatment for microtrade would be distinguished from the other preferential trade schemes for imports from developing countries in that these other schemes provide preferences on a particular country- and product-group basis, whereas the preferential treatment for microtrade offers preference for LPPs that excludes mass-produced industrial products. This exclusion is necessary; because the point of preference for microtrade is providing assistance for LDC producers with limited productive capabilities, there is no need to provide the microtrade preference for products that are mass-produced at industrial facilities. So far no GSP schemes seem to offer preference based on the distinction between products produced locally on small scales and those mass-produced at industrialized facilities. The question is whether preferential treatment can be offered on the basis of this type of distinction. Two issues need to be considered: a legal issue under relevant WTO rules and a logistical issue of classification.

As for the legal issue, the relevant rules authorizing GSPs under the WTO disciplines are the GATT Enabling Clause[53] and the 1971 GSP Decision,[54] with the

[50] WTO, *The Results of the Uruguay Round of Multilateral Trade Negotiations* (Cambridge: Cambridge University Press, 2003), p. 424.

[51] GSPs are approved as an exception to the MFN principle under the "Enabling Clause." GATT, *Differential and More Favourable Treatment Reciprocity and Fuller Participation of Developing Countries*, Decision of 28 November 1979 (L/4903). Preferential treatment to LDC trade has been also provided by other WTO decisions. WTO, *Preferential Tariff Treatment for Least-Developed Countries – Decision on Waiver*, WT/L/304 (June 15, 1999), and WTO, *Decision on Measures in Favour of Least-Developed Countries*, LT/UR/D-1/3 (April 15, 1994).

[52] The EBA scheme is an exemplary trade concession scheme for LDCs. It allows all imports to the European Union from the LDCs to be admitted duty-free and quota-free, with the exception of armaments. The EBA scheme is incorporated into the GSP Council Regulation (EC) No. 2501/2001.

[53] Supra note 51.

[54] The Decision of the CONTRACTING PARTIES of June 25, 1971, relating to the establishment of "generalized, non-reciprocal and non discriminatory preferences beneficial to the developing countries" (BISD 18S/24) (L/3545).

former incorporating GSPs described in the latter.[55] The preamble of the 1971 GSP Decision describes a GSP as a "generalized, non-discriminatory, nonreciprocal preferential tariff treatment in the markets of developed countries for products originating in developing countries."[56] Recent WTO jurisprudence has interpreted the elements described in the preamble of the 1971 Decision "generalized," "non-discriminatory," and "nonreciprocal" as binding requirements for GSPs.[57] Thus, it is necessary to consider whether the provision of a GSP based on the proposed production distinction of LPPs is consistent with these requirements.

Two selection criteria in the microtrade preference need to be reviewed against the GSP requirements. One is the product restriction to LPPs, excluding mass-produced industrial products, and the other is the restriction of beneficiaries to LDCs. First, the product limitation to LPPs is a generalized product classification rather than a specialized one in accordance with the product origin.[58] Although some of the positive conditionalities of the GSPs have been challenged and declared inconsistent with WTO requirements by WTO dispute settlement panels and the WTO Appellate Body,[59] product selections by GSP schemes have been widely practiced without challenge. The product restriction for the microtrade preference is distinguished from the product selections in the other GSP schemes, because the preference based on LPPs depends on the manner in which a product in question has been produced: mass-produced products at industrial facilities will be excluded. Nothing in the relevant GSP rules[60] or in the WTO jurisprudence[61] seems to suggest that this type of product selection is inconsistent with the rules.[62] Second, limiting the beneficiaries of the microtrade preference to LDCs is consistent with GSP requirements, because paragraph 2(d) of the Enabling Clause authorizes special treatment to LDCs among developing countries. The preceding examination suggests that the microtrade preference scheme is consistent with the GSP requirements.

The logistical issue of the preference limited to LPPs is a different issue that requires further discussion. Although it may make sense to limit the preference to

[55] Enabling Clause, supra note 51, para. 2(a), footnote 3.

[56] Supra note 54.

[57] WTO, *European Communities – Conditions for the Granting of Tariff Preferences for Developing Countries*, Report of the Panel, WT/DS246/R (1 December 2003), para. 7.38, WTO, *Report of the Appellate Body*, WT/DS246/AB/R (7 April 2004), paras. 142–147. See also Lorand Bartels, "The WTO Enabling Clause and Positive Conditionality in the European Community's GST Program" (2003) 6(2) *Journal of International Economic Law* 507–532.

[58] The term, "classification" is used in a generic sense and does not mean product classifications under the Harmonized System Code.

[59] WTO (2003), supra note 57.

[60] Supra notes 51, 54.

[61] Supra note 57.

[62] However, Professor Won-Mog Choi opined that the GSP applied only to LPPs is inconsistent with the nondiscrimination requirement because it favors products produced on small scales. He has suggested that a separate decision or waiver will be necessary.

LPPs traded on a small scale and not to the mass-produced industrial products,[63] setting clear standards to distinguish between these two types of products will be a considerable challenge. The same product – for instance, a chair – that will be classified identically under the Harmonized System Codes (HS Codes) may or may not benefit from the preference depending on the manner in which it has been produced. A chair produced manually in small quantities may pass for the LPP qualification for the microtrade preference, whereas mass-produced chairs may not. The current product classification system, such as the HS Codes, used to impose tariffs does not classify products on the basis of the manner of production. Thus, different classification criteria are necessary to determine qualified LPPs.

A possible classification method may be certification by a third party or approval by the importing countries following self-declaration by the LDC producer or trader based on the manner of production as well as production and trade volumes and values in a given period of time. Other possible elements for the determination of LPPs may include the impact that the imported products may have on domestic producers, general income levels of the place of the product origin, and the extent of contribution by the microtrade of the particular product toward improving the economic conditions of the LDC producer. It is recommended that sovereign states adopt liberal and lenient approaches in determining qualified LPPs for the microtrade preference because LDCs have minimal capacity to export mass-produced products. Thus, it is unlikely that their exports will have significant adverse economic impact on domestic producers in developed countries.

The ideal regulatory treatment is the adoption of a duty-free, quota-free GSP scheme for LDCs on all products, such as the EBA scheme of the European Union.[64] Under this type of GSP scheme, which is applied to all products, the potentially complex classification and approval of the qualified LPPs are not necessary for customs purposes. The EBA scheme is a positive step toward achieving

63 The necessity of the separate preferential microtrade scheme may lie in the distinction between the purpose of microtrade and that of the other GSPs: the former is to provide assistance for elimination of poverty among the populations in LDCs that can engage in small-scale productions, whereas the latter is to provide assistance for economic development of developing countries at national levels. The present country- and product-based GSP preferences often exclude products that can threaten domestic producers in the importing countries. Mass-produced textile products are a good example. The separate preference scheme for LPPs that are produced and traded on a small scale are thus unlikely to pose a significant threat to the domestic producers of importing countries and will provide LDC producers with another channel for access to developed-country markets where other country- and product-based preferential schemes may not be available for the particular product.

64 Supra note 52. The proposed separate preference for microtrade is a second-best measure if the duty-free, quota-free preferential trade scheme in favor of LDCs is not available. LDC exporters will lose the preference limited to microtrade if LPP exports do not meet the requisite criteria for microtrade. A concern has then been raised that it would put a cap on the economies of scale that can be enjoyed by LDC exporters. Given that a fear for increased importation that may result from the economies of scale is an important reason not to allow the general, EBA-type preference in the first place, the preferential scheme for microtrade will have to put an inherent limitation on the economies of scale by limiting traded values and quantities.

the WTO objective of assisting developing countries with economic development through trade[65] and should be adopted by all developed countries and participating developing countries.[66] The share of world trade by LDCs remains minuscule,[67] and additional support in favor of LDC trade needs to be considered. For instance, as mentioned earlier, exemption of products of LDC origins, including microtraded LPPs, from any applicable domestic fees and taxes would help facilitate LDC trade.

IV. CONCLUSION: TRADE RATHER THAN AID

Former U.S. President Bill Clinton, Microsoft founder Bill Gates, and many other prominent individuals have emphasized the importance of giving.[68] Aid is indeed important and has saved many lives in places of extreme poverty. Nonetheless, severe poverty will not be eliminated unless the populations in LDCs achieve the level of economy that will bring them out of poverty through economic development. Economic development cannot be achieved solely by aid and requires the development of viable industries. Unfortunately, many LDCs do not have the requisite educational, industrial, financial, and political capabilities to initiate large-scale economic development projects that have been undertaken successfully by some East Asian countries. Economic development has not been successful in most of the LDCs, and crushing poverty still exists.

I suggest microtrade as an alternative way to improve the economic status of impoverished people in LDCs that cannot meet industrial and political conditions to initiate economic development at a national level. Small-scale productions of LPPs can help LDC producers when LPPs are exported into the markets of developed countries in which those products can be sold at much higher prices.[69] There are potentially complex logistical issues in microtrade with substantial cost implications. It is hoped that voluntary assistance will reduce the costs to the extent that earnings from microtrade will enable people in LDCs to reduce or eliminate the most extreme forms of poverty. The advent of the Internet and the accessibility of an online database are essential to the success of the microtrade scheme. Microcredit can be a useful device to finance production of LPPs and microtrade.

65 The preamble to the WTO Agreement provides in relevant part: "*Recognizing* further that there is a need for positive efforts designed to ensure that developing countries, and especially the least developed among them, secure a share in the growth of international trade commensurate with the needs of their economic development." WTO (2003), supra note 50, p. 4.

66 Y. S. Lee (2009), supra note 1, p. 38.

67 The share of world trade by LDCs was mere 0.9% in 2007. *International Trade Statistics 2008* (Geneva: WTO, 2009).

68 See Bill Clinton, *Giving: How Each of Us Can Change the World* (New York: Knopf, 2007). Bill Gates has also founded the largest private foundation in the world, the Bill and Melinda Gates Foundation, with the aim of enhancing health care and reducing extreme poverty (http://www.gatesfoundation.org).

69 Supra note 27.

Regulatory issues are also important for the facilitation and promotion of microtrade. The proposed preferential treatment in favor of microtrade may be authorized under the existing exceptions to the MFN requirement of WTO disciplines, such as GSP schemes. Indeed, the current environment in international trade places considerable emphasis on development, as reflected in the Doha Development Agenda,[70] and it is also hoped that support can be found for microtrade in this new environment.

Microtrade is not proposed as a preferred means of economic development if other, more efficient economic opportunities exist. As shown in the preceding discussion, there is no point to engaging in microtrade if the domestic sale of goods and services can yield more profits for LDC producers or if other economic opportunities, such as employment opportunities arising from large-scale international trade based on mass-production of manufactured products or primary products, provide higher income for LDC residents.[71] Microtrade is an important alternative device to reduce or eliminate poverty in LDCs where such opportunities do not exist. They do not seem to exist in many LDCs, and extreme poverty has persisted for several decades. The basic premise of microtrade is that the higher prices and higher purchasing power of consumers in developed countries justify export efforts,[72] as shown during the economic development process of the East Asian countries. Microtrade is conceived and promoted in this context, albeit on a much smaller scale, to improve the economic status of impoverished people in LDCs.

The proposed microtrade scheme and the large-scale economic development initiatives at national levels, such as those undertaken by the East Asian countries in the past, have different scopes and objectives: the purpose of the latter development initiatives is industrialization of the nation and improvement of the economic level on a national scale. All of the newly industrializing countries had attained the level of a developed economy by the 1990s through economic development on a national scale.[73] However, this is not the objective of microtrade. Microtrade does not aim to replace large-scale economic development initiatives undertaken at national levels. The aim of microtrade is a much more modest one: to generate a level of sustainable income through small-scale trade, which will be sufficient to bring LDC people out of poverty on an individual, family, or perhaps a community basis. Thus, the microtraded LPPs would be products that do not require a high level of capital or mass-production capacities but those that can be manufactured inexpensively with low levels of technology and shipped and sold in developed

70 For the Doha Development Agenda, see WTO, *Doha Development Agenda: Negotiations, Implementation and Development*, available at: http://www.wto.org/english/tratop_e/dda_e/dda_e.htm.

71 Large-scale export industries provided a large number of employment opportunities for the local residents in the East Asian countries during their rapid development periods starting in the 1960s.

72 Supra notes 27, 32.

73 Supra note 7.

countries for a profit. Microtrade can be promoted separately from, or concurrently with, large-scale economic development initiatives.

On a final note, I acknowledge that the economic efficiency of microtrade may be questioned even in cases in which transactions of microtrade appear successful and generate income for LDC producers beyond the poverty level. In economic terms, voluntary assistance is a cost, even if it is not a financial one for LPP producers. Thus, the microtrade scheme may be challenged on the ground that the income generated by microtrade may not justify the associated costs, including voluntary assistance, that may arise from the inefficiency of production and trade on a small scale. The economic efficiency of microtrade needs to be assessed on case-by-case basis, but even where microtrade does not appear economically efficient in the beginning, trade, rather than simply giving handouts, is still a better way to provide productive assistance. The economic case for microtrade can also be made on the ground that successful microtrade will create market demands for LPPs, which may over time reduce costs as demand grows and production and trade volume increases. As a result, a transition from microtrade to larger-scale international trade may occur, lifting LPP producers from poverty onto the path of higher economic development. As mentioned earlier, if no other economic option that would be more viable and profitable for LDC residents is available, microtrade can offer an alternative,[74] and those producing LPPs and gaining income from microtrade will not develop passive reliance on external aid. A meaningful start to overcoming poverty should begin by overcoming such reliance, and microtrade can provide a way to achieve lives free from poverty.

REFERENCES

Aghion, De, Beatriz Armendáriz, and Jonathan Morduch, *The Economics of Microfinance* (Cambridge, MA: MIT Press, 2005).

Amsden, Alice H., *Asia's Next Giant: South Korea and Late Industrialization* (New York: Oxford University Press, 1989).

______, *Escape from Empire: The Developing World's Journey through Heaven and Hell* (Cambridge, MA: MIT Press, 2007).

Bartels, Lorad, "The WTO Enabling Clause and Positive Conditionality in the European Community's GST Program" (2003) 6(2) *Journal of International Economic Law*.

Clinton, Bill, *Giving: How Each of Us Can Change the World* (New York: Knopf, 2007).

Findlay, R., "Growth and Development in Trade Models," in R. W. Jones and P. B. Kenen (eds.), *Handbook of International Economics*, Vol. 1 (New York: North-Holland, 1984).

GATT, Differential and More Favourable Treatment Reciprocity and Fuller Participation of Developing Countries, Decision of 28 November 1979 (L/490).

Harmer, Adele, Katherine Haver, and Abby Stoddard, *Providing Aid in Insecure Environments: Trends in Policy and Operations*, Humanitarian Policy Group Report, Overseas Development Institute (London, September 2006), available at: http://www.cic.nyu.edu/internationalsecurity/docs/hpgreport23.pdf.

74 $E_m = (P_f \times Q_f) - C_{p,d,s,r}$, where $E_m \geq E_d$ and $E_m \geq E_o$. See the preceding analysis in Section II.B.

Helleiner, G. K. (ed.), *Trade Policy, Industrialization, and Development* (Oxford: Oxford University Press, 1992).

Helms, Brigit, *Access for All: Building Inclusive Financial Systems* (Washington, DC: Consultative Group to Assist the Poor, 2006).

Heston, Alan, Robert Summers, and Bettina Aten, *Penn World Table Version 6.2*, Center for International Comparisons of Production, Income and Prices at the University of Pennsylvania (September 2006).

Hirschland, Madeline (ed.), *Savings Services for the Poor: An Operational Guide* (Bloomfield, CT: Kumarian Press, 2005).

Howse, R., and M. J. Trebilcock, *The Regulation of International Trade* (3rd ed., Oxford: Routledge, 2005).

Hudec, Robert, *Developing Countries in the GATT Legal System* (Aldershot, United Kingdom: Gower, 1987).

Inama, Stefano, "Market Access for LDCs: Issues to Be Addressed" (2002) 36(1) *Journal of World Trade*.

Karns, Margaret P., and Karen A. Mingst, *International Organizations: The Politics and Processes of Global Governance* (Boulder, CO: Lynne Rienner Publishers, 2004).

Khandker, Shahidur R., *Fighting Poverty with Microcredit* (Bangladesh edition, Dhaka: The University Press, 1999).

Kim, Kwang-Suk, and Joon-Kyung Park, *Sources of Economic Growth in Korea: 1963–1981* (Seoul: Korea Development Institute, 1985).

Krueger, A. O., "Trade Policies in Developing Countries," in R. W. Jones and P. B. Kenen (eds.), *Handbook of International Economics*, Vol. 1 (New York: North-Holland, 1984).

Lamb, Gregory M., "A Closer Look at What '$100 Laptop' Will Be," *The Christian Science Monitor*, January 29, 2007, available at: http://www.csmonitor.com/2007/0129/p13s01-stct.html.

Ledgerwood, Joanna, and Victoria White, *Transforming Microfinance Institutions: Providing Full Financial Services to the Poor* (Washington, DC: World Bank, 2006).

Lee, Y. S., *Reclaiming Development in the World Trading System* (New York: Cambridge University Press, 2009).

______, "Development and the World Trade Organization: A Proposal for the Council for Trade and Development and the Agreement on Development Facilitation (ADF)" (2006) 6 *Asper Review of International Business and Trade Law*.

Leeson, Peter, and Claudia Williamson, "Anarchy and Development: An Application of the Theory of Second Best" (2009) 2(1) *The Law and Development Review*.

Mangeni, Francis, "How Far Can LDCs Benefit from Duty Free and Quota Free Market Access? The Case of Uganda with Respect to the EU Market," in Y. S. Lee (ed.), *Economic Development through World Trade: A Developing Country Perspective* (The Hague: Kluwer Law International, 2008).

Matsushita, M., T. J. Schoenbaum, and P. C. Mavroidis, *The World Trade Organization: Law, Practice and Policy* (2nd ed., Oxford: Oxford University Press, 2006).

Mavroidis, Petros C., *The General Agreement on Tariffs and Trade: A Commentary* (Oxford: Oxford University Press, 2005).

Moore, Mike, "Ten Years of the WTO: A Success Story of Global Governance" (2005) 2 *Zeitschrift: Internationale Politik und Gesellschaft*.

Moyo, Dembisa, *Dead Aid: Why Aid Is Not Working and How There Is a Better Way for Africa* (New York: Farrar, Straus & Giroux, 2009).

Organization for Economic Cooperation and Development, *International Development Statistics*, available at: http://stats.oecd.org.

Pangestu, Mari, "Industrial Policy and Developing Countries," in Bernard Hoekman, Aaditya Mattoo and Philip English (eds.), *Development, Trade, and the WTO: A Handbook* (Washington, DC: World Bank, 2002).
Petrone, A. F. (ed.), *Causes and Alleviation of Poverty* (Hauppauge, NY: Nova Science Publications, 2002).
Rodrik, Dani, *Industrial Policy for the Twenty-First Century*, paper prepared for UNIDO (September 2004), available at: http://www.hks.harvard.edu/fs/drodrik/UNIDOSep.pdf.
Sen, Amartya, *Culture and Development*, World Bank Paper (December 13, 2000), available at: http://info.worldbank.org/etools/docs/voddocs/354/688/sen_tokyo.pdf.
Srinivasan, T. N., "Trade, Development, and Growth," *Princeton Essays in International Economics*, No. 225 (December 2001).
UNCTAD Secretariat, *The Least Developed Countries Report* 2008 (Geneva: United Nations Commission on Trade and Development).
United Nations Development Program, *U.N. Human Development Report 2003* (New York: Oxford University Press, 2003).
United Nations Office of the High Representative for the Lease Developed Countries, *Selected Economic and Social Indicators for LDCs (2005)*.
Ustorf, Werner, "Response to Wilhelm Dupre" (1998) 1(1) *Implicit Religion*.
Wade, Robert, *Governing the Market: Economic Theory and the Role of Government in East Asian Industrialization* (Princeton, NJ: Princeton University Press, 2003).
World Bank, *Poverty: At A Glance*, available at: http://web.worldbank.org/WBSITE/EXTERNAL/TOPICS/EXTPOVERTY/EXTPA/0,,contentMDK:20040961~isCURL:Y~menuPK:435040~pagePK:148956~piPK:216618~theSitePK:430367,00.html.
______, *The East Asian Miracle* (New York: Oxford University Press, 1993).
World Trade Organization, Doha Development Agenda: Negotiations, Implementation and Development, available at: http://www.wto.org.
______, *European Communities – Conditions for the Granting of Tariff Preferences for Developing Countries*, Report of the Panel, WT/DS246/R (1 December 2003), *Report of the Appellate Body*, WT/DS246/AB/R (7 April 2004).
______, *Implementation of Special and Differential Treatment Provisions in WTO Agreements and Decisions – Note by Secretariat*, WT/COMTD/W/77 (25 October 2000).
______, *International Trade Statistics* 2009 (Geneva, 2009).
______, *The Results of the Uruguay Round of Multilateral Trade Negotiations* (Cambridge: Cambridge University Press, 2003).
Wright, Graham A. N., *Microfinance Systems: Designing Quality Financial Services for the Poor* (Dhaka: The University Press, 2000).
Yunus, Muhammad, *Creating a World without Poverty: Social Business and the Future of Capitalism* (New York: Public Affairs, 2008).

2

Development Disputes in International Trade

Tomer Broude

I. INTRODUCTION

A central "law and development" perspective on international economic law relates to the effective participation of developing countries in the international economic and legal system – in the World Trade Organization (WTO), regional trade agreements (RTAs), bilateral investment treaties (BITs), and other international economic legal mechanisms. In this field, considerable attention has been given over the past decade or so to two overarching legal issues. Substantively, there is the seemingly intractable difficulty in concretizing and enforcing fluid concepts such as "development,"[1] "special and differential treatment" (SDT),[2] and "common but differentiated responsibilities (CDR)"[3] as firm legal rules and principles. In terms of process and procedure, there is the question of the diminished capacity of developing countries (and associated private economic actors) to use rules-based dispute settlement, such as in the WTO, or under RTAs and BITs, to their advantage.[4]

[1] On the position of developing countries in the world trade system, see, most comprehensively, Robert E. Hudec, *Developing Countries in the GATT/WTO Legal System*, Chantal Thomas and Joel Trachtman, eds. (New York: Oxford University Press, 2009; 1st ed., 1987). On the particular issue of defining "development," see Tomer Broude, "The Rule(s) of Trade and the Rhetos of Development: Reflections on the Functional and Aspirational Legitimacy of the WTO" (2006) 27(4) *Columbia Journal of Transnational Law* 221 at section IV.2.

[2] See, e.g., Bernard Hoekman, "Operationalizing the Concept of Policy Space in the WTO: Beyond Special and Differential Treatment" (2005) 8(2) *Journal of International Economic Law* 405; and Andrew D. Mitchell and Tania Voon, "Operationalizing Special and Differential Treatment in the WTO: Game Over?" (2009) 15 *Global Governance* 343.

[3] See Duncan French, "Developing States and International Environmental Law: The Importance of Differentiated Responsibilities" (2000) 49 *International and Comparative Law Quarterly* 35.

[4] The literature on this topic is vast. See, e.g., Marc L. Busch and Eric Reinhardt, "Developing Countries and GATT/WTO Dispute Settlement" (2003) 37(4) *Journal of World Trade* 719; and Gregory Shaffer, "Can WTO Technical Assistance and Capacity Building Serve Developing Countries?" (2005) 23 *Wisconsin International Law Journal* 643.

This chapter relates to both of these issues, but it is neither about the "evolving"[5] or "emerging"[6] – and ever elusive – substance of the international law of development as such nor about dispute settlement from the perspective of developing countries.[7] Rather, as its title suggests, it seeks to characterize some international disagreements as disputes that are in themselves "international development disputes" and in this way to provide a new prism for assessing the problem of enhancing the sensitivity of international dispute settlement to development. The chapter establishes that despite the well-acknowledged vagueness of "development" as an operative legal concept, there exists a set of international legal differences (primarily international economic disputes but not exclusively so) that should be identified as international disputes *about* development. Recognizing them as such has implications for the ways in which such disputes are dealt with. In particular, the effectiveness and legitimacy of using judicial methods to address development disputes should be reconsidered.[8]

Generally defined, international development disputes can be understood as a discrete category of international disputes that, in terms of jurisdiction and applicable law, arise under fairly "hard" rules of international law, such as trade and investment treaties, but in a more practical sense are actually concerned with reviewing the development policies of states, which are regulated on the international level only in very "soft" terms, if at all.[9] In other words, international development disputes are disputes that involve fundamental disagreements between international actors about "how to develop" even though the law that applies in such disputes is not designed or particularly equipped to cope with this question, many aspects of which are riven with doubt and controversy among economists and policy analysts.[10]

Seen in this way, international disputes relating to development issues are surprisingly and increasingly common, and the avenues of their settlement (or lack thereof) are diverse. Nonetheless, in many cases, judicial and quasi-judicial forums are precluded from considering development needs and concerns as normative factors in their decisions in any more than the most general of terms (or at least it would appear that they prefer to refrain from doing so) because of political, legal, and

5 See Oscar Schachter, "The Evolving International law of Development" (1976) 15 *Columbia Journal of Transnational Law* 1.

6 See Francisco V. García-Amador, *The Emerging International Law of Development: A New Dimension of International Economic Law* (New York: Oceana, 1990).

7 See, e.g., Gary Horlick, "Nonconclusions," Chapter 17 of this volume.

8 These implications are not fully developed within the limited scope of this chapter. The idea here is more modestly to explore the viability of "international development disputes" as a definitional concept.

9 For a recent exposition of hard versus soft law in international legal systems and the interaction between them, see Gregory Shaffer and Mark A. Pollack, "Hard vs. Soft Law: Alternatives, Complements and Antagonists in International Governance" (2010) 94 *Minnesota Law Review* 706.

10 See, e.g., Dani Rodrik, *One Economics, Many Recipes: Globalization, Institutions and Economic Growth* (Princeton, NJ: Princeton University Press, 2007), for a critique of both orthodox and critical approaches to international development economics.

structural constraints. Most development-related international dispute settlement avoids frontally engaging with development dilemmas by resorting to legal tools, rules, and doctrines that are formally and teleologically exogenous to development.[11] This phenomenon effectively restricts or even neutralizes the legal effect of development law and development considerations rather than enforcing or empowering them. This chapter suggests that it would be conducive to the integration of development into international law if international development disputes were recognized as a distinct field that necessitates distinct treatment.

The chapter is structured as follows. In the next section, I explain in more detail what is meant by "international development disputes," refining and justifying the concept and distinguishing it from "development law" and "developing countries" as related terms. In the subsequent section, I provide a general typology of disputes that should be considered "international development disputes" in that they relate to development in three interrelated yet distinct senses: economic development, rights-based development, and sustainable development. In the fourth section, in keeping with the volume's focus on international trade, I discuss central examples of international development disputes in the WTO. On this basis, in the fifth and final section, I briefly evaluate the overall impact of development disputes, actual and potential, on the evolution of international development law and ways in which the concept of "international development disputes" might be leveraged from a law and development perspective.

II. WHAT ARE INTERNATIONAL DEVELOPMENT DISPUTES?

The term "international development disputes" as referred to in this chapter requires some clarification and elaboration. After all, it is certainly not a term in common usage.[12] Rather than providing a rigid definition, let us consider some of the relevant alternative dimensions.

A. *Development Disputes Transcend International Development Law*

First, we might pursue a restrictive *ratione materiae* approach, linking disputes to the substantive law they address. Development disputes would then include those

[11] To be sure, international trade law – that area of law most closely related to economic development – has, as its ideal goal, "raising standards of living," "sustainable development," and "the needs of [developing countries] economic development" (see Preamble, Marrakesh Agreement Establishing the WTO), but the world trading order is hardly designed as a fully liberalized system or with the advancement of developing countries firmly in mind; for a comprehensive critique, see Joseph E. Stiglitz, *Making Globalization Work* (New York: W. W. Norton, 2006).

[12] A standard Google.com (May 1, 2010) search for the term "international development disputes" yielded only 11 hits, mostly irrelevant, in contrast to the term "international investment disputes," which yielded 889,000 hits; the term "international trade disputes," which yielded 609,000 hits; and the term "international environmental disputes," which yielded 192,000 hits.

international disputes involving differences over the interpretation and application of a predetermined area of "international development law," just as international trade disputes relate to international trade law or international maritime disputes relate to international maritime law. This would then depend on the substantive scope of international development law and would assume that such an area of law, composed of international development rights and obligations, is clearly identifiable. However, international development law thus construed has always been difficult to delimit in juridically meaningful terms, despite lawmaking and academic efforts to do so.[13]

International development law has, for example, been defined as an "emerging" international legal order based on two principal substantive elements, the "right to development" and the "duty to cooperate for development."[14] To these we must add the evolving international norms of sustainable development.[15] This approach would therefore regard these international legal principles as the applicable law of international development, from which a slew of particular legal claims could be derived, directly informing the international regulation (and litigation) of aid, trade, investment, economic and social rights, as well as environmental and natural resource issues. This approach would be analytically neat and doctrinally attractive. International development disputes would be deemed as all disputes that involve legal applications and interpretations of the right to development, the duty to cooperate for development, principles of sustainable development, and other applicable norms of international development law.

However, such an approach would be narrow and not very instructive. These principles are sparsely cited before international tribunals and even more rarely applied by them, and a basic (and related) criticism that can be leveled against them reflects on their juridical disutility and normative fuzziness. Following this approach would then either leave us with little to study, oblivious to the broader effects that disputes in other areas of international law have on development, or would require us, in a rather contrived fashion, to read the substantive normative principles of international development law into specific judicial cases despite their explicit absence or minor role in practice. Quite simply, international development disputes arise under a broader range of norms than the (unclearly) applicable law of development, *de lege lata*.

[13] Oscar Schachter's seminal essay on the topic begins with the words "[To] talk about an evolving international law of development requires us to identify that law. This compels us to think about fundamentals, an activity not always congenial to practical lawyers who have difficulty enough with the uncertainties of international law and its elusive sources." Schachter (1976), supra note 5, p. 1. Although the international law that relates to development has no doubt become more robust since these lines were written thirty-five years ago, they ring just as true today.

[14] See García-Amador (1990), supra note 6, p. 31 et seq.

[15] For a state-of-the-art collection of essays on the international law of sustainable development, see Nico Schrijver and Friedl Weiss (eds.), *International Law and Sustainable Development: Principles and Practice* (Dordrecht, the Netherlands: Martinus Nijhoff Publishers, 2004).

B. *Development Disputes Transcend Developing–Developed Country Disputes over Differential Treatment*

Another possible alternative approach (strongly related to the first) would be to adopt a definition of international development law as based on the "duality of norms" that derives from "the emergence of a special type of subjects in international law – the category of developing countries,"[16] an approach that would be familiar to many proponents from earlier times. Georges Abi-Saab has described this approach concisely as one that

> postulates as its basis the common interest of all states in the development of the weakest and most vulnerable, which justifies according them preferential treatment in the form of special protection or targeted aid. From this derives the principle of the duality of norms as the principal axis and common denominator of legal regulation, which is formulated differently according to the different sectors of North-South economic relations: commodities, manufactured goods, technology transfers, financial flows, etc.[17]

With respect to international development disputes, this approach would include all disputes relating to international rules that establish legally differential relations between developed and developing countries, such as SDT in the WTO, or CDR under international environmental law, or commitments toward "North–South" technology transfer, for example, in Part XIV of the United Nations Convention on the Law of the Sea. Development disputes would then primarily be disputes over the extent of this duality, the scope of this differential treatment. Indeed, we might even simply consider "development disputes" *ratione personae* as all disputes that arise between developing countries and developed countries. Both of these directions – the narrow and the broad – might be based on the common perception of international development law as "the law regulating the relations among sovereign but economically unequal states."[18] In the context of international disputes, this approach would also relate well to the logic of the important contemporary debate over the relative capacity of developing countries to participate in international dispute settlement and strategies for its enhancement, as already mentioned.[19]

Although international development law is clearly inseparable from international economic disparity, between the so-called North and South, these approaches, too,

[16] Maria Magdalena Kenig-Witkowska, "Development Ideology in International Law," in Subrata Roy Chowdhury, Erik M. G. Denters, and Paul J. I. M. de Waart (eds.), *The Right to Development in International Law* (Dordrecht, the Netherlands: Martinus Nijhoff Publishers, 1992), p. 39.

[17] See Georges Abi-Saab, "Wither the International Community?" (1998) 9 *European Journal of International Law* 263.

[18] See Milan Bulajić, *Principles of International Development Law* (2nd rev. ed., Dordrecht: Martinus Nijhoff, 1993), pp. 43; and Edward Kwakwa, "Emerging International Development Law and Traditional International Law: Congruence or Cleavage?" (1987) 17 *Georgia Journal of International and Comparative Law* 431–432.

[19] See supra note 4.

would seem to be problematic and unenlightening when applied to the area of international disputes. Technically, they would assume that a satisfactory definition of "developing countries" exists, when in fact this is a continuing problem in development law.[20] These definitions would also exclude all South–South disputes that may be highly relevant to development,[21] as well as North–North disputes that may not involve economic inequality or legal differentiation but apply universally applicable legal rules and interpretations that are also pertinent to development and North–South situations.[22] Such definitions would also exclude disputes involving nonstate parties, such as international organizations, especially international financial institutions (IFIs), the important roles and responsibilities of which in international development are indisputable;[23] corporations, in the case of investment disputes, or cases involving accountability for violations of components of the right to development; and indeed individuals, wherever they possess standing or their rights are directly affected. On the other hand, definitions that focus on the differential status or legal treatment of states might include disputes that do not involve development issues. Arguably, not all economic disputes between developing and developed countries, not even all trade disputes that peripherally revert to SDT, involve questions of international development,[24] and clearly, many North–South noneconomic disputes do not relate to development.[25]

In sum, international development disputes do not necessarily relate to the application of differential treatment, nor should the concept be defined as disputes between developed and developing countries.

C. *Development Disputes Are Disputes That Affect Development Policy*

These formal definitions (which focus on international development law or on developing countries) are therefore inadequate for an inquiry into international development disputes. Indeed, they appear to suffer from the general failings of international

[20] See Guglielmo Verdirame, "Definition of Developing Countries under the GATT and other International Law" (1996) 39 *German Yearbook of International Law* 164; and Broude supra note 1.

[21] For example, the Brazil-Uruguay dispute in MERCOSUR on import prohibitions of retreaded tyres (MERCOSUR, Tribunal Permanente de Revision, Laudo No. 1/2005, *Prohibicion de Importacion de Neumaticos Remoldeados Procedentes del Uruguay*; or the Argentina-Uruguay Pulp Mills dispute; ICJ, *Pulp Mills on the River Uruguay (Argentina v. Uruguay)*, Judgment of 20 April 2010.

[22] For example, ICJ, *Gabčikovo-Nagymaros Project (Hungary/Slovakia)*, Judgment of September 25, 1997; and PCA, *Belgium/Netherlands (Iron Rhine Arbitration)*, Award of September 20, 2005.

[23] Of particular relevance are IFI accountability mechanisms such as the World Bank Inspection Panel, which reviews adverse developmental and human rights effects of Bank-financed projects; see World Bank, *Accountability at the Bank: The Inspection Panel at 15 Years* (2009).

[24] This point is elaborated on in Section III.A below.

[25] For example, although a dispute between Mexico and the United States over the treatment of Mexican nationals in the United States upon arrest as suspected criminals (ICJ, *Avena and Other Mexican Nationals [Mexico v. United States of America]*, Judgment of March 31, 2004) has distinct political North–South dimensions, it cannot seriously be considered a development dispute in the absence of ramifications for development policy.

development law, as a field. A more object-oriented, integrated, and functional definition could be proposed in which "international development disputes" are broadly understood as disagreements between international actors (including both states and nonstate actors), *requiring determinations under international law that have significant ramifications for the design and implementation of development policy at the national or international level*, whether involving international development law or developing countries (however defined) or not. So described, international development disputes are in essence legal disagreements on issues that have repercussions for the overarching policy question of *how to develop* and its more specific derivatives.

Thus, an investor–state arbitration under a BIT between a corporation from developed country A and the government of developing country B over an infrastructure contract might in certain circumstances be considered a development dispute, if the contested nationalization were related to A's development policy.[26] A World Bank Inspection Panel review relating to the effects of a World Bank–financed project on the land rights of indigenous peoples would likely be a development dispute.[27] Furthermore, a trade dispute at the WTO over national import restrictions imposed for the sake of environmental sustainability, even if no SDT provisions were involved, would also be considered as an "international development dispute" to the extent that it could affect development policy by providing legal imperatives or constraints. These might all be development disputes, although they might have been excluded by the previously discussed definitions, either because they did not strictly involve "development law" (but rather, investment protection law, World Bank operational policies or procedures, and the general law of the multilateral trading system, respectively), because they were not disputes between developing and developed countries, as the case may be, or both.

This definition of international disputes can be criticized because it appears to be dependent on a clearly defined and widely accepted definition of the term "development," just as the ones discarded earlier in the chapter were reliant on delimitations of "development law" or the identification of "developing countries." This might have been the case, had it required a legal delimitation of development, say, for the purpose of establishing jurisdiction or to determine the applicable law. This definition, however, depends on no such term. It refers to the potential *effects* of a dispute, not to the law that regulates it or to the North–South identity of its parties. Further, it refers to development *policy*, which can be defined more loosely than development law. Development policy is taken here to include the courses of action pursued by governments and international organizations to promote development in a broad sense – namely, a combination of economic growth and poverty alleviation, furtherance of collective and individual social rights, and environmental

[26] One might consider a dispute such as ICSID, *Biwater Gauff (Tanzania) Ltd. v. United Republic of Tanzania*, ICSID Case ARB /05/22, Award of July 24, 2008, to be such a case.

[27] For example, World Bank Inspection Panel, IPN Request RQ97/1, *Brazil: Itaparica Resettlement and Irrigation Project* (1997).

sustainability. International development disputes are thus not related to a single, particular area of substantive law but to the behavior of international actors aimed at development, so defined.

This functional, integrated approach to development is not without legal basis, if one considers the language of the Declaration on the Right to Development,[28] the Rio Declaration,[29] the Doha Declaration,[30] and other sources, but for present purposes, it does not need it. To be sure, "development law" might itself be defined as all international law that significantly influences development policy – a possibility certainly worth entertaining, but this would be more far reaching than is necessary here. International development disputes are disputes that have repercussions for development policy, regardless of how we define development law. In the next section, this approach will be refined by examining particular ways in which disputes may have an impact on development policy.

III. TYPES OF INTERNATIONAL DEVELOPMENT DISPUTES

The integrated definition of international development disputes is useful because it allows us to look at disagreements over development "through the cases," rather than through the narrower lens of law as it is prescribed. In this respect, and to prevent the definition from overreaching itself, it is useful to disaggregate the concept into a few categories. At least three such categories of international development disputes may be identified. These should not be confused with areas of substantive law or with the jurisdictions of particular forums, because none of them is exclusively associated with any; neither are these categories mutually exclusive, because a given development dispute may fall into more than one category. These categories are (a) disputes relating to economic development policy, (b) disputes relating to rights-based development policy, and (c) disputes relating to sustainable development policy.

A. *Disputes Relating to Economic Development Policy*

Economic development disputes are disputes over international rights and obligations that guide or constrain domestic or international policies aimed at promoting

[28] The declaration views development as a process; therefore, development policy is policy aimed at contributing to this process: "[D]evelopment is a comprehensive economic, social, cultural and political process, which aims at the constant improvement of the well-being of the entire population and of all individuals on the basis of their active, free and meaningful participation in development and in the fair distribution of benefits resulting therefrom"; see UNGA, *Declaration on the Right to Development*, Doc. A/RES/41/128 (December 4, 1996), Annex, second preambular paragraph.

[29] The Rio Declaration also views sustainable development as a process, aimed not only at economic development but also environmental concerns. See, e.g., Principle 4 (referring to the "development process"); see UNGA, *Report of the United Nations Conference on Environment and Development*, Annex I, *Rio Declaration on Environment and Development*, Doc. A/CONF.151/26 (Vol. I) (August 12, 1992).

[30] See WTO, *Ministerial Declaration*, Doc. WT/MIN(01)/DEC/1 (November 20, 2001), paras. 2, 6.

development as measured by economic indicators (e.g., GDP per capita, economic measures of poverty). Disputes of this type arise mainly under international economic law, such as trade and investment law, and are often found in the respective forums, for example, the dispute settlement systems of the WTO and RTAs or in the International Center for the Settlement of Investment Disputes. These are sets of international rules and institutions that clearly may affect national and international economic development policy. Thus, if a state objects to another state's use of subsidies on the basis of international trade law, because of their negative effect on its economic development,[31] or because it considers that for developmental reasons it should be eligible for trade preferences granted by another state,[32] these cases can be understood as economic development disputes. Investment disputes that arise out of changes in economic policy and differences over the terms under which international development aid and finance are provided are also, at root, disputes relating to economic development policy. Economic development disputes may also involve other dimensions of development policy, such as social rights or environmental issues (e.g., disputes over the use of child labor in industry or adherence to environmental standards),[33] but at their core, they are economic.

However, should this description appear too expansive, it is crucial to understand that not all international trade disputes, let alone all economic disputes, should be considered international development disputes.

First, many economic disputes arise for reasons that are not related to development and address measures that are not part of development policy. Most trade disputes relate to disagreements over international competitive conditions and are driven by competition between private economic actors over access to markets. When a government decides to shield a domestic industry from foreign competition or to support its production and export capacity, a dispute over compliance with trade disciplines may arise. Targeted protection of certain industries may be a component of deliberate development policy, especially if it is embedded in a broader economic and social policy context, even though such policies may, nonetheless, be controversial in economic and political terms. These controversies, and the effects of development policy on competition, may give rise to disagreements on "how to develop" – the very domain of international development disputes, as understood here. However, in many – perhaps even most – cases, such protection or support is not the outcome of informed development policy but rather the result of protectionist pressures by private economic actors concerned with their own stakes in international trade. These cases should not be considered international development disputes but rather classical trade disputes.

31 See, e.g., WTO Appellate Body Report, *US – Subsidies on Upland Cotton*, WT/DS267/AB/R (3 March 2005).

32 See, e.g., WTO Appellate Body Report, *EC – Conditions for the Granting of Tariff Preferences to Developing Countries*, WT/DS246/AB/R (April 7, 2004).

33 The initial complaint in the *EC–GSP* dispute (ibid.) included reference to labor rights, but this aspect of the complaint was later abandoned by India, the complainant.

To be sure, the line between protectionism driven by domestic interest-group lobbying on one hand and economic measures that are part of development policy on the other can be a difficult one to draw. This is but a reflection of the lack of consensus on legitimate development policy, which is itself a necessary reason for examining development disputes. Notably, existing international trade and investment law does not include a "general exception" for development policy that would permit divergence from trade liberalization and investment protection disciplines where necessary for development.[34] This should not in itself present an obstacle to the conceptual distinction between disputes that are development related and those that are not, which is not a distinction based on applicable law, as explained earlier.

Second, many economic disputes emerge as a result of barriers to trade and investment that are not necessarily motivated by protectionism but relate to public policy considerations that lie outside the sphere of development policy, such as public morals. Such disputes should also not be considered development disputes unless they simultaneously relate to development.

B. *Disputes Relating to Rights-Based Development Policy*

Beyond (and in parallel to) economic variables, development is recognized as a concept that aims to promote the "human condition," to be equated with and derived from human freedom.[35] This has fed into to the idea of rights-based development,[36] which is strongly associated with social justice as well as particular social and economic rights, such as the right to food, the right to health, the right to work, the right to water, and the right to education, in addition to the right to development itself.[37] Many, if not all, international disputes that affect the scope of these rights are hence international development disputes. These might include not only relevant decisions by regional human rights tribunals and reports by international human rights bodies but also investment disputes relating to social rights (e.g., the privatization or nationalization of an essential facility such as water works or sewerage),

34 This option is rarely floated (but see, e.g., in the investment context, United Nations Conference on Trade and Development [UNCTAD], *International Investment Agreements: Flexibilities for Development*, Doc. UNCTAD/ITE/IIT/18 (2000), p. 96 (proposing a general exception for development in investment protection agreements). Indeed, conservative economists would consider such an exception to be an internal contradiction in any trade liberalization scheme, with the understanding that all trade liberalization promotes economic development.

35 See Amartya Sen, *Development as Freedom* (Oxford: Oxford University Press, 2001).

36 See, e.g., Stephen P. Marks, "The Human Rights Framework for Development: Seven Approaches" in Arjun Sengupta, Archna Negi, and Moushumi Basu (eds.), *Reflections on the Right to Development* (New Delhi: Sage Publications India, 2005), p. 23.

37 See UN Economic and Social Council, *Mainstreaming the Right to Development into International Trade Law and Policy at the World Trade Organization*, UN Doc. E/CN.4/Sub.2/2004/17 (June 9, 2004) (Study by Prof. Robert L. Howse).

IFI accountability procedures that examine human rights effects of development projects, or trade disputes affecting access to medicines for epidemic diseases.[38]

However, just as not all economic disputes are development disputes, not all disputes over social rights infringements relate to development but only those that are derived from, or may influence, development policy. For example, disputes over the scope of the right to education may arise because of racial discrimination in ways that cannot be the result of informed development policy.[39]

C. *Disputes Relating to Sustainable Development Policy*

A crucial element of development policy is its environmental sustainability, the principles of which are perhaps most concisely enumerated by the Rio Declaration.[40] Most international disputes over sustainable development policy involving environmental or national or international resource management should be viewed as international development disputes. In this category, a dispute based on international trade law and the international law of the sea with respect to the regulation of fishing[41] may be regarded, for example, at least in part, as a development dispute. An investment dispute that relates to environmental policy[42] may also be deemed a development dispute. This is the case even if the disputes in question are concurrently economic development disputes or otherwise relate to social rights. Some environmental or resource allocation disputes should not, however, be considered development disputes if they have no implications for development policy, but it is difficult to envision transnational environmental disputes that do not have developmental implications.[43]

[38] Such as the dispute over the seizure in the EU of generic pharmaceuticals manufactured in India for use in Brazil; see International Center for Trade and Sustainable Development, "Brazil Slams EU for Seizure of Generic Drugs" (February 4, 2009), available at: http://ictsd.org/i/news/bridgesweekly/39772.

[39] See European Court of Human Rights, Grand Chamber, *Case of Oršuš and Others v. Croatia*, Application No. 15766/03, Judgment of March 16, 2010.

[40] See UNGA, A/Conf.151/26 (Vol. I), Report of the UN Conference on Environment and Development, Annex I, Rio Declaration on Environment and Development (August 12, 1992).

[41] Such as the Chile–EU Swordfish dispute, which set off proceedings both at the WTO and at the International Tribunal for the Law of the Sea but has been suspended through settlement; see Marcos Orellana, "The EU and Chile Suspend the Swordfish Case Proceedings at the WTO and ITLOS," *ASIL Insights* (February 2001), available at: http://www.asil.org/insigh60.cfm.

[42] See, e.g., the NAFTA Chapter 11 investment arbitration in *Methanex Corp. v. United States of America*, Final Award of the Tribunal on Jurisdiction and Merits, August 3, 2005, available at: http://www.state.gov/documents/organization/51052.pdf.

[43] This is true with respect to cases that involve North–North engagement, such as the classical *Trail Smelter Case* between the United States and Canada. *Trail Smelter Arbitration (United States v. Canada)*, (1938) 3 *Review of International Arbitral Awards* 1911, reprinted in (1939) 33 *American Journal of International Law* 182, 3 Review of International Arbitral Awards (1941), 1938, reprinted in (1941) 35 *American Journal of International Law*, 684, and the recently concluded *MOX Plant Case* between Ireland and the United Kingdom. See Nikolaos Lavranos, "The Epilogue in the MOX Plant Dispute: An End without Findings" (2009) *European Energy and Environmental Law Review*.

To be sure, there are many overlaps between these categories of development disputes, and the definitional lines are not bright ones, reflecting the functional and integrative nature of development. The typology's main purpose is to illustrate the scope of international development disputes, not as defined in relation to the substantive law that may govern them but in relation to development policy.

IV. INTERNATIONAL DEVELOPMENT DISPUTES IN THE WTO

As we have already seen, international development disputes can arise in many forums – from the WTO to human rights tribunals – and may be governed by many branches of international law. Given this volume's focus on international trade law, it makes sense to elaborate on the development disputes that make their way to the WTO.

Because of its comprehensive, indeed, almost universal membership,[44] highly active and binding dispute settlement system, and, above all, its focus on international trade regulation, many significant international development disputes have reached the WTO. WTO law includes rules that affect not only on border measures such as industrial and agricultural tariffs but also "behind the border" measures that are especially pertinent to sophisticated national development policy, such as domestic regulation, taxation, subsidies, and environmental protection. As already mentioned, the WTO also incorporates many rules reflective of international development policy, such as SDT provisions and the Generalized System of Preferences (GSP). All of these factors contribute to the WTO's considerable experience with international development disputes, many of which involve developing countries as parties and address high-profile development issues.

However, WTO jurisprudence only partially reflects the potential coverage of development disputes in the WTO. Many developing countries have proven dispute-averse, and in fact least developed countries have yet to take part in a WTO dispute. This clearly constrains the impact of WTO dispute settlement on international development policy and might be a form of "adverse selection" as far as it relates to the states with the most problematic development. Furthermore, disputes relating to rights-based development have not as of this writing been settled in the WTO, although it is likely that such disputes may occur in the future;[45] disputes that involve sustainable development have arisen[46] and will probably increase in the future.

Consequently, the contribution of the WTO to the field of international development disputes, however important, has thus far been mainly restricted to economic development disputes relating to the industrial development policies of economically significant developing countries such as Korea, Brazil, India, and China and

44 As of this writing (May 2010), the membership of the WTO includes 153 States and Separate Customs Territories.

45 See supra notes 33 and 38 for examples.

46 See Section IV.D, infra.

to the developmentally sensitive areas of textiles and agriculture, with a handful of sustainable development disputes as well. To be sure, as explained in the previous section, in areas of economic development, it is difficult – although necessary – to make a clear distinction between trade disputes that stem from members' domestic sectoral political economy preferences and disputes that directly relate to national economic development policy. For example, antidumping duties are usually related to the protectionist needs of domestic industries but in principle may also be part of national import-substitution development strategies, although this might be an abuse of antidumping disciplines. A subsidy may in some cases be granted to preserve the position of an industry in the domestic economy in the face of external competition, but in other cases, it may be part of an export-based economic development policy. All antidumping, subsidies, and countervailing measure disputes jurisprudence may therefore be indirectly relevant to development policy, but a dispute should be considered to be a development dispute only if it requires determinations that can be shown to be related to national or international development policy.

Thus construed, development disputes settled in the WTO generally fall into the following groups. First, there are disputes in which a WTO member challenges an element of another member's economic development policy on the basis of WTO rules; these may be called "constraining development disputes," because they may have the effect of constraining a state's development policy. Second, there are cases in which a WTO member complains against a measure of another WTO member because it constrains its own development policy. These may be called "enabling development disputes," because they may have the effect of increasing the effectiveness of development policy. Third, there are disputes in which a complaint is lodged against a WTO member's measure that is harmful to the economic development of the complaining party. These may be described as "defensive development disputes"; they are distinct from "enabling development disputes" because they do not relate to the development policy of the complaining party but rather to the externalities imposed by one member on the development of another member. Fourth, there are disputes that are concerned with the sustainable environmental policies of members; these are referred to as "sustainable development disputes." A fifth, rights-based type of development dispute may arise in the future, but as mentioned earlier, such disputes have not yet been properly adjudicated in the WTO.

A. *Constraining Development Disputes: Challenges to Members' Economic Development Policy as WTO-Inconsistent*

These are cases in which an element of a WTO member's economic development policy has been challenged by another member as incompatible with WTO obligations. Many of these disputes relate to what is generally referred to as "industrial policy," including the subsidization of infant industries, the protection of domestic industry as part of import-substitution policies, tax manipulation, local content requirements, and weak intellectual property protection. A survey of WTO disputes that reached the full panel adjudication process in the first decade of the WTO's existence has shown that a high proportion of WTO disputes – approximately 25% – have dealt with such developmental policies, as enacted by both developing countries and developed countries.[47] An indicative list of such constraining development disputes in the WTO would include the following:

- WT/DS46 *Brazil – Export Financing Programme for Aircraft*
- WT/DS54, 55, 59, 64 *Indonesia – Certain Measures Affecting the Automotive Industry*
- WT/DS96 *India – Quantitative Restrictions on Imports of Agricultural, Textile and Industrial Products*
- WT/DS146 *India – Measures Affecting the Automotive Sector*
- WT/DS273 *Korea – Measures Affecting Trade in Commercial Vessels*
- WT/DS339, 340, 342 *China – Measures Affecting Imports of Automobile Parts*

The *Indonesia-Autos* example demonstrates the character of development disputes as disputes over "how to develop." In the mid-1990s, Indonesia pursued a "National Car Program" that included local content incentives applicable to imported automobiles. The policy was similar to pre-WTO policies successfully followed by Brazil in the establishment of its local automobile industry. The *Indonesia-Autos* panel found that Indonesia's policies were in violation of particular provisions of GATT Article I (Most-Favored-Nation treatment) and Article III (National Treatment), the Trade-Related Investment Measures, and the WTO Agreement on Subsidies and Countervailing Measures.[48] Indonesia therefore had to amend its automobile policy to bring it into conformity with WTO disciplines. Indeed, as with any such industrial policy, the predispute policy was prone to criticism as an inefficient development policy.[49] The role of government intervention in development presents a legitimate controversy in development economics. What is important to note, for present purposes, is that in the WTO such "constraining development disputes" are adjudicated strictly under international trade disciplines, without addressing the core question of the development effect of the measure and policy under review.[50]

47 See Alisa DiCaprio and Kevin P. Gallagher, "The WTO and the Shrinking of Development Space: How Big Is the Bite?" (2006) 7(5) *Journal of World Investment and Trade* 795.

48 See WTO, *Indonesia – Certain Measures Affecting the Automotive Industry*, WT/DS54, 55, 59, 64 (Panel Report, July 2, 1998).

49 See Haryo Aswicahyono, "How Not to Industrialize? Indonesia's Automotive Industry" (2000) 36(1) *Bulletin of Indonesian Economic Studies* 209.

50 Indeed, in *Indonesia-Autos*, Indonesia invoked some SDT provisions, but these arguments were rejected by the panel. In any case, the panel did not conduct (and to be sure, would not conduct, under prevalent readings of WTO jurisdictional rules and practice) any analysis of the development impact of Indonesia's policy.

B. *Enabling Development Disputes: Challenges to Members' Measures Constraining the Economic Development Policy of Other Members*

These are cases in which a WTO member (typically a developed country) has taken unilateral action targeting an element of another WTO member's economic development policy (typically that of a developing country), and the latter tries to push back through WTO dispute settlement. If the complaint is successful, the removal of the measure therefore enables the development policy of the complaining member.

Disputes in this category are relatively rare for two reasons. First, they are a priori limited to cases in which a WTO member may take unilateral action under WTO rules (in goods, these are primarily countervailing duties, or in some cases, safeguard measures or antidumping duties); second, they often require initiation of the complaint by a developing country, the legal capacity of which might be insufficient.

An example of an enabling development dispute is South Korea's struggle against countervailing measures on Dynamic Random Access Memory Semiconductors (DRAMS) imposed by both the United States and the European Union. Korea's support for its DRAMS industry has been a strategic element of its postindustrial technological policy since the 1990s.[51] Korea's policy has met with resistance in the form of antidumping measures and countervailing duties in the United States and the European Union, both of which have given rise to WTO disputes.[52] By finding that some EU and U.S. measures were WTO-inconsistent, the WTO dispute settlement system largely enabled the continuation of Korea's relevant economic development policy. However, it is noteworthy that the fundamental questions of permissible economic development were not at issue in these cases, but rather, at least primarily, it was the arcane technicalities of countervailing duty procedures and their imposition.[53]

Another example, in trade in services, can be found in the *US-Gambling* dispute.[54] Like other Caribbean states, Antigua and Barbuda encouraged liberalization of Internet gaming based in its territory with the goal of economic development and

51 See Cheng-Fen Chen and Graham Sewell, "Strategies for Technological Development in South Korea and Taiwan: The Case of Semiconductors" (1996) 25(5) *Research Policy* 759. For an economic justification of this extended "learning period," see Staffan Jacobsson, "The Length of the Infant Industry Period: Evidence from the Engineering Industry in South Korea"(1993) 21(3) *World Development* 407.

52 WT/DS99 *United States – Anti-Dumping Duty on Dynamic Random Access Memory Semiconductors (DRAMS) of One Megabit or Above from Korea*; WT/DS296 *United States – Countervailing Duty Investigation on DRAMS from Korea*; WT/DS299 *European Communities – Countervailing Duties Measures on DRAM Chips from Korea*; WT/DS336 *United States – Countervailing Duties on DRAMs from Korea*.

53 See also Dukgeun Ahn, "Korea in the GATT/WTO Dispute Settlement System: Legal Battle for Economic Development" (2003) 6(3) *Journal of International Economic Law* 597.

54 See WTO Appellate Body Report, *US – Measures Affecting the Cross-Border Supply of Gambling and Betting Services*, WT/DS285/AB/R (April 7, 2005).

diversification.[55] The enforcement by the United States (and some of its constituent states) of restrictive gaming laws threatened to disrupt this developmental impact. Antigua's complaint, often seen through the technical prism of services classification and substantive rules[56] or the important question of public morals exceptions to trade liberalization,[57] may therefore also be seen as a development dispute.

C. *Defensive Development Disputes: Challenges to Members' Measures Harmful to the Economic Development of Other Members, in Particular, Developing Countries*

In defensive development disputes, measures taken by one WTO member produce externalities that harm or impede another WTO member's economic development. The developmental focus here is not the policy of the complainant, but the effects – or externalities – of the respondent's policy on the economic development (and alleviation of poverty, as the case may be) of the complainant. Characteristic cases deal with import restrictions imposed by developed countries that deny market access to goods from developing countries in sectors that are crucial to the economic well-being of the latter; subsidies granted to producers in developed countries that suppress world prices and compete unfairly with products from developed countries; and preferences granted by developed countries that discriminate among different developing countries. The following are examples of such defensive development disputes:

- WT/DS27EC – *Regime for the Importation, Sale and Distribution of Bananas* (and related disputes)
- WT/DS33 *US – Measures Affecting Imports of Woven Wool Shirts and Blouses from India*
- WT/DS231 *EC – Trade Description of Sardines*
- WT/DS246 *EC – Conditions for the Granting of Tariff Preferences to Developing Countries*
- WT/DS263,266, 283 *EC – Export Subsidies on Sugar*
- WT/DS267 *US – Subsidies on Upland Cotton*

The "poster child" of this category of disputes is, without a doubt, the *US-Cotton* dispute, in which Brazil challenged U.S. subsidies for cotton producers, with the effect of depressing world prices and denying competitive advantages from Brazil and other developing cotton producers. Notably, the legal focus in cases of this type

55 See Mark Wilson, "Chips, Bits and the Law: An Economic Geography of Internet Gambling" (2003) 35(7) *Environment and Planning* 1245

56 See Joost Pauwelyn, "*Rien ne Va Plus?* Distinguishing Domestic Regulation from Market Access in GATT and GATS"(2005) 4 *World Trade Review* 131.

57 See, e.g., Jeremy C. Marwell, "Trade and Morality: The WTO Public Morals Exception after Gambling" (2006) 81 *New York University Law Review* 802.

is not on the respondent's compliance with trade rules. The effects of its policies on the economic development of the respondent are considered only insofar as they constitute an element of the violation, for example, the question of "serious prejudice" in subsidies cases.[58]

D. *Sustainable Development Disputes: Challenges to Sustainable Development Policies of Members as WTO-Inconsistent*

This special category of development disputes shows most clearly that disputes over development are not the exclusive domain of developing countries. At times, the environmental policy of a developed country comes into conflict with the economic development needs of a developing country; at other times, it is the sustainable development policy of a developing country that is under scrutiny. Examples of sustainable development disputes in the WTO include the following:

- WT/DS332 *Brazil – Measures Affecting Imports of Retreaded Tyres*
- WT/DS58 *US – Import Prohibition of Certain Shrimp and Shrimp Products*
- WT/DS2 *US – Standards for Reformulated and Conventional Gasoline*

Importantly, in some of these disputes WTO adjudicators have taken into account sustainable development considerations.[59] This may be attributed to the specific toeholds relating to sustainable development in the WTO agreements themselves (such as in the Preamble to the Agreement establishing the WTO, and Article XX(g) GATT) and to the existence of "hard," non-WTO sources of sustainable development law, such as the Convention on International Trade in Endangered Species.[60]

V. ASSESSING THE IMPACT OF DEVELOPMENT DISPUTES IN THE WTO

In trade circles, one often hears the truism that "the WTO is not a development organization."[61] The stagnant so-called Doha Development Round makes this abundantly clear; the WTO is not providing an effective negotiating environment conducive to development concerns. Nevertheless, the WTO and its members cannot avoid the inconvenient truth: much of what it actually does in the trade arena relates strongly to development. Focusing on the concept of development disputes elaborated on in this chapter suggests that a large proportion of WTO disputes that are

58 See *US-Cotton* (2005), supra note 31, p. 146 et seq.

59 Particularly in WT/DS58/AB/R *US – Import Prohibition of Certain Shrimp and Shrimp Products*, para. 129 et seq.

60 Ibid.

61 See, e.g., "Trade, Poverty and the Human Face of Globalization," Speech by WTO Director-General Mike Moore, June 16, 2000, available at: http://www.wto.org/english/news_e/spmm_e/spmm32_e.htm.

ostensibly about the enforcement of trade rules are actually "about" development and the perennial question, "how to develop?"

Yet despite the subdued prominence of development issues in WTO disputes, the WTO dispute settlement system regularly treats development disputes of all kinds as if they were simply run-of-the-mill trade disputes driven by regular political economy factors relating to international competitiveness. Thus, issues that should properly be classified as fundamental differences over development policy are dealt with through technical rules of international trade that pay only lip service to development concerns. At best, development is promoted indirectly, when trade disciplines coincide with a development cause, as in the *US-Cotton* case. At worst, this dissonance may result in severe restrictions of development policy space that is necessary at the national level, as in some of the "constraining development disputes" discussed earlier.

The standard responses to this state of affairs have, so far, been calls to make WTO dispute settlement friendlier to developing countries or to revise substantive WTO law to make it more amenable to development concerns. Neither of these approaches, however well motivated, has so far amounted to much, and thus development disputes continue to be adjudicated by the WTO dispute settlement system (and in other tribunals or institutional systems) despite its insensitivity to their development aspect, in a way that is ultimately detrimental to the legitimacy of the WTO, and the contribution of the resultant jurisprudence to the evolution of international development law is scattered and easily distinguished, almost *ad nullum*.

In these circumstances, it seems appropriate to ask whether development disputes should not be treated differently. States have agreed to trade disciplines, but there is little agreement on fundamental principles of development policy. Perhaps it would be better for development, developing countries, and the WTO itself, if "development disputes" as discussed here were recognized as disputes that can also be settled by softer means, such as good offices, mediation, or conciliation, and not through rules-based adjudication, the rules of which do not address the developmental heart of the disputes. The potential advantages of such recourse to alternative dispute resolution, as well as the methods to be pursued, need to be carefully considered and will be left for another chapter. Moreover, it would perhaps be through such a process, and the practices that it would spawn, that development law – a genuine law of development, not simply trade-related development law or investment-related development law, would truly emerge.

REFERENCES

Abi-Saab, Georges, "Wither the International Community?" (1998) 9 *European Journal of International Law*.

Ahn, Dukgeun, "Korea in the GATT/WTO Dispute Settlement System: Legal Battle for Economic Development" (2003) 6(3) *Journal of International Economic Law*.

Aswicahyono, Haryo, "How Not to Industrialize? Indonesia's Automotive Industry" (2000) 36(1) *Bulletin of Indonesian Economic Studies*.

Broude, Tomer, "The Rule(s) of Trade and the Rhetos of Development: Reflections on the Functional and Aspirational Legitimacy of the WTO" (2006) 27(4) *Columbia Journal of Transnational Law*.

Bulajić, Milan, *Principles of International Development Law* (2nd rev. ed., Dordrecht: Martinus Nijhoff Publishers, 1993).

Busch, Marc L., and Eric Reinhardt, "Developing Countries and GATT/WTO Dispute Settlement" (2003) 37(4) *Journal of World Trade*.

Chen, Cheng-Fen, and Graham Sewell, "Strategies for Technological Development in South Korea and Taiwan: The Case of Semiconductors" (1996) 25(5) *Research Policy*.

DiCaprio, Alisa, and Kevin P. Gallagher, "The WTO and the Shrinking of Development Space: How Big Is the Bite?" (2006) 7(5) *Journal of World Investment and Trade*.

French, Duncan, "Developing States and International Environmental Law: The Importance of Differentiated Responsibilities" (2000) 49 *International and Comparative Law Quarterly*.

García-Amador, Francisco V., *The Emerging International Law of Development: A New Dimension of International Economic Law* (New York: Oceana, 1990).

Hoekman, Bernard, "Operationalizing the Concept of Policy Space in the WTO: Beyond Special and Differential Treatment" (2005) 8(2) *Journal of International Economic Law*.

Hudec, Robert E., *Developing Countries in the GATT/WTO Legal System*, Chantal Thomas and Joel Trachtman, eds. (New York: Oxford University Press, 2009; 1st ed., 1987).

International Center for Trade and Sustainable Development, "Brazil Slams EU for Seizure of Generic Drugs," February 4, 2009, available at: http://ictsd.org/i/news/bridgesweekly/39772.

Jacobsson, Staffan, "The Length of the Infant Industry Period: Evidence from the Engineering Industry in South Korea" (1993) 21(3) *World Development*.

Kenig-Witkowska, Maria Magdalena, "Development Ideology in International Law," in Subrata Roy Chowdhury, Erik M. G. Denters, and Paul J. I. M. de Waart (eds.), *The Right to Development in International Law* (Dordrecht: Martinus Nijhoff Publishers, 1992).

Kwakwa, Edward, "Emerging International Development Law and Traditional International Law: Congruence or Cleavage?" (1987) 17 *Georgia Journal of International and Comparative Law*.

Lavranos, Nikolaos, "The Epilogue in the MOX Plant Dispute: An End without Findings" (2009) *European Energy and Environmental Law Review*.

Marks, Stephen P., "The Human Rights Framework for Development: Seven Approaches," in Arjun Sengupta, Archna Negi, and Moushumi Basu (eds.), *Reflections on the Right to Development* (New Delhi: Sage Publications India, 2005).

Marwell, Jeremy C., "Trade and Morality: The WTO Public Morals Exception after Gambling" (2006) 81 *New York University Law Review*.

Mitchell, Andrew D., and Tania Voon, "Operationalizing Special and Differential Treatment in the WTO: Game Over?" (2009) 15 *Global Governance*.

Moore, Mike, "Trade, Poverty and the Human Face of Globalization," WTO Director-General speech, June 16, 2000, available at: http://www.wto.org/english/news_e/spmm_e/spmm32_e.htm.

Orellana, Marcos, "The EU and Chile Suspend the Swordfish Case Proceedings at the WTO and ITLOS," *ASIL Insights*, February 2001, available at: http://www.asil.org/insigh60.cfm.

Pauwelyn, Joost, "*Rien ne Va Plus*? Distinguishing Domestic Regulation from Market Access in GATT and GATS" (2005) 4 *World Trade Review*.

Rodrik, Dani, *One Economics, Many Recipes: Globalization, Institutions and Economic Growth* (Princeton, NJ: Princeton University Press, 2007).

Schachter, Oscar, "The Evolving International law of Development" (1976) 15 *Columbia Journal of Transnational Law*.

Schrijver, Nico, and Friedl Weiss (eds.), *International Law and Sustainable Development: Principles and Practice* (Dordrecht: Martinus Nijhoff Publishers, 2004).

Sen, Amartya, *Development as Freedom* (Oxford: Oxford University Press, 2001).

Shaffer, Gregory, "Can WTO Technical Assistance and Capacity Building Serve Developing Countries?" (2005) 23 *Wisconsin International Law Journal*.

Shaffer, Gregory, and Mark A. Pollack, "Hard vs. Soft Law: Alternatives, Complements and Antagonists in International Governance" (2010) 94 *Minnesota Law Review*.

Stiglitz, Joseph E., *Making Globalization Work* (New York: W. W. Norton, 2006).

Verdirame, Guglielmo, "Definition of Developing Countries under the GATT and other International Law" (1996) 39 *German Yearbook of International Law*.

Wilson, Mark, "Chips, Bits and the Law: An Economic Geography of Internet Gambling" (2003) 35(7) *Environment and Planning*.

World Bank, *Accountability at the Bank: The Inspection Panel at 15 Years* (Washington, DC: World Bank, 2009).

3

Intellectual Property Rights, Trade, and Economic Development

Bryan Mercurio

I. INTRODUCTION

Governments and scholars have for some time grappled with the question of whether there is a connection between intellectual property (IP) and economic development, and if so, how strong the link is.[1] Economic literature is equivocal, with some studies concluding that the connection is strong while others conclude it to be fairly weak (and that there may not even be a connection for least developed countries [LDCs]).[2] What is clear is that countries have historically shaped and amended their IP regimes to promote domestic needs and objectives.[3] It is also clear that several countries with weak IP policies have achieved rapid economic growth and development over the past five decades. For these countries, the strengthening of IP rights (IPRs) occurred after the initial stages of increased growth and development. These countries include the majority of the first generation of newly industrializing economies, including Korea and Taiwan, and other developing nations, such as Brazil, India, and Malaysia.[4] The Japanese developmental experience is similar,

[1] Maskus summarizes the evidence linking IP rights to economic development as "complex and difficult to measure," having an "absence of definitive results," and notes that they "may be interpreted in various ways." Keith E. Maskus, "Incorporating a Globalized Intellectual Property Rights Regime into an Economic Development Strategy," in Keith Maskus (ed.), *Intellectual Property, Growth and Trade* (Oxford: Elsevier, 2008), p. 500. See also Carsten Fink and Keith E. Maskus (eds.), *Intellectual Property and Development: Lessons from Recent Economic Research* (Washington, DC: World Bank, 2004).

[2] See, e.g., Keith E. Maskus, *Intellectual Property Rights in the Global Economy* (Washington, DC: Institute for International Economics, 2000), p. 169; Maskus (2008), supra note 1, pp. 498–499; Judith Chin and Gene Grossman, *Intellectual Property Rights and North–South Trade*, NBER Working Paper (Cambridge, MA: National Bureau of Economic Research, 1998), available at: http://www.nber.org.

[3] For an economic examination of the history of patent protection, see Josh Lerner, *Patent Protection and Innovation over 150 Years*, NBER Working Paper 8977 (Cambridge, MA: National Bureau of Economic Research, 2002), available at: http://www.nber.org/papers/w8977.

[4] See Chin and Grossman, supra note 2, p. 1 (FN 2) and 5; Commission on Intellectual Property Rights (CIPR), *Integrating Intellectual Property Rights and Development Policy* (London, 2002), p. 20,

with the nation quickly developing in the 1960s and 1970s and only adopting strong IPRs protection in the 1980s.[5] Even the United States, now one of the strongest proponents of strong IP protection, did not fully embrace high levels of IP protection until the early 1980s.[6]

This is unsurprising, because it is well known that countries adopt stronger, broader IPRs as they develop from lower- to higher-income countries.[7] This is not to say that IP laws do not assist development.[8] One of the more recent economic studies found that increased IPRs lead to lower prices (by shifting production to lower-cost locations), higher real wages in developing countries, and potentially increased industrial capacity in developing countries through the introduction of advanced technologies.[9] It is also well known that countries failing to protect IP adequately

available at: http://cipr.org.uk/papers/pdfs/final_report/CIPR_Exec_Sumfinal.pdf; Nagesh Kumar, *Intellectual Property Rights, Technology and Economic Development: Experiences of Asian Countries*, RIS Discussion Paper 25/2002, especially pp. 22–23 (Korea), pp. 23–24 (Taiwan); Claudio Frischtak, *The Protection of Intellectual Property Rights and Industrial Technology Development in Brazil*, World Bank, Industry and Energy Working Papers No. 13 (1989); Roberto Mazzoleni and Luciano Martins Costa Póvoa, "Accumulation of Technological Capabilities and Economic Development: Did Brazil's Regime of Intellectual Property Rights Matter?" in Hiroyuki Odagiri, Akira Goto, Atsushi Sunami, and Richard R. Nelson (eds.), *Intellectual Property Rights, Development, and Catch-Up* (Oxford: Oxford University Press, 2010); Lim Heng Gee, Ida Madieha bt Abdul Ghani Azmi, and Rokiah Alavi, *Impact of the Intellectual Property System on Economic Growth: Fact-Finding Surveys and Analysis in the Asian Region Country Report – Malaysia* (undated), World Intellectual Property Association (WIPO)–United Nations University Joint Research Project, available at: http://www.wipo.int/export/sites/www/about-ip/en/studies/pdf/wipo_unu_07_malaysia.pdf.

5 See Janusz A. Ordover, "A Patent System for Both Diffusion and Exclusion" (1991) 5(1) *Journal of Economic Perspectives* 43; Kumar, supra note 4, pp. 20–21.

6 Throughout much of the nineteenth century, U.S. patents and copyright were restricted to U.S. nationals and remained unduly restrictive to foreigners well into the twentieth century. See CIPR, supra note 4, p. 18. Reichman summarizes: "until 1982, the United States had one of the developed world's most precompetitive patent laws (i.e., least protective); until 1978, it had relatively weak copyright laws; and until the 1980s, it had an aggressively interventionist competition law along with a robust doctrine of patent misuse." Jerome H. Reichman, "Intellectual Property in the Twenty-First Century: Will the Developing Countries Lead or Follow?" (2009) 46 *Houston Law Review* 1116.

7 See, e.g., Maskus (2008), supra note 1, pp. 503–504; Maskus (2000), supra note 2, pp. 102–109. For a case study on Taiwan's IP and development, see Yao-Jen Liu and Shang-Jyh Liu, "The Intellectual Property Policy of Taiwan: A Strategic Viewpoint" (2004) *Proceedings of the 2004 IEEE International* 42. Studies have also demonstrated that the significance of IPRs increase with the economic development of a nation. See Richard Rapp and Richard Rozek, "Benefits and Costs of Intellectual Property Protection in Developing Countries" (1990) 24(5) *Journal of World Trade* (1990), 75 (linking economic development to patent protection as a result of increased investment and innovation). See also David M. Gould and William C. Gruben, "The Role of Intellectual Property Rights in Economic Growth" (1996) 48 *Journal of Development Economics* 323.

8 McDorman states: "[t]he problem is that it is unclear whether industrialization precedes, or follows, intellectual property protection." Ted L. McDorman, "U.S.–Thailand Trade Disputes: Applying Section 301 to Cigarettes and Intellectual Property" (1992–1993) 14 *Michigan Journal of International Law* 90, at 117.

9 Lee Branstetter and Kamal Saggi, *Intellectual Property Rights, Foreign Direct Investment and Industrial Development*, NBER Working Paper 15393 (Cambridge, MA: National Bureau of Economic Research, 2009) (finding stronger IPRs discourages imitators but that increased foreign direct investment more than offsets the losses, and increased purchasing power offsets losses as a result of higher prices). This

limit the upside of their economic development.[10] To maximize economic development, countries must align their laws with the prevailing international IP norms and standards. Bringing local laws in line with the international IP norms and standards contained in the Agreement on Trade-Related Aspects of Intellectual Property Rights (TRIPS Agreement) is, according to Professor Jerome H. Reichman, necessary to "reach the frontiers of [the knowledge economy], [and] convert their economies intangible, nonrivalrous outputs into tradeable knowledge goods."[11] Moreover, the experience of successful economic development since the 1960s demonstrates that IPRs are merely one contributing factor to economic growth along with other necessary factors, including governance, stability, agriculture and industrial policy, wider trade, competition, education, and health policies.[12]

Domestically implementing the obligations set out in the TRIPS Agreement provides stability, assists domestic inventors, and sends a positive signal to foreign investors. Of course, implementing TRIPS also has its downside – namely, forcing countries to pay a higher price for technology. Herein lies the dilemma, in which developing countries raise IP standards to fulfill international obligations and attract foreign investment[13] but at the same time potentially stifle economic, financial, and

study takes account of and directly contradicts earlier studies finding that stronger IPRs lead to an overall net welfare loss. See, e.g., Phillip McCalman, "Reaping What You Sow: An Empirical Analysis of International Patent Harmonization" (2001) 55 *Journal of International Economics* 161; Shubham Chaudhuri, Pinelopi K. Goldberg, and Panle Jia, "Estimating the Effects of Global Patent Protection in Pharmaceuticals: A Case Study of Quinolones in India" (2006) 96 *American Economic Review* 1477.

10 See Jonathan M. Barnett, "Property as Process: How Innovation Markets Select Innovation Regime" (2009) 119 *Yale Law Journal* 349.

11 Reichman (2009), see supra note 6, pp. 1115, 1118 (stressing the need not only for IPRs but also appropriate economic and political foundations).

12 See, e.g., Keith E. Maskus, "Intellectual Property Rights and Economic Development" (2000) 32 *Case Western Reserve Journal of International Law* 476–495 (reviewing the empirical literature and concluding that the limited evidence suggests that stronger IPRs promote economic growth and development, but only as "part of a coherent and broad set of complementary" trade, competition, and other economic policies). See also Bryan Mercurio, "Growth and Development: Economic and Legal Conditions" (2007) 30 *University of New South Wales Law Journal* 437.

13 It is often posited that there is a positive relationship between increased IPRs and investment and that exceedingly weak IP protection can even have a negative effect on investment on low-income countries. See, e.g., Organization for Economic Cooperation and Development, *Policy Framework for Investment: A Review of Good Practices* (2006), p. 72, available at: http://www.oecd.org/dataoecd/1/31/36671400.pdf; Bernard M. Hoekman, Keith E. Maskus, and Kamal Saggi, *Transfer of Technology to Developing Countries: Unilateral and Multilateral Policy Options*, World Bank Policy Research Working Paper No. 3332 (2004), available at: http://papers.ssrn.com/sol3/papers.cfm?abstract_id=610377; Vichai Ariyanuntaka, "Rethinking Intellectual Property Rights Enforcement in the Light of TRIPS and Specialized Intellectual Property Court in Thailand," paper presented at the Hong Kong-WIPO IPR Enforcement Symposium (June 1998), available at: http://www.malaysianbar.org.my/index.php?option=com_docman&task=doc_view&gid=133&Itemid=119; Maskus (2008), supra note 1, p. 505. For an overview of investment regulation in the WTO (including TRIPS), see Phillipe Gugler and Julien Chaisse, "Foreign Investment Issues in the WTO – Dealing with Fragmentation while Waiting for a Multilateral Framework" in Julien Chaisse and Tiziano Belmelli (eds.), *Essays on the Future of the World Trade Organization*, Vol. 1 (Geneva: Editions Interuniversitaires Suisses, 2008).

social development by increasing payments to the developed world for superior (and sometimes essential) technologies. Some argue that the "development dilemma"[14] is only a short-term problem and that developing countries that effectively cultivate and harness innovative strengths, abilities, and capacities will eventually be able to capitalize on the high level of protection granted in the TRIPS Agreement.[15] In fact, in combination with other factors, such as advantages relating to global competitiveness (i.e., location and availability of cheap labor), developing countries that successfully become technology innovators could in the future use the higher global IP standards to erode the technological comparative advantage of the developed world.[16]

This chapter thus argues that IP is critical to full-scale technological and economic development for developing countries. Linking IPRs and economic development is not often a popular perspective in developing countries.[17] However, it is clear that developing countries must now operate from the perspective of TRIPS being the minimum level of protection mandated by the international community – substantially deviating from the TRIPS standard is not a viable option. With IPRs and protection being raised in almost every free trade agreement (FTA) negotiated by developed countries, as well as through the negotiation of new multilateral treaties, such as the proposed Substantive Patent Law Treaty (SPLT) and the Anti-Counterfeiting Trade Agreement (ACTA),[18] the time is ripe for developing countries to revisit the role of IP and economic development. Countries must seek the answers to a number of questions: Have increased IPRs had an impact on poverty-reduction strategies? Have IPRs encouraged or led to increased growth? How have IPRs affected access to information, knowledge, education, and research? Is the IP policy coherent with other public policy issues, such as investment, public health, trade, and competition?

[14] Robert L. Osterard, Jr., *The Development Dilemma: The Political Economy of Intellectual Property Rights in the International System* (El Paso, TX: LFB Scholarly Publishing, 2003), p. 77.

[15] Reichman (2009), supra note 6, pp. 1119–1120.

[16] Ibid. A recent example is the United States relying on Asian technology to build high-speed rail networks because of a lack of local industrial capacity. See Joan Lowy, "Many High-Speed Rail Jobs Could Go to Foreign Companies with Fast-Train Experience," *Los Angeles Times*, January 28, 2010; Toh Han Shih, "GE Wants China's Fast-Rail Technology: Beijing May Supply the Skills to Fulfil Obama's Dream of High-Speed Network across US," *South China Morning Post*, February 17, 2010, p. A1.

[17] It should thus be made clear at the outset that this chapter does not treat all "developing countries" including least developed countries (LDCs) equally. This chapter does not advocate a one-size-fits-all strategy; instead, the discussion and analysis contained in this article recognizes technological differences between "developing" countries and therefore is more so aimed at upper-middle-income developing countries such as India and China as well as those in Southeast Asia and parts of Central and South America. For an interesting analysis of the issue of differentiating between developing countries in IP and development, see Shamnad Basheer and Annalisa Primi, "The WIPO Development Agenda: Factoring in the 'Technically Proficient' Developing Countries," in Jeremy de Beer (ed.), *Implementing the World Intellectual Property Organization's Development Agenda* (Waterloo, Canada: Wilfrid Laurier University Press, 2009).

[18] See WIPO, *Substantive Patent Law Harmonization Law*, available at: http://www.wipo.int/patent-law/en/harmonization.htm.

The chapter is structured as follows: Section II briefly traces the internationalization of IP, particularly focusing on both the transition from the treatiies administered by the World Intellectual Property Organization (WIPO) to the WTO TRIPS Agreement and on the consistent effort of some nations to raise international IP standards, predominantly through FTAs. Section III questions whether developing countries should continue following the policies of developed countries. It calls on developing countries to create an IP and development framework that adequately balances the needs of users and innovators. Focusing on patents, the section offers several suggestions to assist in the development of the framework.[19] Section IV concludes with the recommendation that developing countries not only resist pressures to surrender the right to use the flexibilities built into the TRIPS Agreement but also to explore and better utilize the flexibilities in a manner that allows IPRs to be part of a broader developmental framework.

II. INTERNATIONALIZATION OF INTELLECTUAL PROPERTY

The internationalization of IP law, regulation, and policy began in the eighteenth and nineteenth centuries, when IPRs appeared in Friendship, Commerce and Navigation (FCN) treaties.[20] The multilateralization of international IP quickly followed in the latter part of the nineteenth century through the negotiation and adoption of two important treaties – the Paris Convention for the Protection of Industrial Property (1883) and the Berne Convention for the Protection of Literary and Artistic Works (1886). Importantly, both treaties multilateralized the principles of national treatment and most favored nation (MFN) to signatory states. In addition, the treaties introduced certain minimum standards and other regulations that increased certainty and predictability to the IP community. Both treaties, however, merely serve as a framework for developing IP policy. Signatories retained wide scope to draft and implement their own laws. Moreover, despite providing for recourse to the International Court of Justice (ICJ) in the event of a dispute, the treaties lacked a true dispute settlement and enforcement mechanism (there has never been a dispute filed with the ICJ). Thus, despite the conclusion of both treaties, IPRs and protection varied widely between countries.

Developing country involvement in the Paris and Berne Conventions was limited, and it was not until the mid-twentieth century that developing countries began

[19] Other areas of IP are equally important to development (i.e., trademark and its effect on FDI and licensing of production and distribution rights; copyright and its effect on local cultural activities; access to information and educational needs; and the protection of geographic indications) but are not discussed in this chapter because of space considerations.

[20] A 1778 FCN between France and the United States is reputed to be the first such treaty. M. Sornarajah, *The International Law on Foreign Investment* (Cambridge: Cambridge University Press, 2004), p. 209. See also Daniel J. Gervais, "The Internationalization of Intellectual Property: New Challenges from the Very Old and the Very New" (2002) 12 *Fordham Intellectual Property, Media and Entertainment Law Journal*.

influencing the direction of international IPRs protection. This, of course, is not surprising because many developing countries only became fully independent, decolonized nation-states in the decades following the Second World War. As part of an ambitious independence strategy stressing self-reliance and the creation of a "New International Economic Order" (NIEO), developing countries sought to influence the system to suit their own particular developmental priorities.[21] These countries not only sought greater access for their goods in the world market but also greater access to the goods and services of developed countries in the form of aid and assistance to develop industrial capacity. In terms of IP, developing countries stressed the need for transfers of technology from the developed world and liberal use of compulsory licenses to promote local production of goods. Although it was thought that such policies would counter monopoly prices and lead to greater economic development, in reality, many developing countries were left with even more expensive, inferior products and several inefficient industries operating without the threat of competition. Public health declined, educational needs remained unmet, and shortages of basic necessities (as well as luxuries) were commonplace.

The developing-country resurgence did produce some results internationally and certainly influenced the future direction of international IP. For instance, the Stockholm Protocol of 1967 (revising the Berne Convention) contained special rights for developing countries, including special reservations regarding translations, reproduction, broadcasting, and educational use of copyrighted works.[22] Developing countries also repeatedly pressed for the revision of the Paris Convention, but their efforts were less successful because developed countries refused to agree to the demands.[23]

At the same time, developed countries began to realize that their economic future lay not in industrial production but in advancement through information, knowledge, and intellectual creation. With the development of burgeoning technologies (i.e., the invention of the computer and satellite technology) and the emergence

[21] For more on NIEO, see Jagdish N. Bhagwati (ed.), *The New International Economic Order: The North–South Debate* (Cambridge, MA: MIT Press, 1977); M. P. Rao, *The "New International Economic Order"* (2004); Robert Looney, "New International Economic Order," in *Routledge Encyclopedia of International Political Economy* (1999), available at: http://www.chicagobooth.edu/faculty/selectedpapers/sp49.pdf.

[22] See, generally, Sam Ricketson, *The Berne Convention for the Protection of Literary and Artistic Works: 1886–1986* (London: Centre for Commercial Law Studies, Queen Mary College, 1987). The copyright interests in developed countries, however, opposed the amendments and through successful lobbying essentially rendered the adopted Stockholm Protocol ineffective – most developed countries failed to ratify the Protocol.

[23] See, for instance, developing-country efforts at the Diplomatic Conference on the Revision of the Paris Convention in 1980, 1981, and 1984, available at: http://www.wipo.int/mdocsarchives/AB_XV_1984/P_A_IX_1_E.pdf. See also Paul S. Haar, "Revision of the Paris Convention: A Realignment of Private and Public Interests in the International Patent System" (1982) 8 *Brooklyn Journal of International Law*; Regina A. Loughran, "United States Position on Revising the Paris Convention: Quid Pro Quo or Denunciation" (1982) 5 *Fordham International Law Journal* 411; Susan K. Sell, "Intellectual Property as a Trade Issue: From the Paris Convention to GATT" (1989) 13 *Legal Studies Forum* 407.

of the knowledge economy on the horizon, developed countries recognized that to exploit innovative advantages fully, stronger laws were necessary to avoid misappropriation through counterfeiting and piracy. Of course, stronger domestic laws would do little to combat misappropriation outside of a nation's territorial borders, and with international agreements not designed for or capable of providing the desired level of protection, developed countries began acting unilaterally and seeking an alternative forum to address IP policies.

The United States first began unilaterally enforcing IPRs by virtue of the authority of the United States Trade Representative (USTR) under Section 301 of the U.S. Trade Act of 1974.[24] More specifically, the United States initiated litigation against other countries in the U.S. Court of International Trade (USITC) under its domestic unfair trade practices laws, even though the respondent countries had not violated any international agreement. The United States filed cases against several developing countries – most notably Brazil, Argentina, India, China, and Taiwan – and extracted concessions from the respondents in a number of cases.[25] In doing so, it effectively promoted the linkage of IP and international trade.

At the same time, the United States (and other developed countries) sought to provide multilateral backing to their efforts by directly linking IP protection to international trade. These countries based their arguments for the direct linkage on the fact that a country with weak or otherwise insufficient IP protection engages in unfair competition because it can benefit through the cheap production and sale of fake and counterfeited goods. This, in turn, could drive the costlier original goods out of the market. Developed countries also attempted to convince developing country governments that effective IP protection would lead to substantial gains through

[24] Section 301–310 of the Trade Act of 1974 (P.L. 93–618) authorizes the U.S. president to take all appropriate action (including retaliation) to obtain the removal of any foreign government act, policy, or practice that violates an international trade agreement or is unjustified, unreasonable, or discriminatory and that burdens or restricts U.S. commerce. The USTR and/or interested firms and industries can initiate Section 301 investigations. See Jasper Womach, *Agriculture: A Glossary of Terms, Programs, and Laws*, Congressional Research Service Report for Congress (2005), p. 230. See also Report of the Panel, *United States – Section 301–310 of the Trade Act of 1974*, WT/DS152/R (December 22, 1999). In 1988, the United States created Special 301 to examine and identify the "adequacy and effectiveness of intellectual property rights" in other countries. If problems exist, countries are monitored and can be categorized as a "Priority Foreign Country" or included in the "Watch List" or "Priority Watch List."

[25] Alan O. Sykes, "TRIPS, Pharmaceuticals, Developing Countries, and the Doha 'Solution,'" (2002) 3(1) *Chicago Journal of International Law* 47n10; Alan O. Sykes, "Constructive Unilateral Threats in International Commercial Relations: The Limited Case for Section 301" (1992) 23 *Law & Policy in International Business* 318–19. Likewise, and partly in response to the United States' provision, the European Economic Community (EEC) adopted Council Regulation 2641/84 to counter "illicit" trade practices against European exporters. For more detailed information, see Wolfgang W. Leirer, "Retaliatory Action in United States and European Union Trade Law: A Comparison of Section 301 of the Trade Act of 1974 and Council Regulation 2641/84" (1994) 20 *North Carolina Journal of International Law & Commercial Regulation* 41. The EEC repealed the regulation upon the creation of the WTO. See Council Regulation 3286/94, available at: http://eur-lex.europa.eu/LexUriServ/LexUriServ.do?uri=CONSLEG:1994R3286:20080305:EN:PDF.

increased investment, which would provide jobs, technology, and necessary foreign currency (i.e., the export of goods would improve balance of payment issues).

In seeking to include IP as a negotiating topic in the Uruguay Round of trade negotiations, the United States and other developed countries used the carrot-and-stick approach to achieve the objective of improving the global system of intellectual property protection. The stick came as a threat of continued unilateral action that could potentially threaten the trade and aid flowing from developed countries to the developing world.[26] The carrot for negotiating and agreeing to the inclusion of IP in the Uruguay Round were concessions in other trade areas, notably increased access to developed country agriculture and textiles markets.[27] Developing countries were also granted several important TRIPS-related concessions, most notably deferred implementation of the substantial portions of the agreement and in promises of technology transfer and assistance.[28] After initial opposition, developing country objections waned, and attention turned to negotiating the agreement.[29]

The resulting compromise, the TRIPS Agreement, is comprehensive in coverage and includes seven sectors of IPRs (i.e., copyright and related rights, trademarks, geographic indications, industrial designs, patents, layout designs of integrated circuits, protection of undisclosed information).[30] Like other covered agreements,

[26] In 1992, the United States first implemented sanctions and withdrew Generalized System of Preferences concessions on Indian pharmaceutical products. Michael Blakeley, *Trade-Related Aspects of Intellectual Property Rights: A Concise Guide to the TRIPS Agreement* (Sweet & Maxwell, 1996), p. 6. Developing country opposition to the inclusion of IPRs into the General Agreement on Tariffs and Trade weakened as the United States continued to threaten and implement Section 301 and Special 301 sanctions. This is especially true of larger developing countries, notably Brazil and Korea. Perhaps more important, continued use of the unilateral retaliatory measures prevented the formation of effective coalitions against IPRs as a negotiating topic. Duncan Matthews, *Globalising Intellectual Property Rights: The TRIPS Agreement* (Oxford: Routledge, 2002), p. 33. The "stick" of Special 301 thus succeeded in convincing developing countries to adopt higher levels of domestic IP protection in exchange for continued preferential access to the U.S. market. See ibid.

[27] See, i.e., Esperanza Durán and Constantine Michalopoulos, "Intellectual Property Rights and Developing Countries in the WTO Millennium Round" (1999) 2 *Journal of World Intellectual Property* 853, and Christopher May and Susan K. Sell, *Intellectual Property Rights: A Critical History* (Boulder, CO: Lynne Rienner Publishers, 2005).

[28] The benefits of the concessions are debated. See, e.g., Duncan Matthews and Viviana Munoz-Tellez, "Bilateral Technical Assistance and TRIPS: The United States, Japan and the European Communities in Comparative Perspective" (2006) 9 *Journal of World Intellectual Property* 629; Timothy P. Trainer, "Intellectual Property Enforcement: A Reality Gap (Insufficient Assistance, Ineffective Implementation)?" (2008) 8 *John Marshall Review of Intellectual Property Law* 47.

[29] Matthews, supra note 26, chaps. 1 (origins) and 2 (negotiations). For more detailed background on the TRIPS Agreement, see Susan Sell, *Power and Ideas: North–South Politics of Intellectual Property and Antitrust* (Albany: State University of New York Press, 1998).

[30] TRIPS also requires Members to provide for the protection of plant varieties, either by patent or an effective sui generis system such as the plant breeder's rights established in the International Union for the Protection of New Varieties of Plants convention.

the basis of TRIPS is MFN and national treatment (NT). The TRIPS also establishes minimum levels of protection and enforcement provisions. In formulating minimum standards, TRIPS incorporates the substantive obligations of the Paris and Berne Conventions and certain provisions of the Treaty on Intellectual Property in Respect of Integrated Circuits, and the Rome Convention. In addition, TRIPS also sets standards in areas that were either not addressed in or, according to Members, were not sufficiently covered in the WIPO Agreements. The fact that the TRIPS Agreement favors larger, IP-exporting countries is well known.[31] What is now also clear is that developed countries did not achieve all that they sought in the Uruguay Round and that they are now attempting to raise the standards through bilateral or regional FTAs or through regime shifting (and forum shopping) at the multilateral level.

The TRIPS Agreement facilitates such attempts to raise minimum IP standards by allowing Members to apply higher levels of IP protection as long as the principles of MFN and NT are respected. Not only does this allow countries to adopt higher standards of protection domestically, it also allows them to negotiate for higher standards in FTAs and other forums (so called TRIPS-Plus). Furthermore, as the MFN clause in TRIPS (Article 4) states that any Member that grants "any advantage, favour, privilege or immunity" to the nationals of *any* other country must accord the same treatment to the nationals of other TRIPS Members, TRIPS-Plus obligations assist in the process of recalculating and resetting international IP standards.[32] Unlike Article XXIV of the GATT, Article 4 operates in a relatively unqualified way and does not exempt FTAs from the operation of MFN. In other words, the principle of MFN applies to FTAs. Thus, if enough FTAs are negotiated containing similar TRIPS-Plus provisions, these provisions could become the new minimum standard from which any future WTO negotiating round proceeds.[33]

31 See, e.g., Jerome H. Reichman, "Securing Compliance with the TRIPS Agreement after U.S. v India" (1998) 1 *Journal of International Economic Law* 586 (stating that TRIPS represents "the standards of protection on which the industrial countries could agree among themselves"); Phillip McCalman, "Who Enjoys 'TRIPs' Abroad? An Empirical Analysis of Intellectual Property Rights in the Uruguay Round" (2005) 38 *Canadian Journal of Economics* 574. See also World Bank, *World Development Report 1998/99: Knowledge for Development*, which suggests developed countries would benefit more from TRIPS, with the United States receiving the biggest gains ($19 billion) and Korea incurring the biggest losses ($15 billion).

32 Peter Drahos coined the term "global ratchet" for IPRs. Peter Drahos, *Expanding Intellectual Property's Empire: the Role of FTAs* (2003), p. 7, available at: http://www.grain.org.

33 See ibid.; Bryan Mercurio, "TRIPS-Plus Provisions in Regional Trade Agreements," in Lorand Bartels and Federico Ortino (eds.), *Regional Trade Agreements and the WTO Legal System* (New York: Oxford University Press, 2006), pp. 215–238. See contra, Robert Burrell and Kimberlee Weatherall, "Exporting Controversy? Reactions to the Copyright Provisions of the U.S.–Australia Free Trade Agreement: Lessons for U.S. Trade Policy" (2008) 2 *University of Illinois Journal of Law, Technology and Policy* 310–316.

TRIPS-Plus provisions now appear in almost every comprehensive FTA involving a developed-country party and extend rights and protections in all areas of IP.[34] Provisions effecting IPRs also appear in bilateral investment treaties (BITs) and in other specialist multilateral agreements, most controversially the ACTA.[35] In most cases, these provisions restrict or eliminate flexibilities existing in the TRIPS Agreement.

This constant push for higher levels of international protection is, of course, driven by the corresponding push for higher levels of protection at the domestic level. The detriments to a continual increase in IPRs, however, have begun to effect leading IP exporters such as the United States and European Union. In fact, some in the developed world are now questioning whether these countries now harmfully overprotect IPRs in such a way that slows basic research, technological developments, and true innovation. This is especially true in the United States, where the courts have recently begun tightening patent standards.[36] The clearest evidence of this trend is in the Federal Court of Appeals decision in *In re Bilski*, which rejected claims for a patent involving a method of hedging risks in commodities trading and in so doing called into question the validity of the business method patent.[37] While awaiting the U.S. Supreme Court to rule on the matter,[38] U.S. courts applied the core holdings in *In re Bilski* to reject business method patents.[39] Another example

[34] See Michael Handler and Bryan Mercurio, "Intellectual Property," in Simon Lester and Bryan Mercurio (eds.). *Bilateral and Regional Trade Agreements: Commentary and Analysis* (Cambridge: Cambridge University Press, 2009).

[35] See Rosa Castro, "Intellectual Property Rights in Bilateral Investment Treaties" (2006) 9 *Journal of World Intellectual Property* 548; Susan K. Sell, *The Global IP Upward Ratchet, Anti-Counterfeiting and Piracy Enforcement Efforts: The State of Play* (2008), available at: http://twnside.org.sg/title2/intellectual_property/development.research/SusanSellfinalversion.pdf; Charles R. McManis, "The Proposed Anti-Counterfeiting Trade Agreement (ACTA): Two Tales of a Treaty" (2009) 46 *Houston Law Review* 1235.

[36] See, e.g., KSR *Int'l Co. v Teleflex Inc.* (No. 04-1350), 119 Fed. Appx. 282 (2007), which overruled the Federal Circuit's rigid approach and held that a claimed invention cannot be held "obvious" (and thus unpatentable under 35 U.S.C. § 103(a)) in the absence of some proven "teaching, suggestion, or motivation" that would have led a person of ordinary skill in the art to combine the relevant prior art teachings in the manner claimed.

[37] 545 F.3d 943, 88 U.S.P.Q.2d 1385 (Fed. Cir. 2008). Business method patents have flourished in the United States since the decision of *State Street Bank & Trust Co. v. Signature Financial Group, Inc.*, which held that a claimed invention was eligible for patent protection if it involved some practical application and "produces a useful, concrete and tangible result." *In re Bilski* rejected the useful-concrete-tangible test as "inadequate." See also *In re* Ferguson, which stated: "In *In re Bilski*, this court considered whether this 'test' is valid and useful and concluded that it is not."

[38] The Supreme Court issued its ruling on *Bilski v. Kappos* (Supreme Court 2010) (08–964) on June 28, 2010. The decision upheld the conclusion of the lower court that the invention was an unpatentable abstract idea but was narrow in scope and did not preclude the patentability of business methods as a general proposition. Thus, the longer-term effect of the decision is unclear, and lower courts are now forced to decide the issue of patentability on a case-by-case basis. For up-to-date analysis, see Bilski Blog, available at http://www.bilskiblog.com.

[39] See, e.g., *In re Ferguson* (upholding the U.S. Patent and Trademark Office [USPTO] rejection of a "paradigm," that is, a pattern for business marketing, as eligible for patent protection). See contra,

of a pullback in the United States can be seen by the U.S. Supreme Court decision in *eBay, Inc. v. MercExchange*, which overruled the long-standing position of the Federal Circuit Court that a permanent injunction should issue when a patent owner obtains a judgment of infringement, absent "exceptional circumstances" or in "rare instances" to protect the public interest.[40]

IP and development are at a crossroads; developing countries are struggling to formulate a coherent strategy that incorporates IPRs and advances developmental objectives. Developing countries are unsure whether and to what extent they should follow the developed world. In parts of Asia and Latin America, technological development is increasing, and intraregional trade is growing with each passing year. On one hand, these governments still desire (and need) foreign investment, not least for job creation, and a growing number of domestic innovator industries now clamor for higher IP standards. On the other hand, governments also desire increased technology transfers and "space" to enable them to "catch up" to the developed world.

Although many believe the TRIPS Agreement fails to account for the needs of developing countries,[41] the agreement is the international standard, and it is not going to disappear or undergo substantial revision.[42] Developing countries must therefore seek to position their laws and policies strategically to both abide by TRIPS and facilitate economic development. Section III provides a brief road map

the patent recently granted to the social networking Web site Facebook for its method for displaying a news feed in a social network environment. See *US Patent Zuckerberg, et al.* (February 23, 2010), available at: http://tacticalip.com/wp-content/uploads/2010/03/pat7669123.pdf.

40 *eBay Inc. v. MercExchange, L.L.C.*, 126 S. Ct. 1837 (2006). In so holding, the Supreme Court confirmed that the traditional four-factor test used to determine whether an injunction should issue whenever such relief remains relevant. The Court stated: "That test requires a plaintiff to demonstrate: (1) that it has suffered an irreparable injury; (2) that remedies available at law are inadequate to compensate for that injury; (3) that considering the balance of hardships between the plaintiff and defendant, a remedy in equity is warranted; and (4) that the public interest would not be disserved by a permanent injunction. The decision to grant or deny such relief is an act of equitable discretion by the district court, reviewable on appeal for abuse of discretion." The Court also held that an injunction should not be denied simply on the basis that the plaintiff does not practice the patented invention. Since the decision, federal district courts have denied more than 20% of the (once almost automatically granted) requests for permanent injunctions. The first post-*eBay* decision in which a permanent injunction was issued where the patent holder did not practice the invention is in *Commonwealth Scientific & Industrial Research Organisation v. Buffalo Technology, Inc.*, No. 6:06-324, 2007 U.S. Dist. Lexis 43832 (E.D. Tex. June 15, 2007).

41 See, e.g., Keith Maskus and Jerome H. Reichman, "The Globalization of Private Knowledge Goods and the Privatization of Global Public Goods" (2004) 7 *Journal of International Economic Law* 279–320; Carlos M. Correa, "Can the TRIPS Agreement Foster Technology Transfer to Developing Countries?" in Keith E. Maskus and Jerome H. Reichman (eds.), *International Public Goods and Transfer of Technology under a Globalized Intellectual Property Regime* (Cambridge: Cambridge University Press, 2005).

42 On the difficulty of amending a WTO agreement, see Bryan Mercurio, "The WTO and Its Institutional Impediments" (2007) 8 *Melbourne Journal of International Law* 198. On decision making at the WTO, see Claus-Dieter Ehlerman and Lothar Ehring, "Decision-Making in the World Trade Organization" (2005) 8 *Journal of International Economic Law* 51.

of flexibilities that developing countries could consider exploiting when formulating an IP and development policy.

III. DESIGNING AN IP AND DEVELOPMENT FRAMEWORK

A. *Overview*

Although simply following developed country trends may be administratively simple and initially costless, such an approach fails to meet the needs of developing countries. Simply stated, such a strategy lacks clear direction and is not based on well-thought-out developmental aims and objectives. Instead, developing countries must determine the most appropriate IP policy for their respective national context. As mentioned in Section II, developing countries must work within an existing framework – deviating from the international norms of the TRIPS Agreement is not feasible (nor would it contribute to increased growth or sustainable development). Unlike the early industrializing countries, countries can no longer utilize weak IPRs protection to facilitate rapid industrial development. That being said, countries retain the flexibility to develop policies to meet developmental needs and increase their technological capacities. Although developing countries should work together to develop an IP developmental framework – perhaps from within the WIPO Development Agenda – individual countries must also realize that what is in the interests of one country may not be in the short-, medium-, and long-term interests of another country.[43] In essence, the aim is to stimulate a bottom-up approach in which individual developing countries can experiment and the by-product of successful innovations can be adopted to other nations while ensuring the system is appropriate to their needs.[44]

Every development strategy should be formulated in the spirit of paragraph 1 of Article 8 of the TRIPS Agreement, which states:

> Members may, in formulating or amending their laws and regulations, adopt measures necessary to protect public health and nutrition, and to promote the public interest in sectors of vital importance to their socio-economic and technological development, provided that such measures are consistent with the provisions of this Agreement.

Every development strategy will also likely involve certain amendments, interpretations, and maximization of flexibilities in the TRIPS Agreement. It is also likely that a developmental IP strategy will maximize competition in the marketplace, which will better allow for building on the inventions of others than is currently the norm

[43] For more on the WIPO Development Agenda, see Neil W. Netanel (ed.), *The Development Agenda: Global Intellectual Property and Developing Countries* (New York: Oxford University Press, 2009).

[44] Graeme Dinwoodie and Rochelle Dreyfuss, "Designing a Global Intellectual Property System Responsive to Change: The WTO, WIPO and Beyond" (2009) 46 *Houston Law Review* 1190.

in the developed world. For these reasons, the trend toward increasing substantive rights and areas of protection is worrying.[45] To date, developing countries have not effectively resisted pressure from trading partners to implement higher IP standards in FTAs.[46] Even without such external pressures, designing a framework that uses IPRs to encourage development is difficult. The task becomes impossible if countries negotiate away the flexibilities existing within the TRIPS Agreement.

It is not within the scope of this chapter to attempt to design an IP and development framework. The aims of the chapter are more modest, and the remaining part of this section briefly reviews four areas in which developing countries have scope to shape and formulate IP and development policy: granting patent protection, exhaustion of IPRs, exceptions to owner rights and transfer of technology, and competition issues.[47]

In many instances, governments will be faced with a push-pull of, on the one hand, access to knowledge for its citizens and industries, and on the other hand, increased protection for its knowledge creating industries.[48] The challenge for developing countries is to create and implement policies which understand that IPRs are only a means to an end. The goal is not simply to protect IPRs but to foster creativity and innovation in a manner that promotes human endeavors and encourages development.

45 See, e.g., the European Union's sui generis scheme for database protection and the U.S. patent protection for software: *Directive 96/9/EC of the European Parliament and of the Council of March 11, 1996 on the Legal Protection of Databases*, available at: http://eur-lex.europa.eu/LexUriServ/LexUriServ.do?uri=CELEX:31996L0009:EN:NOT. In terms of database protection, it is debatable whether Europe has benefited from the enhanced protection. Database protection has not resulted in increased database production, and the European Commission's first review of the Directive characterized the economic impact of protection as "unproven." DG Internal Market and Services, *First Evaluation of Directive 96/9/EC on the Legal Protection of Databases*, Working Paper, Brussels, December 12, 2005, p. 6, available at: http://ec.europa.eu/internal_market/copyright/docs/databases/evaluation_report_en.pdf. It should be noted, however, that despite the unknown economic impact: "most respondents to an online survey believed that the 'sui generis' right has brought about legal certainty, reduced the costs associated with the protection of databases, created more business opportunities and facilitated the marketing of databases" (Ibid., p. 6). For developing countries, unduly restricting access to information does not appear to be beneficial, and any database protection offered must attach a high standard of creativity to prevent overprotection. See Jerome H. Reichman, "Database Protection in a Global Economy (2002) *Revue Internationale de Droit Economique* 457, 479–80. On software patents, see Wendy H. Schacht, *Patent Reform: Issues in the Biomedical and Software Industries*, Congressional Research Service (April 7, 2006), available at: http://sharp.sefora.org/wp-content/uploads/2007/12/rl33367.pdf.

46 For background, see generally Handler and Mercurio (2009), supra note 34.

47 There are, of course, many other areas that merit discussion but because of space considerations cannot be included in this chapter. Such areas include government research and gene patenting.

48 For example, India is aware that its pharmaceutical patent policy affects not only its successful generic pharmaceutical industry but also its burgeoning innovative pharmaceutical industry. See, e.g., *Mashelkar Committee Report on Pharma Patenting*, March 2009, available at: http://www.patentoffice.nic.in/RevisedReport_March2009.doc. For a brief summary of the history surrounding the report, see the excellent blog postings at SpicyIP. See also Centad, Mashalkar Committee Report: A Critique, available at: http://www.centad.org/focus_33.asp.

B. *Granting Patent Protection*

The first area in which developing countries can tailor their laws to meet developmental needs is through setting stringent standards and requirements for granting patent protection. The TRIPS Agreement provides the minimum standards required for obtaining a patent (Article 27) by separating the requirements into four distinct areas: subject matter, novelty, inventive step (nonobviousness), and capable of industrial application (useful).[49] Article 27.1 is drafted in very broad terms:

> [P]atents shall be available for any inventions, whether products or processes, in all fields of technology, provided that they are new, involve an inventive step and are capable of industrial application.... [P]atents shall be available and patent rights enjoyable without discrimination as to the place of invention, the field of technology and whether products are imported or locally produced.

Such language effectively prohibits Members from excluding pharmaceutical, chemical, and process patents (as many countries did before the TRIPS Agreement); however, Members do have the discretion to tailor their laws to meet their developmental (and other) needs. For instance, patentable subject matter can exclude inventions "necessary to protect *ordre public* or morality, including to protect human, animal or plant life or health or to avoid serious prejudice to the environment"[50] and also exclude medical and surgical methods and plants and animals (other than microorganisms) from patentability.[51] Although untested, it seems reasonably clear that Members are free to determine whether, and to what extent, they will protect business methods as patentable subject matter (i.e., the process of conducting an online auction). In 1998, *State Street & Trust Co. v. Signature Financial Group, Inc.*,[52] overturned existing jurisprudence in the United States by allowing business methods to be patentable subject matter when applied in a practical manner to produce "a useful, concrete and tangible thing."[53] In subsequent years, the number of business patent methods applications significantly increased.[54] Other countries, however, have not embraced business method patents as enthusiastically. For instance, the European Union does not "as such" grant patents for methods of "doing business."[55] There are exceptions, however, such as those for business methods with a "technical character."[56] Other countries do not deem business methods to be patentable

[49] Other standards exist elsewhere, such as Article 29 (enablement) TRIPS.

[50] Article 27.2 TRIPS.

[51] Article 27.3 TRIPS.

[52] 149 F.3d 1368 (Fed. Cir. 1998).

[53] Ibid., p. 1373.

[54] Applications for business method patents have grown from 927 filed in 1997 to an annual average of 7,215 applications for the years 2000–2004. See Brian Boscaljon, "Information Content of Business Methods Patents" (2006) 41(3) *The Financial Review* 391. As noted in Section II, the future of business method patents is in doubt following the decision of *In re Bilksi*.

[55] European Patent Convention, Article 52.

[56] See, e.g., *Hitachi, Ltd.*, Technical Board of Appeal, European Patent Office, T 0258/03–3.5.1 (April 21, 2004). For P more information, see European Patent Office, *Patents for software?* December 30, 2008,

processes.[57] Such differing perspectives provide developing countries wide scope in deciding whether, and to what extent, they should grant patent protection to business methods.

Article 27.1 of the TRIPS Agreement also limits patentable inventions to that which are "new, involve an inventive step and are capable of industrial application." A footnote to Article 27.1 clarifies that the terms "inventive step" and "capable of industrial application" may be deemed by a Member to be synonymous with the terms "non-obvious" and "useful," respectively.[58] The Agreement does not define these terms. Moreover, although some direction can be found in the internationally agreed standards contained in the Patent Cooperation Treaty (PCT), the PCT is not incorporated into TRIPS nor are all WTO Members signatories. Thus, Members are free to set and apply their own substantive conditions. Such discretion has allowed two distinct concepts of novelty to coexist – the majority of nations place no geographic limitation on prior art,[59] whereas others (most prominently, the United States) limits prior art to their own territory. In response to the European Community questioning whether the U.S. patent act (35 U.S.C. 102(a)), in which only knowledge or use in the United States is sufficient for the purposes of defeating novelty is consistent with Article 27.1, the United States defended its law by stating:

> There is no definition of the term "new" in the TRIPS Agreement or in the Paris Convention. In addition, Article 1.1 of the TRIPS Agreement states that "Members shall be free to determine the appropriate method of implementing the provisions of this Agreement within their own legal system and practice." In view of these facts, there is no prescription as to how WTO Members define what inventions are to be considered "new" within their domestic systems.[60]

Members therefore have considerable discretion to tailor the novelty requirement in their domestic laws in a manner that promotes developmental objectives – of course,

available at: http://www.epo.org/topics/issues/computer-implemented-inventions/software.html. For more on patenting software in the European Union, see *Denial of the European Union Software Patent Directive by the European Parliament in July 2005* (Proposal for a Directive on the Patentability of Computer-Implemented Inventions, OJC151E, 25/06/2002, available at: http://ec.europa.eu/internal_market/indprop/comp/index_en.htm. On current uncertainties, see Aloys Huttermann and Ulrich Storz, "A Comparison between Biotech and Software Related Patents" (2009) 31(12) *European Intellectual Property Review* 589.

57 Countries that exclude business methods as patentable subject matter are, for example, the members of the European Patent Convention (article 52 (2)c EPC), Brazil (article 10 III Law 9279, May 14, 1996), Canada (Article 1(2)(c) Patent Law 1977), and India (Patents Amendment Act 2002, Act 38 of 2002).

58 The footnote was seen as necessary because "industrial application" was the standard used in most European countries, whereas "utility" was used in the United States and Canada.

59 See, e.g., European Patent Convention, Article 54.

60 Council for TRIPS, *Review of Legislation in the Fields of Patents, Layout-Designs (Topographies) of Integrated Circuits, Protection of Undisclosed Information and Control of Anti-Competitive Practices in Contractual Licences*, IP/Q3/USA/1 (May 1, 1998), p. 4. The European Community also questioned whether the U.S. provision was consistent with Article 3 of the TRIPS Agreement and GATT Article III, "given that [the provision] affords rights with respect to US inventions that it does not afford to others and that these rights overwhelmingly rebound to the benefit of US nationals."

whether novelty is destroyed through written or publicly available prior art or oral prior art existing anywhere in the world depends entirely on the circumstances and objectives of each nation. Likewise, setting a high standard for inventive step and obviousness can assist developing countries in promoting IPRs as a developmental tool rather than harmful monopolistic right.[61] In this regard, Members can refuse to grant patent protection for new uses of known products, which are often used to extend patent protection for pharmaceutical products for anticompetitive purposes. In this regard, India has taken the affirmative decision to draft legislation that defines what is not patentable; for instance, Section 3(d) of the Indian Patent Act limits patent protection for pharmaceutical derivatives only if it enhances the efficacy of the known substance (i.e., new forms of an existing drug does not qualify as an "invention").[62] Countries choosing to allow "evergreening" of patents still retain flexibilities and the right to regulate, such as by not granting an automatic injunction when an "evergreening" claim is made for additional patent protection[63] and through legislation penalizing spurious or frivolous patent claims and extensions.[64]

Other ways in which developing countries can use IPRs to their developmental advantage involve such measures as developing procedures to encourage the rapid publication of patent applications and ensuring easy and fast opposition (pre and post) procedures at reasonable cost. Countries should also use IPRs to encourage local innovation through such measures as setting the level of patent application and renewal fees within the means of local small and medium-sized enterprises,

61 Here again, the U.S. approach (date of invention or reduction to practice) differs from that of the European Union (first to file).

62 Section 3(d) states: "the mere discovery of a new form of a known substance which does not result in the enhancement of the known efficacy of that substance or the mere discovery of any new property or new use for a known substance or of the mere new use of a known process, machine or apparatus unless such known process results in a new product or employs at least one new reactant." For discussion, see Shamnad Basheer and T. Prashant Reddy, "The 'Efficacy' of Indian Patent Law: Ironing Out the Creases in Section 3(d)" (2008) 5 SCRIPTed, available at http://www.law.ed.ac.uk/ahrc/script-ed/vol5-2/basheer.asp. See also Shamnad Basheer and T. Prashant Reddy, "Ducking TRIPS in India: A Saga Involving Novartis and the Legality of Section 3(d)" (2008) (2) *National Law School of India Review* 131, available at: http://papers.ssrn.com/sol3/papers.cfm?abstract_id=1329201.

63 Some nations grant an automatic injunction against generic competition when an evergreening claim is made. See, for instance, the United States under the Drug Price Competition and Patent Term Restoration Act 1984 (better known as the Hatch-Waxman Act), which allows patent holders to gain a injunction of up to thirty months from generic competition by filing a patent infringement suit. Unsurprisingly, a 2002 report by the U.S. Federal Trade Commission found that evergreening was a major factor in the high price of American drugs and was anticompetitive. The report recommended that manufacturers be limited to only one "claim" per drug. Federal Trade Commission, *Generic Drug Entry Prior to Patent Expiration: An FTC Study* (2002).

64 See, e.g., Australia's Therapeutic Goods Act 1989 (Cth) ss 26C and 26D, which requires patent holders to certify that infringement proceedings are being commenced in good faith, have reasonable prospects of success (as defined in s26C(4)), and will be conducted without unreasonable delay. If the certificate is found to be false or misleading, the patent holder can be fined up to AUS 10 million and the attorney-general may join an action to recoup losses to the Pharmaceutical Benefits Scheme.

formulating a liberal policy on reverse engineering (while adequately protecting business confidential information),[65] and facilitating locals to invent around patents by providing for, inter alia, utility and design patents. Utility patents, which encourage companies (and particularly small and medium-sized enterprises) to undertake minor incremental adaptations and innovations, have been shown to increase innovation and access to new information in such diverse conditions as Brazil, the Philippines, and postwar Japan.[66]

C. *Exhaustion of Intellectual Property Rights*

Another area in which the TRIPS Agreement provides flexibility is in the exhaustion of IPRs. Nothing in the TRIPS Agreement prohibits the parallel importation of products; instead, Article 6 allows Members the freedom to incorporate national, international, or regional exhaustion of rights. Adopting a system of international exhaustion – whereby the first sale of the goods anywhere in the world exhausts IPRs – would allow for the importation of so-called gray-market (also called "parallel importation") goods. The benefit of such a system is that goods sold in a foreign market may be less expensive than those sold domestically. Gray-market goods, however, compete with the goods of the domestic rights owner. By contrast, the rights owner can object to the importation of the otherwise legitimate goods under national and regional exhaustion. Most countries do not approach exhaustion to every IPR in a uniform fashion, meaning that they may allow for parallel imports of some or all copyrighted works, restrict the entry of trademarked goods, and prohibit all or most patented goods. This is true in both developed and developing countries, but it is puzzling that more developing countries (and especially LDCs) do not instigate a more pro-competition approach to exhaustion.

Of particular importance is the value parallel importation may have in reducing the cost of procuring pharmaceuticals and health-related inventions. In many countries, this may allow for more people to have access to pharmaceuticals and medical products.[67] For this reason, many commentators believe developing

65 See Maskus, stating such a policy could "promise dynamic benefits." Maskus, "Using the International Trading System to Foster Technology Transfer for Economic Development" (2005) 1 *Michigan State Law Review* 229. See also Pamela Samuelsson and Suzanne Scotchmer, "The Law and Economics of Reverse Engineering" (2002) 111 *Yale Law Journal* 1575.

66 See Robert E. Evenson and Larry E. Westphal, "Technological Change and Technology Strategy," in Hollis Chenery and T. N. Srinivasan (ed.), *Handbook of Development Economics* (Amsterdam: Elsevier, 1988); Keith E. Maskus and C. R. McDaniel, "Impacts of the Japanese Patent System on Productivity Growth" (1999) 11 *Japan and the World Economy* 557; CIPR (2002), supra note 4, p. 21. See also World Bank, *Global Economic Prospects and Developing Countries* 2002, p. 134.

67 Importantly, safeguards would have to be in place to ensure that discounted or donated pharmaceuticals are not diverted from their intended destination. Moreover, an argument could be made that differential pricing of pharmaceuticals benefits low-income countries, in that the richer nations effectively subsidize poorer countries. Parallel importation of pharmaceuticals could significantly harm those efforts if the poorer nations simply export the drugs to other nations (i.e., Vietnam pays less

countries should adopt the "widest scope" of flexibilities in this regard.[68] India again is considered in this context to be at the forefront of establishing a country-specific approach that fits into a pro-development framework.[69]

However, it could be argued that differential pricing ensures that higher-income countries pay more than lower-income countries. In this regard, it seems unfair for countries such as Brazil to parallel import medicine sold into the Guyana market at cheaper prices. If such actions occur on a large-scale basis, pharmaceutical companies could end all differential pricing schemes and possibly raise the costs of medicines in some of the poorer markets. The recent findings of Flynn, Hollis, and Palmedo, however, indicate that profit-maximizing pricing in the pharmaceutical sector often results in medicines being sold at a high price, affordable to only the few wealthy citizens in a nation, rather than selling at a lower price to more people.[70] Allowing for the parallel importation of pharmaceuticals could potentially alleviate such pricing strategies.

Finally, it should be noted that some developing countries at present only allow for the parallel importation of pharmaceutical products but not for other patented products.[71] This limitation is likely inconsistent with Article 27.1 of the TRIPS Agreement, which prevents discrimination as to the field of technology. The inconsistency can be remedied by permitting parallel importation for patented goods in all fields of technology, and not only for pharmaceuticals and health-related inventions.

D. *Exceptions to Owner Rights*

Another key step toward building a developmentally based IP framework will be to take advantage of the explicit exceptions contained in the TRIPS Agreement. Foremost, developing countries must draft legislation that allows for government use of a patent without the consent of the rights holder (i.e., public, noncommercial use) and more general compulsory license provisions that could be used for a multitude of purposes (i.e., combat anticompetitive behavior, provide access to

than Malaysia for a particular drug, but instead of providing the drug to its citizens, Vietnam exports the drug at a profit to Malaysia). Parallel importation of pharmaceuticals also increases the risks of corruption.

68 See, e.g., Sisule F. Musungu and Cecilia Oh, *The Use of Flexibilities in TRIPS by Developing Countries: Can They Promote Access to Medicines Study 4C?*, Commission on Intellectual Property Rights, Innovation and Health, World Health Organization (August 2005), p. 30.

69 For discussion and analysis of, and suggested amendments to, India's legislative framework (Section 107A of the Patents (Amendment) Act, 2005), see Shamnad Basheer and Mrinalini Kochupillai, "TRIPS, Patents and Parallel Imports: A Proposal for Amendment" (2009) 2 *Indian Journal of Intellectual Property Law* 63.

70 Sean Flynn, Aidan Hollis, and Mike Palmedo, "An Economic Justification for Open Access to Essential Medicine Patents in Developing Countries" (2009) 37 *Journal of Law, Medicine and Ethics* 184 (showing that compulsory licenses may increase social welfare, increase access, and lower costs of essential medicines in developing countries where highly convex demand curves are the norm).

71 See, e.g., South Africa, Medicines and Related Substances Control Act, Section 15C.

medicines at reasonable cost, etc.).[72] Compulsory licenses can also be granted if the rights owner fails to locally "work" the patent; in other words, a compulsory license can be issued not only when rights owners fail to use the patent (i.e., import the product) but also when they fail to locally produce the product subject to the patent protection.[73] Importantly, developing countries must ensure their laws are drafted to allow ample scope for the issuance of compulsory licenses under the broadest conditions allowable under Article 31 of the TRIPS Agreement.[74] Article 31 does not limit the grounds on which a compulsory license may be granted but only sets out the (mainly procedural) conditions to be applied when granting a compulsory license. The point is not to draft broad legislation to enable widespread use of compulsory licenses; on the contrary, use of compulsory licenses could lead (and have led) to economically punishing reprisals. Moreover, and unlike foreign direct investment (FDI) that brings with it advanced technologies and managerial and technical know-how, developing countries that issue compulsory licenses must possess the capabilities to utilize the license effectively. Thus, compulsory licenses should not be viewed as a developmental solution but more as simply a tool as part of a broader developmental strategy. This cannot occur, however, if laws are not in place to allow for compulsory license.[75]

Developing countries can also better utilize the flexibilities by crafting laws that promote the object and purpose of IPRs and the TRIPS Agreement,[76] including the promotion of the transfer of technology, the prevention of abuse of IPRs, and the promotion of public health. In this regard, developing countries should ensure that their laws make use of Article 30 of the TRIPS Agreement allowing for undefined exceptions to patent rights, as long as the exceptions meet the three-step

72 See TRIPS Agreement Article 31 and the yet to be ratified amendment, Article 31bis. On the use of licenses to promote access to medicines, see Aidan Hollis and Thomas Pogge, *The Health Impact Fund: Making New Medicines Accessible for All, A Report of Incentives for Global Health* (2008); Sisule F. Musungu and Cecilia Oh, *The Use of Flexibilities in TRIPs by Developing Countries: Can They Promote Access to Medicines?* (Geneva: South Centre, 2006); Katri Paas, "Compulsory Licensing under The TRIPS Agreement – A Cruel Taunt for Developing Countries?" (2009) 31 *European Intellectual Property Review* 609. Other steps to lower the cost of access of medicines, such as improving infrastructure, education, governmental coherence, and perhaps even imposing price controls on essential medicines, should also be investigated. See, e.g., Bryan Mercurio, "Health in the Developing World: The Case for a New International Funding and Support Agency" (2009) 4 *Asian Journal of WTO & International Health Law and Policy* 27.

73 See Paris Convention, Article 5A (incorporated into the TRIPS Agreement by Article 2). For discussion on this controversial issue, see Bryan Mercurio and Mitali Tyagi, "Treaty Interpretation in WTO Dispute Settlement: The Outstanding Question of the Legality of Local Working Requirements" (2010) 19 *Minnesota Journal of International Law.*

74 To facilitate the process and maximize the benefits of the license, laws should provide for simple, predictable guidelines and procedures promoting efficient use of compulsory licenses.

75 In this regard, it is somewhat surprising that a large percentage of developing countries do not have sufficient legal measures in place to enable both the import and export of drugs under compulsory license as needed under the waiver (and in the future Article 31bis). Numerous developed countries likewise have failed to implement legislation necessary to facilitate the export of drugs under compulsory license.

76 See TRIPS Agreement, Preamble, Article 7 ("Objectives") and Article 8 ("Principles").

test of being (a) limited, (b) do not unreasonably conflict with the normal exploitation of the patent, and (c) do not unreasonably prejudice the legitimate interests of the patent owner, taking account of the legitimate interests of third parties.[77] A particularly useful exception in the area of public health is the so-called Bolar (early working) provision that allows generic manufacturers to import, manufacture, and test a patented product before the expiry of the patent to gain regulatory approval to market the product, thus facilitating its production and sale soon after the expiry of the patent.[78] Another available flexibility related to marketing approval is the extent to which countries protect test data. Article 39.3 only requires Members to protect against unfair commercial use of confidential data, which leaves scope for Members to allow generic manufacturers to "rely on" the test data to facilitate the entry of generic products onto the market. Another related area in which developing countries could craft exceptions to patent rights is when researchers more broadly utilize patented products or processes for noncommercial experimental purposes. Although this exception is narrowly construed in the United States, there is scope to widen the applicability of the exception through careful drafting and implementation.[79] In this regard, India again can serve as a model because it has drafted a provision that mandates full disclosure and allows for effective study and experimentation in a manner that is likely to be consistent with Article 30 of the TRIPS Agreement.[80]

E. *Technology Transfers and Competition Policy*

Acquisition of advanced technologies is crucial to the development of a nation; for this reason, developing countries must facilitate the international transfer of

[77] Article 13 of the TRIPS Agreement provides for an equivalent standard for copyright. The standard was discussed and interpreted in Report of the Panel, US – Section 110(5) Copyright Act, June 15, 2000, WTO Doc. WT/DS/160/R. Academic literature heavily criticizes the panel's interpretation. See Jane C. Ginsburg, "Toward Supranational Copyright Law? The WTO Panel Decision and the 'Three Step Test' for Copyright Exemptions" (2001) 187 *Revue Internationale du Droit d'auteur* 17; Rochelle Cooper Dreyfuss, "TRIPS – Round II: Should Users Strike Back?" (2004) 71 *University of Chicago Law Review* 21; Rochelle Cooper Dreyfuss and G. Dinwoodie, "TRIPS and the Dynamics of Intellectual Property Lawmaking" (2004) 36 *Case Western Reserve Journal of International Law* 95; Bernt P. Hugenholtz and Ruth L. Okediji, *Conceiving an International Instrument on Limitations and Exceptions to Copyright, Final – Report*, 6, March 2008, pp. 16–27, available at: http://www.ivir.nl/publicaties/hugenholtz/finalreport2008.pdf.

[78] Such a provision was interpreted to comply with the conditions of Article 30 in WTO Panel Report, *Canada-Patent Protection of Pharmaceutical Products*, April 7, 2000, WTO Doc. WT/DS114/R. Surprisingly, the majority of developing countries do not directly provide for such rights in legislation. See Phil Thorpe, *Study on the Implementation of the TRIPS Agreement by Developing Countries*, Commission on Intellectual Property Rights Study Paper 7 (undated), available at: http://www.iprcommission.org/papers/pdfs/study_papers/sp7_thorpe_study.pdf.

[79] See Carlos Correa, "Reforming the Intellectual Property Rights System in Latin America" (2000) 23 *The World Economy* 851.

[80] See Section 47(3) of the Indian Patents Act 1970. For discussion and a developing-country perspective on the issue, see Shamnad Basheer and Prashant Reddy, "The 'Experimental Use Exception' through a Developmental Lens" (2010) 50 *The Intellectual Property Law Review* 831.

technology (ITT) from the developed world. Economic studies link increased IPRs to ITT through FDI and licensing, increased incentives to invest in local research and development, and increased local knowledge and capabilities.[81]

The TRIPS Agreement contains several provisions promoting the ITT, including Article 7 (stating IPRs should "contribute to the promotion of technological innovation and to the transfer and dissemination of technology"), Article 8 (stating "appropriate measures... may be needed to prevent... the resort to practices which unreasonably restrain trade or adversely affect the international transfer of technology"), and Article 40 (recognizing some licensing practices and conditions "may have adverse effects on trade and may impede the transfer and dissemination of technology"). These provisions, however, are vague and appear to be either hortatory in nature or have a limited scope for implementation. In contrast, Articles 66.2 and 67 perhaps provide legal obligations on developed countries. Article 66.2 reads:

> Developed country Members *shall provide* incentives to enterprises and institutions in their territories for the purpose of promoting and encouraging technology transfer to *least-developed country* Members in order to enable them to create a sound and viable technological base. (Emphasis added.)

Moreover, Article 67 TRIPS states that developed-country Members:

> *shall provide*, on request and on mutually agreed terms and conditions, technical and financial cooperation in favour of developing and least-developed country Members. Such cooperation shall include assistance in the preparation of laws and regulations on the protection and enforcement of intellectual property rights as well as on the prevention of their abuse, and shall include support regarding the establishment or reinforcement of domestic offices and agencies relevant to these matters, including the training of personnel. (Emphasis added.)

Apart from these provisions, TRIPS does not require WTO Members to take any measures to promote or achieve ITT.[82] Even Article 66.2 is limited to developed-country

[81] See United Nations Conference on Trade and Development (UNCTAD), *Fostering Technological Dynamism: Evolution of Thought on Technological Development Processes and Competitiveness* (Geneva/New York: United Nations, 1996); B. Javorcik, "The Composition of Foreign Direct Investment and Protection of Intellectual Property Rights: Evidence in Transition Economies" (2004) 48 *European Economic Review* 39; L. Branstetter, R. Fisman, F. Foley, and K. Saggi, *Intellectual Property Rights, Imitation, and Foreign Direct Investment: Theory and Evidence*, NBER Working Paper 13033 (Cambridge, MA: National Bureau of Economic Research, 2007); Lee Branstetter and Kamal Saggi, *Intellectual Property Rights, Foreign Direct Investment and Industrial Development*, NBER Working Paper 15393 (Cambridge, MA: National Bureau of Economic Research, 2009). The link is greater for larger and higher-income developing countries and weak for LDCs, which are not viewed as potential competitors for a host of factors, including poor investment climate, infrastructure, governance, and limited skill and expertise. Others remain skeptical that increased IPRs lead to increased FDI. See, e.g., Carlos Correa, *Intellectual Property Rights, the WTO and Developing Countries: The TRIPS Agreement and Policy Options* (London: Zed Books, 2000).

[82] The IPRs Commission concluded that the provisions are based on provisions in the failed *Draft Code of Conduct on Technology Transfer* and outdated because developing-country policies have

Members offering incentives to private companies – private companies cannot be forced into transferring technology. With no concrete obligations or effectiveness test, the power of the TRIPS-ITT provisions seem a priori limited; there does not appear to be any firm obligations in TRIPS for developed countries to actually provide or facilitate ITT.[83] Furthermore, although a growing body of literature exists on the potential scope of provisions such as Article 7 and 8,[84] researchers have given scant attention to the potential scope of the ITT provisions.[85] There has also been little sustained research on the corollary issue of if, and to what extent, the provisions have led to effective technology transfers – that is, what incentives have been provided and how did they produce results – or on why the private sector has played an insignificant role in facilitating ITT.[86] Developing countries should study these issues further with a view to making better use of the TRIPS provisions on technology

dramatically shifted since the 1980s (i.e., from promoting import substitution to trade liberalization). CIPR, supra note 4, p. 25.

83 The IPRs Commission calls Article 66.2 TRIPS "ineffective" and states that "[d]eveloped countries do not appear to have taken additional measures to encourage technology transfer by their firms and institutions." CIPR, supra note 4, p. 26.

84 Keith E. Maskus, *Encouraging International Technology Transfer*, International Centre for Trade and Sustainable Development (ICTSD) & UNCTAD Issue Paper No. 7 (2004); Hoekman, Maskus, and Saggi (2004), supra note 13; Maskus, supra note 63, p. 219.

85 UNCTAD, *The Least Developed Countries Report 2007: Knowledge, Technological Learning and Innovation for Development* (Geneva: United Nations, 2007), available at: http://www.unctad.org/en/docs/ldc2007_en.pdf. In fact, it is common for governmental statements/reports merely to criticize IPRs as a stumbling block to ITT and harmful to development; see, e.g., *Report on Technology Transfer and the WIPO Development Agenda*, A/HRC/15/WG.2/TF/CRP.1, November 19, 2009, p. 5, available at: http://www2.ohchr.org/english/issues/development/right/docs/A-HRC-15-WG2-TF-CRP1.pdf. For more detailed analysis of whether IPRs harm developing countries in absorbing foreign technologies, see Maskus, supra note 2.

86 See Maskus, supra note 2; Keith E. Maskus, Kamal Saggi, and Thitima Puttitanun, "Patent Rights and International Technology Transfer through Direct Investment and Licensing," in Keith E. Maskus and Jerome H. Reichman (eds.), *International Public Goods and Transfer of Technology under a Globalized Intellectual Property Regime* (Cambridge: Cambridge University Press, 2004); Maskus, supra note 80; Fink and Maskus, supra note 1, p. 360; Correa, supra note 75, chap. 2. WTO Members are required to issue reports as to their implementation of commitments. For analysis and criticism of the vague and opaque nature of the reports, see Suerie Moon, *Does TRIPS Art. 66.2 Encourage Technology Transfer to LDCs? An Analysis of Country Submissions to the TRIPS Council (1999–2007)*, UNCTAD-ICTSD Project on IPRs and Sustainable Development, Policy Brief Number 2 (2008), available at: http://www.iprsonline.org/unctadictsd/docs/New%202009/Policy%20Briefs/policy-brief-2.pdf; Juan S. Blyde and Cristina Acea, *The Effects of Intellectual Property Rights on Trade and FDI in Latin America*, InterAmerican Development Bank (2002); Maskus, supra note 80; R. Kumar Rai, "Effect of the TRIPS-Mandated Intellectual Property Rights on Foreign Direct Investment in Developing Countries: A Case Study of the Indian Pharmaceutical Industry" (2008) 11 *Journal of World Intellectual Property* 404; Linsu Kim, *Technology Transfer and Intellectual Property Rights: Lessons from Korea's Experience*, ICTSD & UNCTAD Working Paper (2002), available at: http://ictsd.net/i/publications/11772/; Pedro Roffe, David Vivas-Eugui, and Gina Vea, *Maintaining Policy Space for Development: A Case Study on IP Technical Assistance in FTAs*, ICTSD Issue Paper No. 19 (2007), available at: http://www.iprsonline.org/resources/docs/Roffe-Vivas-Vea%20Blue19.pdf; UNCTAD, supra note 82. On private sector involvement in ITT, see Maria Fyodorova, *Engaging the Private Sector in Technology Transfer Programs*, Business Council for Sustainable Energy (2000); Hoekman, Maskus, and Saggi (2004), supra note 13.

transfer. However, the broader point is that ITT will not meaningfully occur without patents and know-how receiving adequate protection and investment incentives. For these reasons, any ITT initiative must be part of broader policy that also provides a proper environment to encourage and absorb ITT. Restrictive ITT requirements and improperly formulated IP laws may discourage FDI and licensing arrangements. Moreover, it must be remembered that acquiring knowledge via ITT is only part of the equation – a means to an end, with the end being increased development. It is critical that the country acquiring the technology is able to benefit from the ITT; this can only occur when a host of other factors are met, including managerial know-how and trained staff. For this reason, it should again be noted that compulsory or even voluntary licenses can only go so far in assisting development and that ITT via investment (which provides not only the IP but also the capital, experience, know-how, and training) is necessary to long-term development strategies.

Another interconnected and important aspect of the development framework should be finding ways to limit the monopoly powers and potential abuses associated with IPRs by increasing the competitive environment within their territories. At present, an imbalance exists as a result of the TRIPS Agreement strengthening IP protection without effectively addressing competition issues. This is the case despite the TRIPS Agreement providing that appropriate measures can be taken to prevent the abuse of IPRs and anticompetitive practices (see Articles 8, 31, and 40). The IPRs Commission states: "TRIPS has strengthened the global protection offered to suppliers of technology, but there is no international framework to ensure that the transfer of technology takes place within a competitive framework which minimizes the restrictive technology licensing practices."[87]

Without an international competition agreement (whether inside or outside of the WTO), developing countries are left to search for ways to utilize the TRIPS flexibilities allowing for competition law exceptions to prohibit abusive IP and ITT practices. To some extent, this involves issuing compulsory licenses under Article 31, as discussed earlier. In the past, the United States was a frequent user of compulsory licenses to remedy anticompetitive practices. However, there is more to countering anticompetitive practices than compulsory licenses. This underexplored area is one in which developing countries can take a lead in shaping the direction of IPRs into the future by designing laws that facilitate the transfer of advanced foreign technologies and know-how on reasonable terms, conditions, and prices to remain open and affordable to local industry.[88] In short, developing countries should facilitate the use of the technology transfer provisions in TRIPS to increase competition in the marketplace.

[87] CIPR (2002), supra note 4, p. 25.

[88] See Keith E. Maskus and Jerome H. Reichman (eds.), *International Public Goods and Transfer of Technology under a Globalized Intellectual Property Regime* (Cambridge: Cambridge University Press, 2005); Jerome H. Reichman, "Nurturing a Transnational System of Innovation" (2007) 16 *Journal of Transnational Law & Policy* 161.

IV. CONCLUSION

This chapter argues that developing countries should seek ways both to comply with the obligations and maximize the flexibilities of the TRIPS Agreement. In so doing, developing countries should be seeking to create frameworks in which IPRs are viewed not merely as an obligation but also as a developmental tool. Such a strategy will undoubtedly be difficult to develop and employ. Developed countries have not only continued to strengthen domestic IP protection since the creation of the TRIPS Agreement but have also exported such increased standards to others via FTAs and other international agreements.[89] Ideally, developing countries would benefit from the increased standards in the developed world by profiting from the additional protection abroad while guarding against overprotection domestically. Developing countries, however, are under an immense amount of pressure to agree to the increased standards (and corresponding removal of flexibilities) in exchange for the promise of greater market access for goods to developed-country markets. Before committing to increased IP protection, countries must analyze whether any potential increases in market access for goods or services are worth increased standards of IP protection and less flexibility in governmental policy. Developing countries should also remain vigilant in ensuring that the maximization of IPRs does not contravene other provisions of the TRIPS Agreement. Article 1.1 of the TRIPS Agreement is clear in stating that Members may only implement more extensive protection than is required "provided that such protection does not contravene the provisions of this Agreement." This often overlooked and underemphasized part of Article 1.1 could be utilized to limit the extent to which IPRs extend beyond the minimum standards set forth in the TRIPS Agreement.[90]

Above all, developing countries should resist following the path to overprotection, as much of the developed world has done since the late 1990s. Such overexpansion of IP protection has several negative consequences, including the granting of patent protection for basic research, low standards of nonobviousness, and the creation of patent "thickets," all of which can block downstream research.[91] Thus,

[89] For instance, it is clear that the proposed SPLT will remove existing flexibilities in the area of eligibility standards for patent protection by harmonizing standards to the developed-country norm.

[90] See Graeme B. Dinwoodie, "The International Intellectual Property Law System: New Actors, New Institutions, New Sources" (2006) *Marquette Intellectual Property Law Review* 214; Henning Grosse Ruse-Khan and Annette Kur, *Enough Is Enough – The Notion of Binding Ceilings in International Intellectual Property Protection*, Max Planck Institute for Intellectual Property, Competition & Tax Law Research Paper Series No. 09-01 (2008), available at: http://ssrn.com/abstract=1326429.

[91] On restrictions to basic research and knowledge as a global public good, see Joseph E. Stiglitz, *Knowledge as a Global Public Good*, Graduate School of Business, Columbia University (1999), available at: http://cgt.columbia.edu/files/papers/1999_Knowledge_as_Global_Public_Good_stiglitz.pdf. On the excesses of the patent system, see Adam Jaffe and Loshua Lerner, *Innovation and Its Discontents: How Our Broken Patent System Is Endangering Innovation and Progress, and What to Do about It* (Princeton, NJ: Princeton University Press, 2008).

although overprotection can benefit those who receive the patent protection,[92] costs of litigation and anticompetitive behavior increase, and society as a whole suffers as innovation is stifled. Evidence also suggests that meeting the TRIPS standard, combined with properly formulated laws, regulations, and incentives, is sufficient to attract FDI and ITT. In other words, it is unclear whether increased IPRs will actually attract additional FDI and ITT.

Developing countries must confront these issues and tailor innovative laws that work within the existing TRIPS framework but also fit within strategies of and work toward economic development. In this regard, retaining and making use of the flexibilities are critical to any IP and development strategy. The four areas discussed in Section III highlight the opportunities and difficulties of utilizing flexibilities as part of an IP framework for development. Maximizing flexibilities will undoubtedly attract scrutiny both from IP maximalist trading partners and domestic interests, but it is the only option for countries seeking to prevent the protection of IPRs from becoming a completely one-sided proposition that benefits developed countries at great cost to the developing world.

Finally, and importantly, it must also be remembered that IP laws and regulations (whether strong or weak) in isolation will not greatly assist development. Certain policy choices and standards may be necessary to further a developmental agenda, but they are certainly not sufficient. Instead, governments seeking to develop an IP and development strategy must analyze a host of policies to use IPRs successfully for developmental purposes, including those pertaining to a proper regulatory framework, trade, investment, education, and health. Sustainable growth and development will only be achieved when governments recognize the interconnectedness of sectors in coordinating government policy.

REFERENCES

Ariyanuntaka, Vichai, "Rethinking Intellectual Property Rights Enforcement in the Light of TRIPS and Specialized Intellectual Property Court in Thailand," paper presented at the Hong Kong-WIPO IPR Enforcement Symposium, June 1998, available at: http://www.malaysianbar.org.my/index.php?option=com_docman&task=doc_view&gid=133&Itemid=119.

Barnett, Jonathan M., "Property as Process: How Innovation Markets Select Innovation Regime" (2009) 119 *Yale Law Journal*.

Basheer, Shamnad, and Mrinalini Kochupillai, "TRIPS, Patents and Parallel Imports: A Proposal for Amendment" (2009) 2 *Indian Journal of Intellectual Property Law* 63.

[92] This has especially been the case of software and biotech industries. Dinwoodie and Dreyfuss state: "The TRIPS Agreement's strong commitment to a particular vision of proprietary rights – and, on the patents side, to technological neutrality – makes it difficult to revise the law to deal with such matters as the thickets of rights created in the software and biotechnological sectors, open source innovation, and new opportunities for serial and collaborative production." Dinwoodie and Dreyfuss (2009), see supra note 43, p. 1189.

Basheer, Shamnad, and Annalisa Primi, "The WIPO Development Agenda: Factoring in the 'Technically Proficient' Developing Countries," in Jeremy de Beer (ed.), *Implementing the World Intellectual Property Organization's Development Agenda* (Waterloo, Canada: Wilfrid Laurier University Press, 2009).

Basheer, Shamnad, and T. Prashant Reddy, "Ducking TRIPS in India: A Saga Involving Novartis and the Legality of Section 3(d)" (2008) 20(2) *National Law School of India Review*, available at http://papers.ssrn.com/sol3/papers.cfm?abstract_id=1329201.

______, "The 'Efficacy' of Indian Patent Law: Ironing out the Creases in Section 3(d)," (2008) 5 SCRIPTed, available at http://www.law.ed.ac.uk/ahrc/script-ed/vol5-2/basheer.asp.

______, "The 'Experimental Use Exception' through a Developmental Lens" (2010) 50 *IDEA – The Intellectual Property Law Review*.

Bhagwati, Jagdish N. (ed.), *The New International Economic Order: The North–South Debate* (Cambridge, MA: MIT Press, 1977).

Blakeley, Michael, *Trade-Related Aspects of Intellectual Property Rights: A Concise Guide to the TRIPS Agreement* (Andover, United Kingdom: Sweet & Maxwell, 1996).

Blyde, Juan S., and Cristina Acea, *The Effects of Intellectual Property Rights on Trade and FDI in Latin America* (Washington, DC: InterAmerican Development Bank, 2002).

Boscaljon, Brian, "Information Content of Business Methods Patents" (2006) 41(3) *The Financial Review*.

Branstetter, Lee, Raymond Fisman, C. Fritz Foley, and Kamal Saggi, *Intellectual Property Rights, Imitation, and Foreign Direct Investment: Theory and Evidence*, NBER Working Paper 13033 (Cambridge, MA: National Bureau of Economic Research, 2007).

Branstetter, Lee, and Kamal Saggi, *Intellectual Property Rights, Foreign Direct Investment and Industrial Development*, NBER Working Paper 15393 (Cambridge, MA: National Bureau of Economic Research, 2009).

Burrell, Robert, and Kimberlee Weatherall, "Exporting Controversy? Reactions to the Copyright Provisions of the U.S.–Australia Free Trade Agreement: Lessons for U.S. Trade Policy" (2008) 2 *University of Illinois Journal of Law, Technology and Policy*.

Castro, Rosa, "Intellectual Property Rights in Bilateral Investment Treaties" (2006) 9 *Journal of World Intellectual Property*.

Chaudhuri, Shubham, Pinelopi K. Goldberg, and Panle Jia, "Estimating the Effects of Global Patent Protection in Pharmaceuticals: A Case Study of Quinolones in India" (2006) 96 *American Economic Review*.

Chin, Judith, and Gene Grossman, *Intellectual Property Rights and North–South Trade*, NBER Working Paper (Cambridge, MA: National Bureau of Economic Research, 1998), available at: http://www.nber.org.

Commission on Intellectual Property Rights, *Integrating Intellectual Property Rights and Development Policy* (London, 2002), available at: http://cipr.org.uk/papers/pdfs/final_report/CIPR_Exec_Sumfinal.pdf.

Correa, Carlos M., "Reforming the Intellectual Property Rights System in Latin America" (2000) 23 *The World Economy*.

______, *Intellectual Property Rights, the WTO and Developing Countries: The TRIPS Agreement and Policy Options* (London: Zed Books, 2000).

______, "Can the TRIPS Agreement Foster Technology Transfer to Developing Countries?" in Keith E. Maskus and Jerome H. Reichman (eds.), *International Public Goods and Transfer of Technology under a Globalized Intellectual Property Regime* (Cambridge: Cambridge University Press, 2005).

Dinwoodie, Graeme, "The International Intellectual Property Law System: New Actors, New Institutions, New Sources" (2006) *Marquette Intellectual Property Law Review*.

Dinwoodie, Graeme, and Rochelle Dreyfuss, "Designing a Global Intellectual Property System Responsive to Change: The WTO, WIPO and Beyond" (2009) 46 *Houston Law Review*.

Drahos, Peter, *Expanding Intellectual Property's Empire: The Role of FTAs* (2003), available at: http://www.grain.org.

Dreyfuss, Rochelle Cooper, "TRIPS – Round II: Should Users Strike Back?" (2004) 71 *University of Chicago Law Review*.

Dreyfuss, Rochelle Cooper, and Graeme Dinwoodie, "TRIPS and the Dynamics of Intellectual Property Lawmaking" (2004) 36 *Case Western Reserve Journal of International Law*.

Durán, E., and C. Michalopoulos, "Intellectual Property Rights and Developing Countries in the WTO Millennium Round" (1999) 2 *Journal of World Intellectual Property*.

Ehlerman, Claus-Dieter, and Lothar Ehring, "Decision-Making in the World Trade Organization" (2005) 8 *Journal of International Economic Law*.

European Union, DG Internal Market and Services, *First Evaluation of Directive 96/9/EC on the Legal Protection of Databases*, Working Paper, Brussels, December 12, 2005, p. 6, available at: http://ec.europa.eu/internal_market/copyright/docs/databases/evaluation_report_en.pdf.

Evenson, Robert E., and Larry E. Westphal, "Technological Change and Technology Strategy," in Hollis Chenery and T. N. Srinivasan (ed.), *Handbook of Development Economics* (Amsterdam: Elsevier, 1988).

Fink, Carsten, and Keith E. Maskus (eds.), *Intellectual Property and Development: Lessons from Recent Economic Research* (Washington, DC: World Bank, 2004).

Flynn, Sean, Aidan Hollis, and Mike Palmedo, "An Economic Justification for Open Access to Essential Medicine Patents in Developing Countries" (2009) 37 *Journal of Law, Medicine and Ethics*.

Frischtak, Claudio, *The Protection of Intellectual Property Rights and Industrial Technology Development in Brazil*, World Bank, Industry and Energy Working Papers No. 13 (1989).

Fyodorova, Maria, *Engaging the Private Sector in Technology Transfer Programs*, (Washington, DC: Business Council for Sustainable Energy, 2000).

Gervais, Daniel J., "The Internationalization of Intellectual Property: New Challenges from the Very Old and the Very New" (2002) 12 *Fordham Intellectual Property, Media and Entertainment Law Journal*.

Ginsburg, Jane C., "Toward Supranational Copyright Law? The WTO Panel Decision and the 'Three Step Test' for Copyright Exemptions," (2001) 187 *Revue Internationale du Droit d'auteur*.

Gould, D., and W. Gruben, "The Role of Intellectual Property Rights in Economic Growth" (1996) 48 *Journal of Development Economics*.

Gugler, Phillipe, and Julien Chaisse, "Foreign Investment Issues in the WTO – Dealing with Fragmentation while Waiting for a Multilateral Framework," in Julien Chaisse and Tiziano Belmelli (eds.), *Essays on the Future of the World Trade Organization*, Vol. 1 (Geneva: Editions Interuniversitaires Suisses, 2008).

Haar, Paul S., "Revision of the Paris Convention: A Realignment of Private and Public Interests in the International Patent System" (1982) 8 *Brooklyn Journal of International Law*.

Handler, Michael, and Bryan Mercurio, "Intellectual Property," in Simon Lester and Bryan Mercurio (eds.), *Bilateral and Regional Trade Agreements: Commentary and Analysis* (Cambridge: Cambridge University Press, 2009).

Hoekman, Bernard M., Keith E. Maskus, and Kamal Saggi, *Transfer of Technology to Developing Countries: Unilateral and Multilateral Policy Options*, World Bank Policy Research Working Paper No. 3332 (2004), available at: http://papers.ssrn.com/sol3/papers.cfm?abstract_id=610377.

Hollis, Aidan, and Thomas Pogge, *The Health Impact Fund: Making New Medicines Accessible for All* (New Haven, CT: Incentives for Global Health, 2008), available at: http://www.yale.edu/macmillan/igh/hif_book.pdf.

Hugenholtz, Bernt P., and Ruth L. Okediji, *Conceiving an International Instrument on Limitations and Exceptions to Copyright, Final Report*, March 6, 2008, available at: http://www.ivir.nl/publicaties/hugenholtz/finalreport2008.pdf.

Human Rights Council, *Report on Technology Transfer and the WIPO Development Agenda*, A/HRC/15/WG.2/TF/CRP.1, November 19, 2009, p. 5, available at: http://www2.ohchr.org/english/issues/development/right/docs/A-HRC-15-WG2-TF-CRP1.pdf.

Huttermann, Aloys, and Ulrich Storz, "A Comparison between Biotech and Software Related Patents" (2009) 31 *European Intellectual Property Review*.

Jaffe, Adam, and Loshua Lerner, *Innovation and Its Discountents: How Our Broken Patent System Is Endangering Innovation and Progress, and What to Do about It* (Princeton, NJ: Princeton University Press, 2008).

Javorcik, B., "The Composition of Foreign Direct Investment and Protection of Intellectual Property Rights: Evidence in Transition Economies" (2004) 48 *European Economic Review*.

Kim, L., *Technology Transfer and Intellectual Property Rights: Lessons from Korea's Experience*, International Centre for Trade and Sustainable Development & United Nations Conference on Trade and Development Working Paper (2002), available at: http://ictsd.net/i/publications/11772.

Kumar, Nagesh, *Intellectual Property Rights, Technology and Economic Development: Experiences of Asian Countries* RIS Discussion Paper 25/2002 (2002), available at: http://www.ris.org.in/dp25_pap.pdf.

Lerner, Josh, *Patent Protection and Innovation over 150 Years*, NBER Working Paper 8977 (Cambridge, MA: National Bureau of Economic Research, 2002), available at: http://www.nber.org/papers/w8977.

Leirer, Wolfgang W., "Retaliatory Action in United States and European Union Trade Law: A Comparison of Section 301 of the Trade Act of 1974 and Council Regulation 2641/84" (1994) 20 *North Carolina Journal of International Law & Commercial Regulation*.

Lim, Heng Gee, Ida Madieha bt Abdul Ghani Azmi, and Rokiah Alavi, *Impact of the Intellectual Property System on Economic Growth: Fact-Finding Surveys and Analysis in the Asian Region Country Report – Malaysia* (undated) WIPO – UNU Joint Research Project, available at: http://www.wipo.int/export/sites/www/about-ip/en/studies/pdf/wipo_unu_07_malaysia.pdf.

Liu, Yao-Jen, and Shang-Jyh Liu, "The Intellectual Property Policy of Taiwan: A Strategic Viewpoint" (2004) *Proceedings of the 2004 IEEE International*.

Looney, Robert, "New International Economic Order," in *Routledge Encyclopedia of International Political Economy* (1999), available at: http://www.chicagobooth.edu/faculty/selectedpapers/sp49.pdf.

Loughran, Regina A., "United States Position on Revising the Paris Convention: Quid Pro Quo or Denunciation" (1982) 5 *Fordham International Law Journal*.

Lowy, Joan, "Many High-Speed Rail Jobs Could Go to Foreign Companies with Fast-Train Experience," *Los Angeles Times*, January 28, 2010, available at: http://www.latimes.com.

Mashelkar Committee, Report on Pharma Patenting, March 2009.

Maskus, Keith E., *Encouraging International Technology Transfer*, International Centre for Trade and Sustainable Development & United Nations Conference on Trade and Development Issue Paper No. 7 (2004).
______, "Using the International Trading System to Foster Technology Transfer for Economic Development" (2005) 1 *Michigan State Law Review*.
______, "Intellectual Property Rights and Economic Development" (2000) 32 *Case Western Reserve Journal of International Law*.
______, *Intellectual Property Rights in the Global Economy* (Washington, DC: Institute for International Economics, 2000).
______, "Incorporating a Globalized Intellectual Property Rights Regime into an Economic Development Strategy," in Keith Maskus (ed.), *Intellectual Property, Growth and Trade* (Oxford: Elsevier, 2008).
Maskus, Keith E., and C. R. McDaniel, "Impacts of the Japanese Patent System on Productivity Growth" (1999) 11 *Japan and the World Economy*.
Maskus, Keith E., and Jerome H. Reichman, "The Globalization of Private Knowledge Goods and the Privatization of Global Public Goods" (2004) 7 *Journal of International Economic Law*.
______, (eds.), *International Public Goods and Transfer of Technology under a Globalized Intellectual Property Regime* (Cambridge: Cambridge University Press, 2005).
Maskus, Keith E., K. Saggi, and T. Puttitanun, "Patent Rights and International Technology Transfer through Direct Investment and Licensing," in K. E. Maskus and J. H. Reichman (eds.), *International Public Goods and Transfer of Technology under a Globalized Intellectual Property Regime* (Cambridge: Cambridge University Press, 2004).
Matthews, Duncan, *Globalising Intellectual Property Rights: The TRIPS Agreement* (Oxford: Routledge, 2002).
Matthews, Duncan, and Viviana Munoz-Tellez, "Bilateral Technical Assistance and TRIPS: The United States, Japan and the European Communities in Comparative Perspective" (2006) 9 *Journal of World Intellectual Property*.
May, Christopher, and Susan K. Sell, *Intellectual Property Rights: A Critical History* (Boulder, CO: Lynne Rienner Publishers, 2005).
Mazzoleni, Roberto, and Luciano Martins Costa Póvoa, "Accumulation of Technological Capabilities and Economic Development: Did Brazil's Regime of Intellectual Property Rights Matter?" in Hiroyuki Odagiri, Akira Goto, Atsushi Sunami, and Richard R. Nelson (eds.), *Intellectual Property Rights, Development, and Catch-Up* (Oxford: Oxford University Press, 2010).
McCalman, Phillip, "Reaping What You Sow: An Empirical Analysis of International Patent Harmonization" (2001) 55 *Journal of International Economics*.
______, "Who Enjoys, 'TRIPS' Abroad? An Empirical Analysis of Intellectual Property Rights in the Uruguay Round" (2005) 38 *Canadian Journal of Economics*.
McDorman, Ted L., "U.S.–Thailand Trade Disputes: Applying Section 301 to Cigarettes and Intellectual Property" (1992) 14 *Michigan Journal of International Law*.
McManis, Charles R., "The Proposed Anti-Counterfeiting Trade Agreement (ACTA): Two Tales of a Treaty" (2009) 46 *Houston Law Review*.
Mercurio, Bryan, "TRIPS-Plus Provisions in Regional Trade Agreements," in Lorand Bartels and Federico Ortino (eds.), *Regional Trade Agreements and the WTO Legal System* (New York: Oxford University Press, 2006).
______, "Growth and Development: Economic and Legal Conditions" (2007) 30 *University of New South Wales Law Journal*.

———, "The WTO and Its Institutional Impediments" (2007) 8 *Melbourne Journal of International Law*.

———, "Health in the Developing World: The Case for a New International Funding and Support Agency" (2009) 4 *Asian Journal of WTO & International Health Law and Policy*.

Mercurio, Bryan, and Mitali Tyagi, "Treaty Interpretation in WTO Dispute Settlement: The Outstanding Question of the Legality of Local Working Requirements" (2010) 19 *Minnesota Journal of International Law*.

Moon, Suerie, *Does TRIPS Art. 66.2 Encourage Technology Transfer to LDCs? An Analysis of Country Submissions to the TRIPS Council (1999–2007)*, United Nations Conference on Trade and Development–International Centre for Trade and Sustainable Development Project on IPRs and Sustainable Development, Policy Brief Number 2 (2008), available at: http://www.iprsonline.org/unctadictsd/docs/New%202009/Policy%20Briefs/policy-brief-2.pdf.

Musungu, Sisule F., and Cecilia Oh, *The Use of Flexibilities in TRIPS by Developing Countries: Can They Promote Access to Medicines?* (Geneva: South Centre, 2006).

Netanel, Neil W. (ed.), *The Development Agenda: Global Intellectual Property and Developing Countries* (New York: Oxford University Press, 2009).

Ordover, Janusz A., "A Patent System for Both Diffusion and Exclusion," (1991) 5 *Journal of Economic Perspectives*.

Organization for Economic Cooperation and Development, *Policy Framework for Investment: A Review of Good Practices* (2006), available at: http://www.oecd.org/dataoecd/1/31/36671400.pdf.

Osterard, Robert L., Jr., *The Development Dilemma: The Political Economy of Intellectual Property Rights in the International System* (El Paso, TX: LFB Scholarly Publishing, 2003).

Paas, Katri, "Compulsory Licensing under the TRIPS Agreement – A Cruel Taunt for Developing Countries?" (2009) 31 *European Intellectual Property Review*.

Rai, R. Kumar, "Effect of the TRIPS-Mandated Intellectual Property Rights on Foreign Direct Investment in Developing Countries: A Case Study of the Indian Pharmaceutical Industry" (2008) 11 *Journal of World Intellectual Property*.

Rapp, R., and R. Rozek, "Benefits and Costs of Intellectual Property Protection in Developing Countries" (1990) 24 *Journal of World Trade*.

Reichman, Jerome H., "Securing Compliance with the TRIPS Agreement after U.S. v India" (1998) 1 *Journal of International Economic Law*.

———, "Database Protection in a Global Economy" (2002) *Revue Internationale de Droit Économique* 457, 479–480.

———, "Nurturing a Transnational System of Innovation" (2007) 16 *Journal of Transnational Law & Policy*.

———, "Intellectual Property in the Twenty-First Century: Will the Developing Countries Lead or Follow?" (2009) 46 *Houston Law Review*.

Ricketson, Sam, *The Berne Convention for the Protection of Literary and Artistic Works: 1886–1986* (London: Centre for Commercial Law Studies, Queen Mary College, 1987).

Roffe, P., D. Vivas, and G. Vea, *Maintaining Policy Space for Development: A Case Study on IP Technical Assistance in FTAs*, International Centre for Trade and Sustainable Development Issue Paper No. 19 (2007), available at: http://www.iprsonline.org/resources/docs/Roffe-Vivas-Vea%20Blue19.pdf.

Ruse-Khan, Henning Grosse, and Annette Kur, *Enough Is Enough – The Notion of Binding Ceilings in International Intellectual Property Protection*, Max Planck Institute for Intellectual Property, Competition & Tax Law Research Paper Series No. 09-01 (2008), available at: http://ssrn.com/abstract=1326429.

Samuelsson, Pamela, and Suzanne Scotchmer, "The Law and Economics of Reverse Engineering" (2002) 111 *Yale Law Journal*.

Schacht, Wendy H., *Patent Reform: Issues in the Biomedical and Software Industries*, Congressional Research Service (April 7, 2006), available at: http://sharp.sefora.org/wp-content/uploads/2007/12/rl33367.pdf.

Sell, Susan K., "Intellectual Property as a Trade Issue: From the Paris Convention to GATT" (1989) 13 *Legal Studies Forum*.

______, *Power and Ideas: North–South Politics of Intellectual Property and Antitrust* (Albany: State University of New York Press, 1998).

______, *The Global IP Upward Ratchet, Anti-Counterfeiting and Piracy Enforcement Efforts: The State of Play* (2008), available at: http://twnside.org.sg/title2/intellectual_property/development.research/SusanSellfinalversion.pdf.

Shih, Toh Han, "GE Wants China's Fast-Rail Technology: Beijing May Supply the Skills to Fulfil Obama's Dream of High-Speed Network across US," *South China Morning Post*, February 17, 2010.

Sornarajah, M., *The International Law on Foreign Investment* (Cambridge: Cambridge University Press, 2004).

Stiglitz, Joseph E., *Knowledge as a Global Public Good*, Graduate School of Business, Columbia University (1999), available at: http://cgt.columbia.edu/files/papers/1999_Knowledge_as_Global_Public_Good_stiglitz.pdf.

Sykes, Alan O., "Constructive Unilateral Threats in International Commercial Relations: The Limited Case for Section 301" (1992) 23 *Law & Policy in International Business*.

______, "TRIPS, Pharmaceuticals, Developing Countries, and the Doha 'Solution,'" (2002) 3 *Chicago Journal of International Law*.

Thorpe, Phil, *Study on the Implementation of the TRIPS Agreement by Developing Countries*, Commission on Intellectual Property Rights Study Paper 7 (undated), available at: http://www.iprcommission.org/papers/pdfs/study_papers/sp7_thorpe_study.pdf.

Trainer, Timothy P., "Intellectual Property Enforcement: A Reality Gap (Insufficient Assistance, Ineffective Implementation)?" (2008) 8 *John Marshall Review of Intellectual Property Law*.

United Nations Conference on Trade and Development, *The Least Developed Countries Report 2007: Knowledge, Technological Learning and Innovation for Development*, (Geneva: United Nations, 2007), available at: http://www.unctad.org/en/docs/ldc2007_en.pdf.

______, *Fostering Technological Dynamism: Evolution of Thought on Technological Development Processes and Competitiveness* (Geneva/New York: United Nations, 1996).

United States Federal Trade Commission, *Generic Drug Entry Prior to Patent Expiration: An FTC Study* (Washington, DC: U.S. Federal Trade Commission, 2002).

Womach, Jasper, *Agriculture: A Glossary of Terms, Programs, and Laws*, Congressional Research Service Report for Congress (2005).

World Bank, *World Development Report 1998/99: Knowledge for Development*.

______, *Global Economic Prospects and Developing Countries 2002*.

World Intellectual Property Association, *Substantive Patent Law Harmonization Law*, available at: http://www.wipo.int/patent-law/en/harmonization.htm.

World Trade Organization, Council for TRIPS, *Review of Legislation in the Fields of Patents, Layout-Designs (Topographies) of Integrated Circuits, Protection of Undisclosed Information*

and Control of Anti-Competitive Practices in Contractual Licences, IP/Q3/USA/1, 1 May 1998.
———, Report of the Panel, *United States – Section 301–310 of the Trade Act of 1974*, WT/DS152/R, 22 *December* 1999.
———, Report of the Panel, US – Section 110(5) Copyright Act, 15 June 2000, WTO Doc. WT/DS/160/R.
———, Panel Report, *Canada-Patent Protection of Pharmaceutical Products*, April 7, 2000, WTO Doc. WT/DS114/R.

4

Trade, Border Security, and Development

Maureen Irish

I. INTRODUCTION

How are developing countries to react to recent changes in border security procedures that are detrimental to their interests? Since the terrorist attacks of September 11, 2001, on the United States, border measures for goods have become part of the new security environment. Defending against possible attacks on ports and harbors is a difficult challenge when tiny amounts of chemical, biological, or nuclear substances can cause devastating harm. In response to the threat, governments adopted new approaches in border administration. For oceangoing cargo, security inspections are no longer limited to the place of importation but have shifted to the place of export where goods are loaded into large shipping containers and placed onto vessels. Exporting countries are expected to have facilities, equipment, and personnel ready to scan these containers using X-ray and gamma-ray technology, and radiation detection devices.

Countries wanting to resist these changes in border administration have had to deal with unilateral actions by importing countries, with negotiations in a maritime treaty and with a standardization process at the World Customs Organization. It would be difficult for a developing country to act alone to argue against the new measures. Sonia E. Rolland has examined alliances among developing countries at the World Trade Organization (WTO) and advocates increased support for

This paper is part of a project on border security that has benefited from the assistance of Robert Shapiro, Rahim Punjani, Michelle Oliel, Gia Williams, Shannon Derrick, Angela Papanicolopoulou, Slawomir Szlapczynski, Zlatina Georgieva, and Christopher Fitch. I would like to express my appreciation to Annette Demers, Reference Librarian, Paul Martin Law Library, University of Windsor. Financial support for the project from the Law Foundation of Ontario is gratefully acknowledged. I am also grateful for discussions on border security issues with participants in the 2009 World Customs Organization's Partnerships in Customs Academic Research and Development (PICARD) conference in San Jose, Costa Rica, in particular, Carol West, Hans-Michael Wolffgang, and Mariya Polner. Any errors or omissions are mine.

coalitions, especially regional ones.[1] To enhance the position of developing countries within the WTO, Yong-Shik Lee has recommended elevating the current Committee on Trade and Development to full Council status and negotiating a new set of rules to reform the provisions on special and differential treatment that appear throughout several agreements.[2] Border security is a particularly daunting issue for developing countries to address because discussions take place in several settings. Now that the solidarity of the New International Economic Order (NIEO) era in the 1970s has faded, there is an absence of structure for those countries whose interests are negatively affected by the new regime.

This chapter discusses the new security measures for oceangoing transport in light of the entitlement of developing countries to special and differential treatment. The chapter first outlines the changes in maritime shipping rules in response to the new security concerns. It then analyzes legal arguments based on WTO law, including provisions available only to developing countries. The following section considers the scope of a national security defense and comments on the role of general public international law in WTO dispute settlement. The chapter identifies some issues of extraterritoriality and possible noncompliance with WTO law, including a failure to reflect special and differential treatment for developing countries in the establishment of the new framework.

Security is one of the traditional responsibilities of customs enforcement, the duty to protect the territory from dangerous goods, plants, animals, and harmful imports of all kinds. All countries, developed and developing, share an interest in combating terrorism and ensuring security. National security matters are, of course, of the highest order. When the protection of national security requires the cooperation of outsiders, the security interests of all the participating countries are implicated. The new border measures place an economic burden on developing countries for security concerns that may not match their own national security priorities.

If the new measures are to fit within modern customs administration, their conformity with international trade law must be addressed. This could be done through dispute settlement at the WTO or possibly through negotiation of new provisions that would address the need to protect security and also recognize the special position of developing countries. Developing countries have an opportunity to use their legal rights in the WTO, but questions remain over the most effective way to advance their interests.

[1] Sonia E. Rolland, "Developing Country Coalitions at the WTO: In Search of Legal Support" (2007) 48 *Harvard International Law Journal* 483. She has also argued in favor of recognition of differentiation among WTO Members in the negotiating structures. Sonia E. Rolland, "Redesigning the Negotiation Process at the WTO" (2010) 13(1) *Journal of International Economic Law* 65.

[2] Yong-Shik Lee, "Development and the World Trade Organization: Proposal for the Agreement on Development Facilitation and the Council for Trade and Development in the WTO," in Yong-Shik Lee (ed.), *Economic Development through World Trade: A Developing World Perspective* (The Hague: Kluwer Law International, 2008), p. 3.

II. OCEAN TRANSIT

Large shipping containers have transformed the world of maritime carriage of goods, saving the time and expense previously involved in the handling, loading, and unloading of packages. After the attacks of September 11, 2001, the United States Customs Service adopted a major change in its approach to the treatment of imports in shipping containers. Commissioner Robert C. Bonner announced the change in a speech to the Center for Strategic and International Studies on January 17, 2002.[3] Rather than accepting the usual practice of preparation of the ship's manifest and the entry documents during the voyage,[4] Customs would instead demand that the information be filed before the loading of the goods into the container. Through agreements with host governments at the place of export, Customs Service officers would assist in identifying and inspecting high-risk containers to prevent dangerous weapons and possibly people[5] from reaching U.S. shores.

The Container Security Initiative (CSI) was put into place starting in 2002 at the most significant sources of imports arriving in the United States.[6] It was gradually expanded to other ports so that it covered approximately 86% of containerized cargo imports into the United States by the end of 2007.[7] To qualify for CSI, a port must have gamma-ray or X-ray equipment and radiation detection devices. The arrangements with other governments are reciprocal. Other nations are invited to station their customs officers in U.S. territory to deal with inspections of containers bound for their countries. After a container is sealed and scanned, it does not have to be inspected again on arrival in the country of import. For exports to the United States, information must be filed at least twenty-four hours before loading.[8] Filing

3 U.S. Customs Commissioner Robert C. Bonner, *Speech before the Center for Strategic and International Studies* (Washington, DC, January 17, 2002), available at: http://www.cbp.gov/xp/cgov/newsroom/commissioner/speeches_statements/archives/2002/jan172002.xml, accessed April 3, 2010.

4 Gregory W. Bowman, "Thinking Outside the Border: Homeland Security and the Forward Deployment of the U.S. Border" (2007) 44 *Houston Law Review* 198, 208; United Nations Conference on Trade and Development, *Container Security: Major Initiatives and Related International Developments*, Report by the UNCTAD Secretariat, UNCTAD/SDTE/TLB/2004/1 (February 26, 2004), paras. 20, 21.

5 In October 2001, authorities in Italy found a suspected terrorist in a container destined for Halifax, Canada. The container was equipped with a bed and bathroom for the journey. See U.S. Customs Commissioner Robert C. Bonner, January 17, 2002, supra note 3.

6 Security and Accountability for Every Port Act of 2006 (SAFE Port Act), Pub. L. No. 109-347, 120 Stat. 1884 (2006), Sec. 205.

7 U.S. Customs and Border Protection, Fact Sheet, *CSI in Brief* (March 3, 2008), available at: http://www.cbp.gov/xp/cgov/trade/cargo_security/csi/csi_in_brief.xml, accessed April 3, 2010. For a description of the gradual expansion of coverage, see Marjorie Florestal, "Terror on the High Seas: The Trade and Development Implications of U.S. National Security Measures" (2007) 72 *Brooklyn Law Review* 392–394.

8 19 C.F.R. § 4.7(b)(2).

of information and any inspection cover all containers, even if some are to be transhipped to third countries.[9]

In December 2002, the International Maritime Organization (IMO) adopted the International Ship and Port Facility Security Code (ISPS Code) as amendments to the International Convention for the Safety of Life at Sea (SOLAS Convention).[10] The ISPS Code entered into effect on July 1, 2004. Its application is mandatory for all contracting governments to the SOLAS Convention.[11] The Code calls for security plans for ships and port facilities, international ship security certificates from the flag state of the ship, and identification of personnel responsible for security.[12] Ship and port facility security plans involve three possible levels of security, the details of which are approved following security assessments.[13] If a ship enters or plans to enter a port that is at a lower level of security than the ship, it shall so advise the port authorities and the government in which the port is located.[14]

Governments supervise compliance with the Code.[15] SOLAS Regulation XI-2/9 gives governments the authority to monitor ISPS compliance by ships that visit their ports. Governments may inspect them, delay them, detain them, restrict their operations within the port, or even expel them from the port.[16] Ships must provide information on request when they intend to enter a port and must keep records for their last ten calls in port. If the government of a port has clear grounds to believe a ship to be in noncompliance with the ISPS Code, the government may inspect, demand a rectification of the noncompliance, or deny permission to enter the port.[17] In addition, ISPS compliance for ships and ports could be linked to authorized economic operator programs that are used by some governments to give preferred status to commercial supply chain participants who meet certain security requirements. In the U.S. program C-TPAT (Customs-Trade Partnership Against Terrorism), the criteria for marine and port terminal operators note that ISPS certification is accepted as satisfying the relevant requirements for physical access and security controls. As well, the criteria state that C-TPAT members may only use terminals that are in

[9] United Nations Conference on Trade and Development (UNCTAD) 2004, para. 21. For discussion of the provision of information, see ibid., paras. 22–39. See further SAFE Port Act, supra note 6, Sec. 203(b).

[10] *International Convention for the Safety of Life at Sea*, November 1, 1974, in force May 25, 1980, 1184 U.N.T.S. 3, 14 Int'l Legal Materials 959 (SOLAS Convention). The ISPS Code is not available on the IMO Web site but must be purchased from the International Maritime Organization or from a commercial supplier. This is an unfortunate arrangement for an organization taking part in global public-policy making.

[11] SOLAS Convention, Article I(b). As of February 28, 2010, there are 159 parties to the convention (http://www.imo.org). The amendment was adopted pursuant to Article VIII(c). Note that the convention applies to bulk trade as well as containers.

[12] See UNCTAD, *Review of Maritime Transport* (2005), pp. 85–87.

[13] ISPS Code, Part A, sections 7, 8, 14, 15.

[14] ISPS Code, Part A, section 7.7.

[15] ISPS Code, Part A, section 4.

[16] Regulation XI-2/9, section 1.3.

[17] Regulation XI-2/9, section 2.

compliance with the ISPS code.[18] C-TPAT membership includes importers, carriers (highway, rail, air, and sea), foreign manufacturers, customs brokers, marine port and terminal operators, and third-party logistics providers.

In June 2005, the World Customs Organization (WCO) adopted the SAFE Framework of Standards at its annual meeting.[19] The SAFE Framework provides standards designed to secure and facilitate trade, particularly in relation to global supply chains. The standards apply to relations between governments and to their dealings with the private sector. One of the standards supports the CSI approach to inspection. It states that "[t]he Customs administration should conduct outbound security inspection of high-risk containers and cargo at the reasonable request of the importing country."[20] As well, the technical specifications for Standard 1 on customs control procedures state that "[t]he exporter . . . has to submit an advance electronic export Goods Declaration . . . prior to the goods being loaded onto the means of transport or into the container being used for their exportation."[21] The World Customs Organization (WCO) model convention for mutual administrative assistance between governments also supports advance exchange of information for security reasons. Article 10 of the convention permits mutual arrangements for the exchange of cargo information before the arrival of imports at a territorial border.[22] Since 2005, the International Organization for Standardization (ISO) has had industry guidelines for supply chain management. In 2007, these were upgraded from publicly available specifications to international standards. The standards are intended to set out

[18] C-TPAT, Minimum-Security Criteria, U.S. and Foreign-Based Marine Port Authority and Terminal Operator (MPTO), August 2007, p. 2, available at: http://www.cbp.gov/xp/cgov/trade/cargo_security/ctpat/security_criteria/; follow the links for maritime port authority and terminal operators.

[19] World Customs Organization, *Framework of Standards to Secure and Facilitate Global Trade* (2005). The framework was reissued and updated to add standards for supply chain participant programs such as C-TPAT in June 2007. World Customs Organization, *WCO SAFE Framework of Standards* (2007).

[20] Customs-to-Customs Standard 11, *WCO SAFE Framework of Standards*, pp. 9, 24.

[21] *WCO SAFE Framework of Standards* at 11, technical specifications for Customs-to-Customs Standard 1. As well, the carrier has to submit an advance electronic cargo declaration that "should be lodged" in advance of the loading of the goods or container onto the ship (ibid., p. 13).

[22] WCO, *International Convention on Mutual Administrative Assistance in Customs Matters (Johannesburg Convention)*, opened for signature June 27, 2003, Article 10. The information listed is as follows: consignor or consignor code or exporter or exporter code; description of goods or tariff code number; UNDG number (dangerous goods code); type of packages identification; number of packages; measure unit qualifier; total gross weight; total invoice amount; currency code; place of loading or place of loading code; carrier identification or carrier name; equipment identification number; equipment size and type identification; seal number; identification of means of transport crossing the border of the territory of the Contracting Party or code; nationality of means of transport crossing the border of the territory of the Contracting Party or code; conveyance reference number; transport charges method of payment or code; Customs office of exit or code; country(ies) of routing or code; first port of arrival or code; date and time of arrival at first port of arrival in the territory of the Contracting Party or code; consignee or consignee code or importer or importer code; notify party or notify party code; delivery destination; agent or agent code; Unique Consignment Reference Number (Article 10(2)). A similar list of information is included in the technical specifications in the WCO SAFE Framework for the export goods and cargo declarations (*WCO SAFE Framework of Standards*, pp. 11–14).

practices that will assist in compliance with the ISPS Code and the WCO SAFE Framework.[23]

Further changes are under discussion. In particular, as of July 1, 2012, U.S. legislation is set to ban entry of any containers that were not "scanned by nonintrusive imaging equipment and radiation detection equipment" at the port of export.[24] This requirement of 100% scanning has been strongly criticized by U.S. trading partners and by the World Customs Organization.[25] Critics point to the cost and disruption at ports of export and see the impending change as a rejection of risk-based management that would produce few, if any, security benefits.[26]

III. CLAIMS IN WTO LAW

Developing countries may conclude that the recent changes in border security are not designed with their priorities in mind. The CSI involves a financial burden for any exporting country that participates. Scanning equipment must be purchased and maintained. Space must be found for a facility to do the scanning. Extra staff time is required for inspections and coordination with customs officers from the importing country. The United States as the importing country does not shoulder the burden but expects the exporting country to cover the costs.[27] It is not surprising that the areas of the world left out of CSI tend to consist of developing and least developed countries.[28] Their trading opportunities are diminished for any exports that would be shipped by container.

[23] UNCTAD, *Review of Maritime Transport* (2008), p. 117 (referring to ISO 20858 concerning maritime port facility security assessments and security plan development, and the ISO 28000 series of standards for supply chain management).

[24] Implementing Recommendations of the 9/11 Commission Act, Pub. L. 110-53, 121 Stat. 266 (2007), Sec. 1701. The section provides for possible two-year delays in the implementation date in certain circumstances, including technical inadequacies of available equipment and significant impacts on flow of trade and cargo. Sec. 1701(4).

[25] Robert Ireland, "The WCO SAFE Framework of Standards: Avoiding Excess in Global Supply Chain Security Policy" (2009) 4 *Global Trade and Customs Journal* 341.

[26] European Commission Staff Working Document, Secure Trade and 100% Scanning of Containers, February 2010, SEC (2010) 131 final; Policy Research Corporation, The Impact of 100% Scanning of U.S.-Bound Containers on Maritime Transport, April 24, 2009, report commissioned by the European Commission, Directorate-General Energy and Transport; D. Widdowson and S. Holloway, "Maritime Transport Security Regulation: Policies, Probabilities and Practicalities" (2009) 3(2) *World Customs Journal* 17.

[27] An exception was made in the case of Greece, the host of the 2004 Summer Olympics. On this occasion, the United States provided the technology on loan. See Marjorie Florestal, "Terror on the High Seas: The Trade and Development Implications of U.S. National Security Measures" (2006–2007) 72 *Brooklyn Law Review* 394n35. The U.S. government also donated an X-ray machine for scanning at the port of Santos in Brazil. Lyndon B. Johnson School of Public Affairs, the University of Texas at Austin, *Port and Supply-Chain Security Initiatives in the United States and Abroad*, report prepared for the Congressional Research Service, Policy Research Project Report No. 150 (2006), p. 101.

[28] Eric J. Lobsinger, "Post-9/11 Security in a Post-WWII World: The Question of Compatibility of Maritime Security Efforts with Trade Rules and International Law" (2007) 32 *Tulane Maritime Law Journal* 100–103.

The new ISPS Code imposes burdens on countries that are members of the SOLAS Convention, because ports must prepare and follow security plans, and governments must certify and monitor them. The Code is not limited to container traffic but applies to ships involved in all types of trade. There is no provision of special and differential treatment for developing countries. A United Nations Conference on Trade and Development (UNCTAD) study examined the costs of implementing the ISPS Code between 2003 and 2005. The study observed scale effects showing that expenses were relatively higher at small ports.[29] The ISPS Code is costly, but being outside the Code is also a clear disadvantage for any country with export interests.

There are several possible WTO claims over the changes in ocean transit, including some provisions available only to developing countries. This section discusses those claims. Potential defenses are examined in the following section.

Article I of the General Agreement on Tariffs and Trade (GATT) provides for most-favored-nation (MFN) treatment for products originating in or destined for WTO member countries. The obligation applies to "all rules and formalities in connection with importation or exportation." The obligation has wide scope, covering "any advantage, favour, privilege or immunity." Assume two shipments of toys, one from country A that has CSI ports, and the other from country B that does not have CSI ports. The toys originating in A can be loaded onto a container that is sealed and inspected if necessary and then shipped twenty-four hours after the filing of all relevant information. The container will not have to be inspected again when it arrives at the port in the United States or other importing country that applies a similar CSI rule. The toys from country B, however, will need to transit to another country of export to have the same treatment. If they leave from a port in B, they risk more complex and lengthy formalities on arrival, even if they meet the rules regarding entry information filing before loading and even if the port in B complies with the requirements of the ISPS Code. There could be delays before the cargo is permitted to unload, as well as the possibility of penalties, extra expenses, and further delays. CSI ports seem to have advantages over non-CSI ports. It appears that the toys from A receive better treatment than the toys from B, contrary to GATT Article I. In response, it could be argued that the difference is based on the place of shipment rather than the country of origin. At the very least, producers in country B would have an extra expense for transportation to deliver goods to a port in another country first before shipping them to the intended destination. In addition, because the MFN treatment obligation also applies to exports, there is a likely breach of GATT Article I by country A, the country of origin with CSI ports, if its export rules and formalities for goods destined for the United States or another CSI partner country are different from the export rules and formalities that apply to goods destined for other WTO Members, assuming such rules and formalities count as an "advantage, favour, privilege or immunity."

[29] *Maritime Security: ISPS Code Implementation, Costs and Related Financing*, Report by the UNCTAD Secretariat, UNCTAD/SDTE/TLB/2007/1 (March 14, 2007).

Assume a further shipment of toys from country C, whose ports are not ISPS-certified. Goods shipped from those ports could encounter additional delays and even be turned away on arrival at their destination, pursuant to the SOLAS Convention. Even if the ship has a valid ISPS certificate from its own flag state, it might have moved to a higher level of security because it stopped at the non-ISPS port in country C. If this is a question of the origin of goods rather than their place of shipment, there could be a breach of Article I or possibly GATT Article XI, should the goods be denied entry altogether. Article XI prohibits import restrictions other than duties, taxes, and other charges.[30] Analysis is similar but a bit more complicated if the ship had other cargo on board before it stopped at the port in C, because all the cargo would receive whatever treatment is given to the toys from C, even if the other cargo was in containers loaded and sealed previously in CSI-compliant circumstances. Articles I or XI could be implicated, depending on whether the effect of the lack of ISPS certification for the port in C leads to delays and penalties or to denial of entry altogether. If the destination country is one that links its authorized economic operator program to the exclusive use of ISPS ports, then whatever benefits flow from membership in that program would also be affected for all the goods on board (and possibly for other activities of members of the program). Those benefits are likely to be matters such as speedier customs processing and reduced likelihood of secondary inspections, all issues that would qualify for GATT Article I coverage as advantages, favors, privileges, or immunities in connection with importation.

GATT Article V on freedom of transit of goods through the territory of a WTO member country would also be relevant. Pursuant to Article V:2, goods are to have freedom of transit without distinction based on "the flag of vessels, the place of origin, departure, entry, exit or destination." Article V:5 contains an MFN obligation requiring that all traffic in transit to or from a WTO Member be treated no less favorably than traffic to or from any other country. Because Article V prohibits distinctions based on the place of shipment, differences in treatment related to CSI compliance or ISPS compliance could be problematic.[31] The obligation of Article V:5 applies to all charges, regulations, and formalities in connection with the transit, which would cover matters such as delays, penalties, and denial of entry.

Further, Article V:6 states that goods that have been in transit through the territory of a WTO Member shall receive treatment no less favorable than the treatment they would have had if they had come directly from their country of origin without the period in transit. If goods receive less favorable treatment because they were on a ship that later called at a non-ISPS certified port, there would likely be a breach of Article V:6. Distinctions based on CSI-compliance or the twenty-four-hour rule might also

[30] If a 100% scanning requirement is put into effect, analysis of Articles I and XI would be similar, depending on whether a failure to scan all cargo leads to delays and penalties or results in denial of entry of the ship.

[31] Justin S. C. Mellor, "Missing the Boat: The Legal and Practical Problems of the Prevention of Maritime Terrorism" (2002) 18 *American University International Law Review* 394.

be vulnerable to Article V:6, because transit as defined in Article V:1 could include warehousing, breaking bulk, and changing the mode of transportation. If the transit involves reloading of the goods at an intermediate port, then treatment might differ depending on the circumstances of that reshipment and might be less favorable than the treatment they would have received if they had been transported directly from the country of origin.

Special and differential treatment for developing countries has been part of international trade law since at least the negotiation of GATT in October 1947.[32] Part IV was added to GATT in 1965 to recognize trade as a means of achieving economic development. In Part IV, Article XXXVII:3 commits developed countries to have special regard to the trade interests of developing countries and to "explore all possibilities of constructive remedies before applying . . . measures . . . [that] would affect essential interests" of developing countries.[33] Developed countries are also to consider collaborating in international action to "provide greater scope for the development of imports" from developing countries.[34] Developed countries are obliged to "refrain from . . . increasing . . . nontariff import barriers on products . . . of particular export interest" to developing countries.[35] Article XXXVIII contains a number of obligations to collaborate in GATT and elsewhere to promote economic development through trade, including through "international harmonization and adjustment of national policies and regulations" and through "technical and commercial standards affecting . . . transportation."[36] These Part IV obligations are significantly at odds with the establishment of a new system for border clearances that increases the economic burdens on developing countries and creates obstacles for their exports.

The Enabling Clause of 1979 reaffirms the objectives of Part IV[37] and, in two paragraphs, emphasizes the special economic difficulties of the least developed countries.[38] Paragraph 8 requires that "particular account" be taken of the position of the least developed countries "in view of their special economic situation and their development, financial and trade needs." Although this is a somewhat more general commitment, it does appear that the least developed countries have fared badly in the new rules for security inspections since 2001.

Potential arguments are also available in other agreements in the WTO system, including the Agreement on the Application of Sanitary and Phytosanitary Measures (SPS Agreement), the Agreement on Technical Barriers to Trade (TBT Agreement),

[32] GATT Article XVIII allows developing countries extra flexibility in providing governmental assistance for economic development. Raj Bhala, "Mercy for the Third World through GATT Article XVIII" (2002) 6 *Singapore Journal of International & Comparative Law* 498.

[33] GATT, art. XXXVII:3(c).

[34] GATT, art. XXXVII:3(b).

[35] GATT, art. XXXVII:1(b).

[36] GATT, art. XXXVIII:2(e).

[37] *Differential and More Favourable Treatment, Reciprocity and Fuller Participation of Developing Countries*, Doc. L/4903, BISD 26S/203 (November, 28 1979), para. 7.

[38] Ibid., paras. 6, 8.

and the General Agreement on Trade in Services (GATS). As well, the provisions of the Agreement on Preshipment Inspection will be relevant.[39]

The SPS Agreement applies to measures that protect human, animal, or plant life from toxins and disease-causing organisms. The measures covered include processes and production methods, packaging, testing and inspection procedures, and requirements associated with the transport of animals or plants.[40] The definition thus could apply to some security concerns over biological or chemical substances, or even nuclear weapons. If the agreement applies, the inspections must be based on international standards (Article 3.1), which might include WCO and ISO standards. The measures will apply only to the extent necessary to protect health (Article 2.1). As well, they must not discriminate arbitrarily or unjustifiably among WTO Members or be applied in a manner that would constitute a disguised trade restriction (Article 2.2).

The SPS Agreement contains detailed provisions in favor of developing countries, including technical assistance.[41] Article 9.2 is as follows:

> Where substantial investments are required in order for an exporting developing country Member to fulfil the . . . requirements of an importing Member, the latter shall consider providing such technical assistance as will permit the developing country member to maintain and expand its market access opportunities for the product involved.

If this obligation applies to aspects of the border security regime, it would support efforts to enhance technical assistance for adaptation to the new requirements.

Use of the TBT Agreement would also depend on interpretation of threshold definitions. In the agreement, technical regulations and standards are defined as relating to processing and production methods of goods, including packaging requirements. The mention of processing and production methods in the definition of a technical regulation refers to "applicable administrative provisions."[42] The obligations of the agreement could be relevant to security inspections and scanning if any of the WCO or ISO standards on supply chain security are found to be sufficiently linked to processing and production. If the agreement applies, technical regulations are to be based on international standards (Article 2.4) and would be subject to an MFN obligation (Article 2.1). They could not create unnecessary obstacles to international trade or be more trade restrictive than necessary to fulfill a legitimate objective (Article 2.2). There are explicit provisions in favor of special and differential treatment in the agreement. In Article 11, technical assistance is obligatory if requested.

39 For a thorough analysis of WTO law as applied to the container security initiative, see Christopher Dallimore, "Securing the Supply Chain: Does the Container Security Initiative Comply with WTO Law?" dissertation, University of Muenster (2008), available at: http://miami.uni-muenster.de/servlets/DocumentServlet?id=4577.

40 SPS Agreement, Annex A, section 1.

41 SPS Agreement, art. 9.1.

42 TBT Agreement, Annex I.

Article 12 makes differential and more favorable treatment obligatory in the preparation and application of technical regulations and standards (Article 12.1, 12.2), with a view to ensuring that the regulations and standards "do not create unnecessary obstacles to the expansion and diversification of exports from developing country Members" (Article 12.7) including special problems relating to infrastructure (Article 12.8).

The argument based on the GATS would relate to the obligation of MFN treatment for all WTO member countries in Article II, if any aspects of maritime security are found to discriminate on the basis of the country of service suppliers, such as customs brokers, freight forwarders, or transportation services. Should it apply, GATS also has provisions to encourage the participation of developing countries in world trade.[43]

The Agreement on Preshipment Inspection provides obligations that are especially relevant to CSI inspections. The inspection activities covered in the agreement include verification of the "quality" of the goods (Article 1.4), which should include some issues of border security. Governments requiring preshipment inspection are responsible for ensuring that it is carried out in a nondiscriminatory and transparent manner (Article 2.1, 2.5). The agreement is directed primarily to the situation of developing countries that contract with private entities to do preshipment inspections of goods being exported to the developing country, usually for valuation, classification, and customs entry purposes. It covers any entity "mandated" to do preshipment inspections. Whether this definition would include a mandate given to an exporting government for some inspections is not clear, and it is possible that the independent review procedure in Article 4 would not be available for exporters in that situation. The agreement does at least impose obligations of nondiscrimination and transparency on exporting governments concerning preshipment inspection activities in their territory (Article 3).

In the Doha Round, negotiations on trade facilitation have produced a tentative text that would amend the Agreement on Preshipment Inspection. In the current Doha Round, developing countries reluctantly agreed to negotiate on trade facilitation issues relating to the movement and clearances of goods. Annex D to the General Council Decision of August 1, 2004, deals with these negotiations and supports the principle of special and differential treatment, including the recognition that "the extent and the timing of entering into commitments shall be related to the implementation capacities of developing and least developed Members."[44] In December 2009, a draft agreement was reached on trade facilitation.[45] Ironically, while preshipment inspections were being imposed on developing countries through

[43] GATS, art. IV.

[44] Decision Adopted by the General Council on August 1, 2004, WT/L/579, August 2, 2004, Annex D, para. 2.

[45] Negotiating Group on Trade Facilitation, *Draft Consolidated Negotiating Text*, TN/TF/W/165 (December 14, 2009).

changes in border security procedures outside the WTO, the trade facilitation talks moved in the opposite direction, away from preshipment inspections. Article 10.6 of the draft text, which is subject to some qualifications and bracketing, prohibits countries from imposing a requirement of preshipment inspection for customs related matters such as valuation and classification. It is hard to know what to make of Article 10.6.4 in the draft text, which would prohibit any new requirements of preshipment inspection after the effective date of any amendments. The draft provision covers all Members and appears to limit security inspections.

In summary, in WTO law, developing (and other) countries wishing to contest the changes in border administration would have several arguments available, based on the obligations of MFN treatment in GATT Article I and freedom of transit in GATT Article V. Claims might also be made under the SPS Agreement, TBT Agreement, and GATS. In addition to arguments available to all Members, developing countries can bolster their position by relying on provisions in Part IV of GATT, the Enabling Clause, the SPS Agreement, the TBT Agreement, and GATS. The Agreement on Preshipment Inspection could have particular relevance, especially in the form of the proposed amendments as drafted during the Doha Round of negotiations.

IV. NATIONAL SECURITY AND PUBLIC INTERNATIONAL LAW

If the new security measures involve breaches of WTO law, could such breaches be justified by exemption clauses in the relevant agreements or perhaps by other rules of public international law? The defense commonly advanced is the national security exemption in GATT Article XXI(b):

> Article XXI.
>
> Nothing in this Agreement shall be construed . . .
>
> (b) to prevent any Member from taking any action which it considers necessary for the protection of its essential security interests
> (i) relating to fissionable materials or the materials from which they are derived;
> (ii) relating to the traffic in arms, ammunition and implements of war and to such traffic in other goods and materials as is carried on directly or indirectly for the purpose of supplying a military establishment;
> (iii) taken in time of war or other emergency in international relations

The exemption is potentially quite wide, and the self-judging language gives a member leeway over its interpretation, or at least the interpretation of parts of it.[46]

[46] If a national security defense is not effective, the exemption in GATT Article XX(b) for measures "necessary to protect human, animal or plant life or health" might also be advanced. That exemption is not examined in this chapter.

Subparagraphs (i) and (ii) clearly apply to trade in nuclear materials and various armaments and would cover controls or bans on such trade. If an action has additional purposes, there could be a question about whether these exemptions would be available. In other words, general cargo inspections may not be in the same category as a ban on trade in specific goods, particularly if the inspections are to check for other possible threats. A WTO Member may have discretion to decide on the necessity of an action and what its essential security interests are. Such discretion, however, would not extend to the issue of whether an action relates to the matters covered by subparagraphs (i) and (ii). If those subparagraphs fail to provide a defense for all claims, then analysis would turn to the exemption in subparagraph (iii) for actions "taken in time of war or other emergency in international relations."

In the past, there was debate in GATT over whether the national security exemption of Article XXI was justiciable. Some Members argued that a national security defense was political only and beyond the competence of dispute settlement panels.[47] In the WTO, the Dispute Settlement Understanding (DSU) makes the establishment of a panel automatic, unless the Dispute Settlement Body decides by consensus against establishment.[48] A panel has standard terms of reference, unless the parties to the dispute agree otherwise, subject to control by the Dispute Settlement Body.[49] In the WTO context, it is now unlikely that a panel, the Appellate Body, or the Dispute Settlement Body as a whole would decide that a responding member could take an issue of interpretation of a covered agreement entirely outside the jurisdiction of the DSU simply by invoking the Article XXI exemption.

Andrew Emmerson has analyzed the security exemption in Article XXI as reflecting both a purely realist notion of unfettered sovereignty and now a modified concept of sovereignty defined within the WTO legal process. Whether one adopts an institutionalist approach that looks to the framework of interdependence or a constructivist approach that examines how national identities are formed within that framework, he argues that legal formalism shifts the debate toward an ideal of cooperation and constraint. There are suggestions in the academic literature that WTO panels could review the good faith and proportionality of any use of the exemption.[50] Emmerson

47 Contracting Parties to the General Agreement on Tariffs and Trade, *Analytical Index: Guide to GATT Law and Practice* (6th ed., Geneva: WTO, 1994), pp. 553–564.

48 Understanding on Rules and Procedures Governing the Settlement of Disputes (DSU), Article 6.1.

49 DSU, art. 7.

50 Michael J. Hahn, "Vital Interests and the Law of GATT: An Analysis of GATT's Security Exception" (1991) 12 *Michigan Journal of International Law* 583, 599–602; Hannes L. Schloemann and Stefan Ohlhoff, "'Constitutionalization' and Dispute Settlement in the WTO: National Security as an Issue of Competence" (1999) 93 *American Journal of International Law* 424; Dapo Akande and Sope Williams, "International Adjudication on National Security Issues: What Role for the WTO?" (2003) 43 *Virginia Journal of International Law* 365. Dallimore would also review for reasonableness. Christopher Dallimore, supra note 39, pp. 288–294.

notes that "at the very least, panels are competent to determine whether a 'war or other emergency in international relations' actually exists."[51] As Michael Hahn has pointed out, the meaning of the reference to an emergency cannot be "so vague as to encompass any tension between [s]tates."[52] The terrorist threat is clearly a crucial one, but the fact that a risk is important does not turn it automatically into an emergency, especially if the risk appears likely to continue for some period of time.

Whatever the meaning of the Article XXI defense in GATT, it would likely also cover the provisions of the SPS Agreement, which is linked to GATT by the statement in its Preamble that the Agreement is intended to be an elaboration of GATT rules. Article XIV*bis* of the GATS provides a national security exemption in language similar to the terms of GATT Article XXI. Most of the obligations examined earlier supporting special and differential treatment for developing countries are contained in GATT and are thus subject to Article XXI, except for the 1979 Enabling Clause. Like the SPS Agreement, the Enabling Clause refers to GATT and thus may also be tied to Article XXI.

There is no direct linkage between GATT and the Agreement on Preshipment Inspection, which lacks its own national security exemption. The TBT Agreement is also a separate freestanding agreement without a national security exemption, although its Preamble recognizes that "no country should be prevented from taking measures necessary for the protection of its essential security interest."[53] For these two agreements, it might be argued that they are so closely connected to GATT and GATS that the same national security exemption should be available as well. If that argument is not successful or if GATT Article XXI and GATS Article XIV*bis* are not interpreted in a way that provides a complete defense for all claims, then attention would turn to general public international law.

The possible use of non-WTO public international law by WTO panels and the Appellate Body is controversial. In the DSU, claims must be based on WTO-covered agreements.[54] DSU Article 3.2 makes it clear that those agreements are to be interpreted in accordance with the customary rules of interpretation of public international law. Joost Pauwelyn argues that, like all other treaties, the WTO agreements were born into the system of public international law. Unless the negotiators of the WTO agreements contracted out of general international law on particular topics, he maintains that responding Members may use rules of that system to defend themselves against WTO complaints. In this view, non-WTO law can be used to shape the interpretation of WTO provisions and could take priority in case

[51] Andrew Emmerson, "Conceptualizing Security Exceptions: Legal Doctrine or Political Excuse?" (2008) 11(1) *Journal of International Economic Law* 146.

[52] Hahn (1991), supra note 50, p. 592.

[53] National security is also listed as a legitimate objective of regulation: TBT Agreement, Articles 2.2, 2.10, 5.4.

[54] DSU Articles 7, 11.

of a conflict.[55] If a member supplements its national security defense with public international law analysis beyond the provisions of GATT Article XXI and GATS Article XIV*bis*, it would not be arguing that there is a conflict with WTO law, but merely that non-WTO law offers it a wider defense. A panel and potentially the Appellate Body would have to decide whether that argument is available or whether the WTO national security exemptions are all-encompassing and contract out of non-WTO law.[56]

If general public international law is available, the recent changes in maritime security would raise issues of extraterritoriality and jurisdiction. Posting customs officers to foreign territory is an intrusion on sovereignty[57] and thus requires consent from the foreign government. Even though the visiting officers from the intended country of import apply their own country's criteria to identify containers for inspection, officials of the exporting country will not necessarily agree, and the container may leave the port without being inspected. The protective principle for jurisdiction in international law provides a basis for the importing country to attempt to regulate extraterritorially to protect its vital interests, such as security, immigration, and protection of the currency.[58] Jurisdiction to regulate, however, does not give the importing country jurisdiction to enforce outside its own territory.[59] On its own, the country of import does not normally have authority to require equipment to be made available and scanning or other inspections to be done in the country of export. All of these enforcement activities require the action, or at least the authorization, of the country of export.

A comparison is sometimes made between CSI and the granting of visa applications at an embassy in foreign territory,[60] but the two situations are not fully analogous. CSI does not simply apply at the entry point into the country of import,

55 Joost Pauwelyn, "The Role of Public International Law in the WTO: How Far Can We Go?" (2001) 95 *American Journal of International Law* 535.

56 Andrew Mitchell emphasizes that this step in the reasoning requires careful interpretation of the WTO-covered agreement in accordance with customary rules of treaty interpretation, in light of the presumption that dispute settlement must be effective. Andrew D. Mitchell, *Legal Principles in WTO Disputes* (Cambridge: Cambridge University Press, 2008), p. 95; Andrew D. Mitchell, "The Legal Basis for Using Principles in WTO Disputes" (2007) 10(4) *Journal of International Economic Law* 795.

57 Antonio Cassese, *International Law* (2nd ed., New York: Oxford University Press, 2005), pp. 51–52; Jessica Romero, "Prevention of Maritime Terrorism: The Container Security Initiative" (2003) 4 *Chicago Journal of International Law* 603; Justin S. C. Mellor, "Missing the Boat: The Legal and Practical Problems of the Prevention of Maritime Terrorism" (2002) 18 *American University International Law Review* 358.

58 Ian Brownlie, *Principles of Public International Law* (6th ed., New York: Oxford University Press, 2003), p. 302; Vaughan Lowe, "Jurisdiction," in Malcolm D. Evans (ed.), *International Law* (New York: Oxford University Press, 2003), p. 342; Rosalyn Higgins, *International Law and How We Use It* (Oxford: Clarendon Press, 1994), p. 74.

59 Vaughan Lowe, supra note 58, p. 351; Malcolm N. Shaw, *International Law* (5th ed., Cambridge: Cambridge University Press, 2003), p. 573.

60 Gregory W. Bowman, supra note 4, pp. 229–230.

but requires various official actions to occur within foreign territory. As those actions become more onerous – including, perhaps, a requirement to scan all cargo – the question becomes whether such requirements are sufficiently tied to a vital interest to be covered by the protective principle, in the absence of consent.

The controversy over 100% scanning involves questions of the effectiveness of inspections and other aspects of container security. Any scanning requirement is limited to containers and does not cover other cargo that is shipped in bulk or separately because of its size or weight. The container must be sealed with a tamper-proof seal at the time of scanning. Inspecting for radiation could reveal the presence of nuclear substances, but X-ray or gamma-ray scanning would not directly reveal chemical or biological substances.[61] To supplement scanning, containers and vessels with other cargo could be equipped with devices measuring changes in temperature, pressure, and acidity to detect other harmful substances.[62]

Importing countries may wish to push the border outward to avoid the risk of bombs being detonated in a harbor on arrival. For some risks, however, such as the terrorist hidden in a container, scanning at the port of import is at least as effective as scanning elsewhere. If the importing country receives advance customs filings electronically, it can analyze the information in its own territory and decide whether to scan some or even all containers. Scanning on entry keeps the importing country in charge of its own security measures and their costs.[63] The question in public international law would be how far the protective principle extends and how much is left to the importing country to decide as a matter of its vital security interests. Depending on the assessment of the risks, the conclusion may be less deferential to the views of the importing country than GATT Article XXI and GATS Article XIV*bis*.[64]

If the national security defense in either WTO-covered agreements or non-WTO law fails to resolve all claims, there is one further question involving public international law that could arise. This issue addresses the relationship between the ISPS Code and the WTO. Because these are both treaty-based obligations, public international law might assist in determining which one has priority in case of a conflict.

[61] European Commission Staff Working Document, Secure Trade and 100% Scanning of Containers, February 2010, SEC (2010) 131 final at 11.

[62] Carsten Weerth, "The Cross-border Detection of Radiological, Biological and Chemical Active and Harmful Terrorist Devices" (2009) 3(2) *World Customs Journal* 101.

[63] Joshua A. Lindenbaum, "Assuring the Flow: Maritime Security Challenges and Trade between the U.S. and China" (2006–2007) 6 *Richmond Journal of Global Law and Business* 95; K. Lamar Walters III, "Industry on Alert: Legal and Economic Ramifications of the Homeland Security Act on Maritime Commerce" (2006) 30 *Tulane Maritime Law Journal* 311.

[64] For a recent restrictive interpretation of a national security exemption in a treaty (although differently worded), see *Oil Platforms (Islamic Republic of Iran) v. United States of America*, Judgment, ICJ Reports 2003, p. 161.

The customary international law rules on treaty interpretation are reflected in the Vienna Convention on the Law of Treaties.[65] According to Article 31(3)(c) of the Vienna Convention, interpretation shall take account of "any relevant rules of international law applicable in the relations between the parties."[66] This phrase is wide enough to support the idea that a panel and the Appellate Body have jurisdiction to consider non-WTO treaty obligations such as the ISPS Code. Should they conclude that non-WTO law conflicts with a WTO rule, there is debate over their power to respond.

Article 19.2 of the DSU states that the findings and recommendations of panels and the Appellate Body "cannot add to or diminish the rights and obligations provided in the covered agreements."[67] Does this mean that they could never give a non-WTO rule priority over a WTO agreement? Lorand Bartels concludes that panel and Appellate Body jurisdiction is restricted in just this way and that WTO-covered agreements must have priority.[68] Andrew Mitchell disagrees, on the basis that if using non-WTO law is the correct interpretation of a covered agreement, then doing so neither adds to nor diminishes the provisions of the agreement.[69] Pauwelyn argues that the DSU restrictions do not prohibit Members themselves from creating new treaty obligations and that subsequent bilateral agreements remain possible between WTO Members.[70] Gabrielle Marceau accepts that there are limits on panel and Appellate Body rulings. She suggests it would be difficult for Members to enter into separate bilateral agreements without affecting third-party rights.[71]

65 Vienna Convention on the Law of Treaties (1969) 8 *International Legal Materials* 679.

66 There is debate over whether "the parties" refers to the parties to a given dispute or whether all parties to the treaty being interpreted must also be party to an external treaty before Article 31(3)(c) applies to a rule from the external treaty. If full membership must be in common, any defense based on the ISPS Code would fail. Twenty-one WTO Members are not party to the SOLAS Convention: Armenia, Botswana, Burkina Faso, Burundi, Central African Republic, Chad, Costa Rica, El Salvador, European Union, Former Yugoslav Republic of Macedonia, Guinea Bissau, Kyrgyz Republic, Lesotho, Liechtenstein, Mali, Nepal, Niger, Rwanda, Swaziland, Uganda, and Zimbabwe (Members and Observers, http://www.wto.org; Status of Conventions, http://www.imo.org, both Web sites accessed September 28, 2010). The full common membership requirement, however, is difficult to reconcile with Article 41 of the Vienna Convention, which permits bilateral modifications of multilateral treaties.

67 DSU Article 3.2 is to the same effect concerning recommendations and rulings of the Dispute Settlement Body.

68 Lorand Bartels, "Applicable Law in WTO Dispute Settlement Proceedings" (2001) 35(3) *Journal of World Trade* 499.

69 Andrew D. Mitchell, *Legal Principles in WTO Disputes* (Cambridge: Cambridge University Press, 2008), p.96.

70 Joost Pauwelyn, "How to Win a World Trade Organization Dispute Based on Non-World Trade Organization Law? Questions of Jurisdiction and Merits" (2003) 37(6) *Journal of World Trade* 1003.

71 Gabrielle Marceau, "Conflicts of Norms and Conflicts of Jurisdictions: The Relationship between the WTO Agreement and MEAs and other Treaties" (2001) 35(6) *Journal of World Trade* 1116, 1129. See *Vienna Convention on the Law of Treaties*, art. 30(5).

Mitsuo Matsushita states there is no easy answer to the question and notes the problems of conflicting rights and obligations for parties.[72]

If both treaties are considered, they would be interpreted carefully to see whether they are in conflict. If the WTO-covered agreement prohibits a trade barrier that a non-WTO treaty seeks to permit, perhaps there is no conflict because it is possible to comply with both by obeying the prohibition. Pauwelyn rejects this narrow notion of conflict and emphasizes that the intent to permit in the non-WTO treaty should not be overridden lightly. He would apply the conflict rule of the Vienna Convention giving priority to the obligation later in time.[73] In contrast, Marceau would use a *lex specialis* approach earlier in the interpretation to give priority to a specific obligation over a more general one.[74] Concerning the changes in maritime security, some of the possible claims in WTO law are not prohibitions. The obligations of special and differential treatment, which are specific to developing countries, are potentially compatible with the ISPS Code. A panel or the Appellate Body might decide that they apply cumulatively with the ISPS Code even if there is no finding or recommendation on other claims.

It is inconvenient that a WTO panel or the Appellate Body could be prohibited from ruling on a conflict between WTO-covered agreements and non-WTO law, especially because all claims over breach of WTO obligations are supposed to be made through the DSU process.[75] Did Members intend to modify WTO agreements when they entered into the ISPS Code? Did they assume there was no incompatibility? Between two active treaty-based international institutions with wide membership, it is difficult to see how frictions can be resolved adequately using a rule that favors the obligation later in time. The answer could change with each amendment to part of one system or the other.[76] Perhaps there is need for new rules on how to interpret such overlapping obligations, assuming that panels or the Appellate Body have jurisdiction to address the issue.

In summary, the national security defense in GATT Article XXI and GATS Article XIV*bis* may be effective for some aspects of the new maritime security regime. If WTO complaints are brought, a panel and potentially the Appellate Body may have to consider arguments based on non-WTO public international law that would raise issues of their mandates as set out in the DSU.

[72] Mitsuo Matsushita, "Governance of International Trade under World Trade Organization Agreements – Relationships Between World Trade Organization Agreements and Other Trade Agreements" (2004) 38(2) *Journal of World Trade* 199.

[73] *Vienna Convention on the Law of Treaties*, art. 30(3); Joost Pauwelyn, *Conflict of Norms in Public International Law: How WTO Law Relates to other Rules of International Law* (Cambridge: Cambridge University Press, 2003). He hesitates, however, over whether WTO panels should make rulings on non-WTO law: Joost Pauwelyn, supra note 70, p. 1027.

[74] Gabrielle Marceau, supra note 71, p. 1086.

[75] DSU Article 23.

[76] Joost Pauwelyn, "Bridging Fragmentation and Unity: International Law as a Universe of Inter-Connected Islands" (2004) 25 *Michigan Journal of International Law* 903.

V. CONCLUSIONS

In the field of securitization studies, political scientists examine how states define and behave in national security crises. Securitization moves an issue outside usual politics. Its general hallmarks are an existential threat, some emergency action, and a tendency to break free from the ordinary rules.[77] As customs authorities coped with the threat of terrorism, new security measures were developed.

With the passage of time, customs administration is moving away from the securitized climate and politics of shock that followed the attacks of September 2001. Counter-terrorism security measures are now a regular feature of border responsibilities. Attention is not solely on the point of entry but also on the place of export and the full supply chain for goods.[78] This chapter has argued that the changes in maritime security present several potential breaches of WTO law, including the obligation of special and differential treatment for developing countries. The measures chosen involve significant capital costs for equipment and ongoing maintenance, as well as the expenditure of administrative resources on tasks that might not otherwise be a high priority for a poor country.

David Kennedy has characterized the era since 1995 in law and development thinking as "postneoliberal," a time when law is seen as the central rhetoric and when some are revisiting themes of bargaining power from the 1970s.[79] The new security concerns are real and important and need to take their place as part of global public policy. It would be challenging for WTO panels and the Appellate Body to deal with matters of national security presented in the new system of border administration, but the legal arguments are clearly available, and issues surrounding customs procedures are within the traditional competence of GATT.

It will be for developing countries (and possibly other countries) to decide whether to bring complaints through the WTO over the changes that have taken place in border administration. In addition, wider negotiations on border security may be in order, encompassing the debate over 100% scanning, along with a possible rethinking of security measures and the effectiveness of inspections. Any such negotiations would present an opportunity to recognize special and differential treatment for developing countries, through the design of any new substantive rules and through enhanced support for financing and technical assistance. Within the WTO, if not in other venues, the presence of a strong dispute settlement system provides constraints

77 Michael C. Williams, "Words, Images, Enemies: Securitization and International Politics" (2003) 47 *International Studies Quarterly* 514. See B. Buzan, O. Waever, and J. De Wilde, *Security: A New Framework for Analysis* (Boulder, CO: Lynne Rienner, 1998), pp. 23–26.

78 See further Maureen Irish, "Supply Chain Security Programs and Border Administration" (2009) 3(2) *World Customs Journal* 43.

79 David Kennedy, "The 'Rule of Law,' Political Choices, and Development Common Sense," in David M. Trubek and Alvaro Santos (eds.), *The New Law and Development: A Critical Appraisal* (New York: Cambridge University Press, 2006), pp. 158, 161, 163, 166.

on bargaining positions. Whatever the strategic choice, developing countries have the option of using WTO legal rights to affect outcomes.

REFERENCS

Akande, Dapo, and Sope Williams, "International Adjudication on National Security Issues: What Role for the WTO?" (2003) 43 *Virginia Journal of International Law*.

Bartels, Lorand, "Applicable Law in WTO Dispute Settlement Proceedings" (2001) 35(3) *Journal of World Trade*.

Bowman, Gregory W., "Thinking Outside the Border: Homeland Security and the Forward Deployment of the U.S. Border" (2007) 44 *Houston Law Review*.

Dallimore, Christopher, "Securing the Supply Chain: Does the Container Security Initiative Comply with WTO Law?" dissertation, University of Muenster, 2008, available at: http://miami.uni-muenster.de/servlets/DocumentServlet?id=4577.

Emmerson, Andrew, "Conceptualizing Security Exceptions: Legal Doctrine or Political Excuse?" (2008) 11(1) *Journal of International Economic Law*.

Florestal, Marjorie, "Terror on the High Seas: The Trade and Development Implications of U.S. National Security Measures" (2007) 72 *Brooklyn Law Review*.

Hahn, Michael J., "Vital Interests and the Law of GATT: An Analysis of GATT's Security Exception" (1991) 12 *Michigan Journal of International Law*.

Ireland, Robert, "The WCO SAFE Framework of Standards: Avoiding Excess in Global Supply Chain Security Policy" (2009) 4 *Global Trade and Customs Journal*.

Lee, Yong-Shik, *Economic Development through World Trade: A Developing World Perspective* (The Hague: Kluwer Law International, 2008).

Lyndon B. Johnson School of Public Affairs, the University of Texas at Austin, *Port and Supply-Chain Security Initiatives in the United States and Abroad*, Report prepared for the Congressional Research Service, Policy Research Project Report No. 150 (2006).

Marceau, Gabrielle, "Conflicts of Norms and Conflicts of Jurisdictions: The Relationship between the WTO Agreement and MEAs and other Treaties" (2001) 35(6) *Journal of World Trade*.

Matsushita, Mitsuo, "Governance of International Trade Under World Trade Organization Agreements – Relationships Between World Trade Organization Agreements and Other Trade Agreements" (2004) 38(2) *Journal of World Trade*.

Mellor, Justin S. C., "Missing the Boat: The Legal and Practical Problems of the Prevention of Maritime Terrorism" (2002) 18 *American University International Law Review*.

Mitchell, Andrew D., *Legal Principles in WTO Disputes* (Cambridge: Cambridge University Press, 2008).

Pauwelyn, Joost, "The Role of Public International Law in the WTO: How Far Can We Go?" (2001) 95 *American Journal of International Law*.

______, *Conflict of Norms in Public International Law: How WTO Law Relates to other Rules of International Law* (Cambridge: Cambridge University Press, 2003).

______, "How to Win a World Trade Organization Dispute Based on Non-World Trade Organization Law? Questions of Jurisdiction and Merits" (2003) 37(6) *Journal of World Trade*.

______, "Bridging Fragmentation and Unity: International Law as a Universe of Inter-Connected Islands" (2004) 25 *Michigan Journal of International Law*.

Rolland, Sonia E., "Developing Country Coalitions at the WTO: In Search of Legal Support" (2007) 48 *Harvard International Law Journal*.

———, "Redesigning the Negotiation Process at the WTO" (2010) 13(1) *Journal of International Economic Law*.

Schloemann, Hannes L., and Stefan Ohlhoff, "'Constitutionalization' and Dispute Settlement in the WTO: National Security as an Issue of Competence" (1999) 93 *American Journal of International Law*.

United Nations Conference on Trade and Development, *Container Security: Major Initiatives and Related International Developments*, Report by the UNCTAD Secretariat, UNCTAD/SDTE/TLB/2004/1 (February 26, 2004).

———, *Maritime Security: ISPS Code Implementation, Costs and Related Financing*, Report by the UNCTAD Secretariat, UNCTAD/SDTE/TLB/2007/1 (March 14, 2007).

Weerth, Carsten, "The Cross-border Detection of Radiological, Biological and Chemical Active and Harmful Terrorist Devices" (2009) 3(2) *World Customs Journal*.

Widdowson, David, and Stephen Holloway, "Maritime Transport Security Regulation: Policies, Probabilities and Practicalities" (2009) 3(2) *World Customs Journal*.

PART II

Law and Development in the World Trade Organization

5

World Trade Organization and Developing Countries

Reform Proposal

Yong-Shik Lee

I. INTRODUCTION

In today's world where developing countries comprise the vast majority of nations and where a significant portion of the world's population is still suffering from crushing poverty,[1] economic development is one of the most important global issues. The importance of international trade for successful economic development, as shown in the cases of South Korea, Taiwan, Singapore, Hong Kong, and, more recently, China, has been well documented,[2] and it is important that the international governance and regulatory framework for international trade is structured in a way to facilitate, rather than hamper, the economic development of developing countries.

[1] It has been estimated that in 2005, 1.4 billion people had consumption levels below USD 1.25 a day and 2.6 billion (48% of the world population) under USD 2 per day.

[2] See A. O. Krueger, "Trade Policies in Developing Countries," in R. W. Jones and P. B. Kenen (eds.), 1 *Handbook of International Economics* (New York: North-Holland, 1984), pp. 519–569; 1 R. Findlay, "Growth and Development in Trade Models," in R. W. Jones and P. B. Kenen (eds.), *Handbook of International Economics* (New York: North-Holland, 1984), pp. 185–236; T. N. Srinivasan, "Trade, Development, and Growth," *Princeton Essays in International Economics No. 225* (December 2001); G. K. Helleiner (ed.), *Trade Policy, Industrialization, and Development* (Oxford: Oxford University Press, 1992); World Bank, *The East Asian Miracle* (New York: Oxford University Press, 1993). See also Alice H. Amsden, *Escape from Empire: The Developing World's Journey through Heaven and Hell* (Cambridge, MA: MIT Press, 2007); Alice H. Amsden, *Asia's Next Giant: South Korea and Late Industrialization* (New York: Oxford University Press, 1989); Robert Wade, *Governing the Market: Economic Theory and the Role of Government in East Asian Industrialization* (Princeton, NJ: Princeton University Press, 2003).

Earlier versions of this chapter have been published in 6 *Asper Review of International Business and Trade Law* (2006), 177–208; *Reclaiming Development in the World Trading System* (New York: Cambridge University Press, 2006); *Economic Development through World Trade: A Developing World Perspective* (The Hague: Kluwer Law International, 2008), 3–32; *Developing Countries in the WTO Legal System* (New York: Oxford University Press, 2009), 291–319.

The World Trade Organization (WTO) represents the international governance and regulatory framework for international trade today.[3] The WTO membership includes as many as 153 countries,[4] including all major economies and trading nations, except perhaps Russia, and WTO legal disciplines are mandatory on all WTO Members.[5] WTO rules lay down the fundamental legal principles that govern conduct on international trade by member states. The WTO dispute settlement body adjudicates trade dispute cases raised by a member state and rule violations alleged to be committed by another. Various report mechanisms of the WTO monitor conduct of member states on international trade and ensure their compliance with WTO disciplines. Thus, the WTO has become the "United Nations" of international trade, and its rules constitute international law of trade that can be specifically enforced.[6]

This chapter considers the current governance system in the WTO as well as WTO disciplines and examines whether they are structured adequately to support and facilitate the economic development of developing countries. The WTO may not be a development institution per se: its primary objective is to create and maintain an integrated, more viable, and durable multilateral trading system.[7] Yet the WTO also acknowledges the importance of international trade for the economic development of developing countries and recognizes the "need for positive efforts designed to ensure that developing countries, especially the least developed among them, secure a share in the growth in international trade commensurate with the needs of their economic development."[8] Also, the core agenda of the current WTO trade negotiation round, the Doha Round, is the facilitation of development (Doha Development Agenda, "DDA").[9]

Thus, it is necessary to examine the adequacy of the current governance in the WTO and WTO disciplines in relation to development facilitation. The governance in the WTO should adequately address the importance of economic development in the international trading system. Given the significant impact that the rules on international trade have on economic development, such as those on trade-related subsidies, such relevant trade rules should facilitate, not inhibit, adoption of effective economic development policies. This chapter looks to assess whether the current WTO governance and rules are consistent with development interests

3 The WTO was established in 1994 by the Marrakech Agreement Establishing the World Trade Organization (hereinafter the "WTO Agreement"), succeeding the earlier General Agreement on Tariffs and Trade regime, which had continued since 1947.

4 The WTO Web site, http//www.wto.org.

5 The WTO Agreement, art. 14:4–5.

6 WTO disciplines are included in the WTO Agreement and its annexes. WTO, *The Legal Texts: The Results of the Uruguay Round of Multilateral Trade Agreements* (Geneva: WTO, 1999).

7 The WTO Agreement, Preamble, para. 5. The WTO (1999), supra note 6, p. 4.

8 Ibid., para. 2.

9 For the detailed description of the DDA, see the WTO Web site, http://www.wto.org/english/tratop_e/dda_e/dda_e.htm.

and makes proposals to close gaps between the current system and the need to facilitate economic development.

II. RECLAIMING DEVELOPMENT IN WTO GOVERNANCE

A. *Current Organization*

The major organizational body that concerns trade and development within the WTO is the Committee on Trade and Development (CTD). The CTD is established under the General Council with a mandate to handle issues on trade and development. Its mandate is also to address related issues, such as implementation of preferential provisions for developing countries, guidelines for technical cooperation, increased participation of developing countries in the trading system, least developed countries (LDCs) issues, notifications of Generalized System of Preferences (GSP) programs, and preferential trade arrangements among developing countries.

Current WTO assistance to developing countries focuses on capacity-building. In this area, the WTO offers assistance through its Training and Technical Cooperation Institute. Assistance includes providing regular training sessions in Geneva on trade policy, organizing approximately 400 technical cooperation activities annually, including seminars and workshops in various countries and courses in Geneva, and offering legal assistance to some developing countries.[10] These capacity-building activities are undoubtedly helpful to developing countries, but the scope of assistance is rather limited, because the focus is on technical capacity-building. The WTO needs to consider other essential areas concerning trade and development, such as technology transfer, financial mechanism, and debt relief.

The CTD does not have the mandate to address these other essential issues, and thus developing countries have requested that the WTO discuss these issues. The need for a new round to address a development agenda resonated widely. The 2004 report on the implementation of the United Nation Millennium Declaration emphasized the responsibility of developed countries to meet development goals, stating specifically that developed countries must fulfill their responsibilities "by increasing and improving development assistance, concluding a new development-oriented trade round, embracing wider and deeper debt relief and fostering

[10] For legal assistance, thirty-two WTO governments created an Advisory Centre on WTO Law in 2001. Its members consist of countries contributing funding and those receiving legal advice. LDCs are automatically eligible for advice, whereas other developing countries and transition economies must be fee-paying members. For further information, see http://www.wto.org. In addition, The WTO Reference Center program was also initiated in 1997 with the objective of creating a network of computerized information centers in LDCs and developing countries. The International Trade Center, a joint body with United Nations Conference on Trade and Development (UNCTAD), also helps developing countries expand export and to improve their import operations.

technology transfer."[11] In response to this demand, the new round includes a series of development issues in its agenda (Doha Development Agenda; DDA). In addition, the DDA established two working groups: "Trade, Debt and Finance" and "Trade and Transfer of Technology."[12] The CTD met in special sessions to handle work under the DDA.

B. *Case for the Council for Trade and Development*

The current organizational apparatus of the WTO is rather insufficient to address complex and long-term development issues on trade and development.[13] The mandate of the CTD is limited, as described earlier, and the WTO's activities to assist developing countries have also been rather limited in scope. This problem of insufficiency can be answered by elevating the existing Committee to full Council status, thus strengthening the organizational apparatus.

The need for such an institutional elevation can be explained by comparison with the treatment of trade-related aspects of intellectual property rights promoted by developed countries. Although trade and development issues concern the vast majority of WTO Members, a relatively limited number of countries promoted intellectual property rights in the Uruguay Round negotiations. Nonetheless, the importance of intellectual property rights was emphasized during the negotiations and led to the establishment of the full Council, not a Committee, and a separate agreement (the Agreement on Trade-Related Aspects of Intellectual Property Rights, or "TRIPS Agreement") to address complex and long-term intellectual property issues in the WTO.[14]

As mentioned earlier, trade and development issues concern a vast number of developing countries, and there is consensus in the WTO that these issues should be addressed within the WTO. The current DDA reflects this consensus, and the present round is called the "development round." If these trade and development issues, which concern the majority of WTO membership, are considered as important as TRIPS, which was promoted by a smaller number of developed countries, it is fair and proper that trade and development issues be accorded the same institutional attention and weight by elevating the present Committee to full Council status. This proposed institutional reform would help resolve the worry that

[11] *Implementation of the United Nations Millennium Declaration*, UN 59th Sess., UN Doc. A/59/282 (2004), para. 43.

[12] The DDA addresses the issues of trade, debt, and finance; trade and transfer of technology; technical cooperation and capacity building; LDCs; and special and differential treatment. WTO, *Ministerial Declaration*, WT/MIN(01)/DEC/1 (November 20, 2001).

[13] The current organizational apparatus consists of the CTD and the Subcommittee on LDCs aided by the Training and Technical Cooperation Institute under the WTO Secretariat.

[14] The Council for Trade-Related Aspects of Intellectual Property Rights is organized under Article IV of the WTO Agreement.

trade and development issues have not received due attention and have been set aside.[15]

The suggested elevation will not only make a statement recognizing the essential importance of development issues but will also meet practical needs. Such needs include the replacement of current working groups with separate committees. WTO working groups are established to address important trade and development issues, such as trade, debt and finance, and trade and technology transfer. These issues are complex and require continued attention within the WTO. Separate committees, rather than limited subcommittees, are necessary to incorporate these important issues as a working agenda in the WTO. To oversee the effective operation of these committees, a separate council would need to be established within the WTO. In addition, individual developing countries face unique problems resulting from increased participation in the WTO and securing full benefits of WTO membership. Therefore, an additional committee is necessary to bring adequate institutional attention to these problems and assist with the needs of developing countries more effectively on an individual-country basis. The current Advisory Centre on WTO Law[16] may be expanded and incorporated into this body to render legal advice to developing-country members.

In summary, the lack of due organizational status and the resulting appearance of insufficient institutional attention to development issues have created a widespread perception that the WTO represents the interests of developed countries and multinational corporations rather than those of its majority members – developing countries. One way to resolve this issue is to elevate the current body in charge of development issues to Council level. Instituting a new Council could also serve important functions that the current CTD is not mandated to serve. Such functions could include addressing specific complex and long-term issues of development with a better organizational apparatus. The new Council, with a specific role as described in the following section, will have a wider mandate to implement all necessary measures to promote trade and development and a capacity to address essential development issues that concern the majority of WTO Members.

C. *Role of the Council for Trade and Development*

The primary objective of the new Council is to set a development agenda and promote development interests in the trading system. Its role can include the following:

1. promotion of a development agenda and implementation of trade-related development assistance policies;

[15] WTO, *Report of the WTO's High-Level Symposium on Trade and Development on 17–18 March 1999*, available at: http://www.wto.org/english/tratop_e/devel_e/summhl_e.htm.

[16] Supra note 10.

2. regulatory monitoring concerning development; and
3. instituting and supervising development assistance activities, including those of subcommittees.

a. Development Assistance Policy Implementation

The Council should create a regulatory environment in the trading system that allows and facilitates the implementation of effective development policies by developing-country members. In doing so, the Council should identify problems and gaps in the current trading system in facilitating development and, accordingly, set a trade and development agenda on a regular basis. This agenda may be discussed at the Ministerial Conferences and trade rounds to develop a more development-supportive regulatory system and modify relevant rules when necessary. In promoting a trade and development agenda, the Council may cooperate with relevant international bodies, such as the United Nations Committee on Trade and Development (UNCTAD) and the United Nations Industrial Development Organization (UNIDO). Through such cooperation, the trade and development agenda set by the WTO would be promoted and coordinated more effectively and consistently throughout the world.

In addition, a mechanism should be devised for developed-country members and participating developing-country members to file a mandatory Trade-Related Development Assistance Report (TDAR) on a regular basis. It would report members' activities that are in compliance with the trade and development agenda set by the Council. The Council may receive and examine TDARs on a regular basis and consult with relevant members to discuss their development assistance activities. The Council and developed-country members may agree on specific commitments to be fulfilled by the latter to promote the trade and development agenda; the Council may further examine, within a certain time period, whether these commitments are being met.

The point of this proposal is to have a full Council to set a relevant trade and development agenda on a regular basis and, through the reporting mechanism, impose specific commitments on each developed- and participating developing-country member to assist with development. The enforceability of these commitments may be questioned, because the WTO may not always be able to apply effective sanctions against violating members. The authorization of retaliatory measures may not be an effective sanction if developing countries do not have leverage against the violating developed-country member. Nonetheless, the Council's actions to identify the relevant trade and development agenda and to identify and monitor members' specific obligations in the trading system will still promote development interests. Since the implementation of the WTO, WTO Members have largely complied with the specific obligations imposed by the WTO, even without the threat of sanctions.

b. Regulatory Monitoring

The Council may also monitor compliance of relevant WTO provisions on development assistance, including the existing provisions in WTO rules offering special and differential treatment (SDT) in favor of developing countries (SDT provisions),[17] General Agreement on Tariffs and Trade (GATT) Articles[18] XXXVI–XXXVIII, and the pro-development provisions proposed in the following section of this chapter. Part of these monitoring elements can be incorporated in the aforementioned TDAR. Violations of these provisions should be reported to the Council if the violations are detrimental to the trade interests of developing-country members. The Council may subsequently consult with the violating member to seek a resolution. The commitments of developed-country members in GATT Article XXXII can be monitored by the TDAR. Compliance with these commitments may require a broader policy adjustment by the developed-country member, which may necessitate the monitoring by the Council. The Council may publish an annual report on the compliance status of these development assistance provisions and provide monitoring of any systematic compliance failure. The Council may also include such a problem in the trade and development agenda for possible rule modification.

c. Instituting and Supervising Committees

The Council may institute standing or ad hoc committees to address specific issues of trade and development that require long-term attention, such as technological transfer among developed- and developing-country members. There should be at least one committee specifically devoted to the problems of LDCs and another to assist with building capacities of developing countries to participate fully in the trading system and realize the benefits. Assistance should be provided to developing-country members involved in costly and time-consuming trade disputes, and the current WTO Advisory Centre[19] needs to be expanded to offer assistance to every developing-country member in need of assistance with respect to the panel or Appellate Body proceedings. Consideration can be given as to whether it would better serve the need of developing-country members by assigning the function of the existing WTO Advisory Centre to a committee under the Council for Trade and Development.

III. RECLAIMING DEVELOPMENT IN WTO DISCIPLINES

The current governance structure in the WTO is inadequate to address development, and the current WTO disciplines are also ineffective to promote development

[17] See Section III.B.b infra.

[18] The old GATT articles have been incorporated in the WTO Agreement in Annex 1A: Multilateral Trade Agreements in Goods.

[19] Supra note 10.

interests and, in some important areas, they inhibit the adoption of effective development policies. This section examines the inadequacy of the current rules and makes reform proposals.

A. *Current Rules and Limitations*

The major development assistance provisions in WTO disciplines include GATT Articles XVIII, XXXVI–XXXVIII, the Enabling Clause, and SDT provisions in various WTO agreements. Part IV of GATT (Articles XXXVI–XXXVIII) titled "Trade and Development," provides a set of provisions attempting to assist economic development.

a. Article XVIII

Article XVIII of GATT, "Governmental Assistance to Economic Development,"[20] facilitates the establishment of industries by authorizing relevant trade measures. This Article supports the infant-industry promotion policy,[21] which uses tariff protection to promote domestic industries in the early stages of development. Article XVIII allows developing countries to establish a particular industry by authorizing them to maintain a flexible tariff structure (e.g., increase tariff rates by modifying the Schedule of Concessions). This flexibility enables developing countries to grant tariff protection for infant industries. Article XVIII also acknowledges the need for trade measures for balance-of-payment (BOP) purposes.[22]

Reciprocity is required for a modification of the Schedule of Concessions to facilitate an industry: the modifying WTO Member is required to negotiate with other members with which the relevant concession was initially negotiated having a substantial interest (paragraph 7(a) of Section A). Therefore, this modification under Article XVIII may require a compensatory measure by the modifying member to reach agreement with other members. If an agreement is not reached within sixty days after the WTO is notified of the modification, the member may still unilaterally modify the concession in question. This can occur only on the condition that the

[20] General Agreement on Tariffs and Trade, October 30, 1947, 58 U.N.T.S. 187, Can.T.S. 1947 No. 27 (entered into force January 1, 1948) available at: http://www.wto.org/english/docs_e/legal_e/gatt47_e.pdf.

[21] Friedrich List (1789–1846) is widely known as the father of infant-industry promotion, which was proposed in his famous work, *The National System of Political Economy*, trans. by Sampson S. Lloyd, available at: http://socserv2.socsci.mcmaster.ca/~econ/ugcm/3ll3/list/national.html.

[22] Section B of Article XVIII authorizes BOP measures for development purposes. Paragraph 8 of the Article provides, "The contracting parties recognize that contracting parties coming within the scope of paragraph 4(a) of this Article [i.e., developing countries in the early stages of development] tend, when they are in rapid process of development, to experience balance of payment difficulties arising mainly from efforts to expand their internal markets as well as from the instability in their terms of trade." GATT (1948), supra note 20.

WTO finds that the compensatory adjustment offered by the modifying member is adequate and that every effort was made to reach an agreement.[23] In addition, the modifying member must give effect to the compensatory adjustment at the same time as the modification.[24] However, if the WTO finds that the compensatory adjustment offer is not adequate, other members with a substantial interest are free to adopt retaliatory measures by modifying or withdrawing substantially equivalent concessions against the modifying member.[25]

Article XVIII relaxes the requirement of binding concessions under Article II and authorizes developing-country members to modify their Schedule of Concessions to facilitate an infant industry. However, the requirement of consultations and negotiations may cause considerable delays in implementing trade measures for development purposes. The requirement of reciprocal concessions (compensation) may also impose a burden on the economy of the modifying developing country. Although the effectiveness of infant-industry facilitation policies has been questioned in economic circles, the cases of recent development history indicate that the facilitation of industry by government has contributed to successful economic development.[26] Thus, the provisions of Article XVIII can play a positive role in assisting economic development, but the requirements of negotiations and compensation may diminish the effectiveness.

b. GATT Articles XXXVI–XXXVIII

The provisions in GATT Articles XXXVI–XXXVIII set out an array of measures, commitments, and collaborations on the part of developed countries and the WTO in support of economic development.

Article XXXVI[27] addresses the vital role of export earnings in economic development, possible authorization of special measures to promote trade and development, the need for more favorable and acceptable conditions of access to world markets for primary products (on which many developing countries depend), the need to diversify the economic structure in developing countries and to avoid excessive dependence on the export of primary products, and the important relationship between trade and financial assistance to development.[28] The Article also clarifies that there should be no expectation of reciprocity by developed countries for commitments made by them in trade negotiations to reduce or remove tariffs and other trade barriers for developing members.[29]

23 GATT (1948), supra note 20, art. XVIII, para. 7(b).

24 Ibid.

25 Ibid.

26 For more discussion on this point, see Y.S. Lee, *Reclaiming Development in the World Trading System* (New York: Cambridge University Press, 2009), chap. 3.

27 GATT (1948), supra note 20.

28 Ibid.

29 Ibid., para. 8.

Article XXXVII[30] elaborates developed-country members' commitment to assist developing countries with economic development. Methods include:

- according high priority to the reduction and elimination of import barriers to products of particular export interest to developing members;
- refraining from introducing or increasing import barriers to such products;[31] and
- according high priority to the reduction and elimination of policies specifically applicable to primary products wholly or mainly produced in developing countries, which hamper the growth of consumption of those products.[32]

Developed-country members are also required to make efforts to maintain trade margins for developing-country members at equitable levels when a government directly or indirectly determines the resale price of products wholly or mainly produced in developing countries.[33] They are also obligated to adopt measures providing a greater scope for the development of imports from those developing countries.[34] Special regard is to be given to the trade interests of developing countries in the application of trade measures against imports (paragraph 3). Article XXXVIII[35] provides for joint action and calls for an institutional effort by the WTO to assist with the development of developing countries.

Critics have argued that the provisions of Articles XXXVI–XXXVIII are declaratory rather than obligatory because they are not enforced by effective sanctions. Article XXXVII excuses developed-country members from the various commitments set out in the Article for "compelling reasons," thus further weakening the effectiveness of these provisions.[36] These compelling reasons may include domestic legal obligations, in which case developed countries may avoid their "commitments" by legislating against them. Thus, it is doubtful that the commitments under Articles XXXVI–XXXVIII have actually affected the policies of developed countries in any significant way to accord more favorable treatment to developing countries.

c. Enabling Clause

A set of policy statements made in the GATT decision on November 28, 1979, in favor of developing-country members, referred to as the "Enabling Clause," also

[30] GATT, supra note 20. Also with respect to this commitment, para. 1 of Article XXXVII provides in relevant part: "The developed contracting parties shall to the fullest extent possible – that is, except when compelling reasons, which may include legal reasons, make it impossible – give effect to the following provisions." This provision allows developed countries to avoid this commitment by, for instance, legislating for import restraints from developing countries.

[31] Ibid., para. 1(b).

[32] Ibid., para. 1(c).

[33] Ibid., para. 3(a).

[34] Ibid., para. 3(b).

[35] GATT (1948), supra note 20.

[36] Ibid., art. XXXVII, para. 1.

provides development assistance provisions.[37] The Enabling Clause approves the GSP and the exchange of preferences among developing-country members.[38] It also provides for differential and preferential treatment for developing countries with respect to nontariff measures,[39] as well as special treatment for LDCs.[40] The Enabling Clause also states that developed countries should not expect reciprocity for the commitments they make in trade concessions[41] and should exercise utmost restraint in seeking concessions from the LDCs.[42] As in the case of Articles XXXVI–XXXVIII discussed earlier, the Enabling Clause is not mandatory in that there is no effective sanction against a violation of these commitments. The Enabling Clause *enables* developed countries to provide preference for developing countries, but it does not *obligate* them to do so.

d. Special and Differential Treatment Provisions

There are other provisions in the WTO disciplines, the majority of which are found in the various agreements in the Uruguay Round,[43] which provide SDT in favor of developing countries.[44] One hundred and forty-five such provisions are scattered throughout several WTO agreements, understandings, and GATT articles, among which twenty-two are applied exclusively to LDCs. These provisions relax current discipline requirements for the benefit of developing countries, require protection of the interests of developing countries, or give more compliance time for developing countries (transitional period).

Currently, however, this SDT is not sufficient to meet the development needs of developing countries for several reasons. First, protection is often not sufficient. For instance, Article 9.1 of the Agreement on Safeguards requires the exemption of imports originating in a developing country from safeguards in which the portion of such imports does not exceed 3%, provided that the collective share of imports from all such developing-country members (under 3%) accounts for not more than 9%.[45] Article 9.2 of the Agreement also allows developing-country members to apply safeguards for an additional two years beyond the maximum duration and to reapply

37 *Differential and More Favourable Treatment, Reciprocity and Fuller Participation on Developing Countries*, GATT C.P. Nov. L/4903, 26th Supp. B.I.S.D. (1980) 203.

38 Ibid., para. 2(a).

39 Ibid., para. 2(b).

40 Ibid., para. 2(d).

41 Ibid., para. 5.

42 Ibid., para. 6.

43 Annex 1 of the WTO Agreement includes various agreements supplementing the old GATT rules. WTO (1999), supra note 6, pp. 3–353.

44 For a review of the SDT provisions in the WTO, see WTO, *Implementation of Special and Differential Treatment Provisions in WTO Agreements and Decisions – Note by Secretariat*, WTO Doc. WT/COMTD/W/77 (October 25, 2000).

45 WTO, *Agreement on Safeguards*, available at http://www.wto.org/english/docs_e/legal_e/25-safeg.pdf.

safeguards to the same product after shortened intervals.[46] Critics have argued that the ceilings (the individual 3% and collective 9%) are too tight and the small extensions are not very helpful for developing countries.[47] Similarly, these provisions do not relieve developing countries of the WTO disciplines in any significant way or give substantial protection in the areas where their trade interests are significantly affected, such as tariff bindings, subsidies, and antidumping rules.

The transition period, provided as a preference for developing countries, is not helpful either. The SDT expires after a stipulated period for transition, although the need of development that may justify the SDT may remain. When permanent exceptions are given, the number of beneficiary developing countries is often too limited; for example, when exemptions are allowed in subsidy rules to permit export subsidies, only a handful of LDCs benefit from this exemption on a permanent basis.[48] In addition, current SDT does not provide differentiated treatment to developing countries of widely different development status other than LDCs. A recent study has pointed out the need for greater differentiation in SDT.[49]

B. *Reform Proposals*

a. The Agreement on Development Facilitation

As discussed in the preceding section, the current rules are inadequate to facilitate economic development. Substantively, permanent SDT should be given to developing countries in the areas that affect economic development, such as tariff bindings, subsidies, antidumping, trade-related intellectual property rights, and trade-related investment measures. In addition, provisions offering SDT to developing countries are scattered throughout various WTO disciplines without any coherent regulatory standard, when the need for such is clearly evident. A separate agreement should be put in place that provides a coherent standard to determine which developing-country members can benefit from certain SDT and set out principles underlying the provisions of SDT. This agreement could be called the Agreement on Development Facilitation (ADF).

Under the current system, the developing-country status is self-declaratory, and the absence of definition for developing-country members seems to create regulatory ambiguity.[50] In addition, the current system provides the same level of SDT to

46 Ibid.

47 Jai S. Mah, "Injury and Causation in the WTO Agreement on Safeguards" (2001) 4(3) *Journal of World Intellectual Property* 380–382.

48 For instance, only LDCs are exempted from the prohibition of export subsidies. See Section III.B.c infra for a relevant discussion.

49 Michael Hart and Bill Dymond, "Special and Differential Treatment and the Doha 'Development' Round" (2003) 37(2) *Journal of World Trade* 409.

50 Fan Cui, "Who Are Developing Countries in the WTO?" (2008) 1(1) *The Law and Development Review*.

developing-country members with widely different levels of development status and economic need for SDT. A recent study emphasizes the need for greater differentiation in SDT.[51] The ADF should provide a definition for a developing-country member and also differentiate SDT for developing-country members to enhance the clarity and rationality of the system.[52] The ADF may also include substantive, permanent SDT provisions as suggested in the remainder of this section.[53]

b. Adjustment to Tariff Bindings[54]

The WTO system requires members to maintain their commitments on import concessions in the form of tariff bindings stipulated in the Schedule of Concessions.[55] Although this principle provides essential stability to the international trading system, the tariff commitments remove the ability of developing countries to use trade protection to facilitate their industries at early stages of development (infant industries). There is considerable debate on the validity of infant-industry promotion policies. Nonetheless, a recent study recognizes that fundamental economic restructuring seldom takes place in the absence of governmental intervention,[56] and the case for state-supported industrial facilitation has already been made in some literature.[57]

51 Supra note 49.

52 What standard can be adopted to determine developing-country status? Individual income levels can be considered. The World Bank uses gross national income per capita to categorize nations into different income groups. This economic indicator can be used as a primary determinant for development status. Methods for differentiating SDT for various developing-country members should also be sought, and the subcategorization of the developed-country members, such as the one used by the World Bank, can be adopted for such differentiation. For instance, Article 9.2 of the Agreement on Safeguards authorizes a longer duration of a safeguard measure to be applied by a developing-country member. This additional duration can be differentiated in accordance with the developed status of the particular developing-country member (perhaps extended for poorer developing countries and shortened for richer ones) identified by the subcategorization discussed earlier.

53 Developed-country members were reluctant to provide extensive SDT, whereas developing-country members insisted on such treatment. Some types of SDT simply buy developing-country members more time to comply with WTO obligations, whereas others provide permanent preferential treatment. The reluctance on the part of developed-country members to provide extensive SDT may represent their preference for "one rule for all nations." In other words, eventually one rule should apply to all trading nations, both developed and developing, and SDT that offers temporary preference should not be extended in time. In addition, SDT that offers a permanent preference to a limited number of developing-country members, such as LDCs, should not be expanded to benefit more developing-country members. It would be necessary to reconsider whether this one-rule policy is justifiable. If the development needs of developing-country members justify preferential treatment in the first place, then this treatment should not expire until they attain developed economy status, and therefore, this one-rule policy is not tenable from the perspective of economic development.

54 The proposal to adjust binding concessions to facilitate development was first made in Y. S. Lee, "Facilitating Development in the World Trading System: A Proposal for Development Facilitation Tariff and Development Facilitating Subsidy" (2004) 38(6) *Journal of World Trade* 935.

55 GATT (1948), supra note 20, art. II.

56 Dani Rodrik, *Industrial Policy for the Twenty-First Century* (paper prepared for UNIDO, September 2004), p. 15.

57 Y. S. Lee (2004), supra note 54, pp. 938–939.

Regardless of the debate, a developing country should be allowed to choose policies that are best suited for its development, fully considering the ramifications of the proposed tariff increases. If it finally determines that its industrial promotion policy demands tariff increases, its previous import commitments should not tie its hands. The provisions of GATT Article XVIII allow modification of the schedule to aid the facilitation of infant industries, but these provisions require members to undergo potentially time-consuming and complicated negotiations with other interested members before the application of higher tariffs. Thus, more flexible treatment should be available to developing countries with respect to binding concessions authorizing additional tariffs beyond their scheduled commitments to facilitate industries for economic development.[58]

This additional tariff applied for the purpose of infant-industry promotion can be called Development-Facilitation Tariff (DFT).[59] In brief, the DFT allows a developing country to apply tariff rates above the scheduled commitments unilaterally when the country can demonstrate a development need for such a tariff with a concrete plan for industrial facilitation. The application of a DFT should require procedural safeguards to minimize the possibility of abuse. Safeguards could include a formal investigation and hearing requirement, notices to other interested members, consultations, and a maximum duration for its application. The maximum applicable rate of the DFT should also be systematically differentiated according to the development stage of a particular developing country, as determined by the level of its per capita income.[60] For example, the maximum DFT rate applicable by wealthier developing countries should be lower than that of a less affluent developing country, measured by per capita income.[61]

Some may argue that the introduction of DFT in the world trading system will undermine the import concessions made by developing countries and disrupt the balance of concessions achieved through trade negotiations. Although these concessions are important, the need for economic development should be given priority. The impact of DFT on world trade will be rather limited because the majority of world trade is conducted among developed economies and not subject to

58 Arguably, the need for tariff protection should have been contemplated by developing countries when they agreed to specific tariff bindings in the multilateral trade negotiations. Nonetheless, their economic needs and national goals may have changed following political shifts (e.g., election of a new government, end of a dictatorship, etc.), and therefore, development initiatives may begin long after the conclusion of trade negotiations. If so, the developing country should not be prohibited from offering trade protection to its infant industry because of its previous import commitments, and it should be allowed to do so without prolonging negotiations and the burden of compensations or the threat of retaliations.

59 Y. S. Lee (2004), supra note 54, for the details of the proposed DFT.

60 Ibid., pp. 946–947.

61 There will likely be some concern that this liberal treatment may lead to rampant protectionism by developing countries without either a genuine need or a constructive plan for infant-industry promotion. The procedural safeguards introduced earlier counter this possibility of abuse.

DFT applications.[62] In addition, because of demands by developed countries with more powerful economies, developing countries with limited negotiating power are often compelled to make concessions beyond the levels that they are prepared to offer or accept.[63] Consequently, when there are clear development plans that demand import protection, it would be fair to allow import restraints to meet those development needs.

c. Subsidy Treatment[64]

Another essential element of industrial promotion policies for economic development is a government subsidy. Strategically planned government subsidization has contributed to the successful development of some developing countries, such as South Korea. Under the Agreement on Subsidies and Countervailing Measures (SCM Agreement), export subsidies (subsidies that are contingent on export performance) and import-substitution subsidies (subsidies that are contingent on the use of domestic over imported goods) are prohibited because they have adverse effects on international trade.[65] In addition, a subsidy is "actionable" (i.e., the other country may retaliate against the subsidy with countermeasures) when certain conditions are met.[66] Countervailing duties (CVDs), which are additional tariffs imposed on imports to offset the effect of subsidies,[67] are also an applicable remedy when subsidization causes or threatens material injury to an established domestic industry or materially retards the establishment of a domestic industry.[68]

Current WTO subsidy provisions prohibiting export subsidies and import-substitution subsidies, as well as those authorizing countervailing measures against

[62] Organisation for Economic Co-operation and Development, OECD.StatExtracts, available at: http://stats.oecd.org.

[63] On developing countries and trade negotiations, see Anne Krueger, "The Developing Countries and the Next Round of Multilateral Trade Negotiations" (1999) 22(7) *The World Economy* 909.

[64] Y. S. Lee (2004), supra note 54, pp. 948–953.

[65] Agreement on Subsidies and Countervailing Measures, April 15, 1994, LT/UR/A-1A/9, available at: http://www.wto.org/english/docs_e/legal_e/24-scm.pdf. Annex I of the SCM Agreement includes the illustrative list of prohibited export subsidies.

[66] These conditions are as follows: (a) the subsidy is specifically limited to an enterprise or group of enterprises, an industrial sector or group of industries, or a designed geographic region within the jurisdiction of the granting authority (specificity requirement); and (b) the subsidy causes adverse effects to the interests of other members. Adverse effects include (a) injury (material injury) to the domestic industry of the importing country, (b) nullification or impairment of benefits of bound tariff rates, or (c) serious prejudice to the domestic industry (ibid., arts. 2 and 5).

[67] Part V of the SCM Agreement (arts. 10–23) provides for substantive and procedural rules for the application of countervailing duties. According to art. 18, exporters can also avoid CVDs by undertaking to increase their export prices (price undertaking). This price undertaking is voluntary on the part of the exporters, and the importing country may consider the acceptance of the undertaking impractical, for instance, where the number of actual or potential exporters is too great (ibid.).

[68] GATT, supra note 20, art. VI, para. 6.

actionable subsidies,[69] reduce the key ability of developing countries to provide support to promote their industries in the early stages of development.[70] Infant industries in developing economies often need export markets because of a limited domestic market. Government support is called on to improve their competitiveness in the foreign market, as well as in their own. The SCM Agreement recognizes this and affirms, "subsidies may play an important role in economic development programmes of developing country Members."[71] The SCM Agreement also provides certain special and differential treatment to developing countries, that is, LDC members are not prohibited from applying export subsidies,[72] and other developing countries are permitted to apply export subsidies for a period of eight years from the date of entry into force of the WTO Agreement in 1995, which has already expired.[73] These prohibited or otherwise actionable subsidies should be allowed for developing countries if they demonstrate a need for such subsidies with a concrete development plan. Such subsidy, specially authorized to facilitate development, could be labeled Development-Facilitation Subsidy (DFS).[74]

As is the case for the DFT, procedural safeguards should be provided to minimize the abuse of DFS applications. The maximum applicable DFS rate should also be differentiated in accordance with the per capita income level of a particular developing country, because the development need would be greater for poorer developing countries. A question may arise as to whether the availability of a DFS would lead to a subsidy race among developing countries, thus diminishing the effect of the subsidy for the industrial promotion of individual developing countries and causing only a distortion of resources. The answer is that a developing country should be trusted with its own best judgment as to whether subsidization would be necessary. Many economic and political factors would affect a government decision to grant a subsidy, and a prudent government would consider the existence and even the possibility of similar subsidies that may be applied by competing countries in the future. A developing country will subsidize those export industries that it believes will have the best potential for success, and the possibility of these competing subsidies will be part of that equation.

[69] Supra notes 65 and 66.

[70] It has been observed that the current subsidy rules have made "a significant dent in the ability of developing countries to employ intelligently-designed industrial policies." Rodrik (2004), supra note 56, pp. 34–35. Note that today's developed countries provided extensive subsidies during their development stages, which would have been either prohibited or actionable under the SCM. Ha-Joon Chang, *Kicking Away the Ladder: Development Strategy in Historical Perspective* (London: Anthem Press, 2002), chap. 2.

[71] SCA Agreement, supra note 65, art. 27.1 (emphasis added).

[72] Ibid., art. 27.2(a). This preference ceases to apply to any of these LDC members when it reaches USD 1,000 GNP per capita (ibid., Annex VII).

[73] Ibid., art. 27.2(b).

[74] Y. S. Lee (2004), supra note 54, pp. 948–953.

d. The Suspension of Antidumping Measures, Trade-Related Investment Measures (TRIMs) Agreement, and TRIPS Agreement

Elements of the ADF may also include suspension of antidumping (AD) measures and the Trade-Related Investment Measures (TRIMs) and TRIPS Agreements in favor of developing countries.[75] AD actions[76] that are applied against "dumped imports" in the form of increased tariffs are the most frequently applied import measures in the world today. From 1995 to 2008, as many as 2,190 AD measures were been applied.[77] Exports from developing countries have been the primary target of AD measures, because the vast majority of the AD measures have been applied to the exports from developing countries.[78]

Most economists doubt that solid economic justifications exist for AD measures. Also, inherent complexity and arbitrariness in the determination of dumping[79] have created a breeding ground for abuse of AD actions.[80] National authorities can adopt

75 An argument may be made that these elements can be included in the corresponding agreements and not in the ADF. Their regulatory placement requires further discussion. In this chapter, these elements are introduced to discuss their substantive merits.

76 For the specific determination of dumping margins and the imposition and collection of antidumping duties, see WTO, *The WTO Agreement on Implementation of Article VI of the General Agreement on Tariffs and Trade 1994*, arts. 6.10 and 9, available at: http://www.wto.org/english/docs_e/legal_e/19-adp.pdf. Price undertakings are also allowed as in the application of CVD actions. Supra note 67; ADP Agreement, art. 8. For the origin of antidumping measures, see Congressional Budget Office, *How the GATT Affects Antidumping and Countervailing-duty Policy* (1994), p. 18. Antidumping actions include both antidumping duties and price undertakings.

77 WTO, *Annual Report 2009*, pp. 39–40, available at: http://www.wto.org/english/res_e/booksp_e/anrep_e/anrep09_e.pdf.

78 Ibid. However, increasingly more AD measures are being applied by developing countries, notably India.

79 Dumping is defined as the sale at a price under "normal value" that needs to be first determined. ADP Agreement, supra note 76, art. 2.1. The complexity and arbitrariness in the determination of normal value are easily seen. For example, there may not be a single home market price to compare, and the complex adjusted average may have to be calculated to come up with a reference home price. The home country may not completely be a market economy (e.g., transitional economy), and therefore, the home price may not represent the true market price. Or the product in question may not even be sold in the home market, or too few of the product are sold to be the basis of a valid home price. In all these cases, the price needs to be "constructed" by an evaluation of cost (constructed cost) plus reasonable profit. Finding the "export price" that is necessary to determine the existence of dumping by comparison with the home price can be equally complex because a number of adjustments to the transaction price may be necessary to keep the comparison with the home price fair. These adjustments may include complex calculations involving numerous items, such as warranty services, advertising costs, etc. Y. S. Lee (2009), supra note 26, chap. 4.

80 Depending on a specific methodology adopted to calculate costs and average prices, the result can be vastly different, not to mention that the measure of "reasonable profit" can also vary. A study has revealed that in the case of the United States, the vast majority of national AD practices do not actually even identify either price discrimination or sales below cost. Brink Lindsey, "The U.S. Antidumping Law: Rhetoric versus Reality," Cato Institute Trade Policy Analysis No. 7 (August 16, 1999), available at: http://www.cato.org/pub_display.php?pub_id=3650.

a methodology that will yield the least desirable result for exporters[81] and then come up with a finding of dumping.[82] Depending on their choice of methodology and calculation, the authorities will also be able to find different dumping margins.[83] This arbitrariness in the current AD rules and its significant adverse effect on trade have led to the inclusion of AD rules in the new Doha Round agenda, with a possibility for rule modifications.[84] Nonetheless, it is unlikely that the inherent arbitrariness in determining dumping could be reduced to a satisfactory level.[85]

AD measures cause a critical problem for trade of developing countries. The competitiveness of their product is normally based on low prices, reflecting lower labor costs. Developing countries should be allowed to use this advantage to achieve economic development through international trade. AD measures targeting inexpensive products have been major impediments to the exports of developing countries.[86] Although a lower price alone is not a sufficient ground for the application of AD measures,[87] the current provisions permitting the "construction" of costs and reference prices make it relatively easy for national authorities to find dumping and apply AD measures against exports from developing countries. Yale economist T. N. Srinivasan has characterized antidumping as the equivalent of a "nuclear weapon in the armory of trade policy" and suggested its removal at the 1999 WTO High-Level Symposium on Trade and Development.[88] Indeed, considering the economic needs of developing countries, AD measures should not be applicable to their trade. Safeguard measures[89] can respond to the predatory dumping that results in the

[81] Article 2 of the ADP Agreement authorizes such leeway in the determination of dumping. ADP Agreement, supra note 76.

[82] Although the provisions of the ADP Agreement attempt to provide disciplines on AD actions, "in common parlance, it is usual to designate all low-cost imports as dumped imports." International Trade Centre UNCTAD/WTO and Commonwealth Secretariat, *Business Guide to the Uruguay Round* (Geneva: ITC/CS, 1995), p. 181.

[83] ADP Agreement, supra note 76.

[84] WTO, *Ministerial Declaration*, WT/MIN(01)/DEC/1 (November 20, 2001), para. 28. Reform proposals have been made to reduce the abuse and arbitrariness in the application of AD measures. See Brink Lindsey and Dan Ikenson, "Reforming the Antidumping Agreement: A Road Map for WTO Negotiations," Cato Institute Trade Policy Analysis No. 21 (December 11, 2002), available at: http://www.cato.org/pub_display.php?pub_id=3636.

[85] This is because the very attempt to determine the "normalcy" of a price in a market economy, in which prices are determined by market forces and not by any normative rules, is inherently arbitrary no matter what standard is applied. It was pointed out that "[t]he primary justification for the antidumping law is really more political than economic. The guiding precept is *legitimacy* rather than *efficiency*" (emphasis in original). Brink Lindsey, supra note 80, p. 3.

[86] Supra note 82.

[87] Dumping should also *cause* or *threaten* material injury to the domestic industry for the application of an AD measure. GATT, supra note 20, art. VI, para. 6. Unlike the serious injury standard required for the application of a safeguard measure (*Agreement on Safeguards*, supra note 45, art. 4), the threshold for material injury is not considered high.

[88] Report 1999, supra note 15.

[89] Article 2.1 of the *Agreement on Safeguards* sets out the general requirement for the application of a safeguard measure. See supra note 45.

displacement of domestic products, which may be the only justification for AD rules.[90]

Another area that has significant relevance to the economic development and trade of developing countries is foreign investment. Foreign direct investment (FDI) may provide developing countries with resources necessary for the development that these countries typically lack, including financial capital, technological resources, production facilities, and managerial expertise. FDI also offers employment opportunities for local populations. In accepting FDI, the host developing countries may be inclined to set a series of conditions to steer FDI to maximize its contribution to their development objectives. For example, to facilitate export industries, these governments may adopt investment measures requiring foreign investors to export a certain portion of products produced in the host country. Investment measures may have significant implications on trade. For instance, if the host country adopts investment measures requiring foreign investment to export a certain portion of their products in an attempt to promote exports and reduce competition with other domestic producers, this foreign company may be compelled to export more than it otherwise would. Similarly, if investment measures require foreign investments to purchase domestic products, this may reduce the importation of these products from other countries that it may have imported from in the absence of such measures. The WTO TRIMs[91] attempts to regulate certain investment measures that affect trade – namely, those that are inconsistent with Articles III and XI of GATT.[92]

As mentioned, TRIMs are often adopted in pursuing development objectives. Although there was some doubt as to the industrial promotion effects of TRIMs,[93] TRIMs may nevertheless play an important role in industrial promotion because they can help facilitate infant domestic industries by promoting exports and encouraging the use of domestic products. Note that all of today's developed countries also adopted investment measures to meet their development objectives during their own development.[94] The TRIMs Agreement seems to mainly target the investment

90 For more discussion, see Yong-Shik Lee, *Safeguard Measures in World Trade: The Legal Analysis* (2nd ed., The Hague: Kluwer Law International, 2005), chap. 14.2.

91 WTO, *Agreement on Trade-Related Investment Measures*, available at: http://www.wto.org/English/docs_e/legal_e/18-trims.pdf.

92 GATT, supra note 20, arts. III and XI.

93 The criticism includes the following: TRIMs are economically inefficient because investment terms are controlled by investment measures rather than by market forces; the governments of the hosting countries may abuse TRIMs politically, for instance, to serve the interests of selected producers that are not necessarily relevant to the needs for development; and the restrictive terms of TRIMs may also discourage investors from making investments in developing countries adopting these measures and thereby deprive the host developing countries of the opportunities to benefit from the investment that can provide necessary resources for their development. This criticism about TRIMs is in line with the objections to state industrial promotion discussed earlier. See also supra note 26, chap. 3.1.

94 Ha-Joon Chang and Duncan Green, *The Northern WTO Agenda on Investment: Do as We Say, Not as We Did* (Geneva: South Centre and London: Catholic Overseas Development Agency, June 2003), p. 33. TRIMs can be either effective or counter-effective to the development interest of a particular developing country depending on the economic conditions and the developmental stage of

regulations of developing countries, but there is no clear need for such multilateral control on investment. For instance, major investors are often in a position to negotiate the terms of their investment with the host developing country. In addition, more than 2,600 bilateral investment treaties around the world already require national treatment in favor of foreign investors and prohibit a wider range of TRIMs than those restrained by the TRIMs Agreement. If a developing country is ready to give up certain TRIMs, it will do so bilaterally or unilaterally, even without treaty obligations. However, if a developing country considers the adoption of TRIMs as necessary to meet its development objectives, then mandatory trade rules should not prohibit their adoption. Therefore, the multilateral control on TRIMs needs to be lifted in favor of developing countries.[95]

Lastly, the application of the TRIPS Agreement to developing countries should be reconsidered. Advanced knowledge, such as new technology and production techniques, is essential to facilitating industries. Historically, the ability to copy technologies developed in advanced countries has been one of the most essential elements in determining the ability of developing countries to catch up.[96] Today, developed countries attempt to prevent unauthorized use of advanced technology by assigning a propriety right called an intellectual property right (IPR). Thus, the enforcement of IPRs affects the ability of developing countries to acquire advanced technology for the purpose of development. The introduction of the TRIPS Agreement in trade disciplines is one of the important attempts to enforce IPRs around the world.

The introduction of the TRIPS Agreement was an ambitious undertaking in the Uruguay Round.[97] This agreement, comprising seventy-three articles in seven parts, is one of the most extensive provisions in the WTO Agreement. It establishes mandatory standards for the protection of various IPRs, including copyrights, trademarks, geographic indications, industrial designs, patents, and layout designs of integrated circuits, providing substantial minimum terms of protection (e.g., fifty years for copyright, twenty years for patent, and indefinite renewal of trademark with a minimum

the individual country. For instance, an imposition of a local content requirement may be unnecessary and economically inefficient at a time when the domestic industry can compete with imports. On the other hand, this particular investment measure may be useful and facilitate domestic infant industries in the initial stages of development where domestic industries require some protection. This suggests that TRIMs can provide a means to facilitate development.

95 Reflecting this concern, twelve countries proposed to change the text of the TRIMs Agreement to make commitments under the agreement optional and not mandatory. WTO, *Preparations for the 1999 Ministerial Conference*, WTO Doc. WT/GC/W/354 (1999).

96 Richard R. Nelson, "The Changing Institutional Requirements for Technological and Economic Catch Up," paper presented at the Danish Research Unit for Industrial Dynamics Summer Conference 2004 on Industrial Dynamics, Innovation and Development, available at: http://www.druid.dk/conferences/summer2004/papers/ds2004–280.pdf.

97 WTO, Agreement on Trade-Related Aspects of Intellectual Property Rights, available.

of seven years for each registration).[98] In addition to providing effective enforcement procedures under its own laws,[99] the TRIPS Agreement also requires members to apply national treatment and most-favored-nation treatment to protect foreign IPRs.[100] Rules of other major IPRs conventions are also incorporated by reference in the relevant provisions of the TRIPS Agreement.[101]

The adoption of the TRIPS Agreement as part of trade disciplines raises important concerns. First, the TRIPS Agreement attempts to establish a regulatory regime to protect IPRs within all WTO member states. This includes those member states whose economic and social developments do not yet embrace the concept of IPRs and whose judicial systems have not yet developed sufficiently to recognize and enforce IPRs.[102] It is doubtful that the imposition of an economic and legal system, such as an IPRs regime, should be the role of trade disciplines. Their role should be limited to remedying trade injury resulting from IPRs violations where such injury has been demonstrated. The adoption of the TRIPS Agreement in the WTO, primarily for the effectiveness of enforcement, is not a desirable precedent.

The imposition of an IPRs regime may prematurely set economic and legal barriers to acquiring advanced technology for development.[103] This concern is amplified because the current TRIPS provisions require long durations of IPRs protections.[104] One may argue that the protection of IPRs provides an incentive for creations and innovations that may contribute to economic development, but in today's world where technological gaps between developed and developing countries are wider than ever, developing countries cannot close this gap by relying on their own "creativity" alone.[105] They need access to advanced knowledge and technology. In this respect, developing countries today are at a considerably larger disadvantage than those of the past, because no international IPRs regime was imposed on them, or at least certainly not to the extent imposed by the TRIPS Agreement today.

98 Ibid.

99 Ibid., art. 41.

100 Ibid., arts. 3–4.

101 The Paris Convention (1967), the Berne Convention (1971), the Rome Convention (1961), and the Treaty on Intellectual Property in Respect of Integrated Circuits (1989) are incorporated by reference. TRIPS, art. 1.

102 A historical study shows that IPRs began to be recognized and protected when considerable economic and social developments had taken place. Chang, supra note 70, pp. 83–85.

103 In addition, concern was raised that the compliance requirement of the TRIPS Agreement will impose a considerable financial burden on developing countries, particularly LDCs. According to a study, implementing the TRIPS obligations would require "the least developed countries to invest in buildings, equipment, training, and so forth that would cost each of them $150 million – for many of the least developed countries this represents a full year's development budget." J. Michael Finger, "The WTO's Special Burden on Less Developed Countries" (2000) 19(3) *Cato Journal* 425.

104 TRIPS, supra note 97.

105 On the other hand, if a developing country considers that the extensive protection of IPRs is in its own interest, this country, rather than the WTO, should be trusted to set its own standards for protection under its own laws and regulations. Supra note 26, chap. 5.

Although the trade effect of IPRs violations may need to be addressed, the imposition of an IPRs regime clearly and unnecessarily impedes the development interest of developing countries. The need to acquire advanced knowledge and technology on the part of developing countries does not mean that developed countries have to give up their IPRs interests entirely. Alternative provisions that enable developed countries to apply trade sanctions where they demonstrate that a violation of their IPRs has led to significant injury to their trade can be devised, rather than the current provisions that attempt to establish a uniform IPRs regime throughout the world.[106] In the meantime, the provisions of the TRIPS Agreement should be suspended in favor of developing countries to the extent that it imposes on these countries the establishment of an IPRs regime that they are not ready for.

e. Extension of Special Treatment for LDCs

Some developed countries have offered preferential treatment to LDCs greater than that provided under the existing GSP (preferential tariff rates in favor of qualifying developing countries) scheme. For instance, the European Union has introduced the Everything-but-Arms (EBA) initiative, offering duty-free and quota-free treatment to products currently exported by LDCs.[107] Other countries, such as the United States and Canada, offer similar preferential treatment to LDCs, although less comprehensive and more limited in scope than the EBA initiative.[108] Considering the dire economic need of LDCs, an EBA-type of duty- and quota-free treatment to the trade of LDCs needs to be implemented by developed countries and participating developing countries in the WTO. While implementing this initiative in favor of LDCs, a transitional period can be established for the complete removal of trade barriers to sensitive products.[109] Members would also have to ensure that nontariff measures do not undermine the trade benefit of these preferences for LDCs.[110]

[106] The general exceptions of Article XX already allow trade sanctions to protect IPRs. What seems necessary is to set detailed rules for the substantive and procedural requirements for the application of a trade measure to remedy injury cased by an IPRs violation. A member should be authorized to apply trade measures only where a violation of its IPRs *causes injury* to its domestic industry through trade. An injury test, such as the one found in Article 4.2(a) of the Agreement on Safeguards, should be required to ensure that the measure is applied based on a reasonable assessment of injury caused by IPRs violations and not on an arbitrary determination by national authorities. This way, developed countries will be able to protect their own IPRs interests by applying their own laws, as well as the rules of relevant international IPRs conventions, without imposing regulatory burden on developing countries such as the one currently imposed by the TRIPS Agreement. Supra note 26, chap. 5.

[107] For an initial evaluation of the EBA initiative, see Paul Brenton, "Integrating the Least Developed Countries into the World Trading System: The Current Impact of European Union Preferences Under 'Everything but Arms'" (2003) 37(3) *Journal of World Trade* 623.

[108] For instance, the United States has implemented the Africa Growth and Opportunity Act, which offers improved access to certain African, but not Asian, LDCs. Ibid., pp. 644–645.

[109] In the EBA initiative, trade liberalization is complete as of 2010.

[110] It has been observed that nontariff measures, as well as stringent rules of origin, continue to limit exports from LDCs significantly. Stefano Inama, "Market Access for LDCs: Issues to Be Addressed"

IV. CONCLUSION

To facilitate economic development effectively in trade disciplines, it is important to examine the current institutional apparatus and regulatory structure in the WTO. The current Committee on Trade and Development and the development assistance provisions scattered throughout the GATT/WTO disciplines are not sufficient to meet this objective. Regulatory and organizational reforms are thus necessary to effectively meet the development agenda and implement development assistance policies. This reform should include the elevation of the CTD to the new Council for Trade and Development and the establishment of a coherent body of rules that facilitate development (ADF).

The proposed expansion of the current organizational apparatus means an expansion of staff and an increase in resources available to assist developing countries. Financial assistance from some members has allowed trade ministers and representatives from developing countries to participate in WTO meetings and negotiations. The financial assistance necessary to enable the participation of developing countries should not be left to the generosity of individual members but should be provided systematically by the WTO. The WTO Advisory Centre on WTO Law should also be supported by the WTO budget. The WTO budget allocation to the activities and functions of trade and development should be significantly increased to meet these needs.

Logistics must be improved to address the needs arising from the limited financial and human resources of developing countries. The scarcity of these resources often prevents developing countries from participating in the trade organization fully, so WTO meetings and negotiation schedules should also be set to allow maximum participation of developing countries.[111] The use of modern technology, such as Web technology, should be adopted to increase participation of developing countries, who cannot afford to station experts in Geneva to participate in these meetings, without having to travel to Geneva from their home countries. The lack of participation by developing countries in WTO processes has often been pointed out as a reason for the poor representation of the interests of developing countries; thus, ways to relieve these difficulties, such as the foregoing proposals, should be sought.

The monitoring and enforcement mechanism of the development assistance provisions and policies should also be devised. The requirement of a Trade-Related Development Assistance Report can be considered. Developed-country members

(2002) 36(1) *Journal of World Trade* 115. Applications of administered protection, such as antidumping measures, countervailing duties, and safeguards, can also diminish the beneficial effect of preference for LDCs.

[111] Renato Ruggiero, the former director-general of the WTO, acknowledged that some developing and least developed countries had difficulty participating fully in the organization, mainly because there were too many meetings. He believed that it was an objective problem, not the result of a deliberate policy of exclusion. Report 1999, supra note 15.

should be required to make this report regularly, subject to review by the Council for Trade and Development. Developing-country members may also participate in the reporting process on a voluntary basis. This report requirement will be consistent with the objectives of development facilitation manifested in Part IV of GATT. The proposed organizational and regulatory reform, as well as this suggested improvement of practical logistics, would help to turn what many have seen as merely "rhetoric for development assistance" into real and effective actions to assist developing countries.

REFERENCES

Amsden, Alice H., *Escape from Empire: The Developing World's Journey through Heaven and Hell* (Cambridge, MA: MIT Press, 2007).

______, *Asia's Next Giant: South Korea and Late Industrialization* (New York: Oxford University Press, 1989).

Brenton, Paul, "Integrating the Least Developed Countries into the World Trading System: The Current Impact of European Union Preferences Under 'Everything but Arms'" (2003) 37(3) *Journal of World Trade*.

Chang, Ha-Joon, *Kicking Away the Ladder: Development Strategy in Historical Perspective* (London: Anthem Press, 2002).

Chang, Ha-Joon, and Duncan Green, "The Northern WTO Agenda on Investment: Do as We Say, Not as We Did" (Geneva: South Centre and London: Catholic Overseas Development Agency, June 2003).

Findlay, R., "Growth and Development in Trade Models," in R. W. Jones and P. B. Kenen (eds.), *Handbook of International Economics*, Vol. 1 (New York: North-Holland, 1984).

Finger, J. Michael, "The WTO's Special Burden on Less Developed Countries" (2000) 19(3) *Cato Journal*.

Helleiner, G. K. (ed.), *Trade Policy, Industrialization, and Development* (Oxford: Oxford University Press, 1992).

International Trade Centre UNCTAD/WTO and Commonwealth Secretariat, *Business Guide to the Uruguay Round* (Geneva: ITC/CS, 1995).

Inama, Stefano, "Market Access for LDCs: Issues to Be Addressed" (2002) 36(1) *Journal of World Trade*.

Krueger, A. O., "Trade Policies in Developing Countries," in R. W. Jones and P. B. Kenen (eds.), *Handbook of International Economics*, Vol. 1 (New York: North-Holland, 1984).

Krueger, Anne, "The Developing Countries and the Next Round of Multilateral Trade Negotiations" (1999) 22(7) *The World Economy*.

Lee, Yong-Shik, "Facilitating Development in the World Trading System: A Proposal for Development Facilitation Tariff and Development Facilitating Subsidy" (2004) 38(6) *Journal of World Trade*.

______, *Safeguard Measures in World Trade: The Legal Analysis* (2nd ed., The Hague: Kluwer Law International, 2005).

______,*Reclaiming Development in the World Trading System* (New York: Cambridge University Press, 2009).

Lindsey, Brink, and Dan Ikenson, "Reforming the Antidumping Agreement: A Road Map for WTO Negotiations," Cato Institute Trade Policy Analysis No. 21 (December 11, 2002).

Nelson, Richard R., "The Changing Institutional Requirements for Technological and Economic Catch Up," paper presented at the Danish Research Unit for Industrial Dynamics

Summer Conference Summer Conference 2004 on Industrial Dynamics, Innovation and Development.
Rodrik, Dani, *Industrial Policy for the Twenty-First Century*, paper prepared for United Nations Industrial Development Organization, September 2004.
Srinivasan, T. N., "Trade, Development, and Growth," *Princeton Essays in International Economics No*. 225 (December 2001).
United Nations, *Implementation of the United Nations Millennium Declaration*, UN 59th Sess., UN Doc. A/59/282 (2004).
Wade, Robert, *Governing the Market: Economic Theory and the Role of Government in East Asian Industrialization* (Princeton, NJ: Princeton University Press, 2003).
World Bank, *The East Asian Miracle: Economic Growth and Public Policy, World Bank Policy Research Reports* (New York: Oxford University Press, 1993).
World Trade Organization, *Annual Report* 2009 (Geneva: WTO).
———, *Ministerial Declaration*, WT/MIN(01)/DEC/1 (November 20, 2001).
———, *The Legal Texts: The Results of the Uruguay Round of Multilateral Trade Agreements* (Geneva: WTO, 1999).
———, *Report of the WTO's High-Level Symposium on Trade and Development on 17–18 March* 1999, available at: http://www.wto.org/english/tratop_e/devel_e/summhl_e.htm.
———, *Preparations for the 1999 Ministerial Conference*, WTO Doc. WT/GC/W/354 (1999).

6

Rediscovering the Role of Developing Countries in the GATT

Faizel Ismail

I. INTRODUCTION

At the launch of the Doha Round, developing countries were skeptical that the round would address the issues of concern to developing countries. Their skepticism was based on their experience of the past eight rounds of the General Agreement on Tariffs and Trade (GATT) that failed to address adequately the interests and concerns of developing countries. The Doha Round has witnessed developing countries play an active role, through the formation of several developing-country coalitions, based on specific issues, for example, the G20, Non-Agricultural Market Access (NAMA) 11, G33, and regional groups, such as the African Caribbean and Pacific (ACP) and groups that represented developing countries at lower levels of development, for example, least developed countries (LDCs) and small and vulnerable economies (SVEs). These groups have tended to be relatively organized and articulate in expressing their interests and advancing their negotiating positions. Some of the major developing-country groups such as the G20, NAMA 11, and G33 are technically competent and have been able to match the capacity of the major developed countries in the Doha negotiations. The unfolding history of this process has been recorded elsewhere, and this chapter does not intend to address this issue here.[1]

Since the formation of the GATT, developing countries have been arguing for their particular development situations and interests to be taken into account.[2]

[1] F. Ismail, *Mainstreaming Development in the WTO: Developing Countries in the Doha Round* (Geneva: CUTS International and Friedrich Ebert Stiftung, 2007).

[2] Robert Hudec records that the proposal of developing countries in the International Trade Organization negotiations to include a provision taking "into account the special conditions which prevail in countries whose manufacturing industry is still in the initial stages of development" was ignored by the United States. See R. E. Hudec, *Developing Countries in the GATT Legal System* (Brookfield, VT: Gower, 1987).

An earlier version of this chapter was published in the inaugural edition of *The Law and Development Review* (2009).

However, the demand by developing countries for increased market access for products of export interest to them, such as agricultural products and textiles, were largely ignored. Instead, these products faced ever-increasing protection in developed countries for the more than fifty years since the formation of GATT/World Trade Organization (WTO). At its inception in 1947, the newly formed GATT did not recognize the special situation of developing countries. The fundamental principle of the agreement, referred to as the most-favored-nation (MFN) treatment, provided for in Article 1 of the GATT, was that rights and obligations should apply uniformly to all contracting parties.

Thus, in the early period of the GATT (1948–1955), developing countries participated in tariff negotiations and other aspects of GATT activities as equal partners. However, the GATT went on to incorporate a number of exceptions to its general principles of MFN[3] and national treatment[4] through the so-called special and differential treatment (SDT) provisions. Nonetheless, these provisions were considered to be largely ineffective. The WTO, and the GATT before it, has thus been criticized by developing countries and civil society groups as being unfair, unbalanced, and prejudicial to the interests of developing countries.[5]

Why has the GATT failed to address the development needs of developing countries? A large number of writers on the history of the GATT have ascribed this to at least three reasons: (a) the passive and defensive role of developing countries in the GATT, (b) the lack of participation of developing countries in the exchange of concessions, and (c) the focus of developing countries on SDT for developing countries as their main objective. This perspective has become the conventional wisdom in the academic literature and has shaped the perspectives of contemporary students of the GATT.

With regard to the first reason, consider the view of an eminent writer on the subject in a recent article. Michael Finger[6] states, "through GATT's Tokyo Round, which ended in 1978, developing-country participation in multilateral trade negotiations was either passive or defensive. Developing countries that had joined the GATT had in large part remained by-standers; many had acceded under Article

3 GATT, art. I, provides that "any advantage, favour, privilege or immunity granted by any contracting party to any product originating in or destined for any other country shall be accorded immediately and unconditionally to the like product originating in or destined for the territories of all other contracting parties." This rule prohibits members from discriminating against imports according to their source.

4 GATT, art. III.i, provides: "The contracting parties recognize that internal taxes and other internal charges, and laws, regulations and requirements affecting the internal sale, offering for sale, purchase transportation, distribution or use of products, and internal quantitative regulations requiring the mixture, processing or use of products in specified amounts or proportions, should not be applied to imported or domestic products so as to afford protection to domestic production." This national treatment provision requires members to accord nondiscriminatory treatment to imports vis-à-vis domestic products once they have passed through customs.

5 See J. Stiglitz, *Globalization and Its Discontents* (New York: W. W. Norton, 2002).

6 J. M. Finger, "Implication and Imbalance: Dealing with Hangover from the Uruguay Round" (2007) 23 *Oxford Review of Economic Policy* 440–460.

XXVI.1 (c), which exempted them from having to negotiate concessions in order to enter." Finger goes on to state, however, that in "the Uruguay Round things were different. Already in the run-up to the Round, many developing countries took an active role." However, Finger and other writers recognized that the Uruguay Round was unbalanced and that "developing countries had given more than they got – a concern that the basic GATT/WTO ethic of reciprocity had been violated." The main reasons for this outcome have been ascribed to the "lack of assessment of the impacts of the agreement" and that the Uruguay Round Agreements were "poorly understood and certainly not quantified."[7]

Some developing-country writers on the subject have also taken a pessimistic view of the role of developing countries in the GATT and have argued that although developing countries have had a numerical advantage in the GATT/WTO, this has not helped them and ascribe this to a number of weaknesses.[8] These weaknesses are identified as "victims of traps and pitfalls," "victims of harassment," indifference, and silence because of their ignorance of the issues or fear of developed-country response or at best "stiff resistance and sudden collapse."[9]

This chapter shows that these observations do not do justice to the active role developing countries played in shaping the architecture of the international trade organization (ITO) and the GATT by continuing to assert their demands for increased market access for products of export interest to developing countries, and for the special needs and interests of the developing countries to be provided for in the GATT. This was achieved in the early period of the GATT, notwithstanding their export pessimism and political weakness as they emerged from the ravages of colonialism. However, developing countries did lack the technical capacity and organization to build their bargaining power and gain negotiating leverage in the multilateral negotiations. This was only to emerge in the Doha Round from the formation of strong coalitions based on their development interests. Despite this, the Uruguayan case against fifteen Organization for Economic Cooperation and Development members of the GATT in 1961 illustrates that developing countries were not merely passive participants in the GATT subsequent to its formation. This argument is discussed further in Section II.

The second reason for the failure of the GATT to address the needs of developing countries has been ascribed to their lack of participation in the exchange of concessions. Will Martin and Patrick Messerlin state that "the fact that developing countries were not actively participating in the Kennedy and Tokyo Rounds made

[7] S. Ostry, "The Uruguay Round North–South Grand Bargain: Implications for Future Generations," in D. M. Kennedy and J. D. Southwick (eds.), *The Political Economy of International Trade Law: Essays in Honour of Robert E. Hudec* (Cambridge: Cambridge University Press, 2002).

[8] B. L. Das, *The WTO and the Multilateral Trading System: Past, Present and Future* (Penang, Malaysia/London: Third World Networks and Zed Books, 2003).

[9] See also F. Jawara and A. Kwa, *Behind the Scenes at the WTO: The Real World of International Trade Negotiations* (London: Zed Books, 2003).

it much easier for the industrial countries to create mechanisms such as the Multi-Fibre Arrangement (MFA) targeted against exports from developing countries, to continue to exclude agriculture, to exclude other labour-intensive products from full formula-based liberalization, and to offer tariff preferences only at the discretion of the importer."[10] They argue further that "had emerging and developing countries been active participants in the exchange of market-access concessions in the Kennedy Round, it may have required more time to negotiate, and its measured productivity might have been lower, but it would likely have been much more successful in meeting the needs of developing countries."

This chapter argues that this perspective fails to recognize that in the early rounds of the GATT, the developing countries were excluded from participation by the insistence of the United States and the European Economic Community (EEC – now referred to as the European Union, EU) on the principal supplier rule, the exclusion of internal taxes and quotas that effectively excluded tropical products from the negotiations, and reciprocity. Thus, developing countries were not unwilling to participate in the negotiations but were rendered unable to do so.[11] However, notwithstanding this, developing countries did make some relatively significant concessions in the early GATT Rounds, including the Tokyo and Kennedy Rounds. These issues are discussed further in Section III.

The third argument that many writers ascribe to the poor treatment of developing countries in the GATT is their apparent focus on SDT. Martin and Messerlin explain this argument as follows: "Prior to the Uruguay Round, most developing countries had sought to achieve their objectives primarily through special and differential treatment provisions. This was partly a result of the widespread belief in import substitution as a path to development, and partly to the power of the interest groups in import-substituting firms in developing countries."[12] These writers go on to assert that many of these countries resisted the use of key GATT approaches, such as reciprocal liberalization and the principle of nondiscrimination and that "the introduction of these provisions reflected a move away from the original GATT objective of providing a forum for exchanging market access towards one of making transfers to developing countries."

This chapter argues that these writers fail to problematize the concepts of MFN and reciprocity that were debated in the ITO. Developing countries in the ITO were of the view that these concepts required taking into account the different levels of development and special needs of developing countries. In addition, I argue that Part IV of the GATT (1965) and the subsequent Enabling Clause (1979) that created the basis for the special and differential treatment provisions of the Tokyo

[10] W. Martin and P. Messerlin, "Why Is It So Difficult? Trade Liberalization under the Doha Agenda" (2007) 23 *Oxford Review of Economic Policy* 347–366.

[11] R. Wilkinson and J. Scott, "Developing Country Participation in the GATT: A Reassessment" (2008) 7 *World Trade Review* 1–18.

[12] W. Martin and P. Messerlin (2007), supra note 10, pp. 347–366.

Round were partly a response to the failure of the developed countries to address the key interests of developing countries because of their own domestic protectionist interests in products of export interest to developing countries, particularly in areas such as agriculture and textiles.

This chapter elaborates on the three themes just discussed by raising three questions on the role of developing countries in the GATT. First, did developing countries play a passive and defensive role in the GATT (Section II)? Second, did they exchange concessions? Had they provided more concessions, could they have extracted more concessions from the developed countries (Section III)? Third, was SDT the main objective and focus of developing countries that participated in the GATT negotiations (Section IV)? Finally, the chapter also discusses the perspectives of writers cited earlier on the role of developing countries in the Uruguay Round (Section V). In this section, I assess the role of developing countries in the launching of the Uruguay Round and the contribution of developing countries to the Uruguay Round on four of the negotiating issues, including agriculture, textiles and clothing, Agreement on Trade-Related Aspects of Intellectual Property Rights (TRIPS), and services. The conclusion of the chapter summarizes the main arguments (Section VI).

II. DID DEVELOPING COUNTRIES PLAY A PASSIVE AND DEFENSIVE ROLE IN THE GATT?

A. *Overview*

Of the twenty-three original contracting parties of the GATT, ten were developing countries.[13] By 1960, of the thirty-seven contracting parties, twenty-one were developed and only sixteen were developing. However, by 1970, this trend changed significantly; of the seventy-seven contracting parties, twenty-seven were developed and fifty-two were developing countries. By 1987, of the ninety-five contracting parties, twenty-nine were developed and sixty-six were developing countries.[14] Thus, the number of developing countries participating in the GATT Rounds increased progressively: twenty-five in the Kennedy Round, sixty-eight in the Tokyo Round, and seventy-six in the Uruguay Round; in the Doha Round, more than 70% of the 153[15] participating Members were developing countries.[16]

[13] See R. E. Hudec (1987), supra note 2. The countries were Brazil, Chile, Cuba, China, India, Lebanon, Myanmar, Pakistan, Sri Lanka, and Syria. China (also Syria and Lebanon) withdrew after the first few years. At the time, some countries, such as Australia, New Zealand, and South Africa, were also regarded as developing countries. However, the latter were to be regarded as developed countries much later. Until the Uruguay Round, South Africa was still regarded as a developed country in the GATT.

[14] By early 1995, the GATT had 128 members.

[15] WTO, *World Tariff Profiles* (2008).

[16] WTO, *Annual Report* (2001).

At the time of the creation of the GATT, the vast majority of developing countries were still under colonial rule.[17] In some cases their interests were spoken for by the developed countries or "represented" by their colonizers during the early GATT Rounds. In some cases, they were satellite regimes of their colonial states, as was the case of Southern Rhodesia (now Zimbabwe) and South Africa. In addition, the developed countries, or the colonial countries, tended to regard the GATT as their "property" and "they did not have to accommodate the interests of the rest of the world."[18] Thus, as many developing countries became independent in the late 1950s and early 1960s, their perspectives were shaped by this colonial experience and the particular development needs of their newly independent countries.

B. *The ITO*

However, notwithstanding their political weakness, the developing countries did participate actively, both in the GATT negotiations and especially in the process toward creating the ITO. Developing countries were already actively involved in the negotiations on the formation of the ITO, which was abandoned because of the failure of the U.S. Congress to ratify the ITO Charter. Even in the first negotiations on the ITO Charter, the developing countries were vigorously engaged and "tabled a wide range of proposals" in the negotiations on the ITO charter. The first draft of the ITO Charter proposed by the United States in December 1945 had "no provisions on economic development, nor were there any special rules or exceptions for developing countries."[19]

Much of the debate about the GATT took place in the negotiations toward the creation of the ITO because it was understood that the GATT would be incorporated into the ITO once it was created. Thus, the debates about the nature and underlying principles that governed the trading system took place in the ITO negotiations rather than the GATT. The principle of reciprocity was debated in the ITO negotiations with developing countries raising concerns that they lacked the bargaining power to enable them to extract concessions of value from developed countries on a reciprocal basis, and therefore there should be some consideration for the reality that developing countries were not able to grant reciprocal tariff cuts of equal value to that of the more advanced developed countries.[20] Despite these objections, this principle was adopted as a core principle in the GATT and incorporated in the preamble of GATT 1947.

[17] See Annex A, B, C, D, of the Havana Charter for a list of territories of the United Kingdom; France; Belgium, Luxembourg, and the Netherlands; and the United States, respectively.

[18] R. E. Hudec, *The GATT Legal System and World Trade Diplomacy* (2nd ed., New York: Cambridge University Press, 1990).

[19] WTO, *Background Document, High Level Symposium on Trade and Development* (Geneva, March 17–18, 1999).

[20] R. Wilkinson and J. Scott (2008), supra note 11.

During the first meeting of the negotiations on the ITO Charter, held in London in 1947, the United States put forward its proposed Charter (which had been agreed between the United States and the United Kingdom much earlier). Notably, the Brazilian delegation had also presented its "Proposed Charter." The Brazilian Charter engaged with the U.S. proposal on the MFN principle by stating that this should be adhered to unconditionally only by countries in the advanced stage of development. Although both charters called for a general prohibition on quantitative restrictions, the U.S. proposal provided for a broad range of exemptions on the ban for any agricultural product.

The Brazilian proposal also called for recognition of the problems faced by less developed countries as well as the need for special measures to assist these countries with their development.[21] During the debate on the ITO Charter in the United Nations Economic and Social Council, developing countries were able to insert an amendment that called for the ITO negotiations to "take into account the special conditions which prevail in countries whose manufacturing industry is still in the initial stages of development." The United States rejected this proposal, and thus it did not get into the ITO Charter.

However, on the issue of the voting method, the developing countries were more successful. For decision making in the ITO, the U.S. delegation proposed the same method of weighted voting that was used in the recently created International Monetary Fund (IMF). A similar proposal was made by the United Kingdom to take into account the economic size of the country in its share of the vote – a system of weighted voting. Developing countries voiced their opposition to such a system of voting because they feared that this would institutionalize their secondary status. A number of developing countries[22] voiced strong opposition to weighted voting and came out in favor of consensus. As a consequence, the ITO did not adopt a system of weighted voting. On this issue, developing countries did succeed in shaping the voting procedures of the ITO and the GATT.

Developing countries were active participants in the negotiations on the ITO and did succeed in getting some of their concerns into the finally agreed Charter at the Havana Conference in early 1948. It was partly for this reason and the fact that the United States did not succeed in reflecting all of its interests in the ITO Charter that the Havana ITO Charter was rejected by the U.S. Congress and thus never came into force.[23]

C. *The Uruguayan Case*

Developing countries were not merely passive participants in the GATT subsequent to its formation either. This can be illustrated by the Uruguayan case. In 1961,

[21] Ibid.
[22] Such as Czechoslovakia, Turkey, Lebanon, Iraq, El Salvador, Venezuela, and Mexico.
[23] WTO (1999), supra note 19.

Uruguay filed a legal complaint against fifteen developed countries (the entire developed-country membership of GATT) that listed 576 restrictions in the fifteen markets against its exports. The point of the Uruguayan complaint was to draw attention to the commercial barriers facing exports from developing countries.[24] Most of the provisions that Uruguay pointed to were GATT illegal, and the case pointed to the GATT's lack of effectiveness in protecting the interests of developing countries at the time. Thus, the Uruguayan case illustrates that the developing countries did participate and did attempt to shape the architecture of the trading system. In some cases, they succeeded and in some cases they failed to make the changes they sought. However, their failure to effect changes in the GATT should not be mistaken for a lack of participation and engagement.

III. DID DEVELOPING COUNTRIES EXCHANGE CONCESSIONS? HAD THEY PROVIDED MORE CONCESSIONS, COULD THEY HAVE EXTRACTED MORE CONCESSIONS FROM THE DEVELOPED COUNTRIES IN RETURN?

This section further explores the issue of developing-country participation in the GATT in the context of developing countries' willingness to participate in the exchange of concessions during the early GATT Rounds and the later Dillon, Kennedy, and Tokyo Rounds of negotiations.

A. *Early GATT Rounds*

During the early period of the GATT, there were at least three major obstacles to developing-country participation in the process of tariff bargaining or exchange of concessions. These include the principle of reciprocity, the principal supplier rule, and the focus on tariffs only in the negotiations.

During the debate on the ITO negotiations, the United States made it clear that it required the principle of reciprocity to be the foundational principle of the GATT. This required that any tariff cuts that were made by the United States would have to be paid for by reciprocal concessions for the benefit of U.S. manufactured goods. Developing countries such as India argued that because of the limited size of their domestic market, their bargaining power was inadequate to induce concessions from developed countries; moreover, they wanted to protect their infant industries, which were at the early stage of industrialization.[25]

During the negotiations on the ITO, many members had preferred a system of bargaining that was formula based – across-the-board tariff negotiations – but the U.S. Congress indicated that this would be unacceptable. The United Kingdom supported this method because it would have led to the leveling of high U.S. tariffs. The U.S. delegation, however, argued for a system of reciprocal bargaining over

[24] See R. E. Hudec (1987), supra note 2, pp. 46–47.
[25] R. Wilkinson and J. Scott (2008), supra note 11.

specific tariff lines that required a product-by-product, principal supplier method of tariff negotiations through which a country could only be requested to make tariff cuts on a particular product by the principal supplier of that product to that country.[26] This meant that for any particular product, the importing country negotiates its tariff rate with its principal supplier and not with all suppliers of the same product. Developing countries at the time were seldom principal suppliers of any product, except raw materials that entered industrialized countries duty-free. Only at the Fourth Geneva Round of GATT in 1956 was this rule modified to allow developing countries to negotiate collectively in requesting concessions. However, they were still effectively prevented from requesting concessions in any products that they did not produce in large quantities. Thus, the principal supplier rule had the effect of locking out developing countries from the tariff-cutting negotiations.

Furthermore, for those developing countries that exported tropical products, the primary impediments to their exports were more often internal taxes in importing markets rather than tariffs. These internal taxes were as high as 500% for products such as sugar. However, internal taxes were not on the agenda of the GATT and could not be negotiated. In addition, quotas were also not part of the early GATT negotiations, and as the GATT evolved, these growing quotas in developed countries increased the barriers to entry for the products of interest to developing countries.

Thus, Wilkinson[27] observes that by the mid-1960s, the evolution of the GATT led to two experiences. For the industrialized countries, "liberalization under the GATT had seen the volume and value of trade in manufactured, semi-manufactured and industrial goods increase significantly." In addition, "they had also managed to protect their agricultural and textile and clothing sectors through a blend of formal and informal restrictions." To give effect to this, a number of GATT waivers existed to protect developed-country agricultural markets and the exclusion of textiles and clothing from liberalization in developed countries. For developing countries, this meant that the products of interest to them were excluded from liberalization.[28] Thus, the argument that developing countries' were not willing to provide concessions in the early rounds of the GATT must be seen in the context of the many obstacles that prevented developing countries' effective participation in the tariff bargaining process and that excluded them from the negotiations. This was to shape their approach to the unfolding rounds of negotiations in the GATT.

B. *Haberler Report*

The export interests and demands of developing countries were again clearly articulated in the 1950s (at a Ministerial Meeting in 1957 and the Haberler Report in

[26] Ibid.

[27] R. Wilkinson, *The WTO: Crisis and Governance of Global Trade* (London: Routledge, 2006).

[28] Ibid.

1958) and placed firmly on the agenda of the Kennedy Round in 1964. Developing countries, although still a minority in the GATT, by the mid-1950s asserted the need for market access in developed countries for products in which they had a comparative advantage. Thus, a GATT Ministerial Meeting convened to discuss this issue in November 1957 noted "the failure of the trade of less developed countries to develop as rapidly as that of developed countries, excessive short-term fluctuations in prices of primary products, and widespread resort to agricultural protection."[29] This meeting led to a study of these issues that produced the Haberler Report in October 1958.[30]

The Haberler Report found that there was some substance in the feeling of disquiet among primary goods–producing countries at the time that the rules and conventions about commercial policies were relatively unfavorable to them. As a result, the contracting parties adopted a Declaration on the Promotion of Trade of Less-developed Countries in December 1961. The Declaration called for action in seven areas: the removal of those quantitative restrictions that affect the export trade of less developed countries; special attention to tariff reductions of direct and primary benefit to less developed countries; removal, or considerable reduction, of fiscal duties in developed countries; improved access for developing countries in purchases made by state agencies; preferences in market access for developing countries; limitation of subsidies on production or export of primary products; and careful observance of GATT- or UN-mandated limitations on disposal of commodity surpluses or strategic stocks. The Declaration also called for a "sympathetic attitude to the question of reciprocity by developing countries." Finally, it called for more attention to be given in developed countries' technical assistance programs to efforts by developing countries to improve production and marketing methods and for the expansion of trade among developing countries themselves.

C. *Dillon Round*

The Haberler Report had recommended the inclusion of internal taxes in the negotiations. This – together with strong pressure from developing countries, particularly, India and Brazil – led to the inclusion of internal taxes in the Dillon Round (1960–1961). The inclusion of internal taxes in the Dillon Round was met with fierce opposition from the United States and the newly formed EEC. The increasing use of nontariff barriers (NTBs) to protect the agricultural markets of developed countries and the exclusion of agriculture from the negotiations, together with the use of the principal supplier rule, resulted in poor and disappointing results for agricultural exporting developing countries.[31]

[29] WTO (1999), supra note 19.

[30] See Annex 2 for further elaboration.

[31] R. Wilkinson and J. Scott (2008), supra note 11.

Thus, in 1963 a Nigerian-led group of developing countries (G21) proposed a program of action urging the contracting parties to focus their attention on targeting those barriers to trade identified as directly affecting the less developed countries. This program was adopted as a resolution at the May 1963 GATT Ministerial Meeting. The resolution called for a standstill on new tariff and nontariff barriers. However, the EEC obtained an exception for its emerging common external tariff. Austria and Japan stated that they were not able to meet the deadline of December 1965, and the United States stated that its national legislation required its tariffs to be reduced over a five-year period and thus it could not comply. The 1963 resolution only resulted in a committee to investigate the revision of the GATT with a view to safeguarding the interests of developing countries in their international and development programs.[32]

D. *The Kennedy Round*

The Kennedy Round thus was to remedy some of these deficiencies in the GATT and was "advertised as the long-awaited answer to demands by developing countries for improved access to developed-country markets."[33] The tariff reductions that were required to be made by developed countries on tropical products that were of export interest to developing countries did not materialize. The Kennedy Round (1963–1967), that had promised to prioritize the issues of interest to developing countries (agriculture and textiles), thus failed to make any real progress on these issues.

The U.S. Trade Expansion Act passed by the U.S. Congress in 1962 provided the United States with the basis to negotiate across-the-board, formula-based negotiations. However, the approach the United States chose was a hybrid one that utilized a formula combined with substantial bilateral bargaining over the exceptions list. This bargaining usually took place between the principal suppliers of the product in question to ensure reciprocity. Thus, in this process, developing countries were still hampered by their lack of bargaining power and the ability to offer reciprocal tariff concessions. Thus, the Kennedy Round also resulted in the previous pattern of achieving far greater concessions for products of export interest to developed countries.

In contrast to the approximately 35% average tariff reductions achieved for developed-country manufactured goods, tariff cuts on cotton textile products only achieved an 18% cut from the United States and 22% from the EEC. In addition, both the United States and the EEC made their textiles sector offer conditional on the renewal of the Long-Term Arrangement (LTA), rendering these tariff cuts irrelevant due to the LTA quotas, imposed against the largest supplying developing countries into these developed-country markets.[34] In addition, little progress was

[32] Ibid.

[33] WTO (1999), supra note 19.

[34] R. Wilkinson and J. Scott (2008), supra note 11.

made on agriculture because the agriculture support programs of the United States and the EEC remained highly restrictive, and developing countries continued to face high tariffs on finished and semifinished industrial products.[35]

However, despite this, developing countries did participate in the tariff reduction process with at least twenty-three developing countries having declared themselves as participating countries for the purpose of making a contribution, with about fourteen making tariff bindings or concessions that were included in their GATT schedules.[36]

E. *Tokyo Round*

Again, in the Tokyo Round, developing countries did participate by making proposals for agreement and agreeing to implement restrictions in certain areas. The Tokyo Round went beyond tariff cuts and went on to negotiate rules on NTBs. For developing countries, one of the most important issues was the so-called Voluntary Export Restraints (VERs). These VERs dominated the cotton sector and several other products of importance to developing countries. By the time of the Tokyo Round, there were more than 850 NTBs in force. The committee charged with examining Quantitative Restrictions (QRs) with a view to restricting their use produced two reports, with one synthesizing the proposals of developing countries, represented by Brazil and the three Chairs – of the GATT contracting parties, the Council, and the Committee on Trade and Development. It called for the gradual liberalization and elimination of QRs. The other report was presented by the United States, which made a distinction between legal and illegal restrictions, with the illegal QRs being subject to negotiations. However, few countries accepted the U.S. distinction or definition of what was legal or illegal. Thus, the multilateral approach to the negotiations on QRs was abandoned in favor of a bilateral request and offer approach.

As in the Kennedy Round, in the Tokyo Round, the developed countries made the extension of the MFA a precondition for any reduction of tariffs on textiles. In addition, the United States restricted the growth of its quotas for developing-country textiles even further, from 6% to 1 to 3% a year. The EEC went further and required the major developing-country exporters to reduce their textile and clothing exports to below 1976 levels, requiring cuts of 9%, 7%, and 25%, for Hong Kong, Korea, and Taiwan, respectively.[37]

On the issue of safeguards in which the developing countries had a major interest, Brazil and Nigeria, on behalf of the majority of developing countries, presented proposals. However, the negotiations broke down because developing countries refused to accept the EEC's demand that each member should have the right to

35 Ibid.
36 Ibid.
37 Ibid.

impose unilateral safeguards on individual countries without multilateral approval. Even in other areas of the negotiations, such as customs valuation and subsidies and countervailing duties, developing countries played an active role, but their views were largely ignored.

Thus, on many of the negotiations on NTBs codes and in the negotiations on tariffs and agriculture, developing countries played an active role but were largely ignored in the process. The United States and the EEC negotiated a mutually acceptable outcome and then included other members of the Quad (Japan and Canada). The rest of the GATT membership were thus faced with a fait accompli, with developing countries lacking the political and economic bargaining power to determine the outcome.[38]

However, notwithstanding this lack of negotiating power, developing countries did make concessions in the Tokyo Round. The Tokyo Round Schedules include concession bindings from several developing countries.[39] In the supplementary protocol to the Tokyo Round in November 1979, concessions were made by a large number of other developing countries.[40] Thus, the contention that developing countries were not active participants in the Kennedy and Tokyo Rounds and were not willing to make tariff concessions does not take into account the active role that developing countries played in attempting to negotiate agreements in their interest and the tariff concessions that they actually did make.

Although these concessions may not have been very significant, they should be considered in the context of the refusal of developed countries to engage fully or respond in a positive manner to the negotiating proposals put forward by developing countries and the poor results achieved by developing countries on both tariff and nontariff barriers against products of export interest to them. Given the growing protectionism in the developed countries on agriculture and textiles and clothing products of interest to developing countries, the relatively small markets of developing countries, the principal supplier tariff reduction techniques adopted by developed countries, and the relatively poor political and economic bargaining power of developing countries, it is unlikely that they could have achieved better results had they made more robust tariff-cutting concessions for the products of export interest to developed countries of the GATT.

IV. WAS SPECIAL AND DIFFERENTIAL TREATMENT THE MAIN OBJECTIVE AND FOCUS OF DEVELOPING COUNTRIES IN THE GATT?

This chapter engages with the assertion that developing countries "sought to achieve their objectives primarily through special and differential treatment provisions"

38 Ibid.

39 Czechoslovakia, Yugoslavia, Argentina, Jamaica, Romania, and Hungary.

40 Brazil, Chile, the Dominican Republic, Egypt, Haiti, India, Indonesia, Ivory Coast, Korea, Malaysia, Pakistan, Peru, Singapore, Uruguay, and Zaire.

before the Uruguay Round. As the GATT advanced with each GATT Round, developing countries were willing and did in fact contribute to the process of tariff reduction and exchange of concessions. However, developing countries also sought to create provisions in the GATT that addressed their particular development situation and needs. This section discusses the gradual adoption of these special and differential measures by the GATT, Article XVIII, Part IV of the GATT, and the Enabling Clause, and argues that they were often not fully responsive to the demands of the developing countries and, in most cases, dressed up in best endeavor language, without legal effect. The section begins with a discussion of the contention that developing countries simply resisted "the use of key GATT approaches, such as reciprocal liberalization and the principle of non-discrimination" and that "the introduction of these provisions reflected a move away from the original GATT objective of providing a forum for exchanging market access towards one of making transfers to developing countries." I argue that this fails to problematize these concepts as being inadequate to address the very real differences that existed and still remain today between the levels of development and different development needs of developing countries.

A. *Reciprocity and MFN*

The debates about the nature and underlying principles that governed the trading system took place in the ITO negotiations rather than the GATT. The first draft of the ITO Charter proposed by the United States in December 1945 had "no provisions on economic development, nor were there any special rules or exceptions for developing countries."[41]

The principle of reciprocity was debated in the ITO negotiations, with developing countries arguing that they were unable to negotiate with developed countries on a reciprocal basis because of their lack of bargaining power. Notwithstanding these objections, this principle was adopted as a core principle in the GATT.[42]

The Brazilian Charter critiqued the U.S. proposal on the MFN principle, arguing that this was only appropriate for countries that were at a more advanced stage of development. In addition, the efforts of developing countries to insert an amendment in the ITO Charter that recognized the special situation of developing countries in the early stages of development were rejected by the United States.[43]

Thus, the principles of reciprocity and MFN were highly contested by developing countries during the negotiations in the ITO. The adoption of these principles by the GATT without the full support of developing countries and without any qualification

41 WTO (1999), supra note 19.

42 R. Wilkinson and J. Scott (2008), supra note 11.

43 Ibid.

should thus be highlighted by academic observers of the GATT. These concepts were thus to be continuously challenged by developing countries in the early period of the GATTs formation, during the early and later rounds of the GATT, and up to and including in the Doha Round.

The need for the concepts of reciprocity and MFN to take into account the special needs of developing countries led to the adoption of a number of development provisions in the GATT. In addition, a number of provisions went beyond this to provide for positive measures to be adopted by the developed countries of the GATT to assist developing countries with their development needs, especially with regard to capacity building and technical assistance. These measures were agreed to by developed countries partly because of the increasing pressure that developing countries created in the GATT for them and also because the recognition by developed countries that the prevailing techniques of negotiation, the increasing protectionism in developed countries for products of interest to developing countries, and the outcomes of the early rounds were not resulting in market access gains for developing countries.

B. *Article XVIII*

At the review of the GATT in 1954–1955, developing countries again criticized the failure of the GATT to meet their needs, particularly with regard to the exclusion of agriculture from the ambit of the GATT and the exemption of agricultural products from the ban on quantitative restrictions. Developing countries argued that they required to be afforded the use of trade-restricting measures to protect their infant industries. Thus, Article XVIII of the GATT was revised to provide developing countries additional flexibility with regard to their obligations. It enabled developing countries to raise their bound tariffs for the purposes of economic development and, with certain conditions, to use any measure that was not inconsistent with other provisions of GATT for the purpose of promoting a particular industry.

C. *Part IV of the GATT*

It was in response to this criticism of the GATT and its failure to address the concerns of developing countries that at a special session of the GATT in Geneva, November 1964, the contracting parties drew up a protocol amending the GATT and introduced a fourth protocol known as Part IV of the GATT, which dealt with trade and development issues. Part IV, however, was the result of significant negotiations by developing countries that had submitted a large number of proposals. However, the result was a significantly reduced version of provisions submitted by the less developed countries. Part IV of the GATT did commit developed countries to (a) giving high priority to the reduction and elimination of trade barriers to trade for goods of export interest to developing countries, (b) refraining from introducing or increasing tariffs or NTBs on these products, (c) removing the requirement for reciprocity, and (d) creating the Committee on Trade and Development to monitor progress being made in these areas.

Part IV of the GATT also created the basis for preferences for developing countries, both between developed and developing countries and between developing countries. Developing countries took advantage of the latter provision, and on December 8, 1971, a protocol relating to trade negotiations between developing countries was finalized, along with some trade concessions between developing countries. Developed countries did use the former provision to introduce the Generalized System of Preferences (GSP) schemes in favor of developing countries. Developing countries had created the pressure for a firmer legal basis for these legal arrangements than the GATT waiver that had been used for this purpose.

D. *Enabling Clause*

During the Tokyo Round, both the earlier-mentioned preferential arrangements were provided with a firmer legal basis through the adoption of the Enabling Clause in 1979. The agreement by the United States[44] to expand the preference system (the European countries had brought their colonial preferences into the GATT at its formation) led to the formal legal recognition of such derogations from the MFN principle of the GATT. The Enabling Clause gave permanent legal authorization for the GSP, preferences between developing countries, special treatment for developing countries from GATT rules, and special treatment for the least developed countries. Developing countries had refused to sign any of the agreements or "codes" reached in the Tokyo Round until agreement was reached to include special and differential treatment provisions for developing countries. This was therefore agreed to by the United States and the other developed countries in the GATT and took the form of nonbinding assurances of technical assistance to help developing countries comply with the new rules or exemptions from the new obligations.

Thus, Part IV of the GATT (1965) and the subsequent Enabling Clause (1979) that created the basis for the special and differential treatment provisions of the Tokyo Round were a direct response to the failure of the developed countries to address the key interests of developing countries in their markets because of the ever-increasing protection in their markets of products of interest to developing countries. Developing countries did attempt to negotiate the opening of developed-country markets but were obstructed from doing so, as the foregoing sections have shown. In addition, developing countries were willing and did in fact contribute to the process of tariff reduction and exchange of concessions. Developing countries

[44] Hudec notes that the United States agreed in 1969 to expand the GSP system and to create its own GSP for developing countries that the EEC already had in place. See R. E. Hudec (1987), supra note 2.

thus could not be said to have "sought to achieve their objectives primarily through special and differential treatment provisions" prior to the Uruguay Round.

However, developing countries also sought to create provisions in the GATT that addressed their particular development situation and needs. The special and differential measures that were gradually adopted by the GATT were often not fully responsive to the demands of the developing countries and, in most cases, dressed up in best endeavor language without legal effect.[45] Thus, the assertion by these writers that developing countries simply resisted "the use of key GATT approaches, such as reciprocal liberalization and the principle of non-discrimination" does not recognize that these concepts do not address the real issues of the different levels of development and needs of developing countries.

The failure of the GATT during the first eight rounds to address the issues of the appropriate balance between the principles of reciprocity and MFN on one hand and the special development needs of developing countries on the other continues to haunt the members of the WTO in the Doha Round.[46]

V. THE URUGUAY ROUND (1986–1993)

The Uruguay Round was to be concluded in four years, with a midterm review to be held at a Ministerial Conference in Montreal in 1988, and its final concluding Ministerial Conference to be held in Brussels in 1990. The round had a large set of issues to be negotiated, including tariffs, nontariff measures, tropical products, natural resource–based products, agriculture, textiles and clothing, GATT Articles, Safeguards, the MTN Agreement and arrangements (i.e., the codes negotiated in the Tokyo Round), subsidies and countervailing measures, dispute settlement, trade-related aspects of intellectual property rights (including trade in counterfeit goods), trade-related investment measures, functioning of the GATT system, and services.

The Trade Negotiating Committee was set up and chaired by GATT Director-General Arthur Dunkel. At the beginning of the negotiations, these issues were negotiated in fifteen separate negotiating groups. Fourteen negotiating groups were under the Group of Negotiations on Goods (GNG), and Services fell under the Group of Negotiations on Services (GNS). However, the round was to take three more years to conclude after the Brussels Ministerial Conference held in December 1990. The round was finally concluded on December 15, 1993, in Geneva and was formally brought to an end at the Marrakech Ministerial Meeting held in April 1994.

In this section, I assess the role of developing countries in the launching of the Uruguay Round. I then proceed to assess the contribution of developing countries

[45] Srinivasan is quoted as stating that under Part IV, the "less developed countries achieved little by way of precise commitments . . . but a lot in terms of verbiage"; quoted in R. Wilkinson and J. Scott (2008), supra note 11.

[46] F. Ismail, "How Can Least Developed Countries and Other Small, Weak and Vulnerable Economies Also Gain from the WTO Doha Development Agenda on the Road to Hong Kong?" (2006) 40 *Journal of World Trade* 37–68.

to the Uruguay Round on four of the previously noted negotiating issues. The scope of this chapter does not allow the undertaking of a detailed assessment of all fifteen of the negotiating issues. Instead, I discuss two of the most important issues of the round for developing countries in which those countries were the *demandeurs*, that is, agriculture and clothing and textiles, and two of the issues that were firmly opposed by developing countries at the beginning of the Uruguay Round, that is, TRIPS and services. The contribution of developing countries on these four issues is discussed for each of the three periods subsequent to the launching of the Uruguay Round: (a) from the launch of the Uruguay Round (December 1986 to Montreal (December 1988), (b) from Montreal to Brussels (December 1990), and (c) from Brussels to Marrakech (April 1994).

A. *Launching the Uruguay Round (Punta del Este, December 1986)*

Although many writers ascribe a passive and defensive role to developing countries in previous rounds of the GATT, they acknowledge that in "the Uruguay Round things were different. Already in the run-up to the Round, many developing countries took an active role."[47] However, these writers recognized that the Uruguay Round was unbalanced and that "developing countries had given more than they got."[48] These writers maintain that the main reason for this outcome was the developing countries' lack of technical capacity.[49] Some developing-country writers also take a pessimistic view of the role of developing countries in the GATT. They have argued that the lack of these countries' success was due to their lack of capacity and their fear of developed countries.[50]

This section discusses the role of developing countries during the attempts to launch the Uruguay Round to illustrate that this description is not entirely accurate. Developing countries did understand the dangers posed by the new issues that were proposed by the United States for inclusion into the new round. This is why they opposed the inclusion of these issues in the agenda of the negotiations. In addition, the description of the role of developing countries as "stiff resistance and sudden collapse" is not accurate. Developing countries were engaged in the negotiations until the last minute and did secure some gains in shaping the agenda of the launch of the Uruguay Round.

Two years after the end of the Tokyo Round, the United States initiated a process toward launching a new round. The majority of developing countries were opposed to the proposed extension of the GATT's remit into services, intellectual property, and investment. Developing countries such as India and Brazil argued that previous rounds had not yielded gains for developing countries and that action should first be

47 J. M. Finger (2007), supra note 6.
48 Ibid.
49 Ibid.
50 See also F. Jawara and A. Kwa (2003), supra note 9.

taken to remove VERs restrictions, the MFA, and restrictions in agriculture.[51] This opposition was a major factor that resulted in the collapse of the November 1982 Ministerial Meeting that had been called to launch the round.

The United States pursued the objective of launching a new round with threats to impose unilateral import restrictions under Section 301 (of the 1974 U.S. Trade Act). The United States also introduced new export subsidies to challenge the EEC.[52] The support for a new round grew to include all the developed countries and a number of developing countries by 1985. However, a group of twenty-four developing countries[53] were firmly opposed to the agenda of the round. They insisted on progress being made first on the removal of the GATT-inconsistent measures and the MFA. They opposed the new agenda of services, TRIPS, and investment, and instead called for a round that was confined to industrial products and agriculture, together with a standstill and roll back of protectionist measures that were inconsistent with the GATT.[54]

The group of twenty-four developing countries that opposed the round was eventually reduced to a group of ten.[55] However, the group of ten eventually agreed to the launch of the round that included the new agenda, after having secured agreement that these new issues would be pursued on a separate track from the negotiations on goods. Croome[56] records that the new issues involved long negotiations, at Punta del Esta, in which the United States, India, and Brazil were the principal participants. The major result that emerged was a detailed procedural agreement that ensured coverage of all three subjects but separated them sufficiently from the traditional areas of GATT negotiations to be acceptable to Brazil, India, and their allies.

Thus, although the developing countries did not succeed in pushing the new issues off the agenda of the GATT, they did succeed in shaping the agenda to some extent. Nevertheless, the fact that the Uruguay Round was only launched in 1986, at Punta del Este, Uruguay, about five years later than the United States had wanted, was a result of the opposition that developing countries had waged and their insistence that the issues of interest to them should be adequately addressed. Developing countries therefore played an active role in the launching of the Uruguay Round and shaping its agenda. The fact that they had not succeeded in removing the new issues from the negotiating agenda was not a result of lack of technical capacity but the superior negotiating power of the United States (and other developed members of the GATT),

[51] C. Croome, *Reshaping the World Trading System: A History of the Uruguay Round* (2nd ed., The Hague: Kluwer Law International, 1999).

[52] The United States raised its export subsidies from zero in 1984 to USD 256 million in 1986. The EEC already had export subsidies amounting to USD 47,094 million. R. Wilkinson and J. Scott, supra note 11.

[53] They included Argentina, Bangladesh, Brazil, Burma, Cameroon, Columbia, Core d'Voire, Cuba, Cyprus, Egypt, Ghana, India, Jamaica, Nicaragua, Nigeria, Pakistan, Peru, Romania, Sri Lanka, Tanzania, Trinidad and Tobago, Uruguay, Yugoslavia, and Zaire.

[54] C. Croome (1999), supra note 51.

[55] Argentina, Brazil, Cuba, Egypt, India, Nicaragua, Nigeria, Peru, Tanzania, and Yugoslavia.

[56] C. Croome (1999), supra note 51, p. 24.

reflected in its threats to use its unilateral Section 301 actions. Developing countries were, however, engaged and negotiating until the last moment in shaping the agenda of the Uruguay Round. The characterization of developing-country participation as "stiff resistance and sudden collapse" is not an accurate description of the role of developing countries in launching the Uruguay Round.

B. *From the Launch of the Uruguay Round to Montreal (December 1988)*

a. Agriculture

At the beginning of the round, the United States took an aggressive approach to agriculture liberalization, calling for the elimination of domestic support and export subsidies within ten years. The Cairns Group,[57] which was closely allied to the United States, took a more realistic approach, calling for significant reform of developed-country protectionist policies in agriculture and substantial reduction of their subsidies and increased market access. The Cairns Group was an alliance made up of developing countries from Latin America and Asia, with some developed countries, including Australia, New Zealand, and Canada. The EEC resisted these pressures to liberalize its highly protectionist agriculture policies and was only willing to entertain a gradual phase out of its protectionist programs. By the time of the Montreal Ministerial Conference, the EEC had failed to make any proposals in the agriculture negotiations despite pressure from both the United States and developing-country agriculture exporting countries.

b. Textiles

At the launch of the Uruguay Round, a highly ambiguous set of the objectives for the textiles and clothing negotiations were agreed on "to formulate modalities that would permit the eventual integration of this sector into GATT on the basis of strengthened GATT rules and disciplines, thereby also contributing to the objective of further liberalization."[58] About twenty developing-country exporters of textiles and clothing came together in the International Textile and Clothing Bureau (ITCB) to coordinate their efforts in the negotiations. The ITCB made proposals for the staged abolition of the MFA. The EEC and Canada argued that the liberalization of textiles and clothing would require a strengthening of all GATT rules and disciplines. However, by the time of the Montreal midterm review there was to be no recommendations that could be sent to Ministers because the members had failed to agree on the basis for the negotiations.

57 The Cairns Group was created in August 1986 at a meeting in Cairns, Australia, of representatives from fourteen predominantly exporting countries, including Argentina, Australia, Brazil, Canada, Chile, Colombia, Fiji, Hungary, Indonesia, Malaysia, Philippines, New Zealand, Thailand, and Uruguay. J. Croome (1999), supra note 51, p. 23.

58 J. Croome (1999), supra note 51, p. 90.

c. TRIPS

At the beginning of the round, there were vastly different perspectives on the agenda for the negotiations on TRIPS. Developing countries were under the impression that the agreement would be restricted to counterfeit goods. However, the developed countries insisted that the agreement would need to cover all intellectual property rights (IPRs), including copyright, patents, trademarks, design, geographic indicators, industrial designs, and trade secrets.[59] By Montreal, there was no real breakthrough on TRIPS. Developing countries were engaged in the negotiations on standards. They insisted, however, that such negotiations must recognize public-interest objectives, including health, development, and the availability of technology.

d. Services

By the time of the Montreal Ministerial Meeting, considerable progress had been made on the services negotiations, with agreement reached on the list of concepts, principles, and rules that needed to be applied to the multilateral framework for the services agreement (General Agreement on Trade in Services; GATS), which was meant to be the centerpiece of the results for this part of the round. Latin American countries had submitted a draft text that emphasized MFN treatment and special provisions for developing countries, including flexibility to open fewer sectors or liberalize fewer types of transactions and the right to regulate the provision of services within their territories to implement national policy objectives.[60] This proposal was supplemented by a proposal from seven Asian and African countries, including India, China, and Egypt, which foresaw that mainly the developed countries would initially undertake liberalization. They proposed that developing countries should join later when the benefits of developed-country liberalization began to flow to developing countries. Developing countries also argued that cross-border movement of labor should also be included in the agreement, whereas developed countries argued that this was an immigration issue.

The United States and the EEC approach to the services negotiations began to harden with their insistence on a negative-list approach to the negotiations (all except a specified list should be covered by the agreement), whereas the developing countries favored a positive-list approach (coverage should be established by building up a list of sectors for inclusion).

There were also sharp differences between developed and developing countries on the scope of the negotiations, with developing countries arguing that the negotiations were to conclude with a general framework of rules and principles, leaving

59 J. P. Singh, "The Evolution on National Interests: New Issues and North–South Negotiations during the Uruguay Round," in John S. Odell (ed.), *Negotiating Trade: Developing Countries in the WTO and NAFTA* (New York: Cambridge University Press, 2006), p. 61.

60 J. Croome (1999), supra note 51, p. 211.

the negotiations to specific commitments to later in the round. Developed countries insisted that the agreement would require a substantial first package of specific commitments, with further liberalization to be negotiated in subsequent rounds.[61]

e. Assessment of the Role of Developing Countries

The Montreal Ministerial Meeting failed to make any progress on agriculture because of the failure of the EEC to make proposals and the aggressive position taken by the United States. However, some progress had been made at Montreal on the issue of tropical products (which was negotiated in a separate but related negotiating group). The main impetus for this progress came from the agreement among developing countries to also make a contribution to liberalization of tropical products.[62] Croome notes that this created the basis for agreement on at least six of the fifteen issues in Montreal (tropical products, antidumping, and two of the institutional issues). However, the Latin American countries were adamant that until there was real progress in agriculture, which they regarded as the core issue of the Uruguay Round, there could be no agreement at all on the other issues. Developing countries were thus already influencing the process of the negotiations for the first time.

On clothing and textiles, developing-country exporters had begun to coordinate their efforts in the negotiations though the ITCB but were still to await detailed proposals from developed countries.

On TRIPS, the United States had begun to put concerted unilateral pressure on developing countries to negotiate a TRIPS agreement in the GATT. The United States was to use its bilateral leverage by linking GSP treatment to IPRs protection and to publish "priority watchlists" under its Section 301 legislation that listed countries that in the United States' view granted unfair access to U.S. firms as a result of their intellectual property practices. Developing countries were thus under pressure to negotiate on the basis of the proposals put forward by the United States to avoid unilateral action.

On services, there was a shift in attitude of developing countries in the services negotiations from a defensive to a more active search for solutions. Thus, by the time of the Montreal meeting, the "battle lines of the services negotiations ceased to be drawn on exclusively North–South lines." Instead, "there was a sharpening of differences on many issues among the developed countries."[63] At this stage of the negotiations, however, developing countries were not in a position to limit the developed-country agenda or to form effective alliances in either the TRIPS or the services negotiations.

[61] Ibid., p. 210.
[62] Ibid., p. 144.
[63] Ibid., p. 207.

C. *From Montreal to Brussels (December 1990)*

a. Agriculture

After the failed Montreal Ministerial Meeting, the Uruguay Round was relaunched in April 1989 with the chairs of the negotiating groups drafting new texts. This time, the United States and the Cairns Group each made detailed proposals on domestic support, export subsidies, and minimum market access. In response, the EEC rejected these proposals of the United States and Cairns Group and instead made a general proposal to negotiate average target reductions. Just one month before the December 1990 Brussels Ministerial Conference, which was intended to bring the round to a close, the EEC produced a more detailed proposal on agriculture that offered a mere 30% reduction in its domestic subsidies and made no offer to reduce its export subsidies.[64] The chair of the agriculture negotiating group thus was unable to produce a text before the Brussels Ministerial Meeting. The Latin American countries were left with no option but to resist any progress elsewhere in the round. This resulted in an impasse in the Uruguay Round negotiations.

b. Textiles

There were no new proposals on textiles and clothing until a few months before the Montreal meeting. The ITCB made detailed proposals that called for the phase out of the MFA within six and a half years. The EEC made proposals for the staged integration of textiles and clothing into GATT with gradual liberalization but refrained from making proposals on how long the phase out should take. Thus, as the Brussels meeting approached, there was a long list of unresolved questions, including the time span for the phaseout of the MFA. At the Brussels Ministerial Conference, there were considerable negotiations on the clothing and textile issues but no agreement on "length of the transitions for the phase out of the MFA and the rates at which products would be integrated."[65]

c. TRIPS

Developing countries were unable to limit the U.S. agenda on intellectual property at the initial stages of the round but did succeed in forming effective coalitions, including on specific aspects of the negotiations with the EEC and Japan. A group of fourteen developing countries assisted by the United Nations Conference on Trade and Development developed a set of proposals (the Talloires Text) on intellectual property in response to the March 1990 proposals of the United States, the EEC, Japan, and Switzerland. The negotiations then moved to include a group of ten developed and ten developing countries to draft a new text. Developing countries made some

[64] Ibid., p. 205.
[65] Ibid., p. 243.

gains in alliance with the EEC, Japan, and Canada on several issues. India's proposal to merge government use and compulsory licensing was supported by the EEC, Japan, and Canada, which became part of the now famous Article 31 of TRIPS.[66]

The insistence by developing countries that the TRIPS Agreement should include negotiations on "the availability, scope and the use of intellectual property rights" was agreed on as an objective for further negotiations in the April 1989 draft text. The United States and the EEC (largely representing the manufacturers) argued that the high research costs incurred by the pharmaceutical companies and long delays in approval justified lengthy patent protection. As the negotiations proceeded, developing countries were to insist that they should obtain explicit recognition of their special need to have flexibility in providing protection to intellectual property so as to be able to pursue important national policy objectives including their public health needs.[67]

d. Services

There was considerable progress in the services negotiations after the Brussels Ministerial Conference. By December 1991, the main framework agreement had been substantially settled with a few outstanding issues, including the question of MFN treatment. The United States held up the negotiations for several months with its insistence that it was not prepared to grant "MFN treatment in its offers to countries whose offers it judged to be inadequate."[68]

e. Assessment of the Role of Developing Countries

Again at the Brussels Ministerial Conference, the failure of the EEC to make detailed proposals on agriculture led to the breakdown of the negotiations. Developing countries, led by the Latin Americans, decided to veto any further progress on other issues if there was to be no progress in the agriculture negotiations. Notwithstanding this position that developing countries had taken, they did participate in advancing the negotiations on several other issues, including the textiles and clothing negotiations. Here, too, the developed countries had not made detailed proposals on the phaseout of the MFA and its transitional period.

On TRIPS, developing countries, although initially resistant to any outcome, began to build their organization, develop alliances, and negotiate to advance provisions that reflected their interests. This effort was to pay dividends in securing several provisions in the agreement that reflected developing-country interests. In the services negotiations, the developing countries had begun to engage in discussions of the framework of the GATS and were successful in influencing the architecture of the agreement to a significant extent.

66 Singh (2006), supra note 59, p. 67.
67 J. Croome (1999), supra note 51, p. 216.
68 Ibid., p. 289.

D. *From Brussels to Marrakech (April 1994)*

a. Agriculture

It was only in July 1991 that the Negotiating Groups began to meet again, six months after the breakdown of the round in Brussels. The dire situation of the round prompted Arthur Dunkel to write his own draft compromise text on agriculture (Dunkel was also the chair of the agriculture negotiating group) and, with the help of the chairs of the negotiating groups, on each of the other negotiating issues. This comprehensive set of draft texts, produced on December 20, 1991, became known as the Dunkel Text. This text was supported by the Cairns Group but firmly rejected by the EC. The inability of the United States and the EEC to resolve their differences created an impasse in the round for most of 1992.

As the term of the Bush administration was coming to an end in 1992, the United States and the EEC intensified their bilateral efforts to find common ground in the latter part of the year. On November 20, 1992, their Uruguay Round negotiators, meeting at Blair House (the U.S. president's Washington guest house for foreign dignitaries), produced a bilateral agreement on agriculture that was to later shape the Uruguay Round agreement.[69] Although agricultural exporters were disappointed at the further weakening of the level of ambition of the agriculture negotiations, even from the compromise proposed in the Draft Final Act, they were prepared to accept the settlement. However, soon after this meeting, the EEC was forced to retreat from the agreement because of France's rejection of the Blair House Agreement.

b. Textiles

The final bargaining on the textiles and clothing negotiations were to take place at the end of 1991 and were incorporated into the Draft Final Act. The phaseout period was to be divided into three phases and was set for ten years in the text.

c. TRIPS

Negotiations on TRIPS had effectively been concluded by December 1991 when Dunkel drafted his Draft Final Text. However, the TRIPS agreement that required governments to provide patent protection for pharmaceuticals and seeds aroused fierce controversy in India, where protestors burned effigies of Dunkel.[70]

d. Services

The services negotiations progressed much faster than the negotiations on goods, despite its slow start and earlier resistance by developing countries. By November 1993, eighty-one countries had made offers to open their services markets, a large

69 Ibid., p. 295.
70 Ibid., p. 293.

number of these were developing countries. Both the United States and the European Union, however, began to raise major concerns. The United States insisted that it would not provide MFN treatment for its offers in financial services unless equivalent benefits were granted to its financial sector, and it was unable to make offers in maritime services. The EEC wanted a carve out for cultural matters from the services sectors. In the final stages of the round, up to the first week of December 1993, the United States and the EEC haggled over the services package in bilateral meetings between U.S. Trade Representative (USTR) Mickey Kanto and Sir Leon Brittan, the European Community Commissioner for Trade. The United States refused to recognize the "special cultural character" on audiovisual services, and the EEC thus made no offers in this sector. The United States withdrew its offer on maritime services.

e. Conclusion of the Uruguay Round

The new U.S. administration, under President Clinton, renewed its fast-track authority in April 1992 to continue until December 15, 1993. U.S. Trade Representative Carla Hills had been replaced by Mickey Kantor, and the GATT was to replace Dunkel in June 1993 with Peter Sutherland as its new director-general. A series of intense bilateral negotiations between Kantor and Brittan in November and the first weeks of December 1993 led to a breakthrough in the round. On December 8, 1993, the European Community (EC; formerly the EEC) and the United States reported on the agreements reached between themselves. Developing countries were to criticize the U.S.–EC deal for having diluted the ambition of the agriculture deal substantially and for providing no new concessions in cotton, textiles, leather, or tropical products.[71]

Even as late as November–December 1993, the United States began to insist on major changes to some of the Uruguay Round agreements. Eleven major changes were proposed by the United States to the Anti-Dumping Agreement. Mickey Kantor and Brittan continued to negotiate maritime services and civil aircraft until the morning of December 15. The United States continued to negotiate for tighter restrictions on compulsory licensing for semiconductor technology and the earlier introduction of patent protection for pharmaceuticals in developing countries. Thus, the majority of participants "had no clear idea only hours before the final offers were due of what the two largest participants would offer."[72] Notwithstanding this lack of transparency in the offers made by the major players, the United States and the EC, Peter Sutherland brought down the gavel to conclude the Uruguay Round at 7:30 p.m. on December 15, 1993. The Uruguay Round agreements were to come into effect on January 1, 1995, when the GATT was to be transformed into the World Trade Organization (WTO).

[71] Ibid., p. 325.
[72] Ibid., p. 328.

f. Assessment of the Role of Developing Countries

Developing countries' initial assessment of the agreements reached by December 3, 1993, "insisted that the market openings that they had received from developed countries for their main exports fell far short of their own offers to liberalize."[73] However, they continued to make reforms in their economies, and by April 1991, about thirty developing countries had unilaterally reduced their tariffs. This prompted the Brazilian delegation to state that "developing countries had walked the extra mile, first by negotiating in a flexible and constructive spirit on issues like services and secondly by opening their markets without waiting for the conclusion of the round," but had not received any recognition for their efforts from the major trading partners.[74]

In the agriculture sector more broadly, developing countries' offers to make concessions in the tropical products negotiation gave impetus to an early settlement of this issue. The negotiations had created a framework that was to include agriculture in the GATT for the first time but yield little market access benefits or strengthened disciplines to limit developed-country subsidization of their agriculture. Developing countries in the Latin American Group as well as in alliance with the Cairns Group had played an important role in the negotiations. In textiles and clothing, the round had begun to integrate this sector within the GATT framework for goods but was only fully to integrate about half of the MFA in the final year of a ten-year transition period. In the textiles and clothing sector, developing countries had also agreed to make concessions. Developing countries were organized in the ITCB and participated actively in shaping the outcome of the final agreement.

Even with regard to the two issues that developing countries had totally opposed for inclusion in the Uruguay Round (i.e., TRIPS and services), they had still played an important role in shaping the outcomes of the TRIPS Agreement and GATS by engaging actively in the negotiations and forming issue-based coalitions.[75] Although developing countries had failed to block the introduction of an expansive agenda related to intellectual property rights by the developed countries, they did succeed in negotiating some provisions, including longer phase-in periods and compulsory licensing provisions for public-interest purposes. They succeeded in these efforts through the use of broader alliances that included the EC, Japan, and Canada. In services, developing countries succeeded in inserting a number of development-friendly provisions in the final GATS framework. These included the adoption of a positive-list approach rather than the negative-list approach insisted on by the United States and the EC. A large number of developing countries did make concessions in the market access offers as part of the services negotiations, although their initial understanding was that the mandate only required creation of a framework. Ironically, it was the developed countries that were to become recalcitrant in the latter

[73] Ibid., p. 324.
[74] Ibid., p. 254.
[75] Singh (2006), supra note 59, p. 78.

stages of the round. The United States and the EC began to limit their market access offers and demand carve outs for specific sectors from the GATS agreement.

Developing countries had clearly participated in each stage of the Uruguay Round negotiations, they shaped the negotiating architecture, they succeeded in inserting provisions in the agreements that would benefit their economies, and they made concessions on market access and took on binding rules. In effect, developing countries were required to accept all the Uruguay Round agreements, whether they negotiated to accept obligations or not, through the concept of the "single undertaking" that was employed in a GATT round for the first time.

Developing countries did succeed in building a number of special and differential provisions into the Uruguay Round agreements, but they negotiated shaping the agreements as a whole rather than focusing exclusively on SDT provisions. Despite these efforts, developing countries were unable to make significant gains from the Uruguay Round.[76] They inherited an imbalanced outcome that created more obligations and provided little real market access opportunities in developed countries for their products. Part of this outcome was due to the poor level of organization and transient nature of developing-country alliances in the Uruguay Round and the fact that the United States and the EC exerted enormous (asymmetric) economic power and leverage, including through aggressive bilateral measures (e.g., the U.S. Super 301 legislation), to pressure developing countries to succumb to their interests.[77] Developing countries were to learn the lessons well and build more effective coalitions in the Doha Round of negotiations.[78]

VI. CONCLUSIONS

At the launch of the Doha Round, it was widely accepted that the results of the Uruguay Round were imbalanced. There was also recognition that the products of interest to developing countries, especially in agriculture, were not adequately addressed in the previous rounds. Even in the area of special and differential provisions for developing countries, the complaint of developing countries that these provisions did not adequately address their purpose was acknowledged, and thus the Doha Round mandate agreed to review these provisions with a view to making these SDT provisions "precise, effective, and operational."[79]

The issues that this chapter has sought to explore are the explanations provided for this imbalance in the GATT, in particular, why the GATT failed to address the

76 J. M. Finger (2007), supra note 6.

77 R. Wilkinson (2006), supra note 27.

78 A. Narlikar and D. Tussie, "The G20 at the Cancun Ministerial: Developing Countries and Their Evolving Coalitions in the WTO" (2004) 27 *World Economy* 947–966.

79 See WTO, *Ministerial Declaration*, WT/MIN(10)/DEC/1, adopted on 14 November 2001 (20 November 2001), paras. 12, 44.

development interests of developing countries. There are some standard explanations for this outcome that have been provided in the academic history of the GATT. This chapter has identified three major themes in the literature that have been argued as reasons for developing countries' failure to advance their interests in the GATT. Three main reasons have been provided: (a) that developing countries did not play an active role in the GATT until the Uruguay Round, and this participation was characterized as passive and defensive; (b) that the developing countries were unwilling and failed to make concessions to their developed-country negotiating partners in the exchange of tariff reduction bargaining; and (c) that the developing countries' main objective and focus in the GATT negotiations was on special and differential provisions.

This chapter has explored each of these themes and argued that such assertions are not an accurate description of the role that developing countries played both in the ITO negotiations and in the GATT. First, developing countries played an active role in the negotiations on the ITO, within which the GATT was to be located. Despite the superior negotiating power of the United States and the other developed countries, the developing countries made some significant advances in including their interests in the ITO Charter. It is partly for this reason that the U.S. Congress refused to adopt the Charter and the creation of the ITO. This chapter also illustrates the active role that developing countries played in the early years of the GATT with the Uruguayan case that was filed in the GATT against fifteen of the developed members of the GATT.

Second, the argument as to the participation of developing countries in the GATT is explored further in the context of developing-country participation in tariff concessions, in the early period of the GATT, and in the later rounds of negotiations, including the Dillon Round, the Kennedy Round, and the Tokyo Round. In each case, the evidence that emerges is that developing countries were excluded from the negotiation process by the negotiating techniques and approach adopted by the GATT (principal supplier and reciprocity) or by the reluctance of the United States and the EEC to negotiate on issues of interest to developing countries (such as agriculture, clothing and textiles, and internal taxes and restrictions).

Third, the argument that developing countries focused on SDT and that this was their main objective in the GATT is also not accurate. The foregoing discussion points to the active role that developing countries played in asserting their demands for increased market access for products of interest to developing countries throughout the history of the GATT.

Developing countries did, however, call for provisions in the GATT that took account of their special situations. In this regard, they debated the concepts of reciprocity and MFN during the ITO negotiations and argued for these concepts to be balanced against the different levels of development and their special development needs. Despite this, developing countries were treated as equals in the early GATT years, and they were required to reciprocate with tariff concessions of their own, notwithstanding their less competitive situations. However, they continued to campaign for provisions to be included in the GATT that addressed their particular development needs. A series of special and differential provisions were gradually included in the GATT providing for derogations from the above GATT principles, in Article XVIII, Part IV of the GATT, and the Enabling Clause.

However, these provisions did not fully take on board the proposals of developing countries. They were at best attempts by developed countries to mitigate for the high and ever-increasing levels of protection in developed countries against the products of interest to developing countries, and they were at best framed in language that was not binding on developed countries. The frustration of developing countries with the ineffectiveness of these provisions resulted in the Doha mandate to agree to review these provisions with a view to making them "more precise, effective and operational." Thus, the argument that these SDT provisions "reflected a move away from the original GATT objective of providing a forum for exchanging market access towards one of making transfers to developing countries" does not resonate in the experience of developing countries.

Most writers on the Uruguay Round now recognize that the results of the round were unbalanced and that developing countries did play an active role in the negotiations. However, these writers either argue that developing countries lacked the technical capacity to assess the results of the round or that their opposition was characterized by "stiff resistance and sudden collapse." A brief discussion of the negotiations leading up to the 1986 launch of the Uruguay Round at Punta del Este suggests that developing countries, although not successful in removing the new issues that the United States and other developed countries insisted on to be part of the agenda of the Uruguay Round, did succeed in shaping the agenda of the round and were engaged in the negotiations until the last moments of the round in Punta del Este. Thus, the description of "stiff resistance and sudden collapse" is not a fitting description of their role in the launch of the Uruguay Round.

In the three periods of the Uruguay Round subsequent to its launch, this assessment has shown that developing countries did play an active role in shaping the outcomes of the agreements: they did make concessions, and they did not focus exclusively on obtaining SDT provisions. However, the lack of stronger organization among developing countries, the dominance of the United States and the EEC in the negotiating process, and their asymmetric power limited the ability of developing countries to make significant gains in the Uruguay Round.

The role of developing countries in the current Doha Round is clearly unprecedented. They are more organized, they have gained significant technical capacity, they are engaged in the process of bargaining and exchange of concessions, they are offensive in areas of export interest to them, and they have developed powerful alliances in the form of the G20 on agriculture and NAMA 11 on industrial tariffs. Even the smaller developing countries, such as the LDCs, the so-called SVEs, and interest groups that are more defensive on agriculture (the G33) or on cotton (the Cotton Four) have been making proposals and shaping the outcome of the Doha negotiations. Thus, developing countries in the Doha Round are influencing not only the content of the Doha Round and its outcome but are also shaping the architecture and trajectory of the multilateral trading system. The current and future generation of developing-country trade negotiators will become increasingly curious about the role that developing countries played in the GATT since its inception. Rediscovering the history of the GATT will become an essential part of their attempts to shape the future architecture and content of the multilateral trading system.

REFERENCES

Croome, C., *Reshaping the World Trading System: A History of the Uruguay Round* (2nd ed., The Hague: Kluwer Law International, 1999).

Das, B. L., *The WTO and the Multilateral Trading System: Past, Present and Future* (Penang, Malaysia/London: Third World Networks and Zed Books, 2003).

Finger, J. M., "Implication and Imbalance: Dealing with Hangover from the Uruguay Round" (2007) 23 *Oxford Review of Economic Policy*.

Hudec, R. E., *Developing Countries in the GATT Legal System* (Brookfield, VT: Gower, 1987).

______, *The GATT Legal System and World Trade Diplomacy* (2nd ed., New York: Cambridge University Press, 1990).

Ismail, Faizel, *Mainstreaming Development in the WTO: Developing Countries in the Doha Round* (Geneva: CUTS International and Friedrich Ebert Stiftung, 2007).

Jawara, F., and A. Kwa, *Behind the Scenes at the WTO: The Real World of International Trade Negotiations* (London: Zed Books, 2003).

Martin, W., and P. Messerlin, "Why Is It So difficult? Trade Liberalization under the Doha Agenda" (2007) 23 *Oxford Review of Economic Policy*.

Narlikar, A., and D. Tussie, "The G20 at the Cancun Ministerial: Developing Countries and Their Evolving Coalitions in the WTO" (2004) 27 *World Economy*.

Ostry, S., "The Uruguay Round North–South Grand Bargain: Implications for Future Generations," in D. M. Kennedy and J. D. Southwick (eds.), *The Political Economy of International Trade Law: Essays in Honour of Robert E. Hudec* (Cambridge: Cambridge University Press, 2002).

Singh, J. P., "The Evolution on National Interests: New Issues and North–South Negotiations during the Uruguay Round," in John S. Odell (ed.), *Negotiating Trade: Developing Countries in the WTO and NAFTA* (New York: Cambridge University Press, 2006).

Stiglitz, J., *Globalization and Its Discontents* (New York: W. W. Norton, 2002).

Wilkinson, R., *The WTO: Crisis and Governance of Global Trade* (London: Routledge, 2006).

Wilkinson, R., and J. Scott, "Developing Country Participation in the GATT: A Reassessment" (2008) 7 *World Trade Review*.

World Trade Organization, *Background Document, High Level Symposium on Trade and Development* (Geneva, March 17–18, 1999).

______, *Annual Report* (2001).

______, *Ministerial Declaration*, WT/MIN(10)/DEC/1, adopted November 14, 2001 (November 20, 2001).

______, *World Tariff Profiles* (2008).

7

WTO Dispute Settlement from the Perspective of Developing Countries

Gary N. Horlick and Katherine Fennell

The law, in its majestic equality, forbids rich and poor alike to sleep under bridges, beg in the streets or steal bread.

Anatole France (1844–1924), *The Red Lily*, chap. 7 (1894)

I. INTRODUCTION

The balance between developed and developing countries in the international trade regime has been a matter of great concern since the inception of the World Trade Organization (WTO). As the WTO's foundational document, the Marrakech Agreement, states, "there is need for positive efforts designed to ensure that developing countries, and especially the least developed among them, secure a share in the growth in international trade commensurate with the needs of their economic development."[1] Mediating between the interests of developed and developing countries in the WTO has been a constant struggle, as highlighted most recently by the continued stalling of the Doha Round over issues such as agriculture and services.[2]

In light of these continued struggles, the question of whether the world trading system in its current form benefits or disadvantages developing countries has been the subject of considerable controversy. Historically, there has been much debate over whether free trade fosters economic development. In the 1960s and 1970s, numerous scholars advocated protectionist policies for developing countries on the basis of the belief that these countries were exploited in the world economy and that international trade only perpetuated developing countries' specialization in primary

[1] Marrakech Agreement, Preamble, available at: http://www.wto.org/english/docs_e/legal_e/04-wto_e.htm, accessed August 29, 2009.

[2] See, e.g., "EU and U.S. Try to Rekindle Trade Talks," *New York Times*, January 24, 2008.

This chapter is based in part on G. Horlick and N. Mizulin, "Developing Countries and WTO Dispute Settlement" (2005) 23 *Integration & Trade Journal* 125–133.

commodities and thereby stymied their economic development.[3] Many developing countries followed this advice during those decades and instituted high tariffs and import substitution models to encourage development. As these policies failed in many countries, however, countries increasingly began to move away from this model and embrace the benefits of trade. Although some scholars still espouse the view that high tariffs are better for economic development, most economists and trade practitioners today agree that trade liberalization in fact encourages economic growth, and they point to the results of trade liberalization policies in numerous developing countries over the past two decades to bolster this claim.[4]

Even assuming support for the benefits of trade liberalization for economic development, however, there is still a great deal of debate about the structure of the world trading system and of institutions such as the WTO. As Kent Jones noted, "the theoretical benefits of trade do not necessarily imply that WTO membership has always done an adequate or sufficient job of promoting economic development in poor countries."[5] Although development concerns have not been ignored in the WTO, as evidenced by the special and differential treatment given to developing countries, there are some scholars who believe that development concerns should assume an even higher profile in the WTO. One such scholar, Dani Rodrik, stated, "[t]he problem with current trade rules is not that they over-emphasize trade and growth at the expense of poverty reduction, but that they over-emphasize trade at the expense of poverty reduction *and* growth."[6] There are others who criticize the rules-based nature of the WTO.[7] Robert Howse, arguing that it is no longer possible to ignore the lack of a clear demarcation between what belongs inside the world trading system and what belongs outside, advocated dismantling some of the WTO structures and allowing for a "genuine transnational democratic deliberation" to restructure the trading system.[8]

The WTO Dispute Settlement Mechanism, one of the most significant developments in the WTO, is also the subject of debate with regard to the position of

[3] See D. Irwin, *Free Trade under Fire* (2nd ed., Princeton, NJ: Princeton University Press, 2005) 160. See also F. H. Cardoso and E. Faletto, *Dependencia y Desarrollo en America Latina: Ensayo de Interpretación Sociológica* (Mexico City: Siglo Veintiuno Editores, 1969); and R. Prebisch, *Change and Development – Latin America's Great Task: Report Submitted to the Inter-American Development Bank* (New York: Praeger, 1971).

[4] See K. Jones, *Who's Afraid of the WTO?* (New York: Oxford University Press, 2004), p. 147; Irwin (2005), supra note 3, p. 161 (noting that countries that have pursued trade liberalization have experienced greater economic development and have not been trapped into producing only raw materials).

[5] Jones (2004), supra note 4, p. 148.

[6] See D. Rodrik, "The Global Governance of Trade: As If Development Really Mattered," background paper to the United Nations Development Programme project on Trade and Sustainable Human Development (New York, October 2001), p. 6.

[7] See, e.g., R. Howse, "From Politics to Technocracy – and Back Again: The Fate of the Multilateral Trading Regime" (2002) 96 *American Journal of International Law* 94; D. Trubek and M. P. Cottrell, "Robert Hudec and the Theory of International Economic Law: The Law of Global Space," in C. Thomas and J. Trachtman (eds.), *Developing Countries in the WTO Legal System* (New York: Oxford University Press, 2009), pp. 143–146.

[8] Howse (2002), supra note 7, pp. 108–109, 113–117.

developing countries in the world trading system. Although those, like Howse, who take issue with the rules-based nature of the WTO, see the dispute settlement mechanism as one of the more rigid and potentially objectionable aspects of the system,[9] many scholars see the rules-based dispute settlement system as particularly beneficial for developing countries.[10] The binding nature of the dispute settlement mechanism allows developing countries to address WTO violations when they might not otherwise have the political or economic power to challenge developed countries, such as the United States and the European Union (EU).[11] Eduardo Perez Motta, chairman of the Mexican Federal Competition Commission and former ambassador of the Permanent Mission of Mexico to the WTO, asserted that "developing, and especially least developed countries are going to benefit more from a strong and solid dispute settlement mechanism."[12]

Whatever the theory, in practice developing countries face greater difficulties in bringing cases and enforcing rulings in the WTO dispute settlement system. Although in theory it would appear that the system offers developing countries equal opportunity, in practice there has been an imbalance in access to WTO dispute settlement. This chapter explores (a) the causes of this imbalance, (b) how recent developments in the world economy and shifts in the economic balance of power among nations might affect this imbalance, and (c) how this imbalance could be addressed.

II. CAUSES OF THE IMBALANCE

The imbalance in WTO dispute settlement has several causes. First, developing countries often lack the resources to participate in the litigation. Second, they may lack leverage to enforce the WTO rulings. Third, there are high indirect costs to bringing a WTO dispute that often act as a deterrent for developing countries.

Notably, the extent to which these causes affect a given developing country often depends on its size and its level of development. Much of the debate about the treatment of developing countries in the WTO fails to differentiate between middle-income and least developed countries. Particularly in the context of dispute settlement, the barriers to participation for developing countries have been disproportionately higher for the smallest, least developed countries. Although there is an imbalance in access more generally for developing countries, it is important to

9 Ibid., 113.

10 See J. Jackson, W. Davey, and A. Sykes, *Legal Problems of International Economic Relations: Cases, Materials and Text* (5th ed., St. Paul, MN: Thomson/West, 2008), pp. 336–337.

11 See, e.g., Jones (2004), supra note 4, p. 150; Jackson, Davey, and Sykes (2008), supra note 10.

12 Eduardo Perez Motta, chairman, Mexican Federal Competition Commission, former ambassador of the Permanent Mission of Mexico to the WTO, panel remarks at the American Society of International Law Centennial Regional Meeting: International Trade Under Rule of Law (March 23, 2006), in Occasional Papers, Dean Rusk Center, University of Georgia School of Law, Andre Barbric, ed., p. 47; see also Jones (2004), supra note 4, p. 150 ("the DSU gives all countries their day in court, a fair hearing of their case, and a decision by an independent panel of judges").

differentiate among the diverse developing countries and to recognize that there are certain so-called developing countries that have made greater use of WTO dispute settlementthan others.

Perhaps the most prominent group of developing countries – Brazil, Russia, India, and China, the so-called BRICs – present an interesting subset of larger, more economically potent developing countries that approach WTO dispute settlement in different ways.[13] Brazil, in many ways, is the exception to the tendency of developing countries to participate less in WTO dispute settlement; some would argue that Brazil in fact makes the greatest (and best) use of the WTO dispute settlement mechanism. India, although not as active as Brazil, has become an increasingly prominent player in the dispute settlement system. China, which only joined the WTO in 2001, has been reluctant to bring cases in WTO but in 2007–2010 filed several important cases against both the United States and the EU. Russia's interaction with the WTO in general has been the most hesitant, with accession talks still ongoing. The more active participation of these developing countries compared with others in the WTO dispute settlement system coincides with their higher economic power and the possibility of obtaining full benefits from their formal developing-country status under the WTO-covered agreements, regardless of their actual level of economic development, which is substantially higher than that of the rest of the developing world.[14]

In this section, we explore three main causes of the imbalance in access to the WTO dispute settlement: lack of resources, lack of leverage to enforce WTO rulings, and high indirect costs of bringing a dispute. In doing so, we differentiate between smaller, least developed countries and larger, more economically potent countries, using the BRICs as our primary examples for the latter.

A. *Lack of Resources*

Developing countries that consider bringing a WTO dispute face a disadvantage in terms of resources. The two largest developed WTO Members, the United States and the EU, by virtue of having the largest economies also tend to have the largest number of WTO disputes. Because both the United States and the EU can foresee that they will have a large and continuing number of WTO disputes, each is in a position to hire specialized lawyers in relatively large numbers on an ongoing

[13] Two Goldman Sachs economists coined the term "BRIC" in a 2003 paper. See D. Wilson and R. Purushotha, *Dreaming with the BRICs: The Path to 2050*, Goldman Sachs Global Economics Paper No. 99 (New York, 2003). Sometimes South Africa is included in this subset, and the group is referred to instead as the BRICS.

[14] For a further explanation on the different categories of developing countries, see A. Mitchell and J. Wallis, *Pacific Countries in the WTO: Accession and Accommodation, The Reality of WTO Accession* chap. 8; and P. Kleen and S. Page, *Special and Differential Treatment of Developing Countries in the World Trade Organization* (2005), Report of the Swedish Ministry of Foreign Affairs Global Development Studies 2, pp. 79–95.

basis. Depending on counting methodology, the United States has between twenty and thirty such lawyers and the EU nearly as many (albeit through more complex bureaucratic arrangements). In addition, both the United States and the EU can draw on a large number of other "in-house" WTO specialists.

By contrast, St. Lucia, which can reasonably foresee only one case every few years (in the event, *Bananas*), does not even have a mission in Geneva and could not reasonably hire as permanent staff a large core of WTO specialists. St. Lucia is not the only country in this position; as recently as 2007, approximately one-quarter of WTO Members did not have a WTO mission.[15] Even those that do have a mission often lack staff with training in international trade.[16] Not all developing countries, however, lack WTO missions with trade expertise. Brazil, by many accounts, is one of the most successful participants in the WTO dispute settlement system, and a large part of Brazil's success derives from the Brazilian government's organization with respect to international trade matters.[17] Brazil's Ministry of Foreign Affairs is professionalized and meritocratic, and it prioritizes international trade.[18] In addition to its mission in Geneva, Brazil has a specialized unit in Brasilia that specializes in dispute settlement and supports the Geneva mission.[19] This dedication of resources has facilitated much of Brazil's success.

Although the disparity in the resources that individual countries dedicate to WTO matters is a problem for the functioning of the WTO as a whole, it has a particularly large impact in dispute settlement. This is because the short deadlines in the dispute settlement mechanism – which are necessary to maintain confidence in the system and which, indeed, are being ignored to a point where the system is losing its credibility[20] – mean that doing the best work on a WTO case requires a high degree of dedication to that case. After the first submission is filed with the panel by the Complainant (which, at least in theory, has had unlimited time to prepare that submission, because the Complainant chooses when to start the case), the rhythm of work is far more intense than in normal court litigation or the predecessor GATT dispute settlement system. In one of the authors' experience with an early WTO dispute, we prepared drafts for a government based on the government's instructions, sent them off to Geneva around midnight for the government to revise, got back in the morning, and started working on our replies to the arguments that we *expected*

15 See K. Bohl, "Problems of Developing Country Access to the WTO Dispute Settlement" (2009) 9 *Chicago-Kent Journal of International & Comparative Law* 162 (citing N. Meagher, "Representing Developing Countries in WTO Dispute Settlement Proceedings," in G. Bermann and P. Mavroidis (eds.), *WTO Law and Developing Countries* (New York: Cambridge University Press, 2007), p. 219).

16 See Bohl (2009), supra note 15, p. 162.

17 G. Shaffer, M. R. Sanchez, and B. Rosenberg, "The Trials of Winning at the WTO: What Lies behind Brazil's Success" (2008) 41 *Cornell International Law Journal* 388.

18 Ibid., pp. 424–429.

19 Ibid.

20 WTO, *Negotiations on Improvements and Clarifications of the DSU*, Proposal by Mexico, WTO Document, TN/DS/W/23 (4 November 2002).

the other government to make in reply to the submission, which was filed later that day. This intense pace continues for most of the panel process with a few very short breaks at the end, and then repeats itself during the Appellate Body process.

Very few countries can dedicate staff more or less full time to that process. Most must rely on their relatively few WTO experts. The experts in Geneva are already responsible for numerous committee meetings a day as well as for dealing with the ministries back home on a wide range of issues. Their counterparts back home have to deal with ministers, other politicians, and the usual daily debris of public service. Thus, many WTO governments are forced to rely, for at least some litigated cases, on outside lawyers who can throw themselves into the project with the same dedication as U.S. or EU inside lawyers. In business terms, this is referred to as a "make or buy" decision – it is rational for the United States and the EU to have large staffs of inside lawyers, because of the expected large volume of cases, and it is equally logical for other countries to "outsource."

The first disparity this presents is that for the United States and the EU, virtually all the financial costs of participating in a WTO dispute are fixed costs – they are unrelated to the particular dispute, and thus the U.S. Trade Representative and the EU can decide to start a case, or decide to defend one rather than settle immediately, without having to consider the cost of lawyers. By contrast, cost is one of the first questions for many, if not most, WTO Members confronted with a WTO dispute (even the Advisory Center on WTO Law is not gratis when it comes to litigation). Hiring outside counsel for a WTO case costs at least USD 250,000 – and doubles if the United States or the EU is on the other side of the case (because neither has any cost beyond their inside lawyers' time, they both tend to throw up a lot of obstacles during litigation). Similarly, a small, poor country, faced with a claim of WTO inconsistency by the United States or the EU, asks itself, as one of several questions, where it will get the money to defend itself. Perhaps this is why smaller countries are more likely than the United States or the EU to settle cases as defendants during the initial consultations than are the United States and the EU, and why the United States and the EU are relatively successful at settling cases as plaintiffs during those consultations. As the representative of Antigua and Barbuda stated, "many small, developing countries had made ... informal settlements that were beneficial to United States economic interests after being told their laws were in violation of WTO law."[21]

Developed countries, however, do not always have an advantage in terms of resources. This advantage disappears when the domestic industry of a developing country is strong and active enough in defending its interest before the WTO by hiring an external legal counsel. That makes domestic affected industry a major source

[21] WTO, *Statement by Sir Ronald Michael Sanders, Chief Foreign Affairs Representative of Antigua and Barbuda to the WTO Dispute Settlement Body* (June 24, 2003), WTO Document WT/DSB/M/151 (August 12, 2003).

of funding the WTO litigation. Among the prominent examples of such support are Ecuador's complaint in *Bananas*, Guatemala's defense in *Cement*, Antigua and Barbuda's representation in *Online Gambling*, as well as the case brought by Brazil against U.S. *Cotton Subsidies*.[22] Brazil, in particular, has been successful at utilizing industry financial support in bringing WTO disputes.[23] In fact, Brazil's successful use of public–private partnerships in WTO dispute settlement has at times put the United States (*Cotton Subsidies*) and the EU (*Sugar*) at a disadvantage, demonstrating that the involvement of domestic industry can have so great an impact as to reverse the imbalance in favor of developing countries.[24]

However, reliance by a government on industry's resources carries its own complications. The ability to bring cases in such a situation, or defend them well, could become more a function of local industries' particular interest in a case, rather than a national interest.[25] If the EU was fully dependent on its industries, it probably would have never brought the *Foreign Sales Corporations* complaint.[26] The case was started without industry pressure – indeed, many European companies' U.S. affiliates received Foreign Sales Corporation (FSC) treatment. Thus, although domestic industry funding may permit developing countries to bring WTO disputes in some cases, such funding will only be a viable option when the domestic industry and national interests are aligned.

B. *Lack of Leverage to Enforce WTO Rulings*

Another major constraint for smaller developed countries is the belief that they cannot retaliate against larger developed countries. Under the WTO rules, if a member does not voluntarily comply with a WTO ruling, the burden of enforcement falls on a complainant, which has a right to raise its tariffs or otherwise suspend WTO obligations against the products of a noncomplying member. There are several reasons for the belief that it is impossible for the developing countries to retaliate against large developed WTO Members such as the United States and the EU.

Economically, smaller countries calculate that if they raise tariffs against the imports from a developed country, it will raise costs in the developing country

22 *European Communities – Regime for the Importation, Sale and Distribution of Bananas*, WT/DS27; *Guatemala – Anti-Dumping Investigation Regarding Imports of Portland Cement from Mexico*, WT/DS60; *Guatemala – Definitive Anti-dumping Measure regarding Grey Portland Cement from Mexico*, WT/DS156; *United States – Measures Affecting Cross-Border Supply of Gambling and Betting*, WT/DS285; *United States – Subsidies on Upland Cotton*, WT/DS267.

23 See Shaffer et al. (2008), supra note 17, pp. 456–464.

24 See *United States – Subsidies on Upland Cotton*, WT/DS267; *European Communities – Export Subsidies on Sugar*, WT/DS265.

25 See, e.g., Shaffer et al. (2008), supra note 17, p. 464 ("The private sector is not always willing to fund a case that the Foreign Ministry believes Brazil should pursue or that it must defend as a respondent, particularly cases of a systemic nature for which the Ministry believes that it needs outside legal assistance.").

26 *United States – Tax Treatment for "Foreign Sales Corporations,"* WT/DS108.

(and many argue that their imports tend to be either necessities such as food or medicine or fuel or inputs for local manufacturers). By contrast, a larger economy is less dependent on imports of any particular item and often produces a much wider range of the inputs. Politically, developing countries calculate that any foreseeable retaliation they could impose on the developed country will be a "pinprick" politically to the developed country, whereas WTO-authorized retaliation permits a developed country to impose politically impossible levels of retaliation on a developing country.

Additionally, on a more systemic level, developing countries understand the fragility of the world trading system and recognize that a rules-based system constrains the most powerful country more than it does the smaller countries. In consequence, some developing countries are willing to forgo retaliation, even if the largest country practices it, to maintain a system that most believe is favorable to them overall. Indeed, even the EU was noticeably more reluctant to impose WTO-authorized retaliatory measures against the United States than vice versa (the EU waited years to push forward its retaliation on the *FSC* case, but the United States "jumped the gun" in *Bananas* by three weeks).

That said, developing countries do have effective means of retaliation – most notably the ability to suspend their TRIPS obligation in cross-retaliation – that some countries, such as Ecuador, Antigua, and Brazil, have shown some interest in pursuing.[27] As Gabriel Slater noted, "[f]or developing countries, suspending United States and European IP [intellectual property] rights offers a powerful stick in their trade with developed countries."[28] The willingness to follow through on the retaliation may, however, differ for smaller, less developed countries and middle-income developing countries, such as the BRICs. Ecuador, in the *Bananas* case, received authorization from the WTO Dispute Settlement Body to suspend its TRIPS obligations in retaliation for violations. Ecuador did not actually suspend its TRIPS obligations, however; rather, it used the threat of such retaliation to help its position in negotiations with the EU and possibly to obtain EU support in its Club of Paris debt renegotiation.[29] Brazil also has threatened to cross-retaliate with the suspension of its TRIPS obligations in *United States – Subsidies on Upland Cotton*. Although it has not yet done so, Brazil's relatively stronger position and its lack of debt vulnerabilities may make it more likely that Brazil would find such retaliation to be in its strategic interest.

[27] See G. Slater, "The Suspension of Intellectual Property Obligations under TRIPS: A Proposal for Retaliating against Technology-Exporting Countries in the World Trade Organization," (2009) 97 *Georgetown Law Journal* 1368–1370; see also J. Reichmann, "Universal Minimum Standards of Intellectual Property Protection under the TRIPS Component of the WTO Agreement" (1995) 29 *International Lawyer* 345.

[28] Slater (2009), supra note 277, p. 1370.

[29] J. M. Smith, "Compliance Bargaining in the WTO: Ecuador and the Bananas Dispute," Conference on Developing Countries and the Trade Negotiation Process, UNCTAD (Geneva, November 6–7, 2003).

C. *High Indirect Costs*

Insufficient litigation resources and lack of leverage to enforce a WTO ruling are not the only reasons developing countries are less active in the context of the WTO dispute settlement. They, for example, do not explain why Egypt dropped out of the U.S.-led coalition against the EU's de facto Genetically Modified Organisms ban. In that case, Egypt would not have been the main complainant and could largely free ride on the U.S. arguments. Also, the U.S. retaliation alone would probably have been sufficient to induce compliance by the EU in the event of a victory at the WTO. Egypt nevertheless abstained from taking part in the complaint, even though this might have hurt prospects for an Egypt-U.S. free trade agreement.[30] The main reason seems to be that, under a cost-benefit analysis, initiating a dispute was not in Egypt's best interest. Egypt would have brought a WTO complaint if the benefits from pursuing it would have outweighed any losses in current or potential trade flows to the EU or development aid from the EU as a result of its decision to go to the WTO.

The key to understanding this analysis is that the initiation of a WTO dispute is considered to be a hostile act toward defendants. Members complained against normally "deplore," "deeply regret," or express "great dissatisfaction and concern" in connection with requests for the establishment of a panel. They can also respond to the initiation of a WTO case by either filing a counter-complaint or undertaking other unfriendly steps. Examples of such behavior are the EU filing a complaint against Australian quarantine regime as a tit-for-tat move following a complaint by Australia against EU protection of geographic indications[31] or Korea initiating a dispute against EU shipbuilding subsidies following the EU challenge to Korean shipbuilding subsidies.[32]

Although this approach to dispute settlement is not at all unique to trade relations between developed and developing countries, developed countries possess greater persuasive force as a function of their degree of economic development when dealing with developing countries. The result is that developing countries would think twice before bringing a WTO complaint against a developed country. For example, even though according to the president of the Mozambican Cotton Association, "the quality of life of millions of Mozambicans is being dramatically eroded by the low price of cotton," Mozambique did not participate in the WTO dispute against

[30] "U.S. Interest in FTA Cools after Egypt Fails to Join GMO Complaint," *Inside U.S. Trade*, July 4, 2003; "U.S. Announces Panel on EU GMO Moratorium, as Grassley Warns Egypt," *Inside U.S. Trade*, June 20, 2003; "Egypt Tells EU It Will Not Be Co-complainant on U.S. GMO Case," *Inside U.S. Trade*, May 30, 2003.

[31] "U.S., Australia Secure WTO Panel to Rule on EU Protection of Geographic Indications," *Daily Report for Executives* (BNA), October 3, 2003.

[32] "South Korea Files Tit-for-Tat Complaint at WTO Against EU Shipbuilding Subsidies," *Daily Report for Executives* (BNA), September 4, 2003.

U.S. Cotton Subsidies.[33] One of the reasons may be that it was anxious to preserve untouched its benefits in trade with the United States, including such sensitive matters as sugar quotas, as well as other forms of development aid, the existence of which depends on the U.S. goodwill alone.[34]

The same rationale might explain why the four major victims of U.S. cotton subsidies – Benin, Burkina Faso, Mali, and Chad – were not complainants in the challenge to those subsidies (although Benin and Chad did take part as third parties). These countries may have worried that unnecessary hostility toward the United States might diminish their chances of success in the parallel-to-the-WTO-litigation Doha Round agricultural negotiations where those countries seek financial compensation to offset the income they are losing as a result of the U.S. cotton subsidies.[35] Although these negotiations have been stalled, recent Obama administration comments about moving the negotiations forward may continue to give affected countries a reason not to bring disputes against the United States.[36]

By the same token, if a WTO-inconsistent trade restriction against developing-country imports is so great that spoiling relations with a developed country is a worthwhile exercise, then a WTO case will be brought. In *Export Subsidies on Sugar*, Thailand reportedly was not deterred from launching a complaint against the EU when the latter warned that this might result in the reduction of Thai tuna imports under a Generalized System of Preferences (GSP) quota.[37] With the recent onset of the global financial crisis and the emergence of increasingly protectionist policies, it may become increasingly common that the losses from the trade restriction are so great as to justify the bringing of a dispute despite the political and economic risks.

III. THE IMPACT OF RECENT DEVELOPMENTS ON THE IMBALANCE

A. *Global Financial Crisis*

The fall of 2008 marked the onset of a global financial crisis that has affected nearly every country across the world. Already we have begun to see countries implement

[33] "The Cotton Sector in Mozambique: Challenges and Options after the WTO Conference in Cancun," transcript of a speech by João Ribas, president of the Mozambican Cotton Association, at Nairobi Conference "Business for Development – Challenges and options for Government and Business after the WTO Conference in Cancun" (March 30–31, 2004).

[34] For the proposition that small nations may fear that developed countries would retaliate by decreasing its development aid, see D. Collins, "Efficient Breach, Reliance and Contract Remedies at the WTO" (2009) 43 *Journal of World Trade* 228.

[35] WTO Negotiations on Agriculture, *Poverty Reduction: Sectoral Initiative in Favor of Cotton, Joint Proposal by Benin, Burkina Faso, Chad and Mali*, WTO Document, TN/AG/GEN/4, (16 May 2003).

[36] See "Obama and Trade: Low Expectations Exceeded," *The Economist*, April 30, 2009, available at: http://www.economist.com/world/unitedstates/displaystory.cfm?story_id=13578834.

[37] "Philippines Claims Victory over Europe Using WTO Mediations in Tuna Tariff Spat," *Daily Rep. for Executives* (BNA), June 10, 2003.

protectionist policies in reaction to the economic challenges their industries are facing.[38] Although this turn toward protectionist policies is problematic for international trade in general, it remains to be seen what impact it will have on the imbalance in access to WTO dispute settlement. At first glance, it would seem that developing countries, also suffering from the financial crisis, will be even more limited in the resources they can devote to bringing disputes in the WTO and thus that the imbalance will continue. However, there is another possible scenario: as developing countries' industries are forced to compete with developed countries' industries, which are receiving subsidies that developing-country governments cannot afford to offer, the developing countries may find bringing a WTO dispute to be the most cost-effective response. If bringing a dispute is less costly for developing-country governments than offering subsidies, then an unexpected consequence of the crisis may be that developing countries become more active participants in the WTO dispute settlement system.

Whether this will happen remains to be seen. It is also possible that developed countries, in response to the financial crisis, will bring more WTO disputes against developing countries in an effort to make their own industries more competitive and thereby relegate developing countries to a defendant role. In fact, both China[39] and the United States[40] have taken each other to the dispute settlement system to challenge measures affecting its industries during that period in order to improve industry-specific competitiveness. This set of disputes follows prior cases between countries from the Northern and Southern hemispheres, such as the *Bananas* case between Ecuador and Europe. In sum, the global financial crisis and the resulting protectionist policies are likely to have some impact on the WTO dispute settlement system and on how both developed and developing countries participate in the system.

B. *Climate Change*

The global financial crisis is not the only crisis facing the world economy; climate change has become an increasingly pressing issue, and there is growing political will to address this problem. However, most proposed measures (such as border barriers or massive subsidies) are likely to stretch WTO rules, thus creating a tension between trade law and the environment. In June 2009, the U.S. House of Representatives

[38] See World Trade Organization, *World Trade Report 2009: Trade Policy Commitments and Contingency Measures* (2009), available at: http://www.wto.org/english/res_e/publications_e/wtr09_e.htm; "The Nuts and Bolts Come Apart: As Global Demand Contracts, Trade Is Slumping and Protectionism Rising," *The Economist*, March 26, 2009, available at: http://www.economist.com/displayStory.cfm?story_id=13362027.

[39] *United States – Measures Affecting Imports of Certain Passenger Vehicles and Light Truck Tyres from China* (WT/DS399).

[40] *China – Measures Related to the Importation of Various Raw Materials* (WT/DS394).

passed the Waxman-Markey bill[41] (still not passed by the Senate) that would adopt a cap-and-trade program, which might contravene WTO rules if emission allowances are allocated discriminatorily or for free. The bill also includes the possibility of imposing border adjustment measures that could potentially violate any WTO rule governing border measures.[42] In case of any violation, any developed- or developing-country member of the WTO could challenge the bill at the dispute settlement level. In April 2009, the EU passed legislation imposing new sustainability requirements for biofuels and bioliquids[43] that has angered Malaysia, Indonesia, and Brazil, who have stated these new requirements are "unjustifiably complex" and threatened to "defend their rights at the WTO," as a last resort.[44] This tension is likely to spark WTO disputes, and the dispute settlement mechanism may serve as a primary means for mediating the conflicts that will arise out of climate change policies.

Climate change policies are certain to affect developing countries. They may also affect developing-country attitudes toward WTO dispute settlement. Depending on the magnitude of the impact of climate change policies on developing countries, the adoption of such policies may lead developing countries to initiate WTO complaints to protect their interests. Such complaints, should they be made, could pose a great challenge to the WTO dispute settlement system, and how the system handles these disputes will be critical to the future of the WTO. Although climate change issues may help to ameliorate the imbalance in access to the WTO dispute settlement by incentivizing developing countries to participate actively in the system, at the same time they may also put unsustainable strain on the system as a whole.

C. *Changes in the Economic Balance of Power*

Yet another recent development in the world economy, the rise of certain developing economies, such as the BRICs, will surely have, and has already had, a great effect on the profile and treatment of developing countries in the WTO, and more specifically in the WTO dispute settlement system. Brazil and South Africa, for example, have provided strong support for some developing countries' arguments in the debate over intellectual property rights and access to medicines.

Although the growing prominence of these countries has already contributed to the advancement of the development agenda in WTO negotiations, it may also help

41 American Clean Energy and Security Act of 2009, available at: http://thomas.loc.gov/cgi-bin/query/z?c111:H.R.2454:.

42 G. Hufbauer and J. Kim, *The World Trade Organization and Climate Change: Challenges and Options* (Peterson Institute for International Economics, September 2009), available at: http://www.iie.com/publications/interstitial.cfm?ResearchID=1301. See also B. Condon, "Climate Change and Unresolved Issues in WTO Law" (2009) 12(4) *Journal of International Economic Law* 895–926.

43 Directive 2009/28/EC of 23 April 2009 on the promotion of the use of energy from renewable sources and amending and subsequently repealing Directives 2001/77/EC and 2003/30/EC.

44 *EU's Sustainable Biofuels Push Angers Malaysia, Brazil*, available at: http://news.mongabay.com/2008/1107-biofuels.html, accessed May 31, 2010.

to correct the imbalance in access to the WTO dispute settlement system. Activity by developing countries with greater resources may benefit other developing countries when their interests align and thus give those countries with fewer resources indirect access to the system.

IV. WHAT IS TO BE DONE?

Although these new developments might help ameliorate the imbalance in access to the WTO dispute settlement system, there are also specific proposals that could help address the imbalance. Greg Shaffer, noting that developing countries are less likely than developed countries to be complainants under WTO than under the General Agreement on Tariffs and Trade and more likely to be defendants, identified a number of proposals, including monetary damages and attorneys' fees for developing countries, less costly procedures, and greater legal assistance.[45] These proposals, if adopted, may correct some of the imbalances described earlier in this chapter.

A. *Greater Legal Assistance and Attorneys' Fees*

Legal aid to developing countries may be provided in two forms – by providing developing countries with legal advice for free or at discounted rates or by giving successful developing-country complainants (or defendants) the opportunity to recover legal expenses from the losing side. The first scenario was implemented by the establishment of the Advisory Centre on WTO Law (ACWL), which functions as an independent international organization. In its first years in existence, the ACWL, whose services, although discounted, are not free, has been a remarkable success in terms of assistance to developing countries. There is every reason, therefore, to further support and expand activities of this organization, including by pushing the United States and the EU to become members of the ACWL. Additionally, because some least developed countries cannot afford even the sharply discounted rates of the ACWL, one might think about the creation of regional Advisory Centres on WTO Law, in particular an African Advisory Centre on WTO Law, whose services would be free for its members both for WTO dispute settlement and for legal support in the rounds of multilateral trade negotiations.

The second scenario, securing greater legal assistance through the reimbursement of legal costs, is complementary to the provision of affordable legal services. First, it would allow successful developing countries to get back their expenses, including those spent on the services of the Advisory Centre. Second, it would also allow developing countries to hire outside legal counsel in situations in which, for reasons of confidentiality or expertise, they prefer to do so. This is especially important when

[45] G. Shaffer, *Defending Interests: Public–Private Partnerships in WTO Litigation* (Washington, DC: Brookings Institution Press, 2003).

a WTO case is a sequel to a WTO-inconsistent national trade remedies investigation. In such cases, a private law firm that represented the developing-country producers in the respective national investigation would have significant expertise and, more important, would be able to provide continuity between a national jurisdiction (where the real remedies are) and the WTO in terms of implementation of the WTO ruling in the jurisdiction concerned.

That said, the reimbursement of attorney's fees for the developing countries cannot be accepted without reservations. First, the experience of jurisdictions using the "costs follow the event" rule (such as in England) shows that not capping reimbursable expenses by some sort of reasonability standard can lead to abuse because there is no incentive for a meritorious complainant or defendant to oversee the efficiency of its lawyers. Second, if reimbursable costs are to be reasonable, a special costs arbitrator is needed to avoid a lengthy litigation on costs.

B. *Monetary Damages*

The lack of retaliation capacity with respect to a noncomplying developed member may be corrected by replacing the remedy of retaliation with other remedies such as compulsory compensation. In this context, the compensation may take the form of either a tariff reduction according to the choice of a developing-country plaintiff (as proposed by Joost Pauwelyn)[46] or monetary compensation for the damage caused by a WTO-inconsistent trade restriction.[47] Both remedies are familiar to the WTO membership. The option of compensation (although in a different form) is reflected in Article 22 of the WTO Dispute Settlement Understanding but has not been frequently used, probably because of its nonmandatory nature and the obligation to provide such compensation on a most-favored-nation basis. Monetary damages have been offered in practice (in *Broadcast Music* and *Upland Cotton*) and are being mentioned among the proposals in the ongoing DSU review.[48] It is important to mention that, by promising real relief to a complaining developing country, the remedy of compensation in either form significantly modifies the cost-benefit analysis of initiating a WTO dispute in a way that secures greater participation of developing countries in the WTO dispute settlement system.

[46] See J. Pauwelyn, "Enforcement and Countermeasures in the WTO: Rules Are Rules – Toward a More Collective Approach" (2000) 94 *American Journal of International Law* 337.

[47] For the argument for a monetary remedy, see Collins (2009), supra note 34, p. 228. However, the authors do not agree with Collins's assertions about efficient breach in the context of the WTO (which is quite different from a private commercial contract). See Collins (2009), supra note 34, p. 227n8 (citing to John H. Jackson, *Sovereignty, the WTO and Changing Fundamentals of International Law* (Cambridge: Cambridge University Press, 2006), p. 147).

[48] Dispute Settlement Body – Special Session – Text for the African Group Proposals on Dispute Settlement Understanding Negotiations – Communications from Kenya, WTO Document, TN/DS/W/42, January 24, 2001. It may be necessary for the damages to only be owed by developing countries (or to limit the amount they would owe).

C. *Less Costly Procedures*

Less costly procedures in the WTO dispute settlement system are necessary if the previously described proposals on reimbursement of attorneys' fees and/or monetary compensation are not adopted. Among procedures that can be adopted are obligatory use of mediation and the introduction of a small claims track with simplified procedures and a single panelist.[49] One could also think of penalizing defendants for complicating litigation by putting forward unmeritorious requests for preliminary rulings. The penalty may consist of deducting days of delay caused thereby from the reasonable period of time for compliance, or, if a proposal on reimbursement of attorneys' fees is adopted, of awarding additional costs. Furthermore, enforcing currently established deadlines for the Panel and Appellate Body hearings would reduce the financial burden on the parties to a WTO dispute. This, however, will require an increase in the budget of the WTO Secretariat.

V. CONCLUSION

Developing countries' access to WTO dispute settlement is an issue of great concern, and there is a need for positive efforts to ensure that developing countries are adequately represented when it comes to defending their interests in the WTO. Full-fledged participation of developing countries in the WTO dispute settlement system requires a change in the current rules so as to provide developing countries with the necessary resources and incentives for successful representation of their interests before the WTO Panels and Appellate Body. Greater legal assistance, viable remedies, and faster and streamlined procedures are key to providing that indeed "right perseveres over might."[50]

It is unclear what impact the uncertainty in the world economy will have on the issue of developing countries' access to WTO dispute settlement. The great challenges of today, like the global financial crisis and climate change, could inadvertently ameliorate some of the imbalances in the system or they could make these imbalances more acute. Should these imbalances persist, there may not be the political will to address these issues, given the gravity of the challenges facing the world economy. However, regardless of whether these issues receive attention in this time of crisis, developing countries' access to WTO dispute settlement is important to the health of the WTO as a whole and is deserving of attention in the short and long run.

49 B. Hoekman and P. Mavroidis, "Enforcing Multilateral Commitments: Dispute Settlement and Developing Countries," paper prepared for the WTO/World Bank Conference on Developing Countries in a Millennium Round, WTO Secretariat, Centre William Rappard (Geneva, September 20–21, 1999), available at: http://worldbank.org.

50 J. Lacarte-Muro and P. Gappah, "Developing Countries and the WTO Legal and Dispute Settlement System: A View from the Bench" (2000) 3 *Journal of International Economic Law* 395.

REFERENCES

American Clean Energy and Security Act of 2009, available at: http://thomas.loc.gov/cgi-bin/query/z?c111:H.R.2454:.

Bohl, Kristin, "Problems of Developing Country Access to the WTO Dispute Settlement" (2009) 9 *Chicago-Kent Journal of International & Comparative Law* 130.

Cardoso, Fernando Henrique, and Enzo Faletto, *Dependencia y Desarrollo en America Latina: Ensayo de Interpretación Sociológica* (Mexico City: Siglo Veintiuno Editores, 1969).

Collins, David, "Efficient Breach, Reliance and Contract Remedies at the WTO" (2009) 43 *Journal of World Trade*.

Condon, Bradley, "Climate Change and Unresolved Issues in WTO Law" (2009) 12(4) *Journal of International Economic Law*.

Directive 2009/28/EC of the European Parliament and of the Council of 23 April 2009 on the promotion of the use of energy from renewable sources and amending and subsequently repealing Directives 2001/77/EC and 2003/30/EC (June 5, 2009).

"Egypt Tells EU It Will Not Be Co-complainant on U.S. GMO Case," *Inside U.S. Trade*, May 30, 2003.

"EU and U.S. Try to Rekindle Trade Talks," *New York Times*, January 24, 2008.

Hoekman, Bernard M., and Petros C. Mavroidis, "Enforcing Multilateral Commitments: Dispute Settlement and Developing Countries," paper prepared for the WTO/World Bank Conference on Developing Countries in a Millennium Round, WTO Secretariat, Centre William Rappard, Geneva (September 20–21, 1999), available at: http://worldbank.org.

Horlick, Gary, and Nikolay Mizulin, "Developing Countries and WTO Dispute Settlement" (2005) 23 *Integration & Trade Journal*.

Howse, Robert, "From Politics to Technocracy – and Back Again: The Fate of the Multilateral Trading Regime" (2002) 96 *American Journal of International Law*.

Hufbauer, Gary, and Jisun Kim, "The World Trade Organization and Climate Change: Challenges and Options," *Peterson Institute for International Economics* (September 2009), Working Paper, available at: http://www.iie.com/publications/interstitial.cfm?ResearchID=1301.

Irwin, Douglas, *Free Trade under Fire* (2nd ed., Princeton, NJ: Princeton University Press, 2005).

Jackson, John, W. Davey, and A. Sykes, *Legal Problems of International Economic Relations: Cases, Materials and Text* (5th ed., St. Paul, MN: Thomson/West, 2008).

Jones, Kent, *Who's Afraid of the WTO?* (New York: Oxford University Press, 2004).

Kleen, Peter, and Sheila Page, *Special and Differential Treatment of Developing Countries in the World Trade Organization* (2005), Report of the Swedish Ministry of Foreign Affairs Global Development Studies.

Lacarte-Muro, Julio, and Petina Gappah, "Developing Countries and the WTO Legal and Dispute Settlement System: A View from the Bench," 3 *Journal of International Economic Law* (2000).

"Obama and Trade: Low Expectations Exceeded," *The Economist*, April 30, 2009, available at: http://www.economist.com/world/unitedstates/displaystory.cfm?story_id=13578834.

Pauwelyn, Joost, "Developing Countries and the WTO Legal and Dispute Settlement System: A View from the Bench" (2000) 3 *Journal of International Economic Law*.

"Philippines Claims Victory over Europe Using WTO Mediations in Tuna Tariff Spat," *Daily Rep. for Executives* (BNA), June 10, 2003.

Prebisch, Raul, *Change and Development – Latin America's Great Task: Report Submitted to the Inter-American Development Bank* (New York: Praeger, 1971).

Reichmann, Jerome, "Universal Minimum Standards of Intellectual Property Protection under the TRIPS Component of the WTO Agreement" (1995) 29 *International Lawyer*.

Ribas, João, President of the Mozambican Cotton Association, "The Cotton Sector in Mozambique: Challenges and Options after the WTO Conference in Cancun," transcript of a speech at Nairobi Conference "Business for Development – Challenges and options for Government and Business after the WTO Conference" in Cancun (March 30–31, 2004).

Rodrik, Dani, "The Global Governance of Trade: As If Development Really Mattered," background paper to the United Nations Development Programme project on Trade and Sustainable Human Development (New York, October 2001).

Shaffer, Gregory C., *Defending Interests: Public-Private Partnerships in WTO Litigation* (Washington, DC: Brookings Institution Press, 2003).

Shaffer Gregory C., M. R. Sanchez, and B. Rosenberg, "The Trials of Winning at the WTO: What Lies behind Brazil's Success" (2008) 41 *Cornell International Law Journal*.

Slater, Gabriel, "The Suspension of Intellectual Property Obligations under TRIPS: A Proposal for Retaliating against Technology-Exporting Countries in the World Trade Organization" (2009) 97 *Georgetown Law Journal*.

Smith, James McCall, "Compliance Bargaining in the WTO: Ecuador and the Bananas Dispute," Conference on Developing Countries and the Trade Negotiation Process, UNCTAD (Geneva, November 6–7, 2003).

"South Korea Files Tit-for-Tat Complaint at WTO against EU Shipbuilding Subsidies," *Daily Report for Executives* (BNA), September 4, 2003.

"The Nuts and Bolts Come Apart: As Global Demand Contracts, Trade Is Slumping and Protectionism Rising," *The Economist*, March 26, 2009, available at: http://www.economist.com/displayStory.cfm?story_id=13362027.

Trubek, David M., and M. Patrick Cottrell, "Robert Hudec and the Theory of International Economic Law: The Law of Global Space," in Chantal Thomas and Joel P. Trachtman (eds.), *Developing Countries in the WTO Legal System* (New York: Oxford University Press, 2009).

"U.S. Announces Panel on EU GMO Moratorium, as Grassley Warns Egypt," *Inside U.S. Trade*, June 20, 2003.

"U.S., Australia Secure WTO Panel to Rule on EU Protection of Geographic Indications," *Daily Report for Executives* (BNA), October 3, 2003.

"U.S. Interest in FTA Cools after Egypt Fails to Join GMO Complaint," *Inside U.S. Trade*, July 4, 2003.

Wilson, Dominic, and Roopa Purushotha, *Dreaming with the BRICs: The Path to 2050*, Goldman Sachs Global Economics Paper No. 99 (New York, 2003).

World Trade Organization, *General Agreement on Tariffs and Trade 1994*, LT/UR/A-1A/1/GATT/1 (January 1, 1995).

______, *Marrakesh Agreement Establishing the World Trade Organization*, LT/UR/A/2 (January 1, 1995).

______, Appellate Body Report, *European Communities – Regime for the Importation, Sale and Distribution of Bananas, Complaint by Ecuador*, WT/DS72/AB/R, adopted September 25, 1997, DSR 1997: II, 591.

______, Appellate Body Report, *Guatemala – Anti-Dumping Investigation Regarding Imports of Portland Cement from Mexico*, WT/DS60/AB/R, adopted November 25, 1998, DSR 1998:IX, 3767.

______, Appellate Body Report, *United States – Tax Treatment for "Foreign Sales Corporations,"* WT/DS108/AB/R, adopted March 20, 2000, DSR, 2000:III, 1619.

______, Panel Report, *Guatemala – Definitive Anti-dumping Measure regarding Grey Portland Cement from Mexico,* WT/DS156/R, adopted November 17, 2000, DSR 2000:XI, 5295.

______, *Dispute Settlement Body – Special Session – Text for the African Group Proposals on Dispute Settlement Understanding Negotiations – Communication from Kenya,* TN/DS/W/42 (January 24, 2001).

______, *Negotiations on Improvements and Clarifications of the DSU – Proposal by Mexico,* TN/DS/W/23 (November 4, 2002).

______, *Committee on Agriculture – Special Session – WTO Negotiations on Agriculture – Poverty Reduction: Sectoral Initiative in Favour of Cotton – Joint Proposal by Benin, Burkina Faso, Chad and Mali,* TN/AG/GEN/4 (May 16, 2003).

______, *Dispute Settlement Body – Minutes of Meeting Held in the Centre William Rappard on June 24, 2003,* WT/DSB/M/151 (August 12, 2003).

______, Appellate Body Report, *United States – Subsidies on Upland Cotton,* WT/DS267/AB/R, adopted March 21, 2005, DSR 2005:I, 3.

______, Appellate Body Report, *United States – Measures Affecting Cross-Border Supply of Gambling and Betting,* WT/DS285/AB/R, adopted April 20, 2005, DSR 2005:XII, 5663 (Corr.1 DSR 2006: XII, 5663 (Corr. DSR 2006: XII, 5475).

______, Appellate Body Report, *European Communities – Export Subsidies on Sugar,* WT/DS265/AB/R, WT/DS266/AB/R, WT/DS283/AB/R, adopted May 19, 2005, DSR 2005:XIII, 6365.

______, *World Trade Report 2009: Trade Policy Commitments and Contingency Measures* (2009), available at: http://www.wto.org/english/res_e/publications_e/wtr09_e.htm.

______, *China – Measures Related to the Importation of Various Raw Materials – Request for the Establishment of a Panel by the United States,* WT/DS394/4 (November 9, 2009).

______, United States – Measures Affecting Imports of Certain Passenger Vehicles and Light Truck Tyres from China – Request for the Establishment of a Panel by China, WT/DS399/2 (December 11, 2009).

8

Pacific Countries in the WTO

Accession and Accommodation, the Reality of WTO Accession

Andrew D. Mitchell and Joanne Wallis

I. INTRODUCTION

In the 1990s, three Pacific island countries, Tonga, Vanuatu, and Samoa, applied to join the World Trade Organization (WTO). However, after negotiating for years to join and with membership almost a formality, Vanuatu in 2001 and Tonga in 2006 suspended the process of their accession. Although Samoa has never formally suspended its process, progress has been slow, and negotiations are about to enter their thirteenth year. These developing Pacific countries have small economies that represent only a tiny fraction of world trade. It is easy to ignore these decisions, particularly while countries with very significant economies, such as Russia, are in the accession process. However, the decisions by Vanuatu and Tonga to suspend their accession at such a late stage are unique in WTO history and raise important questions for the WTO and its membership that should not be ignored. Using Tonga, Vanuatu, and Samoa as case studies, this chapter begins by looking at the issue of trade and development in small island developing states (SIDS), and the potential impacts, both beneficial and detrimental, of the international trading system on these countries. It then explores some of the broader questions facing the WTO that are raised by Tonga and Vanuatu suspending their accession. First, it examines equity concerns about the WTO accession process, along with recent attempts to address these concerns. Second, it considers the shortcomings of the "special and differential treatment" (SDT) currently offered to developing countries and how their special needs could be better accommodated in the WTO. Samoa is included in this discussion because it has faced many of the same issues as Tonga and Vanuatu during its accession negotiations.

The authors thank Ms. Elizabeth Sheargold and Associate Professor Tania Voon for their helpful work and comments on an earlier draft of this chapter. This chapter is based on "Pacific Pause: the Rhetoric of Special & Differential Treatment, the Reality of WTO Accession" (2009) 27 (4) *Wisconsin International Law Journal*.

Whereas Tonga and Vanuatu both suspended their accession processes, Tonga later proceeded with WTO accession in July 2007, Vanuatu resumed its accession bid in 2008, and Samoa continues its accession negotiations. However, this chapter concludes that these decisions do not constitute an endorsement of the WTO accession process or SDT as it is presently implemented in the WTO. Rather accession was pursued *despite* these limitations.

II. TRADE AND DEVELOPMENT IN SMALL ISLAND DEVELOPING STATES

A. *Work on Trade, SIDS and Development*

Development has always played an important role in the General Agreement on Tariffs and Trade[1] (GATT)/WTO.[2] The WTO Ministerial Council, at paragraph 2 of the *Doha Declaration* – which launched what has become known as the *Doha Development Agenda* – stated that "international trade can play a major role in the promotion of economic development and the alleviation of poverty."[3] The WTO has also partnered with the International Monetary Fund (IMF) to create the Aid for Trade program, which provides development assistance to least developed countries (LDCs) to improve infrastructure and ensure capacity to respond to new trade opportunities.[4] Despite this, critics claim that confidence in the WTO's ability to promote economic development and alleviate poverty is "waning,"[5] partly because many developing countries have difficulty getting the most out of their WTO membership.[6]

[1] General Agreement on Tariffs and Trade, WTO Doc. LT/UR/A-1A/1/GATT/1 (April 15, 1994; hereinafter GATT 1994).

[2] For example, the preamble to GATT 1947 recognized the objective of "raising standards of living." *General Agreement on Tariffs and Trade*, WTO Doc. LT/UR/A-1A/1/GATT/2 (October 30, 1947; hereinafter GATT 1947). The preamble to the 1994 WTO Agreement expanded this concept, recognizing the "need for positive efforts designed to ensure that developing countries, and especially the least developed among them, secure a share in the growth in international trade commensurate with the needs of their economic development." At the launch of the Doha Round the Ministerial Conference stated: "The majority of WTO members are developing countries. We seek to place their needs and interests at the heart of the Work Programme adopted in this Declaration." WTO, *Ministerial Declaration of 14 November 2001*, WT/MIN(01)/DEC/1, para. 2 (2002; hereinafter Doha Declaration).

[3] Doha Declaration (2002), supra note 2, p. 2.

[4] International Monetary Fund, *Improving Market Access: Toward Greater Coherence Between Aid and Trade*, (March 2002), available at: http://www.imf.org/external/np/exr/ib/2002/032102.htm, accessed 9 August 2009.

[5] Jane Kelsey, "World Trade and Small Nations in the South Pacific Region" (2005) 14 *Kansas Journal of Law and Public Policy* 247.

[6] See, for example, WTO Secretariat, *World Trade Report 2007: Six Decades of Multilateral Trade Cooperation: What Have We Learnt?* (2007), pp. 293–294, available at: http://www.wto.org/english/news_e/pres07_e/pr502_e.htm (hereinafter Trade Report); Meredith Kolsky Lewis, "WTO Winners and Losers: The Trade and Development Disconnect" (2007) 39 *Georgetown Journal of International Law* 165.

The interaction of trade and development is particularly relevant to SIDS[7] such as Tonga, Vanuatu, and Samoa, which exhibit vulnerabilities that should be specifically addressed by the WTO. Indeed, the WTO has recognized the unique position of SIDS within the international trading system and has established a Work Programme on Small Economies that is intended "to frame responses to the trade-related issues identified for the fuller integration of small, vulnerable economies into the multilateral trading system."[8] Moreover, the Doha Development Agenda includes specific provisions concerning trade related issues relevant to small and vulnerable economies.[9] These include the preferential treatment of SIDS, access to markets, and agricultural subsidies. However, negotiations in these areas have not advanced in the manner hoped.[10]

Development organizations have also turned their attention to the effect of WTO law and process on SIDS. This attention received particular focus after the acceptance of the Millennium Development Goals (MDGs) of which targets 12 and 14 are relevant to SIDS.[11] The MDGs have been utilized by SIDS' advocates, who have argued that future trade negotiations should make the multilateral trading system more equitable through recognition of the particular disadvantages of SIDS, in particular, by allowing SIDS to engage in international trade on a more equal footing, gain more secure access to external markets, and participate as equal partners in WTO negotiations.[12]

The most relevant international organization that undertakes development work specifically relating to SIDS and international trade is the United Nations (UN) Office of the High Representative for the LDCs, Landlocked Developing Countries, and SIDS.[13] This office is responsible for coordinating the implementation of

7 The United Nations recognizes 52 SIDS. United Nations (UN), Office of the High Representative for the Least Developed Countries, Landlocked Developing Countries, and Small Island Developing Countries, *List of Small Island Developing States*, available at: http://www.un.org/special-rep/ohrlls/sid/list.htm.

8 WTO, General Council, *Work Programme on Small Economies: Framework and Procedures*, WT/L/447 (March 5, 2002), available at: http://www.wto.org/english/tratop_e/devel_e/dev_wkprog_smalleco_e.htm.

9 Doha Declaration (2002), supra note 2, p. 35.

10 UN, Port Louis, Mauritius, January 10–14, 2005, *Report of the International Meeting to Review the Implementation of the Programme of Action for the Sustainable Development of Small Island Developing States*, UN Doc. A/CONF.207/11 (February 14, 2005; hereinafter Mauritius).

11 Target 12 advocates the need to develop an "open, rule-based, predictable, non-discriminatory" trading system that is committed to development and poverty reduction. Target 14 specifically addresses the special needs of SIDS. UN Secretary-General, *Report of the Secretary-General on the Road Map Towards the Implementation of the United Nations Millennium Declaration*, A/56/326 (September 6, 2001), p. 58.

12 See Mauritius (2005), supra note 10, p. 67.

13 UN, Office of the High Representative for the Least Developed Countries, *Landlocked Developing Countries and Small Island Developing States*, available at http://www.unohrlls.org.

the Barbados Programme of Action, which was produced at the 1994 world conference, "The Sustainable Development of Small Island Developing States."[14] The UN Development Program has also studied and proposed measures to manage the economic vulnerability of SIDS.[15] The UN Conference on Trade and Development (UNCTAD) is similarly concerned with promoting international trade, with a specific view to accelerating economic development.[16] The World Bank and Commonwealth Secretariat have also been particularly active in respect of SIDS, setting up a Joint Task Force on Small States.[17]

Despite this work, SIDS continue to experience a number of challenges that limit their ability to participate in the world trading system. This section considers the situation of Tonga, Vanuatu, and Samoa and argues that they and other Pacific SIDS exhibit particular vulnerabilities that the WTO should specifically address.

B. *Tonga, Vanuatu, and Samoa: Economic Background*

Like other Pacific SIDS, Tonga, Vanuatu, and Samoa face special challenges that hinder their participation in international trade. These challenges stem from their physical, geographic, economic, and demographic characteristics, which result in a degree of inherent vulnerability that must be taken into account in strategies for their development,[18] including membership of the WTO. Tonga is a developing

[14] UN, General Assembly, *Report of the Global Conference on the Sustainable Development of Small Island Developing States*, A/CONF.167/9 (Bridgetown, Barbados, April 25–May 6, 1994). A five-year follow-up to the Barbados conference was held in 1999 (UN, General Assembly, *Report of the Ad Hoc Committee of the Whole of the Twenty-Second Special Session of the General Assembly*, A/S-22/9/Rev.1, September 27–28, 1999), and a further international meeting to review progress was held in January 2005 (*Report of the International Meeting to Review the Implementation of the Programme of Action for the Sustainable Development of Small Island Developing States, Mauritius*, A/CONF.207/11 (January 10–14, 2005).

[15] Michael Witter, Lino Briguglio, and Assad Bhuglah, *Measuring and Managing the Economic Vulnerability of Small Island Developing States* (May 2002; unpublished paper), available at: http://www.sidsnet.org/docshare/other/economic_vulnerability_paper.pdf.

[16] UN, Conference on Trade and Development, *About UNCTAD*, available at: http://www.unctad.org/Templates/Page.asp?intItemID=1530&lang=1.

[17] This Task Force prepared a report in 2000 (Commonwealth Secretariat/World Bank Joint Task Force on Small States, *Small States: Meeting Challenges in the Global Economy* (April 2000), available at: http://siteresources.worldbank.org/PROJECTS/Resources/meetingchallengeinglobaleconomyl.pdf. In 2002 the Commonwealth Secretariat reported on the implementation of the recommendations made in that report (Commonwealth Secretariat, *Progress in the Implementation of the Recommendations of the Commonwealth Secretariat/World Bank Joint Task Force Report: Small States: Meeting the Challenges in the Global Economy* (August 2002), available at: http://www.thecommonwealth.org/Shared_ASP_Files/UploadedFiles/6157EAA5-9071-4993-A413-EE6BE4152E9D_FMM2003-Small-States-Paper.pdf.

[18] Barbara von Tigerstrom, "Small Island Developing States and International Trade: Special Challenges in the Global Partnership for Development" (2005) 6 *Melbourne Journal of International Law*; Kelsey, supra note 5, p. 247.

country, and Vanuatu and Samoa are both classified as LDCs by the UN.[19] The following table provides a basic outline of the economic position of these countries:

	Tonga[20]	Vanuatu[21]	Samoa[22]
Population (2010)	103,000	247,000	182,000
GDP per capita (2009)	US$3,032	US$2,643	US$3,078
Major sources of imports (2007)	New Zealand (33.8%) Singapore (21.3%) Australia (11.6%)	Australia (20.7%) Singapore (11.8%) New Zealand (11.2%)	New Zealand (29.0%)* Australia (23.6%)* United States (13.2%)*
Major export destinations (2007)	New Zealand (33.3%) United States (30.7%) Japan (13.1%)	Thailand (58.3%) India (18.5%) Japan (11.3%)	Australia (68.9%)* New Zealand (18.3%)* American Samoa (6.3%)*

* 2009 data.

Although agriculture accounts for only approximately 23% of GDP in Tonga, 18% in Vanuatu, and 14% in Samoa, subsistence farmers whose cash income comes largely from remittances make up a significant proportion of the population of these countries.[23] As SIDS, each country is subject to seasonal and external factors over which it has little control, and all have high inflation and trade deficits.[24] Historically, each country has relied on tariffs for government revenue, although each has introduced a consumption tax to reduce this reliance.[25] The effect of the

[19] UN, Office of the High Representative for the Least Developed Countries, *Landlocked Developing Countries and Small Island Developing States, List of Least Developed Countries*, available at: http://www.unohrlls.org/en/ldc/related/62/, accessed 21 August 2009.

[20] Australian Government, Department of Foreign Affairs and Trade, *Country Fact Sheet: Tonga*, available at: http://www.dfat.gov.au/geo/fs/tnga.pdf.

[21] Australian Government, Department of Foreign Affairs and Trade, *Country Fact Sheet: Vanuatu*, available at: http://www.dfat.gov.au/geo/fs/vanu.pdf.

[22] Australian Government, Department of Foreign Affairs and Trade, *Country Fact Sheet: Samoa*, available at: http://www.dfat.gov.au/geo/fs/samo.pdf.

[23] New Zealand House of Representatives, Foreign Affairs, Defence and Trade Committee, *Inquiry into New Zealand's Relationship with the Kingdom of Tonga: Report of the Foreign Affairs*, 47th Parliament (August 2005), p. 13; see supra notes 20–22.

[24] New Zealand House of Representatives (2005), supra note 23.

[25] See Ibid.; and Roman Grynberg and Roy Mickey Joy, "The Accession of Vanuatu to the WTO: Lessons for the Multilateral Trading System," in Roman Grynberg (ed.), *WTO at the Margins: Small States and the Multilateral Trading System* (Cambridge: Cambridge University Press, 2006), pp. 693, 695; and Nella Tavita-Levy, Principal Trade Policy Officer, Samoa Ministry of Foreign Affairs and Trade, *Samoa: Accession to the WTO*, Presentation at the ADB Intensive Course on Accession (Bangkok, March 7–10, 2006).

lower bound tariff rates agreed by each country as a consequence of their WTO accession negotiations on government revenue is uncertain. One possibility is that the lower tariff amount received on a particular value or quantity of imports might be offset by an increase in imports, which may result from lower tariffs[26] or from other sources of tax revenue.

During their accession negotiations, WTO members requested that Tonga, Vanuatu, and Samoa make extensive concessions. The terms of Tonga's accession to the WTO as agreed in 2005, the terms of Vanuatu's accession at the point at which it suspended its negotiations in 2001, and the current terms of Samoa's accession, as set out in the Draft Working Party Report circulated in November 2006, include the following:

- Tonga makes a commitment to eliminate all prohibited industrial subsidy schemes by the date of accession (however, actionable subsidies will be allowed).[27] Vanuatu and Samoa agree that any future subsidies will comply with the Agreement on Subsidies and Countervailing Measures.[28]
- Tonga accepts a transition period to implement the Customs Valuation Agreement until January 1, 2008,[29] Vanuatu and Samoa agree to no transition period to comply with the Customs Valuation Agreement, on the basis that their regimes are already in compliance, or close to compliance.[30]
- In Tonga's case, a transition period to implement the Agreement on Trade Related Aspects of Intellectual Property Rights[31] (TRIPS Agreement) until June 30, 2008,[32] in Vanuatu's case a two-year transition period from accession to comply with the TRIPS Agreement,[33] and in Samoa's case, a request that it has until January 2013 before it is required to comply with the TRIPS Agreement.[34]

[26] Carlos Primo Braga and Olivier Cattaneo, "Introduction," in Carlos Primo Braga and Olivier Cattaneo (eds.), *WTO and Accession Countries* (Cheltenham: Edward Elgar Publishing, 2009), p. 29.

[27] WTO, Sixth Session of the Ministerial Conference, *Report of the Working Party on the Accession of Tonga to the World Trade Organization*, WTO Doc. WT/ACC/TON/17, WT/MIN(05)/4 (2 December 2005), p. 115.

[28] Agreement on Subsidies and Countervailing Measures, WTO Doc. LT/UR/A-1A/9 (April 15, 1994); WTO, Working Party on the Accession of Vanuatu, *Draft Report of the Working Party on the Accession of Vanuatu to the World Trade Organization*, WTO Doc. WT/ACC/VUT/13 (16 October 2001), p. 73; WTO, Working Party on the Accession of Samoa, *Draft Report of the Working Party on the Accession of Samoa to the World Trade Organization*, WTO Doc. WT/ACC/SPEC/SAM/4/Rev.1 (November 8, 2006), p. 92.

[29] Agreement on Implementation of Article VII of the General Agreement on Tariffs and Trade 1994 (Customs Valuation Agreement), WTO Doc. LT/UR/A-1A/4 (April 15, 1994); WTO, Sixth Session of the Ministerial Conference, supra note 27, p. 89.

[30] WTO, Working Party on the Accession of Vanuatu, supra note 28, p. 61.

[31] Agreement on Trade Related Aspects of Intellectual Property Rights, WTO Doc. LT/UR/A-1C/IP/1 (April 15, 1994).

[32] WTO, Sixth Session of the Ministerial Conference, supra note 27, p. 169.

[33] WTO, Working Party on the Accession of Vanuatu, supra note 28, p. 108.

[34] WTO, Working Party on the Accession of Samoa, supra note 28, p. 132.

- In each country's case, an undertaking to implement the Agreement on Technical Barriers to Trade[35] (TBT Agreement) from accession.[36]
- In Tonga and Vanuatu's cases, an undertaking to implement the *Agreement on the Application of the Sanitary and Phytosanitary Measures* (SPS Agreement) from accession,[37] and in Samoa's case, a request that it be granted a transition period until January 2012 before it is required to comply with the SPS Agreement.[38]
- Both Vanuatu and Tonga have agreed to, and Samoa has offered, comprehensive schedules of sector specific services commitments.[39]
- In Tonga's case, an agreement to bind all tariff lines at 15 or 20%,[40] and in Vanuatu's case an agreement to bind all tariff lines at an average rate of 49%.[41] In anticipation of its WTO accession in 2003, Samoa unilaterally lowered its tariffs, from a maximum of 60% to 20%. Tariffs of 10% were also lowered to 8%. Two other tariff bands of 0% and 5% were also adopted.[42]

It is interesting to note that Tonga, Vanuatu, and Samoa agreed to implement the WTO agreements within much shorter time frames than other recently acceded countries, such as Cambodia and Nepal.[43] Each country also made services commitments that cover a much higher number of specific subsectoral entries than other Pacific SIDS.[44] Moreover, Oxfam notes that Tonga has agreed to bind tariffs at levels

35 Agreement on Technical Barriers to Trade, WTO Doc. LT/UR/A-1A/10 (April 15, 1994).

36 WTO, Sixth Session of the Ministerial Conference, supra note 27, p. 116; and WTO, Working Party on the Accession of Vanuatu, supra note 28, p. 76.

37 Agreement on the Application of Sanitary and Phytosanitary Measures, WTO Doc. LT/UR/A-1A/12 (April 15, 1994); WTO, Sixth Session of the Ministerial Conference, supra note 27, p. 126; and WTO, Working Party on the Accession of Vanuatu, supra note 28, p. 87.

38 WTO, Working Party on the Accession of Samoa, supra note 28, p. 106.

39 WTO, Sixth Session of the Ministerial Conference, supra note 27, Add. 2; WTO, Working Party on the Accession of Vanuatu, supra note 28, Add. 2; and WTO, Working Party on the Accession of Samoa, supra note 28.

40 WTO, Sixth Session of the Ministerial Conference, supra note 27, p. 55.

41 WTO, Working Party on the Accession of Vanuatu, supra note 28, Add. 1.

42 Tavita-Levy, supra note 25; WTO, Statement by the Honourable Hans Joachim Keil, Minister of Trade, Government of Samoa, WTO Ministerial Conference, Fifth Session, Cancun, WTO Doc. WT/MIN(03)/ST/155 (September 13, 2003).

43 For example, Cambodia and Nepal were granted a three-year transition period under the TRIPS Agreement in respect of pharmaceuticals. See WTO, Working Party on the Accession of Cambodia, *Report of the Working Party on the Accession of Cambodia*, WTO Doc. WT/ACC/KHM/21 (August 15, 2003), p. 206; WTO, Working Party on the Accession of Nepal, *Report of the Working Party on the Accession of Nepal*, WTO Doc. WT/ACC/NPL/16 (August 28, 2003), p. 138. Moreover, Cambodia and Nepal were each granted a three-year transition period for the TBT Agreement, and Cambodia was given a five-year transition period for the SPS Agreement. See WTO, Working Party on the Accession of Cambodia, pp. 131, 142; WTO, Working Party on the Accession of Nepal.

44 For example, Solomon Islands, which has made commitments in six sub-sectors, and Fiji, which has made commitments in one subsector. See Solomon Islands: General Agreement on Trade in Services – Schedule of Specific Commitments, WTO Doc. GATS/SC/117 (April 1, 1996); Fiji: General Agreement on Trade in Services – Schedule of Specific Commitments, WTO Doc. GATS/SC/32 (April 15, 1994).

"lower than any other country in the history of the WTO, with the sole exception of Armenia."[45] Similarly, with a view to its WTO accession, Samoa unilaterally adopted comparatively low tariff rates. Of course, it is often more meaningful to compare pre- and postaccession *applied* rather than *bound* tariffs rates to access the extent of liberalization.[46] However, Tonga's and Samoa's accession commitments both required significant changes to *applied* tariff rates. Each country did reject some demands during their accession negotiations. Both Tonga and Samoa rejected attempts to secure commitments on competition policy,[47] and each country rejected accession to the plurilateral Agreement on Government Procurement.[48] Tonga also refused to bind tariffs at zero for civil aircraft and parts, on the ground that this would be inconsistent with the proposed single-tariff regime.[49]

Commentators have questioned Tonga's ability to comply with the terms of its accession.[50] In particular, at the time it agreed to the terms of its accession Tonga had no legislation for antidumping, countervailing duty, or safeguard measures but guaranteed that any future measures of this type will comply with the relevant WTO agreements.[51] In addition, Tonga did not have technical regulations, standards or certification procedures, yet agreed to comply fully with the TBT Agreement.[52] Cambodia faced similar implementation problems following its accession to the WTO.[53] Both Vanuatu and Samoa have embarked on extensive structural adjustment programs under the guidance of the Asian Development Bank, an element of which is WTO accession.[54] Although this means that they are in a better position to comply with the WTO agreements if they accede to the WTO, in both countries, the implementation of the reform programs has been costly, and their long-term benefits are uncertain. In particular, both countries run consistent trade deficits that have undermined public support for the reform program, including WTO accession.[55]

[45] Oxfam International, *Blood from a Stone* (December 2005), available at: http://www.oxfam.org/en/files/bn051215_tonga_bloodfromastone/download.

[46] Braga and Cattaneo, supra note 26, p. 23.

[47] Sixth Session of the Ministerial Conference, supra note 27, p. 37; WTO, Working Party on the Accession of Samoa, supra note 28, pp. 31–33.

[48] Agreement on Government Procurement, WTO Doc. LT/UR/A-4/PLURI/2 (April 15, 1994); WTO, Sixth Session of the Ministerial Conference, supra note 27, p. 138; WTO, Working Party on the Accession of Vanuatu, supra note 28, p. 98.

[49] Kelsey, supra note 5, p. 271.

[50] See, for example, Oxfam International, supra note 45.

[51] Sixth Session of the Ministerial Conference, supra note 27, p. 100.

[52] Kelsey, supra note 5, p. 271.

[53] Samnang Chea and Hach Sok, "Cambodia's Access to WTO: 'Fast-Tracked' Accession by a Least-Developed Country," in Peter Gallagher, Patrick Low, and Andrew L. Stoler, *Managing the Challenges of WTO Participation: 45 Case Studies* (Cambridge: Cambridge University Press, 2005), p. 120.

[54] Roman Grynberg and Roy Mickey Joy, "The Accession of Vanuatu to the WTO: Lessons for the Multilateral Trading System," in Roman Grynberg (ed.), *WTO at the Margins: Small States and the Multilateral Trading System* (Cambridge: Cambridge University Press, 2006), pp. 693, 696; Tavita-Levy, supra note 25.

[55] Daniel Gay, "Vanuatu's Suspended Accession Bid: Second Thoughts?" in Peter Gallagher, Patrick Low, and Andrew Stoler, *Managing the Challenges of WTO Participation: 45 Case Studies*

Despite the challenges it faces, at the time it concluded its accession negotiations the Tongan government rejected criticism of its decision to accede to the WTO as "erroneous."[56] Moreover, despite the difficulties it experienced during its accession negotiations Vanuatu has restarted its accession process.[57] Samoa is also continuing its accession negotiations and appears likely to proceed with accession once the terms are agreed.[58]

Yet the wider political context in which these decisions have been made must be borne in mind. Tonga, Vanuatu, and Samoa all rely on foreign aid to fund their development. In the Pacific, multilateral aid is primarily funneled through the Asian Development Bank,[59] and the largest bilateral aid donors are Australia[60] and New Zealand.[61] Both donors advocate the positive developmental effects of trade

(Cambridge: Cambridge University Press, 2005), pp. 590, 591; and Oxfam New Zealand, *Submission of Oxfam New Zealand to Ministry of Foreign Affairs on the WTO Accession Negotiations of Samoa* (September 2005), available at: http://www.oxfam.org.nz/imgs/whatwedo/mtf/onz%20on%20samoa%20wto%20accession.pdf.

56 "Oxfam's Criticism "Outrageous," says Tonga's WTO Delegation," *Matangi Tonga Online*, December 19, 2005, available at: http://www.matangitonga.to/scripts/artman/exec/view.cgi?archive=4&num=1529.

57 Vanuatu Trade Minister James Bule met with WTO Director-General Pascal Lamy in July 2006 in Geneva to discuss ways in which to restart Vanuatu's accession process. Shirley Joy, "WTO to Reopen Dialogue on Vanuatu Membership," *Vanuatu Daily Post*, July 11, 2006. Vanuatu then held bilateral consultations with selected delegations in late 2008, with the current plan that its Working Party will be reactivated once these consultations are completed. United States Trade Representative, *Accessions of Least Developed Countries*, available at: http://www.ustr.gov/trade-agreements/wto-multilateral-affairs/wto-accessions/accessions-least-developed-countries; Australian Government, Department of Foreign Affairs and Trade, *Vanuatu Country Brief*, available at: http://www.dfat.gov.au/geo/vanuatu/vanuatu_brief.html; New Zealand Ministry of Foreign Affairs & Trade, Republic of Vanuatu, available at: http://www.mfat.govt.nz/Countries/Pacific/Vanuatu.php.

58 The first revision of Samoa's Draft Working Party Report was circulated in November 2006. WTO, Working Party on the Accession of Samoa, supra note 28. Samoa has also recently concluded bilateral negotiations with Australia and New Zealand. Australian Government, Department of Foreign Affairs and Trade, *Samoa Country Brief*, available at: http://www.dfat.gov.au/GEO/samoa/samoa_brief.html; New Zealand Ministry of Foreign Affairs & Trade, *Samoa Country Information Paper*, available at: http://www.mfat.govt.nz/Countries/Pacific/Samoa.php.

59 Asian Development Bank, *ADB's Pacific Approach 2010–2014* (2009), available at: http://www.adb.org/Documents/Books/ADB-Pacific-Approach-2010–2014/ADB-Pacific-Approach-2010–2014.pdf.

60 *Partnership for Development between the Government of Australia and the Government of Tonga*, signed in Cairns (August 7, 2009), available at: http://www.ausaid.gov.au/hottopics/pdf/Australia_Tonga_Partnership_for_Development.pdf; *Partnership for Development between the Government of Australia and the Government of Vanuatu*, signed in Canberra (May 27, 2009), available at: http://www.ausaid.gov.au/hottopics/pdf/Australia_Vanuatu_Partnership_for_Development.pdf; *Partnership for Development between the Government of Australia and the Government of Samoa*, signed in Niue (August 20, 2008).

61 *Joint Tonga/New Zealand Country Programme Strategy 2008–2018* (September 2008), available at: http://www.nzaid.govt.nz/library/docs/nzaid-jnt-tonga-nz-country-prog-strategy-2008-2018.pdf; *NZAID/Vanuatu Development Programme Strategy 2006–2010* (June 2006), available at: http://www.nzaid.govt.nz/library/docs/nzaid-vanuatu-strategy-0610.pdf; *Joint Samoa Programme Strategy, Government of Samoa, Government of Australia and Government of New Zealand* (November 2006), available at: http://www.nzaid.govt.nz/library/docs/samoa-jsps-prog-strategy-2006-2010.pdf.

liberalization and seek to drive their recipients toward it via placing conditionalities on aid and by providing direct assistance to implement trade-related policy reforms.[62]

C. *Special Problems of SIDS*

Pacific SIDS such as Tonga, Vanuatu, and Samoa possess a number of characteristics that affect their ability to engage in – and benefit from – international trade. These include small land area, which places pressure on natural resources; narrow resource base, which leads to the production of a narrow range of goods and services; limited opportunities for diversification; vulnerability to natural disasters and environmental change; rising sea levels, which threaten their long-term viability; small populations, which often means limited institutional capacity in the public and private sectors; difficulty achieving economies of scale; high transport costs (both externally and internally); limited sources of revenue, which has historically led to a reliance on tariffs for a substantial proportion of public revenue; limited access to external capital;[63] and in many cases, remoteness and isolation.[64]

These characteristics both impede their integration into global markets, and create cost disadvantages for firms that operate within SIDS.[65] However, because SIDS generally score highly on some development indicators, such as education and health, the international community often overlooks the problems they experience. Indeed, many SIDS have more poverty per capita than their income suggests.[66]

Commentators have identified a number of problems that SIDS experience when participating in the WTO system. These include limited experience in WTO negotiations, limited capacity to mainstream WTO obligations into national laws, limited funds to implement structural adjustments necessitated by WTO rules, limited expertise and lack of scientific infrastructure to implement WTO technical obligations,[67]

[62] AusAID, *Pacific Regional Aid Strategy 2004–2009*, available at: http://www.ausaid.gov.au/publications/pubout.cfm?Id=7085_5949_6483_1791_1576; NZAID, *Annual Review 2007/08: Pacific Overview* (2008), available at: http://www.aid.govt.nz/library/annual-review/ar-2007-08/annual-review-nzaid-2008-3-pacific-overview.pdf.

[63] Tigerstrom, supra note 18, p. 402; Prema-chandra Athukorala, "Trade Policy in a Small Island Economy: The WTO Review of the Maldives" (2004) 27 *The World Economy* 1401; Harvey W. Armstrong and Robert Read, "Trade and Growth in Small States: The Impact of Global Trade Liberalisation" (1998) 21 *The World Economy* 563; Witter, Briguglio and Bhuglah (2002), supra note 15; Mauritius, supra note 10.

[64] See Stephen Redding and Anthony J. Venables, "The Economics of Isolation and Distance," in Roman Grynberg (ed.), *WTO at the Margins: Small States and the Multilateral Trading System* (Cambridge: Cambridge University Press, 2006), p. 145.

[65] Roman Grynberg, "A Theory of Trade and Development of Small Vulnerable States," in Roman Grynberg (ed.), *WTO at the Margins: Small States and the Multilateral Trading System* (Cambridge: Cambridge University Press, 2006), pp. 11, 14.

[66] Commonwealth Secretariat/World Bank Joint Task Force on Small States, supra note 17, pp. 1, 14.

[67] Mauritius, supra note 10.

and difficulty conducting negotiations with more powerful members.[68] Although these problems are experienced by many developing countries, their impact is magnified in SIDS because of their small size, which imposes additional limits on their capacity to participate in the WTO system.

However, it might be more advantageous to SIDs to negotiate within the system, where they have access to the WTO's trading rules. This is because the WTO dispute settlement procedures provide four important mechanisms that can improve the capacity of SIDS (and developing countries more generally) to gain concessions from other states. These mechanisms are "a guarantee for the right to negotiate, a common standard for evaluating outcomes, the option for several countries to join a dispute, and incentives for states to change a policy found to violate trade rules."[69] The difference between the resources and expertise available to SIDS and larger states can lead to a power imbalance during the dispute settlement process. However, the WTO dispute process at least provides a rule-based procedure – as well as the potential for negative publicity – to keep the worst excesses of larger states in check, compared with private negotiations between states. In addition, commentators have argued that the role played by small states in delaying the Doha Round negotiations indicates that, "through the formation of a range of alliances, small developing states have become central to the process and form of multilateral trade negotiations."[70] However, given that small states have merely delayed these negotiations rather than secured a favorable outcome, this conclusion may be optimistic. Moreover, a particular problem facing Pacific SIDS in their interaction with WTO members is their limited human capital and inability to afford permanent representation in Geneva.[71] To some extent, the WTO has attempted to ameliorate this through the Work Programme on Small Economies, which is aimed at framing a response to the trade-related problems of small vulnerable economies such as those of Pacific SIDS.[72] The Advisory Centre on WTO Law, which is partially funded by developed-country WTO members, also provides legal advice, support in dispute settlement proceedings, and training to developing-country members.[73] Moreover, the WTO

68 For example, Davis discusses the difficulties experienced by Peru when conducting its negotiations with the United States. Christina L. Davis, "Do WTO Rules Create a Level Playing Field? Lessons from the Experience of Peru and Vietnam," in John S. Odell (ed.), *Negotiating Trade: Developing Countries in the WTO and NAFTA* (New York: Cambridge University Press, 2006), p. 219.

69 Ibid., p. 220.

70 Donna Lee and Nicola J. Smith, "The Political Economy of Small African States in the WTO" (2008) 97 *The Round Table* 259.

71 Chakriya Bowman, "The Pacific Island Nations: Towards Shared Representation," in Peter Gallagher, Patrick Low, and Andrew L. Stoler, *Managing the Challenges of WTO Participation: 45 Case Studies* (Cambridge: Cambridge University Press, 2005), p. 450.

72 WTO, General Council, supra note 8.

73 WTO, Advisory Centre on WTO Law, *Quick Guide to the ACWL*, available at: http://www.acwl.ch/pdf/acwl_page_imp.pdf.

has assisted in the establishment of a shared representative office for member nations of the Pacific Islands Forum.[74]

Despite these difficulties, commentators have identified a number of consequences of WTO membership that may be particularly beneficial for SIDS, including that WTO membership provides access to technical assistance to build institutional infrastructure; provides shelter from unilateral pressure by more powerful countries through the ability to publicize conflicts at the WTO; encourages the opening of markets through a period of "free riding," leading to greater allocative efficiency and lower consumer process and input costs for exports; improves attractiveness to foreign investors;[75] provides formerly marginalized countries, such as SIDS, the opportunity to "further integrate into the world economy and to better harness the benefits of international trade"; reduces the cost of trade negotiations by automatically passing on all market access improvements negotiated at the WTO to all members; and provides members with the ability to participate in trade rule making.[76]

However, the benefits of WTO membership can only be measured by analyzing its impact after a country has acceded to the WTO. Few empirical studies have been conducted that consider the effects of WTO accession, with one commentator concluding that "little is known about the impact on economic performance and well-being of the other economies that have joined the WTO since 1995."[77] This is because much research focuses on preparation for WTO accession, with "authors typically focused on *estimating the potential* of WTO accession rather than *measuring its effects*."[78] Whereas one commentator has concluded that GATT/WTO membership did not have a statistically significant effect on the value of bilateral trade flows,[79] other studies have disputed this finding and identified that the WTO has had a positive effect on world trade.[80]

Tonga acceded to the WTO in July 2007, but its new income tax, customs, and excise legislation implementing the terms of its accession only became effective

74 Bowman (2005), supra note 71, p. 450.

75 Rolf J. Langhammer and Matthias Lucke, "WTO Accession Issues" (1999) 22 *The World Economy* 837.

76 Braga and Cattaneo, supra note 26, p. 8.

77 Simon J. Evenett, Jonathan Gage, and Maxine Kennett, *WTO Membership and Market Access: Evidence from the Accessions of Bulgaria and Ecuador*, Universitat St. Gallen Working Paper (2004), p. 4, available at: http://www.alexandria.unisg.ch/Publikationen/22175.

78 Braga and Cattaneo, supra note 26, p. 13.

79 Andrew K. Rose, "Do We Really Know That the WTO Increases Trade?" (2004) 94 *The American Economic Review* 98.

80 Arvind Subramanian and Shang-Jin Wei, "The WTO Promotes Trade, Strongly, but Unevenly" (2007) 72 *Journal of International Economics* 151; and Michael Tomz, Judith L. Goldstein and Douglas Rivers, "Membership Has Its Privileges: The Impact of the GATT on International Trade" (2007) 97 *The American Economic Review* 2005.

in February 2008.[81] Therefore, it is too early to access data from which to draw conclusions concerning the impact of WTO accession on Tonga's economy. Despite this, in his 2008 Budget Statement, the Tongan minister of finance noted that although taxes on international trade provided 53% of the Tongan government's revenue in 2003–4, he estimated that only 10% of government revenue will come from import duties now its process of WTO-related tax reform is complete, with the rest coming from domestic taxes, including taxes on income, consumption, and excise.[82]

D. *Conclusion*

In light of the challenges faced by Pacific SIDS when they participate in international trade, it is important to consider how WTO accession affects their development needs. This chapter now considers two specific aspects of WTO law and process that illustrate the complex development needs of Pacific countries in the context of their participation in the international trading regime – namely, the WTO accession process and SDT.

III. ACCESSION

A. *Introduction to the Accession Process*

Seventy-seven new members have joined the WTO since it was established, bringing its total membership to 153.[83] Currently, twenty-nine countries are in the process of WTO accession.[84] Of these countries, thirteen are LDCs,[85] and ten are countries in

[81] *Income Tax Act 2007, No. 10* (Tonga); *Income Tax Regulations 2008* (Tonga); *Consumption Tax Act 2003* (Tonga); *Customs Act 2007, No. 5* (Tonga); *Customs Regulations 2008* (Tonga); *Customs and Excise Management Act 2007, No. 4* (Tonga); Revenue Services, Government of Tonga, available at: http://www.revenue.gov.to.

[82] Hon. Siosiua 'Utoikamanu Tupou, *Budget Statement for Year Ending 30th June 2008*, Ministry of Finance and Planning Government of Tonga, [5]–[6], available at: http://www.finance.gov.to.

[83] WTO, *Members and Observers*, available at: http://www.wto.org/english/thewto_e/whatis_e/tif_e/org6_e.htm.

[84] WTO, *Summary Table of Ongoing Accessions*, available at: http://www.wto.org/English/thewto_e/acc_e/status_e.htm (Afghanistan, Algeria, Andorra, Azerbaijan, Bahamas, Belarus, Bhutan, Bosnia and Herzegovina, Comoros, Equatorial Guinea, Ethiopia, Iran, Iraq, Kazakhstan, Lao People's Democratic Republic, Lebanese Republic, Republic of Liberia, Libyan Arab Jamahiriya, Montenegro, Russian Federation, Samoa, Sao Tome and Principe, Serbia, Seychelles, Sudan, Tajikistan, Uzbekistan, Vanuatu, and Yemen).

[85] WTO, *Least-developed Countries*, available at: http://www.wto.org/English/thewto_e/whatis_e/tif_e/org7_e.htm (Afghanistan, Bhutan, Cape Verde,* Comoros,* Equatorial Guinea, Ethiopia, Lao People's Democratic Republic, Republic of Liberia, Samoa,* Sao Tome and Principe,* Sudan, Vanuatu,* and Yemen). Applicants marked with with an asterisk (*) are also SIDs.

transition to a market economy.[86] Accession to the WTO is a complex, lengthy, and difficult process.

B. *Provisions on Accessions*

Article XII of the Marrakesh Agreement governs accession to the organization. Article XII.1 provides that:

> Any State or separate customs territory possessing full autonomy in the conduct of its external commercial relations and of the other matters provided for in this Agreement and the Multilateral Trade Agreements may accede to this Agreement, on terms to be agreed between it and the WTO.[87]

That accession is a process of negotiation on the "terms to be agreed" immediately distinguishes the process of accession to the WTO from many other international organizations, such as the IMF, which are largely automatic. The article gives no guidance on the "terms to be agreed" or the procedures to be used for negotiating these terms. In this it closely follows the corresponding Article XXXIII of GATT 1947.[88] Article XII.2 goes on to state:

> Decisions on accession shall be taken by the Ministerial Conference. The Ministerial Conference shall approve the agreement on the terms of accession by a two-thirds majority of the Members of the WTO.

There are also a number of other WTO provisions that are relevant to accession.[89]

[86] Azerbaijan, Belarus, Bosnia and Herzegovina, Kazakhstan, Montenegro, Russian Federation, Serbia, Tajikistan, Ukraine, and Uzbekistan.

[87] Marrakesh Agreement Establishing the World Trade Organization, Article XII.1, WTO Doc. LT/UR/A/2 (April 15, 1994).

[88] GATT 1947 Article XXXIII; Marrakesh Agreement Establishing the World Trade Organization, supra note 87, at Article XII.2.

[89] These provisions include Article XVI.1, which lays down that "[e]xcept as otherwise provided under this Agreement or the Multilateral Trade Agreements, the WTO shall be guided by the decisions, procedures and customary practices followed by the CONTRACTING PARTIES to GATT 1947 and the bodies established in the framework of GATT 1947"; Article XII:2, which states that "[d]ecisions on accession shall be taken by the Ministerial Conference"; Article IV:2, which makes it clear that "[i]n the intervals between meetings of the Ministerial Conference, its functions shall be conducted by the General Council"; and Article IX, which deals with decision making. On November 15, 1995, the General Council agreed to procedures regarding decision making under Articles IX and XII of the WTO Agreement that clarified the relation between these two provisions (WT/GC/M/8, page 6); Article XIII provides that: "1. This Agreement and the Multilateral Trade Agreements in Annexes 1 and 2 shall not apply as between any Member and any other Member if either of the Members, at the time either becomes a Member, does not consent to such application. . . . 3. Paragraph 1 shall apply between a Member and another Member which has acceded under Article XII only if the Member not consenting to the application has so notified the Ministerial Conference before the approval of the agreement on the terms of accession by the Ministerial Conference." WTO, *Accessions: The Mandate, Relevant WTO Provisions*, available at: http://www.wto.org/english/thewto_e/acc_e/acc7_3_e.htm.

Membership Has Its Benefits

In addition to the particular benefits to SIDS discussed earlier, Constantine Michalopolous has identified three general benefits of WTO membership.[90] The first benefit is that accession tends to improve domestic policies and institutions, because it requires them to be strengthened and made more certain. For example, accession requires members to lock in relatively liberal trade regimes, which can be important in countries where political decisions are vulnerable to capture by certain interest groups.[91] This is relevant in Tonga, which is still undergoing its transition to full democracy and where traditional ruling elites can exert influence for their commercial advantage. The transparent and binding nature of the reforms mandated by WTO accession can help to counteract these influences. Accession also provides a degree of policy certainty to domestic producers, foreign exporters, and investors that can increase productivity and efficiency. Acceding members may find the WTO commitments they have made a useful excuse to resist domestic protectionist influences. In addition, the transparency and certainty offered by the regulatory and administrative reforms mandated by WTO membership may improve institutional functioning and reduce rent-seeking behavior and corruption.[92] This is particularly relevant to Tonga, Vanuatu, and Samoa, where tariff and other trade concessions are often unevenly distributed according to traditional or family relationships.[93] Improvements to the regulation of "backbone services," such as telecommunications, banking and transport, as well as the regulation of technical, sanitary, and phytosanitary measures, mandated by the WTO agreements, can also improve internal governance and make countries more attractive to foreign investment.[94]

The second is improved market access. Accession to the WTO provides permanent and unconditional most-favored nation (MFN) treatment to the new member.[95]

90 Constantine Michalopoulos, "WTO Accession," in Bernard M. Hoekman, Aaditya Mattoo, Philip English (eds.), *Development, Trade, and the WTO: A Handbook* (Washington, DC: World Bank, 2002), p. 61.

91 Kent Jones, "The Political Economy of WTO Accession: The Unfinished Business of Universal Membership" (2009) 8 *World Trade* Review 279, 281.

92 Zdenek Drabek and Marc Bacchetta, "Trading the Effects of WTO Accession on Policy-making in Sovereign States: Preliminary Lessons from the Recent Experiences of Transition Countries" (2004) 27 *The World Economy* 1083.

93 Peter Larmour, *Corruption and Governance in the South Pacific*, State Society and Governance in Melanesia Discussion Paper 97/5 (1997), available at: http://rspas.anu.edu.au/papers/melanesia/discussion_papers/ssgm97–5.pdf.

94 Joseph Francis, "External Bindings and the Credibility of Reform," in Ahmed Galal and Bernard Hoekman (eds.), *Regional Partners in Global Markets: Limits and Possibilities of the Euro-Med Agreements* (London: CEPR and ECES, 1997), p. 35.

95 Economies, which are not WTO members, may be granted MFN treatment by trading partners, but if this occurs, it is on a voluntary basis. In certain circumstances when a country joins the WTO, it may still not be afforded full MFN treatment. For example, when Georgia, Mongolia, and Kygyz Republic became WTO Members, the United States invoked Article XIII of the Marrakesh Agreement, "Non-Application of Multilateral Trade Agreements between Particular Members." (Under this article, a member can notify the Ministerial Conference (before the Ministerial Conference approves the

This "protection against arbitrary protectionist measures of major trading partners"[96] can be particularly valuable to SIDS and other small states that may experience significant imbalances when negotiating with their trading partners. The multilateral system of bargaining in the WTO also reduces trade negotiation transaction costs,[97] which are acutely felt by SIDS. Finally, there is some evidence that more antidumping measures are imposed on non-WTO members than WTO members.[98]

The third is access to the WTO dispute settlement system, which is seen as impartial. The binding nature of WTO dispute settlement and the high compliance rates with Dispute Settlement Understanding[99] ("DSU") recommendations is seen as an important benefit for many small acceding countries.[100] This is so despite the difficulties that many developing countries may have in taking advantage of the system.

The Accession Process

As this chapter will explore, negotiations in accessions are in one direction only and concern two key questions. The first is how the acceding country intends to meet its WTO obligations (there is no negotiation on the obligations themselves or whether existing WTO members are meeting their WTO obligations). The second is how the acceding country will reduce its level of protection in its markets (there is almost never discussion on how existing members will lower theirs).

The accession process can be divided up into a procedural phase and three substantive phases. The procedural phase involves a country sending a communication to the director-general of the WTO indicating its desire to join. This request is then considered by the WTO General Council. The General Council then will often[101] decide to set up a working party to consider the accession application and nominate the chairman of the working party.[102] Membership of the working party is open to

agreement on the terms of accession of a new member) that it does not consent to the application of the Marrakesh Agreement and the Multilateral Trade Agreements in Annexes 1 and 2 between it and the new member.) The United States later accepted the membership of these countries. 1 WTO Analytical Index 97; Peter Van Den Bossche, *The Law and Policy of the World Trade Organization* (Cambridge: Cambridge University Press: 2008; 1st ed., 2005), p. 174.

96 Braga and Cattaneo, supra note 26, p. 8.

97 Jones, supra note 91, p. 281.

98 Michalopoulos, supra note 90, p. 62.

99 See *Understanding on Rules and Procedures Governing the Settlement of Disputes*, LT/UR/A-2/DS/U/1, (1995), available at: http://docsonline.wto.org/gen_search.asp?searchmode=simple (search WTO official documents for "LT/UR/A-2/DS/U/1" by Document Signal; then click on the Preview (HTML) hyperlink).

100 Braga and Cattaneo, supra note 26, pp. xi, xiv.

101 United States objections led to significant delays in the establishment of the working party on the accession of Iran. "WTO sets up Working Party on Accession of Iran, after U.S. Backs EU by Lifting Veto," *International Trade Reporter*, June 2, 2005.

102 Before making the formal request for accession, a country may request (and will generally obtain) observer status at the WTO to familiarize itself with the institution. The terms of reference for working parties, in general, are "to examine the application of the Government of [name of applicant]

all interested members. When the accession concerns a significant economy, such as China, many members will participate in its activities.

The first substantive phase is the preparation of a memorandum on the Foreign Trade Regime by the applicant in which the applicant describes in detail its foreign trade regime and provides relevant statistical data for circulation to all members. This can be a large task because of the width and depth of issues that the memorandum is supposed to cover,[103] including policies affecting trade in goods and services, the trade-related intellectual property regime, customs valuation, technical barriers to trade, state trading, and foreign trade in goods and services. Some technical assistance is provided by the WTO secretariat and on occasion by other members, bilateral aid agencies, and the World Bank. However, the preparation of the report, and any delays in its preparation, is the responsibility of the applicant. These delays can be substantial, and because they are caused by either capacity constraints or weak follow-up, are particularly likely to affect small developing states such as SIDS. For example, in Tonga's case, there was a delay of more than three years between the establishment of a working party and the submission of a memorandum.

The second substantive phase is a fact-finding one by WTO members, in which members of the working party submit written questions designed to clarify the operation of the applicant's foreign trade regime. As a rule, answers are provided in writing. Two common issues arise at this stage. The first is "the degree of privatization in the economy and the extent to which government agencies involved in the regulation of economic activity do so on the basis of transparent rules and criteria as opposed to administrative discretion."[104] The second is one of governance and concerns "the jurisdiction and capacity of national agencies to implement policies on which commitments are being made"[105] and the capacity of other authorities to nullify those commitments. This phase can take anywhere from a few months to, in Tonga's case, over a year. The applicant's institutional weakness means that there are often long delays in governments ascertaining the consistency between existing legislation and regulations and WTO requirements.

In the third substantive phase, members submit requests, and the applicant responds by tabling its offer or draft schedule for goods and services. Alternatively, the applicant expedites the work by beginning the process by tabling a draft schedule for goods and services and interested members make requests.[106] Then, each interested

to accede to the World Trade Organization under Article XII and to submit to the General Council/Ministerial Conference recommendations which may include a draft Protocol of Accession." Peter Wieter Williams, *A Handbook on Accession to the WTO* (Cambridge: Cambridge University Press,2008), pp. 26, 28.

[103] See WTO Secretariat, *Accession to the World Trade Organization: Procedures for Negotiations under Article XII*, WT/ACC/1 (24 March 1995).

[104] Michalopoulos, supra note 90, p. 63.

[105] Ibid.

[106] The goods schedule contains a detailed schedule of tariffs the applicant intends to impose on goods and the level at which it will "bind" its tariffs. The services schedule contains the commitments

WTO member conducts a specific bilateral negotiation with the applicant on its schedules. Negotiations may also occur regarding whether the applicant's policies and institutions are consistent with WTO obligations. This negotiation phase may overlap a little with the second substantive phase because it may begin before all the points raised by members of the working party have been answered.

Applicants adopt different strategies during these negotiations. One is a "minimal liberalization" strategy in which the applicant offers to liberalize to the minimal extent necessary to secure its accession.[107] This strategy can be based on the belief that maintaining protection provides a bargaining chip to obtain improved market access in future rounds, and significant levels of protection are necessary when going through a transition period. The danger of this strategy is that the country may have little leverage in market access negotiations so its protection is not a valuable bargaining chip but acts simply to impose costs on its own economies. Other applicants have adopted a liberal trade strategy,[108] which means: "(a) binding tariffs at the usually low currently prevailing levels or to agree to reduce and bind tariffs at low levels as part of the accession negotiations; (b) agreeing to a liberal trade regime in agriculture and services; (c) at an early date after accession, participating in such agreements as the government procurement code – which increases competition and transparency in the operation of their markets."[109] This strategy is based on the benefits of liberal trade and investment but also has a number of other advantages: "it tends to facilitate the negotiations for accession; it provides governments political cover against domestic protectionist interests which may otherwise succeed in subverting an existing liberal trade regime; and, the legally binding WTO commitments 'lock-in' reforms by making it more difficult for future governments to reverse the liberalization."[110]

During these negotiations, demands will be made of applicants that exceed those made of existing members. These higher demands may include binding all tariffs (normally at close to applied rates and often at relatively low rates), making significant General Agreement on Trade in Services (GATS) commitments, meeting all WTO commitments at entry without any transition period (China is a counterexample), committing to a timetable to join plurilateral agreements (e.g., the Agreement on Government Procurement); and transitioning to a market economy (often while maintaining anti-dumping procedures that would maintain a "non-market economy" designation of the Applicant). However, there are two reasons to explain the extended scope of these demands: "(1) the level of tariffs bound/applied

(and limitations) that a member wishes to maintain in its services market. It includes horizontal commitments, which involve market access, and national treatment commitments, which apply to all service sectors and specific commitments and limitations for particular service sectors and subsectors in different modes of supply. Williams, supra note 102, pp. 113–132.

107 Michalopoulos, supra note 90, pp. 65–66.

108 See, for example, Albania, Estonia, Georgia, the Kyrgyz Republic, Latvia, and Mongolia. Ibid., p. 66.

109 Ibid.

110 Ibid.

by incumbent members has dramatically dropped as a result of the successive rounds of multilateral trade negotiations (i.e. the standard of admission is higher), and (2) the WTO Agreements extended the coverage of the GATT to include agriculture, textiles etc. that are particularly sensitive sectors in most countries."[111]

After the negotiations are concluded, the working party submits its Report to the General Council or Ministerial Conference. After the General Council or Ministerial Conference adopts the report, and the draft decision is approved by a two-thirds majority of the WTO members' positive vote, "the Protocol of Accession enters into force thirty days after acceptance by the Applicant, either by signature or by deposit of the Instrument of Ratification, if Parliamentary approval is required."[112]

C. *A Commitment Too Far: Vanuatu*

The length and complexity of the accession process is clearly demonstrated by the experience of Vanuatu. Vanuatu made its application for accession to the WTO in July 1995.[113] Its memorandum was completed in November 1995, and two working party meetings were held in July 1995 and October 1999.[114] Its accession package was completed in October 2001.[115] However, just before the Doha Ministerial Conference, at which Vanuatu was due to accede, the minister of trade withdrew a finalized working party report, citing "technical reasons."[116]

A number of reasons have been given for Vanuatu's suspension. One is insufficient internal communication. For example, it has "been suggested that when the Minister of Trade suspended the accession process in 2001 it was the first time that he was fully aware of the contents of the accession package."[117] Another is the limited resources available in Vanuatu: only five staff members dealt with the accession, and there were no resources available for a social or economic impact study. It was also difficult to secure ownership of the process, because Vanuatu had nine governments during its accession negotiations, and each had difficulty familiarizing itself with the details of the accession package. This also undermined the confidence of civil society because the government provided the public with little information regarding the accession process.[118] Finally, a number of members sought significant concessions from Vanuatu, which some have termed WTO-Plus.[119] On goods, Vanuatu agreed to

[111] Braga and Cattaneo (2009), supra note 26, p. 19.
[112] WTO Secretariat, supra note 103.
[113] WTO, *Accession Status: Vanuatu*, available at: http://www.wto.org/english/thewto_e/acc_e/a1_vanuatu_e.htm.
[114] Ibid.
[115] Ibid.
[116] Gay, supra note 55, citing WTO, Working Party on the Accession of Vanuatu, supra note 28.
[117] Ibid., p. 593.
[118] Ibid., pp. 592–593.
[119] Ibid., p. 593.

bind 100 % of tariffs, with a tariff peak of 75% and an average tariff rate of 40%.[120] On services, Vanuatu agreed to ten of a possible eleven general areas, which included fifty specific commitments.[121]

D. *Changes in Accessions Policy*

The agenda set out by the Doha Ministerial Conference in November 2001 included several mentions of the accessions process. Paragraph 9 of the Ministerial Declaration states that:

> We note with particular satisfaction that this conference has completed the WTO accession procedures for China and Chinese Taipei. We also welcome the accession as new members, since our last session, of Albania, Croatia, Georgia, Jordan, Lithuania, Moldova and Oman, and note the extensive market-access commitments already made by these countries on accession. These accessions will greatly strengthen the multilateral trading system, as will those of the 28 countries now negotiating their accession. We therefore attach great importance to concluding accession proceedings as quickly as possible. In particular, we are committed to accelerating the accession of least-developed countries.[122]

Paragraph 42, in the Section on LDCs states that:

> Accession of LDCs remains a priority for the Membership. We agree to work to facilitate and accelerate negotiations with acceding LDCs. We instruct the Secretariat to reflect the priority we attach to LDCs' accessions in the annual plans for technical assistance.[123]

The commitment in this Ministerial Declaration led to the subcommittee on LDCs agreeing to Guidelines on LDC Accessions,[124] which were adopted by the General Council at its meeting in December 2002.[125] These guidelines aim to ensure that the accession of LDCs is "facilitated and accelerated" and include commitments that WTO members will exercise restraint in seeking concessions and commitments on trade in goods and services from acceding LDCs; SDT provisions will be applicable to all acceding LDCs; targeted and coordinated technical assistance and capacity building will be provided on a priority basis by the WTO and other relevant multilateral, regional, and bilateral development partners to assist acceding LDCs; and the good offices of the director-general will be available to assist acceding LDCs

[120] Ibid., p. 600.

[121] Ibid.; WTO, Working Party on the Accession of Vanuatu, supra note 28.

[122] Doha Declaration, supra note 2.

[123] Ibid.

[124] *Subcommittee on Least Developed Countries Communication to the General Council, Accession of Least Developed Countries*, WTO Doc. WT/COMTD/LDC/12 (2002) (Draft Decision for submission to the General Council).

[125] WTO, General Council, *Accession of Least-Developed Countries – Decision of 10 December 2002*, WTO Doc WT/L/508 (2002) (Decision of the General Council).

in implementing the new guidelines decision.[126] There are indications that several members have chosen not to enter into bilateral negotiations with acceding LDCs, and when they have, they followed the guidelines by exercising restraint. Transition periods have also been granted to recently acceded LDCs, such as Nepal, Cambodia, and Cape Verde, as has technical assistance to assist implementation of their WTO obligations. There have also been efforts made to improve the accession process, particularly through the exchange of documentation, utilizing information technology, and through scheduling negotiations around Geneva Week, to minimize the costs of traveling to negotiations.[127]

Of the forty-nine LDCs identified by the United Nations, thirty-two are already members of the WTO, and another twelve are in the process of accession, indicating that these guidelines will continue to be tested.[128]

The Hong Kong Ministerial Declaration adopted on December 18, 2005 stated:

> 59. We reaffirm our strong commitment to making the WTO truly global in scope and membership. We welcome those new Members who have completed their accession processes since our last Session, namely Nepal, Cambodia and Saudi Arabia. We note with satisfaction that Tonga has completed its accession negotiations to the WTO. These accessions further strengthen the rules-based multilateral trading system. We continue to attach priority to the 29 ongoing accessions with a view to concluding them as rapidly and smoothly as possible. We stress the importance of facilitating and accelerating the accession negotiations of least-developed countries, taking due account of the guidelines on LDC accession adopted by the General Council in December 2002.[129]

E. *Conclusion*

Negotiating the "terms to be agreed" for WTO accession is a lengthy, costly, and complex process. The experience of Vanuatu demonstrates that this process is particularly burdensome for small developing countries, such as SIDS, and reinforces the need for change of the accession process in order to assist LDCs. Both the Doha Ministerial Declaration and the Hong Kong Ministerial Declaration recognized that the accession process for LDCs needs to move rapidly and be streamlined, following the new guidelines for LDC accession. It is unclear whether these intentions to simplify accession negotiations for LDCs have, or will, lead to an increase in the rate of small developing countries able to join the WTO. This chapter now considers the limited success of preferential treatment for developing countries in the WTO through an examination of SDT.

126 Ibid.

127 WTO, *Accession of Least-Developed Countries to the WTO*, WTO Doc. WT/COMTD/LDC/W/44 (2009).

128 Ibid.

129 WTO, *Ministerial Declaration of 18 December 2005*, WT/MIN(05)/DEC (2005), p. 59.

IV. SPECIAL AND DIFFERENTIAL TREATMENT

A. *Introduction*

Central to the recognition of development needs in the WTO is the notion of SDT for developing countries. SDT involves discrimination in favor of developing countries and is therefore a departure from MFN treatment, one of the two key nondiscrimination principles of the WTO regime. SDT takes two forms, providing either differential rights or obligations under the WTO Agreements, or according differential treatment to developing countries by other members.[130] Several commentators have argued that SDT provisions would assist Pacific SIDS to participate in international trade by helping to deal with their economic and political marginalization.[131]

SDT is based on the belief that the trade needs of developing countries are substantially different from those of developed countries and therefore that the two types of economies should not be subject to the same trade rules.[132] The most significant benefit of SDT is that it aims to address the challenges that developing countries face in the international trading system and to ensure that developing countries benefit from increased trade liberalization. SDT attempts to "resolve the competing demands for trade liberalization and equitable socioeconomic development."[133] This is particularly relevant to Pacific SIDS, which as discussed earlier, face a number of challenges that hinder their participation in the world trade system.

The principle of SDT emerged partly from the rhetoric of postcolonialism, as it was argued that some developing countries were in an unequal position because of the legacy of colonial oppression.[134] The principle of SDT is the translation of the concept that unequals should benefit from different treatment through the operation of redistributive mechanisms.[135] Indeed, SDT has three primary rationales. The first

[130] WTO, Committee on Trade and Development, *Implementation of Special and Differential Treatment Provisions in WTO Agreements and Decisions: Mandatory and Non-Mandatory Special and Differential Treatment Provisions – Note by the Secretariat (Corrigendum)*, WT/COMTD/W/77/Rev.1/Add.1/Corr.1 (February 4, 2002), 1. For an analysis of how WTO Panels and the Appellate Body have interpreted special and differential treatment provisions, see Edwini Kessie, "The Legal Status of Special and Differential Treatment Provisions under the WTO Agreements," in George Bermann and Petros Mavroidis (eds.), *WTO Law and Developing Countries* (New York: Cambridge University Press, 2007), pp. 22–35.

[131] Roman Grynberg, "WTO Issues for Small Vulnerable States," in *Small States: Economic Review & Basic Statistics* (London: Commonwealth Secretariat, 2000), p. 17.

[132] Endre Ustor, "Most-Favoured-Nation Clause," in Rudolf Bernhardt (ed.), *Encyclopaedia of Public International Law* (Amsterdam: North Holland, 2003), pp. 468, 471.

[133] Peter Lichetenbaum, "'Special Treatment' vs. 'Equal Participation': Striking a Balance in the Doha Negotiations" (2002) 17 *American University International Law Review* 1008.

[134] Frank J. Garcia, "Trade and Inequality: Economic Justice and the Developing World" (2000) 21 *Michigan Journal of International Law* 982–983.

[135] Ibid., pp. 1028–1029; Frank J. Garcia, "Building a Just Trade Order for a New Millennium" (2001) 21 *George Washington International Law Review* 1027–1029.

is based on principles of justice and reflects a "strong link with notions of justice and morality," including "protection of the weak and disadvantaged, compensation for past injustices, and social justice."[136] The second is based on "existing economic development disparities among countries and regions," which have "vastly increased over time."[137] The third is aimed at "ensuring proportionality in the commitments undertaken between developed and developing countries, reflecting their different levels of development and gains from the trading system."[138]

B. *Drawbacks of SDT*

Despite these benefits, there are a number of potential difficulties with SDT, and these are particularly relevant to Pacific SIDS such as Tonga, Vanuatu, and Samoa.

Tariff Preferences

One of the major benefits of SDT is the provision of preferential access to developed-country markets, especially with respect to agricultural products, in which many Pacific SIDS specialize. This preferential access is granted via the Enabling Clause,[139] which allows developed-country members to establish a Generalized System of Preferences (GSP), which grants tariff preferences to developing-country members. Most Pacific SIDS – including Tonga, Vanuatu, and Samoa – are beneficiaries of GSP schemes from Australia, New Zealand, the European Community, and United States. However, although tariff preferences may be beneficial to Pacific SIDS in the short term, they have been criticized as temporary, voluntary, and often subject to policy-motivated conditions and costly implementation requirements.[140] The previous director-general's Consultative Board expressed scepticism about the value of preferential market access, observing that the GSP and other schemes have not always been structured for the benefit of recipients. Indeed, donors of preferential treatment have often determined the range of products that reflect the

[136] Philippe Cullet, *Differential Treatment in International Environmental Law* (Aldershot, England: Ashgate, 2003), p. 36.

[137] Ibid., p. 45.

[138] Faizel Ismail, "A Development Perspective on the WTO July 2004 General Council Decision" (2005) 8 *Journal of International Economic Law* 378–379.

[139] *Decision on Differential and More Favourable Treatment, Reciprocity, and Fuller Participation of Developing Countries*, WTO Doc. L/4903, BISD 26S/203 (November 28, 1979; "Enabling Clause"), [2(a)]. The Enabling Clause is part of GATT 1994 by virtue of paragraph (1)(b)(iv) of the introductory wording to GATT 1994, which states that GATT 1994 incorporates "decisions of the CONTRACTING PARTIES to GATT 1947."

[140] Alexander Keck and Patrick Low, "Special and Differential Treatment in the WTO: Why, When and How?" in Simon Evenett and Bernard Hoekman (eds.), *Economic Development and Multilateral Trade Cooperation* (Washington, DC: The World Bank; New York: Palgrave Macmillan, 2006); Bernard Hoekman and Susan Prowse, "Policy Responses to Preference Erosion: From Trade as Aid to Aid for Trade," paper presented at the OECD Global Forum on Trade, *Special and Differential Treatment: Thinking Outside the Box* (Bridgetown, Barbados, June 28–29, 2005), p. 1.

donor's – rather than the recipient's – interests and have imposed conditions and obligations on their receipt.[141] Similarly, donors have imposed increasingly stringent conditions for the receipt of preferential treatment, "requiring the recipient country to change fundamental national policies in order to get the preferences."[142] Preferences may also "retard trade liberalized in beneficiary countries . . . because GSP preferences can reduce the incentive that export industries in developing countries have to lobby for trade liberalization."[143] Studies have concluded that most beneficiaries have not gained much from trade preferences because of "uncertainty/costs created by 'political conditionality,' product exclusions and rules of origin."[144] Finally, according to one school of thought, "effective integration into the global trading system is a major . . . key to accelerating growth and eradicating poverty in developing countries";[145] this suggests that moves to delay full liberalization, and therefore, full integration, may actually postpone development.

Some commentators argue that preferences are important to Pacific SIDS because, given their special vulnerabilities, market access on equal terms is unlikely to be enough to enable them to increase exports. In particular, it has been argued that a quasi-rent, generally in the form of preferences, has been required to cover the inherent cost disadvantage faced by those who invest in SIDS.[146] However, the problems arising from tariff preference schemes appear to outweigh these benefits. Moreover, even if preferences do benefit Pacific SIDS, these preferences are only transitory[147] because GSP donors typically exclude beneficiaries once they reach a certain stage of development.[148] This is particularly relevant to Pacific SIDS, whose preferential access is currently being threatened in two ways. First, through preference erosion, as the value of preferences is gradually being eroded as MFN tariffs decrease as envisaged in the WTO Agreements.[149] Second, it is threatened through

[141] WTO, Consultative Board, *The Future of the WTO: Addressing Institutional Challenges in the New Millennium* (2004), para. 93.

[142] Peter M. Gerhart and Archana Seema Kelia, "Power and Preferences: Developing Countries and the Rule of the WTO Appellate Body" (2005) 30 *North Carolina Journal of International Law and Commercial Regulation* 532–533.

[143] Caglar Özden and Eric Reinhardt, "The Perversity of Preferences: GSP and Developing Country Trade Policies, 1976–2000" (2005) 78 *Journal of Development Economics* 1–2.

[144] See for example, Paul Brenton, "Integrating the LDCs into the World Trading System: The Current Impact of EU Preferences under Everything but Arms" (2003) 37 *Journal of World Trade* 623–646; Bernard Hoekman, "Operationalizing the Concept of Policy Space in the WTO: Beyond Special and Differential Treatment" (2005) 8 *Journal of International Economic Law* 405, 407.

[145] The Warwick Commission, *The Multilateral Trade Regime: Which Way Forward? The Report of the First Warwick Commission* (2007), p. 38, available at: http://www2.warwick.ac.uk/research/warwickcommission/archive/worldtrade/report.

[146] Roman Grynberg, "Introduction," in Roman Grynberg (ed.), *WTO at the Margins: Small States and the Multilateral Trading System* (Cambridge: Cambridge University Press, 2006), p. 1.

[147] Keck and Low (2004), supra note 140, p. 8.

[148] Ibid., p. 12; Gene Grossman and Alan Sykes, "A Preference for Development: The Law and Economics of GSP" (2005) 4 *World Trade Review* 61.

[149] Hoekman and Prowse (2005), supra note 140, pp. 1, 4–11, 25; Frank Garcia, "Beyond Special and Differential Treatment" (2004) 27 *Boston College International & Comparative Law Review* 291, 304.

the elimination of preference arrangements, following challenges within the WTO based on the MFN principle (for example, the *EU-Bananas* dispute and the *EU-Sugar* dispute).[150] This phenomenon will be enhanced now that the Economic Partnership Agreements between the African, Carribean and Pacific (ACP) regions and the EU are starting to conclude.[151] These agreements are a response to the *EU-Bananas* dispute and will result in ostensibly free trade between the ACP states (including Tonga, Vanuatu, and Samoa) and the EU.[152] In response, advocates for Pacific SIDS have argued that preferences should be maintained because, given their small share of world trade, granting them preferences would result in only minimal distortion and little impact on their trading partners.[153] Indeed, the most significant trading issue currently occupying Pacific SIDS is how to deal with the expected end of preferential relationships.[154] As both Fiji and Papua New Guinea have entered into Economic Partnership Agreements,[155] it is likely that this process will accelerate.

Longer Transition Periods

Another drawback of SDT arises from extended transition periods for implementation of WTO rules by developing countries. Although these are generally seen as "less problematic" and as "mak[ing] eminent sense,"[156] it has been noted that the longer the time taken for implementation, the longer the time to realize the gains from trade[157] and the benefits of the principle of reciprocity, which is the "engine of the WTO."[158] Indeed, it has been argued that nonreciprocity is the "reason why tariff peaks today are largely on goods produced in developing countries."[159] Longer transition periods have also been criticized as "an inadequate response," because they are "arbitrary and not accompanied by or based on an objective assessment

[150] Roman Grynberg and Jan Yves Remy, "Small Vulnerable Economy Issues and the WTO," in Roman Grynberg (ed.), *WTO at the Margins: Small States and the Multilateral Trading System* (Cambridge: Cambridge University Press, 2006), pp. 281, 284.

[151] On November 29, 2007, Fiji and Papua New Guinea entered into Interim Economic Partnership Agreements with the European Union, effective January 1, 2008. European Commission, *Update: Interim Economic Partnership Agreements*, available at: http://trade.ec.europa.eu/doclib/docs/2007/november/tradoc_136959.pdf. Both countries have been criticized for breaking Pacific solidarity by signing the agreements, because other Pacific states had hoped to negotiate as a regional bloc. Because these two countries represent the largest economies in the region, it is expected that other Pacific states will be in a less favorable bargaining position when negotiating their own agreements. "PNG Defends Signing of Economic Partnership Agreement," *Pacific Magazine*, April 30, 2008.

[152] Grynberg, supra note 146, p. 6.

[153] Tigerstrom, supra note 18, p. 402.

[154] Andrew L. Stoler, "Fiji: Preparing for the End of Preferences?" in Peter Gallagher, Patrick Low, and Andrew L. Stoler, *Managing the Challenges of WTO Participation: 45 Case Studies* (Cambridge: Cambridge University Press, 2005), p. 189.

[155] European Commission, supra note 151.

[156] WTO Consultative Board, supra note 141, para. 102.

[157] Ibid., para. 287.

[158] Hoekman, supra note 144, p. 409.

[159] Ibid.

of whether (and when) implementation of a specific set of (proposed) rules will be beneficial to a country."[160] Moreover, many developing countries "now view the transition periods as unrealistic and not commensurate with the concurrent need for capacity building to implement the agreements."[161] Indeed, most of the implementation periods provided in the Uruguay Round agreements have expired, yet many developing countries have still not been able to integrate the requirements of those agreements into their domestic laws.[162] In this regard, there are possibilities in the "GATS scheduling" approach, through which certain commitments can be "made in a manner and at speed which squares with development and other national policy priorities."[163]

The issue of transition periods arose in respect of each of Tonga's, Vanuatu's, and Samoa's accession negotiations. Most important, WTO members argued that, because these countries were not members, they could not utilize SDT provisions. This meant that they could not take full advantage of transition periods for the TRIPS Agreement or customs valuation.[164] Indeed, it has been noted that the decision on the accession of LDCs adopted by the WTO General Council on December 10, 2002, was "partly a response to Vanuatu's predicament both as a capacity-constrained country experiencing difficulties in negotiations and in its inability to take advantage of" SDT.[165]

Technical Assistance

A third drawback of SDT arises from the provision of "technical assistance" to developing-country members by the WTO Secretariat, developed-country members, and other organizations. This assistance is typically conducted through seminars and workshops on WTO law and practice, held in Geneva or locally.[166] Despite the fact that it appears straightforward, this assistance has given rise to numerous problems. Although many developing countries have significant technical assistance needs, developed countries may only be prepared to provide assistance on an ad hoc basis and without accepting legal obligations to contribute specified amounts. In addition, developed countries may tend to construct technical assistance programs that pursue their own interests, such as "Singapore issues" and geographic indications, regardless of the direction of the negotiations.[167] Some commentators also emphasize that technical assistance should cover more than just the narrow WTO rules and needs

[160] Ibid., p. 406.

[161] Lichetenbaum (2002), supra note 133, p. 1019.

[162] Ibid.

[163] WTO, Consultative Board, supra note 141, para. 301.

[164] Gay, supra note 55, p. 601.

[165] Ibid., p. 602.

[166] WTO, *General WTO-related Technical Assistance and Training*, available at: http://www.wto.org/english/tratop_e/devel_e/train_e/general_courses_e.htm.

[167] Olivier Cattaneo, "Has the WTO Gone Too Far or Not Far Enough? Some Reflections on the Concept of 'Policy Space,'" in Andrew Mitchell (ed.), *Challenges and Prospects for the WTO* (London:

to extend to matters such as technology transfer, adjustment assistance, and capacity building.[168] Donors have also failed to coordinate adequately, leading to duplication and inefficiencies in the delivery of technical assistance.[169]

The question of whether technical assistance and capacity building serve developing countries' interests is particularly relevant following the expiration of transition periods for developing countries' implementation of obligations under the 1995 Uruguay Round agreements. This is because when the transition periods were drawing to an end, "many developing countries balked at implementing WTO requirements on account of the costs of doing so, and the perception that they had not benefited from market access as promised."[170] A number of economists and development specialists have criticized the expanded scope of the WTO rules beyond GATT 1947, arguing that "WTO regulations reflect little awareness of development problems and little appreciation of the capacities of least developed countries to carry out the functions."[171] Members committed to address these issues as part of the Doha Development Round, with the Doha Declaration incorporating four paragraphs on technical assistance, one paragraph on trade and technology transfer, two paragraphs on LDCs, and other references throughout the document.[172] It remains to be seen whether these declarations are appropriately tailored toward serving developing-country interests, because many promises of technical assistance were in exchange for developing countries agreeing to negotiate over the "Singapore Issues."[173] Although problems with technical assistance inspired the announcement of a "new strategy" in 2001, which outlines region- and issue-specific strategies for the coordination of assistance aimed at mainstreaming trade-related reforms into national policy,[174] this strategy has been criticized for "continu[ing] to focus on the

Cameron May, 2005), pp. 82–83. See also Mari Pangesu, "Special and Differential Treatment in the Millennium: Special for Whom and How Different?" (2000) *The World Economy* 1285, 1298.

168 Bernard Hoekman, Constantine Michalopoulos, and Alan Winters, "Special and Differential Treatment of Developing Countries in the WTO: Moving Forward after Cancun" (2004) *World Economy* 501–502.

169 Frabizio Zarcone, Carsten Fink, and Carlos A. Primo Braga, "Technical Assistance and WTO Accessions: Lessons from Experience," Draft manuscript prepared after a Joint World Bank-GTZ workshop on WTO accession matters (Berlin, November 17–19, 2004)., pp. 30–31.

170 Gregory Shaffer, "Can WTO Technical Assistance and Capacity-Building Serve Developing Countries?" (2005) 23 *Wisconsin International Law Journal* 645.

171 J. Michael Finger and Philip Schuler, "Implementation of Uruguay Round Commitments: The Development Challenge" (2000) 23 *The World Economy* 511.

172 Paragraphs 38–41 of the Doha Ministerial Declaration address overall technical assistance and capacity building. Paragraphs 42–43 focus on assistance to LDCs. Paragraphs 2, 20–21, 23–24, 26–27, 33, 42–43 address assistance in respect of trade and investment, trade and competition policy, transparency in government procurement, trade facilitation, and trade and environment. Specific technical assistance provisions are also included in paragraphs 2.2, 3.5, 3.6, 5.1 and 14 of the *WTO Ministerial Decision on Implementation-Related Issues and Concerns*, WTO Doc. WT/MIN(01)/17 (14 November 2001).

173 Shaffer (2005), supra note 170, p. 647.

174 WTO, *A New Strategy For WTO Technical Cooperation: Technical Cooperation for Capacity Building, Growth and Integration*, Note by the Secretariat, WTO Committee on Trade and Development, WTO Doc. WT/COMTD/W/90 (21 September 2001).

more limited objectives of trade liberalization and rule implementation."[175] Despite this criticism, since the launch of the Doha Round, donors have provided a greater amount of funding for trade-related technical assistance and the WTO Secretariat has also improved its delivery.[176]

The utility of technical assistance is particularly relevant to Pacific SIDS such as Tonga, Vanuatu, and Samoa, which are largely unprepared to implement obligations under the WTO agreements and underresourced to engage in negotiations in the WTO. Therefore, it is vitally important to Tonga, Vanuatu, Samoa, and other Pacific SIDS that the criticisms of the current technical assistance regime are addressed. Although the WTO has assisted in the establishment of a shared representative office for Pacific SIDS in Geneva to represent the member nations of the Pacific Islands Forum,[177] more assistance will be required to help Pacific SIDS comply with their WTO obligations.

Categorization of "Developing Countries" and "LDCs"

A final drawback of SDT is that it does not provide a clear and defensible means to distinguish between developing countries at different levels of development.[178] The WTO agreements recognize three main categories of WTO members: developed countries, developing countries, and LDCs.[179] LDCs form a subcategory of developing countries and are identified by the UN according to a low-income criterion, a human resource weakness criterion, and an economic vulnerability criterion.[180] At present, 49 LDCs exist, most of which are WTO members or in the process of WTO accession.[181] Other non-LDC WTO members that wish to take advantage of special WTO provisions for developing countries are left to identify themselves as such, subject to challenge by other members. This means not only that there are no clear criteria for establishing developing-country status but also that the development status of members lacks transparency. The WTO Secretariat has described the membership as comprising two-thirds developing countries (when there were

[175] Shaffer (2005), supra note 170, p. 661.

[176] Ibid., p. 678.

[177] Bowman (2005), supra note 71, p. 450.

[178] On distinguishing between developing countries to determine eligibility for SDT, see Peter Kleen and Sheila Page, *Special and Differential Treatment of Developing Countries in the World Trade Organization*, Report – Swedish Ministry for Foreign Affairs Global Development Studies 2 (February 2005), pp. 79–95.

[179] A fourth category could be described as economies in transition. See, for example, *General Agreement on Trade in Services*, WTO Doc. LT/UR/A-1B/S/1 (April 15, 1994), Art XII:1; TRIPS Agreement, Art 65.3; *Agreement on Subsidies and Countervailing Measures*, supra note 28, Art 29.

[180] UN, Economic and Social Council, Committee for Development Policy, *Report on the Sixth Session*, E/2004/33 (March 29–April 2, 2004), para. 15.

[181] WTO, *Least-developed Countries*, available at: http://www.wto.org/English/thewto_e/whatis_e/tif_e/org7_e.htm.

146 members),[182] but it does not publish a list identifying those members. In any case, these developing countries represent an extremely wide spectrum of economies and interests, ranging from those of SIDS such as Tonga, Vanuatu, and Samoa, to those of much larger countries such as Brazil, China, and the Ukraine.[183]

Therefore, although more extensive SDT is available to LDCs, several Pacific SIDS (including Tonga) are classified as developing countries and are not able to fully utilize SDT provisions. In addition, those Pacific SIDS that are classified as LDCs (Vanuatu, Samoa, Papua New Guinea, and the Solomon Islands) face the problem of graduation from LDC status, which could lead to the erosion of market access preferences.[184] Indeed, Samoa was scheduled to graduate from LDC status by the end of 2010, which emerged as a factor driving its accession process.[185] However, in October 2010 Samoa's graduation was delayed until 1 January 2014, in recognition of the disruption caused by the Pacific Ocean tsunami of 29 September 2009.[186] Furthermore, both Tonga and Fiji face the prospect of graduating from developing to developed-country status, which would deprive them of access to SDT entirely. This is despite the fact that the Pacific SIDS face challenges that limit their ability to participate in the international trading system, which has motivated calls for the recognition of SIDS as specific subcategory of WTO members.[187] Indeed, submissions under the Work Programme on Small Economies include suggested criteria for identifying small economies[188] and a proposal that small economies be granted duty- and quota-free access to the markets of developed-country members.[189] In addition to the separate work on "small economies," several groups of developing countries have also sought recognition for the special difficulties they face. This has

[182] WTO, *Understanding the WTO* (3rd ed., 2003), p. 93. Currently, 153 countries (incorporating Tonga) are WTO members. WTO, supra note 83.

[183] Jean-Christophe Bureau, Sébastien Jean, and Alan Matthews, "The Consequences of Agricultural Trade Liberalization for Developing Countries: Distinguishing between Genuine Benefits and False Hopes" (Institute for International Integration Studies, Discussion Paper No. 73, April 2005), p. 14; The Warwick Commission (2007), supra note 145, p. 40.

[184] Mauritius, supra note 10, p. 7; Athukorala, supra note 63, p. 1417.

[185] UN Economic and Social Council, Committee for Development Policy, *Report on the Eighth Session*, UN Doc. E/2007/L.35 (July 2–27, 2007); UN General Assembly Resolutions 59/209, UN Doc. A/RES/59/209 (December 20, 2004) and 62/97, UN Doc. A/RES/62/97 (December 17, 2007); WTO, supra note 127.

[186] General Assembly Resolution 64/295, UN Doc. A/RES/64/295 (13 October 2010).

[187] Grynberg, supra note 131, p. 19.

[188] WTO, Committee on Trade and Development, *Work Programme on Small Economies: Communication from Antigua and Barbuda, Barbados, Bolivia, Cuba, Dominican Republic, El Salvador, Fiji, Guatemala, Honduras, Jamaica, Mauritius, Mongolia, Nicaragua, Paraguay, Sri Lanka, Trinidad and Tobago*, WTO Doc. WT/COMTD/SE/W/12 (February 21, 2005), p. 2.

[189] WTO, Committee on Trade and Development, *Proposals Submitted by the Landlocked Developing Countries: Work Programme on Small Economies*, WTO Doc. WT/COMTD/SE/W/10 (April 27, 2004), p. 2.

included not only SIDS[190] but also "landlocked developing countries,"[191] "newly acceded members,"[192] or "net food-importing developing countries."[193] The latter two of which would also include Pacific SIDS.

Although the Doha Round Work Programme did recognize the concerns of SIDS, with paragraph 35 resolving to establish a specific programme to "frame responses to the trade-related issues identified for the fuller integration of small, vulnerable economies into the multilateral trading system,"[194] it did not go so far as to advocate the recognition of SIDS as a new category of WTO member. Indeed, the Work Programme on Small Economies is intended to promote the "fuller integration of small, vulnerable economies into the multilateral trading system, and not to create a sub-category of WTO Members."[195] Thus, it explicitly states that it does not intend to introduce a new category of SIDS in addition to the recognized categories or to address the issue of graduation. Despite this, there are precedents for the recognition of subcategorization of WTO members, including small economies, which may lend support for the recognition of a category of SIDS.[196]

An alternative to recognizing SIDS as a discrete category of WTO members is to link SDT more closely to the needs of individual countries.[197] This would not necessarily require creating new categories of WTO members or classifying each member in one particular way for the purposes of the WTO agreements as a whole, because this may disadvantage certain developing countries that do not fit into

190 WTO, Committee on Agriculture, *WTO Negotiations on Agriculture: Proposals by Small Island Developing States (SIDS)*, G/AG/NG/W/97 and Corr.1 (December 29, 2000); WTO, Committee on Agriculture, *WTO Negotiations on Agriculture: Proposals by Small Island Developing States (SIDS)*, G/AG/NG/W/97/Corr.1 (February 14, 2001).

191 Committee on Trade and Development, *Communiqué of the Fifth Annual Ministerial Meeting of Landlocked Developing Countries (LLDCs)*, WTO Doc. WT/L/585, WT/COMTD/SE/2 (October 7, 2004); WTO, Committee on Trade and Development, supra note 187.

192 WTO, Negotiating Group on Market Access, *Market Access for Non-Agricultural Products – The Issue of Newly-Acceded Members: Submission by the Separate Customs Territory of Taiwan, Penghu, Kinmen and Matsu*, WTO Doc. TN/MA/W/19/Add.1 (16 May 2003); WTO, General Council, *Doha Work Programme*, Annex A, para. 47, Annex B, para. 11, WTO Doc. WT/L/579 (August 2, 2004; hereinafter Doha Work Programme.

193 WTO, Ministerial Conference, *Decision on Measures Concerning the Possible Negative Effects of the Reform Programme on Least-Developed and Net Food-Importing Developing Countries*, WTO Doc. LT/UR/D-1/2 (March 15, 1994); WTO, Committee on Agriculture, *WTO African Group: Joint Proposal on the Negotiations on Agriculture*, WTO Doc. G/AG/NG/W/142 (March 23, 2001), pp. 7, 19–20.

194 Doha Declaration, supra note 2, p. 53.

195 Ibid.; Doha Work Programme, supra note 191, [1(d)].

196 Examples include the Agreement on Agriculture provisions for net food-importing countries; the *de minimus* provisions in the Agreement on Subsidies and Countervailing Measures, the Agreement on Implementation of Article VI of GATT 1994, the Agreement on Safeguards, and the Agreement on Textiles and Clothing; and the rules stipulating that the minimum contributions by members will be less than 0.015% of world trade, set out in the rules setting contributions to the WTO budget. Roman Grynberg and Jan Yves Remy, "Small Vulnerable Economy Issues and the WTO," in Grynberg and Remy, supra note 150, p. 285.

197 Hoekman (2005), supra note 144, pp. 413, 415.

such groups. Moreover, choosing a single classification may also be too arbitrary, excluding some countries that deserve to be included and including some that should be excluded.[198] Instead, there are proposals that classification according to specific criteria might better operate at the level of individual WTO agreements or even at the level of specific provisions, such that the criteria chosen reflect the development implications of each provision.[199] This may be useful to Pacific SIDS, which could seek SDT in respect of those specific WTO agreements that disadvantage them but that would otherwise fully accept the application of the other agreements.

This raises the broader issue of who should determine the criteria for distinguishing developing countries. Ideally, members would carry out this task,[200] although this has not yet occurred. In the context of tariff preferences, where there is no agreement, it is left to developed-country GSP donors to determine whom to be included as beneficiaries and on what grounds. Although this may be better than having WTO tribunals establish the criteria, it presents "the danger of a return to the pre-UNCTAD days of widespread discrimination"[201] and therefore a further incursion into the general principle of nondiscrimination. Of concern is the fact that the Appellate Body endorsed this situation in *EC-Tariff Preferences*,[202] holding that "preference-granting countries must make available identical tariff preferences to all *similarly-situated beneficiaries*,"[203] and that additional preferences may be granted to respond positively to a particular "development, financial [or] trade need," provided that they are made available to all beneficiaries that share that need.[204] In the *EC-Tariff Preferences* decision, the Appellate Body established two principles: first, that footnote 3 of the Enabling Clause is a binding legal obligation, requiring "generalized, non-reciprocal and non-discriminatory preferences"[205] and second, donor countries may nevertheless afford differential treatment to beneficiary nations based on differences in their "development, financial and trade needs."[206] A number of problems with these principles have been identified. Primarily, the question of

[198] Keck and Low (2004), supra note 140, p. 27.

[199] Hoekman, supra note 144, p. 413; Keck and Low, supra note 140, pp. 9–10; Bernard Hoekman and Carlos Braga, "Special and Differential Treatment and the Doha Development Agenda: Beyond Tariff Preferences," paper presented at the OECD Global Forum on Trade, *Special and Differential Treatment: Thinking Outside the Box* (Bridgetown, Barbados, June 28–29, 2005), p. 13; Thomas Cottier, *From Progressive Liberalisation to Progressive Regulation in WTO Law*, National Center for Competence in Research Working Paper IP 3 (March 2006), p. 14.

[200] Keck and Low (2004), supra note 140, p. 30.

[201] Grossman and Sykes (2005), supra note 148, p. 66.

[202] WTO, Appellate Body Report, *European Communities – Conditions for the Granting of Tariff Preferences to Developing Countries*, WT/DS246/AB/R (April 7, 2004).

[203] Ibid., p. 154 (emphasis added).

[204] Ibid., p. 165.

[205] Ibid., pp. 143–147.

[206] Ibid., pp. 159–162.

"what counts as a development, financial or trade need" arises.[207] In addition, there is the issue of whether a "constraint must exist on the *magnitude* of the differential treatment that is permissible to address heterogeneous development, financial, and trade needs."[208] The question of whether "donor countries have unfettered discretion to select the "needs" that they will address through differential treatment and to ignore others" also arises.[209] This has led to the conclusion that the decision "puts into question many prominent features of the US, European and other GSP schemes."[210] Again, this issue is of particular concern to Pacific SIDS, most of which are major beneficiaries of such GSP schemes.

C. *Conclusion*

There are a number of potential difficulties with SDT that affect Pacific SIDS, including Tonga, Vanuatu, and Samoa. These difficulties arise from the uncertainties and inconsistencies of tariff preference schemes, the distorting effect of long transition periods to implement WTO rules, the ineffectiveness of much technical assistance provided to developing-country members, and the WTO's failure to categorize – let alone recognize – SIDS as a group of members that experience specific challenges that should entitle them to SDT. These difficulties are particularly relevant to Pacific SIDS, most of which derive the biggest share of their government revenue from import duties[211] and the biggest share of their export revenue from agricultural products and services.[212] Therefore, participation in the international trading regime is critical to their future development and economic stability.

V. REVISITING MEMBERSHIP AND THE SINGLE UNDERTAKING

A. *WTO-Lite – Differentiated Undertakings*

One of the major achievements of the Uruguay Round was the extent to which the rules governing international trade were multilateralized. All WTO members are required to join all the agreements administered by it, except for the two plurilateral agreements.[213] This concept of the single undertaking remains important

[207] Grossman and Sykes (2005), supra note 148, p. 55.
[208] Ibid., p. 56.
[209] Ibid.
[210] Ibid., p. 57.
[211] Gay (2005), supra note 55, p. 590.
[212] New Zealand House of Representatives, supra note 23, p. 13.
[213] *Agreement on Trade in Civil Aircraft*, WTO Doc. LT/UR/A-4/PLURI/1 (April 15, 1994); and *Agreement on Government Procurement*, supra note 50.

in the current round, because the Doha Ministerial Declaration states that "the conduct, conclusion and entry into force of the outcome of the negotiations shall be treated as part of a single undertaking."[214] The concept of the single undertaking has advantages including constraining the ability of members to "free ride" on the liberalization of others, and permitting trade-offs across issues that seem otherwise unrelated.[215] However, is it time to revisit this concept? We think it might be.

The current Geneva jargon is of "variable geometry,"[216] a term borrowed from the EU. In the European context, the term is used to describe "the idea of a method of differentiated integration that acknowledges that there are irreconcilable differences within the integration structure and therefore allows for a permanent separation between a group of Member States and a number of less developed integration units."[217] If this term were applied to the WTO, it would mean that new disciplines could be plurilateral, whereby the WTO could serve as "an umbrella institution for agreements, not all of which would be binding on the whole membership."[218] Peter Gallagher and Andrew Stoler similarly propose that agreements could be applied in different ways to different product groups and countries, as determined by the agreement of a "critical mass" of members.[219]

Yet these proposals would pose the same difficulties outlined earlier with respect to identifying developing countries for the purposes of SDT. In addition, they raise the question of which commitments would be covered by these plurilateral agreements. Most members would agree that core issues such as tariff bindings, market access, and nondiscrimination commitments must remain multilateral commitments.[220] Yet the range of views concerning which commitments should become plurilateral is likely to be vast and controversial. A concept of associated membership could also be introduced, in which certain members opt out of full membership and only participate in certain key disciplines. However, we think it is unlikely that this kind of proposal would be accepted. It raises difficult questions about existing members' obligations, graduation (or the movement out of this particular category)

[214] Doha Declaration, supra note 2.

[215] Philip Levy, "Do We Need an Undertaker for the Single Undertaking? Considering the Angles of Variable Geometry," in Simon J. Evenett and Bernard M. Hoekman (eds.), *Economic Development and Multilateral Trade Cooperation* (Washington, DC: World Bank, 2006), pp. 417–418.

[216] The Warwick Commission, supra note 145, p. 30.

[217] Europa Glossary, *Variable Geometry*, available at: http://europa.eu/scadplus/glossary/variable_geometry_europe_en.htm.

[218] Andrew Cornford, *Variable Geometry for the WTO: Concept and Precedents*, United Nations Conference on Trade and Development Discussion Paper No. 171, UNCTAD/OSG/DP/2004/5 (May 2004), p. 8.

[219] Peter Gallagher and Andrew Stoler, "Critical Mass as an Alternative Framework for Multilateral Trade Negotiations" (2009) 15 *Global Governance* 375.

[220] Cornford (2004), supra note 217, p. 8.

and whether it would entrench existing disadvantages faced by these members by taking them out of negotiations.

At the same time, the fact that these proposals would pose difficulties does not necessarily mean that they should be immediately dismissed. Several WTO rules, such as those relating to antidumping,[221] do not make general economic sense, but they are tolerated by the WTO membership as a temporary trade-off to achieve broader trade liberalization. Using the same logic, proposals relating to a plurilateral approach to certain disciplines or a form associated membership could be adopted as a similar short-term trade-off to ensure that developing countries accede to the WTO on terms that they can reasonably be expected to meet.

B. *Accessions Disciplines*

According to Constantine Michalopolous:

> While the insistence of WTO members on a liberal commercial policy at entry is likely to serve both acceding countries long term development interests as well as WTO members' commercial objectives, insistence on adherence to all the WTO commitments at entry and without transition periods in areas such as customs valuation, TRIPS, TBT and SPS where there are obvious institutional weakness in LDCs and transition economies raises serious problems: acceding countries, because of their strong desire for membership, may agree to obligations which they cannot implement, leaving them open to subsequent complaints. Alternatively providing generous transition periods, while transition periods for other countries which are already WTO Members may have expired, would create inequities between existing and new members. The solution to this problem may be the substantial extension of some of these periods for both existing WTO low income members and for acceding LDCs and transition economies, as these transition periods were set arbitrarily in the first place.[222]

Acceding members should also not be required to accept any obligations above general WTO disciplines. For example, acceding countries should not be required to provide higher intellectual property protection than that provided by the TRIPS Agreement or sign on to any plurilateral agreement.

Thus, it seems clear that a "set of basic rules and disciplines would help overcome capacity limitations. These rules could – at least – lay down fixed transition periods for adoption of the TRIPS, Customs Valuation and SPS Agreements; suggest

[221] See, for example, Michael Finger, Francis Ng, and Sonam Wangchuk, *Antidumping as Safeguard Policy*, World Bank Policy Research Working Paper 2730 (2001); Alan Sykes, "Comparative Advantage and the Normative Economics of International Trade Policy" (1998) 1 *Journal of International Economic Law* 80–1.

[222] Michalopoulos (2002), supra note 90, p. 61.

guidelines on import tariff reduction commitments; and put in place maximum required service-sector commitments."[223]

C. *Operationalizing SDT*

Proposals to introduce discipline into the accession procedure are connected to the idea of "operationalizing" SDT, whereby SDT would be made a formal, enforceable part of the WTO system.

This proposal is controversial, and Michael Finger argues that SDT cannot be operationalized.[224] There are also disagreements over how operationalization would occur. Bernard Hoekman has proposed that when the policy measures of developing countries are alleged to be contrary to WTO rules, an independent body could be created to mediate their rationale and development impact.[225] However, this proposal risks "hollowing out" the WTO's dispute settlement procedures (which Hoekman acknowledges)[226] and elevating economic analysis above WTO law. Similarly, Joel Trachtman has proposed that an independent body could assess whether a developing country's measures satisfied "a simple blanket exception." If they did, that member would not be "required to fulfil any commitment that is detrimental to their development or poverty alleviation."[227] However, this proposal raises the same questions as those posed by Hoekman's proposal, with the additional complication that it could significantly impact SDT, either by expanding it to all WTO commitments or by limiting it to only those measures that could be justified on the basis of "sound" economic policy. With these limitations in mind, Andrew Mitchell and Tania Voon favor "merg[ing] economics and law so that the economic criteria are agreed by the Members and written into the WTO rules."[228] This is similar to a proposal, made by Alexander Keck and Patrick Low, that members analyze individual agreements, provisions and countries according to measurable economic criteria.[229] This approach would ensure that the criteria applied to each specific provision are

[223] Gay (2005), supra note 55, pp. 602–603.

[224] Michael Finger, "Developing Countries in the WTO System: Extending Robert Hudec's Historical Analysis to the Doha Round," paper presented at the Cordell Hull Institute Trade Policy Roundtable: Lessons of the Doha Round for Developing Countries (Washington, DC, October 1, 2007), pp. 6, 11, 13.

[225] Hoekman (2005), supra note 144, pp. 416–7, 422.

[226] Ibid., p. 417.

[227] Joel Trachtman, "Ensuring a Development-friendly WTO" (2008) 12 *Bridges Monthly Review* 18.

[228] Andrew Mitchell and Tania Voon, "Operationalizing Special and Differential Treatment in the World Trade Organization: Game Over?" (2009) 15 *Global Governance* 343.

[229] Alexander Keck and Patrick Low, "Special and Differential Treatment in the WTO: Why, When, and How?" in Simon Evenett and Bernard Hoekman (eds.), *Economic Development and Multilateral Trade Cooperation* (2006), pp. 147, 175–176, 178–179, 182.

linked to the rationale for SDT and prevent involving an "independent body" in the process.[230]

D. *Linking Undertakings to Technical Assistance*

Another proposal is to require developing and least developed countries to implement obligations only after they have received the technical assistance to do so. For example, the July 2004 Framework Agreement[231] created such a link in relation to future trade facilitation obligations.[232] This could be expanded to encompass other new obligations or even certain existing obligations. Of course, this raises the difficult questions of the mechanism through which developing countries could seek and receive technical assistance and when they would be considered to have received sufficient assistance for their obligations to become operative. One option has been put forward by a number of developed and developing countries[233] in the context of trade facilitation. The paper proposed that, upon entry into force of the agreement, developing countries would ensure that any measures they already had in place would conform with the agreement and implement any minimal "core" disciplines that might arise from the agreement. For other obligations, in which capacity self-assessment has identified that they require additional time or technical assistance, they would notify the WTO. For measures that would be impossible to implement without technical assistance, the paper suggests having developing countries "formulate a capacity-building plan in cooperation with donors and international organizations, and notify it along with specific implementation periods."

VI. CONCLUSION

Although economic characteristics of SIDS are unique, the experiences of Tonga, Vanuatu, and Samoa in their negotiations to join the WTO reflect broader problems of the organization's treatment of developing countries. The WTO is a rules-based organization, but in relation to accessions, it has no rules. The WTO aspires to assist developing countries, but one of the key vehicles to achieve this, SDT, is ineffective.

[230] Mitchell and Voon (2009), supra note 227, p. 350.

[231] Doha Work Programme, supra note 191, [1d].

[232] Trade facilitation is one of the so-called Singapore issues. Walter Goode, *Dictionary of Trade Policy Terms* (5th ed., 2007), p. 387. "Members are specifically mandated to clarify three articles of the GATT 1994: freedom of transit from other Member states (Article V), trade-related fees and formalities (Article VIII), and transparency in the regulation and administration of trade regulations (Article X)." International Center for Trade and Sustainable Development, "Members Table Draft Articles for Future Agreement on Trade Facilitation," *Bridges Weekly Trade News Digest* (June 14, 2006), available at: http://ictsd.net/i/news/bridgesweekly/6329.

[233] International Center for Trade and Sustainable Development, supra note 231. Non-paper prepared by Canada, Chile, China, the EU, Guatemala, Honduras, Japan, Mexico, Pakistan, Paraguay, Sri Lanka, and Uruguay.

We consider that the accession of countries such as Tonga, Vanuatu, and Samoa to the WTO would largely represent a positive development. Nevertheless, we believe the accessions process should be reformed to better meet the development needs of developing countries and that these reforms should be combined with reforms to SDT. The great need for these reforms is demonstrated by the unprecedented choice of Tonga and Vanuatu to suspend their WTO accession processes.

Reform of the accession process is not only in the interests of those parties seeking to accede; "the ultimate test of the fairness and adequacy of the terms of accession is the capacity of acceding countries to fully implement their commitments."[234] If Tonga – and Vanuatu and Samoa if they finalize their accession – finds that its commitments under the WTO agreements were unrealistic and that it is unable to meet them, "the credibility of the system is then at risk."[235] If new members are unable to fully implement their WTO commitments, then confidence in the enforceability of the WTO agreements could be undermined, and older members may also be encouraged to step away from fully implementing their commitments or to seek alternative bilateral or regional trade forums.

REFERENCES

Armstrong, Harvey W., and Robert Read, "Trade and Growth in Small States: The Impact of Global Trade Liberalization" (1998) 21 *The World Economy*.

Asian Development Bank, *ADB's Pacific Approach 2010–2014* (2009), available at: http://www.adb.org/Documents/Books/ADB-Pacific-Approach-2010–2014/ADB-Pacific-Approach-2010–2014.pdf.

Athukorala, Prema-chandram, "Trade Policy in a Small Island Economy: The WTO Review of the Maldives" (2004) 27 *The World Economy*.

AusAID, *Pacific Regional Aid Strategy 2004–2009* (2004), available at: http://www.ausaid.gov.au/publications/pubout.cfm?Id=7085_5949_6483_1791_1576.

______, Department of Foreign Affairs and Trade, *Country Fact Sheet: Samoa*, available at: http://www.dfat.gov.au/geo/fs/samo.pdf.

______, Department of Foreign Affairs and Trade, *Country Fact Sheet: Tonga*, available at: http://www.dfat.gov.au/geo/fs/tnga.pdf.

______, Department of Foreign Affairs and Trade, *Country Fact Sheet: Vanuatu*, available at: http://www.dfat.gov.au/geo/fs/vanu.pdf.

______, Department of Foreign Affairs and Trade, *Samoa Country Brief*, available at: http://www.dfat.gov.au/GEO/samoa/samoa_brief.html.

______, Department of Foreign Affairs and Trade, *Vanuatu Country Brief*, available at: http://www.dfat.gov.au/geo/vanuatu/vanuatu_brief.html.

Bossche, Peter Van Den, *The Law and Policy of the World Trade Organization* (2nd ed., Cambridge: Cambridge University Press: 2008).

Bowman, Chakriya, "The Pacific Island Nations: Towards Shared Representation," in Peter Gallagher, Patrick Low, and Andrew L. Stoler, *Managing the Challenges of WTO Participation: 45 Case Studies* (Cambridge: Cambridge University Press, 2005).

[234] Braga and Cattaneo (2009), supra note 26, p. xliii.
[235] Ibid.

Braga, Carlos Primo, and Olivier Cattaneo, "Introduction," in Carlos Primo Braga and Olivier Cattaneo (eds.), *WTO and Accession Countries* (Cheltenham: Edward Elgar Publishing, 2009).

Brenton, Paul, "Integrating the LDCs into the World Trading System: The Current Impact of EU Preferences under Everything but Arms" (2003) 37 *Journal of World Trade*.

Bureau, Jean-Christophe, Sébastien Jean, and Alan Matthews, "The Consequences of Agricultural Trade Liberalization for Developing Countries: Distinguishing Between Genuine Benefits and False Hopes" (Institute for International Integration Studies, Discussion Paper No. 73, April 2005).

Cattaneo, Olivier, "Has the WTO Gone Too Far or Not Far Enough? Some Reflections on the Concept of 'Policy Space,'" in Andrew Mitchell (ed.), *Challenges and Prospects for the WTO* (London: Cameron May, 2005).

Chea, Samnag, and Hach Sok, "Cambodia's Access to WTO: 'Fast-Tracked' Accession by a Least-Developed Country," in Peter Gallagher, Patrick Low, and Andrew L. Stoler (eds.), *Managing the Challenges of WTO Participation: 45 Case Studies* (Cambridge: Cambridge University Press, 2005).

Commonwealth Secretariat, *Progress in the Implementation of the Recommendations of the Commonwealth Secretariat/World Bank Joint Task Force Report: Small States: Meeting the Challenges in the Global Economy* (August 2002), available at: http://www.thecommonwealth.org/Shared_ASP_Files/UploadedFiles/6157EAA5–9071-4993-A413-EE6BE4152E9D_FMM2003-Small-States-Paper.pdf.

Commonwealth Secretariat/World Bank Joint Task Force on Small States, *Small States: Meeting Challenges in the Global Economy* (April 2000), available at: http://siteresources.worldbank.org/PROJECTS/Resources/meetingchallengeinglobaleconomyl.pdf.

Cornford, Andrew, *Variable Geometry for the WTO: Concept and Precedents*, United Nations Conference on Trade and Development Discussion Paper No. 171, UNCTAD/OSG/DP/2004/5 (May 2004).

Cottier, Thomas, *From Progressive Liberalization to Progressive Regulation in WTO Law*, National Center of Competence in Research Working Paper IP 3 (March 2006).

Cullet, Philippe, *Differential Treatment in International Environmental Law* (Aldershot, England: Ashgate, 2003)

Davis, Christina L., "Do WTO Rules Create a Level Playing Field? Lessons from the Experience of Peru and Vietnam," in John S. Odell (ed.), *Negotiating Trade: Developing Countries in the WTO and NAFTA* (New York: Cambridge University Press, 2006).

Drabek, Zdenek, and Marc Bacchetta, "Trading the Effects of WTO Accession on Policy-making in Sovereign States: Preliminary Lessons from the Recent Experiences of Transition Countries" (2004) 27 *The World Economy*.

Europa Glossary, *Variable Geometry*, available at: http://europa.eu/scadplus/glossary/variable_geometry_europe_en.htm.

European Commission, *Update: Interim Economic Partnership Agreements*, available at: http://trade.ec.europa.eu/doclib/docs/2007/november/tradoc_136959.pdf.

Evenett, Simon J., Jonathan Gage, and Maxine Kennett, *WTO Membership and Market Access: Evidence from the Accessions of Bulgaria and Ecuador*, Universitat St. Gallen Working Paper (2004), available at: http://www.alexandria.unisg.ch/Publikationen/22175.

Finger, Michael, "Developing Countries in the WTO System: Extending Robert Hudec's Historical Analysis to the Doha Round," paper presented at the Cordell Hull Institute Trade Policy Roundtable: Lessons of the Doha Round for Developing Countries, Washington, DC, October 1, 2007.

Finger, Michael, Francis Ng, and Sonam Wangchuk, *Antidumping as Safeguard Policy*, World Bank Policy Research Working Paper 2730 (2001).

Finger, J. Michael, and Philip Schuler, "Implementation of Uruguay Round Commitments: The Development Challenge" (2000) 23 *The World Economy*.

Francis, Joseph, "External Bindings and the Credibility of Reform," in Ahmed Galal and Bernard Hoekman (eds.), *Regional Partners in Global Markets: Limits and Possibilities of the Euro-Med Agreements* (London: CEPR and ECES, 1997).

Gallagher, Peter, and Andrew Stoler, "Critical Mass as an Alternative Framework for Multilateral Trade Negotiations" (2009) 15 *Global Governance*.

Garcia, Frank J., "Trade and Inequality: Economic Justice and the Developing World" (2000) 21 *Michigan Journal of International Law*.

______, "Building a Just Trade Order for a New Millennium" (2001) 21 *George Washington International Law Review*.

______, "Beyond Special and Differential Treatment" (2004) 27 *Boston College International & Comparative Law Review*.

Gay, Daniel, "Vanuatu's Suspended Accession Bid: Second Thoughts?" in Peter Gallagher, Patrick Low, and Andrew Stoler, *Managing the Challenges of WTO Participation: 45 Case Studies* (Cambridge: Cambridge University Press, 2005).

Gerhart, Peter M., and Archana Seema Kelia, "Power and Preferences: Developing Countries and the Rule of the WTO Appellate Body" (2005) 30 *North Carolina Journal of International Law and Commercial Regulation*.

Goode, Walter, Dictionary of Trade Policy Terms (5th ed., 2007).

Grossman, Gene, and Alan Sykes, "A Preference for Development: The Law and Economics of GSP" (2005) 4 *World Trade Review*.

Grynberg, Roman, "WTO Issues for Small Vulnerable States," in *Small States: Economic Review & Basic Statistics* (London: Commonwealth Secretariat, 2000).

______, "A theory of trade and development of small vulnerable states" in Roman Grynberg (ed.), *WTO at the Margins: Small States and the Multilateral Trading System* (Cambridge: Cambridge University Press, 2006).

______, "Introduction," in Roman Grynberg (ed.), *WTO at the Margins: Small States and the Multilateral Trading System* (Cambridge: Cambridge University Press, 2006).

Grynberg, Roman, and Roy Mickey Joy, "The Accession of Vanuatu to the WTO: Lessons for the Multilateral Trading System," in Roman Grynberg (ed.), *WTO at the Margins: Small States and the Multilateral Trading System* (Cambridge: Cambridge University Press, 2006).

Grynberg, Roman, and Jan Yves Remy, "Small Vulnerable Economy Issues and the WTO," in Roman Grynberg (ed.), *WTO at the Margins: Small States and the Multilateral Trading System* (Cambridge: Cambridge University Press, 2006).

Hoekman, Bernard, Constantine Michalopoulos and Alan Winters, "Special and Differential Treatment of Developing Countries in the WTO: Moving Forward after Cancun" (2004) *World Economy*.

Hoekman, Bernard, "Operationalizing the Concept of Policy Space in the WTO: Beyond Special and Differential Treatment" (2005) 8 *Journal of International Economic Law*.

Hoekman, Bernard, and Carlos Braga, "Special and Differential Treatment and the Doha Development Agenda: Beyond Tariff Preferences," paper presented at the OECD Global Forum on Trade, *Special and Differential Treatment: Thinking Outside the Box* (Bridgetown, Barbados, June 28–29, 2005).

Hoekman, Bernard, and Susan Prowse, "Policy Responses to Preference Erosion: From Trade as Aid to Aid for Trade," paper presented at the OECD Global Forum on Trade, *Special and Differential Treatment: Thinking Outside the Box* (Bridgetown, Barbados, June 28–29, 2005).

International Center for Trade and Sustainable Development, "Members Table Draft Articles for Future Agreement on Trade Facilitation," *Bridges Weekly Trade News Digest* (June 14, 2006), available at: http://ictsd.net/i/news/bridgesweekly/6329.

International Monetary Fund, *Improving Market Access: Toward Greater Coherence Between Aid and Trade*, March 2002, available at: http://www.imf.org/external/np/exr/ib/2002/032102.htm.

Ismail, Faizel, "A Development Perspective on the WTO July 2004 General Council Decision" (2005) 8 *Journal of International Economic Law*.

Jones, Kent, "The Political Economy of WTO Accession: The Unfinished Business of Universal Membership" (2009) 8 *World Trade Review*.

Joy, Shirley, "WTO to reopen dialogue on Vanuatu membership," *Vanuatu Daily Post*, 11 July 2006.

Keck, Alexander, and Patrick Low, "Special and Differential Treatment in the WTO: Why, When, and How?" in Simon Evenett and Bernard Hoekman (eds.) *Economic Development and Multilateral Trade Cooperation* (Washington, DC: The World Bank; New York: Palgrave Macmillan, 2006).

Kelsey, Jane, "World Trade and Small Nations in the South Pacific Region" (2005) 14 *Kansas Journal of Law and Public Policy*.

Kessie, Edwini, "The Legal Status of Special and Differential Treatment Provisions under the WTO Agreements," in George Bermann and Petros Mavroidis (eds.), *WTO Law and Developing Countries* (New York: Cambridge University Press 2007).

Kleen, Peter, and Sheila Page, *Special and Differential Treatment of Developing Countries in the World Trade Organization*, Report – Swedish Ministry for Foreign Affairs Global Development Studies 2 (February 2005).

Langhammer, Rolf J., and Matthias Lucke, "WTO Accession Issues" (1999) 22 *The World Economy*.

Larmour, Peter, *Corruption and Governance in the South Pacific*, State Society and Governance in Melanesia Discussion Paper 97/5 (1997), available at: http://rspas.anu.edu.au/papers/melanesia/discussion_papers/ssgm97–5.pdf.

Lee, Donna, and Nicola J. Smith, "The Political Economy of Small African States in the WTO" (2008) 97 *The Round Table*.

Levy, Philip, "Do We Need an Undertaker for the Single Undertaking? Considering the Angles of Variable Geometry," in Simon J. Evenett and Bernard M. Hoekman (eds.), *Economic Development and Multilateral Trade Cooperation* (Washington, DC: The World Bank; New York: Palgrave Macmillan, 2006).

Lewis, Meredith Kolsky, "WTO Winners and Losers: The Trade and Development Disconnect" (2007) 39 *Georgetown Journal of International Law*.

Lichetenbaum, Peter, "'Special Treatment' vs. 'Equal Participation'": Striking a Balance in the Doha Negotiations" (2002) 17 *American University International Law Review*.

Michalopoulos, Constantine, "WTO Accession," in Bernard M. Hoekman, Aaditya Mattoo, Philip English (eds.), *Development, Trade, and the WTO: A Handbook* (Washington, DC: World Bank, 2002).

Mitchell, Andrew, and Tania Voon, "Operationalizing Special and Differential Treatment in the World Trade Organization: Game Over?" (2009) 15 *Global Governance*.

New Zealand House of Representatives, Foreign Affairs, Defence and Trade Committee, *Inquiry into New Zealand's relationship with the Kingdom of Tonga: Report of the Foreign Affairs*, 47th Parliament (August 2005).

New Zealand Ministry of Foreign Affairs & Trade, *Republic of Vanuatu*, available at: http://www.mfat.govt.nz/Countries/Pacific/Vanuatu.php.

______, *Samoa Country Information Paper*, available at: http://www.mfat.govt.nz/Countries/Pacific/Samoa.php.

NZAID, (2008) *Annual Review 2007/08: Pacific Overview*, available at: http://www.aid.govt.nz/library/annual-review/ar-2007-08/annual-review-nzaid-2008-3-pacific-overview.pdf.

NZAID/Vanuatu Development Programme Strategy 2006–2010 (June 2006), available at: http://www.nzaid.govt.nz/library/docs/nzaid-vanuatu-strategy-0610.pdf.

Oxfam International, *Blood from a Stone* (December 2005), available at: http://www.oxfam.org/en/files/bn05 1215_tonga_bloodfromastone/download.

Oxfam New Zealand, *Submission of Oxfam New Zealand to Ministry of Foreign Affairs on the WTO Accession Negotiations of Samoa*, September 2005, available at: http://www.oxfam.org.nz/imgs/whatwedo/mtf/onz%20on%20samoa%20wto%20accession.pdf.

"Oxfam's Criticism 'Outrageous,' says Tonga's WTO Delegation," *Matangi Tonga Online*, 19 December 2005, available at: http://www.matangitonga.to/scripts/artman/exec/view.cgi?archive=4&num=1529.

Özden, Caglar, and Eric Reinhardt, "The Perversity of Preferences: GSP and Developing Country Trade Policies, 1976–2000" (2005) 78 *Journal of Development Economics*.

Pangesu, Mari, "Special and Differential Treatment in the Millennium: Special for Whom and How Different?" (2000) *The World Economy*.

"PNG Defends Signing of Economic Partnership Agreement," *Pacific Magazine*, April 30, 2008.

Redding, Stephen, and Anthony J. Venables, "The Economics of Isolation and Distance," in Roman Grynberg (ed.), *WTO at the Margins: Small States and the Multilateral Trading System* (Cambridge: Cambridge University Press, 2006).

Rose, Andrew K., "Do We Really Know that the WTO Increases Trade?" (2004) 94 *The American Economic Review*.

Shaffer, Gregory, "Can WTO Technical Assistance and Capacity-Building Serve Developing Countries?" (2005) 23 *Wisconsin International Law Journal*.

Stoler, Andrew L., "Fiji: Preparing for the End of Preferences?" in Peter Gallagher, Patrick Low and Andrew L. Stoler, *Managing the Challenges of WTO Participation: 45 Case Studies* (Cambridge: Cambridge University Press, 2005).

Subramanian, Arvind, and Shang-Jin Wei, "The WTO Promotes Trade, Strongly, but Unevenly" (2007) 72 *Journal of International Economics*.

Sykes, Alan, "Comparative Advantage and the Normative Economics of International Trade Policy" (1998) 1 *Journal of International Economic Law*.

Tavita-Levy, Nella, Principal Trade Policy Officer, Samoa Ministry of Foreign Affairs and Trade, *Samoa: Accession to the WTO*, Presentation at the ADB Intensive Course on Accession (Bangkok, March 7–10, 2006), document on file with authors.

Tigerstrom, Barbara von, "Small Island Developing States and International Trade: Special Challenges in the Global Partnership for Development" (2005) 6 *Melbourne Journal of International Law*.

Tomz, Michael, Judith L. Goldstein, and Douglas Rivers, "Membership Has Its Privileges: The Impact of the GATT on International Trade" (2007) 97 *The American Economic Review*.

Trachtman, Joel, "Ensuring a Development-friendly WTO" (2008) 12 *Bridges Monthly Review*.

Tupou, Siosiua Utoikamanu, *Budget Statement for Year Ending 30th June 2008*, Ministry of Finance and Planning Government of Tonga, available at: http://www.finance.gov.to.

United States Trade Representative, *Accessions of Least Developed Countries*, available at: http://www.ustr.gov/trade-agreements/wto-multilateral-affairs/wto-accessions/accessions-least-developed-countries.

United Nations, Conference on Trade and Development, *About UNCTAD*, available at: http://www.unctad.org/Templates/Page.asp?intItemID=1530&lang=1.

______, Economic and Social Council, Committee for Development Policy, *Report on the Sixth Session*, E/2004/33 (March 29–April 2, 2004).

______, Economic and Social Council Committee for Development Policy, *Report on the Eighth Session*, UN Doc. E/2007/L.35 (2–27 July 2007).

______, General Assembly, *Report of the Ad Hoc Committee of the Whole of the Twenty-Second Special Session of the General Assembly*, A/S-22/9/Rev.1 (New York, September 27–28, 1999).

______, General Assembly, *Report of the Global Conference on the Sustainable Development of Small Island Developing States*, A/CONF.167/9, (Bridgetown, Barbados, April 25–May 6, 1994).

______, Office of the High Representative for the Least Developed Countries, Land-locked Developing Countries and Small Island Developing States, available at: http://www.unohrlls.org.

______, Office of the High Representative for the Least Developed Countries, *Landlocked Developing Countries and Small Island Developing States, List of Least Developed Countries*, available at: http://www.unohrlls.org/en/ldc/related/62.

______, Office of the High Representative for the Least Developed Countries, Landlocked Developing Countries, and Small Island Developing Countries, "List of Small Island Developing States," available at: http://www.un.org/special-rep/ohrlls/sid/list.htm.

______, Port Louis, Mauritius, January 10–14, 2005, *Report of the International Meeting to Review the Implementation of the Programme of Action for the Sustainable Development of Small Island Developing States*, UN Doc. A/CONF.207/11 (February 14, 2005).

______, Secretary-General, *Report of the Secretary-General on the Road Map Towards the Implementation of the United Nations Millennium Declaration*, A/56/326 (September 6, 2001).

Ustor, Endre, "Most-Favoured-Nation Clause," in Rudolf Bernhardt (ed.), *Encyclopaedia of Public International Law* (Amsterdam: North Holland, 2003).

The Warwick Commission, *The Multilateral Trade Regime: Which Way Forward? The Report of the First Warwick Commission* (2007), available at: http://www2.warwick.ac.uk/research/warwickcommission/archive/worldtrade/report.

Williams, Peter Wieter, A *Handbook on Accession to the WTO* (Cambridge: Cambridge University Press,2008).

Witter, Michael, Lino Briguglio, and Assad Bhuglah, "Measuring and Managing the Economic Vulnerability of Small Island Developing States" (May 2002) (unpublished paper), available at: http://www.sidsnet.org/docshare/other/economic_vulnerability_paper.pdf.

World Trade Organization, *A New Strategy for WTO Technical Cooperation: Technical Cooperation for Capacity Building, Growth and Integration*, Note by the Secretariat, WTO Committee on Trade and Development, WTO Doc. WT/COMTD/W/90 (21 September 2001).

______, *Accession of Least-Developed Countries to the WTO*, WTO Doc. WT/COMTD/LDC/W/44 (2009).

______, *Accession Status: Vanuatu*, available at: http://www.wto.org/english/thewto_e/acc_e/a1_vanuatu_e.htm.

______, *Accessions: The Mandate, Relevant WTO Provisions*, available at: http://www.wto.org/english/thewto_e/acc_e/acc7_3_e.htm.
______, Advisory Centre on WTO Law, *Quick Guide to the ACWL*, available at: http://www.acwl.ch/pdf/acwl_page_imp.pdf.
______, Appellate Body Report, *European Communities – Conditions for the Granting of Tariff Preferences to Developing Countries*, WTO Doc. WT/DS246/AB/R (April 7, 2004).
______, Committee on Agriculture, *WTO African Group: Joint Proposal on the Negotiations on Agriculture*, WTO Doc. G/AG/NG/W/142 (March 23, 2001).
______, Committee on Agriculture, *WTO Negotiations on Agriculture: Proposals by Small Island Developing States (SIDS)*, WTO Doc. G/AG/NG/W/97 (December 29, 2000).
______, Committee on Agriculture, WTO Negotiations on Agriculture: Proposals by Small Island Developing States (SIDS), WTO Doc. G/AG/NG/W/97/Corr.1 (February 14, 2001).
______, Committee on Trade and Development, *Communiqué of the Fifth Annual Ministerial Meeting of Landlocked Developing Countries (LLDCs)*, WTO Doc. WT/L/585, WT/COMTD/SE/2 (October 7, 2004).
______,Committee on Trade and Development, *Implementation of Special and Differential Treatment Provisions in WTO Agreements and Decisions: Mandatory and Non-Mandatory Special and Differential Treatment Provisions – Note by the Secretariat (Corrigendum)*, WTO Doc. WT/COMTD/W/77/Rev.1/Add.1/Corr.1 (February 4, 2002).
______, Consultative Board, *The Future of the WTO: Addressing Institutional Challenges in the New Millennium* (2004).
______, General Council, *Accession of Least-Developed Countries – Decision of 10 December 2002*, WTO Doc. WT/L/508 (2002) (Decision of the General Council).
______, General Council, *Doha Work Programme*, WT/L/579 (August 2, 2004).
______,General Council, *Work Programme on Small Economies – Framework and Procedures*, WT/L/447 (March 1, 2002), available at: http://www.wto.org/english/tratop_e/devel_e/dev_wkprog_smalleco_e.htm.
______, *Least-developed Countries*, available at: http://www.wto.org/English/thewto_e/whatis_e/tif_e/org7_e.htm.
______, *Members and Observers*, available at: http://www.wto.org/english/thewto_e/whatis_e/tif_e/org6_e.htm.
______, Ministerial Conference, *Decision on Measures Concerning the Possible Negative Effects of the Reform Programme on Least-Developed and Net Food-Importing Developing Countries*, WTO Doc. LT/UR/D-1/2 (March 15, 1994).
______, *Ministerial Declaration of 14 November 2001*, WTO Doc. WT/MIN(01)/DEC/1 (2001).
______, *Ministerial Declaration of 18 December 2005*, WTO Doc. WT/MIN(05)/DEC (2005).
______, Negotiating Group on Market Access, *Market Access for Non-Agricultural Products – The Issue of Newly-Acceded Members: Submission by the Separate Customs Territory of Taiwan, Penghu, Kinmen and Matsu*, WTO Doc. TN/MA/W/19/Add.1 (May 16, 2003).
______, Sixth Session of the Ministerial Conference, *Report of the Working Party on the Accession of Tonga to the World Trade Organization*, WTO Doc. WT/ACC/TON/17, WT/MIN(05)/4 (December 2, 2005).
______, Statement by the Honourable Hans Joachim Keil, Minister of Trade, Government of Samoa, WTO Ministerial Conference, Fifth Session, Cancun, WTO Doc. WT/MIN(03)/ST/155 (September 13, 2003).

———, *Subcommittee on Least Developed Countries Communication to the General Council, Accession of Least Developed Countries*, WTO Doc. WT/COMTD/LDC/12 (2002) (Draft Decision for submission to the General Council).

———, *Summary Table of Ongoing Accessions*, available at: http://www.wto.org/English/thewto_e/acc_e/status_e.htm.

———, *Understanding the WTO* (3d ed., 2003).

———, Working Party on the Accession of Cambodia, *Report of the Working Party on the Accession of Cambodia*, WTO Doc. WT/ACC/KHM/21 (August 15, 2003).

———, Working Party on the Accession of Nepal, *Report of the Working Party on the Accession of Nepal*, WTO Doc. WT/ACC/NPL/16 (August 28, 2003).

———, Working Party on the Accession of Samoa, *Draft Report of the Working Party on the Accession of Samoa to the World Trade Organization*, WTO Doc. WT/ACC/SPEC/SAM/4/Rev.1 (November 8, 2006).

———, Working Party on the Accession of Vanuatu, *Draft Report of the Working Party on the Accession of Vanuatu to the World Trade Organization*, WTO Doc. WT/ACC/VUT/13 (October 16, 2001).

———, World Trade Report 2007: Six Decades of Multilateral Trade Cooperation: What Have We Learnt? (2007), available at: http://www.wto.org/english/news_e/pres07_e/pr502_e.htm

World Trade Organization Secretariat, *Accession to the World Trade Organization: Procedures for Negotiations under Article XII*, WTO Doc. WT/ACC/1 (March 24, 1995).

"WTO Sets Up Working Party on Accession of Iran, after U.S. Backs E.U. by Lifting Veto," *International Trade Reporter*, June 2, 2005.

Zarcone, Frabizio, Carsten Fink, and Carlos A. Primo Braga, "Technical Assistance and WTO Accessions: Lessons from Experience," Draft manuscript prepared after a Joint World Bank-GTZ workshop on WTO accession matters (Berlin, November 17–19, 2004).

PART III

Law and Development in Free Trade Agreements

9

North–South Regional Trade Agreements

Prospects, Risks, and Legal Regulation

Moshe Hirsch

I. INTRODUCTION

The recent decade has witnessed an unprecedented increase in the number of regional trade agreements (RTAs; mostly FTAs and customs union) and their scope.[1] Several scholars consider the rapid proliferation of RTAs to be one of the major developments in international relations.[2] Although some kinds of RTAs have existed for centuries,[3] the numbers, as well as the world share of trade covered by RTAs, have been steadily increasing over the past decade. Nearly all countries belong to at least one RTA, with some being parties to numerous agreements.[4] RTAs already account for almost half of world trade, and this is expected to increase if all the RTAs currently in the pipeline are implemented.[5] According to the World Trade Organization (WTO), some 462 RTAs have been notified to the General Agreement on Tariffs and Trade (GATT)/WTO up to February 2010. At the same date, 271 agreements were in force.[6]

1 See, e.g., J. A. Crawford and R. V. Fiorentino, *The Changing Landscape of Regional Trade Agreements* (Discussion Paper, World Trade Organization [WTO], 2005), p. 2; WTO, *WTO Annual Report – 2005* (2005), p. 58; Organization for Economic Cooperation and Development (OECD), *Regionalism and the Multilateral Trading System* (Paris: OECD, 2003), pp. 1–2; J. Whalley, *Recent Regional Agreements: Why So Many, So Fast, So Different and Where Are They Headed?* Working Paper – International Institutional Reform, The Centre for International Governance Innovation (2006).

2 M. Schiff and A. Winters, *Regional Integration and Development* (Washington, DC: World Bank and Oxford University Press, 2003), pp. 1–2. See also J. M. Grether, *Preferential and Non-Preferential Trade Flows in World Trade*, Staff Working Paper ERAD-98-10, Economic Research and Analysis Division, World Trade Organization (1998), p. 2.

3 For an historic survey of RTAs, see K. Anderson and H. Norheim, "History, Geography, and Regional Integration," in K. Anderson and R. Blackhurst (eds.), *Regional Integration and the Global Trading System* (New York: St. Martin's Press, 1993), pp. 19, 26–45; Schiff and Winters (2003), supra note 2, pp. 4–6.

4 See, e.g., Crawford and Fiorentino (2005), supra note 1, p. 1; The World Bank, *Global Economic Prospects: Trade, Regionalism, and Development* (Washington, DC: The World Bank, 2005), pp. 28–29.

5 OECD (2003), supra note 1, pp. 1–2.

6 WTO, *Regional Trade Agreements*, available at: http://www.wto.org/english/tratop_e/region_e/region_e.htm.

Developing countries joined RTAs before the recent wave of regionalism, but the vast majority of agreements that were concluded by these countries during the 1960s and 1970s were established between countries at similar levels of economic development.[7] Most RTAs at that period were formed between either developing or developed countries, and the number of RTAs between developing and developed countries was significantly smaller.[8] One of the main characteristics of the recent wave of regionalism is the increasing number of RTAs[9] between developing and developed countries.[10] The prominent examples are the North American Free Trade Agreement (NAFTA)[11] and trade agreements concluded by the European Union (EU), such as the customs union between the EU with Turkey, and FTAs with many Mediterranean countries.[12]

The ongoing proliferation of RTAs intensifies the long-standing debate among scholars and policy makers regarding the motives and repercussions of RTAs[13] and whether the WTO system should promote or restrict the formation of RTAs. Economic analyses of RTAs do not provide a single answer to the question regarding the desirability or undesirability of such arrangements, and the economic literature provides support for both views.[14] The Vinerian Customs Union theory, which is considered the "orthodox" theory of economic integration, emphasizes not only the

7 D. Ray, *Development Economics* (Princeton, NJ: Princeton University Press, 1998), p. 730; R. Dimova, *Preferential Trade Areas and Global Trade: Friends or Foes?* ICRA Working Paper No. 2, SSRN Library (2000), p. 2.

8 See, e.g., M. Schiff, *Multilateral Trade Liberalization, Political Disintegration and the Choice of FTAs versus Customs Union*, World Bank Policy Research Paper No. 2350, Development Research Department (2000), pp. 14–16.

9 P. de Lombaerde, A. Estevadeordal, and K. Souminen, "Governing Regional Integration for Development: Introduction," in P. de Lombaerde, A. Estevadeordal, and K. Souminen (eds.), *Governing Regional Integration for Development* (Aldershot: Ashgate, 2008), p. 1; Crawford and Fiorentino (2005), supra note 1, pp. 2–7.

10 On RTAs between developing and developed states, see, e.g., M. Hirsch, "The Logic of North–South Economic Integration" (2005) 32 *Legal Issues of Economic Integration* 3.

11 North American Free Trade Agreement (Done at Washington on 8 and 17 December 1992, at Ottawa on 11 and 17 December 1992, and at Mexico City on 14 and 17 December 1992, entered into force 1 January 1994) (1993) 32 *International Legal Materials* 289.

12 See Schiff and Winters (2003), supra note 2, pp. 2–3, 74. On the Economic Partnership Agreements between the EU and ACP countries, see M. Desta, "EC–ACP Economic Partnership Agreements and WTO Compatibility: An Experiment in North–South Inter-Regional Agreements?" (2006) 43 *Common Market Law Review* 1343–1379.

13 On various factors motivating countries to establish RTAs, see M. Hirsch, "The Sociology of International Economic Law: Sociological Analysis of the Regulation of Regional Agreements in the World Trading System" (2008) 19 *European Journal of International Law* 277.

14 See, e.g., R. Z. Lawrence, *Regionalism, Multilateralism, and Deeper Integration* (Washington, DC: The Brookings Institution, 1996), p. 44; J. Bhagwati, "Regionalism and Multilateralism: An Overview," in J. Bhagwati, P. Krishna, and A. Panagariya (eds.), *Trading Blocs: Alternative Approaches to Analyzing Preferential Trade Agreements* (Cambridge, MA: MIT Press, 1999), p. 3; J. Bhagwati and A. Panagriya, "Preferential Trading Areas and Multilateralism – Strangers, Friends, or Foes?" in *The Economics of Preferential Trade Agreements* (The AEI Press, Center for International Economics, University of Maryland, Washington DC, 1996), p. 1; P. Sutherland, J. Bhagwati, K. Botchwey, N. FitzGerald, K. Hamada, J. H. Jackson, C. Lafer, and T. de Montbrial, *The Future of the WTO: Addressing*

prospects of "trade creation" arising from preferential arrangements but also the detrimental impacts of "trade diversion" on third parties.[15] Modern trade theories, which are based on models of imperfect competition, challenge traditional customs union theory. The new approaches lead to a more favorable attitude toward preferential arrangements stemming from the relative insignificance that their proponents attribute to the phenomenon of trade diversion. The latter theories tend to emphasize the role of economies-of-scale opportunities and technology transfer generated by RTAs.[16]

Section II of this chapter outlines the regulation of RTAs in the WTO legal system. The section briefly discusses the relevant legal provisions (Article XXIV of the GATT, Article V of the General Agreement on Trade in Services [GATS], and the "Enabling Clause"), the activities of the WTO oversight mechanism, and the decisions of the GATT/WTO dispute settlement bodies that have dealt with these provisions. Section III discusses the economic prospects of North–South RTAs for developing countries, employing the Heckscher–Ohlin model, the economies of scale theory, and Ethier's approach that views RTAs as a signaling device to foreign investors. Section IV presents certain disadvantages of RTAs for developing countries, especially RTAs that apply restrictive rules to trade in labor-intensive goods (in which developing countries have comparative advantage). This section also explains the deficiencies of such RTAs, prominently those relating to political economy considerations and the parties' asymmetric bargaining positions. Section V briefly discusses some mechanisms that may ameliorate the shortcomings of certain RTAs addressed in Section IV. Section VI briefly recaps the main conclusions drawn from preceding sections and emphasizes the central role of domestic institutions in economic development.

II. THE REGULATION OF RTAS UNDER THE WTO LAW

The formation and enlargement of RTAs are addressed by several WTO legal provisions – mainly, Article XXIV of the General Agreement on Tariffs and

Institutional Challenges in the New Millennium – Report by the Consultative Board to the Director-General Supachai Panitchpakdi (Geneva: WTO, 2004) (hereinafter the Sutherland Report), pp. 19–28, 79; J. J. Schott, "More Free Trade Areas?" in J. J. Schott (ed.), *Free Trade Areas and U.S. Trade Policy* (Washington, DC: Institute of International Economics, 1989), pp. 1, 17–55; P. Wonnacottt and M. Lutz, "Is There a Case for Free Trade Areas?" in J. J. Schott (ed.), *Free Trade Areas and U.S. Trade Policy* (Washington, DC: Institute of International Economics, 1989), pp. 3, 59.

15 In accordance with the Vinerian model, "trade creation" happens when high-cost domestic products are replaced by cheaper products imported from other members of the preferential arrangements. "Trade diversion" happens when imported low-cost products from nonmember states are replaced by higher-cost goods that are imported from a member state of the preferential arrangement. J. Viner, *The Customs Union Issue* (New York: Carnegie Endowment for International Peace, 1950), p. 3.

16 R. Pomfert, *The Economics of Regional Trade Arrangements* (Oxford: Clarendon Press, 1997), p. 207; Lawrence (1996), supra note 14, pp. 37–50, 231–247; Schiff and Winters (2003), supra note 2, pp. 46–54.

Trade[17] (GATT), Article V of the GATS,[18] and the Enabling Clause with regard to RTAs among developing countries. Although RTAs deviate from one of the WTO core objectives, the most-favored-nation principle,[19] WTO law allows members to establish and enlarge such preferential arrangements provided some conditions are fulfilled.

The most important rules are included in Article XXIV of the GATT[20] and the 1994 Understanding on the Interpretation of Article XXIV.[21] These provisions lay out the criteria and procedure for the assessment of new or enlarged RTAs.[22] The central requirements are as follows:

1. "[S]ubstantially all the trade" between the RTA members is to be liberalized.[23] With respect to customs unions, the members are also required to apply substantially the same duties and other trade restrictions to products of third parties.[24]
2. The liberalization of trade among the RTA members is to be achieved "within a reasonable length of time."[25] The 1994 Understanding clarifies that this period "should exceed 10 years only in exceptional cases."[26]
3. Duties and other trade restrictions imposed by RTA members on products from third parties must not be higher or more restrictive than those existing

[17] GATT 1994 (opened for signature April 15, 1994, entered into force January 1, 1995) 1867 UNTS 190; General Agreement on Tariffs and Trade 1947 (signed October 30, 1947) 55 UNTS 194.

[18] GATS 1994 (signed April 15, 1994, entered into force January 1, 1995) 1869 UNTS 183.

[19] GATT, art. I (n 17).

[20] On the legislative history of Article XXIV, see J. H. Mathis, *Regional Trade Agreements in the GATT/WTO* (The Hague: Asser Press, 2002), pp. 31–53.

[21] *Understanding on the Interpretation of Article XXIV of The General Agreement on Tariffs and Trade 1994*.

[22] For a detailed analysis of the GATT, art. XXIV, see M. Matsushita, T. J. Schoenbaum, and P. C. Mavoroidis, *The World Trade Organization: Law, Practice and Policy* (2nd ed., Oxford: Oxford University Press, 2006), pp. 555–578; J. H. Jackson, W. Davey, and A. O. Sykes, *Legal Problems of International Economic Relations* (St. Paul, MN: West Group, 2002), p. 503 et seq.; R. Bhala, *Modern GATT Law* (London: Sweet and Maxwell, 2005), pp. 590–604; N. Lockhart and A. Mitchell, "Regional Trade Agreements under GATT 1994: An Exception and Its Limits," in A. Mitchell (ed.), *Challenges and Prospects for the WTO* (London: Cameron May, 2005), p. 217. See also M. J. Trebilcock and R. Howse, *The Regulation of International; Trade* (3rd ed., London and New York: Routledge, 2005), pp. 199–200; P. Van den Bossche, *The Law and Policy of the World Trade Organization: Text, Cases and Materials* (2nd ed., New York: Cambridge University Press, 2008), pp. 699–709; T. Cottier, "The Challenge of Regionalism and Preferential Relations in World Trade Law and Policy" (1996) 1 *European Foreign Affairs Review* 157–170.

[23] Article XXIV(8)(b) of the GATT (regarding FTAs) and Article XXIV(8)(a)(i) of the GATT (regarding customs unions). This rule requires also the elimination of discriminatory standards included in RTAs. J. P. Trachtman, "Toward Open Recognition? Standards and Regional Integration under Article XXIV of GATT" (2003) 6 *Journal of International Economic Law* 485–486.

[24] Article XXIV(8)(a)(ii) of the GATT. This rule requires also the elimination of discriminatory standards included in customs union agreements. Trachtman, supra note 23, pp. 486–487.

[25] Article XXIV(5)(c) of the GATT (regarding FTAs and customs unions).

[26] Article 2 of *Understanding on the Interpretation of Article XXIV of the General Agreement on Tariffs and Trade 1994*.

prior to the formation of the RTA.[27] If the formation of a customs union leads to an increase of the bound duties (under Article II of the GATT) toward third parties, there is an obligation to provide the latter with compensatory adjustment[28] (regularly in the form of tariff concessions).[29]

4. RTA members must notify the WTO and provide it with the agreements and all relevant information.[30]

Article V of the GATS[31] sets out similar but somewhat weaker requirements for the formation and modification of "Economic Integration" agreements in services:[32]

1. The agreement must have substantial sectoral coverage (in terms of the number of sectors, volume of trade affected, and modes of supply). The agreement should not provide for the a priori exclusion of any mode of supply.[33]
2. The agreement must provide for the absence or elimination of substantially all discrimination among the parties in the sectors covered by the agreement. This requirement must be attained either at the entry into force of that RTA or on the basis of a reasonable time frame.[34]
3. The agreement is to be designed to facilitate trade among the RTA parties and not raise the overall level of trade barriers towards third countries (compared to the level applicable prior to such an agreement).[35]
4. The members must promptly notify any such agreement to the Council for Trade in Services and make available to the Council the relevant information.[36]

RTAs among developing countries that liberalize trade in either goods or services are subject to more lenient criteria. The 1979 Decision on Differential and More Favorable Treatment of Developing Countries (the Enabling Clause),[37] which has

[27] Article XXIV5(b) of the GATT (regarding FTAs) and XXIV(5)(a) (regarding customs unions). See also *Understanding on the Interpretation of Article XXIV*, ibid., para. 2.

[28] Article XXIV(6) of the GATT; see also *Understanding on the Interpretation of Article XXIV*, supra note 21, paras. 4–6.

[29] S. Cho, "Breaking the Barrier between Regionalism and Multilateralism" (2001) 42 *Harvard International Law Journal* 439–440.

[30] Article XXIV(7)(a) of the GATT. See also *Understanding on the Interpretation of Article XXIV*, supra note 21, paras. 7–10.

[31] On Article V of the GATS, see also Van den Bossche (2008), supra note 22, pp. 709–714; Matsushita et al. (2006), supra note 22, pp. 578–581.

[32] B. M. Hoekman and M. M. Kostecki, *The Political Economy of The World Trading System* (2nd ed., New York: Oxford University Press, 2001), p. 355; Lawrence (1996), supra note 14, p. 103.

[33] Article V:1(a) of the GATS.

[34] Article V:1(b) of the GATS.

[35] Article V:4 of the GATS.

[36] Article V:7(a) of the GATS.

[37] Articles 2 and 3 of the *Decision on Differential and More Favourable Treatment Reciprocity and Fuller Participation of Developing Countries* (hereinafter Enabling Clause), available at: http://www.wto.org/english/docs_e/legal_e/enabling_e.doc.

become an integral part of the GATT 1994,[38] lays out less demanding[39] requirements than those included in the GATT and GATS.[40] The Enabling Clause notes that developing countries are not required to liberalize "substantially all of their trade" as long as FTAs between developing countries offer mutual reduction or elimination of tariffs.[41]

Agreements establishing RTAs (and interim agreements) are reviewed by the WTO organs.[42] Following the report of the Committee on Regional Trade Agreements (CRTA),[43] the Council for Trade in Goods may determine whether the particular RTA is consistent with the above criteria. If the Council finds that the RTA is not likely to comply with these conditions, it may make recommendations to the parties of the RTA. In the latter case, the RTA's members shall not put into force or maintain the regional agreement unless they are prepared to modify it in accordance with these recommendations.[44] Similar procedures apply to regional agreements on trade in services.[45] This oversight process has proved to be a weak

[38] See Appellate Body Report, *European Communities – Conditions for the Granting of Tariff Preferences to Developing Countries*, WTO Doc WT/DS 246/R (December 1, 2003), para. 90 and note 192, available at: http://www.wto.org/english/tratop_e/dispu_e/ab_reports_e.htm; see also Matsushita et al. (2006), supra note 22, pp. 221.

[39] See Hoekman and Kostecki (2001), supra note 32, p. 355; Alberta Fabbricotti, *The Asean Free Trade Area (AFTA) and Its Compatibility with GATT/WTO* (October 26, 2009), available at: http://ssrn.com/abstract=1494550; Cho (2001), supra note 29, p. 449; R. Z. Lawrence, "Regionalism and the WTO: Should the Rules Be Changed?" in *The World Trading System: Challenges Ahead* (Washington, DC: Institute of International Economics, 1996), pp. 41, 46; M. Gibbs and S. Wagle, *The Great Maze: Regional and Bilateral Free Trade Agreements in Asia* (Colombo, Sri Lanka: Asia-Pacific Trade and Investment Initiative, United Nations Development Programme Regional Center, 2005), p. 17.

[40] Article 2(c) of the Enabling Clause provides as follows: "Regional or global arrangements entered into amongst less-developed contracting parties for the mutual reduction or elimination of tariffs and, in accordance with criteria or conditions which may be prescribed by the CONTRACTING PARTIES, for the mutual reduction or elimination of non-tariff measures, on products imported from one another." Article 3(a) of this clause provides that "any differential and more favourable treatment provided under this clause ... shall be designed to facilitate and promote the trade of developing countries and not to raise barriers to or create undue difficulties for the trade of any other contracting parties"; Enabling Clause, supra note 37.

[41] M. Matsushita and Y. S. Lee, "Proliferation of Free Trade Agreements and Some Systemic Issues – In Relation to the WTO Disciplines and Development Perspectives" (2008) 1 *The Law and Development Review* 32–33.

[42] In the past, all relevant information was examined by WTO ad hoc working parties that reported to the Council for Trade in Goods. The Singapore Ministerial Meeting called for an end to the ad hoc working party review system by establishing a standing CRTA. The new committee was entrusted to carry out the examination of RTAs, "consider systematic implications of such agreements for the multilateral trading system," and make appropriate recommendations. Decision of the General Council of February 6, 1996 WT/L/127 (February 7, 1996); Mathis (2002), supra note 20, p. 306. See also Mathis (2002), supra note 20, pp. 130–131.

[43] RTAs among developing countries that are subject to the Enabling Clause are reviewed by the WTO Committee on Trade and Development. Van den Bossche (2008), supra note 22, p. 708.

[44] Article XXIV(7)(b) of the GATT; *Understanding on the Interpretation of Article XXIV* (supra note 21), articles 7–11.

[45] See Article V:7 of the GATS. Van den Bossche (2008), supra note 22, p. 713.

enforcement mechanism of the conditions laid out in the WTO agreements.[46] The traditional requirement of consensus for a decision to be adopted by the committee effectively blocked decisions disqualifying RTAs.[47]

Thus, although numerous RTAs were reviewed by the ad hoc working parties and CRTA, no RTA was condemned, and only few[48] were declared as consistent with GATT rules.[49] The new CRTA[50] has made some progress in outlining systemic issues regarding RTAs, but its members have been unable to finalize reports on any of these issues.[51]

The GATT dispute settlement bodies have rarely been involved in the application and interpretation of the foregoing legal WTO provisions, and their jurisprudence is summarized briefly here. The 1985 GATT panel decision on the EC Tariff Treatment of Imports of Citrus Products from the Mediterranean Region showed a restrained approach. The panel concluded that it should abstain from examination

[46] See, e.g., Lawrence (1996), supra note 14, pp. 52–3; Bhala (2005), supra note 22, pp. 604–605; Cottier (1996), supra note 22, pp. 160–161.

[47] Thus, for instance, the 1985 Panel Report "EC – Tariff Treatment on Imports of Citrus from Certain Countries in the Mediterranean Region" (unadopted) includes the following findings: "Given the lack of consensus among contracting parties, there had been no decision by the CONTRACTING PARTIES on the conformity with Article XXIV of the agreements under which the EC grants tariff preferences to certain citrus products originating from certain Mediterranean countries, and therefore the legal status of the agreements remained open." WTO, *Analytical Index: Guide to GATT Law and Practice* (6th ed., Geneva: WTO, 1994), p. 761. As Mathis concludes in his comprehensive study on Article XXIV, "Since any final Contracting party decision would require a consensus in any case, and since those committee members in minority also were Contracting Parties for the purpose of a recommendation by the Contracting Parties, the heart of the institutional difficulty regarding non-complying regional agreements must be laid to rest on the requirement of consensus itself." Mathis (2002), supra note 20, p. 83.

[48] See, for instance, the statement of the Working Party on the Customs Union Agreement between the Governments of the Union of South Africa and Southern Rhodesia: "Taking Note of the Interim Agreement and Taking Note of the undertaking of the two Governments, . . . THE CONTRACTING PARTIES DECLARE that the Governments of the Union of South Africa and Southern Rhodesia are entitled to claim the benefits of the provisions of Article XXIV of the General Agreement on Tariffs and Trade relating to the formation of customs unions." WTO, *Report of Working Party 4 on the South Africa–Southern Rhodesia Customs Union*, WTO Doc GATT/CP3/24 (May 14, 1949), p. 9.

[49] Thus, Mavroidis concludes: "We are simply in the dark as to the consistency of the remaining 99% of all PTAs currently in place." P. C. Mavroidis, *Trade in Goods: The GATT and the Other Agreements Regulating Trade in Goods* (Oxford: Oxford University Press, 2007), p. 167. For an analysis of the practice of the GATT/WTO ad hoc working parties, the CRTA, and WTO Members in this field, see P. Mavroidis, "If I Don't Do It, Somebody Else Will (or Won't)" (2006) 40 *Journal of World Trade* 187. See also C. B. Picker, "Regional Trade Agreements v. the WTO" (2005) 26 *University of Pennsylvania Journal of International Economic Law* 282–284; Cho (2001), supra note 29, pp. 421–423; Mathis (2002), supra note 20, p. 98. On the past practice of GATT's bodies regarding RTAs among developing states, see J. M. Finger, "GATT's Influence on Regional Arrangements," in J. de Malo and A. Panagariya (eds.), *New Dimensions in Regional Integration* (Cambridge: Cambridge University Press, 1993), pp. 128, 140–142.

[50] On CRTA's work, see Mathis (2002), supra note 20, pp. 227–258.

[51] *Report of the Committee on Regional Trade Agreements to the General Council*, WT/REG/8 (September 11, 1999) (as cited in Mathis (2002), supra note 20, pp. 306, 308–309).

of the relevant RTA in the context of Article XXIII (nullification and impairment).[52] The two decisions rendered by the GATT panels in the "Bananas Case"[53] in 1993–1994 displayed a less cautious approach regarding legal review of RTAs under Article XXIV. These panels' decisions indicated that in the absence of an Article XXIV compatibility recommendation by the GATT working groups, RTAs could be subject to legal review by the GATT panels.[54]

The most important decision rendered by the GATT/WTO dispute settlement bodies with regard to Article XXIV is the WTO Appellate Body's decision in the Turkey-Textile case.[55] A controversial question that arose in this case relates to the jurisdiction of the WTO dispute settlement bodies to examine the legality of WTO Members' actions under Article XXIV. The Appellate Body stated that it is not called upon to address this issue in this appeal but the decision indicates that the WTO dispute settlements bodies are competent to review matters that are also committed to the evaluation of political bodies, such as CRTA.[56]

III. THE ECONOMIC PROSPECTS FOR NORTH–SOUTH RTAS

Although the group of "developing countries" is extremely diverse to generalize regarding the effects of RTAs on particular countries, it is clear that RTAs with developed countries may yield some significant economic benefits for developing countries. Some specialists point out that North–South RTAs generally increase international trade more than South–South RTAs.[57] The potential of enhanced intraregional trade arising from RTAs between developing and developed countries may be explained by certain international trade theories.

[52] *European Community – Tariff Treatment on Imports of Citrus Products from Certain Countries in the Mediterranean Region: Report of the Panel*, Section 4.15 GATT/L/5776 (February 7, 1986) (unadopted).

[53] *EEC – Member States' Import Regime for Bananas*, DS32/R (June 3, 1993; hereinafter "the first Bananas Case"); *EEC – Member States' Import Regimes for Bananas*, DS38/R (February 11, 1994; hereinafter "the second Bananas Case"). For a detailed examination of these panels' decisions, see Mathis (2002) supra note 20, pp. 88–100.

[54] The first Bananas Case (1993), supra note 53, paras. 358, 372; the second Bananas Case (1994), supra note 53, para. 158.

[55] DSB, *Turkey – Restrictions on Imports of Textile and Clothing Products, Report of the Appellate Body*, AB-1995-5, WT/DS34/AB/R (November 19, 1999; hereinafter "Turkey-Textile Case"). For a detailed examination of this decision, see Mathis (2002), supra note 20, pp. 193–226.

[56] *Turkey-Textile Case* (1999), supra note 55, para. 60. See J. Trachtman, "Decision of the Appellate Body of the World Trade Organization: Turkey – Restrictions on Import of Textile and Clothing Products" (2000) 11 *European Journal of International Law* 217. See also Mathis (2002), supra note 20, pp. 215–216, 255–257; Cho (2001), supra note 29, pp. 449–450.

[57] Global Prospects – Overview and Global Outlook World Bank 2005, p. x; F. Foroutan, *Does Membership in a Regional Preferential Trade Arrangement Make a Country More or Less Protectionist?* The World Bank, Policy Research Working Paper No. 1898, (1998), pp. 4, 7. See also Ray (1998), supra note 7, p. 743; D. Puga and A. J. Venables, *Trading Arrangements and Industrial Development*, Center for Economic Performance Discussion Paper 319 (1996), pp. 21–22.

According to the Heckscher–Ohlin model, international trade is largely influenced by differences in factor endowments and technology, and countries tend to export products intensive in the factors with which they are abundantly supplied.[58] In this model, the prospects for trade are higher between countries that have different relative factor endowments and technology.[59] Developing and developed countries are generally very different in their factors of production and technology, and the Heckscher–Ohlin model persuasively explains the increase of intraregional trade that is generated by RTAs between these countries.[60] As the World Bank 2005 Global Outlook explains:

> In general, North–South agreements score better on implementation than South–South agreements. Because North–South agreements can integrate economies with distinct technological capabilities and other different factor proportions, and because they usually result in larger post-agreement markets, the potential gains are usually greater.[61]

As shown by Ricardo, international trade induces participating countries to specialize in sectors in which they enjoy comparative advantage. The gains from specialization and trade include improving the economic welfare of the trading countries (i.e., movement to a higher production-possibility curve) and expanding output.[62] Consequently, the prospects for increased trade generated by North–South RTAs also promise improvement of the involved parties' economic welfare. It should be noted that these desirable outcomes are not assured in every case of North–South RTAs. The realization of the potential economic gains of such RTAs necessitates

58 H. Flam and M. J. Flanders (eds.), *Heckscher–Ohlin Trade Theory* (Cambridge, MA: MIT Press, 1991), p. 44; P. R. Krugman and M. Obstfeld, *International Economics: Theory and Policy* (8th ed., Boston: Pearson Addison-Wesley, 2009), p. 54; E. E. Leamer, "The Heckscher-Ohlin Model in Theory and Practice" (1995) *Princeton Studies in International Finance* No. 77; P. K. Schott, "One Size Fits All? Heckscher–Ohlin Specialization in Global Production" (2003) 93 *American Economic Review* 686.

59 See, e.g., M. P. Todaro and S. C. Smith, *Economic Development* (10th ed., Essex, England: Pearson Education, 2009), pp. 600–605.

60 Ray (1998), supra note 7, p. 635–636, 730. See also S. R. Yeaple and S. S. Golub, "International Productivity Differences, Infrastructure and Comparative Advantage" (2007) 15 *Review of Intl. Economics* 223; E. Helpman, "The Structure of Foreign Trade" (1999) 13 *The Journal of Economic Perspectives* 142; H. Lai and S. Chun Zhu, "Technology, Endowment and the Factor Content of Bilateral Trade" (2007) 71 *Journal of International Economics* 391–394. On the RTAs parties' comparative advantages and the impact of RTAs, see also Schiff and Winters (2003), supra note 2, pp. 69–71.

61 The World Bank, *Global Prospects: Overview and Global Outlook* (Washington, DC: World Bank, 2005), p. x.

62 See, e.g., Krugman and Obstfeld (2009), supra note 58, pp. 27–48; P. Brenton, H. Scott, and P. Sinclair, *International Trade* (Oxford: Oxford University Press, 1997), pp. 14–26. For the argument that North–South RTAs might also adversely affect economic development by solidifying the industrial structure of a developing country and by hampering its changes to yield higher economic welfare for the future, see Yong-Shik Lee, *Reclaiming Development in the World Trading System* (New York: Cambridge University Press, 2006), pp. 4–9.

genuine and comprehensive trade liberalization, including in labor-intensive products in which developing countries have a comparative advantage.[63]

The theory of economies of scale argues that international trade is not necessarily the result of comparative advantage between the involved countries but rather the result of the tendency of per-unit costs to decrease as production scale increases. In accordance with this theory, international trade creates an integrated market of the involved countries, which is larger than any one of the trading countries' markets. The enlargement of the market generated by the formation of an RTA allows producers in these countries favored access to a wider market, thus enabling them to increase production, reduce production costs, and lower prices. Consequently, following the establishment of an RTA, consumers in the involved countries are able to purchase a greater range of products at lower prices.[64]

It is important to note that such beneficial effects of large-scale production are likely to arise in large and competitive markets.[65] Where the relevant economy is relatively closed (as happens in some developing countries) or the integrated market is too small, the positive impacts of RTAs are likely to be significantly reduced (or not materialized at all).

In addition, it is noteworthy that RTAs do not necessarily generate symmetric benefits to producers in all RTAs members. In accordance with the economies of scale theory, the size of the home market may significantly influence the benefits accrued to different parties participating in RTAs. Milner argues that if the home market is already large, the pursuit of scale economies through RTAs will be less important for local producers because they may already be close to the efficient scale.[66] This analysis indicates that developing countries, which often have a smaller home market (in terms of purchasing power),[67] are generally more likely to benefit from the formation of North–South RTAs.[68]

[63] For a discussion of additional necessary elements (such as domestic institutions and flanking measures) in the context of future Economic Partnership Agreements between the EU and ACP countries, see S Szepesi, *Coercion or Engagement? Economics and Institutions in ACP–EU Trade Negotiations*, Discussion Paper No. 56 (Maastricht: European Centre for Development Policy Management, 2004), pp. 8–16.

[64] Krugman and Obstfeld (2009), supra note 58, pp. 114–117, 129–132; Ray (1998), supra note 7, pp. 638–640; P. Collier, *The Bottom Billion* (Oxford: Oxford University Press, 2008), p. 82. On the RTAs and economies of scale, see also Schiff and Winters (2003), supra note 2, pp. 50–54.

[65] S. Szepesi (2004), supra note 63, pp. 11–12.

[66] H. Milner, "Industries, Governments, and the Creation of Regional Trade Blocks," in E. D. Mansfield and H. Milner (eds.), *The Political Economy of Regionalism* (New York: Columbia University Press, 1997), pp. 77, 85.

[67] See, e.g., D. Rodrik, "Imperfect Competition, Scale Economies, and Trade Policies in Developing Countries," in R. E. Baldwin (ed.), *Trade Policy Issues and Empirical Analysis* (National Bureau of Economic Research; Chicago: University of Chicago Press, 1988), pp. 109, 134.

[68] Still, RTAs between developed and developed countries are likely to expand the markets available to producers in developed countries. This is particularly clear with regard to RTAs with large developing countries, such as India or Brazil.

On the other hand, many developing countries do not implement comprehensive liberal policies in their domestic markets,[69] and this fact may often lead to reduced benefits generated by RTAs with developed countries. Liberalizing external trade with developed countries is expected to enhance competition in the domestic market, but it is no substitute for competitive policies that are largely determined by the local governments of developing countries[70] (although RTAs may also require the adoption of some competitive policies).

Foreign investments are important for numerous developing countries. Large investors may provide the capital and technological knowledge essential for industrialization.[71] Ethier's influential article, "The New Regionalism" (1998), discusses the impacts of North–South RTAs on foreign investment. Ethier underscores one of the typical features of the new wave of regionalism, which is the linking of one or more small country with a larger country.[72] The new RTAs should be viewed as an instrument through which new or small countries compete among themselves for direct investments. The numerous countries that undertake economic reforms consider the capacity to attract foreign direct investments the key to successful entry into the multilateral trading system. Still, the risk of future reversion to nonliberal policies undermines the long-term credibility of the reform. An establishment of an RTA with a large developed country adds a credible enforcement mechanism and constitutes an external commitment to continued long-term reformed policies. This external commitment "makes the country more attractive for direct investments, relative to similar countries without such external commitments."[73] These facts explain why reforming countries are interested in establishing such arrangements,

[69] See, e.g., with regard to ACP countries, Szepesi (2004), supra note 63, pp. 10–11. With regard to sub-Saharan African countries, see M. L. Tupy, "Trade Liberalization and Poverty Reduction in Sub-Saharan Africa" (2005) *Cato Institute Policy Analysis* no. 557, available at: http://www.cato.org/pubs/pas/pa557.pdf; The Heritage Foundation, *Lack of Economic Freedom Plagues Sub-Saharan Africa, Index Finds* (press release, January 13, 2009), available at: http://www.heritage.org/press/newsreleases/index09a.cfm. See also F. Ng and A. Yeats, *Open Economies Better! Did Africa's Protectionist Policies Cause Its Marginalization World Trade?* (World Bank Policy Research Paper No. 1636, 1996), available at: http://papers.ssrn.com/sol3/papers.cfm?abstract_id=620497; J. Gwartney and R. Lawson, *Economic Freedom of the World: 2007 Annual Report* (2007), available at: http://www.freetheworld.com/2007/EFW2007BOOK2.pdf, p. 4.

[70] Szepesi (2004), supra note 63, pp. 10–11.

[71] On the linkages among trade, foreign investment, and competitiveness in developing countries, see L. T. Katesli, "Investment, Trade and International Competitiveness," in J. H. Dunning and K. A. Hamdani (eds.), *The New Globalism and Developing Countries* (Tokyo: UN University Press, 1997), p. 181. On the role of trade in stimulating international knowledge spillovers between industrialized and developing countries, see Szepsi (2004), supra note 63, p. 12.

[72] According to Ethier, the additional features of the "New Regionalism" are (a) the small countries have recently made, or are making, significant unilateral reforms; (b) the degree of liberalization provided for in the agreements is generally modest; (c) the obligations regarding liberalization apply primarily to the small countries; (d) the regional arrangements often involve "deep" integration and member states are committed to harmonize other economic policies; and (e) The participating states are usually neighbors. W. J. Ethier, "The New Regionalism" (1998) 108 *Economic Journal* 1150–1152.

[73] Ethier (1998), supra note 72, p. 1157.

even though they often receive only minor trade concessions from their partners. Ethier states that his model primarily applies to the developing countries and former communist countries but may also be applied, with modifications, to small industrialized countries.[74]

Ethier's model places the subject of investment at the heart of the new wave of regionalism. He views RTAs as a tool for promoting foreign investments to developing countries. Furthermore, within this model that accords utmost importance to investment, the major role of RTAs is to enhance the *credibility* of economic reforms pursued by developing countries. RTAs are employed in this construction as a signaling device to reveal essential information to foreign investors.

NAFTA is the prime example of Ethier's model. The aspiration to attract foreign investments was one of the primary factors that motivated Mexico to accede to this RTA.[75] Some empirical studies confirm that this goal has been significantly realized.[76] Similar impacts, in terms of foreign investment inflows, were generated by the series of agreements concluded during the 1990s between the EU and Eastern and Central European countries and their impending accession to the union.[77] Likewise, the desire to attract foreign investment played an important role in the negotiations between Chile and the United States toward the establishment of the FTA agreement.[78] The same motivation inspired the negotiations between Central American states and the United States toward the formation of the FTA.[79]

Although Ethier's model sheds new light on the interrelationship between foreign investment and RTAs, it is clear that his scheme should not be considered an exclusive path or an exhaustive list of conditions for investment inflow. Other factors, such as the size of the RTA market, strong commitment to rule of law (including securing private property),[80] skilled labor, and adequate infrastructure are also of prime importance for attracting foreign investments. These factors, which are of major importance for foreign investors, do not exist in some developing countries.[81]

74 Ethier (1998), supra note 72, pp. 1156–1159.

75 S. Haggard, *Developing Nations and the Politics of Global Integration* (Washington, DC: The Brookings Institution, 1995), p. 94.

76 A. Walkdrich, *The "New Regionalism" and Foreign Direct Investment: The Case of Mexico* (Manuscript, SSRN Library, October 2001), pp. 1, 3–5.

77 S. Wagstl, "Investment Goes East Boosting EU Integration Drive," *Financial Times*, October 31, 2002; UNCTAD, *World Investment Report 2003* (New York: United Nations, 2003), pp. xiv, 3–4.

78 "Chile Economy: Going It Alone," *The Economist*, January 4, 2003.

79 See, e.g., "Nicaragua Sees CAFTA as Part of Investment Strategy," *International Trade Reporter*, February 20, 2003, p. 359; "How to Trade Up," *The Economist*, February 15, 2003.

80 See, e.g., Szepesi (2004), supra note 63, p. 13.

81 On the lack of adequate infrastructure and skilled labor force as obstacles to successful regional initiatives and development in the West African Economic Union, see P. Robson, *The Economics of International Integration* (4th ed., London and New York: Routledge, 1998), p. 284; M. N. Jovanovic, *International Economic Integration: Limits and Prospects* (2nd ed., London and New York: Routledge, 1998), p. 328.

IV. THE RISKS OF NORTH–SOUTH RTAS

Some North–South RTAs, and particularly bilateral ones, may favor the interests of the developed party and its domestic groups. Such agreements often apply more restrictive rules to trade in agricultural products (compared with industrial goods)[82] on one hand and liberal rules for trade in industrial goods (and services) on the other.[83] Thus, for instance, the World Bank Global Prospects Report notes that "[t]he practice of excluding many agricultural products is common, and it can limit development payoffs."[84] In addition, stringent rules of origin (RoOs), and particularly more restrictive ones applied to products of importance for developing countries (such as agricultural or textile goods),[85] restrict the economic benefits accruing to developing parties.[86] In addition, developing countries with low labor costs are often more constrained by RoOs, most prominently with regard to domestic content criteria.[87] Furthermore, some trade topics that are of interest to major developed countries, such as investment and competition, were not accepted by the WTO Ministerial Conference in Cancun in 2004 but are included in some recent RTAs between developed and developing countries.[88]

The deficiencies of some North–South RTAs may be explained by political economy analysis (emphasizing the role of domestic groups in trade policy) as well as by asymmetric bargaining positions during the negotiation process. The point of departure for political economy analysis of trade policy is that international trade generates distributional consequences (meaning that there are "winners and losers"). The gains arising from free trade are not equally distributed among the various segments of the population and some groups incur significant losses.[89] Groups suffering losses due to a particular trade policy are likely to oppose it, whereas groups benefiting from such policy are expected to support it. Consequently, the shaping of

[82] See, e.g., The World Bank, *Global Prospects – Overview and Global Outlook* (2005), pp. ix–x.

[83] See, e.g., Gibbs and Wagle (2005), supra note 39, p. 52.

[84] *Global Prospects* (2005), supra note 61, p. xiii; see also R. Newfarmer, *Regional Trade Agreements: Designs for Development*, available at: http://www.ppl.nl/bibliographies/wto/files/6535.pdf. See also Matsushita and Lee (2008), supra note 41, p. 32, and the references therein.

[85] On the significant role agricultural export for developing countries, see, e.g., Todaro and Smith (2005), supra note 59, pp. 591–593.

[86] World Bank (2005) supra note 61, p. x; Matsushita and Lee (2008) supra note 41, p. 28; Szepesi (2004), supra note 63, p. 15. On the restrictive rules of origin included in developed countries' systems of preferences, see A. Portugal-Perez and J. S. Wilson, *Why Trade Facilitation Matters to Africa* (Washington, DC: Development Research Group, World Bank, 2008), section 3.4.

[87] M. Hirsch, "International Trade Law, Political Economy and Rules of Origin: A Plea for a Reform of the WTO Regime on Rules of Origin" (2002) 36 *Journal of World Trade* 187–188.

[88] Crawford and Fiorentino (2005), supra note 1, pp. 5–6; Gibbs and Wagle (2005), supra note 39, pp. 10–11, 52. See also Matsushita and Lee (2008), supra note 41, pp. 26–27.

[89] A. L. Hillman, *The Political Economy of Protection* (Chur, Switzerland: Hardwood Academic Publishers, 1989), pp. 1–3; E. B. Kapstein, "Winners and Losers in the Global Economy" (2000) 54 *International Organization* 359, 364.

trade policy is often perceived in political economy literature as a struggle among domestic interest groups.[90]

The Heckscher–Ohlin model shows that the prospects for trade are maximized between countries with different factors of production and technology – and this is clearly the case with regard to trade between developing and developed countries. The fact that the gains from economic liberalization are not evenly distributed among all groups within a country explains the opposition of some domestic groups (the "losers") to these arrangements. The distributive concerns are intensified because of the expected increase in trade. Thus, RTAs with developing countries often generate fears in developed countries regarding a "flood" of labor-intensive products and increasing unemployment. Such concerns often lead strong interest groups within developed countries to oppose such RTAs vigorously.[91]

Milner employs political economy analysis to explain different patterns of RTAs. She argues that the formation and content of these arrangements reflect political leaders' rational responses to their domestic situation.[92] Consequently, it seems that the limited coverage of RTAs regarding agricultural products (relative to manufactured goods), as well as with regard to various restrictions regarding trade in other labor-intensive products, reflects the pressure of domestic groups within developed countries.

The unfavorable rules toward developing countries included in some North–South RTAs may also be explained by the asymmetric positions of the parties negotiating these agreements. Developing countries are often at a disadvantage in such negotiations. These weaker positions often relate to the unequal economic resources available to the parties,[93] as well as the expertise of the negotiators. The asymmetric bargaining positions are prominent in bilateral RTAs that involve a powerful trading party (such as the EU or the United States) and a small developing country. Such bilateral and asymmetric settings are more susceptible to generate trade rules that favor the interests of domestic groups within developed countries. The position of developing countries is often enhanced in multilateral or global trade forums (such as the WTO), where they may form coalitions. Unification of forces enables

[90] G. M. Grossman and E. Helpman, *Interest Groups and Trade Policy* (Princeton, NJ: Princeton University Press, 2002), p. 111 et seq; Milner (1997), supra note 66, pp. 86–88. On the main factors that affect the shaping of trade policy in the domestic arena, see D. Rodrik, "Political Economy of Trade Policy," in G. M. Grossman and K. Rogoff (eds.), *Handbook of International Economics*, Vol. 3 (Amsterdam: Elsevier, 1995), pp. 1457, 1459.

[91] Ray (1998), supra note 7, pp. 731–733.

[92] Milner (1997), supra note 66, pp. 77–89; Grossman and Helpman (2003), supra note 90, p. 199 et seq.

[93] See, e.g., F. N. Garcia, "Is Free Trade 'Free?' Is It Even 'Trade?' Oppression and Consent in Hemispheric Trade Agreements" (2007), Boston College Law School Legal Studies Research Paper Series, available at: http://papers.ssrn.com/sol3/papers.cfm?abstract_id=957851; Matsushita and Lee (2008), supra note 41, pp. 25–26.

the weaker countries to strengthen their bargaining capacity vis-à-vis the stronger countries in the global economic system.[94]

V. ENHANCING THE PROSPECT OF NORTH–SOUTH RTAS FOR DEVELOPING COUNTRIES

The foregoing sections indicate that although North–South RTAs may significantly contribute to economic development in developing countries, some of them include rules that often decrease the likely benefits of these arrangements to developing countries. Such nondesirable features are prominent with regard to restrictions included in RTAs on trade in labor-intensive products (such as agricultural and textile products). This section briefly discusses some mechanisms that may ameliorate the shortcomings of certain RTAs.

RTAs should be negotiated on the bilateral or regional level, and negotiations on these levels are generally more suitable for this task because they enable the directly involved parties to formulate the particular rules needed in the specific context. Multilateral or global arrangements may, however, play a complementary role in enhancing the contribution of RTAs to the economic development in developing countries. Thus, for instance, if a poorer country lacks the resources for meaningful negotiations with a developed country, multilateral institutions may provide the needed financial resources and legal expertise.[95]

Multilateral institutions may also establish nonbinding principles to guide the negotiating parties. Such guidelines may, for instance, set some substantive principles, prominently with regard to trade in labor-intensive products or regarding the allocation of trade benefits between the developing and developed parties.[96] Multilateral organizations may also set certain principles regarding rules of origin included in North–South RTAs.

Producers in developing countries often rely on low production costs, but this economic advantage may well reduce their capacity to comply with RoOs related to local content.[97] To ameliorate this problem, multilateral institutions may set guidelines regarding progressive origin requirements that assign different local content rates to products of developing and developed countries (or designate a favorable "tolerance rule" for products originating from developing countries) corresponding to their relative production costs. Similarly, global guiding instruments may call

94 See, e.g., Hirsch (2008), supra note 13, section 5.

95 See Matsushita and Lee (2008), supra note 41, p. 27.

96 See, e.g., Matsushita and Lee (2008), supra note 41, p. 27.

97 See, e.g., M. Hirsch, "The Asymmetric Incidence of Rules of Origin" (1998) 32 *Journal of World Trade* 41, 52–53; M. Hirsch, "Agreement on Rules of Origin," in R. Wolfrum, P. T. Stoll, and H. P. Holger (eds.), *WTO – Trade in Goods* (Leiden, the Netherlands: Nijhoff, 2011), pp. 1101, 1106.

negotiating parties to include commulation of origin arrangements (among several developing countries) in RTAs between developing and developed countries.[98]

As noted earlier, the WTO oversight process of RTAs has proved to be a weak enforcement mechanism of the conditions laid out in WTO agreements.[99] Because some North–South RTAs are more susceptible to rules that favor the interests of the more powerful parties, the WTO organs may review such RTAs with enhanced scrutiny.

VI. CONCLUDING REMARKS

The preceding sections indicate that North–South RTAs present some potential benefits to developing countries, prominently because of the differing factors of production, the impact of economies of scale (increasing production and lowering production costs), and the attraction of foreign investment. The establishment of an RTA between developing and developed countries certainly does not guarantee that these advantages will be generated and maintained. Domestic features of many developing countries (relating to size of the market and the level of competitions among producers) as well as external factors (relating to the content of those RTAs), often undermine the realizations of the earlier-noted economic advantages. As discussed, some North–South RTAs favor the interest of stronger developed countries, and they constrain the capacity of the poorer party to export products in which it enjoys a comparative advantage. This is the case, for instance, with regard to restrictive rules regarding trade in agricultural products as well as rules of origin.

Consequently, it is impossible to appraise the prospects of all North–South RTAs and forecast whether they are beneficial to developing countries (and if they are, to what extent). Realizing the potential benefits of RTAs between developing and developed countries hinges to a large measure on the agreements' detailed provisions, including its coverage and rules regarding various nontariff barriers (including rules of origin and rules regarding sanitary standards). Equally important is that although trade agreements may promote economic development in poor countries, certain domestic factors within developing countries are also of major importance for long-term development. As noted earlier,[100] liberalizing external trade with developed countries may help to enhance competition in the domestic market, it is by no means substitute for competitive policies that are largely determined by local governments. Thus, if the market of a developing country is closed and noncompetitive, the potential benefits of RTAs are less likely to be materialized.

[98] For a detailed analysis of such compensatory mechanisms, see M. Hirsch, (1998), supra note 97, section IV.

[99] Ibid., section II.

[100] Ibid., section III.

Finally, recent economic literature suggests that domestic institutions play a pivotal role in economic development[101] and that the quality of institutions is of more significance than international trade.[102] Similarly, studies on the relationship between corruption and economic development have concluded that corruption generates adverse effects on the incentives, prices, and opportunities that private and public agents face.[103] Generally, higher levels of corruption are associated with lower government revenues, lower expenditures on operations and maintenance, and lower quality of public infrastructure.[104]

Thus, it is clear that the quality of domestic institutions in developing countries is also of major importance regarding the realization of the potential of North–South RTAs.

REFERENCES

Anderson, K., and H. Norheim, "History, Geography, and Regional Integration," in K. Anderson and R. Blackhurst (eds.), *Regional Integration and the Global Trading System* (New York: St. Martin's Press, 1993).

Bhagwati, J., "Regionalism and Multilateralism: An Overview," in J. Bhagwati, P. Krishna, and A. Panagariya (eds.), *Trading Blocs: Alternative Approaches to Analyzing Preferential Trade Agreements* (Cambridge, MA: MIT Press, 1999).

Bhagwati, J., and A. Panagriya, "Preferential Trading Areas and Multilateralism – Strangers, Friends, or Foes?" in *The Economics of Preferential Trade Agreements* (The AEI Press, Center for International Economics, University of Maryland, 1996, Washington, DC).

Bhala, R., *Modern GATT Law* (London: Sweet and Maxwell, 2005).

Blackburn, K., N. Bose, and M. E. Haque, *Endogenous Corruption in Economic Development* (2004), available at: http://ssrn.com/abstract=761705.

Brenton, P., H. Scott, and P. Sinclair, *International Trade* (Oxford: Oxford University Press, 1997).

Cho, S., "Breaking the Barrier between Regionalism and Multilateralism" (2001) 42 *Harvard International Law Journal*.

Collier, P., *The Bottom Billion* (Oxford: Oxford University Press, 2008).

Cottier, T., "The Challenge of Regionalism and Preferential Relations in World Trade Law and Policy" (1996) 1 *European Foreign Affairs Review*.

Crawford, J. A., and R. V. Fiorentino, *The Changing Landscape of Regional Trade Agreements*, Discussion Paper, World Trade Organization (2005).

[101] According to North, institutions are "the rules of the game of a society or more formally are the humanly-devised constraints that structure human interaction. They are composed of formal rules (statutes law, common law, regulations), informal constraints (conventions, norms of behavior, and self imposed codes of conduct), and the enforcement characteristics of both." D. C. North, *The New Institutional Economics and Development*, available at: http://www.econ.iastate.edu/tesfatsi/NewInstE.North.pdf, pp. 5–6.

[102] D. Rodrik, A. Subramanian, and F. Trebbi, *Institutions Rule: The Primacy of Institutions over Integration and Geography in Economic Development*, IMF Working Paper WP/02/189 (2002).

[103] K. Blackburn, N. Bose, and M. E. Haque, *Endogenous Corruption in Economic Development* (2004), available at: http://ssrn.com/abstract=761705, pp. 3–4.

[104] V. Tanzi and H. R. Davoodi, *Corruption, Public Investment and Growth*, IMF Working Paper No. 97/139 (1999), p. 1, available at: http://ssrn.com/abstract=882701.

Desta, M., "EC–ACP Economic Partnership Agreements and WTO Compatibility: An Experiment in North–South Inter-Regional Agreements?" (2006) 43 *Common Market Law Review*.

Dimova, R., *Preferential Trade Areas and Global Trade: Friends or Foes?* ICRA Working Paper No. 2, SSRN Library (2000), available at: http://papers.ssrn.com/sol3/papers.cfm?abstract_id=248268.

Ethier, W. J., "The New Regionalism" (1998) 108 *Economic Journal*.

Fabbricotti, A., *The Asean Free Trade Area (AFTA) and Its Compatibility with GATT/WTO* (October 26, 2009), available at: http://papers.ssrn.com/sol3/papers.cfm?abstract_id=1494550.

Finger, J. M., "GATT's Influence on Regional Arrangements," in J. de Malo and A. Panagariya (eds.), *New Dimensions in Regional Integration* (Cambridge: Cambridge University Press, 1993).

Flam, H., and M. J. Flanders (eds.), *Heckscher–Ohlin Trade Theory* (Cambridge, MA: MIT Press, 1991).

Foroutan, F., *Does Membership in a Regional Preferential Trade Arrangement Make a Country More or Less Protectionist?* The World Bank, Policy Research Working Paper No. 1898 (1998).

Garcia, F. N., "Is Free Trade 'Free?' Is It Even 'Trade?' Oppression and Consent in Hemispheric Trade Agreements" (2007), Boston College Law School Legal Studies Research Paper Series, available at: http://papers.ssrn.com/sol3/papers.cfm?abstract_id=957851.

Gibbs, M., and S. Wagle, *The Great Maze: Regional and Bilateral Free Trade Agreements in Asia* (Colombo, Sri Lanka: Asia-Pacific Trade and Investment Initiative, United Nations Development Programme Regional Center, 2005).

Grether, J. M., *Preferential and Non-Preferential Trade Flows in World Trade*, Staff Working Paper ERAD-98-10, Economic Research and Analysis Division, World Trade Organization (1998).

Grossman G. M., and E. Helpman, *Interest Groups and Trade Policy* (Princeton, NJ: Princeton University Press, 2002).

Gwartney, J., and R. Lawson, *Economic Freedom of the World: 2007 Annual Report* (2007), available at: http://www.freetheworld.com/2007/EFW2007BOOK2.pdf.

Haggard, S., *Developing Nations and the Politics of Global Integration* (Washington, DC: The Brookings Institution, 1995).

Helpman, E., "The Structure of Foreign Trade" (1999) 13 *The Journal of Economic Perspectives*.

The Heritage Foundation, *Lack of Economic Freedom Plagues Sub-Saharan Africa, Index Finds* (press release, January 13, 2009), available at: http://www.heritage.org/press/newsreleases/index09a.cfm.

Hillman, A. L., *The Political Economy of Protection* (Chur, Switzerland: Hardwood Academic Publishers, 1989).

Hirsch, M., "The Asymmetric Incidence of Rules of Origin" (1998) 32 *Journal of World Trade*.

______, "International Trade Law, Political Economy and Rules of Origin: A Plea for a Reform of the WTO Regime on Rules of Origin" (2002) 36 *Journal of World Trade*.

______, "The Logic of North–South Economic Integration" (2005) 32 *Legal Issues of Economic Integration*.

______, "The Sociology of International Economic Law: Sociological Analysis of the Regulation of Regional Agreements in the World Trading System" (2008) 19 *European Journal of International Law*.

———, "Agreement on Rules of Origin," in R. Wolfrum, P. T. Stoll, and H. P. Holdger (eds.), *WTO – Trade in Goods* (Leiden, the Netherlands: Nijhoff, 2011).

Hoekman, B. M., and M. M. Kostecki, *The Political Economy of The World Trading System* (2nd ed., New York: Oxford University Press, 2001).

Jackson, J. H., W. Davey, and A. O. Sykes, *Legal Problems of International Economic Relations* (St. Paul, MN: West Group, 2002).

Jovanovic, M. N., *International Economic Integration: Limits and Prospects* (2nd ed., London and New York: Routledge, 1998).

Kapstein, E. B., "Winners and Losers in the Global Economy" (2000) 54 *International Organization*.

Katesli, L. T., "Investment, Trade and International Competitiveness," in J. H. Dunning and K. A. Hamdani (eds.), *The New Globalism and Developing Countries* (Tokyo: UN University Press, 1997).

Krugman, P. R., and M. Obstfeld, *International Economics: Theory and Policy* (8th ed., Boston: Pearson Addison-Wesley, 2009).

Lai, H., and S. Chun Zhu, "Technology, Endowment and the Factor Content of Bilateral Trade" (2007) 71 *Journal of International Economics*.

Lawrence, R. Z., *Regionalism, Multilateralism, and Deeper Integration* (Washington, DC: The Brookings Institution, 1996).

———, "Regionalism and the WTO: Should the Rules Be Changed?" in *The World Trading System: Challenges Ahead* (Washington, DC: Institute of International Economics, 1996).

Leamer, E. E., "The Heckscher-Ohlin Model in Theory and Practice" (1995) *Princeton Studies in International Finance No. 77*.

Lee, Y. S., *Reclaiming Development in the World Trading System* (New York: Cambridge University Press, 2006).

Lockhart, N., and A. Mitchell, "Regional Trade Agreements under GATT 1994: An Exception and Its Limits," in A. Mitchell (ed.), *Challenges and Prospects for the WTO* (London: Cameron May, 2005).

Lombaerde, P. de, A. Estevadeordal, and K. Souminen, "Governing Regional Integration for Development: Introduction," in P. de Lombaerde, A. Estevadeordal, and K. Souminen (eds.), *Governing Regional Integration for Development* (Aldershot, England: Ashgate, 2008).

Mavroidis, P., "If I Don't Do It, Somebody Else Will (or Won't)" (2006) 40 *Journal of World Trade*.

———, *Trade in Goods: The GATT and the Other Agreements Regulating Trade in Goods* (Oxford: Oxford University Press, 2007).

Mathis, J. H., *Regional Trade Agreements in the GATT/WTO* (The Hague: Asser Press, 2002).

Matsushita, M., and Y. S. Lee, "Proliferation of Free Trade Agreements and Some Systemic Issues – In Relation to the WTO Disciplines and Development Perspectives" (2008) 1 *The Law and Development Review*.

Matsushita, M., T. J. Schoenbaum, and P. C. Mavoroidis, *The World Trade Organization: Law, Practice and Policy* (2nd ed., Oxford: Oxford University Press, 2006).

Milner, H., "Industries, Governments, and the Creation of Regional Trade Blocks," in E. D. Mansfield and H. Milner (eds.), *The Political Economy of Regionalism* (New York: Columbia University Press, 1997).

Newfarmer, R., *Regional Trade Agreements: Designs for Development*, available at: http://www.ppl.nl/bibliographies/wto/files/6535.pdf.

Ng, F., and A. Yeats, *Open Economies Better! Did Africa's Protectionist Policies Cause Its Marginalization World Trade?* World Bank Policy Research Paper No. 1636 (1996), available at: http://papers.ssrn.com/sol3/papers.cfm?abstract_id=620497.

North, D. C., *The New Institutional Economics and Development*, available at: http://www.econ.iastate.edu/tesfatsi/NewInstE.North.pdf.

Organization for Economic Cooperation and Development, *Regionalism and the Multilateral Trading System* (Paris: OECD, 2003).

Picker, C. B., "Regional Trade Agreements v. the WTO" (2005) 26 *University of Pennsylvania Journal of International Economic Law*.

Pomfert, R., *The Economics of Regional Trade Arrangements* (Oxford: Clarendon Press, 1997).

Portugal-Perez, A., and J. S. Wilson, *Why Trade Facilitation Matters to Africa* (Washington, DC: Development Research Group, World Bank).

Puga, P., and A. J. Venables, *Trading Arrangements and Industrial Development*, Center for Economic Performance Discussion Paper 319 (1996).

Ray, D., *Development Economics* (Princeton, NJ: Princeton University Press, 1998).

Robson, P., *The Economics of International Integration* (4th ed., London and New York: Routledge, 1998).

Rodrik, D., "Imperfect Competition, Scale Economies, and Trade Policies in Developing Countries," in R. E. Baldwin (ed.), *Trade Policy Issues and Empirical Analysis* (National Bureau of Economic Research; Chicago: University of Chicago Press, 1988).

______, "Political Economy of Trade Policy," in G. M. Grossman and K. Rogoff (eds.), *Handbook of International Economics*, Vol. 3 (Amsterdam: Elsevier, 1995).

Rodrik, D., A. Subramanian, and F. Trebbi, *Institutions Rule: The Primacy of Institutions over Integration and Geography in Economic Development*, IMF Working Paper WP/02/189 (2002).

Schiff, M., *Multilateral Trade Liberalization, Political Disintegration and the Choice of FTAs versus Customs Union*, World Bank Policy Research Paper No. 2350, Development Research Department (2000).

Schiff, M., and A. Winters, *Regional Integration and Development* (Washington, DC: World Bank and Oxford University Press, 2003).

Schott, J. J., "More Free Trade Areas?" in J. J. Schott (ed.), *Free Trade Areas and U.S. Trade Policy* (Washington, DC: Institute of International Economics, 1989).

Schott, P. K., "One Size Fits All? Heckscher-Ohlin Specialization in Global Production" (2003) 93 *American Economic Review*.

Sutherland, P., J. Bhagwati, K. Botchwey, N. FitzGerald, K. Hamada, J. H. Jackson, C. Lafer, and T. de Montbrial, *The Future of the WTO: Addressing Institutional Challenges in the New Millennium – Report by the Consultative Board to the Director-General Supachai Panitchpakdi* (Geneva: World Trade Organization, 2004).

Szepesi, S., *Coercion or Engagement? Economics and Institutions in ACP–EU Trade Negotiations*, Discussion Paper No. 56 (Maastricht: European Centre for Development Policy Management, 2004).

Tanzi, V., and H. R. Davoodi, *Corruption, Public Investment and Growth*, IMF Working Paper No. 97/139 (1997), available at: http://ssrn.com/abstract=882701.

Todaro, M. P., and S. C. Smith, *Economic Development* (10th ed., Essex, England: Pearson Education, 2009).

Trachtman, J., "Decision of the Appellate Body of the World Trade Organization: Turkey – Restrictions on Import of Textile and Clothing Products" (2000) 11 *European Journal of International Law*.

______ , "Toward Open Recognition? Standards and Regional Integration under Article XXIV of GATT" (2003) 6 *Journal of International Economic Law.*

Trebilcock, M. J., and R. Howse, *The Regulation of International Trade* (3rd ed., London and New York: Routledge, 2005).

Tupy, M. L., "Trade Liberalization and Poverty Reduction in Sub-Saharan Africa" (2005) *Cato Institute Policy Analysis* 557, available at: http://www.cato.org/pubs/pas/pa557.pdf.

United Nations Conference on Trade and Development, *World Investment Report 2003* (New York: United Nations, 2003).

Van den Bossche, P., *The Law and Policy of the World Trade Organization: Text, Cases and Materials* (2nd ed., New York: Cambridge University Press, 2008).

Viner, V., *The Customs Union Issue* (New York: Carnegie Endowment for International Peace, 1950).

Wagstl, S., "Investment Goes East Boosting EU Integration Drive," *Financial Times*, October 31, 2002.

Walkdrich, A., *The "New Regionalism" and Foreign Direct Investment: The Case of Mexico* (Manuscript, SSRN Library, October 2001).

Whalley, J., *Recent Regional Agreements: Why So Many, So Fast, So Different and Where Are They Headed?* Working Paper – International Institutional Reform, the Centre for International Governance Innovation (2006).

Wonnacottt, P., and M. Lutz, "Is There a Case for Free Trade Areas?" in J. J. Schott (ed.), *Free Trade Areas and U.S. Trade Policy* (Washington, DC: Institute of International Economics, 1989).

World Bank, *Global Economic Prospects: Trade, Regionalism, and Development* (Washington, DC: World Bank, 2005).

______, *Global Prospects: Overview and Global Outlook* (Washington, DC: World Bank, 2005).

World Trade Organization, *Analytical Index: Guide to GATT Law and Practice* (6th ed., Geneva: WTO, 1994).

______, *WTO Annual Report – 2005* (Geneva: WTO, 2005).

Yeaple S. R., and S. S. Golub, "International Productivity Differences, Infrastructure and Comparative Advantage" (2007) 15 *Review of International Economics.*

10

Free Trade Agreements

WTO Disciplines and Development Perspectives

Mitsuo Matsushita and Yong-Shik Lee

I. PROLIFERATION OF FREE TRADE AGREEMENTS

Free trade agreements (FTAs)[1] are undoubtedly becoming a prominent feature in the world trading system: in 1990, 27 FTAs had been reported to the General Agreement on Tariffs and Trade (GATT), and this number increased to 421 as of December 2008.[2] More than 90% of the members of the World Trade Organization (WTO) are participants in FTAs. Many reasons are attributed to this increase in FTAs. Undoubtedly, this proliferation of FTAs was prompted by the failure of international trade negotiations at the WTO. WTO Ministerial Conferences failed in Seattle (1999) and Cancun (2003). Although the Hong Kong Ministerial (2005) was not a total failure, many have criticized as only half-success. The previously launched Doha Round is still stalemated. In parallel to the unsuccessful events at the WTO, trading nations negotiated FTAs with each other and came up with bilateral and regional agreements. In response to the failure of the WTO to agree on direct investment issues, trading nations also entered into many bilateral investment

[1] An FTA can be a bilateral agreement or regional trade agreement (RTA), an agreement in which several countries participate on a regional basis or on the basis of some economic commonality, such as the North American Free Trade Agreement (NAFTA) and Mercado Común del Sur (MERCOSUR, Southern Common Market). There is an international agreement called an economic partnership agreement (EPA). Generally, EPAs include not only trade concessions, such as reduction and elimination of tariffs and quantitative restrictions, but also other forms of arrangements, such as cooperative relationships in the areas of competition policy, environment, government procurement, energy, and so on. In this chapter, for the sake of brevity, the FTA is used to represent FTA, RTA, and EPA unless a distinction is necessary.

[2] WTO, *Regional Trade Agreements*, available at: http://www.wto.org/english/tratop_e/region_e/region_e.htm.

An earlier version of this chapter was published in 1(1) *Law and Development Review* (2008), 23–49.

agreements (BITs). In 2008, the number of BITs was 2,608,[3] and this number is still increasing.

At the same time, the share of FTAs in total world trade has increased tremendously. At present, the big four FTAs (the European Union [EU], NAFTA, the MERCOSUR, and the Association of Southeast Asian Nations [ASEAN]) account for 57% of the total export trade and 63% of the total import trade in the world.[4] As these statistics show, it is not an overstatement to say that FTAs are not an exception merely to the WTO system but parallel the multilateral trade disciplines in the WTO. The proliferation of bilateral and regional agreements may cause erosion to the disciplines of the WTO, and the effectiveness of the multilateral trading system is in jeopardy.[5]

An FTA may be an easy substitute for a difficult multilateral arrangement. Often nations in close geographic proximity share common interests. There may be common elements in culture, religion, language, history, and social and economic systems among such nations. Members of the EU share not only geographic proximity but also common historical backgrounds and linguistic closeness. Nations may share some other trade interests. For example, Japan and Mexico are far away from each other geographically, but Japan is interested in establishing an economic relationship with Mexico so that Japanese enterprises may gain access to the NAFTA market, and Mexico is interested in diversifying its trade connections and reducing its excessive dependence on the United States and the North American market. Because of these and other reasons, there has been an explosion of the WTO regime in the recent years, including, for instance, a recent noteworthy development in East Asia, that is, the signing of a United States–Korea FTA in 2007.[6]

East Asia has lagged behind Western and Latin American countries in creating FTAs. Recently, however, the trend toward FTAs has intensified in East Asia. For example, until recently, Korea and Japan were the only two industrialized trading nations in East Asia that had not entered into FTAs. Recently, both Korea and Japan, as well as China and other ASEAN countries, have entered into FTAs. China is working toward ASEAN + 3, and Korea recently entered into an FTA with the United States. Japan is proposing ASEAN + 6. Similarly, Japan has entered into an FTA with Singapore, Mexico, Malaysia, Philippines, Thailand, and Indonesia.

[3] United Nations Conference on Trade and Development, *World Investment Report 2009*, p. 32, available at: http://www.unctad.org/en/docs/wir2009_en.pdf.

[4] WTO, *International Trade Statistics 2009*, pp. 178–179, tables A3 and A4, available at: http://www.wto.org/english/res_e/statis_e/its2009_e/its2009_e.pdf.

[5] Some systemic issues with regard to the relationship between the WTO disciplines and FTAs/RTAs are extensively discussed in WTO, *Synopsis of "Systemic" Issues Related To Regional Trade Agreements*, WT/REG/W/37 (March 2, 2000).

[6] For a discussion of the United States–Korea FTA, see Y. S. Lee, "The Beginning of Economic Integration between East Asia and North America? – Forming the Third Largest Free Trade Area between the United States and the Republic of Korea" (2007) 41(5) *Journal of World Trade* 1091–1123.

Bilateral negotiations for an FTA are also underway among Japan, Australia, Chile, India, and Korea.

What is the justification for bilateral or regional FTAs in which there is a multilateral trading system in operation under the auspices of the WTO? Compared with multilateral trade negotiations, bilateral and regional trade negotiations for FTAs are generally easier. FTAs may have an effect of expanding free trade beyond what can currently be agreed in the multilateral trading system: if an FTA is successful, the trade in the areas covered by the FTA is liberalized, and the "zone" for the free trade has been expanded. The trade liberalization may promote economic development of the region by increasing economic efficiency. Economic prosperity achieved by the FTA provides a greater opportunity for enterprises outside the region to trade with the region and invest in it.

However, the proliferation of FTAs presents a serious systemic problem to the WTO regime. An FTA is a preferential trading system in which each participant provides concessions to other participants in one way or another. In this sense, an FTA is essentially a discriminatory system vis-à-vis outside parties. The most fundamental principle of the WTO, in contrast, is nondiscrimination among trading nations, as expressed in Articles I and III of the GATT (most-favored-nation (MFN) treatment and national treatment, respectively). The relationship between FTAs and the WTO is a complicated one. On one hand, there is a complementary relationship between the two in that FTAs can accomplish trade liberalization in the areas in which WTO negotiations are not successful, such as direct investment, competition, environment, and so on. In this way, FTAs can accomplish partial liberalization when trade negotiations at the WTO come to an impasse. One might say that partial liberalization is better than no liberalization.

On the other hand, discriminatory treatment involved in FTAs creates an imbalance in the competitive conditions among trading nations and thereby causes unfairness and inequity in trading relations. This may be especially hard on developing countries outside FTA arrangements, which depend on foreign trade and the inflow of foreign capital for their economic development. Equity might also be a question for developing countries negotiating FTAs with developed countries. In such cases, the former may have no choice but to accept the demands of the partner developed country so that it does not lose the developed-country market, which might be crucial. Developing countries with weak and small economies negotiating bilateral FTAs with developed countries or larger developing countries will not enjoy collective bargaining power that they may have during the multilateral trade negotiations and, as a result, may have to give up some of the multilateral protections provided under the WTO, such as special and differential treatment for developing countries. In this respect, the proliferation of FTAs is a challenge to the multilateral governance of international trading system.

Despite the perceived discrimination and inequity, the WTO, which represents multilateralism in international trade, must learn to live with FTAs because of the fact that multilateral trade negotiations are becoming increasingly difficult and that there are so many FTAs in operation. What is important from the viewpoint of the WTO is to keep FTAs at bay while utilizing the effect of liberalization accomplished by FTAs and perhaps also finding a way to minimize potential disadvantages to developing countries. In other words, an important task for members of the WTO is to ensure that WTO disciplines are effectively applied to prevent FTAs from being too exclusive and discriminatory in relation to outside parties. Article XXIV of the GATT allows FTAs on the condition that certain requirements as specified in that article are met. The meaning of Article XXIV is by no means clear and is amenable to different interpretations. Therefore, clarifications of the key provisions of Article XXIV are needed.

With this situation in view, this chapter takes up some selected issues regarding the relationship between the WTO and FTAs. The chapter's analysis is not a comprehensive review but rather a survey of selected issues. However, the authors hope that the discussions made in the following passages contribute something toward the understanding of the problems surrounding the WTO and FTAs from the development perspective.

II. PROLIFERATION OF FTAS AND THE INTERESTS OF DEVELOPING COUNTRIES

Generally, developing countries may be disadvantaged in negotiating FTAs with developed countries because of differences in economic resources and political influence. In multilateral trade negotiations such as those in the WTO, developing countries can form coalitions in which many developing countries participate and present a united front vis-à-vis developed countries.[7] While negotiating FTAs, however, developing countries, generally speaking, may not be able to rely on such a collective approach. Consequently, they may be subjected to the overwhelming bargaining power of big and powerful trade partners. Powerful developed countries may engage in a "divide and conquer" strategy when negotiating FTAs with developing countries. The position of developing countries is especially vulnerable in bilateral trade negotiations because, in bilateral negotiations, the difference in bargaining power between developed and developing countries may be exploited by developed countries to impose conditions favorable to them and unfavorable to developing countries.

One way to deal with this problem may be to make use of multilateral FTAs in which not only two but several parties participate and in which more than one

[7] On development aspects of the WTO, see Y. S. Lee, *Reclaiming Development in the World Trading System* (New York: Cambridge University Press, 2009). For an analysis of the issues regarding the relationship between FTAs/RTAs and BITs and developing countries, see Y. S. Lee, "Free Trade Agreements and Foreign Direct Investment: A Viable Answer for Economic Development?" Chapter 12 of this volume.

developing country are members. In this way, the existence of more than one developing country in the FTA may effectively check the imposition of hard conditions that a powerful developed country may propose. This type of FTA probably matches the reality of economic activities in the sense that modern enterprises operate not only in one or two but in many countries. In East Asia, for example, large enterprises such as Panasonic and Toshiba have a presence in several countries. In one country, parts and components are produced. Then the parts and components are exported to another country and assembled into a finished product there. In turn, the finished product is exported and consumed in a third country. In view of this multinational economic reality, it makes sense to emphasize the importance of multilateral rather than bilateral FTAs.

Another risk for developing countries when negotiating bilateral FTAs with developed countries is that the developed-country party may impose a high standard on the developing-country counterpart with respect to such matters as environmental protection and foreign direct investment. It is often true, as one can see in bilateral FTAs between Japan and some Asian countries, that a developed country requires a developing country to maintain a certain level of environmental protection rather than relaxing the protection for the purpose of inducing investment from abroad. Although the protection of the environment is an important goal to which every country should strive, the environmental regulations imposed on a developing country may be too high and costly for the developing country. Although it is important for developed countries to ensure that their domestic industries are not disadvantaged in relation to counterparts in developing countries because of the difference in the level of environmental protection, the developed-country party should take into account the fact that an excessively high demand for environmental protection in the developing-country party may hamper its economic development. In the long run, this may even disadvantage the developed-country party because of the slower economic growth of its partner.

In many FTAs, provisions for direct investment are included, and there are many bilateral investment agreements specifically aimed at the promotion of direct investment. Although it is generally true that direct investment from a developed country to a developing country benefits the latter by providing financial resources and transferring technology and other managerial resources, stiff requirements imposed by such provisions may interfere with development policies of the developing-country party. For example, in FTAs and BITs, one often finds the requirement of most-favored treatment and national treatment. Although those are fundamental principles of foreign trade, this may hamper effective execution of development policies of the developing-country party; for example, a developing country may prefer to promote a particular industry such as information technology to make it a catalyst for overall economic growth and, for this purpose, subsidizes a particular group of enterprises within the country. This may run counter to the principle of MFN or national treatment.

These are but two areas in which the imbalance of resources between developed countries and developing countries creates unfavorable conditions for developing countries. To cope with such situations, international organizations such as the United Nations Conference on Trade and Development (UNCTAD) can play a role by giving advice to developing countries that are in the process of negotiating FTAs with developed countries. The UNCTAD can also publish certain principles that govern the relationship between developed countries and developing countries and that parties of FTA negotiations should take into account when negotiating an FTA. Those principles may include equitable terms in respect to environment, investment, intellectual property, and so on. This principle would require that developed countries make certain concessions to developing countries in negotiating FTAs instead of insisting on an absolute and formalistic equality.

More fundamental concerns about FTAs between developed and developing countries should also be considered. By eliminating tariff and some of the nontariff trade barriers, FTAs may increase consumer welfare of both developing and developed countries and thereby lead to a growth in GDP. However, tariff elimination may also hamper the long-term development potential of developing countries by depriving them of the ability to protect their domestic market from foreign competition and promote their infant industries.[8] This exposure has an effect of "locking" the existing competitive structure in trade between developing and developed countries – that is, the latter is able to export more sophisticated, high-value-added manufactured products and services, and the former is limited to exporting primary goods and relatively cheaper, labor-intensive products and services, creating large imbalances in trade gains between developed and developing countries.

Current FTAs do not include GATT Article XVIII–type provisions that allow for trade measures to promote infant industries. FTAs should not be used by developed countries as a means to avoid multilateral protection of the developing-country interest such as that found in GATT Article XVIII. Because many FTAs refer to and adopt some of the WTO provisions, such as the WTO Sanitary and Phytosanitary Measures Agreement (SPS), reference to and adoption of the GATT/WTO pro-development provisions, such as Article XVIII, should also be provided for in FTAs between developed and developing countries. Perhaps, as proposed earlier, UNCTAD principles can also include these references. The WTO should also pay attention to the possible erosion of the multilateral trade disciplines by FTAs, particularly on the interest of developing countries, as noted previously. Consideration should be given to a possible modification of GATT/WTO rules, including Article XXIV of the GATT governing formation of FTAs, which is explained in more detail later in the chapter, to clarify that FTAs between developed and developing countries shall not

[8] Lee (2009), supra note 7. Although many economists criticize the validity of the infant-industry argument, the development history of some of the most successful developing countries, such as South Korea, shows that the combination of infant-industry promotion and aggressive foreign export policy can promote successful economic development.

undermine the developing countries' interests as protected by relevant GATT/WTO provisions.[9]

In cases in which developing countries attempt to increase their exports through FTAs, nontariff barriers of developed-country partners, such as a high level of SPS regulations and complicated technical product requirements, stringent rules of origin requirements, sophisticated licensing requirements, and visa limitations against admittance of labor from developing countries, impose considerable difficulty on developing countries. FTAs between developed and developing countries seldom relax these developed-country requirements, resulting in the products and services from developed countries being exported to developing countries with little or no barrier, thanks to the FTA arrangement, but not those from developing countries to developed countries. Although there may be political difficulties with relaxing those nontariff barriers on the part of developed countries, ways must be sought to enable developing countries to overcome these barriers to export their products and services to developed-country partners. "Cumulation" allowance in the EU preferential schemes with respect to the rules of origin requirement is an example of this effort.[10]

III. FTAS WITHIN THE FRAMEWORK OF THE WTO

A. *An Overview*

Article XXIV of the GATT 1994, which is the governing provision on the relationship between the WTO and FTAs, was incorporated into the GATT when it came into being in 1947. At that time, there were organizations similar to FTAs, such as the British Commonwealth in which preferential tariffs existed among the members. Therefore, the framers of the original GATT felt it necessary to allow room for preferential arrangements, such as the British Commonwealth, while imposing disciplines on the formation of FTAs. To deal with such situations, Article XXIV of the GATT 1947 was incorporated. This provision operates as the basic disciplines

[9] Similar provisions are found in Article 11 of the WTO Agreement on Safeguards, which prohibits any WTO Member from engaging in an agreement to adopt gray-area measures (e.g., voluntary export restraints) used to limit exports from developing countries.

[10] In accordance with the EU's rules of origin principles for GSP products providing for regional cumulation, when a product is manufactured in or with inputs from two or more countries belonging to a group of countries enjoying regional cumulation, inputs from other countries of the same group are treated as if they originated in the exporting beneficiary country. The official EU Web site introduces three regional groups benefiting from regional cumulation: Group I consists of Brunei Darussalam, Cambodia, Indonesia, Laos, Malaysia, the Philippines, Thailand, Vietnam, and Singapore (although Singapore is excluded from the Generalized System of Preferences, it continues to participate to cumulation of this group); Group II consists of Costa Rica, Honduras, Guatemala, Nicaragua, Panama, El Salvador, Bolivia, Colombia, Ecuador, Peru, and Venezuela; and Group III consists of Bangladesh, Bhutan, India, Maldives, Nepal, Pakistan, and Sri Lanka. Caf Dowlah, "Trade Preferences and Economic Growth: An Assessment of the U.S. GSP Schemes in the Context of Least Developed Countries," Chapter 14 of this volume.

over FTAs today. However, as mentioned earlier, the meaning of the provisions in Article XXIV is far from clear, and there is only a trickle of decisions made by WTO panels and the Appellate Body.

B. *Key Provisions of Article XXIV of the GATT*

Provisions of Article XXIV of the GATT are designed to allow formation of FTAs and, at the same time, impose disciplines on them so that their discriminatory features do not distort the multilateral trading system. The key substantive provisions of the GATT 1994 are Article XXIV:4; Article XXIV:5(a), (b), and (c); Article XXIV:6; and Article XXIV:8(a)(i)(ii) and (b).

Article XXIV:4 declares a general principle that the purpose of a customs union or of a free trade area should be to facilitate trade between the constituent territories and not to raise barriers to the trade of other contracting parties with such territories.

Article XXIV:5 sets out the conditions under which an FTA can be formed. Article XXIV:5(a) provides that a customs union can be formed if the duties or other regulations imposed at the institution of such union with regard to commerce with outside parties shall not on the whole be higher or more restrictive than those applicable before the formation of such union. Article XXIV:5(b) provides the same conditions with regard to a free trade agreement.

Article XXIV:6 states that, if a member proposes to increase tariffs above the concession rate as a result of forming a customs union, it must negotiate with other members outside the union under Article XXVIII of the GATT 1994.

Article XXIV:8 defines customs unions and free trade areas. Article XXIV:8(a)(i) states that a customs union is an entity in which duties and restrictions of commerce are eliminated with respect to substantially all the trade between the members of the union except those restrictions permitted under Articles XI, XII, XIII, XIV, XV, and XX. Article XXIV:8(ii) states that a customs union establishes common tariffs and other restrictions of commerce with respect to commerce with Members that are outside parties to the union. Article XXIV:8(b) provides the same requirements with respect to a free trade area except that there is no requirement equivalent to (ii), which applies to a customs union.

In the past, there were many instances in which a working party was established to examine the compatibility of an FTA with GATT/WTO disciplines under Article XXIV of the GATT. However, in almost all of such working parties, there was a sharp difference of views regarding compatibility of the FTA with GATT/WTO rules, and, in the reports of those working parties, usually there are two opposing views listed side by side – one advocating that the FTA is compatible with GATT/WTO rules and the other criticizing that it is not.[11]

[11] Japanese Ministry of Economy, Trade, and Ministry (METI), Industrial Structure Council, *2006 Report on the WTO Consistency of Trade Policies by Major Trading Partners* (2006), p. 495, available at: http://www.meti.go.jp/policy/trade_policy/wto_consistency_report/html/f_y2006e.html.

The issue of how to interpret Article XXIV in relation to the existing FTAs was first raised when the European Economic Community (EEC) Treaty was negotiated in 1957. Between that time and 1994, sixty-nine working parties were established to examine the compatibility of the then existing FTAs under GATT rules. In only six of sixty-nine working parties was a consensus reached.[12] The reason for this poor accomplishment was differing interests among members. Those that had already formed FTAs advocated their interests in maintaining those organizations, and those outside the FTAs criticized them. In part, the difficulty is the vagueness of the text of Article XXIV, such as "substantially all," "other trade restrictions," and "on the whole." Only three panels were established to examine the legality of FTAs in light of Article XXIV, but in all of them, the panel reports were not adopted.[13]

C. *Understanding on the Interpretation of Article XXIV of GATT 1994*

Attempts were made to clarify the meaning of Article XXIV of the GATT 1994 in the Uruguay Round. As the result, a limited number of issues were clarified:

1. General
   a. The level of tariffs should be calculated by using weighted average rates.
   b. The period for the completion of an FTA is, in principle, ten years.
   c. When a member of a customs union raises tariffs above the concession rate as a result of joining the customs union, that member should negotiate with outside WTO Members in accordance with XXVIII of the GATT 1994.
   d. An outside member that enjoys the reduction of tariffs due to the joining of a member in a customs union is under no obligation to offer compensation.
2. Article 4.3 of the Anti-Dumping Agreement
   When the degree of integration of a customs union has reached the level as provided for in Article XXIV:8(a), the totality of an industry in the region covered by the customs union is deemed to be a domestic industry.
3. The principle articulated in point 2, also applies to the application of countervailing duties.
4. Agreement on Safeguards 1, footnote
   No provision in Article XXIV of the GATT 1994 prejudices interpretation of the relationship between Article XIX of GATT and Article XXIV:8 of the GATT 1994.
5. "Substantially all" – the interpretation of Article XXIV:8 of GATT 1994

The meaning of "substantially all" in Article XXIV:8 is a controversial subject in the interpretation of that article. Article XXIV:8 states that "substantially all of trade" must be liberalized if a customs union or a free trade area is qualified for exemption

[12] Ibid.
[13] Ibid.

under Article XXIV. A question is what the phrase "substantially all" means: that is, what the rate of liberalization of internal trade meeting the requirements is and whether it is a quantitative requirement only or both a quantitative and a qualitative requirement. If it is merely a quantitative requirement, there is room to interpret this to mean that "substantially all" is satisfied even if, for example, the agricultural sector of a customs union or a free trade area is not liberalized as long as the trade of the customs union or the free trade area is quantitatively liberalized on the whole. For example, the portion of import of agricultural products from Korea to Japan is about 10% of the total imports from Korea. If the 90% quantitative test is adopted, this may mean that the exclusion of agricultural sector is justified as long as other sectors are totally liberalized.

However, if the test is qualitative as well as quantitative, and if the quantitative liberalization is taken to mean that all major sectors of trade should be liberalized, a mere fact that the trade of a member country is liberalized as the whole may not be sufficient for the customs union or free trade area to be exempted under Article XXIV if a particular sector (e.g., agriculture) is not liberalized. In this view, the total exclusion of Korean imports of agricultural products to Japan would not be justified.[14]

This question was raised many times even before the WTO was founded in 1995. The question was raised once in connection with the European Free Trade Association (EFTA) when the Treaty of Stockholm exempted agriculture from the liberalization. In the Working Party, there was a view that "substantially all" should be interpreted to have not only quantitative but also qualitative features. This view maintained that even if the rate of liberalization of internal trade reached 90% quantitatively, this should not be regarded as an automatic approval of the FTA.[15] The representatives of the EFTA maintained that Article XXIV of the GATT 1947 allowed some restrictions with regard to products by stating "substantially all of trade" instead of "substantially all products." Although no consensus was reached in the Working Party, the prevailing view was that both qualitative and quantitative tests should be used.

Another Working Party that examined the EEC–Finland Free Trade Agreement in 1973 took the view that the "substantially all" test should be interpreted to mean liberalization of all products and that exemptions for particular sectors of the economy should not be allowed.[16] From this view, to exempt an entire sector of the economy from liberalization would be contrary to Article XXIV of the GATT no matter what the quantitative coverage of this sector may be in the total trade. The Preamble of the Understanding on the Interpretation of Article XXIV of the GATT

[14] In fact, it has been known that the Japanese demand for a substantial exclusion of the agricultural sector from trade liberalization is the reason for the current suspension of FTA negotiations between Korea and Japan since November 2004.

[15] GATT, Basic Instrument and Selected Document (BISD), 9S/84–85.

[16] BISD, 21/79.

1994 endorses this view by stating that if main areas of trade are exempted from the obligation to abolish restrictions, the contribution of FTAs toward liberal trade is reduced.

The Working Party that reviewed the U.S.–Canada Free Trade Agreement took a positive view toward the agreement because it did not attempt to exclude the agricultural sector as the whole from liberalization. Some contracting parties did express skepticism to the agreement because some specific agricultural products (such as fresh fruits, vegetables, corn and corn products, eggs, and milk products) were exempted.[17] In those working Parties, a focus of discussion was the treatment of agricultural sectors and products.

In view of this, the WTO Secretariat issued a report in 1998 in which it examined sixty-nine FTAs and RTAs and stated that fifty-six FTA agreements excluded some agricultural products and, in two FTA agreements, all of agricultural products were excluded.[18] As one can see from this finding, agricultural issues are an Achilles' heel for the WTO and FTA.

From the perspective of economic development, the trend against exclusion of agriculture in FTAs can be considered a positive development for developing countries because many tend to have a competitive advantage in agriculture products in trade relations to developed countries, as opposed to manufactured products in which developed countries tend to have a competitive advantage.

There is also certain regulatory advantage to developing countries in formation of FTAs: a GATT decision promulgated on November 28, 1979, which is called the Enabling Clause,[19] relaxed this requirement of "substantially all of trade" by providing exemption from the MFN requirement in GATT Article I with respect to "regional or global arrangements entered into amongst *less-developed contracting parties* for the mutual reduction or elimination of tariffs."[20] The Enabling Clause states that developing countries are not required to liberalize "substantially all of their trade" as long as FTAs between developing countries offer mutual reduction or elimination of tariffs.[21] An argument has been raised that this special and differential treatment under the Enabling Clause is not sufficient because it only applies to FTAs between developing countries and not those between developed and developing countries.[22]

[17] BISD, 38S/73.

[18] WTO document, WT/REG/W/26.

[19] GATT, *Decision on Differential and More Favorable Treatment and Reciprocity and Fuller Participation of Developing Countries*, L/4903 (November 28, 1979).

[20] Ibid., para. 2(c).

[21] See Won-Mok Choi, "Enabling Clause or Disabling Clause? – Legal Problems of Making Regional Trade Agreements with Less-Developed Economies," paper presented at the Society for International Economic Law inaugural conference, Law and Development Panel (July 16, 2008).

[22] Ibid.

D. *"Shall not be on the whole higher or more restrictive than before"*

This phrase is found in Article XXIV:5(a), which requires that tariffs and other trade restrictions imposed by an FTA on outside parties shall not on the whole be higher or more restrictive than those before the formation of the FTA. This provision minimizes the discriminatory impact of FTAs on outside parties by requiring the participants of an FTA to keep the status quo with regard to trade restrictions that the participants adopted before the formation of the FTA.

However, the regulatory restraint from raising tariffs and other trade barriers against outside parties does not mean that the non-FTA parties, particularly vulnerable developing countries, will not suffer from "relative disadvantages" created by the FTA. For instance, if country A, which has signed an FTA with country B, maintains its pre-FTA tariffs on product X at 10%, the FTA has not increased tariffs and other trade barriers under Article XXIV, but the non-FTA party country C that exports product X to country A will then have a disadvantage because country B can produce and export product X to country A tariff free, but country C is still subject to the 10% tariff on product X. The effect of this relative disadvantage will be more significant to many developing countries that rely on export of price-sensitive, labor-intensive products and thus are competing on a narrow price margin.[23] The FTA advantage will eliminate those competitive margins for non-FTA signatory developing countries.

With regard to tariffs, Article 1(a)(i) of the Understanding on Interpretations of Article XXIV of the GATT 1994 provides that, for the purpose of Article XXIV:5(a), the weighted average rate should be used to determine the restrictiveness. The phrase "on the whole" seems to suggest that the weighted average level of tariffs of the members of an FTA before the formation of an FTA should be comparable to that which resulted from the formation of an FTA.

There is another issue of interpretation with regard to "other trade restrictions" in Article XXIV:5(a). For example, rules of origin can be an issue. As to whether rules of origin are "trade restrictions" in the meaning of Article XXIV, there are two opposing views. In the Working Party that examined the compatibility of the NAFTA with GATT rules, the United States argued that rules of origin are not trade restrictions in the same sense as tariffs and quantitative restrictions are.[24] From this view, rules of origin are a test to determine which product benefits from the preferential treatment of an FTA but not a trade restriction in itself. Rules of origin do not erect barriers in the same way that tariffs and quantitative restrictions do. The other view is that rules of origin are an important trade issue and may operate as de facto trade restriction. In the Uruguay Round Negotiation, negotiators tackled the

[23] Hence many developing countries may be pushed to sign an FTA with developed countries that provide major export markets for them with the terms dictated by the latter countries for fear of losing their essential markets.

[24] WTO document, WT/REG/M2 (February 21, 1997), p. 10.

issue of whether or not rules of origin were "other restrictions." However, they were unable to reach any conclusion as to whether they were "other restrictions."[25]

If rules of origin are "other restriction of trade" under Article XXIV, there is a problem. Article XXIV:5(a) requires that trade restrictions after the formation of an FTA shall not be higher or more restrictive than those before its formation. The question here is, what is "before"? If an existing FTA is enlarged to another, more expansive FTA (such as the transformation of the U.S.–Canada Free Trade Agreement into the NAFTA), the answer may be a comparison between the common rules or origin at the time of the U.S.–Canada Free Trade Agreement with that of the NAFTA. However, what if a new FTA is entered into? There were no common rules of origin before. The common rules of origin were created only after the formation of the FTA. Then the question is which rules should be compared with which rules. Should the common rules of origin be compared with those of each member at the time before the formation of the FTA? However, a member may have adopted a "tariff classification rule," whereas others may have adopted "the substantial transformation rule." This would make it difficult to arrive at any consistent comparisons.

In the Uruguay Round Negotiation, negotiators discussed the issue of rules of origin in the context of FTAs. However, the outcome was only a statement that there should be transparency in the enforcement of rules of origin in FTAs. Other issues are left to future negotiations and clarifications. No progress has been made on this issue.

Export by developing countries has been hampered by complex and stringent rules of origin adopted by major developed economies.[26] The stringent rules of origin can also reduce the export opportunities created by FTAs for developing countries. Thus, regional or bilateral FTAs should be used as an opportunity to relax the rules of origin to maximize the benefits from the FTAs and not as one to reinforce them so as to limit them.

IV. ARE FTAS "WTO-PLUS"?

A. *An Overview*

As stated earlier, FTAs provide rules in areas where the WTO has failed to do so. Examples include investment, competition policy, and the environment. FTAs include provisions for trade in services and movement of persons, which are lacking or incomplete in the WTO. When FTAs supply rules in the areas in which the WTO has not successfully addressed, FTAs fills in the lacunae. In this way, FTAs are "WTO-Plus."

[25] See WTO, *Background Note by the Secretariat, Systemic Issues Relating to "Other Regulations of Commerce,"* WT/REG/W17 (October 31, 1997).

[26] Stefano Inama, "Market Access for LDCs: Issues to Be Addressed" (2002) 36(1) *Journal of World Trade* 115.

FTAs also provide rules for the subject matters covered by the WTO. Examples include, inter alia, trade remedies (antidumping, countervailing duties, and safeguards), intellectual property, and dispute settlements. In such areas, complicated problems may occur. On one hand, rules in FTAs on these subjects add new rules. For example, the FTA between Singapore and New Zealand incorporates a de minimis rule that if a dumping margin is less than 5% (instead of 2% as provided for the Anti-Dumping Agreement), an antidumping investigation should be terminated.[27] One may argue that this additional rule is WTO-Plus because this is a new principle that regulates the enforcement of antidumping legislation and that the WTO has not been successful in introducing.

This additional rule applies only to the participants of the FTA and, therefore, it is a discriminatory measure in relation to outside parties. It creates an inequality of treatment among WTO Members and therefore may be problematic.

Dispute settlement procedures are also incorporated into many FTAs. There is a possibility that rules developed through dispute settlement procedures of an FTA may differ from those of the WTO when an FTA and the WTO cover the same areas. In the future, there may be a need for some sort of arrangements between the WTO and FTAs through which such contradictions and inconsistencies are eliminated or minimized. At its conclusion, this chapter proposes an "FTA Network" that participants of various FTAs may join to exchange information with regard to detailed rules of the FTAs and to explore possibilities for reducing or minimizing difference of rules. The WTO could also publish a nonbinding model dispute settlement procedure code. The idea of this code would merely be to show basic principles in international dispute settlement so that drafters of FTAs might take them into consideration.

Although FTAs create new rules that the WTO has not created and, in this way, contribute something toward the liberalization of trade, this liberalization is partial and preferential in that it applies only to the FTA participants. This is a mixed blessing for the multilateral trading order. It liberalizes trade at least partially where the WTO cannot accomplish it, and, in this sense, the total liberalization of the world trade may be greater than otherwise. However, because of the inequality of conditions among WTO Members created by the formation of FTAs, trade may be diverted from its normal flow. Whether advantages created by FTAs outweigh the disadvantages depends on the particular conditions of the FTAs.

In contrast, FTAs between developed and developing countries may be called "WTO-Minus," in the sense that the multilateral protection of developing-country interest, such as GATT Article XVIII mentioned earlier, is not incorporated in its provisions. One may argue that the inclusion of such provisions may not be proper

[27] Ministry of Economy, Trade and Industry of Japan, *2007 Report on Compliance by Major Trading Partners with Trade Agreements – WTO, FTA/EPA, and BIT* (April 2007; hereinafter referred to as "2007 Report"), p. 550, available at: http://www.meti.go.jp/policy/trade_policy/wto_compliance_report/html/f_y 2007 e.html (in Japanese).

for FTAs because the objective of FTAs is to reduce or eliminate trade barriers and not allow developing countries to erect them. However, FTAs should be considered in the overall context of the economic development objectives of developing countries; they should be regarded as a means to improve the economic conditions of developing countries and not the end in itself, thus the ability of developing countries to adopt trade-related development policies should be preserved even after the signing of an FTA.

There might be another argument that developing countries entering into an FTA should consider the implications of joining an FTA, including that they may no longer be able to adopt trade measures to promote their industries vis-à-vis the developed-country partner of the FTA. However, global economic realities are such that many developing countries, particularly those with small and vulnerable economies, cannot afford to be excluded from preferential trade arrangements of powerful developed countries for fear of losing vital export markets, as illustrated earlier. This inequality of bargaining power is an important reason that ways should be sought to ensure that multilateral protection of developing-country interests should not be eliminated by FTAs.

The following passages briefly discuss certain areas to examine the relationship between FTAs and the WTO from the development perspective. These areas include investment, competition policy, trade remedies, and dispute settlement. They are but a few of many that require discussion. Nevertheless, preliminary reviews of those areas reveal the nature of issues involved in the relationship between FTAs and the WTO.

B. *Investment*

Investment issues are part of the Singapore Issues[28] and are included in the Doha Agenda.[29] However, the WTO Ministerial Conference in Hong Kong (2005) decided that investment issues would not be taken up in the upcoming negotiation. Therefore, at least for a while, any agreement on investment is left to BITs, FTAs, or RTAs. Nonetheless, investment-related provisions are found in the WTO. One is the TRIMs Agreement and the other is the GATS. The Trade-Related Investment Measures (TRIMs) cover investment measures that affect international trade such

[28] In the WTO Ministerial Conference held in Singapore in 1997, members agreed to explore the possibility of introducing agreements on investment, competition policy, trade facilitation, and government procurement. Those items are called the Singapore Issues. Working Groups were established to study the relationship between trade and investment and that between trade and competition. However, in the Ministerial Conference held in Hong Kong in 2005, members decided not to take up the Singapore Issues.

[29] On issues of investment in the WTO, see Mitsuo Matsushita, "North–South Issues of Foreign Direct Investments in the WTO: Is There a Middle-of-the-Road Approach?" in Steve Charnovitz, Debra P. Steger, and Peter Van den Bossche (eds.), *Law in the Service of Human Dignity* (New York: Cambridge University Press, 2005), pp. 76–89.

as local content and export performance requirements. The Mode 3 of the GATS directly relates to direct investment issues in services sectors. However, provisions in the WTO dealing with investment issues are piecemeal, and there is no agreement in the WTO regime that deals with investment issues in a comprehensive way. However, as mentioned earlier, there are many FTA and BITs agreements among WTO Members and also nonmembers.

In those FTAs/BITs, several principles relate to conditions of international direct investment.[30] Major ones include, inter alia, principles of national treatment, MFN treatment, and fair and equitable treatment. The national treatment principle requires that the host-country party (the country receiving direct investment) accord to investment and investors from the home-country party treatment in laws, regulations, and other governmental measures that are no less favorable than the treatment it accords to domestic investments and investors. MFN treatment requires that the host-country party accord treatment to investment coming from the home-country party that is no less favorable to that accorded by the host-country party to investment coming from any third parties.

The fair and equitable treatment principle requires that the host-country party provide fair and equitable treatment as well as full protection and security to investments and investors coming from the home-country party.[31] In this principle, the issue is not a relative advantage or disadvantage that investors and investors from the home-country party receive compared with those received by domestic investments or those from third countries. The principle requires that the host-country party give certain standards of fair and equitable treatment to investments and investors coming from the home-country party. In this sense, it sets up an absolute standard as opposed to a relative standard in relation to investments and investors from domestic sources and other countries. The major contents of fair and equitable treatment consist of items including due process of law in dealing with investment, the prohibition of denial of justice and capricious treatment, and the protection of reasonable expectations of investors.

The question has arisen of whether this principle requires any higher standards than those that already exist in public international law. The NAFTA Free Trade Commission decided in 2001 that it did not.[32]

In some FTAs/BITs, there are provisions prohibiting performance requirements. Performance requirements include local content requirements and the export–import balancing requirements as provided in the TRIMs Agreement. However, FTAs/BITs add some more prohibitions, including those against the restrictions imposed on domestic sales in connection with investment, the requirement for transfer of technology, and the requirement that all directors or some directors of

[30] See 2007 Report, supra note 27, pp. 624–625.

[31] 2007 Report, supra note 27, p. 625.

[32] Ibid.

an enterprise established by the investment should be nationals of the host-country party.

Some FTAs adopt the positive-list formulae, in which liberalization of investment and the principles mentioned earlier apply only to those areas stated in the list of liberalization commitment, and some others adopt the negative-list formulae, in which the parties agree to liberalize foreign investment generally, except for the areas listed in the liberalization commitment as excluded from the liberalization. FTAs entered into between developed countries tend to adopt the negative-list formulae, as shown in the NAFTA, and FTAs in which developing countries are parties tend to go along with the positive-list approach, as exemplified by the Australia–Thai Agreement and the India–Singapore Agreement.[33]

Another issue dealt with in FTAs with respect to direct investment relates to expropriation and compensation. The general principles here are that expropriation should be for a public purpose, that it should be nondiscriminatory, that it should be made in accordance with the due process of law, and that an appropriate compensation should be paid.

Provisions for expropriation in FTAs often include those for indirect expropriation. Another name for indirect expropriation is "creeping expropriation" and includes such practices by the host-country party as capricious withdrawal of authorization of enterprise activities and a setting of the maximum level of production allowed for foreign investors. In the Metalclad Case,[34] the issue was whether environmental measures taken by the Mexican government amounted to indirect expropriation under NAFTA, and the NAFTA arbitration panel awarded a judgment favorable to the investor.

Provisions on investment are clearly WTO-Plus. International rules on direct investment have been discussed and negotiated in international forums such as the WTO and the Organization for Economic Cooperation and Development without success. At present, the formation of international rules through BITs and FTAs is the only choice that the international trading system has with regard to investment. Although rules in BITs are partial and piecemeal, they serve to promote international investment.

From the perspective of development interests, the current trend toward the "liberalization of investment" under FTAs protects the interest of developed-country investors rather than that of the host developing countries. For instance, many FTAs and BITs prohibit a wide range of TRIMs that are designed to maximize the contribution of foreign investment toward the economic development of the host developing countries. Investor-state dispute settlement provisions in FTAs and BITs that allow the aggrieved foreign investors to raise claims against the government of the host country through arbitration may also put developing countries under

[33] Ibid., p. 626.
[34] Ibid., p. 627.

pressure by making it difficult to adopt economic development policies and public policies that may adversely affect the interest of foreign investors. Although foreign investment may bring essential capital, technology, and managerial expertise that could contribute to the economic development of the host developing countries, some latitude should be allowed for the host developing countries to regulate foreign investment in a way to increase its contribution toward the goal of economic development.[35]

In general, promotion of "greenfield investment" rather than mergers and acquisitions would be more advantageous to developing countries because it creates productive capacities in the latter countries. Well-structured safeguard and safety net provisions should also be incorporated into investment agreements between developing and developed countries. Positive-list formulae are perhaps more advantageous to developing countries because this approach allows developing countries to identify and open the areas in which foreign investment is most desirable for economic development.

C. *Competition Policy*

Competition policy is one of the items included in the Singapore Issues, and in the Singapore Ministerial Conference in 1996, WTO Members decided to set up a working group to study the relationship between competition policy and trade.[36] Accordingly, the Working Group on Trade and Competition was established within the WTO, and the working group turned out reports.[37] However, the Hong Kong Ministerial Conference held in 2005 decided not to take up trade and competition policy and, as the result, this topic is held outside the scope of negotiation as far as the Doha Agenda is concerned.

Many FTAs include provisions for competition policy, and these provisions supply additional rules concerning trade and competition in international trade. Competition policy provisions incorporated in FTAs generally fall roughly into two categories, for example, the NAFTA type and the EU type. In the former, competition policy provisions do not provide substantive rules such as the prohibition of cartels on a per se illegality basis and the control of vertical restraints on a rule of reason basis but leave them to the national laws of each party. If there is no competition law in a party to the FTA, that party is requested to enact a competition law or to implement it. In the latter, the customs union (such as the European Communities) enforces its own

[35] Supra note 7.

[36] On the relationship between trade and competition generally, see Mitsuo Matsushita, "Basic Principles of the WTO and the Role of Competition Policy" (2004) 3(2) *Washington University Global Studies Law Review* 363–385.

[37] WTO, *Working Group on the Interaction between Trade and Competition Policy*, Report to the General Council, WT/WCTP/1 (November 28, 1997), WT/WGTCP/2 (December 9, 1998), WT/WGTCP/3 (October 11, 1999) and WT/WGTCP/5 (October 8, 2001).

"supranational" competition law with its own enforcement mechanism (such as the European Commission and the European Court of Justice). Most of competition policy provisions incorporated in FTAs belong to the former type.

Many FTA provisions related to competition policy can be likened to those incorporated in bilateral competition policy agreements entered into by some major trading countries. Japan entered into such agreements with the United States, European Communities, and Canada. Major rules incorporated in such competition policy provisions fall into, inter alia, the following categories, that is, negative comity, positive comity, notification and consultation, exchange of information, and cooperation in enforcement. Negative comity is a principle in which a nation that is a party to an agreement on competition policy refrains from enforcing its competition law vis-à-vis conduct that affects the interest of the other party, out of respect for the policy of the other party. Positive comity denotes that a nation that is a party to an agreement on competition policy requests the other party to enforce its competition law vis-à-vis a conduct that affects the interest of the former and occurs in the domain of the former.[38]

As an example, competition policy provisions in the Japan–Singapore Agreement are explained here. Chapter 12 of the Agreement is devoted to competition policy. As set out in this chapter, the basic objective is to take appropriate measures against anticompetitive conducts engaged in by private enterprises to maintain smooth flow of trade and investment and thereby efficiency in international trade. When this agreement entered into effect, there was no competition law in Singapore, and therefore the agreement merely provided that the parties endeavor to enact, review, and amend necessary laws and regulations pertaining to anticompetitive conducts. It is hortatory rather than obligatory and has no legally binding effect on the parties. However, the existence of this provision prompts the participants to enact and enforce competition laws if they do not have them yet and, in this way, contributes toward establishing international competition policy. Article 104 of the agreement provides that both parties cooperate in enforcement of competition policy and laws according to their respective laws and regulations and as much as their resources allow. As to details of cooperation, the agreement provides for notification, exchange of information, technical assistance, use of information in criminal procedures, the scope of application, regular reviews, and expansion of cooperation and consultation. It is to be noted that competition policy matters are excluded from the dispute settlement procedures of the agreement.

In almost all FTAs/EPAs in which Japan is a party, there are provisions pertaining to competition policy, which are similar to the ones mentioned earlier.[39]

[38] On comity issues, see U.S. Department of Justice and Federal Trade Commission, *Antitrust Enforcement Guidelines for International Operations* (April 1995), pp. 22–27.

[39] See 2007 Report, supra note 27, pp. 63–66.

Competition policy promotes free trade by eliminating private anticompetitive conduct that would offset the effect of liberalization achieved through trade negotiation. In this sense, competition policy provisions incorporated into FTAs/RTAs are complementary to the WTO regime and can be characterized as WTO-Plus. Also, it is to be noted that the essence of competition policy and law is nondiscrimination, and there is little danger that competition laws incorporated into FTAs are applied discriminatorily.

Enforcement of competition law by way of FTAs is a mixed blessing for developing countries. On one hand, competition law can be used to control anticompetitive behavior by dominant multinational companies from developed countries and protect smaller and weaker domestic enterprises of developing countries. On the other hand, strict application of competition law may not be consistent with the need of developing countries to adopt industrial policies that will involve mobilization and concentration of resources in large-scale manufacturing-based companies, which will, in turn, enjoy dominant positions in domestic markets. It should be noted that newly industrializing countries in the 1970s and 1980s, including Korea, strategically supported and promoted large-scale manufacturing companies such as Hyundai and Samsung as a means to build internationally competitive industries, and strict application of competition law would have been made this support difficult. A compromise should be sought between competition policy and development policy.

D. *Trade Remedies*

In many FTAs, there are provisions for trade remedies, for example, antidumping, countervailing duties, and safeguards. When parties to an FTA are also WTO Members, this may raise complicated and systemic problems.

In relation to WTO jurisprudence, whether trade remedies can be lawfully applied within an FTA is an important question. Article XXVI:8 of the GATT 1994 states that tariffs and trade restrictions must be liberalized, but measures under Articles XI, XII, XIII, XIV, XV, and XX are exempted from the obligation to liberalize. It is to be noted that Article XIX of the GATT (safeguards) and Article VI (antidumping and countervailing duty measures) are not mentioned here. Does this mean that the obligation to liberalize applies to the trade remedy measures and there is an obligation under Article XXIV:8 of the GATT for a member of a customs union or a free trade area to refrain from applying a safeguard, antidumping, or countervailing duty measures? One view is that a member of a customs union or a free trade area that is also a member of the WTO may apply none of these measures to imports coming from other WTO Members that are not members of the customs union or a free trade area while not applying the same measures to members of the customs union or a free trade area.

However, there is a counterargument that the trade remedy measures, such as safeguards, antidumping, and countervailing duty measures, apply even within the

FTA area. The rationale for this interpretation is that the premise of trade remedy measures is that trade is already liberalized. If trade is not yet liberalized, there is no need for trade remedy measures; such measures apply once trade is open. In this view, trade remedy measures apply within the FTA area since the essence of an FTA is to liberalize trade.

In the past few years, several important decisions were rendered by the WTO Appellate Body in which the issue was whether a WTO Member that is also a member of an FTA can exclude from the application of a safeguard measure imports of the product in question coming from countries that are members of the FTA. Important cases include the Argentina Footwear Case,[40] the United States-Wheat Gluten Case,[41] and the United States Lamb Case.[42] In the Argentina Footwear Case, Argentina took into account the import of footwear from MERCOSUR when determining injury to a domestic industry but excluded the application of a safeguard measure to the import from the members of MERCOSUR. The EC challenged this practice at the WTO, and both the Panel and the Appellate Body ruled that the selective application of safeguard measure by Argentina was contrary to Article I and cannot be exempted under Article XXIV:8 (a)(i) of the GATT 1994.

In all of those cases, the Appellate Body announced that there should be a parallelism between the scope of the investigation for a safeguard measure conducted by a member and the scope of the safeguard that is applied as the result of it. The Appellate Body in the foregoing cases ruled that a WTO Member cannot exclude imports coming from WTO Members that are also members of an FTA from the imposition of a safeguard measure, while applying the safeguard measure to imports of the same or like product coming from other WTO Members that are not members of the FTA, as long as the safeguard investigation was conducted with regard to imports of the product coming from all of the countries. This principle applies unless there is persuasive evidence that the imports coming from the WTO Members that are also members of the FTA did not contribute significantly to the injury to the domestic industry.

However, the parallelism as enunciated by the Appellate Body does not resolve the question of whether Article XXIV can be raised as a defense by a member when challenged for discriminatory treatment in favor of other FTA members with regard to safeguards. This issue was raised in the United States-Line Pipe from Korea Case,[43] in which Korea challenged the imposition of a safeguard measure on imports of line pipe from Korea. The panel held that Article XXIV could be invoked as a defense

[40] See *Argentina-Safeguard Measures on Imports of Footwear*, WT/DS121/R (December 14, 1999).

[41] See *United States-Definitive Safeguard Measures on Imports of Wheat Gluten from the European Communities*, WT/DS166/AB/R (December 22, 2000).

[42] See *United States-Safeguard Measures on Imports of Fresh, Chilled or Frozen Lamb Meat from New Zealand and Australia*, WT/DS177/AB/R and WT/DS178/AB/R (May 1, 2001).

[43] See *United States-Definitive Safeguard Measures on Imports of Circular Welded Carbon Quality Line Pipe from Korea*, WT/DS202/AB/R (February 15, 2002).

to claims of violation of provisions in the GATT 1994, and Korea appealed this finding. The Appellate Body reversed the Panel's finding that the United States did not violate its obligations under Articles 2 and 4 of the Agreement on Safeguards by exempting Canada and Mexico from the line pipe measure. It, however, dismissed the Korean appeal on the ground that the question of whether Article XXIV serves as an exception to the requirement of nondiscrimination under the GATT arises only in two situations: (a) that the administering authority did not consider imports coming from countries that are members of an FTA in determining injury issues and (b) that the administering authority determines that imports coming from members outside the FTA alone are sufficient to cause a serious injury to a domestic industry. The Appellate Body reasoned that because neither of such situations existed in this case, this issue was legally moot.

A legal question that Article XXIV presents in relation to trade remedies to be applied within FTAs is whether trade remedies are allowed if, after applying trade remedies, substantially all of the internal trade of an FTA is still open. Because the language of Article XXIV requires that there should be liberalization within an FTA of "substantially all" of the internal trade but does not require "all" of the internal trade of an FTA to be open, there may be room for some trade restrictions within the FTA as long as substantially all of the internal trade is open. Does this mean that trade remedy measures applied within an FTA are allowed as long as they remain within this limit? The liberal reading of the text seems to allow this interpretation, which was suggested by the Appellate Body in the Argentina Footwear Case.[44] If this interpretation is accepted, it may cast doubt on the legitimacy of an argument that members of the WTO and also members of an FTA are obligated to exclude the internal trade within the FTA from the application of trade remedy measures under Article XXIV of the GATT 1994 and that this exclusion is exempted from the MFN obligations. This is because members of the WTO that are also members of an FTA can apply trade remedy measures as long as substantially all of the internal trade of the FTA remains open.

In another scenario, a trade remedy measure that a WTO Member and also a member of an FTA applies may have such a great impact on the internal trade within the FTA that substantially all of the internal trade of the FTA is no longer open. If this should be the case, an application of a trade remedy measure within an FTA cannot be justified. A determination as to whether a particular trade remedy measure would restrict the trade within an FTA to the extent that substantially all of the internal trade within the FTA is no longer liberalized should be made on a case-by-case basis. In any event, the requirement of this justification will set a serious limitation on the application of trade remedy measures within FTAs.

In some FTAs, provisions containing trade remedies merely incorporate rules declared in the Anti-Dumping Agreement of the WTO and other relevant WTO

[44] See 2007 Report, supra note 27.

agreements. However, in some other FTAs, there are provisions that supply disciplines on invocation of trade remedies that are more stringent than those provided for in WTO agreements. For example, in the agreement between Singapore and Australia, the de minimis antidumping margin and the negligible amount of import below which the enforcement agency cannot impose antidumping duties is set at 5%, as opposed to 2% and 3% in the WTO Anti-Dumping Agreement, respectively.[45]

In the Australia–New Zealand Agreement, the parties decided to abolish antidumping duties in the trade between them and to apply competition rules to anticompetitive conduct that affect trade between those two countries. Similarly, in the agreement between Canada and Chile, antidumping duties were abolished after 2003, and competition laws would apply to control dumping between those two countries.[46]

With respect to safeguard measures, many FTAs incorporate rules of the WTO Safeguard Agreement as well as GATT XIX. However, in some FTAs, more stringent restrictions on advocating safeguards are imposed. For example, in the Japan–Singapore EPA, the application of safeguards is limited to cases in which there is an absolute increase of import and no provisional measures are allowed. Moreover, the application of safeguards is limited to the interim period (ten years since it started).

Negotiations on trade remedies in the WTO are difficult. This is especially true with antidumping matters and, in this respect, FTA provisions that impose higher disciplines on invocation of trade remedies contribute toward further liberalization of trade. In this way, FTAs are WTO-Plus. However, FTAs also create unequal treatment with regard to trade remedies among FTA members and nonmembers and therefore deprive WTO Members outside FTAs of a "level playing field." In this sense, FTAs are both WTO-Plus and WTO-Minus. Whether "Plus" is greater than "Minus" depends on the specific situation. It is submitted that coordination and harmonization among trade remedy systems in the WTO and various FTAs are needed. It is important to note that when harmonization among FTA rules is attempted, the WTO should introduce upgraded trade remedy rules to match more liberal provisions on trade remedies in some FTAs rather than downgrading liberal provisions in FTAs to a less liberal standard of the trade remedy provisions in the WTO.

The trade remedy measures of primary importance to developing countries are antidumping measures. Primary targets of antidumping measures are cheaper exports from developing countries, and antidumping measures have been used as convenient tools to protect domestic producers of developed countries. Because of this interest, developed countries, particularly the United States, had long refused to address the arbitrary nature of antidumping measures or to make any changes until recently when developing countries began to apply an increasing number of antidumping

[45] Ibid., p. 550.
[46] Ibid., p. 553.

measures against exports from developed countries. Despite some of the examples given earlier that heightened the requirements for invocation of antidumping measures, most FTAs between developed and developing countries fail to eliminate or reduce antidumping measures by making their invocations more difficult. The result is that with or without FTAs, developing countries continue to suffer from invocation of antidumping measures against their exports but are obliged to provide market access for exports from developed countries. The same applies to countervailing duty measures. The aforementioned guidelines for FTAs between developed and developing countries should include recommendations to reduce trade remedy measures, including antidumping measures that target exports from developing countries. Replacement of antidumping measures with competition rules, as exemplified in a few FTAs noted earlier, may be considered as an alternative solution to this problem.[47]

E. *Dispute Settlement*

Dispute settlement procedures are incorporated into many FTAs and BITs.[48] A peculiar feature of dispute settlement procedures in BITs is that not only state-to-state disputes but also investor-to-state disputes are dealt with. Disputes in which investors challenge states (host-country governments) are brought before arbitral panels established by the BIT. Generally, the following are the major features of dispute settlement procedures in BITs.

a. Procedures in BITs

I. CONSULTATION. Consultation between disputing parties is obligatory, and the period of three to six months is generally stipulated.

II. REFERRAL TO ARBITRAL PANEL. When a dispute between an investor and the government of the host country is not resolved through consultation, the investor can refer the matter to an arbitral panel. In many BITs, there are provisions in which the host country has given consent that it will submit to an arbitral panel. Also, in many BITs, an investor can choose either the ICSID rules or UNCITRAL rules as applicable laws and sometimes ICC arbitration rules are provided for applicable laws. Referral to an arbitral panel is conditioned on the requirement that the investor does not bring the matter before national courts. Also, a claimant is generally prohibited from bringing the matter before domestic courts after an arbitral award has been issued.

[47] It has also been argued that antidumping measures should be replaced with safeguards and that the former should be banned. Y. S. Lee, "Toward a More Open Trading System: Should Safeguards Replace Antidumping Measures?" (2005) 1(2) *21st Century Law Review* 3–14.

[48] See 2007 Report, supra note 27, pp. 85–88.

III. REMEDY. Unlike state-to-state disputes, awards in an investor-to-state dispute usually grant monetary compensation or restitution. An arbitral award is final and binding on the parties. Generally, after a dispute is resolved through an arbitral panel, it is final, and the claimant is entitled to no further recourse. However, the ICSID Treaty provides for a review and repeal of the award under certain conditions.

b. Procedures in FTAs

Dispute settlement procedures are provided in FTAs. Like the dispute settlement procedures of the WTO, those in FTAs stipulate consultation among the parties, referral to panel, an award that is binding, and that the losing party rectify wrongs, and/or compensation.

In general, there are three types of dispute settlement procedures in FTAs. The first category is the NAFTA type in which a dispute settlement panel is composed on an ad hoc basis when a dispute arises and each party can bring a claim against the other. All of the dispute settlements procedures in which Japan is a party belong to this type. This type of dispute settlement procedure has been adopted, inter alia, in the Korea–Singapore Agreement, the Australia–Singapore Agreement, and the Thai–New Zealand Agreement.[49]

The second category is the EU type in which a dispute is referred to a commission or council composed of representatives of the parties to the FTA, and the council or commission renders decisions and issues recommendations. In addition to the EU, some multilateral agreements adopt this category.[50]

The third category, a hybrid of the first two types, is one in which a dispute is referred to a council or commission as in the second category, but the parties can choose to compose a panel, as in the first category, when the dispute is not resolved through the procedures in the second category. There are many FTAs that adopt this type, including ASEAN and the Andean Community.[51]

In some areas, subject matters covered by an FTA overlap with those covered by WTO agreements. When disputes arise in such areas, both dispute settlement procedures provided for in the WTO regime and those provided for in the FTA may apply at the same time. When this happens, the question is which agreement prevails. On this issue, dispute settlement procedures provided in an FTA can be divided into three categories: (a) those in which the procedures provided in FTA are given priority, (b) those in which the WTO dispute settlement procedures are given priority, and (c) those in which claimants can choose either forum. NAFTA falls under the first category. NAFTA procedures apply when the claimant asserts that the subject matter should be judged under environmental rules, SPS rules, and

49 Ibid., p. 686.
50 Ibid., pp. 686–687.
51 Ibid., p. 687.

technical barrier to trade (TBT) rules provided in the NAFTA Agreement. The EC–Chile Agreement falls under the second category, in which it is provided that when WTO agreements apply to the subject matter of a dispute, WTO agreements should be given priority. Many dispute settlement procedures incorporated into FTAs, such as those in which Japan is a party, belong to the third category, a party to a dispute can choose either the WTO dispute settlement procedures or those provided for in the FTA, but once a party has chosen one procedure, it cannot later resort to other procedures.

Dispute settlement procedures incorporated in BITs can be distinguished from the WTO dispute settlement procedures in that they cover disputes concerning investment in which investors bring claims against a state and, as such, accomplish the result that the WTO is not capable of accomplishing. Likewise, dispute settlement procedures incorporated into FTAs are suitable for resolving disputes on subject matters unique to the FTA. Many FTAs today are focused not only on trade matters but also on investment, movement of persons, and many other matters. Disputes on such matters cannot effectively be resolved through the WTO dispute settlement procedures.

However, when disputes arise in the areas covered by WTO agreements and an FTA, the application of the FTA dispute settlement procedures raises a problem with the WTO disciplines. Article 23 of the DSU states, "When [WTO] Members seek the redress of a violation of obligations or other nullification or impairment of benefits under the covered agreements or an impediment to the attainment of any objective of the covered agreements, they shall have recourse to, and abide by, the rules and procedures of this Understanding." The text of that article seems to prohibit recourse to any dispute settlement procedures other than those incorporated into the dispute settlement procedures in the WTO when the subject matter of a dispute is covered by WTO agreements. How can provisions in NAFTA requiring recourse to its dispute settlement procedures under certain circumstances in exclusion of the WTO procedure be reconciled with this WTO requirement? The existence of different dispute settlement procedures between FTAs and the WTO create confusion and uncertainty in the international trade order through forum shopping when the participants of FTAs are also members of the WTO. In light of this, there arguably should be a principle that the WTO dispute settlement procedure should be given priority over those in FTAs when a subject matter is covered by both.

From the perspective of developing countries, the availability of separate dispute settlement procedures in an FTA can be as much a burden as an opportunity to bring up their own claims in a seemingly more neutral forum than national courts. Developed countries, with more resources and better expertise with the dispute settlement procedure, are more likely users of these procedures than their developing-country counterparts. When multiple forums are available, as illustrated earlier, developed countries that have more experience with different kinds of dispute settlement procedures will have even more of an advantage to put forward their claims than relatively inexperienced developing countries. Perhaps this is another reason to give priority to the WTO dispute settlement procedure in which subject matters are covered by both WTO and the FTA. The specific dispute settlement procedures in FTAs between developed and developing countries, including investor-state dispute settlement procedures, should not be overly complicated, costly, and time-consuming for developing countries with limited resources and expertise.

The dispute settlement procedures in FTAs may also have certain implications for the development policies that they adopt. For instance, dispute settlement procedures that allow private foreign investors to bring claims against the host state and require the latter to submit to arbitrations may deter state effort to promote policies that are necessary for economic development but may adversely affect the interest of foreign investors, such as placing foreign exchange controls and safeguards in the times of financial crisis if the FTA does not specifically allow them. Although the dispute settlement procedures are used to resolve disputes arising from the application and interpretation of an FTA, these procedures should not be used as a systematic deterrence against developing countries that are trying to adopt economic development policies with some adverse effect on the trade interest of developed countries and the investment interest of their citizens.

V. CONCLUSION – SHOULD THERE BE AN FTA NETWORK?

The proliferation of FTAs raises a concern, from the perspective of economic development, that the removal of trade barriers may take away the ability of developing countries to use trade-related policies, such as tariff protection authorized under GATT Article XVIII, to protect and develop their domestic industries. On the other hand, those who advocate for FTAs also argue that the improvement of economic efficiency resulting from the removal of trade barriers should contribute to the economic development of developing countries. The impact of FTAs on economic development thus needs to be assessed and systematically monitored, perhaps by international bodies such as the WTO and UNCTAD, and the study of this impact should facilitate a discussion as to whether the aforementioned UNCTAD principles and the proposed mandatory development-facilitation clause in Article XXIV will be necessary.

The proliferation of FTAs may also result in the formation of different and sometimes conflicting rules of trade among trading nations. Also, some FTA rules may also conflict with WTO rules. In this respect, it is highly desirable that trading nations establish a mechanism or network in which information on various FTA rules are compiled. Such a network could provide a forum in which representatives of different FTAs meet regularly, exchange information regarding the implementation of such rules, and cooperate with each other with a view to prepare for a degree of convergence of such rules. This network may be governmental or nongovernmental and, at the initial stage, may engage only in taking stock of different rules. Ultimately, this network may develop to present models or patterns of trade rules and seek to harmonize the currently different rules in FTAs.

In this connection, it is noteworthy to mention activities of the International Competition Network (ICN).[52] The ICN is a virtual network of government agencies in charge of competition policy and other interested persons. The WTO decided to establish a working group on trade and competition at the 1998 Ministerial Conference in Singapore with the view to draft an agreement to be incorporated in the WTO regime. Due to various reasons, including the opposition of developing countries and the United States, the WTO decided in the Hong Kong Ministerial Conference (2005) that this subject would be dropped from the Doha Development Round. Some developing countries took the position that a binding agreement on competition policy in the WTO could hamper them in designing and executing industrial policies or development policies. The United States also opposed on the grounds that a consensus achieved by all WTO members would represent a low common denominator. Meanwhile, Joe Klein (assistant attorney general of the United States Justice Department) proposed the creation of an informal network of competition policy enforcement agencies instead of a formal international organization in which officials of competition authorities of different nations, practicing attorneys, representatives of business communities, and academics gather together on a regular basis (once in two years) and discuss issues of competition policies. This proposal was accepted by many nations, gathered momentum, and was launched in the 2002 Conference of the ICN held in Naples, Italy.

The main feature of the ICN is that this is not an international organization nor has it any permanent seat. This is a network in which more than 100 nations participate, exchange information, and try to iron out practical ways to establish cooperative relationships among them. The ICN is composed of several working groups: the Merger Working Group, the Cartel Working Groups, and the Competition Advocacy Working Group.[53] Members of the groups engage in joint research in the issues of importance, meet regularly, and issue nonbinding recommendations. However, it is expected that participating enforcement agencies respect these recommendations and adopt them in the enforcement of their laws when it is possible. The ICN has been tremendously successful in promoting convergence of competition policies of the participating nations. Its feature is informality and flexibility. It is an independent network separate from international organizations such as the WTO, the OECD, and the UNCTAD.

One can envision that a similar network would be established in which nations having FTAs participate in an FTA network, regularly meet, and discuss ways to iron out degrees of convergence among FTAs to the extent possible. If there is

[52] For details of the history and current activities of the ICN, see Eleanor M. Fox, "Linked-In: Antitrust and the Virtues of a Virtual Network" (2009) 43(1) *The International Lawyer* 151–174.

[53] For details of activities of the ICN, see http://www.internationalcompetitionnetwork.org.

secretariat of FTAs, it could also participate. Differences of trade rules contained in different FTAs would be discussed and, if there are any inconsistencies among them, there would be discussions as to the reasons for such differences and possible ways to mitigate problems arising from such differences. If one follows the ICN model, there would be no formal organization and nor any binding resolutions and regulations. Such a network is a virtual network, and its recommendations are hortatory. This network may produce binding regulations in the future but, at present, such tight governance is not envisioned or anticipated. It is probably more realistic to establish such a network at this time instead of establishing a formal organization with binding regulations over the participants and aim at virtual convergence of different rules contained in FTAs.

Another question is whether a sponsor is necessary or desirable for this network. One can think of the Asia-Pacific Economic Cooperation or the ASEAN in East Asia. The WTO can play an important role in organizing such an FTA network. The WTO needs a mandate from members to establish a formal organization for monitoring FTAs and converging trade rules in such FTAs. However, even without such a mandate, the WTO can engage in coordinating FTA activities.

One idea is to make use of the Trade Policy Review Mechanism (TPRM), which is Annex 3 of the Marrakech Agreement. The Trade Policy Review Board (TPRB) is established based on Annex 3. The TPRB regularly reviews trade policies of WTO Members, and when it finds that there are problems in their trade policies, it recommends improvements. Recommendations have no compulsory effect, and its recommendations cannot be used in the dispute settlement procedure. However, it can be effective in reminding WTO members of their problems and rectifying them.

Mandate G of the TPRM states: "An annual overview of developments in the international trading environment which are having an impact on the multilateral treading system shall also be undertaken by the TPRB." There may be arguments, both pro and con, as to the scope of the mandate stated in the Mandate G. However, there is no explicit prohibition in Mandate G against the TPRB's engagement in coordinating FTA activities.

If the TPRB is to engage in such activities, it can collect data on different FTA agreements, compare them, and come up with some model rules in areas such as the rules of origin, point out differences among them, and recommend that WTO Members participating in FTAs exercise their best efforts to converge the contents of such rules or reduce differences. The TPRB can review the progress on a regular basis, and, after some years, trade rules in different FTAs may be more harmonized.

The WTO needs to open up a new horizon to break through the deadlock in negotiations and the resulting stagnation. It is time for members to give the WTO a new mission. If this network is successfully developed, it will contribute not only to the convergence of different rules into a meaningful whole but also to the promotion of the interests of developing countries. In the frame of such a network, developing countries can present their common interests and concerns associated with FTAs.

REFERENCES

Choi, Won-Mok, "Enabling Clause or Disabling Clause? – Legal Problems of Making Regional Trade Agreements with Less-Developed Economies," paper presented at the Society for International Economic Law inaugural conference, Law and Development Panel (July 16, 2008).

Dowlah, Caf, "The Generalized System of Preferences of the United States: Does It Promote Industrialization and Economic Growth in the Least Developed Countries?" (2008) 1(1) *The Law and Development Review*, available at: http://www.bepress.com/ldr.

Fox, Eleanor H., "Linked-In: Antitrust and the Virtues of a Virtual Network" (2009) 43(1) *The International Lawyer*.

GATT, *Decision on Differential and More Favorable Treatment and Reciprocity and Fuller Participation of Developing Countries*, L/4903 (November 28, 1979).

______, Basic Instrument and Selected Document, 9S/84–85, 21/79, 38S/73.

Inama, Stefan, "Market Access for LDCs: Issues to Be Addressed" (2002) 36(2) *Journal of World Trade*.

Japanese Ministry of Economy, Trade, and Ministry (METI), Industrial Structure Council, *2006 Report on the WTO Consistency of Trade Policies by Major Trading Partners* (2006), available at: http://www.meti.go.jp/policy/trade_policy/wto_consistency_report/html/f_y2006e.html.

Lee, Y. S., "Foreign Direct Investment and Regional Trade Liberalization: A Viable Answer for Economic Development?" (2005) 39(4) *Journal of World Trade*.

______, "Toward a More Open Trading System: Should Safeguards Replace Antidumping Measures?" (2005) 1(2) *21st Century Law Review*.

______, "The Beginning of Economic Integration between East Asia and North America? – Forming the Third Largest Free Trade Area between the United States and the Republic of Korea" (2007) 41(5) *Journal of World Trade*.

______, *Reclaiming Development in the World Trading System* (New York: Cambridge University Press, 2009).

Matsushita, Mitsuo, "Basic Principles of the WTO and the Role of Competition Policy" (2004) 3(2) *Washington University Global Studies Law Review*.

______, "North–South Issues of Foreign Direct Investments in the WTO: Is There a Middle-of-the-Road Approach?" in Steve Charnovitz, Debra P. Steger, and Peter Van den Bossche (eds.), in *Law in the Service of Human Dignity* (New York: Cambridge University Press, 2005), pp. 76–89.

Ministry of Economy, Trade and Industry of Japan, *2007 Report on Compliance by Major Trading Partners with Trade Agreements – WTO, FTA/EPA, and BIT* (April 2007), available at: http://www.meti.go.jp/policy/trade_policy/wto_compliance_report/html/f_y 2007 e.html (in Japanese).

United Nations Conference on Trade and Development, *World Investment Report* 2009, p. 32, available at: http://www.unctad.org/en/docs/wir2009_en.pdf.

U.S. Department of Justice and Federal Trade Commission, *Antitrust Enforcement Guidelines for International Operations* (April 1995).

World Trade Organization, *Background Note by the Secretariat, Systemic Issues Relating to "Other Regulations of Commerce,"* WT/REG/W17 (October 31, 1997).

______, *Argentina-Safeguard Measures on Imports of Footwear*, WT/DS121/R (December 14, 1999).

______, *Synopsis of "Systemic" Issues Related to Regional Trade Agreements*, WT/REG/W/37 (2 March 2000).

———, *United States-Definitive Safeguard Measures on Imports of Wheat Gluten from the European Communities*, WT/DS166/AB/R (December 22, 2000).
———, *United States-Safeguard Measures on Imports of Fresh, Chilled or Frozen Lamb Meat from New Zealand and Australia*, WT/DS177/AB/R and WT/DS178/AB/R (May 1, 2001).
———, *Working Group on the Interaction between Trade and Competition Policy*, Report to the General Council, WT/WCTP/1 (November 28, 1997), WT/WGTCP/2 (December 9, 1998), WT/WGTCP/3 (October 11, 1999), and WT/WGTCP/5 (October 8, 2001).
———, *United States-Definitive Safeguard Measures on Imports of Circular Welded Carbon Quality Line Pipe from Korea*, WT/DS202/AB/R (February 15, 2002).
———, International Trade Statistics 2009, pp. 178–179, Tables A3 and A4, available at: http://www.wto.org/english/res_e/statis_e/its2009_e/its2009_e.pdf.
———, "Regional Trade Agreement," text available at: http://www.wto.org/english/tratop_e/region_e/region_e.htm.

11

Developing Countries, Trade, and Human Rights

Free Trade Agreements, Development Needs, and the European Union's Generalized System of Preferences

Anthony E. Cassimatis

I. INTRODUCTION

Preferential trade arrangements, principally free trade agreements and trade preferences for developing countries offered pursuant to the Generalized System of Preferences (GSP), have been used by the United States and the European Union to link international trade and human rights formally.[1] Recent developments include the adoption by the Council of the European Union (EU) on July 22, 2008, of Council Regulation (EC) No. 732/2008. This regulation continues, with slight modification, the arrangements established under Council Regulation (EC) No. 980/2005. The 2005 regulation was itself the EU's response to the World Trade Organization (WTO) Appellate Body's decision in *European Communities – Conditions for the Granting of Tariff Preferences to Developing Countries*.[2] Other important developments have

[1] See, e.g., Dr. Roman Grynberg and Veniana Qalo, "Labour Standards in US and EU Preferential Trading Arrangements" (2006) 40(4) *Journal of World Trade* 619. On Canada's attempts at such linkage in free trade agreements, see, e.g., Maureen Irish, "GSP Tariffs and Conditionality: A Comment on EC-Preferences" (2007) 41(4) *Journal of World Trade* 683, 694; and Steve Charnovitz, "The Labour Dimension of the Emerging Free Trade Area of the Americas," in Philip Alston (ed.), *Labour Rights as Human Rights* (Oxford: Oxford University Press, 2005), p. 143.

[2] WT/DS246/AB/R, April 7, 2004. The Dispute Settlement Body adopted the Appellate Body's report and the modified panel report on April 20, 2004. For academic commentary on the panel and Appellate Body reports, see, e.g., Lorand Bartels, "The WTO Enabling Clause and Positive Conditionality in the European Community's GSP Program" (2003) 6 *Journal of International Economic Law* 507; Robert Howse, "Back to Court after Shrimp/Turtle? Almost but Not Quite Yet: India's Short Lived Challenge to Labor and Environmental Exceptions in the European Union's Generalized System of Preferences" (2003) 18 *American University International Law Review* 1333; Steve Charnovitz, Lorand Bartels, Robert Howse, Jane Bradley, Joost Pauwelyn, and Donald Regan, "Internet Roundtable – The Appellate Body's GSP Decision" (2004) 3 *World Trade Review* 239; Lorand Bartels, "The Appellate Body Report in European Communities – Conditions for the Granting of Tariff Preferences to Developing Countries and its Implications for Conditionality in GSP Programmes," in Thomas Cottier, Joost Pauwelyn, and Elisabeth Bürgi Bonanomi (eds.), *Human Rights and International Trade* (Oxford: Oxford University Press, 2005), p. 463; Gregory Shaffer and Yvonne Apea, "GSP Programmes and Their Historical-Political-Institutional Context," in Cottier, Pauwelyn, and Bürgi Bonanomi,

included the continuing evolution of the labor chapters of free trade agreements (FTAs) entered by the United States. The extent of this evolution is apparent when one compares recent FTAs, such as that negotiated with the Republic of Korea in 2007,[3] with earlier FTAs[4] and the North American Agreement on Labor Cooperation (NAALC),[5] which is a side agreement to the North American Free Trade Agreement (NAFTA).[6]

Concerns have been raised about the implications for developing countries of these measures linking trade and human rights.[7] This chapter examines these recent developments. Although there remain grounds for concern in some of these cases, there are also signs of efforts by the United States and the EU to address some of the criticisms of previous initiatives.[8] The chapter concludes with a consideration of the

ibid., p. 488; Jane Bradley, "The Enabling Clause and the Applied Rules of Interpretation," in Cottier, Pauwelyn, and Bürgi Bonanomi, ibid., p. 504; Gene M Grossman and Alan O Sykes, "A Preference for Development: The Law and Economics of GSP" (2005) 4 *World Trade Review* 41; Gregory Shaffer and Yvonne Apea, "Institutional Choice in the Generalized System of Preferences Case: Who Decides the Conditions for Trade Preferences? The Law and Politics of Rights" (2005) 39(6) *Journal of World Trade* 977; Peter M. Gerhart and Archana Seema Kella, "Power and Preferences: Developing Countries and the Role of the WTO Appellate Body" (2005) 30 *North Carolina Journal of International Law and Commercial Regulation* 515; Grynberg and Qalo, supra note 1; Lorand Bartels, "The WTO Legality of the EU's GSP+ Arrangement" (2007) 10 *Journal of International Economic Law* 869 ("Bartels 2007"); Maureen Irish, supra note 1; Stephanie Switzer, "Environmental Protection and the Generalized System of Preferences: A Legal and Appropriate Linkage?" (2008) 57 *International and Comparative Law Quarterly* 113; Anthony E. Cassimatis, "Developing States, the Generalized System of Preferences and Trade Measures Designed to Improve Respect for Human Rights," in Ross Buckley, Vai Io Lo, and Laurence Boulle (eds.), *Challenges to Multilateral Trade – The Impact of Bilateral, Preferential and Regional Agreements* (The Hague: Kluwer Law International, 2008), p. 201; and Dr. Umut Turksen, "The WTO Law and the EC's GSP+ Arrangement" (2009) 43(5) *Journal of World Trade* 927.

3 Free Trade Agreement between the United States of America and the Republic of Korea, done at Washington on June 30, 2007 (not yet in force; US–Korea FTA). U.S. FTAs are available at: http://www.ustr.gov/trade-agreements/free-trade-agreements. The United States–Panama Trade Promotion Agreement (done at Washington on June 28, 2007; US–Panama FTA), and the United States–Colombia Trade Promotion Agreement (done at Washington on November 22, 2006; US–Colombia FTA), which are also not yet in force, include similar labor rights provisions to those set out in the US–Korea FTA.

4 See, e.g., the Agreement between the United States of America and the Hashemite Kingdom of Jordan on the Establishment of a Free Trade Area, done at Washington on October 24, 2000, in force on December 17, 2001 (US–Jordan FTA) and the United States–Chile Free Trade Agreement, done at Miami on June 6, 2003, in force on January 1, 2004 (US–Chile FTA).

5 Reprinted in 32 International Legal Materials 1499 (1993) ("ILM").

6 Reprinted in 32 ILM 289 and 605 (1993).

7 See, e.g., Grynberg and Qalo (2006), supra note 1; and Magda Shahin, "To What Extent Should Labor and Environmental Standards Be Linked to Trade?" (2009) 2(1) *The Law and Development Review*. For a more general assessment of concerns confronting developing countries, see Yong-Shik Lee, *Reclaiming Development in the World Trading System* (New York: Cambridge University Press, 2009). For a general discussion of the legality of human rights related trade measures, see Anthony E. Cassimatis, *Human Rights Related Trade Measures under International Law* (Leiden, the Netherlands: Martinus Nijhoff, 2007). For a discussion of efforts to link trade and environmental protection in the context of the EU's GSP arrangements, see Switzer (2008), supra note 2.

8 Criticisms have come not just from trade law scholars. See, e.g., Philip Alston, "Labor Rights Provisions in U.S. Trade Law – 'Aggressive Unilateralism?'" in Lance A. Compa and Stephen F. Diamond (eds.),

concept of "development," which is invoked in the context of GSP arrangements and more generally under the WTO Agreement through the expressions "development need[s]" and "sustainable development." The human and social dimensions of the concept of development are analyzed. The extent to which the concept extends beyond purely economic considerations potentially has profound implications for any assessment of measures seeking to link trade and human rights.

II. RECENT U.S. INITIATIVES

Since the negotiation of the NAALC in the early 1990s, the United States has been seeking to incorporate labor rights chapters into the FTAs it negotiates.[9] A comprehensive review of the labor rights chapters in FTAs entered by the United States is beyond the scope of this chapter.[10] Instead, four features of the FTA negotiated between the United States and the Republic of Korea in 2007 are considered and contrasted with earlier FTAs entered by the United States. This comparison demonstrates how the labor chapters in U.S. FTAs have evolved. The most recently negotiated FTAs have been drafted to avoid some of the most problematic features, from a developing-country perspective, of earlier FTAs. The four features are: obligations to enact national labor laws; obligations to enforce national labor laws; respect for investigative and prosecutorial discretion and resource constraints at the national level; and dispute resolution procedures under the FTA.

A. *Obligations to Enact National Labor Laws*

Article 19.2.1 of the U.S.–Korea FTA provides that:

> [e]ach Party shall adopt and maintain in its statutes and regulations, and practices thereunder, the following rights, as stated in the *ILO [International Labour Organization] Declaration on Fundamental Principles and Rights at Work and its Follow-Up* (1998) (ILO Declaration): . . .
>
> (a) freedom of association;
> (b) the effective recognition of the right to collective bargaining;
> (c) the elimination of all forms of compulsory or forced labor;
> (d) the effective abolition of child labor and, for purposes of this Agreement, a prohibition on the worst forms of child labor; and
> (e) the elimination of discrimination in respect of employment and occupation.

When compared with earlier FTAs, three aspects of this provision are noteworthy. The first is that the parties have assumed a "hard" obligation to modify national

Human Rights, Labor Rights, and International Trade (Philadelphia: University of Pennsylvania Press, 1996), p. 71.

9 The United States has entered FTAs predominantly with developing countries, but it has succeeded in having labor rights chapters incorporated into FTAs with Singapore and Australia.

10 For a comparative review, see Charnovitz (2005), supra note 1, pp. 151–161.

laws to enshrine the rights contained in the ILO Declaration.[11] By comparison, the equivalent provisions of earlier FTAs such as the U.S.–Chile FTA[12] employ "soft" language, providing instead that the parties "shall strive to ensure" that the "principles" contained in the ILO Declaration "are recognized and protected" by their domestic law.

The second noteworthy aspect of Article 19.2.1 of the U.S.–Korea FTA is the *inclusion* of the prohibition of discrimination in employment or occupation. Contrast this with the *omission* of this right from Article 6.6 of the U.S.–Jordan FTA. The absence, in U.S. trade legislation addressing labor rights, of a right to be free from employment-related discrimination has been traced back to legislative amendments in 1984. It is said to reflect the position taken by the Reagan administration in response to efforts by the Democrat-controlled Congress to incorporate labor rights provisions into amendments to the U.S. GSP legislation.[13] This legislative approach appears to have had an impact on the drafting of the NAALC[14] and other FTAs, such as the U.S.–Chile FTA.[15]

The third aspect of Article 19.2.1 of the U.S.–Korea FTA is the *absence* of an obligation to enact laws generally on working conditions. The following "internationally recognized worker right" was initially incorporated into the 1984 GSP amendments[16] and then included in the NAALC[17] and subsequent FTAs:[18]

> [A]cceptable conditions of work with respect to minimum wages, hours of work, and occupational safety and health.

Understandably, this type of provision (which is better understood as a "bundle" of rights) has drawn criticism from those commentators writing from developing-

[11] The sense of hard and soft international law being used here is different from the more common use of these terms to distinguish instruments that are or are not in and of themselves binding under international law. The distinction being employed here is one made by Professor Condorelli and appears linked to concerns about the justiciability of treaty provisions that are, for example, drafted in aspirational terms; see Luigi Condorelli, "Discussion – *Lex Lata* and *Lex Ferenda*," in Antonio Cassese and Joseph H. H. Weiler (eds.), *Change and Stability in International Law-Making* (Berlin: Walter de Grutyer, 1988), pp. 78–81.

[12] See Article 18.1 of the U.S.–Chile FTA.

[13] See Lance Compa and Jeffrey S. Vogt, "Labor Rights in the Generalized System of Preferences: A 20-Year Review" (2001) 22 *Comparative Labor Law and Policy Journal* 199, 203. Compa and Vogt suggest the following reasons for the approach taken by the Reagan administration:

> Some officials in the administration feared souring relations with allied oil-producing states where discrimination against women and non-Muslims is prevalent. Others did not want to subject Israel to criticism over the treatment of Palestinian workers. Still others had vague unfounded concerns that non-discrimination provisions in U.S. trade laws might revive the recently defeated Equal Rights Amendment to the U.S. Constitution. (ibid., p. 203)

[14] See Article 29.1 of the NAALC.

[15] See Article 18.8 of the U.S.–Chile FTA.

[16] Compa and Voigt (2001), supra note 13, p. 202.

[17] See Article 49 of the NAALC.

[18] See, e.g., Article 6.6(e) of the U.S.–Jordan FTA, and Article 18.8 of the U.S.–Chile FTA.

country perspectives.[19] The provision significantly expanded the opportunity for the United States to undermine the legitimate comparative advantage of developing countries. This type of provision was not included in the 1998 ILO Declaration, no doubt, to avoid the risk of abuse for protectionist purposes. It will be recalled that the 1998 ILO Declaration was adopted, inter alia, as a response to the 1996 Singapore WTO ministerial declaration.[20] The International Labour Conference, which adopted the ILO Declaration, echoed the language of the Singapore WTO Ministerial Declaration when it stressed

> that labour standards should not be used for protectionist trade purposes, and that nothing in this Declaration and its follow-up shall be invoked or otherwise used for such purposes; in addition, the comparative advantage of any country should in no way be called into question by this Declaration and its follow-up.[21]

In apparent recognition of such concerns, the U.S.–Korea FTA does not require the enactment of national laws beyond those rights contained in the ILO Declaration.[22] By way of contrast, the U.S.–Chile FTA, in Article 18.1.2, includes an obligation (albeit soft) on each party to "strive to ensure that its laws provide for labor standards consistent with the internationally recognized labor rights," which are defined to include "acceptable conditions of work with respect to minimum wages, hours of work, and occupational safety and health."[23]

B. *Obligations to Enforce National Labor Laws*

The U.S.–Korea FTA provides in Article 19.2.2 that:

> [n]either Party shall waive or otherwise derogate from, or offer to waive or otherwise derogate from, its statutes or regulations implementing paragraph 1 [which

[19] See, e.g., Grynberg and Qalo (2006), supra note 1, pp. 626–640.

[20] Virginia A. Leary, "The WTO and the Social Clause: Post-Singapore" (1997) 8 *European Journal of International Law* 118, 121.

[21] Declaration on Fundamental Principles and Rights at Work, adopted by the International Labour Conference at its 86th Session Geneva, June 1998, para. 5. The declaration is reprinted in 137 *International Labour Review* (1998), 253. Compare the following paragraph of the WTO Ministerial Declaration adopted at Singapore in 1996:

> We renew our commitment to the observance of internationally recognized core labour standards. The International Labour Organization (ILO) is the competent body to set and deal with these standards, and we affirm our support for its work in promoting them. We believe that economic growth and development fostered by increased trade and further trade liberalization contribute to the promotion of these standards. We reject the use of labour standards for protectionist purposes, and agree that the comparative advantage of countries, particularly low-wage developing countries, must in no way be put into question. In this regard, we note that the WTO and ILO Secretariats will continue their existing collaboration. (Singapore Ministerial Declaration, WT/MIN(96)/DEC/W, December 13, 1996, para IV.)

[22] If a party does have laws dealing with minimum conditions regarding employment or occupation, then the U.S. FTAs require, subject to issues of prosecutorial discretion and resource constraints, the enforcement of those laws. See, e.g., U.S.–Korea FTA Articles 19.3 and 19.8.

[23] See Article 18.8 of the U.S.–Chile FTA.

> sets out the rights enshrined in the 1998 ILO Declaration] in a manner affecting trade or investment between the Parties, where the waiver or derogation would be inconsistent with a fundamental right set out in that paragraph.

This type of provision has significance, in particular, for those developing countries that have established export processing zones. The reference to "investment" also expands the scope of the provision beyond the scope of equivalent provisions in earlier FTAs.[24]

More generally, Article 19.3.1(a) of the U.S.–Korea FTA provides that:

> [n]either Party shall fail to effectively enforce its labor laws, including those it adopts or maintains in accordance with Article 19.2.1, through a sustained or recurring course of action or inaction, in a manner affecting trade or investment between the Parties, after the date this Agreement enters into force.[25]

Unlike earlier FTAs, the U.S.–Korea FTA includes provisions requiring "persons with a recognized interest" be given access to national tribunals for the enforcement of national labor laws.[26] The FTA also requires each party to ensure that "proceedings before such tribunals for the enforcement of its labor laws are fair, equitable, and transparent."[27] Resource issues arise for all States when international legal obligations are assumed to enforce national law. These resource issues can be particularly acute for developing countries. Creating legal remedies for the victims of labor rights violations allows for a broader distribution of the costs of enforcement of labor laws. Poverty is, however, a major factor in determining whether such costs can be carried by victims or those seeking to represent their interests. The U.S. FTAs with Jordan,[28] Chile,[29] and Korea[30] include provisions requiring labor cooperation between the parties.

C. *Respect for Regulatory, Investigative, and Prosecutorial Discretion and Resource Constraints at the National Level*

The U.S.–Jordan FTA includes recognition of these resource issues. Article 6.4(b) provides that:

> [t]he Parties recognize that each Party retains the right to exercise discretion with respect to investigatory, prosecutorial, regulatory, and compliance matters and to make decisions regarding the allocation of resources to enforcement with respect to other labor matters determined to have higher priorities. Accordingly, the Parties

[24] Compare Article 6.2 of the U.S.–Jordan FTA. See Grynberg and Qalo (2006), supra note 1, p. 632.
[25] "Labor laws" are defined in Article 19.8 U.S.–Korea FTA.
[26] Article 19.4.1 U.S.–Korea FTA.
[27] Article 19.4.2 U.S.–Korea FTA. The article then sets out more specific obligations.
[28] Article 6.5 U.S.–Jordan FTA.
[29] Article 18.5 U.S.–Chile FTA.
[30] Article 19.6 and Annex 19-A U.S.–Korea FTA.

> understand that a Party is in compliance with subparagraph (a) [setting out the obligation to effectively enforce national labor laws] where a course of action or inaction reflects a reasonable exercise of such discretion, or results from a *bona fide* decision regarding the allocation of resources.

Although a provision dealing with regulatory discretion and resource issues was included in the U.S.–Korea FTA, there are significant differences compared with the foregoing provision. In particular, Article 19.3.1(b) of the U.S.–Korea FTA provides that:

> [a] decision a Party makes on the distribution of enforcement resources shall not be a reason for not complying with the provisions of this Chapter. Each Party retains the right to the reasonable exercise of discretion and to *bona fide* decisions with regard to the allocation of resources between labor enforcement activities among the fundamental labor rights enumerated in Article 19.2.1, provided the exercise of such discretion and such decisions are not inconsistent with the obligations of this Chapter (Footnote omitted.)

The footnote to this paragraph indicates that this enforcement flexibility extends beyond national laws protecting the rights contained in the 1998 ILO Declaration.[31] Similar provisions appear in other more recent FTAs.[32]

D. *Treaty Dispute Resolution Procedures*

The provisions of the U.S.–Korea FTA requiring protection and enforcement of labor rights under national law are also linked to the international dispute resolution provisions of the FTA. Thus, a panel can be established under Chapter 22 of the U.S.–Korea FTA to hear a claim that a state party has failed to carry out its obligations under Article 19.2.1 to "adopt and maintain in its statutes and regulations, and practices thereunder" the rights enshrined in the 1998 ILO Declaration.[33] Equally, a state party can initiate the panel process to hear a complaint that rights set out in the ILO Declaration have not been enforced under the national law of the other party as required by Articles 19.2.2 and 19.3.1(a). By way of contrast, the NAALC does not permit a panel process to be initiated in respect of alleged violations of freedom of association, the right to collectively bargain, or the prohibition of discrimination in employment or occupation.[34]

[31] The footnote to Article 19.3.1(b) of the U.S.–Korea FTA provides:

> For greater certainty, a Party retains the right to exercise reasonable enforcement discretion and to make *bona fide* decisions regarding the allocation of enforcement resources with respect to labor laws other than those relating to fundamental rights enumerated in Article 19.2.1.

[32] See Article 17.3.1(b) of the U.S.–Colombia FTA, and Article 16.3.1(b) of the U.S.–Panama FTA.

[33] But note the terms of the letters dated June 30, 2007, recording the understanding of the parties in relation to labor chapter of the U.S.–Korea FTA.

[34] See Article 29 of NAALC.

The U.S.–Korea FTA and more recent FTAs also include more robust dispute resolution procedures than some of the earlier FTAs. The U.S.–Jordan FTA, for example, has a relatively unsophisticated dispute resolution procedure that could be frustrated by the refusal of a state party to appoint a panel member.[35]

E. *Conclusions on Recent U.S. FTAs*

The efficacy of the NAALC and the labor provisions of the U.S.–Chile FTA have been seriously questioned.[36] Commentators have, however, suggested that a fundamental shift in the policies of the U.S. government in linking trade and human rights occurred in 2006.[37] Post-2006 FTAs negotiated by the United States appear to support this assessment. Some features of this change of policy appear to offer modest improvements from the perspectives of developing countries. The increased focus in the more recent FTAs on the rights set out in the 1998 ILO Declaration promises greater objectivity than was ever possible under earlier instruments that relied more heavily on references to "acceptable conditions of work with respect to minimum wages, hours of work, and occupational safety and health." Although some controversial issues remain,[38] there is much greater international consensus regarding the international legal status of the rights set out in the ILO Declaration.

Other aspects of the more recent U.S. FTAs are more likely to be of concern to developing countries. Obligations to establish national tribunals having jurisdiction over alleged infringements of labor rights may impose a significant burden on developing countries. Linking such obligations to dispute resolution procedures under the treaties has the potential to compound the problem.

[35] See Article 17.1(c) of the U.S.–Jordan FTA. Note also Article 17.1(e)(ii).

[36] Steve Charnovitz has offered the following assessment:

> The NAFTA labor side agreement has been in effect since January 1994, and in over 10 years, no government has brought a case against another government's lack of enforcement of the covered labor laws. Many informed observers have concluded that the NAFTA parties all live in glass houses with regard to labor rights, and so would be uninterested in amending the side agreement to allow individuals to lodge complaints to an international tribunal. The side agreement does allow individuals to send communications about national enforcement problems, and twenty-eight have been sent. . . . Little has happened as a result, however, except for some joint statements and remedial seminars. Of course, the fact that the enforcement provisions have proved a nullity does not mean that the side agreement is unsuccessful. Overall, the experiment has proved useful in creating an international commission to promote North American labor cooperation. Unfortunately, that institutional centerpiece was omitted from the US–Chile Free Trade Agreement. . . . The only purpose being served by these labor provisions is to satisfy the political need of appearing to use the FTA to safeguard worker rights. (Charnovitz [2005], supra note 1, pp. 155–160.)

[37] According to Aaronson and Zimmerman, "[o]n November 7, 2006, the earth moved for those individuals who follow the U.S. debate over trade and labor rights. After both houses of Congress changed hands from Republican to Democratic control, the leaders of the House Ways and Means and Senate Finance committees promised a new approach to trade policymaking"; Susan Ariel Aaronson and Jamie M. Zimmerman, *Trade Imbalance – The Struggle to Weigh Human Rights Concerns in Trade Policymaking* (New York: Cambridge University Press, 2008), p. 163.

[38] Cassimatis (2007), supra note 7, pp. 87–90.

The question remains whether the post-2006 FTAs, which are not yet in force, will overcome the efficacy problems identified with the labor provisions of the earlier treaties. There also remain more fundamental efficacy-related issues that require consideration.

Past efficacy-based criticisms of U.S. measures have been narrowly focused on the inclusion and operation of dispute resolution structures and procedures in relation to labor rights. What appears to have been missing, however, from the assessments so far undertaken of the efficacy of U.S. measures linking trade and human rights has been a consideration of the broader implications of such policies for the welfare of the population of the developing countries to which these policies apply.

The efficacy of human rights provisions in GSP arrangements has been the subject of greater scrutiny. It is to recent developments in such arrangements that attention is now turned.

III. RECENT EU INITIATIVES

The European Community and member states of the EU have entered into various trade-related treaties with developing countries. These treaties generally include provisions referring to human rights and providing for suspension in cases of serious human rights violations.[39] Perhaps the most significant treaty of this kind is the Cotonou Agreement[40] between the European Community, EU member states, and African, Caribbean, and Pacific states. Article 50 of the Cotonou Agreement refers to the labor-related human rights that are set out in the 1998 ILO Declaration. Article 96 sets out the procedure to be applied, inter alia, in cases of failure to "fulfil an obligation stemming from respect for human rights."[41] Under Article 96(2)(c), suspension of the Cotonou Agreement for such failure is referred to "as a measure of last resort,"[42] and disputes regarding the interpretation of the agreement may be submitted to compulsory arbitration.[43] Recent developments in the

[39] See, generally, Lorand Bartels, *Human Rights Conditionality in the EU's International Agreements* (Oxford: Oxford University Press, 2005), and Dr. Lorand Bartels, *The Application of Human Rights Conditionality in the EU's Bilateral Trade Agreements and other Trade Arrangements with Third Countries, European Parliament*, EXPO-B-INTA-2008–57, PE 406.991 (November 2008).

[40] Partnership Agreement between the Members of the African, Caribbean and Pacific Group of States of the One Part, and the European Community and Its Member States, of the Other Part, done at Cotonou on 23 June 2000, *Official Journal of the European Communities*, L 317/3 (December 15, 2000), entered into force on April 1, 2003.

[41] Article 96 is supplemented by Annex VII, which was agreed to in 2005 – see *Agreement Amending the Partnership* Agreement between the Members of the African, Caribbean and Pacific Group of States, of the One Part, and the European Community and Its Member States, of the Other Part, signed in Cotonou on 23 June 2000, *Official Journal of the European Union*, L 209/27, August 11, 2005.

[42] Article 96 (as amended by agreement in 2005) also provides that measures taken in response to a failure to resolve a dispute by consultation "shall be revoked as soon as the reasons for taking them no longer prevail," and measures taken in response to violations must be "taken in accordance with international law, and proportional to the violation." See Bartels (2005), supra note 39, p. 30.

[43] See Article 98 of the Cotonou Agreement.

application of the Cotonou Agreement have included consultations under Article 96 with Fiji.[44]

Focusing on EU GSP arrangements, the most significant recent development has been the adoption by the Council of the European Union on July 22, 2008, of Council Regulation (EC) No. 732/2008.[45] This regulation extends until December 31, 2011, the arrangements established under Council Regulation (EC) No. 980/2005, which applied until December 31, 2008.[46] As noted earlier, the 2005 regulation was itself a response to the Appellate Body's decision in *European Communities – Conditions for the Granting of Tariff Preferences to Developing Countries*.[47] This decision and the preceding panel report have been the subject of extensive commentary.[48] The focus of this chapter is therefore on Regulation No. 732/2008 and issues surrounding its consistency with the WTO Agreement and the Enabling Clause, as well as the efficacy of such measures.

A. *General Contours of Council Regulation (EC) No. 732/2008*

With one exception,[49] the terms of Regulation No. 732/2008 follow those of the regulation that it superseded. Regulation No. 732/2008 links access to trade preferences for developing countries to respect for human rights[50] in two ways. First, the regulation sets out a "[s]pecial incentive arrangement for sustainable development and good governance" for developing countries that meet the definition of "vulnerable country" in Regulation No. 732/2008.[51] This arrangement allows for more

[44] See, e.g., Council of the European Union, Declaration by the Presidency on behalf of the European Union on Recent Developments in Fiji, Brussels, April 20, 2009, 8772/1/09 REV 1 (Presse 90), P 42/09. For a list of countries that have been subjected to measures under the Lome and Cotonou agreements, see Bartels (2008), supra note 39, p. 11.

[45] Council Regulation (EC) No. 732/2008 of July 22, 2008, applying a scheme of generalized tariff preferences for the period from January 1, 2009, to December 31, 2011, and amending Regulations (EC) No. 552/97, (EC) No. 1933/2006 and Commission Regulations (EC) No. 1100/2006, and (EC) No. 964/2007, *Official Journal of the European Union*, L211/1, August 6, 2008.

[46] For the WTO notification by the European Communities of the measure, see WTO Committee on Trade and Development, *Generalized System of Preferences, Notification by the European Communities*, Addendum, WT/COMTD/N/4/Add.4 (12 March 2009). For questions from WTO Members on the regulation and replies on behalf of the European Communities, see *WTO Trade Policy Review Body, Trade Policy Review, European Communities, Minutes of Meeting*, Addendum, WT/TPR/M/214/Add.1 (2 July 2009), pp. 69–70, 268, and 269.

[47] WT/DS246/AB/R, April 7, 2004.

[48] See, e.g., the references set out in supra note 2.

[49] The exception relates to the number of opportunities provided to developing countries to qualify for the special incentive arrangements under the regulation and whether the list of beneficiaries is in effect closed. See Article 9(1)(a) of Regulation No. 732/2008. This is discussed further later in the chapter.

[50] The regulation also links eligibility for trade preferences to entry into, and compliance with, specified environmental, drug trade, and corruption suppression treaties. A review of this aspect of the regulation is beyond the scope of this chapter.

[51] See Articles 7 to 10 of Regulation No. 732/2008. For the developing countries that are currently benefiting under the special incentive arrangements, see Commission Decision (EC) No. 938/2008 of December 9, 2008, *Official Journal of the European Union*, L 334/90.

favorable access to the EU market than is provided under the standard EU GSP arrangements.[52] These special incentive arrangements are restricted to states that have become (or are becoming) parties to specified multilateral human rights and ILO treaties.[53] The definition of "vulnerable country" under the regulation therefore appears to be based on two broad factors, one explicit and the other implicit. The explicit factor is the absence of World Bank classification as a "high-income country" and a lack of diversification of GSP-covered imports into the EU.[54] The implicit factor, which is suggested by the preamble to the regulation[55] and which has been confirmed by the European Communities in explanations offered within the WTO Committee on Trade and Development,[56] relates to the burdens assumed

[52] Note the two types of general preferences – those for developing countries generally (Article 6 of Regulation No. 732/2008) and preferences for least developed countries (under the "Everything-but-Arms" initiative; Articles 11 and 12).

[53] The relevant treaties are set out in Part A of Annex III of the regulation. The specified treaties are:

1. International Covenant on Civil and Political Rights
2. International Covenant on Economic, Social and Cultural Rights
3. International Convention on the Elimination of All Forms of Racial Discrimination
4. Convention on the Elimination of All Forms of Discrimination Against Women
5. Convention Against Torture and other Cruel, Inhuman or Degrading Treatment or Punishment
6. Convention on the Rights of the Child
7. Convention on the Prevention and Punishment of the Crime of Genocide
8. Convention concerning Minimum Age for Admission to Employment (No. 138)
9. Convention concerning the Prohibition and Immediate Action for the Elimination of the Worst Forms of Child Labour (No. 182)
10. Convention concerning the Abolition of Forced Labour (No. 105)
11. Convention concerning Forced or Compulsory Labour (No. 29)
12. Convention concerning Equal Remuneration of Men and Women Workers for Work of Equal Value (No. 100)
13. Convention concerning Discrimination in Respect of Employment and Occupation (No. 111)
14. Convention concerning Freedom of Association and Protection of the Right to Organise (No. 87)
15. Convention concerning the Application of the Principles of the Right to Organise and to Bargain Collectively (No. 98)
16. International Convention on the Suppression and Punishment of the Crime of Apartheid.

[54] See Article 8(2) Regulation No. 732/2008.

[55] See paragraph 8 of the preamble to Regulation No. 732/2008, which contends that "additional tariff preferences should be granted to those developing countries which, due to a lack of diversification and insufficient integration into the international trading system, are vulnerable *while assuming the special burdens and responsibilities resulting from the ratification and effective implementation of core international conventions on human and labour rights*, environmental protection and good governance" (emphasis added).

[56] In response to a question from the representative of Pakistan in the WTO Committee on Trade and Development regarding Regulation No. 980/2005, the representative of the European Communities made the following observation:

> Vulnerable developing countries which by their own volition assume special burdens and responsibilities due to the ratification and effective implementation of core international conventions on human and labour rights, environmental protection and good governance should benefit from additional tariff preferences. These preferences are designed to promote further economic growth and thereby to respond positively to the internationally recognised need for sustainable development. (See "The EU's Generalized System of Preferences: Responses to

by developing countries that are parties to the particular human rights (including labor-related rights) treaties set out in Regulation No. 732/2008. In effect, the enforcement obligations assumed by developing countries under these treaties are treated as contributing to vulnerability for the purposes of the regulation.[57]

Second, Regulation No. 732/2008 provides a mechanism for the temporary withdrawal of GSP arrangements (both standard and special incentive arrangements), inter alia, in cases of "serious and systematic violations of principles" enshrined in specified multilateral human rights and ILO treaties.[58] Temporary withdrawal is linked to "the conclusions of the relevant monitoring bodies" overseeing compliance with the treaties.[59]

B. *International Legal Rules Applicable to GSP Arrangements*

The legal disciplines under the WTO Agreement relevant to the EU's GSP arrangements can be summarized as follows:

1. For GSP arrangements to comply with the *legal* requirements of the Enabling Clause, the arrangements must involve "generalized, non-reciprocal and non discriminatory preferences beneficial to the developing countries."[60]
2. The obligation of nondiscrimination between developing countries when trade preferences are given under GSP arrangements does not prohibit all forms of distinction between developing countries. In addition to distinctions in favor of least developed countries, the Appellate Body recognized an

Questions Submitted by Brazil, China, India and Pakistan," WT/COMTD/57/Add.5 [June 27, 2006], p. 8).

57 Cf. Bartels (2007), supra note 2, pp. 874–877.

58 Article 15(1)(a) of Regulation No. 732/2008. In subparagraph (b) of Article 15(1), there is reference to the "the export of goods made by prison labour." This provision indicates that a defense of the EU regulation is also likely to include reliance on Article XX of GATT 1994. Before the panel in *European Communities – Conditions for the Granting of Tariff Preferences to Developing Countries*, the European Communities unsuccessfully sought to rely on Article XX(b) of GATT 1994. This aspect of the panel's report was not the subject of appeal to the Appellate Body. Consideration of the prospects of successful reliance on other paragraphs of Article XX is beyond the scope of this chapter. For an analysis of relevant issues, see, e.g., Cassimatis (2007), supra note 7, pp. 334–398 and 415–416.

59 Article 15(1)(a) of Regulation No. 732/2008. See also Article 18. For states being denied preferences, see paragraph 24 of the preamble to Regulation No. 732/2008.

60 The Enabling Clause provides in paragraphs 1 and 2(a) (and in footnote 3 to paragraph 2(a)) that:

1. [n]otwithstanding the provisions of Article I of the General Agreement, contracting parties may accord differential and more favourable treatment to developing countries, without according such treatment to other contracting parties. . . .
2. The provisions of paragraph 1 apply to the following:
   (a) Preferential tariff treatment accorded by developed contracting parties to products originating in developing countries in accordance with the Generalized System of Preferences.
3. As described in the Decision of the CONTRACTING PARTIES of 25 June 1971, relating to the establishment of "generalized, non-reciprocal and non discriminatory preferences beneficial to the developing countries" (Basic Instrument and Selected Document 18S/24).

entitlement to differentiate between developing countries to respond positively to the different development needs of developing countries.[61]

3. To qualify as a relevant development "need" of a developing country, the need must be established according to an "objective standard."[62] According to the Appellate Body, "[b]road-based recognition of a particular need, set out in the WTO Agreement or in multilateral instruments adopted by international organizations, could serve as such a standard."[63] The Appellate Body also spoke of the development need having to be "widely-recognized."[64]
4. Differentiation between developing countries must be based on a nexus between the trade measures and a positive response to the particular developing countries' development, financial or trade needs.[65] Does, for example, the trade preference address a "development . . . need" that, by its nature, is a need that can be addressed by way of trade preferences?

C. *Concerns Regarding the Legality of Council Regulation (EC) No. 732/2008*

Although questions have been raised about the consistency of past EU GSP arrangements with the WTO Enabling Clause obligation of *nonreciprocity* in relation to trade preferences,[66] it has been in the area of *nondiscrimination* between developing

[61] According to the Appellate Body:

> by requiring developed countries to "respond positively" to the "needs of developing countries," which are varied and not homogeneous, paragraph 3(c) [of the Enabling Clause] indicates that a GSP scheme may be "non-discriminatory" even if "identical" tariff treatment is not accorded to "all" GSP beneficiaries. Moreover, paragraph 3(c) suggests that tariff preferences under GSP schemes may be "non-discriminatory" when the relevant tariff preferences are addressed to a particular "development, financial [or] trade need" and are made available to all beneficiaries that share that need. (Paragraph 165 of the Appellate Body report in *European Communities – Conditions for the Granting of Tariff Preferences to Developing Countries*, WT/DS246/AB/R [April 7, 2004].)

[62] Ibid., para. 163.

[63] Ibid.

[64] Ibid., paras. 164 and 179.

[65] According to the Appellate Body:

> the expectation that developed countries will "respond positively" to the "needs of developing countries" suggests that a sufficient nexus should exist between, on the one hand, the preferential treatment provided under the respective measure authorized by paragraph 2 [of the Enabling Clause], and, on the other hand, the likelihood of alleviating the relevant "development, financial [or] trade need." In the context of a GSP scheme, the particular need at issue must, by its nature, be such that it can be effectively addressed through tariff preferences. Therefore, only if a preference-granting country acts in the "positive" manner suggested, in "respon[se]" to a widely-recognized "development, financial [or] trade need," can such action satisfy the requirements of paragraph 3(c). (Ibid., para. 164.)

[66] See Bartels (2003), supra note 2, pp. 526–530, who argues convincingly that these concerns are ultimately unfounded.

countries that most concerns have been raised. Does Regulation No. 732/2008 satisfy the Enabling Clause's requirement of nondiscrimination?

Dr. Lorand Bartels has offered a thoughtful critique of the regulation that preceded Regulation No. 732/2008.[67] With one possible exception,[68] his concerns apply equally to the current regulation.[69] The concerns raised have included whether the regulation responded to a "development need" identified according to some "objective standard." Bartels has argued that "a country that has not ratified a convention may have precisely the same development needs as one that has."[70] The difficulty in linking the giving of trade preferences to the entry into treaties has also been noted. The members of the WTO include autonomous customs areas such as Macao, which may lack independent legal personality to enter into human rights and other treaties.[71]

Related to these concerns, questions have also been raised about the definition of "vulnerable country,"[72] which in Regulation No. 732/2008 includes a requirement that a beneficiary country's GSP covered imports into the European Community "represent less than 1% in value of the total GSP-covered imports into the Community."[73] It is difficult to see how this could be considered an objective criterion of development need. Bartels makes the point succinctly:

> This criterion is not defined in terms of the country at issue, but in terms of EU imports, an entirely independent factor. As such, by definition it *cannot* be a relevant criterion for discriminating between developing countries.[74]

Concerns have also been raised regarding the selectiveness of the EU's designation of treaties that must be ratified to qualify for the special incentive arrangements. For example, the International Convention on the Protection of the Rights of All Migrant Workers and Members of Their Families is not included in the list of treaties that developing countries must become party to in order to benefit from the special incentive arrangements. This treaty is included in the list of "Core International Human Rights Instruments" maintained by the Office of the United Nations High

67 Bartels (2007), supra note 2, pp. 874–882.

68 The exception is his concern regarding the "closed" nature of the list of beneficiaries under Regulation No. 980/2005. Bartels questions how the regulation could meet the Appellate Body's concern about the need to give similarly situated developing countries the opportunity to secure special incentive preferences when the regulation only allowed preferences for those countries meeting the criteria on October 31, 2005; see ibid., p. 882. Regulation No. 732/2008 now offers two opportunities to secure special preferences; see Article 9(1)(a). The list of beneficiaries is therefore restricted but not closed, at least it was not until April 30, 2010.

69 See Bartels (2008), supra note 39, pp. 15–16.

70 Bartels (2007), supra note 2, p. 877. Compare Switzer (2008), supra note 2, pp. 139–145.

71 Bartels (2007), supra note 2, p. 877.

72 Ibid., p. 882.

73 Article 8(2)(b) of Regulation No. 732/2008.

74 Bartels (2007), supra note 2, p. 882 (emphasis in original).

Commissioner of Human Rights.[75] No member state of the EU is currently a party to this treaty.

In addition to selectiveness, it has also been questioned whether the EU's preferences constitute a positive response to development needs when certain beneficiaries do not appear to confront the risk of violations of a number of the conventions.[76] The sequencing of the giving of special preferences after the assumption by developing countries of implementation obligations under the treaties has also been questioned.[77] There also appears to be a risk that some developing countries may be less able to incur these implementation costs and that positive capacity-building measures may be justified.[78]

In relation to the negative measures provided for under Regulation No. 732/2008, Bartels has identified an issue that other commentators appear to have overlooked.[79] In a 2008 study requested by the European Parliament's Committee on International Trade, the issue was explained in the following way:

> [I]n *EC – Tariff Preferences*, the Appellate Body said that any preferential treatment must be a "positive response" to a development need. But once preferences are withdrawn from a country, the additional preferential treatment is being given to the remaining beneficiaries. The question is therefore not whether the withdrawal of preferences is a positive response to the needs of the country from which the preferences are being withdrawn. Rather, it is whether the continuing grant of preferences to the remaining beneficiaries is a positive response to *their* development needs.[80]

A question nonetheless also arises as to whether a developing country being denied preferences under the negative measures provided for in Regulation No. 732/2008 is being discriminated against in a manner prohibited by the Enabling Clause.

75 See http://www2.ohchr.org/english/law.

76 Bartels explains his concern as follows:

> The Appellate Body's references to "improving . . . the situation" and to "alleviating the . . . need" are clearly linked to material situations, most likely with resource implications. Arguably, there would be some flexibility in the degree of risk that a situation will be present in any given country. Some countries clearly have a "need" to prevent damage from foreseeable natural disasters. But this does not mean that every possible risk, no matter how remote, can be considered a "development need" of any given country. . . . Bolivia is at no risk of sustaining direct damage from a tsunami; nor, fortunately, does it appear to be at any risk of suffering apartheid or genocide. This is not to say, of course, that no countries have a relevant "need" to prevent genocide or apartheid, nor that tariff preferences would necessarily be an inappropriate means of meeting such a need. But in the concrete case, it does appear that the EU is granting GSP + preferences to compensate countries for "development needs" that they do not have. (Bartels (2007), supra note 2, p. 880.)

77 Ibid., pp. 881–882.

78 Ibid., p. 881.

79 See, e.g., Cassimatis (2007), supra note 2; and Charnovitz et al. (2005), supra note 2, p. 249.

80 Bartels (2008), supra note 39, p. 16 (emphasis in original).

Whether there has been such discrimination depends fundamentally on the identification of a relevant "development . . . need" that allows differentiation between beneficiary countries and the country that has had its preferences suspended. The centrality of this issue and the potentially broad scope of "development . . . needs" extending beyond issues of economic development requires further consideration. It is to this issue and the related concept of "sustainable development" that attention is now turned. It is contended that some of the concerns raised by Dr. Bartels do not arise if a broad conception of development is adopted and Regulation No. 732/2008 is understood in that context.

D. *"Development . . . Needs," "Sustainable Development," and Human Rights*

Regulation No. 732/2008 invokes the human right to development and the concept of sustainable development in support of the arrangements set out in the regulation.[81] If a link between respect for human rights, sustainable development, and the notion of "development needs" is established, then this has potentially profound implications for efforts to link trade and human rights under the WTO Agreement.

In the present context, it is appropriate to frame the issues in terms of the Enabling Clause and the concept of development needs. Can the costs of ensuring compliance with international human rights obligations be said to give rise to a development need?

An initial issue is the link between human rights and development. Central to understanding this issue is the 1986 Declaration on the Right to Development.[82] The declaration itself represents a change in developing-country strategies following the failure of efforts to establish a "New International Economic Order" in the 1960s and 1970s.[83] An explicit human rights framework was chosen as part of this change in strategy.

The drafters of the Declaration on the Right to Development nonetheless sought to ensure coherence with existing human rights standards under international law. Thus, Article 6(3) of the declaration linked efforts to secure the right to development to respect for other human rights:

> States should take steps to eliminate *obstacles to development* resulting from failure to observe civil and political rights, as well as economic, social and cultural rights.[84]

[81] See paragraph 7 of the preamble to the regulation, which refers, inter alia, to the 1986 Declaration on the Right to Development and to the 1992 Rio and the 2002 Johannesburg declarations, which in turn address the concept of sustainable development. Bartels addresses the broader social conception of development in his discussion of Regulation No. 980/2005. Bartels (2007), supra note 2, pp. 874–877.

[82] See General Assembly resolution 41/128, adopted on December 4, 1986.

[83] See Ian Brownlie, *The Human Right to Development* (London: Commonwealth Secretariat, 1989), pp. 22–23.

[84] Emphasis added.

If failure to observe international human rights obligations results in obstacles to development, then it can readily be contended that ensuring compliance with international human rights obligations removes obstacles to development or, in language of the Enabling Clause, addresses a development need.

Complying with obligations to respect human rights under international law, however, is not without cost. Assistance in meeting the costs of establishing and maintaining the necessary institutional structures and enforcement mechanisms to ensure respect for international human rights obligations can, therefore, on this analysis, be characterized as responding to a development need.

A related point might also be made. A state that has assumed obligations to respect *and to ensure respect* for human rights[85] will necessarily incur costs even if particular international human rights standards, such as those related to the prohibitions of genocide or apartheid, are unlikely to be violated in that state. The obligations in relation to the prohibitions of genocide and apartheid include duties to prevent,[86] and to prosecute persons alleged to have committed, these international crimes.[87]

One of the difficulties that arises when attempting to link respect for international human rights standards with the concept of "development need" appears to be similar to an ambiguity in the human right to development. A prominent aspect of the debates surrounding the human right to development is uncertainty over the extent to which it is a right of individuals or a collective right.[88] This ambiguity appears to have an analogue in the concept of "development need." Are the needs to which there must be a positive response the "needs" of enterprises, sectors, or an entire country? The Declaration on the Right to Development is perhaps best interpreted as setting out a bundle of rights with both individual and collective dimensions.[89] If development, for the purposes of the Enabling Clause, is recognized as having social and human dimensions,[90] then a similar approach appears warranted.

This issue may have a bearing on the requirement, identified by the Appellate Body in *EC-Tariff Preferences*, of a nexus between trade preferences and a positive response to a developing country's development needs. If development needs are accepted

85 See, e.g., Article 2 of the International Covenant on Civil and Political Rights.

86 See, e.g., the decision of the International Court of Justice in the *Case Concerning the Application of the Convention on the Prevention and Punishment of the Crime of Genocide*, Judgment of February 27, 2007, para. 430.

87 In relation to the crime of apartheid, see Article IV of the International Convention on the Suppression and Punishment of the Crime of Apartheid.

88 Brownlie (1989), supra note 83, pp. 15–17.

89 Ibid.

90 Textually, the phrase "development, financial and trade needs" supports a construction of development extending beyond economic considerations. "Development" also appears to be "by definition, evolutionary."; see *Legal Consequences for States of the Continued Presence of South Africa in Namibia (South West Africa) notwithstanding Security Council Resolution 276 (1970), Advisory Opinion*, ICJ Reports 1971, 16, 31–32, para. 53; and *United States – Import Prohibition of Certain Shrimp and Shrimp Products*, WT/DS58/AB/R (October 12, 1998), adopted by the Dispute Settlement Body on November 6, 1998, para. 130.

as including the needs of individual enterprises, then measures providing trade preferences for the benefit of such enterprises might be seen as positive responses to address the costs of compliance with international labor standards.[91] Establishing a nexus of the kind suggested by the Appellate Body appears more difficult, however, when development needs are considered on a national level involving a broader range of international human rights.[92]

A fundamental question that will also have potentially profound implications for the interpretation of the WTO Agreement is whether a link between the human right to development and the concept of sustainable development can be substantiated. The answer appears both reasonably clear and controversial. The Rio Declaration on Environment and Development specifically refers to the right to development in Principle 3.[93] Judge Cançado Trindade referred to the drafting history of the Rio Declaration and the link between international human rights standards and the Rio Declaration in his separate opinion in the 2010 decision of the International Court of Justice in the *Case Concerning Pulp Mills on the River Uruguay*.[94]

The Johannesburg Declaration makes the link between sustainable development and international human rights standards even more explicit than the Rio Declaration.[95] Given the reference to the concept of "sustainable development" and the reliance placed on the Rio Declaration by the Appellate Body, for example, in the *Shrimp Turtle Case*,[96] a link between international human rights standards and the reference to "sustainable development" in the WTO Agreement appears to be unavoidable.

91 Compare Grossman and Sykes (2005), supra note 2, p. 56.

92 Contrast the much narrower range of rights enumerated in the EU's GSP arrangements set out in Article 26(1) of Council Regulation (EC) No. 2501/2001. Compare the doubts expressed by Bartels in relation to the Appellate Body's approach of requiring that "the particular need at issue must, by its nature, be such that it can be effectively addressed through tariff preferences"; Bartels (2007), supra note 2, p. 876.

93 Principle 3 of the Rio Declaration provides that:

> [t]he right to development must be fulfilled so as to equitably meet developmental and environmental needs of present and future generations.

The drafting history of the declaration appears to support the common identity of the "right to development" in Principle 3 of the Rio Declaration and the right to development set out in the Declaration adopted by the General Assembly in 1986; see Report of the United Nations Conference on Environment and Development, Rio de Janeiro, June 3–14, 1992, Volume 2, Proceedings of the Conference, UN Doc A/CONF.151/26/Rev.l (Vol. II); Nicholas A. Robinson (ed.), *Agenda 21 & the UNCED Proceedings*, Vol. 1 (New York: Oceana Publications, 1992), p. cxv; and Patricia Birnie, Alan Boyle, and Catherine Redgwell, *International Law and the Environment* (3rd ed., Oxford: Oxford University Press, 2009), pp. 118–119.

94 *Argentina v. Uruguay*, Judgment April 20, 2010. See the separate opinion of Judge Cançado Trindade at paras. 132–140 and 159–160.

95 See Johannesburg Declaration on Sustainable Development, UN Doc A/CONF.199/L.6/Rev.2 (September 4, 2002), para. 28.

96 *United States – Import Prohibition of Certain Shrimp and Shrimp Products*, WT/DS58/AB/R (October 12, 1998), adopted by the Dispute Settlement Body on November 6, 1998, para. 168.

E. *Efficacy Concerns*

Empirical analysis of preferential trade agreements (including GSP arrangements) suggests that arrangements that provide for concrete market access consequences, dependent on respect for international human rights standards, are more likely to be efficacious when compared with human rights treaties that lack concrete enforcement mechanisms.[97] Nonetheless, more empirical evidence appears necessary. In an important study in 2005, it was noted that in relation to recently negotiated preferential trade agreements, there was "no strong case study evidence to either support or reject the proposition that these [preferential trade agreements] influence members' human rights practices, and further research into these new cases will be crucial in the next few years."[98]

IV. CONCLUDING OBSERVATIONS

United States efforts to incorporate respect for international labor standards have developed in recent years. Some of the more unreasonable features of earlier U.S. FTAs, such as obligations imposed on developing states regarding "acceptable conditions of work" have been addressed in more recent FTAs in a manner that reduces the prospects of protectionist abuse. The U.S. policy of including labor standards into FTAs has, however, been criticized as being ineffective. In contrast, EU efforts to link trade and human rights, by way of positive measures, have been assessed as having been reasonably effective in securing respect for international human rights standards.[99] What has been missing, however, from the assessments so far undertaken of the efficacy of both U.S. and EU measures linking trade and human rights has been a consideration of the broader implications of such policies for the welfare of the population of the developing countries to which these policies apply. There have been calls for such assessments in the context of EU measures linking trade and human rights.[100] In the absence of such assessments, whatever the international legal position might be, it appears impossible to assess properly whether labor-related human rights clauses in U.S. FTAs or the EU's GSP arrangements are actually having a positive impact on the development needs of developing countries.

[97] See Emilie M. Hafner-Burton, "Trading Human Rights: How Preferential Trade Agreements Influence Government Repression" (2005) 59 *International Organization* 593.

[98] Ibid., pp. 613–614.

[99] See, e.g., Bartels (2008), supra note 39, p. 18; and Hafner-Burton, supra note 97; cf. Yaraslau Kryvoi, "Why European Union Trade Sanctions Do Not Work" (2008) 17 *Minnesota Journal of International Law* 209.

[100] Bartels (2008), supra note 39, pp. 1–2, 18–19. Compare Grossman and Sykes (2005), supra note 2, pp. 57–66; and James Harrison and Alessa Goller, "Trade and Human Rights: What Does 'Impact Assessment' Have to Offer?" (2008) 8 *Human Rights Law Review* 587.

REFERENCES

Aaronson, S. A., and J. M. Zimmerman, *Trade Imbalance – The Struggle to Weigh Human Rights Concerns in Trade Policymaking* (New York: Cambridge University Press, 2008).

Alston, P., "Labor Rights Provisions in U.S. Trade Law – 'Aggressive Unilateralism?'" in L. A. Compa and S. F. Diamond (eds.), *Human Rights, Labor Rights, and International Trade* (Philadelphia: University of Pennsylvania Press, 1996).

Bartels, L., "The WTO Enabling Clause and Positive Conditionality in the European Community's GSP Program" (2003) 6 *Journal of International Economic Law* 507.

______, "The Appellate Body Report in European Communities – Conditions for the Granting of Tariff Preferences to Developing Countries and Its Implications for Conditionality in GSP Programmes," in T. Cottier, J. Pauwelyn, and E. Bürgi Bonanomi (eds.), *Human Rights and International Trade* (Oxford: Oxford University Press, 2005).

______, *Human Rights Conditionality in the EU's International Agreements* (Oxford: Oxford University Press, 2005).

______, "The WTO Legality of the EU's GSP + Arrangement" (2007) 10 *Journal of International Economic Law*.

______, *The Application of Human Rights Conditionality in the EU's Bilateral Trade Agreements and Other Trade Arrangements with Third Countries, European Parliament*, EXPO-B-INTA-2008–57, PE 406.991 (November 2008).

Brownlie, I., *The Human Right to Development* (London: Commonwealth Secretariat, 1989).

Cassimatis, A. E., *Human Rights Related Trade Measures under International Law* (Leiden, the Netherlands: Martinus Nijhoff, 2007).

Charnovitz, S., "The Labour Dimension of the Emerging Free Trade Area of the Americas," in P. Alston (ed.), *Labour Rights as Human Rights* (Oxford: Oxford University Press, 2005).

Compa, L., and J. S. Vogt, "Labor Rights in the Generalized System of Preferences: A 20-Year Review" (2001) 22 *Comparative Labor Law and Policy Journal*.

Grossman, G. M., and A. O. Sykes, "A Preference for Development: The Law and Economics of GSP" (2005) 4 *World Trade Review*.

Grynberg, R., and V. Qalo, "Labour Standards in US and EU Preferential Trading Arrangements" (2006) 40(4) *Journal of World Trade*.

Hafner-Burton, E. M., "Trading Human Rights: How Preferential Trade Agreements Influence Government Repression" (2005) 59 *International Organization*.

Harrison, J., and A. Goller, "Trade and Human Rights: What Does 'Impact Assessment' Have to Offer?" (2008) 8 *Human Rights Law Review*.

Irish, M., "GSP Tariffs and Conditionality: A Comment on EC-Preferences" (2007) 41(4) *Journal of World Trade*.

Kryvoi, Y., "Why European Union Trade Sanctions Do Not Work" (2008) 17 *Minnesota Journal of International Law*.

Leary, V. A., "The WTO and the Social Clause: Post-Singapore" (1997) 8 *European Journal of International Law*.

Lee, Y. S., *Reclaiming Development in the World Trading System* (New York: Cambridge University Press, 2009).

Shahin, M., "To What Extent Should Labor and Environmental Standards Be Linked to Trade?" (2009) 2 *The Law and Development Review*.

Switzer, S., "Environmental Protection and the Generalized System of Preferences: A Legal and Appropriate Linkage?" (2008) 57 *International and Comparative Law Quarterly*.

Turksen, U., "The WTO Law and the EC's GSP + Arrangement" (2009) 43(5) *Journal of World Trade*.

12

Free Trade Agreements and Foreign Direct Investment

A Viable Answer for Economic Development?

Yong-Shik Lee

I. REGIONALISM IN INTERNATIONAL TRADE AND INVESTMENT

Although the global multilateral trading system represented by the World Trade Organization (WTO) provides a regulatory framework for international trade today, as of May 2010, 320 regional trade arrangements (RTAs) are also in force.[1] RTAs have a significant impact on international trade today because more than 90% of WTO Members, including developing-country members, have signed at least one or more RTAs. The trade of a majority of developing-country members is thus affected by the terms of RTAs as well as WTO disciplines. The trade of developing countries not participating in particular RTAs may also be affected by the terms of these RTAs because the competitive position of their exports in the markets of RTA members can be relatively weakened by the trade preference offered to the members but not to nonmember developing countries.

Most of these RTAs are free trade agreements (FTAs), eliminating both tariff and nontariff trade barriers and thereby creating a free trade area among the participating countries. FTAs include both bilateral trade arrangements (e.g., the Jordan–U.S. Free Trade Agreement and the Korea–Chile Free Trade Agreement) as well as multilateral arrangements that have created important economic entities, such as the European Union, North American Free Trade Agreement (NAFTA), Association of Southeast Asian Nations (ASEAN), and Mercado Común del Sur (South Common Market, MERCOSUR). The WTO approves the formation of an FTA if it eliminates trade barriers with respect to substantially all the trade among its members *and* does not raise trade barriers to nonmembers after formation of the

[1] WTO, http://rtais.wto.org/UI/PublicAllRTAList.aspx.

An earlier version of this chapter was published in the 39(4) *Journal of World Trade* (August 2005), 701–717, and in *Reclaiming Development in the World Trading System* (New York: Cambridge University Press, 2009), chap. 6. The author is grateful to Professor Gary Horlick for his comment on this chapter.

FTA.[2] The latter requirement is to ensure that these FTAs do not develop into exclusive trade blocs such as those seen in the 1930s[3] that contributed to deepening the worldwide depression and also provided a cause of the Second World War.[4] The rationale for the authorization of an FTA is that a free trade zone created by an FTA would eventually expand to include more countries to benefit from free trade.

In recent years, FTAs have proliferated as multilateral negotiations in the WTO framework have become more difficult; these negotiations have come to deal with increasingly sensitive areas, such as trade and investment, trade and competition policy, intellectual property rights, and epidemics.[5] As an alternative to multilateral negotiations on a global scale that could take years to come to any consensus, nations have begun to resort to trade negotiations among a more limited number of countries sharing common interests in trade and investment, closer economic and cultural ties, and geographic proximity. This trend has led to the formation of a number of FTAs around the world. The four largest free trade areas (the European Union [EU], NAFTA, MERCOSUR, and ASEAN) accounted for more than two-thirds of world trade.[6] More FTAs are being negotiated between developing and developed countries.[7] Concerns have been expressed against this proliferation of FTAs, because it may erode WTO disciplines and distract members from important multilateral negotiations. Yet regional trade liberalization by these FTAs is considered to promote development.[8] The next section of this chapter considers this issue.

Significant increases in foreign direct investment (FDI) are another phenomenon in the scene of international economy in recent decades. Rapid development of transportation and communication and the increasing availability of information across national borders have resulted in great increases in FDI around the world in the past few decades.[9] The increase of multinational businesses and the reduction of restrictions against foreign investors also have contributed to the proliferation of FDI. Nearly all countries, regardless of whether they are of developed or developing economic status, welcome FDI today because it provides employment opportunities

[2] Article XXIV of the GATT authorizes the formation of customs unions and free trade areas. WTO, *The Legal Results of the Uruguay Round of Multilateral Trade Negotiations: The Legal Texts* (Cambridge: Cambridge University Press, reprint, 2003), pp. 457–460.

[3] Major economic powers, such as Britain, France, and the United States, erected trade barriers in their home and colonial markets. As a result, exporters from countries without vast domestic or colonial markets, such as Germany and Italy, were put at a substantial disadvantage.

[4] For the economic causes of the Second World War, see Andrew J. Crozier, *The Causes of the Second World War* (Oxford: Blackwell Publishers, 1997).

[5] Mitsuo Matsushita, "Legal Aspects of Free Trade Agreements in the Context of Article XXIV of the GATT 1994," paper presented at The Way Forward to Successful Doha Development Agenda Negotiation seminar, United Nations University, Tokyo, Japan (May 24–25, 2004).

[6] Ibid.

[7] For instance, the Chile–Korea FTA and the Mexico–Japan FTA have recently been agreed to.

[8] Matsushita (2005), supra note 5.

[9] FDI outflow increased from USD 27 billion in 1982 to USD 1,858 billion in 2008. United Nations Conference on Trade and Development (UNCTAD), *World Investment Report 2009*, table 1.3, Selected Indicators of FDI and International Production, 1982–2008, p. 18.

for the local population and also brings valuable resources to benefit the economy of the host countries, including capital, technology, information, managerial expertise, and sales and marketing networks.

The resources that FDI brings to the host country have particularly important implications for developing countries, which often lack the necessary resources to facilitate development. Many countries have tried to attract FDI by offering favorable incentives to foreign investors, including tax and other financial benefits, infrastructure built for or made available to foreign investors, assistance with complying with domestic regulatory requirements, and one-stop services for the needs of foreign investors, privileged legal status, and even trade protection. To attract FDI, developing countries are also encouraged to create a favorable investment environment for foreign investors (e.g., better infrastructure, more transparent regulatory system). The subsequent section also discusses the feasibility of acquiring FDI by developing countries as well as its viability as a means for development.

Unlike trade, there is no comprehensive multilateral discipline on investment on a global scale. The previous Organization for Economic Cooperation and Development (OECD) attempt to create a multilateral agreement on investment was not successful.[10] The Agreement on Trade-Related Investment Measures (TRIMs Agreement) was created during the Uruguay Round to regulate government measures that affect trade, but its scope and the extent of its application seems rather limited to be considered a comprehensive discipline on investment,[11] although the provisions of the TRIPs have implications on the development of developing countries, as discussed later in this chapter. In the absence of a comprehensive regulatory regime on investment, a number of bilateral arrangements called "bilateral investment treaties" (BITs) regulate FDI.[12] An initiative to create a set of multilateral investment rules as part of the WTO disciplines began,[13] but the likelihood of ratification of such an agreement is not high because of serious objections among WTO Members.

[10] The Organization for Economic Cooperation and Development (OECD) launched negotiation on the Multilateral Agreement on Investment (MAI) in 1995 to be a "free standing international treaty, open to all OECD Members and the European Communities, and to accession by non-OECD Member Countries." Its proposed objective was to "provide a broad multilateral framework for international investment with high standards for the liberalization of investment regimes and investment protection and with effective dispute settlement procedures." A series of intense negotiations ceased in 1998 without reaching an agreement on the final version. The background and negotiations of the MAI are introduced in the official OECD site, http://www1.oecd.org/daf/mai/intro.htm.

[11] The TRIMs Agreement, comprising nine articles and an annex, is brief and only includes a few provisions: the agreement prohibits investment measures that are inconsistent with Articles III and XI of the GATT, which requires national treatment and the general elimination of quantitative restrictions, respectively. WTO, *The Legal Results of the Uruguay Round of Multilateral Trade Negotiations: The Legal Texts*, supra note 2, pp. 143–146. The rationale for this prohibition is that these measures distort trade by requiring investors to make certain export or import commitments.

[12] In 2008, the number of BITs was 2,608, and this number is still increasing. UNCTAD, *World Investment Report 2009*, p. 32, available at: http://www.unctad.org/en/docs/wir2009_en.pdf.

[13] WTO Ministerial Declaration, WTO doc. WT/MIN(01)/DEC/1 (November 20, 2001), paras. 20–22.

II. DEVELOPMENT AND FREE TRADE

It has been discussed that FTAs have initiated regional trade liberalization throughout the world. How does this affect economic development? The answer would become fundamentally different depending on what one believes are the necessary economic conditions to facilitate economic development. One who subscribes to neoclassical ideas[14] that free markets and economies open to foreign trade and investment best foster development would likely support FTAs as a positive instrument in facilitating development and discount state intervention with trade as economically inefficient. According to this view, trade protection, such as tariffs, would only reduce the economic welfare of the importing country[15] and therefore should be systematically reduced, as has been done during the past decades under the auspices of the GATT, and later the WTO.[16]

It is necessary to examine the theoretical basis of this belief; according to the classical trade theories, the elimination of trade barriers would allow specialization in the production of products in which a country has a relative advantage, and this specialization would eventually improve economic efficiency.[17] This rationale

[14] Neoclassical economics, referring to a grouping of economic schools generally favoring free-market approaches, emerged in the late nineteenth century in opposition to Marxism and reaffirmed that the market promotes economic efficiency and fair social distribution. It has become the dominant, mainstream economics in Anglo-American universities since the Second World War and has also influenced the positions of postwar international economic institutions, such as the International Monetary Fund (IMF) and World Bank. Neoclassical economics forms the core of a political-economic philosophy, widely referred to as "neoliberalism," which discourages positive government intervention in the economy and promotes free-market approaches, including privatization and trade liberalization. In this sense, the terms "neoclassical economic stance" and "neoliberal stance" are considered synonymous and are used interchangeably throughout this chapter without distinction. IMF conditionality during the financial crisis in Asia, which caused adverse effects on the economy of the crisis-stricken countries, reflected this stance and imposed restrictions on government trade and industrial policies. Rodrik (2004), *Industrial Policy for the Twenty-First Century* (paper prepared for United Nations Industrial Development Organization, September 2004), p. 33. See also Hider A. Khan, *Global Markets and Financial Crises in Asia* (New York: Palgrave Macmillan, 2004). With respect to trade, the pursuit of free trade, an important part of the neoliberal economic stance, has been the objective of the GATT regime and more so of the subsequent WTO.

[15] For the trade effects of tariffs and quantitative restrictions, see Dominick Salvatore, *International Economics* (8th ed., Hoboken, NJ: John Wiley and Sons, 2003), chaps. 8 and 9.

[16] There were eight multilateral trade negotiations (rounds) during the GATT era (1947–1994). The first round (the Doha Round) in the WTO regime began in November 2001. During the previous GATT rounds, tariffs were reduced by an average of 35% at each round. As a result, the average tariff rates of nonprimary products of industrial countries fell to a mere 3.9% after the Uruguay Round in 1994. John H. Jackson, *The World Trading System* (2nd ed., Cambridge, MA: MIT Press, 1997), p. 74.

[17] A prominent classical economist, David Ricardo, explained that international trade takes place because of the differences in the *relative advantages* of producing products, as defined by the relative cost of producing given products. David Ricardo, *Principles of Political Economy and Taxation* (1817). According to Ricardo's theory, all parties participating in international trade improve their economic welfare, and government intervention with international trade is not necessary; such intervention reduces the economic welfare to be gained by trade. Ricardo's theory and the subsequent Heckscher–Ohlin model that explains the *causes* of the difference in relative advantage formed the cornerstone of

presents the case of promoting free trade for economic development, and trade protection would only reduce the benefit to be gained by trade.[18] Nonetheless, a recent historical study done by Cambridge economist Ha-Joon Chang suggests that this specialization alone did not bring about economic development, and virtually all developed countries today adopted industrial promotion policies[19] to establish some manufacturing basis with the extensive use of subsidies and trade protections.[20] Another study has also concluded that developing economies tend to diversify, rather than concentrate, production patterns in a large cross-section, and this suggests that the driving force of economic development cannot be the forces of comparative advantage as advocated by many neoliberal economists.[21]

The question of conditions to facilitate the development of developing countries, particularly the role of the state in facilitating development, has been debated for centuries[22] and will likely continue into the future. Departing from the conventional neoliberal view that the role of the government should be limited to correcting evident market failures and achieve macroeconomic stabilities,[23] the pendulum has

modern trade theories. The Heckshcr–Ohlin model explains that a country has a relative advantage in a product produced by making the most use of a production factor that is relatively abundant in that country. For instance, countries richly endowed with capital export capital-intensive products, whereas those with labor export labor-intensive products. This theory was presented in Ohlin's master work, *Interregional and International Trade* (1933).

18 Supra note 15.

19 "Industrial promotion policies" or "industrial polices" in this chapter refer to a wide range of government policies targeting facilitation and promotion of a particular industry, including infant-industry promotion policies (i.e., state policies to facilitate industries at early stages of development). One of the author's previous articles discusses infant promotion policy arguments. Y. S. Lee, "Facilitating Development in the World Trading System – A Proposal for Development Facilitating Tariff and Development Facilitating Subsidy" (2004) 38 *Journal of World Trade*, Section II:A. Various policy tools, such as government subsidies and trade protections, are used to promote domestic industries.

20 Chang illustrates the trade and industrial policies of today's major developed economies adopted during their own development periods, which included state subsidization and trade protections for infant-industry promotion. H.-J. Chang, *Kicking Away the Ladder: Development Strategy in Historical Perspective* (London: Anthem Press, 2002), chap. 2, pp. 13–68.

21 Jean Imbs, and Romain Wacziarg, "Stages of Diversification" (2003) 93(1) *American Economic Review* 63–86. The conclusion of this study is also supported by the fact that the number of export products tends to increase, rather than decrease, in the process of economic development. Bailey Klinger and Daniel Lederman, "Discovery and Development: An Empirical Exploration of 'New' Products," World Bank, August 2004.

22 On one hand, economists subscribing to the classical theory founded by Adam Smith (1723–1790) and developed by his successors have favored the market-oriented economy with limited government intervention only to correct market failures and to achieve macroeconomic stabilities (e.g., stable monetary policy to check inflation), whereas others, such as Alexander Hamilton, Daniel Raymond, Friedrich List, and their followers advocated more active state roles to facilitate industries, particularly those in the early stage of development ("infant" industries) through various support and trade protections. See the author's book, *Reclaiming Development in the World Trading System* (New York: Cambridge University Press, 2009) for more discussion on this issue. Classical theory has formed the dominant position in recent decades and has influenced the stance of world economic institutions, as well as many governments. Supra note 14.

23 Ibid.

started to swing back to the other direction, and the stance that there are more active and essential roles for the government in facilitating development seems to be gaining more approval.[24] For instance, it has been observed that industrial restructuring necessary to initiate development rarely takes place without significant government assistance:[25] the unknown risk of expanding into new, nontraditional production activities may deter private sectors from engaging in such activities.[26] This government assistance may take various forms, including bailout guarantees, subsidies, and trade protections, or any combination of these measures, to reduce risks in engaging in new productive pursuits.

Trade protection would be particularly important for developing countries with limited financial resources available for state subsidization. Thus, trade protection, although discounted by many "mainstream" economists for creating economic inefficiency,[27] is closely relevant to development. Trade protection has been used by developing countries in conjunction with other industrial support to facilitate a new industry with some notable success.[28] Infant-industry promotion advocates argue[29] that this short-term inefficiency or welfare loss caused by trade protection is

[24] This movement seems to have been influenced by the success of economic development of certain East Asian countries with extensive state involvement in industrial facilitations, as well as notable failures of policy recommendations (some binding as IMF conditionality) based on the neoliberal economic stance, particularly those caused by the advice of the IMF to the countries that faced financial crisis in the late 1990s. For a discussion of the government role in economic development of the East Asian countries, see Larry E. Westphal, "Industrial Policy in an Export Propelled Economy: Lessons from South Korea's Experience" (in Symposia: The State and Economic Development) (1990) 4(3) *The Journal of Economic Perspectives* 41–59; John Brohman, "Postwar Development in the Asian NICs: Does the Neoliberal Model Fit Reality?" (1996) 72(2) *Economic Geography* 107–130. For a discussion of the IMF treatment of the Asian financial crisis, see Hider A. Khan, *Global Markets and Financial Crises in Asia* (Palgrave Macmillan, 2004). The government measures adopted by the United States and other developed countries in response to the recent financial crisis, which provided direct investments in failing banks, also affirm the changing trend in support of increased government involvement in the economy.

[25] Rodrik, supra note 14, p. 15.

[26] Ibid., pp. 7–8. Even if innovative entrepreneurs bear the risk and become successful, they may have to share their gains with latecomers who benefit from their experience but do not pay for the risk. Ibid., pp. 8–9.

[27] Supra note 15.

[28] Supra note 20. See also Y. S. Lee, supra note 19.

[29] Friedrich List (1789–1846) is widely known as the father of infant-industry promotion, although he was not the first who made this argument. Alexander Hamilton and Daniel Raymond precede List in advocating state facilitation of infant industries. List's famous work, *The National System of Political Economy* (1841), sets out his infant-industry argument, which supports the adoption of trade protections to support domestic industries in early stages of development. Infant-industry promotion policy provides initial support and protection while the new industry goes through the learning curve. The success of this policy is finally achieved when the industry becomes competitive enough to sustain itself without government subsidies, justifying initial economic inefficiencies resulting from the protection. The economic achievement by the outward-oriented policies of the East Asian countries, which emphasized both state industrial support and exports, is a good example of this success. For a discussion of infant-industry arguments, see also Lee (2004), supra note 19.

justified by a greater economic benefit to be gained by the facilitation of development, ultimately leading to a higher standard of living for a majority of the population. Infant-industry promotion arguments are not without critics,[30] but history has shown that it can facilitate development where necessary political and social arrangements are in place,[31] as shown by the successful development cases of some East Asian countries, including South Korea and Taiwan.[32] It has been cautioned that should a developing country exercise trade protection, it would have to ensure internal competition.[33] Indeed, East Asian countries encouraged intense competition among major domestic producers while their industries enjoyed certain trade protection. Article XVIII of the GATT authorizes an application of trade measures to facilitate industries in early stages of development (i.e., "infant" industries).[34]

[30] Lee (2004), supra note 19. For instance, critics argue that governments do not have better information than private sectors as to what are "promising industries" to be facilitated. On the contrary, this is not always the case in developing countries where the availability of information and assessment is limited. Harvard economist Dani Rodrik commented, "Yes, the government has imperfect information . . . so does the private sector." Rodrik (2004), supra note 14, p. 3. Critics have also pointed out other problems associated with state involvement in industrial facilitation, such as bureaucratic inefficiencies, prevalent corruption in many developing countries, and the dependency created by supported industries on state support measures, but these problems are not insurmountable as demonstrated by the successful development cases of the East Asian countries.

[31] These arrangements are the ones that induce effective cooperation and communication between the public and private sectors. A recent work by Dani Rodrik illustrates an ideal institutional arrangement between the public and private sectors to be in place to facilitate development. Rodrik (2004), supra note 14. Failures of development policies of many developing countries are attributed to the lack of this political and social arrangement.

[32] The World Bank noted in its 1993 report that the East Asian experience had been a confirmation of its market-friendly approach to policy because, among other things, their policies showed a strict adherence to market supply and demand. World Bank, *The East Asian Miracle* (New York: Oxford Press, 1993). On the contrary, it has been argued that a closer examination reveals the weaknesses and questions about some of the critical elements of analysis contained in the report and, consequently, that many of the report's conclusions and recommendations, relating to trade and industrial strategy in particular, need to be "heavily" discounted. Dani Rodrik, "King Kong Meets Godzilla: The World Bank and the East Asian Miracle," CEPR Discussion Paper no. 944 (London: Centre for Economic Policy Research, 1994). Perhaps the World Bank Report emphasized one aspect of the East Asian development that did utilize the market mechanism, but as noted, the East Asian countries also adopted extensive government subsidization and trade protection to facilitate industries, which are not exactly the prescriptions of neoclassical/neoliberal economics.

In addition, it is to be noted that the adoption of trade protection is not necessarily indicative of a "closed" economy. It has been commonplace among economists to consider that the success of the East Asian economies resulted from their "openness" as demonstrated by active export activities and that the failure of some others promoting trade protection policies, such as import substitution, in their "closeness" reflected in import barriers. However, this simple analogy is misleading and overlooks an important fact that the former economies, such as South Korea and Taiwan, also adopted extensive trade protection measures to facilitate their infant industries. Westphal (1990), supra note 24, and Brohman (1996), supra note 24.

[33] Professor Gary Horlick has commented that if a (developing) country does not open the market, it needs internal competition and that state ownership or private monopoly impedes that competition. The competition may be non-price, such as quality, as was often the case in Japan.

[34] WTO, *The Legal Results of the Uruguay Round of Multilateral Trade Negotiations: The Legal Texts*, supra note 2, p. 447–453. See also Lee (2004), supra note 19, Section II:B.

The advocating of state-led industrial promotion and trade protection does not mean that industries of developing countries must be closed to international trade for the duration of development. On the contrary, international trade has played an essential role in successful development. It should be noted that the success of the East Asian economies is a result of a link between initial trade protection for infant domestic industries and export facilitation to overcome the disadvantage of limited domestic markets and to utilize overseas markets.[35] This link did not seem to exist or was rather weak in development policies, adopted by some South Asian countries, such as India and Latin American countries, with a primary focus on import-substitution aspects.[36] These policies, in contrast to export facilitation policies, did not achieve the same success enjoyed by the East Asian economies, particularly for those countries with limited domestic markets or the lack of domestic demand. Both export facilitation and trade protection have been a result of deliberate policy choices. This chapter proceeds on a premise that the state has essential roles in the economic development of developing countries in industrial facilitation, and a developing country should be allowed to adopt effective development policies, including infant-industry promotion.

From the perspective of industrial facilitation, free trade between developing and developed countries may actually hamper the facilitation of the manufacturing industries in developing countries that are necessary for development[37] because the elimination of trade barriers by the terms of the applicable FTA will remove the ability of developing countries to offer trade protection for their infant industries. It seems no coincidence that today's developed countries, including the United States, maintained high tariff rates during their own development.[38] Although economies in similar development stages with a complementary industrial makeup might benefit from free trade, free trade between developed and developing countries can limit

[35] Y. S. Lee, supra note 22, chap. 1.

[36] For a review of import-substitution policies, see Ian Little, Tibor Scitovsky, and Maurice Scott, *Industries and Trade in Some Developing Countries* (London: Oxford University Press, 1970); A. O. Krueger, "Alternative Strategies and Employment in LDCs" (1978) 68(2) *American Economic Review* 270–274; H. Bruton, "Import Substitution," in H. B. Chenery and T. N. Srinivasan (eds.), *Handbook of Development Economics*, Vol. 2 (Amsterdam: North-Holland, 1989), pp. 1601–1644; H. Bruton, "A Reconsideration of Import Substitution" (1998) 12 *Journal of Economic Perspective* 903–936.

[37] Economic development, or simply development, is defined as the process of a structural transformation of an economy from one based primarily on the production of primary products (i.e., a product consumed in its primary unprocessed state) generating low levels of income to another based on modern industries that provide higher levels of income. The history of economic development has shown that this transition requires the formation of manufacturing-based industries. Supra note 20.

[38] Supra note 20. For instance, the United States maintained high tariff rates (more than 40% on average) by the end of the Second World War. On this point, Professor Gary Horlick has cautioned that citing the U.S. case might be misleading because the United States at that time (unlike many other developing countries today) could "live off" the U.S. market. However, other "smaller" developing countries that later became advanced industrial countries, such as South Korea, also maintained relatively high tariff rates during economic development since the 1960s to protect growing domestic industries.

the latter's development potential that could be materialized through industrial promotion, including trade protection measures.

It should be noted that in a *static* economic model that considers economic efficiency *at any given point in time*, a developing country engaged in an FTA with a developed country may still benefit from an increase in economic welfare by reducing trade barriers.[39] Nonetheless, this benefit might come at the expense of sacrificing development potential to be realized through industrial promotion. Subsidies may also be considered in place of trade measures that may lead to a distortion of trade. However, as noted earlier, many developing countries may not have sufficient resources for these subsidies; therefore, trade protection might be the only remaining option for industrial promotion, or the protection may still need to be adopted in conjunction with other support programs available to meet the objectives of industrial promotion. South Korea and Taiwan offered both trade protection and subsidies to facilitate domestic industries during their respective development.[40]

Recent regulatory trends in regional trade liberalization raise another concern for development because these trends do not appear consistent with the interest in development. With respect to FTAs, a new breed of FTA, promoted by certain developed countries such as the United States, does not only seek to eliminate tariff and nontariff barriers but also attempts to instill certain regulatory elements in developing countries. These elements include enforcement of intellectual property rights (IPRs), requirement of environment and labor standards, and authorization of uninhibited capital transfers.[41] These new requirements go beyond the facilitation of international trade by reducing trade barriers and are likely to have adverse effects on the development of developing countries because these additional requirements in the new FTAs affect wider aspects of the economic and regulatory systems of the developing country under which development policies are adopted and implemented. For instance, the stringent requirement of IPRs protection will diminish the availability of new information and will make its use costly. The enforcement of IPRs, which requires an administration of a complex IPRs regime, can also be costly and may cause a substantial diversion of scarce human and capital resources that could be used more productively elsewhere.[42] The other requirements, such as the labor and environmental standards, could equally be costly and burdensome on developing countries.

39 Supra note 15.

40 Supra note 32.

41 Alvin Hilaire and Yongzheng Yang, "The United States and the New Regionalism/Bilateralism" (2004) 38 *Journal of World Trade* 609.

42 According to a study, implementing an IPRs regime such as the one required by the WTO's TRIPS (Trade-Related Aspects of Intellectual Property Rights) obligations would cost each of the least developed countries USD 150 million, representing a full year's development budget of many such countries, to invest in buildings, equipment, training, and so forth. J. Michael Finger, "The WTO's Special Burden on Less Developed Countries" (2000) 19(3) *Cato Journal* 435.

III. OPTIMAL COMBINATION WITH FDI?

Are there any circumstances in which free trade can work for economic development without solidifying the existing industrial structure of the developing country thus sacrificing its long-term development potential?[43] An optimal combination of FDI and free trade might create such a circumstance. Free trade may promote development if there is substantial and constant inflow of FDI. If FDI can replace the role of the state in providing resources to facilitate development that the private sectors of the host countries typically lack,[44] trade barriers that cause welfare loss to the economy[45] might not be necessary.[46] In this scenario, FDI and free trade can promote economic development in conjunction with each other, provided that the

[43] As discussed earlier, this long-term development potential was realized through industrial promotion and restructuring in some of the East Asian countries, such as South Korea, which would have been difficult had their infant but growing domestic industries not been allowed to retain their share of domestic market through trade protection measures.

[44] In poor developing countries where private sectors do not have adequate information and resources, only the government may be able to mobilize needed resources as demonstrated in the development process of today's developed countries, such as South Korea. For the role of the government in economic development promoting industrial development and facilitating transfer of resources, see Edward S. Mason, "The Role of Government in Economic Development" (1960) 50(2) *The American Economic Review* 636–641; Anne O. Krueger and Baran Tuncer, "An Empirical Test of the Infant Industry Argument" (1982) 72(5) *The American Economic Review* 1142–1152 (an empirical examination revealed that protection was not warranted in the Turkish case); Larry E. Westphal, supra note 24; John Brohman, "Postwar Development in the Asian NICs: Does the Neoliberal Model Fit Reality?" (1996) 72(2) *Economic Geography* 107–130; Jacques Poot, "A Synthesis of Empirical Research of the Impact on Long-Run Growth" (2000) 31(4) *Growth & Change* 516–546; Martijn R. E. Brons, Henri L. F. DeGroot, Peter Nijkamp, "Growth Effects of Governmental Policies: A Comparative Analysis in a Multi-Country Context" (2000) 31(4) *Growth & Change* 547–572. The following references provide helpful guidance on the role of governments in facilitating infrastructure and in securing necessary capital for development. Barry Eichengreen, *Financing Infrastructure in Developing Countries: Lessons from the Railway Age* (1994; prepared as a background paper for the World Bank's World Development Report on infrastructure issues in developing countries); Ashella Tshedza Ndhlovu, *Mobilization of Capital Funds by Urban Local Authorities: Zimbabwe* (South African Development Community Information Centre on Local Governance, 2001); Dani Rodrik, *Industrial Policy for the Twenty-First Century*, paper prepared for UNIDO, September 2004, available at http://ksghome.harvard.edu/~drodrik/UNIDOSep.pdf.

[45] Supra note 15.

[46] As discussed earlier, FDI may bring essential economic resources to host developing countries that they typically lack, such as financial capital, advanced technology and production techniques, production facilities and machinery, managerial expertise, and foreign sales networks. In addition, utilizing FDI for development may have an advantage over alternative state industrial promotion policies in that FDI is driven by market forces and is therefore less susceptible to domestic political considerations that often diminish the effect of state industrial support. Bureaucratic inefficiencies and possible corruption that are landmark problems with state industrial support may not apply to FDI run by private enterprises. FDI is considered to be a positive stimulus for any economy, including that of developing countries. It is believed to have been a major engine for the rapid economic growth in China since the 1980s. See Kevin H. Zhang, "How Does FDI Affect Economic Growth in China?" (2001) 9(3) *Economics of Transition* 679–693.

FDI seeks to materialize the long-term economic potential of the host country.[47] However, these conditions can hardly be met for the majority of developing countries.

First of all, the majority of FDI has been available only to developed countries[48] and a handful of developing countries.[49] The substantial majority of developing countries have not received FDI in any significant amount to facilitate economic development.[50] As mentioned earlier, developing countries are encouraged to create favorable conditions to attract more FDI. However, it is not likely to be feasible for many of these developing countries to create such conditions that can compete and match those of developed countries or a handful of developing countries. Unlike developed countries or a small number of "advanced" developing countries, the majority of developing countries also lack essential social and physical infrastructures to attract foreign investment, such as efficient communication and transportation systems, ample supplies of utilities (e.g., electricity and water), sufficient markets, a working financial system, an educated workforce, a reliable legal system, and a secure and stable political environment. Many of these conditions come as a result of economic development that developing countries try to achieve in the first place; thus, it is not be likely that most developing countries can attain the conditions that are necessary to attract FDI in any significant amount even if they embark on costly reforms. Thus, FDI is not an option for most developing countries, other than the few, whose economic endowments do not allow themselves to provide attractive incentives and conditions for investment.

Second, FDI may not always serve long-term economic interests of the host developing countries: FDI does not necessarily bring in "patient capital" that can wait for long-term economic potential to materialize.[51] The stability and consistency of

[47] Supra note 51.

[48] In 2008, developed countries received FDI amounting to USD 962.3 billion out of the total FDI of USD 1967.4 billion worldwide. UNCTAD, *World Investment Report 2009*, annex table B.1, FDI inflows, by region and economy, 2006–2008, p. 247.

[49] In 2008, more than 50% of all FDI provided to developing countries was directed to China (USD 108.3 billion), Hong Kong (USD 63 billion), India (USD 41.6 billion), Singapore (USD 22.7 billion), Brazil (USD 45.1 billion), Mexico (USD 22 billion), and Nigeria (USD 20.3 billion). UNCTAD, supra note 48. Note that some of the countries widely considered to be developed economies, such as South Korea, Hong Kong, and Singapore, are classified as developing countries in these statistics, and therefore considerable amounts of FDI that these countries received have also been included in total amount of FDI directed to developing countries.

[50] For instance, the amount of FDI that all African countries received in 2008 was USD 87.6 billion in total, comprising 5.1% of FDI inflows worldwide, which was a substantial increase from 2.7% in 2003. However, more than 60% of the FDI in Africa was concentrated in only four African countries: Nigeria, Angola, South Africa, and Egypt. UNCTAD, supra note 48.

[51] FDI may set a target time frame for the investment return (i.e., may prefer short-term returns) that may not be consistent with the host country's long-term development interests. Multinational companies may not necessarily contribute to FDI in a way that maximizes the economic potential of the host country but that serves the best interest of their worldwide operations.

FDI inflows are also questionable. Although FDI is considered to be more of a long-term investment than a short-term financial investment, such as stock purchases, divestment is nonetheless always possible. A major divestment may leave considerable difficulties to the economy of the host developing country, which depends on foreign investment, and thus disrupt its development plans. In addition to divestment, foreign investors can also easily take the money out of the developing country by borrowing from local banks, using their fixed assets (e.g., factories, machinery) as collateral and change the money into foreign currency in an open capital market. A recent study has revealed that FDI is also affected by the economic cycle of the investors' home countries, which brings elements of instability and increases the vulnerability of the developing countries depending on FDI for economic development.[52]

In addition, political considerations, as well as economic rationale, can affect FDI. FDI may be less susceptible to domestic political considerations in the sense that it is less affected by domestic constituencies of the host country. Yet other political elements may affect FDI. For instance, an emergence of hostile public sentiment in the host country against the investor's country may raise concern for foreign investors and affect their investment decisions, although these sorts of problems would not necessarily affect domestic investors. Changes in the foreign policies of the investors' own governments may also affect investment decisions. Even if foreign investors try to maintain political neutrality in making investment decisions, a serious dispute between the host country and the investor's, such as one that leads to economic embargo, may disrupt investment and make partial or total divestment inevitable. This susceptibility to political elements diminishes the reliability of FDI as an engine for development.

The preceding discussion reveals that the "optimal combination" of FTA and FDI would be hard to achieve in practice, although this suggested combination may have existed in China to some extent. China has been receiving the highest amount of FDI among developing countries, and trade barriers to Chinese exports have been lowered after the entry of China into the WTO.[53] It has been suggested that FDI contributed to China's rapid development,[54] and more liberalized China's trade, since its accession to the WTO, is also considered to have contributed to its economic development.[55] On the other hand, the Chinese government has been actively engaged in industrial facilitation, providing various subsidies to its industries and making huge investments in building infrastructure for industries. At any rate,

[52] Eduardo Levy-Yeyati, Ugo Panizza, and Ernesto Stein, "The Cyclical Nature of North–South FDI Flows," paper presented at the Joint Conference of the Inter-America Development Band and World Bank, *The FDI Race, Who Gets the Prize? Is It Worth the Effort?* (October 2002).

[53] Supra note 49.

[54] Zhang (2001), supra note 46.

[55] Parikshit Basu and Yapa Bandara, *WTO Accession and Socio-Economic Development in China* (Cambridge: Woodhead Publishing, 2009).

as China's ability to attract massive and constant FDI is largely based on its unique market potential and the ability of supply labor thanks to its 1.3 billion population, the case of China seems to have a limited application to the majority of other developing countries.

IV. CONCLUSION

The preceding discussion allows us to conclude whether FDI and regional trade liberalization by FTAs will provide an answer for economic development and effectively replace the need for state industrial support and trade protection. FDI is concentrated on a small number of developing countries,[56] and free trade by itself is not sufficient to promote development, suggesting that neither FDI nor free trade can replace the role of the government in facilitating development. The recent historical study has also revealed that most of today's developed countries have engaged in extensive infant-industry promotion through government subsidization and trade protection.[57] An ideal combination of free trade and FDI can be contemplated as an alternative to state industrial support, but the limited availability of FDI and the lack of its reliability as an engine for development seem to render such a combination remote in practice, at least for the majority of developing countries.

In addition, there is a particular concern when FTAs are used as a means to get around the terms of the multilateral trade agreement of the WTO and impose various regulatory requirements on developing countries that are not directly relevant to the facilitation of trade, such as IPRs enforcement and labor and environmental standards. Of course, a developing country is not required to join FTAs, but it may not be able to afford to stay outside if strong initiatives for FTAs are made bilaterally or regionally by powerful economies where the developing country has an essential economic interest.

Developed countries should refrain from using FTAs as a device to circumvent the rights of developing countries to facilitate development[58] that have been

[56] Supra note 49.

[57] Supra note 20. Professor Junji Nakagawa of Tokyo University has argued that this is a simplistic generalization because the United States after the Civil War, Germany under Bismarck, and Japan after the Second World War cannot be "put in a same basket: international environments were different; market structures were different; governments, and their policy instruments were different; and economic theories were different." In the author's opinion, a discussion of these differences is largely irrelevant to the point of the argument unless it is identified *specifically how* these differences actually preclude the argument of infant-industry promotion. As an analogy, economists accept the essence of the market theory advocated by Adam Smith more than 200 years ago and consider it to still be applicable, although with some variances, to today's economies, which are obviously different from those of Adam Smith's time and from one another.

[58] The authorization of industrial facilitation under GATT Article XVIII through trade measures is an example of these rights.

protected under the multilateral trading system.[59] To prevent this circumvention, consideration should be given to specifying in the relevant WTO provisions that members are prohibited from engaging in any arrangement bilaterally or otherwise that would undermine the rights of developing countries protected under the WTO provisions. The current WTO provision stipulates a similar requirement in which it prohibits members from entering into *any* arrangement that allows *gray-area measures* through which trading countries agree to restrain trade for the benefit of the domestic producers of the importing country.[60]

The effects of an FTA on development would vary, depending on the specific terms of the FTA and certain economic factors, such as the difference in development stages and the industrial makeup of the participating countries. From the development perspective, FTAs may deprive the participating developing country of the ability to protect infant industries that cannot initially compete with the imports from developed countries. On the other hand, FTAs among economies in similar development stages with a complementary industrial makeup may improve the economic welfare and efficiency for the participating countries without undermining their development potential.[61] Some of the notable free trade areas, such as MERCOSUR and ASEAN, comprise the participation of countries in similar development status.

Caution should be taken against the recent proliferation of FTAs around the world. The potential adverse effect on development for developing countries that join FTAs, particularly those with developed countries, has already been noted. In addition, it should also be reiterated that the trade of nonparticipating developing countries can be adversely affected by the proliferation of FTAs because they offer trade preference to their member countries, which may not be available to nonmember countries. Although all nonmember countries may be equally subject to the same disadvantage vis-à-vis the member countries,[62] the adverse trade impact can be harshest on nonmember developing countries where export industries may not be strong enough to compete with those of the member countries, which benefit from the FTAs, or those of nonmember developed countries.

Therefore, the proliferation of FTAs is likely to create a more difficult trade environment for developing countries: they will be under pressure to join FTAs

[59] Of course, this suggested protection may not be applicable to nonmember countries of the WTO. However, WTO membership now includes the vast majority of both developed and developing countries. As of May 2010, membership in the WTO comprised 153 nations. Developing countries constitute two-thirds of WTO membership.

[60] Article 11.1 of the WTO Agreement on Safeguards stipulates such prohibition. WTO, *The Legal Results of the Uruguay Round of Multilateral Trade Negotiations: The Legal Texts*, supra note 2, p. 321.

[61] Friedrich List, who advocated infant-industry promotion, believed that free trade is beneficial among countries at similar levels of industrial development. Friedrich List, supra note 29.

[62] The MFN treatment under GATT Article I is still applied in trade relations with countries outside the FTA. WTO, *The Legal Results of the Uruguay Round of Multilateral Trade Negotiations: The Legal Texts*, supra note 2, pp. 424–425.

so that they are not excluded from these preferential trade clubs, or they would suffer more harshly from the disadvantage of not being a part of one. On the other hand, joining an FTA may subject the developing country to terms that are adverse to their development interests. This can present a double dilemma for developing countries. The late Professor Robert Hudec, an eminent trade scholar, was critical of trade preference regimes because developing countries facing these regimes would be vulnerable. Hudec believed that an MFN-based regime is the only genuine protection available to developing countries as "a legal substitute for economic power on behalf of smaller countries."[63]

In recent years, developing countries have been facing an ever-increasing number of RTAs. How can the dilemma be resolved? One possibility is a gradual elimination of trade barriers within regional trade areas at more or less the same rate and on the same timetable as the lowering of barriers towards nonmembers. Renato Ruggiero, the former director-general of the WTO, has observed this possibility in certain regional trade areas such as the Asia-Pacific Economic Cooperation.[64] Yet others may not necessarily follow this approach.[65] Nonetheless, in the former scenario, the danger of creating trade blocs and the threat to the trade of nonmember developing countries would be minimized.

Another possibility has been suggested by a Yale economist T. N. Srinivasan, who stated in a 1999 WTO high-level symposium on trade and development that a "sunset clause" should be introduced to the issue of regional agreements in which preferences available to the members of the regional agreement would be extended to all WTO Members in five years.[66] The members of the existing FTAs may not be willing to give up trade preferences exclusively shared among the members, making such preferences available to all members of the WTO. Nonetheless, this proposed sunset clause would be ideal to meet the interests of developing countries because it would allow nonmember developing countries to receive trade preferences provided by the FTA, the terms of which may not be consistent with their development interest, without having to join it.

REFERENCES

Basu, Parikshit, and Yapa Bandara, *WTO Accession and Socio-Economic Development in China* (Cambridge: Woodhead Publishing, 2009).

Brohman, John, "Postwar Development in the Asian NICs: Does the Neoliberal Model Fit Reality?" (1996) 72(2) *Economic Geography*.

63 Robert Hudec, *Developing Countries in the GATT Legal System*, Thames Essays (London: Trade Policy Research Centre, 1987), pp. 216–217.

64 WTO News Release (April 26, 1996).

65 Ibid.

66 World Trade Organization, *The Report of the WTO High-level Symposium on Trade and Development* (1999), available at: http://www.wto.org.

Brons, Martijn R. E., Henri L. F. DeGroot, and Peter Nijkamp, "Growth Effects of Governmental Policies: A Comparative Analysis in a Multi-Country Context" (2000) 31(4) *Growth & Change*.

Bruton, H., "Import Substitution," in H. B. Chenery and T. N. Srinivasan (eds.), *Handbook of Development Economics*, Vol. 2 (Amsterdam: North-Holland, 1989).

______, "A Reconsideration of Import Substitution" (1998) 12 *Journal of Economic Perspective*.

Chang, H.-J., *Kicking Away the Ladder: Development Strategy in Historical Perspective* (London: Anthem Press, 2002).

Chang, Ha-Joon, and Duncan Green, *The Northern WTO Agenda on Investment: Do as We Say, Not as We Did*, South Centre/CAFOD, June 2003.

Crozier, Andrew J., *The Causes of the Second World War* (Oxford: Blackwell Publishers, 1997).

Dolzer, Rudolf, and Margrete Stevens, *Bilateral Investment Treaties* (The Hague: Martinus Nijhoff Publishers, 1995).

Eichengreen, Barry, *Financing Infrastructure in Developing Countries: Lessons from the Railway Age* (1994). The World Bank: Policy Research Working Paper Series.

Finger, J. Michael, "The WTO's Special Burden on Less Developed Countries" (2000) 19(3) *Cato Journal*.

Hilaire, Alvin, and Yongzheng Yang, "The United States and the New Regionalism/Bilateralism" (2004) 38 *Journal of World Trade*.

Hudec, Robert, *Developing Countries in the GATT Legal System*, Thames Essays (London: Trade Policy Research Centre, 1987).

Imbs, Jean, and Romain Wacziarg, "Stages of Diversification" (2003) 93(1) *American Economic Review*.

Jackson, John H., *The World Trading System* (2nd ed., Cambridge, MA: MIT Press, 1997).

Khan, Hider A., *Global Markets and Financial Crises in Asia* (New York: Palgrave Macmillan, 2004).

Krueger, A. O., "Alternative Strategies and Employment in LDCs" (1978) 68(2) *American Economic Review*.

______, "Alternative Strategies and Employment in LDCs" (1978) 68(2) *American Economic Review*.

Krueger, A. O., and Baran Tuncer, "An Empirical Test of the Infant Industry Argument" (1982) 72(5) *The American Economic Review*.

Lee, Y. S., "Facilitating Development in the World Trading System – A Proposal for Development Facilitating Tariff and Development Facilitating Subsidy" (2004) 38 *Journal of World Trade*.

Levy-Yeyati, Eduardo, Ugo Panizza, and Ernesto Stein, "The Cyclical Nature of North–South FDI Flows," paper presented at the Joint Conference of the Inter-America Development Band and World Bank, *The FDI Race, Who Gets the Prize? Is It Worth the Effort?* (October 2002).

List, Friedrich, *The National System of Political Economy* (1841).

Little, Ian, Tibor Scitovsky, and Maurice Scott, *Industries and Trade in Some Developing Countries* (London: Oxford University Press, 1970).

Mason, Edward S., "The Role of Government in Economic Development" (1960) 50(2) *The American Economic Review*.

Matsushita, Mitsuo, "Legal Aspects of Free Trade Agreements in the Context of Article XXIV of the GATT 1994," paper presented at the seminar, *The Way Forward to Successful Doha Development Agenda Negotiation*, United Nations University, Tokyo, Japan (May 24–25, 2004).

Ndhlovu, Ashella T., *Mobilization of Capital Funds by Urban Local Authorities: Zimbabwe* (South African Development Community Information Centre on Local Governance, 2001).

Ohlin, Bertil, *Interregional and International Trade* (1933).

Poot, Jacques, "A Synthesis of Empirical Research of the Impact on Long-Run Growth" (2000) 31(4) *Growth & Change*.

Ricardo, David, *Principles of Political Economy and Taxation* (1817).

Rodrik, Dani, *Industrial Policy for the Twenty-First Century*, paper prepared for UNIDO, September 2004, available at http://www.ksghome.harvard.edu/~drodrik/UNIDOSep.pdf.

______, "King Kong Meets Godzilla: The World Bank and the East Asian Miracle," CEPR Discussion Paper no. 944 (London: Centre for Economic Policy Research, 1994).

Salvatore, Dominick, *International Economics* (8th ed., Hoboken, NJ: John Wiley and Sons, 2003).

United Nations Conference on Trade and Development, *World Investment Report 2004*, table 1.3 Selected Indicators of FDI and International Production, 1982–2003.

______, *World Investment Report* 2004, annex table B.1, FDI inflows, by region and economy, 1992–2003.

______, *World Investment Report* 2009.

Westphal, Larry E., "Industrial Policy in an Export Propelled Economy: Lessons from South Korea's Experience" (in Symposia: The State and Economic Development) (1990) 4(3) *The Journal of Economic Perspectives*.

World Bank, *The East Asian Miracle* (New York: Oxford Press, 1993).

World Trade Organization, News Release, April 26, 1996.

______, *The Report of the WTO High-level Symposium on Trade and Development* (1999), available at: http://www.wto.org.

______, WTO doc. WT/GC/W/354 (October 11, 1999).

______, Ministerial Declaration, WTO doc. WT/MIN(01)/DEC/1 (November 20, 2001).

______, *The Legal Results of the Uruguay Round of Multilateral Trade Negotiations: The Legal Texts* (Cambridge: Cambridge University Press, reprint, 2003).

Zhang, Kevin H., "How Does FDI Affect Economic Growth in China?" (2001) 9(3) *Economics of Transition*.

PART IV

Law and Development in Regional Initiatives

13

Islands of Prosperity and Poverty

A Rational Trade Development Policy for Economically Heterogeneous States

Colin B. Picker

I. INTRODUCTION

International law has typically operated at the state-to-state level, as opposed to a substate level. As such, it is states as a whole that are typically the subjects of international law. In contrast, individuals, corporations, and even substate political entities such as municipalities and provinces/states are typically not subjects of international law.[1] Of course, in some fields within international law, such as human rights and international investment law, these substate entities are beginning to have greater rights and obligations as they begin to play a more active participatory role in international law.[2] In international trade and development law, however, the rules and policies still largely operate at the traditional international law level – at the country or state level.[3]

Such an approach fails to take into account adequately the reality of development within countries, a reality that reflects that countries are not homogenous – that development heterogeneity is reflected in the fact that often, within developing countries, there are islands of prosperity and islands of stagnation. Treating a country as one unit and assuming one level of development for the whole country can cause significant distortions to development policy when in fact within many states,

[1] See, e.g., Convention on Rights and Duties of States, art. 2, December 26, 1933, 165 L.N.T.S. 19 (The "Montevideo Convention") ("The federal state shall constitute a sole person in the eyes of international law"). See, generally, Philip C. Jessup, "The Subjects of a Modern Law of Nations" (1947) 45 *Michigan Law Review* 383.

[2] See, e.g., Yishai Blank, "Localism in the New Global Legal Order" (2006) 47 *Harvard International Law Journal* 267. See also, North American Free Trade Agreement (NAFTA), chap. 11; the Universal Declaration of Human Rights.

[3] E.g., the members of the World Trade Organization (WTO) may be "[t]he contracting parties to GATT 1947 . . . and the European Communities" and "[a]ny State or separate customs territory possessing full autonomy in the conduct of its external commercial relations." See Agreement Establishing the World Trade Organization, arts. XI and XII(1).

Special thanks to my research assistant, Yihong "Andrew" Huang.

we see differential or asymmetric interstate development. The problems associated with a failure to take into account substate economic heterogeneity are manifold and include, among other things, the inefficient allocation of scarce development support, exacerbation of problems related to the scope of development policy, and contribution to harmful urbanization. Successful development policies are elusive enough without adding these additional obstacles.

This chapter explores the conflict between the usual unitary development policy and the reality of disparities of economic development across the different regions within states. To highlight the issue, this chapter explores the case of China. China may be one of the most visible examples of the problems inherent in a unitary development approach. The chapter also suggests some alternative development policy approaches that move away from a unitary approach and therefore would take into account the different levels of development within a state.

II. THE PROBLEMS OF A UNITARY DEVELOPMENT POLICY

The vast majority of states in the world are developing. Strikingly, despite being labeled a rich man's club, within the World Trade Organization (WTO), the majority of members are also developing countries. However, developing countries reflect a veritable rainbow of styles and characters. Those countries can be found in Asia, Latin America, Africa, Europe, and the Pacific. Some are small, sometimes very small, and others are among the largest and most populous countries in the world. Their cultures and political systems span the full range encountered in the world. For example, a country like Kenya is clearly different from North Korea in too many respects to list, yet the World Bank classifies both as low-income countries. Similarly, Bhutan and Samoa are not at all alike, and yet they too fall under the same classification employed in the World Bank's development policy.[4] However, we could, if we chose, easily divide these developing countries, even using only economic criteria and not the many other relevant indicia of development. Such divisions could produce criteria such as "'dependent,' 'advanced developing,' 'dynamic emerging economies,' 'transition economies,' 'newly industrialized countries,' 'post colonial states,' and so on."[5] With such diversity visible among the many developing countries of the world, it simply cannot be that they are sufficiently so alike that the rule is to apply to them a "one-size" fits all development policy approach, even if the only criteria were economic.

The same range of diversity also often exists within countries. Countries, especially larger ones, include different geographies, peoples, economies, religions, cultures, histories, and so on. Yet development policy for the most part applies to states

[4] See World Bank Web site, Data & Statistics: Country Groups.

[5] Colin B. Picker, "Neither Here Nor There – Countries That Fall between the Developed and the Developing World in the WTO" (2004) 36 *George Washington International Law Review* 151.

as whole. Of course, there are many development policy issues that need to be applicable to all developing countries, irrespective of their internal characters, for they relate to factors independent of a state's specific internal characteristics. An example of an issue applicable to all developing countries irrespective of their size or culture or demographics might be the issue of balance of payments problems that developing countries encounter all too often.[6] This is clearly national in character and not suited to a substate differentiation.

There are, however, many development policy issues that are affected by a unitary development policy approach. Indeed, if the issue of differential or asymmetric interstate development is ignored, as it largely is in today's development policy, it may too often undermine those same development policies, making them inefficient or even causing them to miss their goals entirely. Furthermore, these problems likely exacerbate some of the common socioeconomic development-related problems developing countries are experiencing.

A. *Inefficiency*

As I noted in a previous discussion of this issue, the simple and traditional problem of inefficiency rises to the fore when one considers a unitary development policy:

> If a country, as a whole, can qualify as developing, yet includes parts that are developed, these parts will receive benefits they do not deserve under the development policy. This is over-inclusion. Similarly, there may be countries that do not qualify or are otherwise not considered developing for WTO purposes, yet in those countries there may be regions that are not receiving the needed developing country benefits. This is under-inclusion. This problem applies to developing countries, transition countries, former developing counties as well as, most heretically, regions in the so-called developed world.[7]

In other words, this is an inefficient application of development policy. Given how difficult it is to muster support for development policies within developed countries, any misallocation of development support can be costly – in political as well as financial terms. A clear and tangible example may be the domestic economic and political cost of providing preferential access under Generalized System of Preferences (GSP)-type development programs to a country that nonetheless has visible "islands of prosperity."[8]

[6] See, e.g., GATT, art. XVIII.

[7] See Picker (2005), supra note 5, p. 153.

[8] "For example, allowing duty-free access for developing country goods is less efficient, in that the more efficient producers in developed countries lose access to that market. In addition, duty-free access results in competition for domestic suppliers of those goods, with resultant lost sales and profits" (Picker (2005), supra note 5, p. 155).

B. *Urbanization*

Aside from the inefficiencies produced by a unitary development policy, there may in fact be developing-country problems that are exacerbated by that same unitary development policy. The most notable problem may be its contribution to the often harmful urbanization that is taking place in many developing countries.[9] A state-centered development policy may result in development of those parts of a state already set up for development – usually the urban parts of a country. Although urbanization may make short-term economic sense, the long- and often short-term consequences for both those urban areas and the rural areas left behind can be devastating. Those rural areas thus end up with less development policy support, further exacerbating their relative lack of economic development.

> [W]hen the percentage of the rural population living under the rural poverty line [in developing countries] is compared with the percentage of the urban population living under the urban poverty line (a higher figure in most countries), it can be clearly seen that in almost all countries the rural population has a higher percentage under its relatively lower poverty line than is present for the urban population. Out of forty-five countries with data, only seven had urban poverty levels that were higher than the rural poverty rates.[10]

However, although the harm to those left behind in the countryside is significant, there is no question that the harm to the cities in developing countries is just as tangible. That harm includes increased congestion, poverty, pollution and other environmental harms, crime, and the gradual creation of permanent slum populations.[11] The cost of these problems, in both the rural and urban environments, is not something that developing countries should bear in addition to all the other challenges and obstacles that they face on the path to development.

C. *Lack of Predictability – Which States Are the Developing Countries?*

One of the goals of regulation is, of course, to provide predictability and certainty in economic interactions. However, a recurrent issue that arises in development policy is the disagreement over which countries should legitimately be considered

[9] For data on urbanization, see the World Bank, Data & Statistics – table 3.10 Urbanization, available at: http://siteresources.worldbank.org/DATASTATISTICS/Resources/table3_10.pdf. "For the first time in human history, more than half of the world's population lives in urban areas. Demographic projections suggest this figure could rise to well over 60% over the next two decades, and the developing world is the locus in which this demographic transformation will have its greatest impact." See World Bank Web site: World Bank Urban Strategy.

[10] See Picker (2005), supra note 5, p. 150.

[11] It is estimated that approximately one-third of urban populations in developing countries (approximately 1 billion people) live in slums. See World Bank Report, *Systems of Cities: Harnessing Urbanization for Growth and Poverty Alleviation*, p. 11, available at: http://siteresources.worldbank.org/INTURBANDEVELOPMENT/Resources/336387-1256765033399/strategy_exec_summary.pdf.

to be developing countries. Clearly, the inability to determine this can introduce a significant level of uncertainty into economic transactions involving such countries. The WTO, however, fails to resolve the issue:

> There are no WTO definitions of "developed" and "developing" countries. Members announce for themselves whether they are "developed" or "developing" countries. However, other members can challenge the decision of a member to make use of provisions available to developing countries.[12]

Under such circumstances, controversy and confusion are inevitable. Over the years, there has been no shortage of calls for rationalization of this issue.[13] However, the very heterogeneity of the hundred-plus countries at issue lies at the heart of the problem in finding common ground for an agreed definition of what is a developing country for purposes of development policy.[14] However, that accepted heterogeneity with its position as one of the intrinsic obstacles to an agreed definition is itself too much of a simplification. For those states are not internally homogenous – hence, the proposal at issue in this chapter.

Within the trade policy context, the discussion that follows on China's developing-country status is perhaps one of the most prominent examples of the problems arising out of the failure of the WTO to resolve this issue adequately – but at the inter- and intrastate level. The tensions between states that arise as a result of such disagreements can be serious and destructive. The present unitary development policy that simply employs a state's aggregate indicators and characteristics to determine whether it qualifies as a developing country is bound to lead to disagreements when the country at issue is both qualitatively different from other developing countries and when it includes within it islands or regions of prosperity or economic stagnation. China is such a county.

However, by moving away from a state-centered development policy and to one more focused on the on-the-ground realities within countries, much of the debate concerning the identification of which countries may be developing and which cannot could be eliminated. No longer will countries be compared with each other in the aggregate, for development policy would be aimed at smaller units within each of those countries. Admittedly, the proposal may perhaps replace that heated and complicated discussion with one that includes all the questions and issues, discussed subsequently, that may arise as a result of a more intrusive analysis of a state's internal development. That more invasive analysis would, however, result in a more nuanced consideration of developing-country status, for it would look at both aggregate state data as well as internal data by region. Surely such an analysis

[12] World Trade Organization, *Who Are the Developing Countries in the WTO?* available at: http://www.wto.org/english/tratop_e/devel_e/d1who_e.htm.

[13] See Fan Cui, "Who Are the Developing Countries in the WTO?" (2008) 1 *Law and Development Review* 122.

[14] Ibid., p. 131.

would lead to a more accurate identification of when and, most crucially, *where* development policy should be applied. As such, it should be less contentious.

III. CHINA AS A DEVELOPING COUNTRY AND THE UNITARY DEVELOPMENT POLICY

The issues discussed in this chapter may be illuminated through consideration of one individual country's intersection with trade and development policy. This examination focuses on China. Previously, this issue of trade and asymmetric interstate development was illuminated through consideration of Russia in the context of its developing-country issues and its accession to the WTO, but the China issues considered here are now much more apt and broadly applicable.[15]

The problem of a unitary development policy is particularly acute for countries that are undergoing rapid industrialization and growth, for that growth typically occurs asymmetrically, as is the case with China's recent development. Indeed, China's impressive growth since the 1980s has led to tremendous disparities. When China emerged from the many ruinous economic and political experiments of its early communist period, experiments that included the devastating "Great Leap Forward" and the Cultural Revolution, it began its modern period of economic development with a significantly impoverished base, with the vast majority of the population living in the countryside. Even then, however, the cities were significantly more productive than the countryside.[16] That economic difference between the countryside and the cities widened during the past few decades, eventually resulting in a "gap in per capita income between rural and urban areas . . . [of] a ratio of three to one."[17] Furthermore, the level of urbanization has more than doubled in the same period.[18] Additionally, wide differences between the various provinces are also now apparent. Thus, "[f]rom 1990 to 2003, the ratio of per capita GDP of the richest to poorest province grew from 7.3 to 13 [whereas in] China, the richest province has more than 8 times the per capita public spending than the poorest province."[19]

[15] See Picker (2005), supra note 5, p. 169 (using the example of Russia's WTO accession and its asymmetric development to highlight the issue raised by a regional approach to developing-country benefits within the WTO; that in Russia there are "islands of prosperity" that might not merit the benefits of developing-country status within the WTO, whereas much of the rest clearly qualifies for those developing-country benefits, perhaps providing one approach for Russia in its accession negotiations).

[16] David Dollar, *Poverty, Inequality and Social Disparities during China's Economic Reform*, World Bank Policy Research Working Paper 4253 (2007), p. 9.

[17] "[T]hree to one is a very high gap by international standards." Dollar (2007), supra note 16, p. 10 (citing T. Sicular, X. Yue, B. Gustafsson, and S. Li, "The Urban-Rural Income Gap and Inequality in China" (2007) 53 *Review of Income and Wealth* 93–126).

[18] Dollar (2007), supra note 16, p. 11.

[19] "In the US, the poorest state has about 65 percent of the revenues of the average state, and in Germany, any state falling below 95 percent of the average level gets subsidized through the 'Finanzausgleich' (and any receiving more than 110 percent gets taxed). In Brazil, the richest state has 2.3 times the revenues per capita of the poorest state. Inequalities in spending are even larger at the sub-provincial

Needless to say, there are real consequences for the people in the poorer provinces. For example, "[b]y 2003, high-school enrollment was nearing 100% in the wealthier provinces while still less than 40% in poor provinces."[20]

The disparities within China, from the modern developed cities on the east coast to the primitive conditions in much of the countryside, have led to considerable but good faith differences of opinion about whether China should be treated as a developing or developed country for purposes of international trade law. Indeed, its developing status was one of its key issues during its accession negotiations to both the General Agreement on Tariffs and Trade (GATT) and the WTO. China consistently argued that it was a developing country and should be treated as such within the WTO.[21] China made this argument despite consistent objections from the European Union and the United States throughout the long accession process.[22]

The final, inconclusive negotiated result of the divergent views on China's status as a developing country within the WTO was "'that for certain purposes, China is a developed country and for certain purposes it is a developing country.'"[23] Perhaps the best work on the status of China as a developing country within the WTO is by Marcia Harpaz.[24] The gist of her analysis is that China is neither a developing nor a developed country as far as its accession commitments and, more crucially today, as far as its participation as a member within the WTO and its perpetual ongoing negotiations are concerned. Thus, the status of China as developing country has been applied differently to different sectors of its economy and to different trade topics.[25] However, these "pragmatic"[26] solutions and analyses are with respect to the whole of China and not to its individual parts, in contrast to the unitary approach to regional

level. The richest county, the level that is most important for service delivery, has about 48 times the level of per capita spending of the poorest county." Dollar (2007) supra note 16, p. 14 (internal citations omitted).

20 Dollar (2007), supra note 16, p. 15.

21 Marcia D. Harpaz, *China and the WTO: New Kid in The Developing Bloc?* Hebrew University International Law Research Paper No. 2-07 (February 1, 2007), p. 5, available at: http://ssrn.com/abstract=961768.

22 Ibid., pp. 10–11.

23 Ibid., p. 13, relying on "U.S. Insists Position Remains Unchanged on China Entry into WTO," *Inside U.S. Trade* (March 17, 1995).

24 Ibid.

25 Ibid., p. 17. In general, Harpaz goes through the various sectors, discussing which were subject to developing- or developed-country rules. For example, for industrial subsidies, agriculture, intellectual property, and the Trade-Related Investment Measures, China generally agreed to the regime applicable to developed countries. In contrast, China managed to retain developing-country benefits in the areas of balance of payments. Ibid., pp. 15–40.

26 "[I]n the final Report of the Working Party: 'Some members of the Working Party indicated that because of the significant size, rapid growth and transitional nature of the Chinese economy, a pragmatic approach should be taken in determining China's need for recourse to transitional periods and other special provisions in the WTO Agreement available to developing country WTO members'" Harpaz, supra note 21, p. 13, quoting Report of the Working Party on the Accession of China, *Report of the Working Party*, WT/ACC/CHN/49 (October 1, 2001), para. 9.

economic difference within China.[27] Nonetheless, as the economic data discussed earlier show, the reality of China's development is that there are clearly parts of China that are like developed countries and clearly parts that are like developing countries. Perhaps it might have been most efficient, from a development policy perspective, to have also accorded developing status to select regions within China.

For example, the common developing-country problem of destructive urbanization, discussed earlier, might be assisted through a development policy that takes into account asymmetric development such as we have seen in China. That urbanization does not only contribute to the impoverishment of the countryside but also leads to cities that are having a difficult time handling their rapid growth. As an initial matter, the Chinese urban centers are now increasingly facing severe environmental problems associated with their rapid and concentrated growth. For example, a recent compilation of air pollution in cities found that among the thirty most polluted, twenty-one were in China.[28] Additional critical problems related to China's urbanization include, among other issues, shortages of urban water,[29] shortages of land,[30] shortages of energy,[31] environmental pollution (air contamination, solid waste disposal, and soil pollution),[32] and insufficient urban infrastructure.[33] China, of course, is not blind to this issue. China has employed different strategies to counter the negative consequences of rapid urbanization. For example, the *Hokuo* system is, among other things, one method to counter the urbanization.[34] However, the problem is

[27] "On the eve of accession in July 2001, China's chief negotiator, Long Yongtu, summed up the Chinese position regarding its status as a developing country to the Working Party, stating that the Chinese '... still firmly believe that China is a developing country ... It has been one of the basic principles we stick to in the negotiations of the past 15 years. However, we have taken a pragmatic attitude towards the various treatments for the developing countries as embodied in the WTO agreements and practices ... In some important areas, we insist on undertaking obligations in consistency with our own development level ... In some areas, however, where China has already had the capability to implement obligations as all WTO Members, we deem not necessary for China to enjoy preferential treatments to the developing countries.'" Harpaz, supra note 21, p. 14.

[28] Economist Books Staff, *Pocket World in Figures 2010 Edition* (London: Profile Books, 2009), p. 105. In contrast, among the top thirty best "quality of living" cities, there was not a single Chinese city. Ibid., p. 24.

[29] "General Report on Sustainable Urbanization Strategy for China," Issues Paper Prepared for the 2005 CCICED Annual General Meeting, at 3.1.3, available at: http://lib-contentdm2.lib.sfu.ca/cgi-bin/showfile.exe?CISOROOT=/cciced&CISOPTR=1283&filename=1284.pdf#search=%22urbanization%22, p. 17. (Among the 661 cities, about 420 or more are short of water, with 114 of them in severe shortage.)

[30] With such associated problems as reduction in needed agricultural land, "insufficient land for public service facilities, infrastructure and ecological environment, whereas industrial land use in cities is proportionally too high," the "squeezing out [of] urban afforested land and transportation space, causing a number of problems including traffic jams, green project land shortage, and urban heat island effects." Ibid.

[31] Ibid. (including "energy shortage, environment pollution and low efficiency in energy usage").

[32] Ibid., at 3.2.

[33] Ibid., at 3.4.

[34] "Each person has a registration (hukuo) in either a rural area or an urban area, and cannot change the hukuo without the permission of the receiving jurisdiction. In practice cities usually give registration to

difficult to handle, and many of China's policies have not proved as successful as its leadership would have liked; in particular, the *Hokuo* system has proven to be rather permeable. To the extent that China's urbanization problems are a consequence of economic development in urban areas and not rural regions, employment of a coordinated development trade policy aimed at China's disadvantaged rural regions would help to counteract that destructive urbanization.

Thus, although China's true status may be somewhere in between developed and developing, or, more accurately, developed for some regions and developing for others, such a status was not permitted during China's accession or under the present unitary development policy. The failure to make provision for this reality has had, as has been shown, negative consequences for China and development policy in general. Perhaps it is time to approach development differently.

IV. A PROPOSAL FOR SUBSTATE REGIONAL TRADE DEVELOPMENT

A few years ago, I made a proposal in an article that would, I believe, rationalize the issue of regionalism within modern trade policy. That proposal, the individual parts of which could be applied separately and independently of each other, suggests the following:

(1) In granting Generalized System of Preferences (GSP)-type benefits, developed countries should provide either:
   (a) GSP benefits to internal regions of countries not previously covered, so long as the region on its own qualifies as "developing" (through employment of the usual criteria), or
   (b) "GSP-Plus" benefits to previously covered but relatively worse off regions within countries;

(2) Countries should be allowed to employ WTO developing country protections for internal regions, so long as the region alone qualifies as developing, even if the country, taken as a whole, is not allowed to employ the WTO protective devises because it is developed.

(3) Countries [previously accorded developing country benefits] should be examined to determine whether the more developed regions within the country should be graduated, while the less developed regions continue to receive WTO developing country benefits.[35]

This proposal counters many of the problems associated with a unitary development policy. As an initial matter, it responds to the likely inefficiencies of a development policy that fails to take into account differing levels of development with countries.

skilled people who have offers of employment, but have generally been reluctant to provide registration to migrants from the countryside." Dollar (2007), supra note 16, p. 10.

35 Picker (2005), supra note 5, p. 147.

The proposal also helps to counter the all-too-often devastating urbanization experienced in those countries through asymmetric internal development. It also may result in greater buy-in by developed countries that then see development policy being applied in a more efficient and targeted way. For example, there are only a handful of countries that provide GSP treatment.[36] Perhaps that number might go up if it was thought that the GSP was more efficiently applied via the GSP-Plus Proposal.

Indeed, if much of the success of development policy resides in the hands of developed countries, as surely it must be given the realities of the world's distribution of wealth and power, then it is critical that developed countries are more easily able to connect development policy with their own self-interest. One way to achieve this goal is through the direct applicability of development policy to "developing" regions in developed countries. After all, there will be voices, often strong political voices, that may impede support for global development policies when those voices see domestic development needs being unmet. Thus, for example, in the United States, it may all too often be asked why an impoverished family business in depressed Louisiana should not receive the same development policy support as a similar impoverished business in Botswana. Specifically, such a business might seek the same GSP access to Europe as their competitor in Botswana enjoys in its trade relations with Europe. The foregoing proposal would permit just that scenario, allowing products from regions designated as "developing" within developed countries a form of GSP access to other developed markets.

True, this may be perceived as a radical departure from traditional development policy. The claim will be that developed countries have their own resources to be able to develop their disadvantaged regions and should not pass that cost on to trade policy. However, as the situation in Louisiana suggests, both pre– and post–Hurricane Katrina, central governments too often fail the politically weak groups that live in those depressed regions.[37] Indeed, the very fact that a region in a developed country is struggling economically may itself be a sign that the central government has already failed to provide for or assist that region. Furthermore, if development is about improving human conditions, then why should someone in Louisiana, for example, suffer for the failings of their central government? Similarly, would we really expect the Chinese government in Beijing fully or even partially to take into account the interests of its poorer far-flung regions – especially if those regions

[36] There are thirteen such programs that have been reported to the United Nations Conference on Trade and Development (UNCTAD). See UNCTAD, *About GSP*, available at: http://www.unctad.org/templates/Page.asp?intItemID=2309&lang=1 (noting the following countries: Australia, Belarus, Bulgaria, Canada, Estonia, the European Union, Japan, New Zealand, Norway, the Russian Federation, Switzerland, Turkey, and the United States of America).

[37] Although tongue in cheek, it is nonetheless telling that it is quite common to see "Louisiana: Third World and Proud of It" on bumper stickers and T-shirts in Louisiana. See, e.g., Dirtycoast.com and its products.

include ethnic minorities, too often viewed as troublesome by central governments? History suggests we should not make those assumptions. Thus, applying development policy to regions in need of development in the developed world may be fraught with difficulties, but difficulties worth handling. This is especially so if a consequence of bringing developed countries within development policy would result in those countries becoming more enthusiastic about the expansion and implementation of development policy.

In addition to describing the benefits of the proposal, the earlier article also went into some detail on the problems that would be faced trying to implement the proposal, including the following:

- The issues associated with the WTO Members' inability to agree to amendments to the WTO agreements or even to conclude the present negotiation round
- Domestic constitutional constraints that would not allow internal regional discrimination[38]
- Rule of origin issues (e.g., ensuring covered products originate in disadvantaged regions within states)
- Identification of suitable regions for developing-region status
- Internal political obstacles

The article then addressed each of those concerns and provided mechanisms that could ameliorate or eliminate the anticipated problems.[39] For example, the rules of origin problem is not an insignificant barrier and yet could be dealt with. Indeed, the whole issue of the "spaghetti bowl" of rules of origin is a major problem in general in international trade law.[40] Thus, customs officials and shippers and all the other participants involved in the "nuts and bolts" of trading goods across borders would be faced with even more rules of origin regulations if the proposal were adopted. However, if those participants can handle the present complicated rules of origin systems, then it does not seem unreasonable to expect that they would be able to master the additional rules of origin issues presented by the proposal. One additional complication, however, is that of ensuring that internal regions benefiting from the proposal are the beneficiaries of the proposal as opposed to their more developed neighbors within the same country. Of course, specific regional marks of origin would need to be applied and suitable rules and enforcement mechanism created

[38] For example, the U.S. Constitution's "uniformity" clause may be relevant. See U.S. Const. art. I, § 8. ("The Congress shall have Power to lay and collect Taxes, Duties, Imposts and Excises . . . but all Duties, Imposts and Excises shall be uniform throughout the United States.")

[39] Picker (2005), supra note 5, pp. 160–167.

[40] See Jagdish Bhagwati, *A Stream of Windows: Unsettling Reflections on Trade, Immigration, and Democracy* (Cambridge, MA: MIT Press, 1998), pp. 290–291.

for the proposal to work. The example employed in the earlier article concerning this proposal is still apt to show how the system would work:

> Assume that within Russia, Siberia was a recipient of GSP-Plus and that a Siberian car manufacturer shipped almost-completed cars to a St. Petersburg finishing plant, where the completed car is then shipped to the United States. If marked appropriately, that car will be identified as "made in Siberia." At the port of entry, the [U.S.] Bureau of Customs and Border Protection (CBP) would normally trust the mark of origin and apply the GSP-Plus preferential access rate of duty. If a U.S. automotive manufacturing company or the CBP is mistrustful, then the Russian car company must prove the actual origin of the car, by both showing the appropriate paperwork and being amenable to inspection at the appropriate foreign sites.[41]

Clearly, the rules of origin problems are not fatal to the proposal. Similarly, the other suggested problems would also prove surmountable.

Of course, given international law's predominant focus on states as a whole, the proposal might be considered too radical for the traditional international law approach of the WTO. However, there has been application of development policy just with respect to a specific sector of the economy within a country.[42] In other words, there is precedent for a recognition that countries have within them parts or features that may be developed country-like and hence not covered by development policy. Thus, it might be that the auto industry within a country is sufficiently developed that it does not merit development assistance, even as the agricultural sector within that same country may still merit development policy support. Surely the equivalent recognition that some geographic sectors are more deserving than other sectors within a county for development policy support is equally valid.

Furthermore, there is WTO precedent for the application of trade law to regions within countries. For example, the WTO's Agreement on Subsidies and Countervailing Measures (SCM Agreement) originally provided "green-light" subsidies for regions that were "disadvantaged" and even provided detailed rules to ensure that "gerrymandering" did not take place.[43] Similarly, the WTO's Agreement on Government Procurement provides for the coverage of substate entities and their

41 Picker (2005), supra note 5, p. 162.

42 See, e.g., S. Lester and B. Mercurio, *World Trade Law: Texts, Materials and Commentary* (Oxford: Hart Publishing, 2008), p. 780, discussing EU contesting Korea's status as a developing country with respect to the Agreement on Agriculture at the Korea Beef case DSB report adoption meeting, WTO Doc. WT/DSB/M/96 (January 10, 2001), para. 14.

43 That agreement provides, in pertinent part, for nonactionable subsidies for

> assistance to disadvantaged regions within the territory of a Member given pursuant to a general framework of regional development and non-specific . . . within eligible regions provided that:
>
> (i) each disadvantaged region must be a clearly designated contiguous geographical area with a definable economic and administrative identity;

procurements.[44] The proposal above, for the creation of a regional trade and development policy, is simply an extension of the same underlying reality – that member states are not internally homogenous.

However, might the proposal result in disputes when some countries are effectively denied previously provided developing-country benefits, because the new policy then focuses that development assistance to only some part of the country, whereas other parts that had previously received those benefits either are graduated or receive relatively less generous development policy support? Indeed, given that urban areas, often the location of the ruling elites, will likely lose benefits in favor of previously underdeveloped regions, and thus probably less politically powerful regions, one can expect discontent within many countries as a result of the implementation of the policy. A dispute may then arise to the extent that the aggrieved country (representing the newly disadvantaged elites) can identify another recipient developing country that has not similarly lost development policy benefits. In this case, there might be a claim of prohibited discrimination between countries. Indeed, the WTO's Appellate Body, in the *EC Tariff Preference Case*, found that WTO developing-country benefits should be provided on a nondiscriminatory basis to "similarly situated" countries.[45] The question is then whether the two countries that are receiving different internal regional development support could be considered to be similarly situated, especially if the two states' aggregate indicators are similar. A determination of similarity based on states' aggregate indicators would clearly undermine the proposal's focus on internal regions. As such, "similarity" should be measured on the basis of the internal regions' characteristics.

The actual mechanics of determining internal regional similarity may at first glance appear to be overwhelming. Yet within the WTO, the determination of when countries are similarly situated for development policy purposes has often

(ii) the region is considered as disadvantaged on the basis of neutral and objective criteria, indicating that the region's difficulties arise out of more than temporary circumstances; such criteria must be clearly spelled out in law, regulation, or other official document, so as to be capable of verification;

(iii) the criteria shall include a measurement of economic development which shall be based on at least one of the following factors:

one of either income per capita or household income per capita, or GDP per capita, which must not be above 85 per cent of the average for the territory concerned;

unemployment rate, which must be at least 110 per cent of the average for the territory concerned;

as measured over a three-year period; such measurement, however, may be a composite one and may include other factors.

(WTO Agreement on Subsidies and Countervailing Measures, April 15, 1994, art. 8.2.)

44 See WTO Agreement on Government Procurement, Annex 2, containing subcentral government entities.

45 WTO Appellate Body Report, *European Communities – Conditions for the Granting of Tariff Preferences to Developing Countries*, WTO Doc. WT/DS246/AB/R (2004).

been resolved through the use of finer detailed classifications. For example, the SCM Agreement arguably uses four such classifications with respect to its application to development policy. Those classifications are least developed countries, specific countries noted in Annex VII of the SCM Agreement that have attained GNP per capita greater than USD 1,000, those moving from centrally planned to market economies, and then the remaining developing countries.[46] Although those classifications apply to states as a whole, there seems to be no reason why those criteria could not be applied to discrete regions. Thus, there may be regions within countries that could be compared with the "least developed countries" (where, e.g., the GNP per capita is below USD 1,000) or even where the economy is in transition (e.g., when a new local government institutes transformative economic [and other] policies). Indeed, employment of other classifications could also be considered, including the UN Industrial Development Organization's "Economic Vulnerability Index," the Friends of the Earth's "Happy Planet Index," the "Human Poverty Index," the UN Development Programme's "Human Assets Index," UN Conference on Trade and Development's "Trade and Development Index," and so on.[47] Although there may be some problems with access to a region's data, most of the proposed development classification methods should be able to be applied to regions within a state – provided there is the will to do so. That "will" would be exhibited through states' abilities and efforts to collect the necessary data at that discrete regional level of detail.

V. CONCLUSION

In the earlier article that first proffered the proposal, it was suggested that the proposal could be applied to Russia and to its WTO accession negotiations. If applied in that context, it could allow Russia to negotiate accession agreements that would have permitted Russia to take advantage of development policy for its less developed regions even as its more developed centers would be covered by the usual WTO rules. This might actually simplify some of the accession issues currently faced by the many participants in Russia's accession negotiations. If employed, the eventual deals struck between Russia and the WTO and between Russia and key WTO Members might then better reflect the realities of Russia's economic conditions. Given the ongoing nature of Russia's accession negotiations, the idea might still have some potency.

In this chapter, however, to illuminate the proposal in a different manner and for a different context, the proposal was applied to China. China is already a member of the WTO, and its status as a developing country is apparently resolved. Nonetheless,

46 Subsidies and Countervailing Measures Agreement, arts. 27(2), 27(3), 29 and Annex VII. See also Cui (2008), supra note 13, p. 137.

47 Cui (2008), supra note 13, p. 146.

the proposal is still relevant in the postaccession China context. The realities of China's asymmetric development still exists and indeed may be getting worse, with potential destabilizing consequences for China and therefore for the rest of the world. As such, it is not too late to try to apply a more efficient and equitable development policy taking into account those realities and contributing to a more balanced and hence stable development within China.

A similar analysis could also be undertaken with respect to Brazil and India – two WTO Members that are also developing countries and that, like Russia and China, also exhibit internal geographic heterogeneity with respect to development. Examination of each of the two would, just as with the examination of China and Russia under the proposal, provide further arguments in favor of the proposal. Brazil, for example, is a country where environmental and development policies may be most starkly in conflict. Might a policy of assisting certain regions more than or differently from others within Brazil, based on economic and sustainability measurements, be productive? Such a policy would further both goals, as opposed to a state-centered development policy that conceivably could hold environmental policies hostage to the development of parts of the country where the environment is not so closely bound up with development policies. Similarly, consideration of India's geographic economic heterogeneity might also prove useful in previously unimagined ways. For example, India is a country of great ethnic and religious diversity. Such diversity can lead to conflict, especially when exacerbated by economic hardship. Might the proposal help to alleviate that conflict by ensuring economic development to those parts of India that are less developed and hence where communal conflict may thrive? In any event, the consideration of the proposal to those and other countries is outside the scope of this chapter, although it is illustrative of the potential benefits of the proposal outside the China and Russia context.

Of course, leaving aside China and the other large developing countries and their asymmetric development, another benefit of the proposal would be to help the ongoing negotiations within the Doha Round – the "Development Round." That Round, started in 2001, is languishing with little hope of completion in sight. The obstacles to a successful completion of Doha are, in significant part, due to disagreements between the developed and the developing world. Application of this proposal within the Doha Round might allow countries to approach the problematic issues in a much more nuanced manner. Because the proposal posits that within many of the countries there are in fact developed and developing regions, regardless of any usual characterization as developed or developing, those countries may then reassess their positions, ones that had been based on their perhaps inaccurate self-perception. As such, it might be easier to find agreement within the WTO when so many of its members, spanning the traditional developed–developing line, would then realize that within their countries they share common problems related to development.

Finally, and perhaps of most significance, is the relationship of the proposal to the ideas of localism and subsidiarity and to the greater representation of peoples' needs and desires reflected in those concepts. Localism and subsidiarity are ideals that are fast becoming emerging features of the international legal landscape.[48] This reflects the trend to grant local authorities and communities within countries an increasing share of power and greater participation in matters both domestic and international. Thus, within Europe we see the principle of subsidiarity assume a central position with the European Union legal framework.[49] Also, globally, such groups as the World Bank and the UN's Centre for Human Settlements have been proponents of a greater role for regions and localities within states.[50] Although international law, and the WTO in particular, has not yet fully moved to the point that regions are full participants, there is clearly a global move toward greater roles for localities, communities, and regions. There might even be a role for this idea in the support of indigenous groups, traditionally groups that have not always benefited as clearly from the international economic system. In any event, this trend is driven both by ideas of efficiencies and by the notion of granting people a more direct and manageable control of their lives through localism and subsidiarity. This proposal supports and advances that move within the WTO, even as it still retains the traditional role of the state.

REFERENCES

Bhagwati, Jagdish, *A Stream of Windows: Unsettling Reflections on Trade, Immigration, and Democracy* (Cambridge, MA: MIT Press, 1998).

Blank, Yishai, "Localism in the New Global Legal Order" (2006) 47 *Harvard International Law Journal*.

China's Sustainable Urbanization: Issues Paper Prepared for the 2005 CCICED Annual General Meeting, at 3.1, available at: http://www.harbour.sfu.ca/dlam/Issues%20Paper%202005.htm.

Cui, Fan, "Who Are the Developing Countries in the WTO?" (2008) 1 *Law and Development Review*.

Dollar, David, *Poverty, Inequality and Social Disparities During China's Economic Reform*, World Bank Policy Research Working Paper 4253 (2007).

Economist Books Staff, *Pocket World in Figures 2010 Edition* (London: Profile Books, 2009).

Harpaz, Marcia D., "China and the WTO: New Kid in the Developing Bloc?" Hebrew University International Law Research Paper No. 2-07 (February 1, 2007).

Jessup, Philip C., "The Subjects of a Modern Law of Nations" (1947) 45 *Michigan Law Review*.

Lester, S., and B. Mercurio, *World Trade Law: Texts, Materials and Commentary* (Oxford: Hart Publishing, 2008).

48 See Blank (2006), supra note 2, p. 267.

49 See, e.g., Protocol on the Application of the Principles of Subsidiarity and Proportionality in the Lisbon Treaty, *Treaty of Lisbon Amending the Treaty Establishing the European Union and the Treaty Establishing the European Community* art. 2, Dec. 13, 2007, O.J. (C 306) 1.

50 See Blank (2006), supra note 2, p. 267, text and notes 11 and 12.

Picker, Colin P., "Neither Here Nor There – Countries That Fall Between the Developed and the Developing World in the WTO" (2004) 36 *George Washington International Law Review*.

World Trade Organization, Doc. WT/DSB/M/96 (January 2001).

———, Appellate Body Report, *European Communities – Conditions for the Granting of Tariff Preferences to Developing Countries*, WTO Doc. WT/DS246/AB/R (2004).

14

Trade Preferences and Economic Growth

An Assessment of the U.S. GSP Schemes in the Context of Least Developed Countries

Caf Dowlah

I. INTRODUCTION

About four decades ago, in the early 1970s, the now-defunct General Agreement on Tariff and Trade (GATT) adopted a special trade mechanism called the Generalized System of Preferences (GSP), which allowed developed countries to grant differential and favorable treatment to less developed countries. A major objective of the initiative was to increase imports into developed countries of semi-manufactured and manufactured goods from developing countries to promote industrialization and economic growth of the latter and thereby enhance greater integration of these countries into the global economy.[1] Such trade preferences, especially tariff concessions, were expected to induce reallocation of factors of production from traditional sectors to more profitable manufacturing activities in developing countries and thus facilitate trade-based, as opposed to aid-based, international resource transfers from the developed to the developing nations.[2]

[1] See GATT, *Basic Instruments and Selected Documents, 18th Supplement* (Geneva: United Nations, 1972).

[2] Nondiscriminatory GSP preferences were believed to be more efficient than foreign aid for transferring resources to developing countries because they would be a subsidy to developing-country production and a tax on developing-country consumption of manufactures; thus, the welfare gains from such export or production subsidy – for both developing countries and the world economy – would be substantial. For greater details, see D. Clark, "Trade versus Aid: Distributions of Third World Development Assistance" (1991) 39(4) *Economic Development and Change*; Ronald I. Meltzer, "The Politics of Policy Reversal: The US Response to Granting Trade Preferences to Developing Countries and Linkages between International Organizations and National Policy Making" (1976) 30(4) *International Organization*; R. McCulloch and J. Pinera, "Trade as Aid: The Political Economy of Tariff Preferences for Developing Countries" (1977) 67(5) *American Economic Review*.

This chapter is an outgrowth of a research project titled "The US Generalized System of Preferences for Developing Countries: How Beneficial Is It for the Industrialization and Economic Growth of the World's Poorest Nations?" The project was funded by the Research Foundation of the City University of New York. The complete project report can be accessed at: http://www.qcc.cuny.edu/SocialSciences/cdowlah/gsp_project.asp. The author is grateful to the anonymous referees for their critical but constructive comments and suggestions that helped to improve the chapter.

Over the course of time, developed countries, especially the United States and the European Union (EU), offered several GSP schemes.[3] However, available literature indicates that, in general, the GSP schemes had been less advantageous for recipient countries than they were touted to be at their inception,[4] and they were more advantageous for some products, some countries, and sometimes only.[5] This chapter supplements this argument by considering the fact that GSP schemes were often directed more at advanced developing countries, which needed them the least, than to the least developed countries (LDCs),[6] which needed them the most.[7] The chapter also argues that some donor-induced factors, such as astute manipulation of product coverage and renewal processes, significantly contributed to the dismal performance of such schemes in respect to the LDCs.[8]

The chapter is organized as follows: in Section II, I briefly discuss the evolution of GSP schemes, mainly in the context of the United States and the EU. In Section III, I evaluate historical performance of U.S. GSP schemes in the context of the LDCs.

3 More than twenty-five industrialized countries currently offer GSP programs. Most prominent among them are Australia, Bulgaria, Canada, the European Union, Japan, New Zealand, Norway, Russian Federation, Turkey, Switzerland, and the United States. For details on recent performance of GSP schemes, see United Nations Conference on Trade and Development (UNCTAD), *Trade Preferences for LDCs: An Early Assessment of Benefits and Possible Improvements* (New York: United Nations, 2003), pp. 8–41.

4 See the first chapter of UNCTAD, *Quantifying the Benefits Obtained by Developing Countries from the Generalized System of Preferences* (New York: United Nations, 1999).

5 Some seminal works that take such a stand include C. Ozden and E. Reinhardt, *The Perversity of Preferences: The Generalized System of Preferences and Developing Country Trade Policies, 1976–2000*, Policy Research Working Paper Series (Washington, DC: World Bank, 2002).

6 The United Nations currently categorizes fifty countries as LDCs on the basis of three criteria: (a) GDP per capita – under USD 900 for inclusion and above USD 1,035 for graduation; (b) Augmented Physical Quality of Life (APQLI) – based on nutrition, health, education, and adult literacy indicators; and (c) Economic Vulnerability Index, based on GDP shares of different sectors. Currently, thirty-five LDCs are in Africa, nine in Asia, one in the Caribbean, and five in the Pacific region. See UNCTAD, supra note 3, p. 113.

7 In 1996, for example, the top ten beneficiaries of the EU GSP were China, India, Indonesia, Thailand, Malaysia, Brazil, Pakistan, Colombia, Mexico, and South Korea – all advanced developing countries. Similarly, in 2004, the top beneficiaries of U.S. GSP schemes, excluding petroleum products, were India, Brazil, Thailand, Indonesia, Turkey, Philippines, South Africa, Venezuela, Argentina, and Russia. None of these are low-income countries or LDCs. For details, see C. Dowlah, *The Generalized System of Preferences of the United States: A Critical Analysis from the Perspectives of the Least Developed Countries* (New York: CUNY Research Foundation, 2005).

8 Some studies, however, argue that East Asian countries, which were granted the fewest preferences, grew the fastest, whereas many other countries, such as those in sub-Saharan African (SSA), which were granted the deepest preferences, achieved little economic progress over the decades. See J. Francois, B. Hoekman, and M. Manchin, *Preference Erosion and Multilateral Trade Liberalization*, World Bank Policy Research Working Paper no. 3730 (Washington, DC: World Bank, 2005). This line of argument, however, ignores the fact that GSP schemes have systematically favored advanced beneficiaries, who were better suited to export GSP-eligible products than poorer beneficiaries (see Clark (1991), supra note 2). Also, scholars tend to agree that trade preferences alone cannot account for rapid growth and development in East Asia; domestic policies and institutions also played considerable role. See, e.g., the March 2006 issue of the *Finance and Development* (Washington, DC: International Monetary Fund).

In Section IV, I focus on some of the major factors responsible for the dismal failure of the GSP schemes, especially in respect to the LDCs, and suggest some plausible remedies. Section V concludes the chapter.

II. EVOLUTION OF THE GSP SCHEMES

The origins of the GSP schemes can be traced to the special and differential treatment (SDT) provisions adopted by the erstwhile GATT in the late 1950s. The STD provisions granted developed countries certain flexibilities with respect to the GATT's fundamental principles of reciprocity and most-favored-nation (MFN) status in trading with developing nations. The GATT contracting parties agreed to such flexibilities considering mainly the mounting terms-of-trade and balance-of-payment problems of developing nations. Considerations were also given to compensate unequal economic status of developing nations and to encourage their greater participation in the multilateral trading system under the GATT.[9] Developing countries also pressed for such flexibilities because, emerging from colonial rules, many of them faced low and unstable prices and highly elastic demand for primary commodities that they exported, while paying significantly higher prices for manufactured goods, capital goods, and machinery that they imported.

The so-called trade gap argument – that is, slow growth of demand for developing nations' primary exports compared with relatively rapid growth of demand for manufactured goods of industrialized nations – came to light when Argentine economist Raul Prebisch pressed the issue before the first session of the United Nations Conference on Trade and Development (UNCTAD) in 1964. Prebisch demanded that the exports of the developing nations be granted temporary duty-free entry into all developed-country markets as a "logical extension of the infant industry argument." He argued that only such trade preferences – preferential access to larger markets in developed countries – could help industries in developing countries build necessary economies of scale to survive in global competition.[10] Subsequently, the second

[9] For greater detail, see C. Dowlah, *Backwaters of Global Prosperity* (New York: Praeger, 2004), pp. 55–67; B. Hoekman and M. Kostecki, *The Political Economy of the World Trading System* (New York: Oxford University Press, 2001); Government Accountability Office, *International Trade: Comparison of US and European Union Preference Programs*, Report to the Subcommittee on Trade, Committee on Ways and Means, House of Representatives (June 2001); and C. Michalopoulas, *The Role of Special and Differential Treatment for Developing Countries in GATT and the World Trade Organization*, World Bank Working Paper Series (Washington, DC: World Bank, 1999).

[10] Raul Prebisch also proposed several safeguards for protecting the firms and workers in GSP-granting countries against any disruptive effects of duty-free import competition. For example, he argued for (a) a single overall limit on the volume of articles eligible for the GSP; (b) preemptory exclusions – each donor country could eliminate from its GSP schemes specific products that would compete with particularly sensitive domestic industries; (c) right of GSP-granting countries to exclude from its GSP articles that were imported in excess of a fixed percentage of domestic consumption of such articles. For greater detail, see T. Graham, "The US Generalized System of Preferences for Developing Countries: International Innovation and the Art of the Possible" (1978) 72(3) *The American Journal of International Law*; and David Wall, "Problems with Preferences" (1971) 47(1) *International Affairs*.

UNCTAD session, held in 1968, called for something termed the "Generalized System of Preferences," under which developed countries could grant trade preferences to developing countries to increase their export earnings, industrialization, and economic growth.[11]

The "GSP Decision" per se, however, was adopted by the GATT in 1971, when the developed countries were granted a ten-year "waiver" from the fundamental GATT principles of reciprocity and MFN. Then, the Enabling Clause, adopted by the GATT in 1979, authorized differential and more favorable treatment toward developing countries and special treatment to the LDCs on a permanent basis.[12] The evolution of the actual GSP schemes is elaborated in this section in the context of the European Union and the United States.

A. *The GSP Schemes of the European Union*

The EU was the first to introduce the GSP schemes in 1971. Initially, it granted tariffs and quota preferences, as well as ceilings for individual countries and products, but it reserved the right to (a) exclude certain less developed countries from the scheme; (b) determine the product coverage, rules of origin, and the duration of the scheme; (c) reduce preferential margins by lowering or removing tariffs on imports from each other; (d) determine the size of the tariff cuts affecting the preferences; and (e) include safeguard mechanisms.[13] The LDCs, however, hardly benefited from these schemes because their main exports – agricultural products – received no preference.[14]

However, the GSP schemes of the EU went through several revisions over the years, and a major overhaul was carried out in 1995. Discarding previous practice of granting quotas and fixing ceilings for individual countries and products, under the 1995 revisions, the EU removed quantitative restrictions altogether and provided for tariff preferences, which varied according to the sensitivity of products on the EU market. Also, the GSP schemes were simplified into four major arrangements: (a) General Arrangement, under which the benefits were extended to all developing countries;[15] (b) Special Scheme for the Protection of Labor Rights – the so-called

[11] See UNCTAD, supra note 3.

[12] The Enabling Clause, however, mandated that the GSP would be nondiscriminatory, nonreciprocal, and autonomous and cautioned that developed countries must "exercise utmost restraint in seeking any concessions or commitments made by them to reduce or remove tariff and other barriers to the trade of such countries." See GATT, *Differential and More Favorable Treatment, Reciprocity and Fuller Participation of Developing Countries* (Geneva: United Nations, 1979).

[13] See C. MacPhee and V. Oguledo, "The Trade Effects of the US Generalized System of Preferences" (1991) 19(4) *Atlantic Economic Journal* 19–26; and D. Wall (1971), supra note 10.

[14] See M. Bronfenbrenner, "Review Article: Predatory Poverty on the Offensive: The UNCTAD Record" (1976) 24 *Economic Development and Change* 825–831.

[15] Generally, G-77 countries are considered as developing countries. But China, which never belonged to the group, has also been considered as a developing country for the purposes of GSP. More recently, several transition economies of the former Soviet Union and Eastern Europe have also been considered eligible for GSP benefits.

social clause – which was made available to all beneficiary countries of the general arrangements who complied with the core labor standards;[16] (c) Special Scheme for the Protection of the Environment, which was made available to all beneficiary countries of the General Arrangement that complied with international standards on forest management, as specified by the International Tropical Convention (ITC); and (d) Special Scheme to Combat Drug Production and Trafficking, or "the drug regime," which was granted to certain countries that combated illicit production and trafficking of drugs.[17] Also, replacing the earlier system of adopting GSP regulations on a yearly basis, since 1995, the EU adopted only one GSP regulation for all products and for all arrangements for a period of at least three years.

One of the offshoots of this new system was the "Everything-but-Arms" (EBA) initiative, adopted in 2001. Under EBA, the EU granted duty-free access to all products from all LDCs, with the exception of arms and ammunition, and thus coverage was extended to all sensitive agricultural products, which in the past were either completely excluded or only granted a small preferential margin. Three sensitive products – fresh bananas, rice, and sugar – however, were slated for gradual liberalization.[18]

In its June 2005 revisions for the period of January 2006 to December 2008, the EU repackaged its GSP schemes into three major categories: a General Scheme, a GSP-Plus scheme, and the EBA.[19] The new schemes, however, made GSP benefits subject to more stringent reviews of core human and labor rights, good governance, and environmental conventions. The General Scheme, available to all beneficiary countries, increased product coverage to 7,200 items, incorporating 300 additional products, mostly in the agriculture and fishery sectors. The GSP-Plus Scheme[20] provides special incentives to beneficiary countries that implemented certain international standards in human and labor rights, environmental protection, the fight

[16] The labor standards, based on ILO conventions, included elimination of forced labor or compulsory labor, freedom of association, right to collective bargaining, elimination of discrimination in employment and occupation, and the abolition of child labor.

[17] Such as Bolivia, Colombia, Costa Rica, Ecuador, El Salvador, Guatemala, Honduras, Nicaragua, Pakistan, Panama, Peru, and Venezuela.

[18] Customs duties on rice and sugar were to be eliminated between 2006 and 2009. During this period, these products were duty-free within the limits of tariff quotas (*UNCTAD GSP Newsletter*, February 2002). UNCTAD/ITCD/TSB/Misc.65. EBA stipulated that the banana regime would be liberalized by January 2006, but it remains unimplemented. In Decemeber 2008, the EU and Latin American leaders, however, reached some understandings for liberlazing banana dispute. See http://ec.europa.eu/agriculture/trade/index_en.htm.

[19] See European Commission, *GSP: The New EU Preferential Market Access System for Developing Countries* (Brussels, June 23, 2005).

[20] The provisions for the "GSP-Plus" program, however, came into force in June 2005. Special incentives include provisions for an additional 20% preference, on top of preferences available under the general arrangements, in the case of textiles and clothing, and an extra preference of 5 percentage points for products that receive 3.5 percentage points of flat preference under the general arrangements.

against drugs, and good governance.[21] Conditions for the EBA, the third component of the new scheme, however, remained unchanged – all beneficiaries are granted duty-free and quota-free access to the EU market.

The 2005 revisions also provided for a modified graduation formula. In contrast to previous the graduation matrix, based on the share of the GSP imports and indexes of development and export specialization, the new matrix was based on a "single straightforward criterion" under which the overall share of the EC market was considered as a share of exports from the GSP countries.[22] The modified graduation formula, however, came with certain caveats. For example, "sensitive" products that are also produced in the EU enjoy a higher border protection. Under the new "tariff modulation," duties on imports of nonsensitive products have been exempted, whereas duties on sensitive products have been reduced to minimize "erosion of preferences."[23] Also, availability of tariff preferences as well as their extent depends on the arrangements enjoyed by the beneficiary country in which the products originate.[24] For example, ad valorem or specific duties on all GSP-covered products under its GSP-Plus program were suspended.[25]

The EU's rules of origin principles for GSP products provide for what is called "regional cumulation," under which when a product is manufactured in or with inputs from two or more countries belonging to a group of countries enjoying regional cumulation, inputs from other countries of the same group are treated as if they originated in the exporting beneficiary country. This regional cumulation is noticeably generous because it does not discriminate whether the inputs are from

[21] Of the twenty-seven conventions, sixteen are on human and labor rights, and seven relate to good governance and protection of environment. All of them had to be ratified by beneficiary countries by December 2008. The Web site of the European Union suggests that sixteen beneficiary countries have been qualified to receive the additional preferences offered under the GSP-Plus incentive arrangement by ratifying all twenty-seven conventions. See http://ec.europa.eu/trade/wider-agenda/development/generalised-system-of-preferences/.

[22] The graduation scheduled for assessment at the end of 2008 excluded textiles and clothing, which is reviewed annually.

[23] GSP preferences suffer from erosions when MFN duties are lowered, but as long as MFN rates are not eliminated completely, GSP preferences remain meaningful. The EU GSP schemes retain considerable worth as they grant "flat-rate reduction," which determines applicable MFN duty for GSP products in absolute terms. Currently, the EU GSP provides a flat rate of 3.5 percentage points reduction on MFN ad valorem duties, which is equivalent to a 14% reduction on MFN rate. See A. Panagariya, "EU Preferential Trade Policies and Developing Countries," EconWPA, International Trade Series number 0308014, available at: http://ideas.repec.org/p/wpa/wuwpit/0308014.html.

[24] For example, of the 10,300 tariff lines of the Common Custom Tariff (CCT), for roughly 2,100 products, the MFN duty rate was zero. Of the remaining 8,200 products, 7,000 were subject to preferences under general arrangements, of which 3,300 were classified as nonsensitive and 3,700 were classified as sensitive products. The special scheme for the LDCs granted duty-free access to about 8,200 tariff lines, but, as mentioned earlier, with the exception of arms and ammunition and the delaying of fresh bananas, rice, and sugar.

[25] For products subject to ad valorem and specific duty, the ad valorem element will be suspended. Such duty suspensions, however, will not apply to sections from which any given country has been graduated.

countries that are beneficiaries of its GSP programs.[26] The new system also gives preferential access to countries that have a lower share of EU imports. For example, groups of products from beneficiary countries that in a given sector account for more than 15% of EU imports from GSP countries are "graduated" and cease to benefit from preferential access. In the case of textiles and clothing, the "graduation threshold" is set at 12.5%.

Currently, the EU provides nonreciprocal trade preferences to 171 countries and territories under its GSP schemes and absorbs approximately 20% of developing-country exports. In 2003, approximately 80% of developing-country exports entered the EU duty-free or at reduced duty rates. In the same year, 63% of exports from the LDCs to the Quad countries (Japan, the EU, the United States, and Canada) was absorbed by the EU. Also, the EU imports more agricultural products from developing countries than the United States, Japan, and Canada combined. The official EU Web site claims that its GSP schemes are "the most generous of all developed-country GSP systems," and during 1999–2003, developing countries' share in total EU imports grew from 33% to 40%.[27]

The EU also offers non-GSP preferential schemes. Initially, its nonreciprocal trade covered the African, Caribbean, and Pacific (ACP) regions under the ACP-EC Lome Convention of 1975, which was replaced by the Contonou Agreement in 2000. Currently, seventy-nine ACP countries are eligible for preferences under the agreement; the unilateral preferences, granted under the Contonou Agreement, are, however, slated for replacement by WTO-compatible reciprocal economic partnership agreements (EPAs) by 2008.[28] Under the agreement, manufactured and processed products from ACP countries are exempt from EU custom duties. For agricultural products, however, different preferences are given – whereas tropical products, which do not compete with European products, enter duty-free, temperate products face exemption or reduction of duties, and fruits and vegetables are subject to seasonal restrictions.[29]

It is also notable that the EU's imports from the ACP countries had been more substantial than the EU's GSP schemes or the EBA. In 2002, for example, agricultural

[26] According to the EU Web site, currently there are three regional groups benefiting from regional cumulation: Group I consists of Brunei Darussalam, Cambodia, Indonesia, Laos, Malaysia, the Philippines, Thailand, Vietnam, and Singapore (although Singapore is excluded from GSP, it continues to participate to cumulation of this group); Group II consists of Costa Rica, Honduras, Guatemala, Nicaragua, Panama, El Salvador, Bolivia, Colombia, Ecuador, Peru, and Venezuela; and Group III consists of Bangladesh, Bhutan, India, Maldives, Nepal, Pakistan, and Sri Lanka.

[27] See http://ec.europa.eu/trade/issues/global/gsp/legis/index_en.htm and http://ec.europa.eu/trade/issues/global/gsp/pr230605_en.htm.

[28] The Contonou Agreement, which came under a WTO waiver approved at the Doha Ministerial Meeting in 2001, was slated for expiration by December 2007 (WTO Document WT/MIN(01)/15, November 14, 2001).

[29] Some agricultural products face quantitative restrictions or are excluded from preferential treatment. For certain products, such as bananas, beef, and sugar, the EU provides special market access through commodity protocols.

products accounted for approximately 10% of the EU GSP and EBA imports, whereas the share of the ACP countries was approximately 30%.[30] In the same year, 18% of the EU textile imports came from the GSP countries, of which 80% came under the EBA.[31] The ACP schemes are, however, less generous in terms of duty reduction and more so in terms of cumulation than the EBA scheme.[32]

B. *The GSP Schemes of the United States*

The United States introduced its GSP schemes under Article 4 of the 1974 Trade Act, which mandated "temporary duty free tariff preferences" to help beneficiary developing countries (BDCs) "compete effectively with industrialized nations in the U.S. market." U.S. GSP schemes, however, came in force in January 1976. Initially mandated for a ten-year period, the schemes were aimed at promoting "broad-based and sustained economic development" of the BDCs through trade rather than aid, because trade was "a more effective and cost-efficient" way of industrialization.[33] The Trade Act empowers the U.S. president to confer the GSP eligibility to any country that does not harbor international terrorism, does not nationalize American property without compensation, and is not a communist country or a member of a commodity export cartel that causes serious disruption in the world economy.

Experience since the 1970s suggests that in granting GSP eligibility of a country, the U.S. president generally considers the following factors: (a) the level of economic development, (b) the record of workers' and human rights, and (c) whether it is a recipient of trade preferences from other countries.[34] In addition, the BDCs must meet the rules of origin and shipping regulations, and the United States reserves the right to make changes in its GSP product and country coverage, competitive need limits, and so on, so that it can adapt to "changing market conditions and the changing needs of producers, workers, exporters, importers and consumers."[35] The president, however, enjoys broad discretion over when and how to apply these

30 Although 95% of ACP exports enjoy free access to the EU, they perform poorly compared with other developing countries – their share in total EU imports fell from 6.7% in 1976 to 3.1% in 2002. See M. Manchin, *Preference Utilization and Tariff Reduction in European Union Imports from Africa, Caribbean, and Pacific Countries*, World Bank Policy Research Working Paper no. 3688 (Washington, DC: World Bank, 2005).

31 See "EU Developing Countries Trade Relations Key facts and Figures," MEMO/04/22 Brussels, Feb. 2, 2004, available at http://europa.eu/rapid/pressReleasesAction.do?reference=MEMO/04/22&format=HTML&aged=0&language=EN&guiLanguage=en.

32 Francois, Hoekman, and Manchin (2005), supra note 8. The EU also offers what is called Autonomous Trade Measures (ATMs) for the Western Balkan – Albania, Bosnia and Herzegovina, Croatia, Yugoslav Republics of Macedonia and Serbia, and Montenegro. ATMs are similar to EBAs. Beneficiary countries get duty- and quota-free access for all products, except quotas for some fish products, wine, and beef. Also, see L. Nilsson, supra note 28.

33 See U.S. Congress Ways and Means Committee, *The President's Report to Congress on the Generalized System of Preferences* (Washington, DC: U.S. Government Press, 1990), pp. 1–2.

34 See Ozden and Reinhardt (2003), supra note 5.

35 See Ways and Means Committee (1990), supra note 33, p. 5.

eligibility conditions. Potential beneficiaries of U.S. GSP facilities also have to guarantee reasonable access to U.S. goods and services, protect intellectual property rights, reduce trade-distorting investment policies, and eliminate trade-distorting exports.

A striking feature of U.S. GSP program, however, has been its on-again, off-again character: between the year of its inception – 1976 – and 2006, the program was sporadically renewed nine times, and eight of those renewals took place after 1993. Usually the schemes are extended for a period of less than fifteen months, and more often than not, they expired in midyear. The latest renewal, signed by President George W. Bush in 2006, reauthorized the program up to 2008.

The U.S. GSP program went through a major overhaul under the Trade and Tariff Act, 1984, which, among others, redefined the criteria for eligibility of the BDCs, provided for general reviews, refixed competitive need limits (CNL), and revised the country income restrictions.[36] The 1984 act split the CNL into upper and lower levels. At the upper level, a beneficiary country could lose GSP eligibility for a product if its exports exceed 50% of the appraised value of the total U.S. imports of that product or the flat level exceeds USD 115 million in 2002, scheduled to increase by USD 5 million each year after that. At the lower level, a beneficiary country could lose eligibility if it is determined that a particular product from that country is "sufficiently competitive" and the product is up to 25% of U.S. imports, or it exceeds the flat amount of 40% of CNL (i.e., USD 42 billion in 2002). The 1984 Act also empowers the president to waive CNL entirely on a product- and country-specific basis.

A second wave of reforms to U.S. GSP schemes came with the renewal of the program in 1997, when GSP product coverage was expanded for the LDCs. Under the Special GSP/LDC program, selected LDCs were granted duty-free treatment on additional 1,783 tariff lines. In particular, horticultural products, such as certain fruits, vegetables, cut flowers, and citrus juices, were brought under duty-free regimes of GSP.

A far-reaching reform of U.S. GSP schemes, however, occurred in 2000, when President Bill Clinton signed the African Growth and Opportunity Act (AGOA) as a part of the Trade and Development Act (TDA 2000),[37] granting expanded GSP benefits to eligible countries of sub-Saharan Africa (SSA). Under AGOA, those SSA countries designated as lesser developed beneficiary countries (LDBCs), were exempted from CNL and made eligible for duty-free benefits for an additional

[36] The concepts of CNL and country income restrictions refer to the provisions, under which GSP-recipient countries might lose their GSP benefits if their national income is higher than occasionally revised income thresholds.

[37] Title I of the TDA extended nonreciprocal trade preferences to a majority of SSA countries under AGOA, and Title II extended such preferences to the Caribbean countries, under the Caribbean Basin Trade Partnership Act (CBTPA). Overall, the TDA granted duty-free and quota-free access, especially for textile and apparel products, to twenty-four Carribean Basin Initiative (CBI) countries and forty-eight SSA countries.

1,200 products not available to other GSP members.[38] Moreover, AGOA beneficiary countries were entitled to receive GSP benefits through September 2008, regardless of whether GSP was extended beyond 2006.[39]

In 2003, President George Bushfurther extended the GSP coverage for AGOA countries to sustain "the momentum behind the economic reform and liberalization."[40] The AGOA Acceleration Act, 2004, (AGOA III) then extended trade preferences for these countries up to 2015. Originally, AGOA countries were eligible for limited duty- and quota-free access to the U.S. market for textile made with U.S. yarn and fabrics. Apparel imports made from fabric and yarn produced in AGOA countries were subject to a cap of 1.5% of overall U.S. apparel imports, growing to 3.5% of overall imports over an eight-year period. In August 2002, AGOA II doubled the applicable percentages of the cap. AGOA III allows the Lesser Developed Beneficiary Countries (LDBCs) to export textiles made from yarn and fabrics coming from any third country to the U.S. duty-free.[41]

Thanks to such exceptionally favorable measures, U.S. imports from AGOA countries increased remarkably in the 2000s. The U.S. imports from AGOA countries were valued at USD 14 billion in 2003, a 55% increase from 2002. In 2004, AGOA imports increased 88% to USD 26.6 billion, including duty-free imports under AGOA as well as preexisting GSP programs. It is, however, notable that about 87% of the import was petroleum products, and imports of nonpetroleum products increased by only 22%. Also, in 2004, AGOA textile and apparel imports increased 35% to USD 1.6 billion, but most benefits went to only a few countries – namely, Nigeria, Angola, Gabon, South Africa, and Chad.

Currently, U.S. GSP preferences are available to more than 10,000 products – about 4,600 of them were eligible for duty-free imports when approximately 5,500 products or product categories (defined at the eight-digit level in U.S. Harmonized Tariff Schedules) are eligible for duty-free entry from more than 140 designated GSP beneficiary countries and territories. However, out of 5,500 products, 1,800 receive duty-free treatment only when imported from the LBDCs and the countries eligible

38 Some AGOA countries, such as Congo, Kenya, Nigeria, and Swaziland – which are not LDCs – are also considered LDCs under AGOA. Also, AGOA grants free access to 215 products that were previously statutorily excluded from the GSP programs, even for the LDCs. These products include watches, electronic articles, steel articles, footwear, handbags, luggage, flat goods, work gloves and leather apparel, and semi-manufactured and manufactured glass products. See *UNCTAD GSP Newsletter*, UNCTAD/ITCD/TSB/Misc.65 (February 2002).

39 The U.S. Trade Act, 2002, extended GSP program for another five years, retrospective from September 30, 2001.

40 See http://www.agoa.gov/agoalegislation/index.asp.

41 AGOA includes thirty-seven of the forty-eight countries in SSA. AGOA III's "third country yarn and fabric provision" is extended to almost all of them, excluding only Botswana, Gabon, Mauritius, Namibia, Seychelles, and South Africa. AGOA products, however, must comply with the rules of origin requirements of a minimum 35% of local content; donor country content may be counted to this 35% requirement up to 15%, and cumulation is allowed among designated AGOA countries. See http://agoa.gov/eligibility/country_eligibility.html.

under the AGOA.[42] Between 1994 and 2001, U.S. GSP imports from effective LDC beneficiaries[43] increased from USD 68 million to USD 2.9 billion, with product coverage rising from 4.9% to 44.1%.[44] In 2003, total imports under the U.S. GSP schemes amounted to USD 21.9 billion.[45]

The U.S. GSP program is, however, the largest in terms of country eligibility. More than 140 countries were eligible for tariff preferences under this program in 2006. However, it provides the least extensive coverage: in general, duty-free treatment is more extensive for manufactured goods than for agricultural products. Several lines of products, which are of export interest to developing countries, especially to the LDCs, remain prohibited under this program. Textiles, watches, footwear, luggage, handbags, work gloves and other apparel made of leather, steel, glass, electronics components, and various other products are either fully or partially prohibited. Also, many agricultural products, such as beef, peanuts, tobacco, sugar, and diary products are subject to tariff-rate quotas.[46]

The graduation methods of U.S. GSP schemes are also remarkable. In general, when a country's per capita gross national product (GNP) exceeds the threshold level of income, it automatically loses its GSP eligibility. Several countries, such as South Korea, Hong Kong, Taiwan, Malaysia, Bahrain, Bermuda, and Brunei, have graduated from the U.S. GSP program under this principle. The United States also has removed some countries, such as Cuba, Iran, and Myanmar, from its GSP programs on political grounds, meaning such grounds are also used to restrict GSP imports.

[42] See *Promoting Economic Growth in Developing Countries*.

[43] The word "effective" refers to LDC beneficiaries that are actively utilizing the GSP schemes.

[44] See UNCTAD (2003), supra note 3, p. 13.

[45] See Global Trade Practice Group, *USTR Announces Request for Public Comments – Extension of GSP Programs* (November 2005), available at: http://www.gtlaw.com.

[46] A recent hearing of the U.S. House Committee on Ways and Means provides a glaring example how exclusion of such products of export interest to LDCs from the trade preference programs of the United States seriously erode trade benefits for many poorer nations. On November 17, 2009, testifying before the subcommittee on trade of the House Committee on Ways and Means, Paul O'Brien of the international development organization Oxfam pointed out that in 2008, for every dollar in aid the United States provided to Bangladesh, the largest of the LDCs in the world, Bangladesh paid nearly USD 4 in tariffs on goods exported to the United States. Bangladeshi exporters paid USD 573 million in tariff to the United States in 2008 but received only USD 151 million in aid. Similarly, other LDCs and poor countries paid tariffs for exports that were many times more than what they received in aid from United States. Also, of all the tariff revenue that United States collected from the LDCs in 2008, Bangladesh paid 58% and Cambodia 40%, whereas only 0.2% of U.S. imports from Cambodia and 0.6% from Bangladesh received preferential market access, thanks to the exclusion of products, such as textiles and ready-made garments, frozen shrimp, and footwear from U.S. preference programs. In 2008, Bangladesh exported products worth USD 3.75 billion to the United States, of which textile and ready-made garments amounted to USD 3.54 billion. Mr. O'Brien also pointed out that although the average tariff rate on imports into the United States is 1.7%, Bangladesh pays more than 15%, whereas France, the United Kingdom, and Saudi Arabia pay an average tariff of less than 1%. Bangladeshi exporters pay more than twice as much in tariff to the United States than the United Kingdom, even though the value of Bangladeshi exports is only one-tenth the value of United Kingdom's exports.

III. THE U.S. GSP SCHEMES AND THE LDCS

As explained in the previous section, although country eligibility of U.S. GSP program is extensive, its product coverage is narrow. Also, the program's duty-free treatment is more extensive for manufactured goods and some nonagricultural primary products, such as oil and petroleum products, whereas its coverage of agricultural products is highly constrained. Imports of some selected lines of products from developing countries are either partially or wholly prohibited, restricted, or subject to tariff-rate quotas. Unfortunately, those are the major products that are products of greater export interest to the LDCs, except for some LDCs that are oil and petroleum exporters. Overwhelming dominance of oil and petroleum products in U.S. GSP schemes can be gauged from the fact that in 2001, for example, although approximately 44% of LDC dutiable exports received U.S. GSP coverage, the share could be as low as 4% if oil and petroleum products were excluded.[47]

Time series data of the U.S. GSP imports also indicate that this narrow access of LDC products to the U.S. market under its GSP programs has also been highly unstable and volatile. For example, during 1980–1988, when the U.S. GSP program was in its infancy, only a few LDCs received GSP benefits, and almost all of them experienced a precipitous fall in those benefits.[48] In 1980, only six LDCs – Haiti, Madagascar, Malawi, Mauritius, Mozambique, and Zambia – received U.S. GSP benefits, and their combined share totaled only 2.7% of the U.S. GSP imports in that year.[49] In 1981, eight LDCs received GSP benefits, but their total share dropped to 2.2% of the total U.S. GSP imports in that year. The overall share of LDCs in the U.S. GSP imports continued to decline throughout the period, totaling 1.3% in 1982 (when only three LDCs – Mali, Mauritius, and Mozambique – received the benefits), 1.3% in 1983 (when five LDCs – Haiti, Ghana, Mauritius, Mozambique, and Zambia – received benefits), and then fell to less than 1% during 1984–1988 period. It is also noticeable that few LDCs received GSP benefits during this period – numbering between two to six,[50] with the annual average share of Haiti (the largest beneficiary) at 0.34%, Zambia (the second largest) at 0.28%, and Mauritius (a distant third) at a 0.14% share.[51]

A main reason for such a poor share of the LDCs in the U.S. GSP imports during 1980–1984 has to do with dismal GSP utilization rates by the LDCs themselves.

47 See UNCTAD, supra note 3, p.13.

48 See Appendix A: "United States Imports Afforded Duty Free Status under GSP, 1980–84 (values in US$)," in Dowlah (2005) supra note 7, available at: http://www.qcc.cuny.edu/SocialSciences/cdowlah/gsp_project.asp.

49 Ibid.

50 Six countries in 1980, four in 1981, five in 1982 and 1983, three in 1984 and 1985, four in 1986, three in 1987, and two in 1982.

51 It should, however, be noted that this declining share of the LDCs occurred when U.S. GSP imports increased from USD 72 billion in 1981 to USD 183 billion in 1988. See Dowlah (2005) supra note 47.

As Appendix B[52] indicates, only five LDCs – Bangladesh, Uganda, Mozambique, Madagascar, and Lesotho – had GSP utilization rates above 70% during the period, whereas three other LDCs – Tanzania, Zambia, and Malawi – had utilization rates around 60%. The utilization rates for other LDCs had been extremely poor. Also, the utilization rates showed considerable volatility. Whereas some LDCs, such as Bangladesh, Guinea, Kirbati, Malawi, Mozambique, Nepal, Niger, Sao Tome and Principe, Tanzania, Uganda, and Vanuatu, increased their utilization rates, other LDCs experienced a decline. For example, Haiti's utilization rate fell from 44.3% in 1984 to 17.7% in 1988, whereas Nepal's share increased from 62% to 80% during the same period. The utilization rate, however, fell most remarkably for the SSA countries – the third world of the Third World.

Obviously, wide-ranging issues are responsible for such a poor record of U.S. GSP utilization rates by the LDCs. One prime suspect, however, is its product coverage, which showed distinct bias toward manufacturing as well as oil and petroleum products. Most of the LDCs, obviously, lacked both. In the 1980s, most of the LDCs were still largely agricultural exporters, few had oil and petroleum resources, and few were catching up with the rudimentary manufacturing activity of producing textiles and apparel products.

The scenario changed, albeit only slightly, during 1989–2005. During this period, as Appendix C[53] shows, thirty-six LDCs had less than 10% of their exports covered by U.S. GSP benefits, and only six LDCs – Angola, Cape Verde, Equatorial Guinea, Malawi, Mozambique, and Zaire – had more than 20% of their exports receiving such benefits. In fact, seventeen LDCs had less than 1% of their exports to U.S. receiving GSP benefits, whereas for twelve LDCs the share was less than 4%.[54]

The period of 2001–2005, which coincides with the AGOA, however, gives a remarkable twist. During this period, the share of the AGOA countries receiving U.S. GSP benefits increased remarkably. For example, Angola's share jumped from 27% in 1989 to 78% in 2005. Similarly, Equatorial Guinea's share jumped to 62% from 25%, Mozambique's share increased to 62% from 46%, and Zaire's share reached 60% from 29% during the period.[55] It is also remarkable that during the same period, the shares of many non-AGOA LDCs fell, indicating that AGOA has already had an impact on the U.S. GSP-supported exports of non-AGOA LDCs.[56]

52 See Apendix B: "United States imports afforded duty free status under GSP, 1985–88 (values in US$)," in Dowlah (2005), supra note 47.

53 See Appendix C: "USA General System of Preferences Utilization Rates, 1984–1988," in Dowlah (2005) supra note 47.

54 For GSP utilization rates for LDC beneficiaries for the period of 1994–2001, see UNCTAD, supra note 3, p.13. The report also suggests that GSP utilization rates in Quad countries fell from 56% in 1996 to 39% in 2001 (table 1).

55 Some other AGOA countries that experienced increased GSP shares include Chad, Ethiopia, and Gambia.

56 It is hardly surprising that economic performance – GDP growth as well as GDP per capita – of African LDCs exceeded that of the Asian LDCs "for the first time" during the 2001–2002 period. See UNCTAD, *The Least Developed Country Report 2004* (New York: United Nations, 2004), p. 6.

Available evidence, therefore, leads to the unavoidable conclusion that GSP schemes have generally underperformed and yielded less-than-expected increases in imports from LDCs. The LDCs are also not doing any better in terms of other professed objectives of GSP, such as acceleration of industrialization, economic growth, and integration into the world economy. Overwhelming evidence indicates that the LDCs are now more marginalized in the world economy than ever in terms of industrialization, economic growth, exports share, foreign aid, inflow of foreign investment, burden of external debt, and poverty.[57]

IV. PROBLEMS WITH GSP SCHEMES AND FEASIBLE REMEDIES

Several factors can be held responsible for the dismal performance of GSP schemes in the context of the LDCs. First, historically, GSP schemes were directed at more advanced developing countries, which were better suited to export GSP-eligible products. Second, the GSP schemes have been voluntary and unilateral in character – they operated outside the purview of the binding GATT-WTO legal system, and thus, GSP-granting countries could modify, direct, or remove such schemes unilaterally suiting their own needs and interests. Third, GSP coverage of developing-country exports has not been robust, and the actual utilization rate has been insignificant. Fourth, often GSP-granting countries disproportionately substituted nontariff barriers on sensitive GSP-eligible products, and almost routinely GSP utilization had been subject to stringent economic and noneconomic conditionalities.[58]

Fifth, there are rules of origin, value-addition requirements, and other conditions of derogation. The U.S. TDA, for example, requires that the beneficiary countries assemble apparel articles from U.S.-made fabrics. The EU GSP rules of origin require two manufacturing processes in the country of export to make it eligible for duty reduction.[59] Moreover, administrative and technical problems related to compliance of the rules of origin requirements are also substantial.[60] Specifications of the rules of origin have become more important in recent years as technological progress and globalization have led to increasing fragmentation of the production

[57] Several authoritative studies have documented the pace and magnitude of marginalization of the LDCs in recent decades. See, e.g., B. Bora, R. Gryberg, and M. Razzaque, *Marginalization of LDCs and Small Vulnerable States in World Trade* (London: Commonwealth Secretariat, 2004); Dowlah (2004), supra note 9, p. 11–27; UNCTAD, supra note 3; WTO, *World Trade Development and Prospects for 2002* (Geneva: WTO, 2002); and WTO, *World Trade Report 2003* (Geneva: WTO, 2003).

[58] For example, the 1974 U.S. Trade Act makes a country ineligible for GSP if it harbors terrorism, violates workers' rights or human rights, or a country is either communist or nationalizes American property without compensation. Similarly, EU GSP regulations envisage enhanced social, labor, drug trafficking, and ecological conditions.

[59] Although in some cases, it allows regional accumulation of derogation, the procedural requirements remain onerous, often prohibiting the recipient countries from deriving full advantage of the GSP schemes.

[60] Preferences are often underutilized because of administrative burden – which has been estimated to be at 4% on average – reducing the magnitude of erosion costs significantly. See Francois, Hoekman, and Manchin (2005), supra note 8.

process into different stages or tasks in different locations. Such administrative tasks also reduce effective preference margins.[61]

Sixth, evidence suggests that GSP-granting countries often severely restrict GSP benefits bowing to domestic protectionist forces. This has been manifested in respect to a number of products in which developing countries have greater export interests, but it has been most pronounced in respect to textiles and agricultural products. For example, the EU GSP, which grants 30% duty reduction for sensitive and 100% duty reduction for nonsensitive products, subjects textile and clothing products to 30% duties as they are classified as sensitive products.

Seventh, the GSP margin has been eroding as a consequence of the MFN tariff reductions in successive GATT rounds[62] and also because of preferential trading arrangements[63] and other forms of trade liberalizations.[64] Recent evidence suggests that proliferation of preferential trading arrangements, including unilateral preferences, such as GSP schemes, that developed countries offer to developing countries, result in a stumbling-block effect[65] on multilateral trade liberalization and hinder a Pareto improvement.[66]

[61] For many developing countries, these costs might be higher because of information disadvantages, institutional weaknesses, and other factors. The costs of documentation and the administration of origin rules was about 3% for European Free Trade Association (EFTA) countries for their exports to the European Community. See, e.g., J. Herin, *Rules of Origin and Differences between Tariff Levels in FETA and in the EC, European Free Trade Association*, Occasional Papers no. 13 (EU Economic Affairs Department, 1986). Another study puts such costs at 6.2% for the NAFTA members. See C. Carrere and J. de Melo, *Are Different Rules of Origin Equally Costly? Estimates from NAFTA*, CEPR Discussion Paper no. 4437 (Washington, DC: Center for Economic Policy and Research, 2004).

[62] For example, as some observers point out, by providing similar duty-free access to a much larger number of developing countries, EBA has eroded effective duty concessions to the LDCs, see *Bridges*, December 12, 2001; and R. Sally, "*Whither the WTO? A Progress Report on the Doha Round* (Washington, DC: Cato Institute, 2003).

[63] Such as the Lome Convention, which granted deeper-than-GSP preferences to ACP countries for markets in the EU countries. See H. Lecomte, *ACP-EU Trade Arrangements in a Post-Lome World: Towards a Successful Partnership*, ICTSD Globalization Dialogues (Geneva: International Centre for Trade and Sustainable Development, 2005).

[64] Often trade liberalizations are so thorough that special preferences such as GSP or Lome preferences appear to be substitutes for liberalization of trade. See D. Brown, "Trade and Welfare Effects of the European Schemes of the Generalized System of Preferences" (1989) 37 *Economic Development and Cultural Change* 757–776; and J. Whalley, "Non-discriminatory Discrimination: Special and Differential Treatments under the GATT for Developing Countries" (1990) 100 *Economic Journal* 1318–1328.

[65] Currently nearly all WTO Members are also members of preferential trade arrangements (PTAs), and trade within PTAs account for one-third of world trade. See J. Bhagwati, J. Krishna, and A. Panagariya (eds.), *Trading Blocs: Alternative Approaches to Analyzing Preferential Trade Agreements* (Cambridge, MA: MIT Press, 1999).

[66] According to a study, switching to an import subsidy scheme would generate an annual net welfare of USD 4.3 billion for 170 countries studied – USD 2.9 billion for the United States, the EU, and Japan; USD 520 million for the LDCs; and USD 900 million for the rest of the world. See N. Limao and M. Olarreaga, *Trade Preferences to Small Developing Countries and Welfare Costs of Multilateral Trade Liberalization*, Policy Research Working Paper Series (Washington, DC: World Bank, 2006).

Eighth, GSP preferences are allegedly revoked when they actually start to boost the recipients' exports. Under the U.S. GSP, of 154 eligible countries, thirty-six have "graduated" so far. The most recent EU GSP graduated Hong Kong (China),[67] North Korea, and South Korea; excluded India and Pakistan from GSP benefits with respect to textile products; and excluded China, Malaysia, and Thailand for clothing products. These processes, often labeled "country graduation" or "product graduation," that allow the GSP-granting countries unilaterally to exclude some countries or some products from GSP benefits, have drawn mixed reactions.

The EU, for example, argues that the graduation process allows the GSP-granting countries to better target preferences on the countries that need them the most and exclude those countries that have succeeded in developing their economy to a point where they are able to face international competition without trade preferences.[68] The United States, as mentioned earlier, also uses CNL and income levels (GNP of beneficiary countries) and authorizes the president broad discretion to the same end. Critics, however, argue that often the process to determine a beneficiary country's international competitiveness or the developmental needs of the exporting country might be subject to subjective, rather than objective, determinations.

Finally, in recent years, disputes over the legal meaning of the GSP conditionalities, especially with respect to the meaning and scope of the Enabling Clause of GATT, added a powerful new dimension to the STD provisions authorized by the so-called GSP Decision of June 25, 1971.[69] In general, the Enabling Clause, adopted in 1979, allows the developed countries to depart from the MFN obligations to provide favorable and differential trade preferences for goods imported from the developing countries and grant even more favorable trade preferences to goods imported from the LDCs.[70] In dispute is Article I:1 of the GATT, which states, "a mutually acceptable system of generalized, non-reciprocal and non-discriminatory preferences beneficial to developing countries in order to increase their export earnings, to promote industrialization, and to accelerate the rate of economic growth of these countries."

In its challenge to the Drug Enforcement Conditions in the European Countries before a WTO Panel in 2002, India had argued that the Enabling Clause authorized the GSP-granting countries to give better tariff treatment to the developing countries as a whole but did not permit differential treatment within a GSP scheme that would enable various developing countries to be treated differently. India's complaint hinged squarely on the requirement of nondiscriminatory preferences outlined in

67 The decision of the graduation of four Asian Tigers – Hong Kong, South Korea, Singapore, and Taiwan – was announced by the U.S. president on January 29, 1988, which came into force on January 1, 1989. At the time of graduation, these countries received GSP treatment for about USD 10 billion. See Ways and Means Committee (1980), supra note 33, p. 27.

68 See http://ec.europa.eu/trade/issues/global/gsp/legis/index_en.htm.

69 See GATT, supra note 1.

70 See GATT, supra note 12.

Paragraph 2(a) of the Enabling Clause. Apparently, India's complaint was prompted by Pakistan receiving special benefits afforded by the EU under its drug-related preferences and thereby suffering from trade diversion from India to Pakistan. The WTO Panel, in December 2003, however, decided in favor of India by stating that the EU's GSP program was discriminatory in character and therefore that it violated the requirement of the Enabling Clause. The WTO Appellate Body also upheld the panel's interpretations of the legal implications of the dispute but did so with "significant modifications."[71] This dispute has also raised a plethora of other legal issues, such as whether GSP preferences are voluntary or constitute a legal commitment to the WTO.[72]

It is clear, however, that the objectives set forth in the GSP Decision of 1971 or the Enabling Clause of 1979 to boost export earnings, promote industrialization, and increase rate of growth through trade preferences – that is, through trade, rather than aid – have not materialized in respect to the LDCs. Available evidence suggests instead that the LDCs are being marginalized in recent decades. At the same time, recent experiences with the EBA and the AGOA suggest that the situation in the LDCs can be improved. There are both built-in and discretionary lapses with the existing GSP schemes. In most cases it is the voluntary and unilateral character of the GSP that allows GSP-granting countries to manipulate their schemes, leaving little or no certainty for the GSP-beneficiary countries about market conditions in developed countries. Although these affect all GSP beneficiaries, the LDCs suffer more starkly. Lacking infrastructures, capital, technology, product quality, industrial skills, as well as labor and ecological standards, they are structurally handicapped for utilizing even the available GSP benefits. Therefore, any improvement of the GSP schemes – to make them more effective for the LDCs – must address at least three issues simultaneously: the voluntary and unilateral character of the GSP schemes, market uncertainty faced by GSP-beneficiary countries, and the structural handicaps of the LDCs.

71 See L. Bartels, "The WTO Enabling Clause and Positive Conditionality in the European Countries GSP Program" (2003) 6(2) *Journal of International Economic Law* 507–532.

72 For insightful discussions on such legal issues, see R. Howse, "India's WTO Challenge to Drug Enforcement Conditions in the European Community Generalized System of Preferences" (2003) 4 *Chicago Journal of International Law*; L. Bartels, "The Appellate Body Report in European Communities – Conditions for the Granting of Tariff Preferences to Developing Countries, WT/DS246/AB/R and Its Implications for Conditionality in GSP Programs," in E. Bürgi, J. Pauwelyn, and T. Cottier (eds.), *Linking Trade and Human Rights: Framework and Case Studies* (Oxford: Oxford University Press, 2005). The paper can be accessed at the Social Science Research Network: http://ssrn.com/abstract=667283; and L. Bartels, "The WTO Enabling Clause and Positive Conditionality in the European Countries GSP Program" (2003) 6(2) *Journal of International Economic Law* 507–532; G. Grossman and A. Sykes, *A Preference for Development: The Law and Economics of GSP*, International Law Workshop Paper no. 6 (Berkeley: University of California, 2004); WTO Penal Report, *European Communities – Conditions for the Granting of Tariff Preferences to Developing Countries*, WT/DS246/R (adopted as modified by the Appellate Body report on April 20, 2004); and WTO Appellate Body Report, *European Communities – Conditions for the Granting of Tariff Preferences to Developing Countries*, WT/DS246/AB/R (adopted April 20, 2004).

A. *Change Voluntary Character of GSP Schemes*

The original rationale and intent for the adoption of the GSP program was to promote economic growth of developing countries through trade rather than aid by increasing their purchasing power in the short run and diversifying their economies in the longer run via exports of manufactured and semi-manufactured products. However, the voluntary and unilateral character of GSP schemes has largely frustrated that objective. Many factors, ranging from bureaucratization to politicization, as well as downright protectionism in the developed world, have contributed to this outcome. Bureaucratization was manifested in stringent rules of origin requirements and cumbersome administrative procedures for utilizing GSP benefits. Politicization of the schemes led to pursuance of noneconomic goals in granting, limiting, and withdrawing GSP benefits. Domestic protectionism has been manifested by stricter labor and environmental standards in GSP-granting countries. As long as the voluntary and unilateral character of GSP schemes remains, there would be little chance to move out of this quagmire. One plausible way out would be to bring the GSP schemes under the binding and transparent rules of the WTO.

B. *Guarantee Market Access*

Quota- and duty-free exports of developing-country products to developed-country markets was the prime motivating force for introduction of the GSP schemes. That objective – after four decades of the adoption of the GSP schemes – remains largely unaccomplished. Instead, evidence shows that GSP benefits were denied, withdrawn, and manipulated at the will of the GSP-granting countries. GSP schemes also experienced considerable uncertainties with respect to product coverage as well as continuation, which often contributed to considerable market uncertainty in GSP-beneficiary countries. With appropriate rules in place for the GSP schemes, enforceable by the WTO, such market uncertainties can largely be eliminated. Also, with such measures in place, political, bureaucratic, and protectionist manipulation of GSP schemes by donors will subside, and beneficiary countries will have a better grasp of both available and forthcoming GSP benefits in developed-country markets.

C. *Supply Constraints in the LDCs*

Although GSP-granting countries, international trade rules, global trends of trade, aid and foreign investment, and many other factors are responsible for the marginalization of the LDCs, the fact that the LDCs themselves are no less responsible for the sad state of affairs can hardly be overemphasized. Almost all these countries are still overwhelmingly primary exporters, only a few of them have succeeded in diversifying into manufacturing exports, almost all of them lack physical infrastructures and human capital, and many are plagued in bureaucratic and political quagmires, such as corruption, inefficiency, civil strife, and unstable governments. Transforming these countries into well-diversified manufacturing economies would be a monumental task by any stretch of the imagination.

The efforts that are currently under way – especially under the so-called Integrated Framework for Trade-Related Technical Assistance for the LDCs, which brought multilateral agencies, such as the International Trade Center (ITC), the International Monetary Fund (IMF), United Nations Development Program (UNDP), the World Bank, and the World Trade Organization (WTO) together to help the LDCs in overcoming technical and institutional constraints in the areas of trade policy, human resources, and export supply EN seem to be largely misdirected.[73] The LDCs need long-term capacity building to reorient their economies to manufactures, diversify their exports, and increase their competitiveness in the world economy. None of these goals can be served through the current approach of Integrated Framework. A well-thought-out, broad-based scheme should focus on some key elements, such as privatization, private sector development, expansion of the role of nongovernmental organizations, diversification of exports, and the implementation of market-based economic and financial policies.

V. CONCLUDING REMARKS

There is little doubt that the available GSP schemes have largely failed with respect to the LDCs. None of the professed objectives that legitimized the adoption of such schemes in the first place – such as industrialization, exports, and economic growth through trade than aid – has materialized for LDCs. Three major factors can be held responsible for such a dismal performance of the GSP schemes: unilateral and arbitrary character of GSP programs, built-in and discretionary lapses that conditioned GSP schemes over the decades, and crippling supply constraints in the LDCs. This chapter suggests the following strategies for overcoming such a depressing state of affairs: (a) implement a thorough structural transformation of GSP beneficiary economies, that is, diversification of their export base with greater focus on exports of manufacturing products that are demanded in global markets; (b) subjecting GSP schemes to binding WTO rules to do away with unilateral and arbitrary manipulation by the GSP-granting countries; and (c) guaranteeing steadfast market access for products of less developed countries to developed-country markets. In the end, the world community must adopt a bold and pragmatic plan to revamp GSP schemes on one hand and remove the supply constraints of the LDCs on the other to lift the LDCs from the morass of poverty and vulnerability.

[73] Scholars and observers have long been pressing these issues. See, e.g., Dowlah (2004), supra note 9, pp. 127–164; and B. Hoekman and M. Kostecki (2001), supra note 9, p. 387.

REFERENCES

Bhagwati, J., P. Krishna, and Arvind Panagariya (eds.), *Trading Blocs: Alternative Approaches to Analyzing Preferential Trade Agreements* (Cambridge, MA: MIT Press, 1999).

Baldwin R., and T. Murray, "MFN Tariff Reductions and LDC Benefits under the GSP" (1977) 87 *Economic Journal.*

Bartels, Lorand, "The Appellate Body Report in European Communities – Conditions for the Granting of Tariff Preferences to Developing Countries, WT/DS246/AB/R and its Implications for Conditionality in GSP Programs," in *Linking Trade and Human Rights: Framework and Case Studies*, E. Bürgi, J. Pauwelyn, and T. Cottier (eds.), (Oxford: Oxford University Press, 2005), available at: http://ssrn.com/abstract=667283.

______, "The WTO Enabling Clause and Positive Conditionality in the European Countries GSP Program" (2003) 6(2) *Journal of International Economic Law.*

Bora, Bijit, Roman Gryberg, and Mohammad A. Razzaque, *Marginalization of LDCs and Small Vulnerable States in World Trade* (London: Commonwealth Secretariat, 2004).

Brenton, P., "Integrating the Least Developed Countries into the World Trading System: The Current Impact of EU Preferences under Everything But Arms" (2003) 37(3) *Journal of World Trade.*

Bronfenbrenner, Martin, "Review Article: Predatory Poverty on the Offensive: The UNCTAD Record" (1976) 24 *Economic Development and Change.*

Brown, Drusilla, "Trade and Welfare Effects of the European Schemes of the Generalized System of Preferences" (1989) 37 *Economic Development and Cultural Change.*

Carrere, C., and J. de Melo, *Are Different Rules of Origin Equally Costly? Estimates from NAFTA*, CEPR Discussion Paper no. 4437 (Washington, DC: Center for Economic Policy and Research, 2004).

Clark, Don P., "Trade versus Aid: Distributions of Third World Development Assistance" (1991) 39(4) *Economic Development and Change.*

Cooper, William H., "Generalized System of Preferences," *Congressional Research Service (CRS)* Report for Congress (Washington, DC: Library of Congress, 2004).

Dowlah, Caf, *Backwaters of Global Prosperity: How Forces of Globalization and GATT/WTO Trade Regimes Contributed to the Marginalization of the World's Poorest Nations* (New York: Praeger, 2004).

______, *The Generalized System of Preferences of the United States: A Critical Analysis from the Perspectives of the Least Developed Countries* (New York: CUNY Research Foundation, 2005).

Francois, Joseph, Bernard Hoekman, and Miriam Manchin, *Preference Erosion and Multilateral Trade Liberalization*, World Bank Policy Research Working Paper no. 3730 (Washington, DC: World Bank, 2005).

Government Accountability Office, "International Trade Issues Concerning the Generalized System of Preferences" (1994), Testimony before the Subcommittee on International Trade, GAO/T-GGD-94-174.

______, *International Trade: Comparison of US and European Union Preference Programs*, Report to the Subcommittee on Trade, Committee on Ways and Means, House of Representative (June 2001).

General Agreement on Tariffs and Trade, *Generalized System of Preferences* (GSP Decision) (Geneva: Basic Instrument and Selected Document 18S/24, 1971).

______, *Basic Instruments and Selected Documents*, 18th Supplement (Geneva: United Nations, 1972).

———, *Differential and More Favorable Treatment, Reciprocity and Fuller Participation of Developing Countries* (Geneva: United Nations, 1979).

Global Trade Practice Group (GTPG), "USTR Announces Request for Public Comments – Extension of GSP Program," *Global Trade Practice Group Newsletter*, November 2005.

Graham, Thomas R., "The US Generalized System of Preferences for Developing Countries: International Innovation and the Art of the Possible" (1978) 72(3) *American Journal of International Law*.

Grossman, Gene M., and Alan O. Sykes, *A Preference for Development: The Law and Economics of GSP*, International Law Workshop Paper no. 6 (Berkeley: University of California Press, 2004).

Herin, J., *Rules of Origin and Differences between Tariff Levels in FETA and in the EC, European Free Trade Association*, EU Economic Affairs Department Occasional Papers no. 13 (1986).

Hoekman, Bernard, and Michael Kostecki, *The Political Economy of the World Trading System* (New York: Oxford University Press, 2001).

Hoekman, Bernard, and Susan Prowse, *Economic Policy Responses to Preference Erosion: From Trade as Aid to Aid for Trade*, World Bank Policy Research Working Paper no. 3721 (Washington, DC: World Bank, 2005).

Howse, Robert, "India's WTO Challenge to Drug Enforcement Conditions in the European Community Generalized System of Preferences" (2003) 4 *Chicago Journal of International Law*.

Hudec, Robert, *Developing Countries in the GATT Legal System* (London: Trade Policy Research Center, 1987).

Lecomte, Henri-Bernard, *ACP-EU Trade Arrangements in a Post-Lome World: Towards a Successful Partnership*, ICTSD Globalization Dialogues (Geneva: International Centre for Trade and Sustainable Development, 2000).

Lederman, Daniel, and Caglar Ozden, 2003 *US Trade Preferences: All Are Not Created Equal*, World Bank Working Paper (Washington, DC: World Bank, 2003).

Limao, Nuno, and Marcelo Olarreaga, *Trade Preferences to Small Developing Countries and Welfare Costs of Multilateral Trade Liberalization*, World Bank Policy Research Working Paper Series (Washington, DC: World Bank, 2005).

MacPhee, Craig R., and Victor I. Oguledo, "The Trade Effects of the US Generalized System of Preferences" (1991) 19(4) *Atlantic Economic Journal*.

Manchin, Miriam, *Preference Utilization and Tariff Reduction in European Union Imports from Africa, Caribbean, and Pacific Countries*, World Bank Policy Research Working Paper no. 3688 (Washington, DC: World Bank, 2005).

Mason, Amy M., "The Degeneralization of the Generalized System of Preferences (GSP): Questioning the Legitimacy of the U.S. GSP" (2004) 54(2) *Duke Law Journal*.

McCulloch, Rachel, and Jose Pinera, "Trade as Aid: The Political Economy of Tariff Preferences for Developing Countries" (1977) 67(5) *American Economic Review*.

Meltzer, Ronald I., "The Politics of Policy Reversal: The US Response to Granting Trade Preferences to Developing Countries and Linkages between International Organizations and National Policy Making" (1976) 30(4) *International Organization*.

Michalopoulas, Constantine, *The Role of Special and Differential Treatment for Developing Countries in GATT and the World Trade Organization*, World Bank Working Paper Series (Washington, DC: World Bank, 1999).

Murray, Tracy, *Trade Preferences for Developing Countries* (New York: John Wiley and Sons, 1977).

Nilsson, Lars, *Comparative Effects of EU and US Trade Policies on Developing Country Exports* (Brussels: European Commission Trade Directorate General, 2005).
Ozden, Caglar, and Erick Reinhardt, *The Perversity of Preferences: The Generalized System of Preferences and Developing Country Trade Policies, 1976–2000*, Policy Research Working Paper Series (Washington, DC: World Bank, 2002).
Page, Sheila, *Preference Erosion: Helping Countries to Adjust*, ODI Briefing Paper (London: Overseas Development Institute, 2004), available at: http://www.odi.org.uk/resources/download/2259.pdf.
Panagariya, A., "EU Preferential Trade Policies and Developing Countries," EconWPA, International Trade series no. 0308014, available at: http://ideas.repec.org/p/wpa/wuwpit/0308014.html.
Reynolds, Kara M., "The Erosion of Tariff Preferences: The Impact of U.S. Tariff Reductions on Developing Countries," SSRN Working Paper Series (2005), available at: http://ssrn.com/abstract=763665.
Romalis, John, *Would Rich Country Trade Preferences Help Poor Countries Grow? Evidence from the Generalized System of Preferences* (Chicago: GSB, 2003).
Sally, Razeen, *Whither the WTO? A Progress Report on the Doha Round* (Washington, DC: Cato Institute, 2003).
Stevens, Christopher, and Jane Kennan, *GSP Reform: A Longer-Term Strategy (with Special Reference to the ACP)* (Brighton, England: Institute of Development Studies, February 2005).
The Trade Partnership, *The US Generalized System of Preferences Program: An Update* (Washington, DC: The Trade Partnership, 2003).
United Nations Conference on Trade and Development, *Quantifying the Benefits Obtained by Developing Countries from the Generalized System of Preferences* (New York: United Nations, 1999).
______, *The Least Developed Country Report 2000* (New York: United Nations, 2000).
______, *Trade Preferences for LDCs: An Early Assessment of Benefits and Possible Improvements* (New York: United Nations, 2003).
______, *The Least Developed Country Report 2004* (New York: United Nations, 2004).
U.S. International Trade Commission, *U.S.–Africa Trade Profile* (2005).
U.S. Trade Representative, 2003 *Comprehensive Report on Trade and Investment Policy Toward Sub-Saharan Africa and Implementation of the African Growth and Opportunity Act* (2003).
Wall, David, "Problems with Preferences" (1971) 47(1) *International Affairs*.
Ways and Means Committee, *Report to the Congress on the First Five Years' Operation of the U.S. Generalized System of Preferences (GSP), Transmitted by the President of the United States* (Washington, DC: US Government Printing Press, 1980).
______, *The President's Report to Congress on the Generalized System of Preferences as Required by Section 505 (B) of the Trade Act of 1974, as amended* (Washington, DC: U.S. Government Press, 1990).
Whalley, John, "Non-discriminatory Discrimination: Special and Differential Treatments under the GATT for Developing Countries" (1990) 100 *Economic Journal*.
World Bank, *World Development Report, 2003* (New York: Oxford University Press, 2004).
World Trade Organization, *World Trade Development and Prospects for 2002* (Geneva: WTO, 2002).
______, *World Trade Report 2003* (Geneva: WTO, 2003).

15

Economic Development of North Korea

Call for International Trade-Based Development Policy and Legal Reform

Yong-Shik Lee, Young-Ok Kim, and Hye Seong Mun

I. INTRODUCTION

The image of the Democratic People's Republic of Korea (hereinafter "North Korea") is that of a hermit closed to the outside world and doing unsavory things, such as developing nuclear arsenals and long-range missiles behind the iron curtain. With this image in mind, one may easily jump to the conclusion that this hermit country would never make a genuine attempt to be part of the international economic and trading system. However, North Korea, for its part, has shown consistent effort to become integrated to the world economy by soliciting international investment and attempting participation in international trade. According to a recent *Newsweek* article, despite various sanctions imposed on North Korea by the international community to deter its nuclear ambitions, Pyongyang today has diplomatic and commercial relations with more than 150 countries, including most European Union member states.[1] Furthermore, with assistance from its closest ally, China, North Korea has adopted many economic measures to improve its lagging infrastructures, including major mining facilities.[2] The recent global financial crisis appears not to have affected the North Korean economy as much as it has the rest of the world.[3]

[1] "How Kim Affords His Nukes," *Newsweek*, June 8, 2009.

[2] Ibid.

[3] Ibid.

This chapter is based on Y. S. Lee, *Strategy for Economic Development in North Korea for the Establishment of Peace in the Korean Peninsula* (in Korean), report to the Ministry of Foreign Affairs and Trade of South Korea (2008). A previous version was also published in the 3(1) *Law and Development Review* (2010), 136–156. The authors are grateful to Dr. Leonid Petrov, University of Sydney, Department of Korean Studies, for insightful comments, and to Flora Ho and Sarah Choe for editorial assistance.

Founded as a communist/socialist[4] country in 1948, the North Korean economic reforms[5] began with an effort to attract foreign investment. In 1984, North Korea had enacted the Joint Venture Law as part of its policy reform to attract foreign investment. The North Korean legislature supplemented this law with more detailed Enforcement Rules, together with the enactment of the Joint Venture Tax Law and Alien Income Tax Law,[6] to deal with tax matters associated with foreign investments. Efforts to induce foreign capital in the 1980s through a number of legislations were nonetheless largely unsuccessful. Some investments came from the Jochongryeon, the pro–North Korea residents' league in Japan, but these investments were mostly political in nature and were used to provide financial support for the North Korean regime.

North Korea continued to implement economic reform policies in the 1990s. A notable result from this period is the designation of the Rajin-Sonbong area as a Free Economic Trade Area (FETA) in 1991. The FETA is located in the port area of North Korea's northeast shore, close to the Russian and Chinese borders. This project included a master plan to develop this area into an international cargo transit center, a manufacturing zone focusing on export processing, and an international center of tourism in Northeast Asia. The outcome of Rajin-Sonbong FETA, however, was not as successful as the regime had wished because of the lack of efficient policy coordination and participation from neighboring countries, such as China and South Korea.

With lessons learned from the failure in Rajin-Sonbong, North Korea announced yet another comprehensive special economic zone development plan in 2002. First, the northwest border city of Sinuiju was designated a special administrative region (Sinuiju Special Administrative Region), with plans to develop the city into an international trade, high-technology, finance, and tourism zone. Second, the Mount Kumgang area was designated as a specialized zone for tourism (Mount Kumgang Special Tourism Zone), which was subsequently opened to some foreign tourists. In particular, it was opened to tourists from its southern neighbor, South Korea, for the first time in their history. Finally, Kaeseong Industrial Complex was set up

4 Throughout this chapter, the terms "communist" and "socialist" are used without distinction.

5 A prominent North Korea expert, Dr. Leonid Petrov, has commented that it would be incorrect to state that North Korea has been trying to "reform" its economy, citing that the very word "reform" is a taboo in North Korean political vocabulary. Nonetheless, the North Korean regime has adopted economic measures that amount to "reform" regardless of the terminology the regime has used. A series of plans to establish special economic zones and the Economic Management Improvement Measures announced in July 2002, discussed in this chapter, are good examples.

6 North Korean laws can be found in *Code of the Democratic People's Republic of Korea* (in Korean) (Pyongyang: Law Publishing, 2004), published by the public publishing corporation of North Korea. The general public may access this code, which includes the full text of more than 100 laws enacted in North Korea.

as a special economic zone focusing on the manufacturing industry (Kaeseong Special Industrial Zone), allowing establishment of manufacturing factories owned by foreign corporations, particularly those of South Koreans. With the exception of the Sinuiju project, these measures have achieved some success in attracting foreign investments and tourists, primarily from South Korea.[7]

This chapter surveys the economic reality of North Korea today and reviews its economic development policies, focusing on its major reform measures.[8] Objectives and limits of those policies are examined. On the basis of this examination, the chapter also proposes a new economic development strategy for North Korea that utilizes international trade as a vehicle for economic development. Finally, the chapter proposes legislative reforms to create a positive regulatory environment for the country's economic development.

II. ECONOMIC REALITY OF NORTH KOREA AND REFORM POLICIES

A. *Earlier Success and Economic Decline of North Korea*

North Korea has a considerably smaller economy than neighboring states, including South Korea. According to economic estimates,[9] its gross domestic product (GDP) is USD 25 billion and its GDP per capita is USD 1,100. These figures alone indicate the serious impoverishment of the North Korean population: the latter figure is close to the level of per capita income for least developed countries identified by the United Nations[10] and only one-eighteenth of the GDP per capita of South Korea.

[7] Soon-Jik, Hong, "Evaluation on North Korea's Policy of Special Economic Zone and Success Cases" (2003) 40 *Study on Unification Issues* 178.

[8] These reforms were initiated to overcome economic difficulties and to provide food and necessities for its impoverished population. Also, after experiencing the shock of the collapse of the Soviet bloc in the late 1980s, the reform policy was thought inevitable for the fear of isolation from the international community altogether.

[9] Press Release, Bank of Korea, June 18, 2008.

[10] Forty-eight countries have been designated as LDCs (thirty-three African countries, fourteen Asian countries, and one Latin America and Caribbean country). The LDCs are determined by the following criteria (available at: http://www.unohrlls.org/en/ldc/related/59/):

1. a low-income criterion, based on a three-year average estimate of the gross national income (GNI) per capita (under $905 for inclusion, above $1,086 for graduation);
2. a human capital status criterion, involving a composite Human Assets Index (HAI) based on indicators of (a) nutrition: percentage of population undernourished; (b) health: mortality rate for children aged five years or under; (c) education: the gross secondary school enrolment ratio; and (d) adult literacy rate; and
3. an economic vulnerability criterion, involving a composite Economic Vulnerability Index (EVI)– based on indicators of: (a) population size; (b) remoteness; (c) merchandise export concentration; (d) share of agriculture, forestry and fisheries in gross domestic product; (e) homelessness owing to natural disasters; (f) instability of agricultural production; and (g) instability of exports of goods and services.

TABLE 15.1. *Average Annual Growth Rates of North Korea, 1946–1960*[11]

	1946	%	1949	%	1953	%	1956	%	1960
National income	100	(27.8)	209	(−7.6)	145	(30.0)	319	(20.4)	683
Gross industrial product	100	(49.9)	337	(−10.5)	216	(41.0)	605	(36.6)	2,105

(Average annual growth percentage rate in parenthesis.)

Recent economic reports also indicate that a significant portion of the North Korean population suffers from serious malnutrition and the lack of basic necessities, including essential medicines and fuel.[12]

The predicament of the North Korean economy is in sharp contrast to its earlier success. In the 1950s, despite the devastation and destruction of the Korean War (1950–1953), North Korea, with the assistance from the old Communist bloc including the Soviet Union, showed remarkable economic growth. The socialist-planned economy in North Korea appeared to be successful in mobilizing the necessary resources for a rapidly growing economy at a time when socialist economic experiments elsewhere, such as the Great Leap Forward in China, had disastrous results, including massive starvation among the population and economic downturns (Table 15.1).

However, the inefficiency of the planned economy the staggering burden of its increased military spending (reaching some 30% of its GDP), and economic sanctions led by the United States began to put pressure on the nation's industrial output. Consequently, the North Korean economy slowed down in the 1970s, staggered in the 1980s, and finally suffered a severe crisis in the 1990s, with food shortages resulting in a large number of deaths from starvation[13] and tens of thousands fleeing the country in search of food and basic necessities (Table 15.2).

Since the 1980s, when the North Korean economy began to stall, Pyongyang has tried various reform measures to tackle the worsening economic difficulties, including the series of legislations to attract foreign investment, as discussed earlier. These efforts largely failed to improve the economic conditions in North

11 Hong Taek, Kim, "Economic Growth of North Korea: 1845–1995" (in Korean), *Study on Economic Development*, p. 85.

12 For a recent study of North Korean economy, see D. K. Nanto and E. Chanlett-Avery, *North Korea: Economic Leverage and Policy Analysis*, Congressional Research Service Report for Congress (January 22, 2010), available at: http://www.fas.org/sgp/crs/row/RL32493.pdf.

13 According to Professor Kyung Sook Park of Seoul National University, the estimated death toll during the food crisis in the 1990s reached to 340,000. *Hanyeorye Newspaper* (in Korean), March 17, 2010, available at: http://www.hani.co.kr/arti/politics/defense/410540.html.

TABLE 15.2. *Estimates of Economic Growth of North Korea since the 1990s*

Unit: %, Economic Growth Rate

Source: Bank of Korea (2008).

Korea. Notably, the reforms attempted in North Korea were limited in scale compared with the economic reform policies of China in the 1980s, and the North Korean regime had underlying problems initiating full-scale reform policies. The next subsection reviews recent economic reform policies in North Korea and their limitations.

B. *North Korea's Economic Reform Policies and Limitations*

Before the 1990s, even with a series of legislative reforms to attract foreign investment, North Korea had been largely unwilling to modify its planned economic system or introduce a market economy. However, affected by long-standing economic downturns in the 1990s and the spread of the market economy elements within the country, such as unauthorized private marketplaces, the North Korean authorities came to realize the inevitability of reform in line with the principles of market economy if they were to deal with the fundamental economic problems created by the old communist system. With this realization, North Korea announced and implemented the Economic Management Improvement Measures on July 1, 2002 (hereinafter, the "July 1 Measures").

The July 1 Measures were significant in that they partially introduced a market economy.[14] Professional business management systems were introduced, decentralizing economic units and allowing individual managers to use business profits.[15] Modern accounting systems were also partially introduced. Moreover, the Measures curtailed socialist sectors, including social security benefits, enhanced the functions of banks, altered labor management systems by encouraging competition among individual workers, and adopted an incentive system that provides better workers with financial compensation. In an effort to attract more foreign investments, North Korea also implemented policies to build additional special economic zones in the Sinuiju, Kaeseong, and Mount Kumgang regions, drawing on past experiences acquired from the running of the Rajin-Sonbong Special Economic Zone.[16]

The July 1 Measures, which adopted elements of the market economy, made some contributions to economic recovery between 2002 and 2005.[17] However, the measures were limited in that they only partially introduced market economy incentives, without adopting the more essential elements, such as private corporate ownership. The framework of the planned economy remained, and production capabilities were not fully recovered. Difficulties caused by the shortage of energy and raw materials also limited the success of the measures. Thus, in 2006, North Korea began to record a negative growth again.[18] Although the July 1 Measures ultimately failed to bring full recovery to the ailing North Korean economy, it allowed some elements of a market economy, including private marketplaces, to take root in North Korea. These roots have proved to be strong: North Korea's more recent attempts to abolish private marketplaces (after the currency reform) have failed, and the private market has now been established as an indispensable part of its economy.[19] Another phenomenon of the North Korean economy during its temporary economic recovery in the early 2000s and its subsequent decline is a deepened dependency on China, in particular, Chinese imports of energy resources and other necessities (Table 15.3).[20]

Following the July 1 Measures, another significant economic reform trial by North Korea was the designation of the Sinuiju Special Administrative Region (SSAR). The Sinuiju region, adjacent to the border with China, provides investors with material advantages in land procurement to build their business operations and factories, supplying them with industrial irrigation, electric power, as well as

[14] *Understanding North Korea*, Education Center for Unification, Ministry of Unification (2008), pp. 155–165.

[15] Y. S. Lee, *Strategy for Economic Development in North Korea for the Establishment of Peace in the Korean Peninsula* (in Korean), report to the Ministry of Foreign Affairs and Trade of South Korea (2008).

[16] Ibid.

[17] Supra note 14.

[18] Y. S. Lee (2008), supra note 15, pp. 6–8.

[19] *New York Times*, February 5, 2010, p. A6.

[20] Y. S. Lee (2008), supra note 15, pp. 6–8.

TABLE 15.3. *North Korea's Trade Dependence on China*

2003	2005	2007	2008
43%	52.6%	67.1%	70.2%

Source: Korea Trade-Investment Promotion Agency.

easy access to North Korea's neighboring economic powerhouse, China. The SSAR was modeled after the Hong Kong Special Administrative Region. As in the case of Hong Kong, SSAR is allowed to pursue self-governance in relation to administrative, judicial, and legislative affairs, as well as economic management, which is to be based on principles of a market economy. The purpose of this radical reform was to promote foreign investments and carry out experiments of a market economy within the confines of the region.

However, the SSAR was another failure: it did not receive support from China, which was essential for its success. China did not welcome the establishment of a Hong Kong–style special economic region so close to its border, which could potentially divert foreign investment from northeast China, a region that is relatively backward compared with other regions and that also needs foreign investments to develop its economy. To inhibit the project, China arrested a Chinese entrepreneur, who had been appointed to be the first head of the SSAR, on corruption charges. North Korea eventually failed to materialize the SSAR project because it did not have concrete plans to attract businesses in the absence of assistance and cooperation from the Chinese government.[21]

Following unsuccessful endeavors with the SSAR, North Korea embarked on the project to build the Kaeseong Industrial Complex (KIC) in cooperation with South Korea. Initiated by an agreement between the two Koreas in 2000, the project aimed at developing, in three stages, 66.1 km^2 of industrial complex in the vicinity of the city of Kaeseong, located close to the border with South Korea. For this project, the North agreed to provide workforces, and the South was to take the helm of its management by providing financial resources and plant facilities, moving management teams from South Korean companies there. In July 2010, 121 South Korean small and medium-sized enterprises (SMEs) were manufacturing textiles, leather goods, chemicals, machinery, and electronics in the first-stage development area (3.3 km^2), employing 44,400 North Korean workers.[22]

The KIC is the first significant outcome of full-fledged economic collaboration between South Korea and North Korea in the area of manufacturing, and it is by far the most successful of the North Korea's economic reform policies. As of July 2010, the KIC had produced a total of USD 647 million worth of products since January 2005, with an annual production of USD 256 million in 2009 – more than 10% of the

[21] Y. S. Lee (2008), supra note 15, pp. 9–10.
[22] Kaeseong Industrial District Management Committee Web site, http://www.kidmac.com.

North Korean GDP. Nonetheless, there remain significant issues with the operation of the KIC, including certain restraints on traffic, telecommunications, and customs clearance imposed by North Korea.[23] Also, the terms of economic sanctions imposed by the international community have prohibited strategic materials that could potentially be used for military production from being brought into the KIC, thus impeding the production of highly sophisticated, cutting-edge industrial goods that require such materials. In addition, the businesses operating in the complex are mainly SMEs, rather than major companies, which is yet another factor limiting the development of the KIC.[24]

Also, there is a question of limited economic return to North Korea. Because North Korea provides only the workforce, employed by South Korean companies at an average rate of around USD 75 per month, the economic return to North Korea is limited to labor wages, which was USD 38.3 million in 2009. There is no joint venture between North and South Korean companies in the KIC, which means that it does not spearhead North Korean economic growth but merely provides its economy, in the form of wages, with less than 15% of the total worth of products produced annually in the KIC. The long-term stability of the KIC is also an issue. Whenever the North–South relationship has deteriorated, both countries have threatened to discontinue the KIC.[25]

North Korea's various reform trials in recent decades have failed to promote economic development. Setting up special economic zones where businesses enjoy preferential treatment and allowing foreign investment in certain limited regions has simply not been enough to earn the trust of overseas investors or attract foreign investment in sufficient amounts to promote economic development. For reform policies to be successful, as has been the case in China since the 1980s, more extensive measures, including private corporate ownership, will have to be adopted.

There are internal political constraints that prevent the North Korean regime from embarking on more extensive economic reforms. As a result of its sixty-year isolation from the outside world and the strict controls that the regime has placed on the amount of information that people may access, economic reform policies, even limited ones, can significantly destabilize the security of the regime by bringing in information from the outside world, including that which may not be supportive of the government's positions. In view of this risk, there is a limit to the scale and extent of the economic reform policy that the North Korean regime is willing to adopt.[26]

Lack of experience in operating a market economy, insufficient infrastructure, and inadequate legal and financial systems have also caused difficulties in attracting and maintaining foreign investments. Since the 1980s, attempts have been made to enact

[23] Y. S. Lee (2008), supra note 15, pp. 9–10.
[24] Ibid.
[25] Ibid.
[26] Ibid., pp. 11–12.

laws and regulations to promote foreign investment and protect the rights of foreign investors, but the absence of a fair and effective dispute resolution process in its judicial system and the socialist economic practices that are at odds with practices of market economy, such as freedom of contracts, have proved to be significant barriers to the successful recruitment of foreign investments.[27] The failure of the July 1 Measures and, more recently, the disastrous failure of the currency reform[28] were also caused in significant part by the inexperience and lack of expertise with the elements of market economy.

Apart from the foregoing concerns, North Korea has created a defense-oriented economy, focusing on production of military commodities and an industrial structure concentrated on heavy industries. As a result of the continued tension with its southern neighbor and much of the Western world, including the United States and Japan, a significant amount of North Korea's scarce resources continues to be devoted to military production, which accounts for almost 30% of the nation's GDP.[29] As long as this continues, reform policies will have only limited, if any, success because of the lack of resources dedicated to nonmilitary production.[30]

Lack of external markets is another issue. South Korea has benefited from the vast consumer markets in the United States and Europe since the beginning of its rapid economic development in the 1960s. Because of the incessant political tensions between North Korea and the Western world, international markets are largely closed to North Korean products. Given North Korea's tense relations with the West, it is also unlikely that international organizations such as the World Bank, which is dominated by Western countries, will provide support for its economic development.[31] North Korea is not yet a member of the World Trade Organization, membership in which is essential to gaining market access to major importing countries in the world.

For North Korea to overcome the aforementioned constraints and successfully undertake economic development, the following conditions need to be established. First, it will be necessary for the North Korean regime to make a political decision to concentrate on economic development and invest necessary resources in it by diverting resources from unproductive military pursuits. The prerequisite for making such a decision is the regime's awareness that the benefits of economic development, for both the regime itself and the North Korean people, would be greater than any loss, including the risk of weakened governmental control over information accessible to the North Korean people that would result from the inevitable inflow

[27] Ibid.

[28] M. Noland, "North Korea's Failed Currency Reform," Op-ed for BBC Online, February 5, 2010.

[29] Central Intelligence Agency, The World Factbook 2003 – Korea, North.

[30] Y. S. Lee (2008), supra note 15, pp. 11–12.

[31] In particular, since the new administration came on board, South Korea has deviated from the so-called Sunshine Policy of engaging the North, which was maintained by the two former presidents, Kim Dae-Jung and Roh Moo-Hyun, and has been taking a hard-line stance on the inter-Korean relationship.

of information from the outside world in the process of economic reform.[32] In the past, North Korea has carried out economic reform only to the extent that it does not threaten the stability of the regime. Ironically, internal stability has been threatened by the recurring economic crises since the 1990s, causing tens of thousands of economic refugees to flee the country. Thus, more extensive economic reform is necessary not only to improve the lives of North Koreans but also to stabilize the nation.

Second, it will be necessary for North Korea to settle its relations peacefully with South Korea, Japan, and the Western world, including the United States, to gain vital foreign investment, access to consumer markets, and economic support from outside the country, particularly from South Korea.[33] The issue of nuclear weapons development in North Korea must be resolved because of its negative effects on North Korea's relations with potential economic supporters and trading partners.[34] If the North Korean regime concentrates its efforts on economic development and improves relations with the rest of the world, cooperation and support from neighboring countries with economic resources and markets would be the remaining vital element to the success of its development. The stability and economic development of North Korea would serve not only its own interest but also that of all neighboring countries and the region as a whole. In this context, China's contribution is essential. China has already supported North Korea politically and economically during difficult times with the other neighbors and the Western world. Its successful economic reforms and development can also serve as a reference for North Korea.[35]

III. STRATEGY FOR NORTH KOREAN ECONOMIC DEVELOPMENT

A. *A New Model for Economic Development*

Even after the failures of earlier economic reform policies in the 1980s and 1990s, North Korea remains interested in new economic development policies that will promote economic growth without threatening its regime. Vietnam's Doi Moi policy is an example. It is an economic reform policy that has been implemented in Vietnam

32 The government control on information in North Korea appears to have already been weakened; a significant number of North Koreans now have access to outside information through various mediums, such as mobile phones. *Epoch Times*, April 20, 2010, available (in Korean) at: http://www.epochtimes.co.kr/news/view.html?section=1&category=102&no=105186.

33 The performance of KIC, which has been the best success of North Korea's economic reform policy, shows how important South Korea's contribution can be in the economic development of North Korea.

34 North Korea and the neighboring nations, including Japan, South Korea, and China, as well as the United States and Russia, are engaged in the six party talks to resolve this issue.

35 China's premier, Wen Ziabao, was known to have advised the head of North Korea, Kim Jong-Il, to consider China's economic reform policy during his recent visit to China. Lin Zhi, "Chinese Premier Meets Kim Jong IL," *Xinhua News*, May 7, 2010, available at: http://news.xinhuanet.com/english2010/china/2010–05/07/c_13281720.htm.

since 1986 in the interest of trade expansion, financial market liberalization, and market economy implementation while maintaining the communist regime. The policy contributed to the rapid growth of Vietnam in the 1980s and the 1990s.[36] North Korea's leader, Kim Jong-il, reportedly showed much interest in the Vietnamese Doi Moi policy when Nong Duc Manh, secretary general of the Central Committee of the Communist Party of Vietnam, visited Pyongyang in October 2007.

Whichever economic development model North Korea wishes to adopt, the conditions discussed in the preceding section, such as the political will to prioritize economic improvement over military buildup and to establish peaceful relations with its neighbors to attain necessary economic and financial support, are essential for the success of economic reform. Also, consideration must be given to the unique characteristics of the North Korean economy, which differ from those of its neighbors, including China, as well as the lessons that can be learned from the failure of the ill-planned radical privatization that took place in Russia and the other Eastern European counties after the fall of the Soviet Union.[37] An economic development model that is not responsive to the economic and political realities of North Korea is unlikely to succeed.

North Korea may require a new type of economic development model that utilizes international trade mechanisms but also allows a measure of control over the inflow of information and personnel from outside to meet the needs of the country's political realities. It is often argued that China's economic reform policy since the 1980s can be a model for North Korea.[38] However, although China's development model can be a useful reference, showing how a centrally planned and managed socialist economy can be transformed into a market economy, it is important to note that the Chinese model is predicated on the abundance of labor and the existence of a huge potential market based on the country's population of 1.3 billion. These have been key incentives for foreign investments. North Korea does not have the comparable domestic market potential and labor base. As such, whereas China's policy and experiences in its reform may give good reference points, it cannot be a model per se for North Korea.[39]

Construction of a new economic development model for North Korea must begin with an assessment of its economic realities. Today the country has a small domestic market and insufficient capital, which is similar to the domestic economic conditions

[36] "North Korea, Abandon 'Game of the Crisis' Strategy," *Media Today*, April 10, 2009.

[37] In the years following the fall of the Soviet Union, Russia's productivity was reduced by half, and the other Eastern European countries in the former Soviet bloc experienced similar economic disintegration and confusion for more than a decade. A. C. Black, "After the Fall," *Swans*, March 22, 2000.

[38] Supra note 35.

[39] For instance, Shenzhen, one of China's early special economic zones, set up as an essential part of its economic development plan, has now achieved great success, partly because of its close proximity to the one of the world's major financial and trade centers – Hong Kong – and partly because of its own significant labor base, which does not exist in North Korea.

of South Korea in early 1960s. As was the case in South Korea, North Korea also has a well-educated labor force and a significant level of administrative ability, unlike many less developed countries in other parts of the world. In addition, North Korea has substantial industrial and technological capabilities, particularly in heavy and chemical industries; although these capabilities were developed from its military pursuits, they can be converted to commercial use. Given the characteristics of the North Korean economy, the export-driven economic development model led by the state, which South Korea adopted to overcome its own small domestic market and insufficient capital, can be considered an applicable development model for North Korea.[40]

There are some obstacles to the implementation of this development model in North Korea. Unlike South Korea, which benefited significantly from foreign markets open to its exports and financial assistance offered by international institutions for its development, North Korea is currently a nonmember of the major trade and financial institutions, including the World Trade Organization and the International Monetary Fund. It does not have normal trade relationships with countries such as the United States and Japan that could offer major export markets for its products, nor does it receive financial assistance from international institutions. In addition, various regulatory issues, including the limited recognition of private property ownership, are currently stifling corporate activities and resulting in the corruption of government officials.[41]

Many of these obstacles could be overcome if North Korea could attain support from South Korea, which has been promoting the reunification of two Koreas[42] as a national objective for the past six decades. South Korea has a legitimate interest in supporting the economic development of North Korea to reduce the enormous financial cost that it would bear should the reunification process proceed without improvement of the North Korean economy.[43] An economically improved and

[40] Y. S. Lee (2008), supra note 15, pp. 13–16.

[41] Ibid.

[42] Korea had been a united nation for more than a thousand years until it was divided into the communist North and the capitalist South after World War II.

[43] The cost of the Korean Reunification was estimated at USD 2 trillion. Peter M. Beck, "Contemplating Korean Reunification," *Wall Street Journal*, January 4, 2010, available at: http://online.wsj.com/article/SB10001424052748704340304574635180086832934.html. Dr. Petrov observes that "this statement reveals the bleak future of North Korea as an inferior party to be absorbed by South Korea in the process of South-led unification. Certainly, this is not acceptable for the DPRK [Democratic People's Republic of Korea] regime, which claims its exclusive legitimacy on the Korean peninsula." However, the history of the North–South economic exchanges seems to suggest otherwise. For instance, the agreement to establish the KIC, under which South Korea provides capital and North Korea provides labor, may well be seen as placing North Korea in the position of an "inferior" party because it merely provides labor to South Korean companies. Nonetheless, North Korea has accepted this arrangement for practical economic reasons. The North Korean leadership has acknowledged the economic superiority of South Korea and its role in the economic development of North Korea. Furthermore, North Korea has demanded more investment and aid from South Korea under the slogan "Cooperation between Our People" (envisioning North and South Koreans as one "people").

politically stable North Korea will make it much easier for South Koreans to pursue, financially and otherwise, reunification should the two nations agree to end the division of the peninsula. South Korea, currently one of the largest trading nations in the world and the thirteenth largest economy in possession of some of the most competitive and technologically sophisticated industries in the world, has sufficient economic capacity to provide what North Korea requires for economic development, including export market, capital, corporate managerial expertise, and industrial technology.

To its economic benefit, North Korea also has a rich endowment of natural resources, including key industrial materials, such as coal, tin, tungsten, zinc, lead, iron ore, uranium, and copper, the value of which is estimated at approximately USD 2 trillion.[44] Coupled with its own industrial capacity, educated labor force, administrative and institutional capacity, and the possibilities of economic cooperation with South Korea, North Korea is better positioned than many other underdeveloped countries to carry out the export-oriented economic development model.

South Korea's economic development history provides useful references for North Korea.[45] For instance, South Korea carried out a series of comprehensive, five-year economic development plans from 1962 to early 1996. These plans could serve as a useful model for North Korea. Each plan listed key policy goals in the corresponding five-year period, functioning as a blueprint for industrial and economic development, as illustrated in Table 15.4. During the period of Five-Year Economic Development Plans, South Korea showed stellar growth in its economy, registering an average annual growth rate of 8.8% from 1962 to 1991. This unprecedented rapid economic development has transformed South Korea from one of the poorest countries in the world into a prosperous and advanced country with a significant share in world trade and massive industrial capacities.

The South Korean Five-Year Economic Development Plans show that its economic growth was initially led by light, labor-intensive industries and manufacturing, maximizing the use of its educated labor force. Later on, the focus was gradually shifted to heavy and chemical industries that produced more value-added, technologically sophisticated products but required substantial facilities and capital (Table 15.4). The transition occurred when South Korea began to acquire a sufficient amount of capital resources and technological expertise to support heavier and more sophisticated industries. This type of transitional development strategy has important implications for North Korea. It may be desirable for North Korea to

[44] In accordance with the estimate by the Korean Chamber of Commerce.

[45] Dr. Petrov points out that the South Korean economy developed under particular circumstances – namely, Cold War politics and a favorable U.S. trade regime that allowed South Korea and Taiwan to grow quickly into Asian Tigers and Dragons. According to Dr. Petrov, North Korea lost its benefactors twenty years ago. South Korea can be a market for North Korea just as the United States was for South Korea during its development era. This of course will only be possible if North Korea builds peaceful and cooperative relationships with South Korea and its allies, including the United States and Japan.

TABLE 15.4. *Key Policies for South Korea's Five-Year Economic Development Plans (1962–1991)*[46]

1st (1962–1966)	2nd (1967–1971)	3rd (1972–1976)
– Promote import-substitute industries – Build petroleum and fertilizer plants – Transition to export-oriented policy (1964)	– Expand export bases – Strengthen international competitiveness of light industries – Produce industrial raw materials – Introduce and adopt new technologies	– Promote heavy and chemical industries – Promote science and technology – Increase exports
4th (1977–1981)	**5th (1982–1986)**	**6th (1987–1991)**
– Attain the status of world's major economy – Rationalize industrial structure – Build key plants	– Promote best quality and precision in products – Export plant facilities – Support private enterprises to develop production technologies	– Promote world-class industries – Promote aviation industry – Expand overseas industrial investments

start with industries that can make better use of its abundant natural resources and existing industrial base as well as its educated labor force.

An effective institutional framework will also be important for the implementation of development policies. The Economic Planning Board (EPB), which South Korea established in 1961, was responsible for the planning and implementation of economic development plans. The EPB was separate from other government ministries and assumed the role of a control tower for the country's economic development, coordinating relevant government ministries and guiding the government toward achieving the objective of economic development. Setting up a similar institution in North Korea may increase efficiency in the planning and implementation of economic development policies.

Along with an effective institutional framework, the existence of an adequate legal system and laws that support, rather than hinder, business and economic activities is also important for economic development, as discussed later in this chapter. Public health is another important issue. During the serious food crisis of the 1990s, North Korea lost a large percentage of its population; tens of thousands of people either died from starvation or fled the country in search of food. Lack of food and medical resources has caused serious public health problems in North Korea. This humanitarian issue is also relevant to economic development, because economic success requires a healthy, educated labor force.

[46] "Challenging Moments in Korean History (2): Five-Year Economic Development Plans," *Korean Economy Daily*, August 2008.

TABLE 15.5. *Health indicators for Democratic People's Republic of Korea*[47]

	1995–1996	2010
Population	22,114,000	22,757,275
Life expectancy	70.1 years	64.13 years
Mortality rate	6.8/1,000	10.6/1,000
Infant mortality	18.6/1,000	50.15/1,000

B. *Public Health in North Korea*

As is general practice in socialist countries, North Korea adopted free education and health care systems. Its constitution requires provision of comprehensive and compulsory free medical care to all its citizens,[48] and the North Korean government has the national policy of universal health care. According to the World Health Organization, North Korea achieved remarkable progress in the development of its health care system before the crisis in the 1990s.[49] It gave priority to primary health care services for children and women and to the improvement of access to preventive and curative health care.[50] Large investments were made in other basic social services, including water, sanitation, and health education, and by the 1980s, the health and nutritional status of the population was among the best in the region.[51]

However, the economic and food crisis of the 1990s took a toll on public health in North Korea. Major economic difficulties and a series of natural catastrophes seriously disrupted the agricultural and energy sectors, and economic sanctions worsened the situation. The food security situation deteriorated, leading to a high level of malnutrition, especially in the period of 1995–2000.[52] The problems in the health sector and in food security were compounded by a decreasing energy supply and reduced access to clean water and sanitation. Furthermore, hospitals and clinics have been rendered less effective by the lack of medications, together with shortages of electricity, water, and heating, especially during the harsh winters.[53] The health indicators in Table 15.5 show the deteriorating public health situation in North Korea since the mid-1990s.

The public health problems have led to a further reduction of North Korea's labor force, a necessary component of economic development. The situation requires

47 *CIA World Factbook 2010*, available at: http://www.cia.gov/library/publications/the-world-factbook/geos/kn.html.

48 Supra note 6, Article 72.

49 WHO, *WHO Country Cooperation Strategy 2004–2008 Democratic People's Republic of Korea* (June, 2003), p. 6.

50 Ibid.

51 Ibid.

52 Supra note 13.

53 Supra note 49.

serious attention. Although international organizations have provided massive food aid and medical support,[54] long-term support is also necessary, particularly with the country's now-disintegrated medical education system, which will result in a serious shortage of doctors in the years ahead. South Korea, which has world-class medical technology and infrastructure, can play a key role. The South Korean government can promote the transfer of medical personnel and technology to North Korea. It can also develop a legal framework that encourages pharmaceutical companies, hospitals, and medical experts to provide support to North Korea with incentives, such as tax abatement and grants.

C. *Legal Reform for Economic Development*

The rule of law may not be a hallmark of an authoritative communist country such as North Korea. In the past, communist regimes placed the will of leadership and that of the party above the rule of law, and there has been controversy as to the role and effectiveness of law in communist countries.[55] However, the necessity for the rule of law has been raised by the North Korean regime itself, evidenced by a number of key legislations since the 1990s, including laws governing civil rights and obligations, foreign investments, and economic and business activities. Most markedly, North Korea enacted the Civil Code in September 1990, as well as the Code of Civil Procedure and the Code of Civil Remedy.[56]

Although these laws recognize private ownership of certain properties such as personal properties and houses[57] and provide legal remedies for the breach of certain individual rights, the key principle of communism – that is, the limitation of private ownership of productive means – has not been removed altogether. According to the North Korean Constitution, only the state may own corporations, and no private ownership of a corporation, in whole or in part, is recognized.[58] The only exception is the foreign ownership of corporations allowed under the terms of relevant legislations.[59] Despite the initial successes in Russia in the 1920s and in North Korea in the 1950s and 1960s, the experiences of communist countries

54 It has been reported that a total of USD 1.2 billion was provided to North Korea between 1995 and 2002 for humanitarian support, including food, medicine, and medical supplies. Lee, Jong-Un, "Current Status of Humanitarian Support to North Korea by International Organizations and Future Assignments" (in Korean), *World Economy*, March 2003.

55 The North Korean regime is known to have recently deleted "communism" from its constitution, which is speculated to be related to the family succession of the position of the North Korea's leader, Kim Jong-il, to his son, Kim Jong-eun.

56 Supra note 6; North Korea also established a law school at its premier university, Kim Il Sung University, in 2001 to meet increasing legal demands in North Korea.

57 Provisions of the Civil Code allow a person to own a private home, household articles, daily necessaries, and other personal items, including automobiles, and also guarantee the right of inheritance (Article 63 of the Civil Code).

58 Supra note 6, Article 21, North Korean Constitution.

59 With the enactment of the Foreign Enterprise Law (1992), foreign individuals or enterprises are now allowed, under certain conditions, to establish and operate a business in North Korea.

in recent decades have clearly shown the limits of central communist economic planning, based on the ideology of "public" or "collective" ownership of property: economic efficiency and productivity remained low when private corporate ownership was not recognized and when private drive for economic enterprises was precluded.

Recognizing this difficulty, China, although still maintaining in its constitution the two pillars of the socialist economic management principle, collective ownership and community ownership, began to allow private ownership of corporations.[60] China first did this through the enactment of specific acts allowing private corporate ownership without amending the constitution,[61] which could have been politically sensitive and raised serious objections from the conservative communist sector. A similar pragmatic approach is found in Hong Kong with respect to land ownership: constitutionally, land could only be owned by the state, but de facto private ownership of land is allowed and protected under the provisions of specific acts.[62] Perhaps this approach could be adopted by North Korea to allow private ownership of productive means, such as corporations.

Recognition of private corporate ownership will be a key element for the successful economic development of North Korea.[63] Although state planning has played an important role in guiding the successful economic development of South Korea, it has by no means replaced the private drive for business enterprise, which is responsible for creating world-class industries and corporations such as Samsung and Hyundai. The South Korean development model presents an effective partnership between the public and private sectors, suggesting that the legal authorization and protection of private corporate ownership are important for increasing productivity and inducing economic development. A legal system that allows individuals to invest in or establish enterprises, grants certain rights to investors and managers of enterprises, and permits distribution of corporate profits as an incentive to enhance productivity is essential for successful economic development.

In addition to property ownership, laws governing enforcement of contracts are also important to reduce uncertainties associated with business activities in North Korea. Although the North Korean Civil Code recognizes debt,[64] it lacks detailed provisions that deal with cases of contractual breach. In an era in which virtually all

60 Y. S. Lee (2008), supra note 15, p. 30.

61 Ibid.

62 Ibid.

63 Dr. Petrov considers this point self-contradictory and something that cannot be taken seriously because North Korea is a communist state and therefore cannot recognize private ownership without damaging its social and economic foundation. Nonetheless, North Korea has, as noted earlier, recognized private ownership, albeit to a limited extent, of items such as houses and agricultural produce grown in small plots around houses. Because "communism" is no longer advocated as the guiding ideology under the constitution, the expansion of private ownership may be possible after North Korea's political leadership recognizes the necessity of economic development.

64 Part III, Civil Code, supra note 6.

business transactions are done through contracts, lack of remedies for contractual breaches and enforcement procedures are a major issue. The lack of land use rights is also of concern, particularly with respect to the foreign use of land in areas such as the KIC and in the event of assignment of such rights to a third party. Foreign investors may also have concerns as to compensation in the event of nationalization, the absence of fair and speedy dispute resolutions, and the complex administrative procedures for obtaining necessary licenses to operate a business in North Korea. Although North Korea has made considerable efforts to attract and protect foreign investments,[65] clearer and more detailed rules are necessary to resolve these concerns.

IV. CONCLUSION

The economic development of North Korea is vital if several issues that concern not only the country itself but also its neighbors are to be resolved. The first issue is the ongoing humanitarian crisis. The food crisis in North Korea in the late 1990s resulted in deaths of hundreds of thousands, many of whom were women and children. It also caused tens of thousands to flee the country. Many still live in northeast China and Mongolia without adequate food and shelter, often chased by border patrols and police forces, which upon capture will send them back to North Korea. Given the gravity of the circumstances, economic assistance must be provided for these people, preferably when they are still in North Korea, regardless of the West's unfavorable view of the country's regime. The only long-term solution to this human tragedy is the successful economic development of North Korea to ensure that its citizens can live with adequate food, shelter, and medical care.

The country's economic development would also help maintain the stability of the Northeast Asian region. Should the North Korean economy collapse completely, millions of refugees would be expected to cross the borders to secure food and safety, disrupting the stability of the region. North Korea reportedly demanded economic aid and a guarantee of the security of its regime as preconditions to discontinue its nuclear weapons production as required by the international community. Economic development would remove at least one element – an economic one – fueling

[65] The Foreign Investment Act (1992) allows a foreign investor to invest in various sectors, such as manufacturing industry, agriculture, construction, transport, telecommunications, science and technology, tourism, commerce, and financial services (Article 6). In addition, the act stipulates that the state particularly encourages investment in sectors that introduce modern technologies, produce internationally competitive goods, develop resources and promote infrastructure construction, and promote scientific research and technical development. Foreign-invested enterprises that invest and operate in these sectors shall receive preferential treatment, including the reduction of or exemption from income and other taxes, favorable conditions for land use, and the preferential supply of bank loans (Article 8). Additionally, the assets invested by foreign investors shall not be subject to nationalization (Article 19), and profits and other incomes earned by a foreign investor in its business may be remitted abroad (Article 20, Article 29 of the Foreign Exchange Control Act).

this dangerous nuclear game. Economic development would also be necessary to reduce the enormous cost that South Korea would have to bear in the event of reunification. For those who wish to see more democracy and freedom in North Korea, successful economic development would also be of benefit because, as history has shown, people with greater economic resources tend to take more interest in their political rights than those with inadequate resources, who must focus on their daily survival.[66]

The North Korean regime has made considerable efforts to improve its economy. Although the regime may not wish to open the country to the outside world to the extent that China has for fear that the inflow of outside information and influence may cause them to lose control over the population, measures can still be taken to embark on economic development. Given the weak purchasing power of the domestic population and the small domestic market, international trade is essential for successful economic development in North Korea. Cooperation with South Korea is a key factor because South Korea, with an interest in reunification, can provide the North with the necessary consumer market, capital resources, industrial technology, business managerial expertise, and, importantly, successful economic development know-how. With an educated labor force, significant production capacities, and the endowment of rich natural resources, North Korea is better equipped than many other developing countries to carry out successful economic development. It can be done particularly in partnership with South Korea, the economy of which can be augmented by North Korean resources, including its inexpensive labor force and natural resources.

The North–South economic partnership has been attempted with the KIC, and it has achieved considerable success as evidenced by the successful operation of South Korean factories in the North for the past several years. If North Korea cannot completely "open" the country to the outside in the near future, it may nonetheless consider expanding the KIC and building additional "industrial parks" to attract more South Korean and other foreign companies. Legal protections and certainties must be guaranteed to foreign investors, including those from South Korea, to ensure security and efficient operation of their businesses. Private corporate ownership should be allowed for North Koreans so that their talents and drive may be deployed to increase national productivity, which is essential for successful economic development. The underlying prerequisite to successful development is the establishment of peaceful and cooperative relations with South Korea and the West, including the United States. North Korea can then divert its considerable military spending to its economic development and be accepted into the international community as a peaceful and contributing member. This would allow international

[66] Cambridge economist Dr. Ha-Joon Chang noted that democracy tends to be promoted as a result of economic development. Ha-Joon Chang, *Kicking Away the Ladder* (London: Anthem Press, 2002), chap. 3.

institutions such as the World Bank to provide support for North Korea's economic development.[67]

REFERENCES

Beck, Peter M., "Contemplating Korean Reunification," *Wall Street Journal*, January 4, 2010, available at: http://online.wsj.com/article/SB10001424052748704340304574635180086832934.html.

Black, A. C., "After the Fall," *Swans*, March 22, 2000.

Central Intelligence Agency, *World Factbook* 2003, North Korea.

______, *World Factbook 2010*, North Korea, available at http://www.cia.gov/library/publications/the-world-factbook/geos/kn.html

Chang, Ha-Joon, *Kicking Away the Ladder* (London: Anthem Press, 2002).

Choi, Y. H., and G. C. Oh, *The Current Affairs and Future Prospects of the Kaeseong Industrial Complex*, Policy Brief No. 17, Gyeonggi Research Institute (May 2009).

Goodby, James, "The Emerging Architecture for Security and Cooperation in Northeast Asia" (2008) 8(3) *Issues and Insights*.

Hong, Soon-Jik, "Evaluation on North Korea's Policy of Special Economic Zone and Success Cases" (2003) 40 *Study on Unification Issues*.

Kim, Hong Taek, "Economic Growth of North Korea: 1845–1995" (in Korean), *Study on Economic Development*.

Kim, Hugo W., "Did South Korea Choose the Best Growth Strategy and Can North Korea Follow the Lessons from the South?" (2002) 3(1) *The Journal of Korean Economy*.

Lee, Y. S., *Strategy for Economic Development in North Korea for the Establishment of Peace in the Korean Peninsula* (in Korean), report to the Ministry of Foreign Affairs and Trade of South Korea (2008).

Nanto, D. K., and E. Chanlett-Avery, *North Korea: Economic Leverage and Policy Analysis*, Congressional Research Service Report for Congress, January 22, 2010, available at: http://www.fas.org/sgp/crs/row/RL32493.pdf.

Noland, M., "North Korea's Failed Currency Reform," Op-ed for BBC Online, February 5, 2010.

Wolf, Charles, Jr., and Norman D. Levin, *Modernizing North Korea: Objectives, Method, and Application* (Rand Corporation, 2008).

World Health Organization, *WHO Country Cooperation Strategy 2004–2008 Democratic People's Republic of Korea*, June 2003.

Zhi, L., "Chinese Premier Meets Kim Jong IL," *Xinhua News*, May 7, 2010.

[67] Dr. Petrov notes the significant sovereign debt borne by North Korea (according to Dr. Petrov, between USD 12 and 24 billion) and cites its poor credit history, which resulted from default on foreign loans in the 1970s, as a disincentive for any international financial institutions, such as the World Bank, to provide development aid to North Korea. Although credit history is indeed important in the decision to provide future aid and credit extensions, the importance of North Korea's economic development – not only for the nation itself but also for the stabilization of the region as a whole – may well overweigh this credit consideration and justify provision of development aid.

16

Applying the "Specificity" Test in Countervailing Duty Cases in the Context of China's Foreign Investment Policies

Xiaojie Lu

I. INTRODUCTION

In constructing subsidy and countervailing duty (CVD) laws, the most difficult task is to distinguish between "legitimate" government activities on one hand, and trade distorting subsidies on the other. The difficulty can be inherent in light of the divergent views on the role of government involvement with industry and on the industrial policies of developing countries.[1] At present, the World Trade Organization (WTO) Agreement on Subsidies and Countervailing Measures (SCM) adopts the specificity requirement, which allows countervailing actions against government programs that aid local enterprises or industries in any manner that would harm foreign industries.[2]

It is believed that subsidies aimed at a specific industry for the sole purpose of helping domestic producers will distort markets and thus are more likely to be the types of subsidies that the General Agreement on Tariffs and Trade (GATT) was designed to discourage.[3] Because the specificity requirement is so important in relation to distinguishing the legitimate government activities and trade-distorting practices, the application and the interpretation of this requirement will determine how much latitude a WTO Member would consider in its policy making. It is thus not surprising to find heated debates on this subject, particularly with regard to the disputes between the United States and Canada concerning Canada's forestry

[1] See GATT Non-Official Report, *The "Leutwiler Report," Trade Policies for a Better Future, the GATT and the Uruguay Round* (1987). See also J. H. Jackson, W. J. Davey, and A. O. Sykes Jr., *Legal Problems of International Economic Relations* (St. Paul, MN: Thomson West, 2002), p. 767.

[2] See Article 2.1 of the SCM Agreement.

[3] See W. K. Wilcox, "GATT-Based Protection and the Definition of a Subsidy" (1998) 16 *Boston University International Law Journal* 155.

The author thanks Julia Ya Qin, James Li, Yong-Shik Lee, and Zhenmin Wang for their valuable observations and comments. In addition, the author thanks Zhenghui Leon Li and Jenny Cheung for their comments on the draft of the chapter. The views expressed in this chapter, as well as any errors and omissions, are solely those of the author.

policy[4] and between China and the United States on the specificity test of China's investment-inducing policy – the "Two Years Free, Three Years Half" program.[5]

According to China's Two Years Free, Three Years Half program, enterprises with a level of foreign investment not less than 25% are exempt from income tax in the first two profitable years and pay half of their applicable income tax rate for the following three years. The U.S. Department of Commerce (USDOC) ruled that the restricted application of the Two Free, Three Half program to a group of enterprises, that is, enterprises that satisfy the minimum foreign investment requirement, makes these tax subsidies specific as a matter of law.

The confirmative determination that the program is de jure specific, and thus "countervailable" raises several technical questions with respect to how to clarify the specificity requirement provided by the U.S. CVD laws and the WTO SCM Agreement. The determination also has broad policy implications for China, India, Vietnam, and other developing countries that adopt the similar investment-inducing policies.[6] Extending the CVD application to those foreign investment policies raises concerns as to the flexibility developing countries can enjoy in formulating their policies for social and economic development through the encouragement of foreign investment.

This study intends to shed light on the above-mentioned problems by reviewing the specificity requirement and its application in the WTO context and the U.S.

[4] See WTO Panel Report, *United States – Final Countervailing Duty Determination with Respect to Certain Softwood Lumber from Canada*, WT/DS257/R (August 29, 2003); WTO Appellate Body Report, *United States – Final Countervailing Duty Determination with Respect to Certain Softwood Lumber from Canada*, WT/DS257/AB/R (January 19, 2004); Panel Report, *United States – Final Countervailing Duty Determination with Respect to Certain Softwood Lumber from Canada Recourse by Canada to Article 21.5 (DS257)*, WT/DS257/RW (August 1, 2005); WTO Appellate Body Report, *United States – Final Countervailing Duty Determination with Respect to Certain Softwood Lumber from Canada Recourse by Canada to Article 21.5 of the DSU*, WT/DS257/AB/RW (December 5, 2005).

[5] The program is provided by China's Foreign Invested Enterprise and Foreign Enterprise Income Tax Law (hereinafter "FIE Tax Law"). In the recent Countervailing Duty Investigation concerning Coated Free Sheet Paper from the PRC (hereinafter "CFS Paper from China"), USDOC determined that the "Two Free/Three Half" program is a de jure specific subsidy on the grounds that it is granted to the specific enterprises – Foreign Invested Enterprises (hereinafter "FIEs"). See USDOC, *Preliminary Affirmative Countervailing Duty Determination: Coated Free Sheet Paper from the People's Republic of China*, 72 FR 17484 (April 9, 2007). *Final Determination in the Countervailing Duty Investigation of Coated Free Sheet from the People's Republic of China*, 72 FR 60645 (October 17, 2007) (Final Determination).

[6] India, Vietnam, and Laos have similar policies. See *Foreign Capital Utilization in China: Prospects and Future Strategy*, World Bank Report (World Bank Beijing Office, 2007). For instance, in India, firms investing in special economic zones are entitled to a fifteen-year income tax break consisting of a 100% exemption for the first five years, a 50% exemption for the second five years, and an exemption on a proportion of export profits for the final five years. See United Nations Conference on Trade and Development (UNCTAD), *FDI from Developing and Transition Economies: Implications for Development*, World Investment Report 38 (2006). ASEAN countries also believe the positive incentives made by the preferential tax policies. See WTO Working Group on the Relationship between Trade and Investment, *Communication from ASEAN*, WT/WGTI/W/41 (July 3, 1998).

CVD practices. The study consists of four parts. The first part is an overview of the specificity requirement set forth in the WTO SCM Agreement, including its definition, history, and application in several panel reports. The second part discusses its establishment in the U.S. CVD laws and inherent problems in the specificity requirement. The third part focuses on the CFS case and analyzes various flaws in the USDOC determination on the specificity test to the Two Free, Three Half program. The fourth part discusses, in a broader sense, the policy implications of the CFS case for developing countries. The study urges the administrative authority to conduct the specificity test carefully to maintain the balance between trade objectives and the autonomy of national development policies.

II. THE SPECIFICITY REQUIREMENT IN THE WTO SCM AGREEMENT

The WTO SCM Agreement includes important improvements on the Tokyo Round Subsidies Code[7] by explicitly defining an actionable subsidy. According to Article 1 of the SCM Agreement, an actionable subsidy, either under WTO dispute settlement procedures or in a domestic CVD proceeding, must have three elements: (a) "a financial contribution" by a government or any public body within the territory of a member; (b) "a benefit" conferred, and (c) be "specific." This section provides a brief overview of the specificity requirement in the WTO SCM Agreement, followed by an examination of the origin of the specificity requirement in WTO history, and then evaluates the panels' interpretation in certain WTO cases.

A. *Definition of the Specificity Requirement*

For the first time, the SCM Agreement introduced the concept of specificity into the context of multilateral trading system. Article 2 of the SCM Agreement provides that a subsidy must be specific to an enterprise or industry or group of enterprises or industries ("certain enterprises") within the jurisdiction of the granting authority to be actionable. For the purpose of determining the specificity of a subsidy, several principles apply.

If the legislation or the granting authority explicitly limits access to a subsidy to certain enterprises, the subsidy is specific.[8] This is often called de jure specificity.[9] However, Article 2 further provides that if eligibility is limited, based on explicit, verifiable, objective criteria (i.e., criteria or conditions that are neutral, do not

[7] See Agreement on Interpretation and Application of Article VI, XVI, and XXIII of the GATT, reprinted in GATT, *Basic Instruments and Selected Documents (BISD)* 9S/84–85, 21/79, 38S/73 (1980), 26th Supp.

[8] See Article 2.1 of the SCM Agreement.

[9] See Terence P. Stewart (ed.), *The GATT Uruguay Round: A Negotiating History (1989–1992)* (Kluwer Law International, 1993), p. 863. See also P. C. Mavroidis, P. A. Messerlin, and J. M. Wauters, *The Law and Economics of Contingent Protection in the WTO* (Cheltenham, England: Edward Elgar Publishing, 2008), p. 354.

favor certain enterprises over others, are economic in nature, and are horizontal in application), the program is not specific as long as eligibility is automatic and the criteria are strictly adhered to.[10]

Even if the subsidy appears to be nonspecific, a WTO Member may determine whether the subsidy is de facto specific[11] if there are reasons to believe that the subsidy may in fact be specific.[12] In doing so, the investigating authority may consider the following factors:

- use of a subsidy program by a limited number of certain enterprises,
- predominant use by certain enterprises,
- the granting of disproportionately large amounts of subsidy to certain enterprises, and
- the manner in which discretion has been exercised by the granting authority in the decision to grant a subsidy.

Specifically, Article 2 provides that in determining de facto specificity, the investigating authority should also take into account the extent of diversification of economic activities within the jurisdiction of the granting authority, as well as the length of time during which the subsidy program has been in operation.[13] Article 2.2 states that a subsidy that is limited to certain enterprises located within a designated geographic region within the jurisdiction of the granting authority shall be specific. Article 2.3 states that all export subsidies and import substitution subsidies within the meaning of Article 3 of the SCM Agreement are automatically deemed to be specific.

Finally, Article 2.4 requires that any determination of specificity shall be clearly substantiated on the basis of positive evidence. It means the investigating authority should presume nonspecificity unless positive evidence of specificity is provided. Thus, the investing authority bears the burden of proof on the specific test.

B. *The History of the Specificity Test in the SCM Agreement*

GATT Article VI and Article XVI illustrate the rules for subsidies and countervailing duties. Article VI contains general rules governing the application of countervailing duties. According to Article VI, for a countervailing duty action to be authorized, the effect of the subsidization must cause or threaten material injury to an established domestic industry or materially slow down the establishment of a domestic industry. Article XVI contains general provisions on subsidies, of which the main purpose is to encourage notification of and consultation on the use of subsidies. It requires parties to notify the GATT of any subsidies that affect imports or exports and to

[10] Article 2.1(b) of the SCM Agreement.

[11] Supra note 9. See also WTO Panel Report, *United States-Softwood Lumber IV*, para. 7.116.

[12] Article 2.1(c) of the SCM Agreement.

[13] Ibid.

consult with any parties whose interests are threatened by or are suffering serious prejudice from such subsidies. Neither of the provisions set out the concept of subsidies or distinguishes legitimate government activities from trade-distorting subsidies. Additionally, the injury requirement does not affect the administration of countervailing duty laws that were already in existence at the time of the signing of the GATT by virtue of the grandfather clause in the Protocol of Provisional Acceptance. This left the U.S. government "free to countervail without demonstrable economic justification."[14]

The amendment of Article XVI in 1955 singled out export subsidies, prohibiting the use of an export subsidy on nonprimary products as of January 1, 1958. An illustrative list of export subsidies was developed to aid parties in interpreting the provisions in the final amendment of Article XVI in 1960. Those amendments acknowledged that export subsidies and domestic subsidies affected trade differently.

Nevertheless, more effort was and still is required to distinguish successfully the widely used specific domestic subsidies because, for most nations, domestic subsidies are frequently used as important instruments for achieving sound social and economic policy objectives. It would be a mistake to apply countervailing duties against domestic subsidies indiscriminately. Negotiations in the later Tokyo Round recognized this and elucidated that contracting parties "do not intend to restrict the right of signatories to use such subsidies to achieve these and other important policy objectives which they consider desirable."[15] If some domestic subsidies are going to be countervailable and others are not, a mechanism is required to distinguish between the "good" and the "bad" domestic subsidies. Accordingly, the Tokyo Round Subsidies Code picks out the subsidies granted "*regionally or by sector*" "with the aim of giving an advantage to *certain enterprises*" and suggests these forms of subsidies be reviewed periodically.[16] However, further clarification on the concept of subsidy was not made in the Tokyo Round negotiations because of the conflict between the United States and other countries.[17] In addition, like other Tokyo Round codes, the Subsidies Code was a side code, which only binds the adopting countries, leaving nonsignatories uncommitted to the disciplines.[18] Nevertheless, the foregoing provisions in the Tokyo Round Subsidies Code were one of the first attempts to distinguish legitimate government activities and trade-distorting subsidies.

Unlike the Tokyo Round Code, the Uruguay Round SCM binds all members as an integral part of the WTO. It also contains a definition of subsidy and introduces the concept of a "specific" subsidy – for the most part, a subsidy available only to an enterprise or industry or group of enterprises or industries within the jurisdiction

14 M. J. Trebilcock and R. Howse, *The Regulation of International Trade* (New York: Routledge, 2005), p. 254n22.

15 See Article XI of the Tokyo Round Subsidies Code, para. 1.

16 Ibid., para. 3.

17 See Trebilcock and Howse (2005), supra note 14, p. 254.

18 Ibid.

of the authority granting the subsidy. Only specific subsidies may be subject to the countervailing duty actions taken by other WTO Members.[19]

The specificity requirement mechanism introduced during the Uruguay Round was previously only used in the United States. U.S. CVD laws date back to 1879 and were amended several times through the Tariff Act of 1930, the Trade Act of 1974, and other legislation.[20] Not until the Trade Agreement Act of 1979, however, was the specificity requirement added to U.S. laws. It limits the classification of the countervailable domestic subsidy to those that are provided "to a specific enterprise or industry, or group of enterprises or industries,"[21] From then on, the specificity requirement has been an important and pivotal concept in the U.S. administration's application of countervailing duties, on which there is considerable jurisprudence both at the administrative level and in court appeals from administrative determinations.[22] A series of cases that relied on the specificity requirement have been developed into a "de facto specificity test" by not only looking at whom the subsidy was intended to benefit but also whom the subsidy benefited in practice.[23]

It should be noted that the specificity requirement in U.S. law constrained the U.S. government in using CVDs and imposed more constrained obligations than required by the international rules (i.e., the Tokyo Round Subsidies Code).[24] One may question the policy grounds supporting the specificity requirement. As noted earlier, subsidies are widely used instruments for governments to achieve certain social and economic policy goals. If a subsidy is generally available to all society and all manufacturing sectors, can one impose CVD against it merely because of its minimal and incidental trade-distorting effect? Some scholars maintain that the specificity test minimizes the distortive economic effects of CVDs by separating subsidies that distort economic efficiency from those that do not.[25]

On the other hand, part of the rationale for the specificity test is that it is useful as a tool of administration to oust a number of cases that should not to be brought into the process of countervailing duty or other international rules.[26] Because all industries in every country receive some direct or indirect government benefits, a practical limit on the number of CVD actions is necessary to eliminate the "actionable" subsidies of general activities undertaken by various governments.

19 See GATT, *Focus Newsletter* (December 1993), pp. 10–11.

20 See Wilcox, supra note 3, p. 135.

21 See 19 USC 1677(5A).

22 See John H. Jackson, *The World Trading System* (Cambridge, MA: MIT Press, 1995), p. 267.

23 See, generally, *PPG Indus., Inc. v. United States*, 928 F.2d 1568, 1571–72 (Fed. Cir. 1986) (following the test created by the court in Cabot Corp.); *Cabot Corp. v. United States*, 620 F. Supp. 722 (Ct. Int'l Trade 1985) (adopting the case by case de facto specificity test).

24 Tokyo Round Subsidies Code provided no specificity requirement for the subsidy determination.

25 James D. Southwick, "The Lingering Problem with the Specificity Test in United States Countervailing Duty Law" (1988) 72 *Minnesota Law Review* 1174.

26 See Jackson, supra note 22, p. 268.

At the beginning when it was introduced to the countervailing investigations, the specificity requirement was not itself free from controversies. The Court of International Trade in the *Bethlehem Steel* case criticized it because it denied American producers protection from imports receiving a government advantage solely on the grounds that the program conferring the advantage was generally available in the competitor's country.[27] In response to similar cases involving natural resource subsidies, members of the U.S. Congress suggested to allow CVD against generally available natural resource programs that discarded the specificity requirement.[28] However, concerns that mirror legislation by other countries would damage U.S. exports if the related country discontinued adherence to the specificity test strongly influenced the Congress's decision not to pass bills eliminating the test.[29]

C. *Inherent Problems in the Concept*

Although the specificity requirement was well-established in U.S. countervailing law and the SCM Agreement, both the U.S. courts and WTO panels have had trouble interpreting it. This is mostly because of the deliberately sketchy language.[30] No guidance was provided with respect to what constitutes a specific enterprise or industry and "group of enterprises or industries." As discussed in the following paragraphs, it remains unclear in several respects, which makes the requirement difficult to apply in practice.

First, in what sense could enterprises or industries be characterized as specific? Does sector-specific, capital-specific, employment-specific, or technology-specific matter when "specific" is examined? Generally, if benefits are conferred according to specified criteria rather than to enterprises or industries in specific sectors, the USDOC will not directly determine the program as a de jure specific subsidy. It will further examine whether the criteria are neutrally or automatically applied rather than at the government's discretion.[31] Specified criteria can be enterprises with "an unemployment level of six or more percent,"[32] projects that introduce new energy-saving technology,[33] projects for pollution control,[34] or companies that employ manual laborers.[35]

[27] *Bethlehem Steel Corp. v. United States*, 590 F. Supp. 1237 (Ct. Int'l Trade 1984), pp. 1241–1245.

[28] See Southwick (1988), supra note 25, p. 1165. See also *Dual Pricing of Natural Resources*, Hearing before the Subcommittee on International Trade of the Comm. on Finance of the United States Senate, 99th Cong., 2d Sess. (1986), p. 39.

[29] Southwick (1988), supra note 25, p. 1159n3.

[30] See Gary N. Horlick et al., *The Countervailability of Subsidies: Specificity*, 372 PLI/COMM 35 (December 2, 1985), p. 44.

[31] See *Certain Steel Products from the Federal Republic of Germany*, 47 Fed. Reg. 39,345, 39,350 (1982).

[32] See Horlick et al. (1985), supra note 30, p. 38.

[33] See *Certain Steel Products from the Netherlands*, 47 Fed. Reg. 39, 372 (1982).

[34] See *Certain Steel Products from France*, 47 Fed. Reg. 39,340 (1982), Comment 4.

[35] See *Certain Steel Products from Belgium*, 47 Fed. Reg. 39,304, 39,309, 39,311 (1982), Comment 10.

Second, what constitutes an "industry" for the purpose of finding specificity? For instance, is a domestic subsidy that is available to the entire agricultural sector nonspecific because there are a number of agriculture subsectors (grain, beef, etc.), and thus agriculture is broad enough to be considered "nonspecific"?[36] The enquiry is also related to the broadness of "group." If a domestic subsidy is conferred to some disparate, but not all, industries, how many disparate industries can be categorized as a "group of . . . industries," or is the grouping is too large? The USDOC has determined that duty deferral to twenty-four disparate industries designated by the Korea Ministry of Finance was not limited to a specific industry or group of industries.[37]

Because the countervailing duty laws provide no guidance with regard to these issues, it leaves the investigation authority with considerable latitude in the assessment of targeting industries. As Horlick once pointed out, "arguably the statutory language on its face would allow Commerce to avoid countervailing any program that applied to the industry under investigation and just a few additional industries (or group of industries). On the other hand, arguably it would enable Commerce to countervail programs that applied to all industries in a particular country but one."[38]

Because the specificity requirement in Article 2 of the SCM Agreement tracks the practices conducted by the USDOC, it gives no guidance on the interpretation of the requirement as it is in the U.S. practices. In the WTO dispute settlement practice regarding the requirement, the issue with respect to specificity is how to establish in practice that the range of beneficiaries of a subsidy is "specific" to "certain enterprises" as opposed to "nonspecific." The term "certain enterprises" refers to "an enterprise or industry or group of enterprises or industries." As a consequence, the identification of an "industry" may be important in establishing specificity in particular cases.[39]

In *United States – Subsidies on Upland Cotton*, the panel noted that "an industry, or group of 'industries,' may be generally referred to by the type of products they produce."[40] The panel found that certain measures at issue were or are available specifically in respect of upland cotton, and these subsidies are "specific" because they are not even available in respect of a number of commodities. However, in *United States – Softwood Lumber IV*, the panel noted that "industry" is defined as "a particular form or branch of productive labor; a trade, a manufacture," and the term "industry" in Article 2 is not used to refer to enterprises producing specific goods or end products.[41] It suggests that the text of Article 2 does not require a detailed analysis of the end products produced by the enterprises involved, nor does it provide that

36 Jackson (1995), supra note 26, p. 269.
37 See 49 Fed. Reg. 46,776 (1984).
38 See Horlick et al. (1985), supra note 30, p. 44.
39 See World Trade Report 2006, p. 198.
40 See *Panel Report, United States – Subsidies on Upland Cotton*, WT/DS267/R (September 8, 2004), paras. 7.1138 and 7.1142.
41 See *Panel Report, United States – Final Countervailing Duty Determination with Respect to Certain Softwood Lumber from Canada*, WT/DS257/R (August 29, 2003), para.7. 119–120.

only a limited number of products should benefit from the subsidy. Thus, the "wood products industries," consisting of the pulp and paper mills and the sawmills and remanufacturers that produce the subject merchandise, used the stumpage programs and were considered by the panel to constitute at most a limited group of industries. However, neither of the panel reports were reviewed by the Appellate Body. The jurisprudence on specificity requirement remains to be limited.

III. SPECIFICITY OF THE TWO FREE, THREE HALF TAX PROGRAM IN THE CFS CASE

The United States previously maintained a long-standing policy of not applying the CVD law to nonmarket economies, including China.[42] However, on November 20, 2006, the USDOC initiated a CVD investigation on imports of coated free sheet (CFS) paper from China.[43] The case is a striking one because it is the first CVD investigation against the imports from China since 1991.[44] Since the CFS Case, many CVD investigations have been initiated against the products originating from China (see Table 16.1).

After nearly one year of investigation, on October 17, 2007, USDOC made a final determination that several subsidies being provided by the Chinese government to producers and exporters of CFS paper are countervailable.[45] The case came to an end without a CVD order because the International Trade Commission (ITC) found no injury to the U.S. industry.[46] Nevertheless, USDOC's policy on the specificity of the Two Free, Three Half program was followed in the subsequent investigations initiated against China's products.[47]

42 Ibid.

43 In the CFS Case, the USDOC selected the two largest, Gold East Paper (Jiangsu) Co. Ltd. (Gold East) and Shandong Chenming Paper Holdings Ltd. (Chenming), as the mandatory respondents, among thirteen Chinese CFS paper producers/exporters alleged by the petitioner, NewPage Corporation. See USDOC, *Final Determination in the Countervailing Duty Investigation of Coated Free Sheet from the People's Republic of China*, 72 FR 60645 (October 17, 2007).

44 U.S. GAO, *US-China Trade: Commerce Faces Practical and Legal Challenges in Applying Countervailing Duties*, GAO-050474, Report to Congressional Committees (Washington, DC, June 2005).

45 See USDOC, *Final Determination in the Countervailing Duty Investigation of Coated Free Sheet from the People's Republic of China*, 72 FR 60645 (October 17, 2007).

46 ITC, *Coated Free Sheet Paper from China, Indonesia, and Korea*, Investigation No. 701-TA-444–446 (Final) and 731-TA-1107–1109 (Final) (Publication No. 3965; December 2007).

47 See, e.g., *Issues and Decision Memorandum for Final Determination in the Countervailing Duty Investigation of Raw Flexible Magnets from the People's Republic of China*, 73 FR 39667 (July 10, 2008), p. 21; *Issues and Decision Memorandum for the Final Determination in the Countervailing Duty Investigation of Lightweight Thermal Paper from the People's Republic of China*, 73 FR 57329 (October 2, 2008), p. 16; *Issues and Decision Memorandum for the Final Determination in the Countervailing Duty Investigation of Citric Acid and Certain Citrate Salts From the People's Republic of China*, 74 FR 16836 (April 13, 2009), p. 15; *Issues and Decision Memorandum for the Final Determination in the Countervailing Duty Investigation of Certain Oil Country Tubular Goods From the People's Republic of China*, 74 FR 64045 (December 7, 2009), p. 16.

TABLE 16.1. *U.S. Countervailing Duty Investigations against the Products Originated from China (through November 18, 2010)*

	Products	Initiation	Preliminary injury determination	Preliminary subsidization determination	Final subsidization determination	Final injury determination
1	Coated Free Sheet Paper	10/31/06	Confirmative	Confirmative	Confirmative	*Negative*
2	Standard Pipe	07/05/07	Confirmative	Confirmative	Confirmative	Confirmative
3	Light-walled Rectangular Pipe and Tube	07/24/07	Confirmative	Confirmative	Confirmative	Confirmative
4	Laminated Woven Sacks	07/25/07	Confirmative	Confirmative	Confirmative	Confirmative
5	Off-the-Road Tires	08/07/07	Confirmative	Confirmative	Confirmative	Confirmative
6	Raw Flexible Magnets	10/18/07	Confirmative	Confirmative	Confirmative	Confirmative
7	Lightweight Thermal Paper	11/02/07	Confirmative	Confirmative	Confirmative	Confirmative
8	Sodium Nitrite	12/05/07	Confirmative	Confirmative	Confirmative	Confirmative
9	Circular Welded Austenitic Stainless Pressure Pipe	02/25/08	Confirmative	Confirmative	Confirmative	Confirmative
10	Circular Welded Carbon Quality Steel Line Pipe	04/29/08	Confirmative	Confirmative	Confirmative	Confirmative
11	Citric Acid and Certain Citrates Salts	05/13/08	Confirmative	Confirmative	Confirmative	Confirmative
12	Tow-Behind Lawn Groomers and Parts	07/21/08	Confirmative	Confirmative	Confirmative	Confirmative
13	Certain Kitchen Appliance Shelving and Racks	08/26/08	Confirmative	Confirmative	Confirmative	Confirmative
14	Certain Oil Country Tubular Goods	05/05/09	Confirmative	Confirmative	Confirmative	Confirmative
15	Prestressed Concrete Steel Wire Strand	06/23/09	Confirmatve	Confirmatve	Confirmatve	Confirmatve
16	Certain Steel Grating	06/25/09	Confirmative	Confirmatve	Confirmatve	Confirmatve
17	Wire Decking	07/02/09	Confirmative	Confirmatve	Confirmatve	*Negative*
18	Narrow Woven Ribbons with Woven Selvedge	08/06/09	Confirmative	Confirmatve	Confirmatve	Confirmatve
19	Certain Magnesia Carbon Bricks	08/25/09	Confirmatve	Confirmatve	Confirmatve	Confirmatve
20	Seamless Carbon and Alloy Steel Standard, Line, and Pressure Pipe	10/14/09	Confirmative	Confirmatve	Confirmatve	TBD
21	Certain Coated Paper	10/20/09	Confirmative	Confirmatve	TBD	TBD
22	Certain Standard Steel Fasteners	10/22/09	*Negative*			
23	Certain Sodium and Potassium Phosphate Salts	10/23/09	Confirmative	Confirmatve	Confirmatve	Confirmatve
24	Drill Pipe	01/27/10	Confirmatve	Confirmatve	TBD	TBD
25	Aluminum Extrusions	04/27/10	Confirmatve	Confirmatve	TBD	TBD

TBD = to be decided.

Source: Compiled by the authors from the U.S. Department of Commerce statistics, available at: http://ia.ita.doc.gov/stats/inv-initiations-2000-current.html.

The alleged subsidies include three groups: Government Policy Lending Program,[48] Income Tax Program,[49] and VAT (value added tax) and Duty Exemption Program.[50] The Two Free, Three Half program is in the second group, which was determined as specific in law and thus countervailable.[51]

The Two Free, Three Half program was one of the most common incentives in China for the purpose of attracting foreign investment. It was also a popular investment-inducing policy adopted by other developing countries.[52] The program was established in the former Foreign Invested Enterprise and Foreign Enterprise Income Tax Law (FIE Tax Law) enacted in 1991. According to Article 8 of the FIE Tax Law, productive FIEs that were scheduled to operate not less than ten years were exempt from income tax in their first two profitable years and pay half of their applicable tax rate for the following three years.[53] The tax holiday started with the first profitable year after the enterprise had commenced operation, and earlier losses have been carried forward and set off against profits.

The Two Free, Three Half program applies to productive FIEs in numerous sectors, including the following:[54]

1. Machine manufacturing and electronics industries;
2. Energy resource industries (not including exploitation of oil and natural gas);
3. Metallurgical, chemical and building material industries;
4. Light industries, and textiles and packaging industries;
5. Medical equipment and pharmaceutical industries;
6. Agriculture, forestry, animal husbandry, fisheries and water conservation;
7. Construction industries;

[48] The USDOC determined that all loans provided to the CFS paper manufacturing enterprises by Policy Banks and State-Owned Commercial Banks in the People's Republic of China constitute government-provided loans. See USDOC, *Final Determination in the Countervailing Duty Investigation of Coated Free Sheet from the People's Republic of China*, 72 FR 60645 (October 17, 2007), Comment 8.

[49] Income Tax Programs in this case include the "Two Free, Three Half" Program, reduced tax rate for FIE's based on location, local income tax exemption for "productive FIEs." See Ibid.

[50] VAT and Duty Exemption Program in this case include VAT rebates on purchases of domestically produced equipment, VAT and tariff exemptions on imported equipment, and Domestic VAT Refunds for companies located in the Hainan Economic Development Zone. See Ibid.

[51] See USDOC, *Final Determination in the Countervailing Duty Investigation of Coated Free Sheet from the People's Republic of China*, 72 FR 60645 (October 17, 2007), Comment 14.

[52] Supra, note 6, p. 7, 24. See communication from ASEAN.

[53] See Article 8 of the Income Tax Law of the People's Republic of China of Foreign Investment Enterprise and Foreign Enterprises, promulgated by the National People's Congress on April 9, 1991.

[54] See Article 72 of the Detailed Implementation Rules of the Income Tax Law of the People's Republic of China of Foreign Investment Enterprise and Foreign Enterprises.

8. Communications and transportation industries (not including passenger transport);
9. Development of science and technology, geological survey and industrial information consultancy directly for services in respect of production and services in respect of repair and maintenance of production equipment and precision instruments;
10. Other industries as specified by the tax authorities under the State Council.

Item 10 was clarified in another regulation promulgated by the State Administration of Taxation in 1992, stating that[55] the following foreign invested enterprises (FIEs), engaging in the following categories of business, shall be regarded as manufacturing FIEs:

(1) construction, installation, assembly engineering design and providing services to engineering projects (including consultation services);
(2) consultation services refer to, for improving performance, efficiency, quality and so forth, providing technical assistance or technical guidance to the reform of the current manufacturing technology of a project construction or enterprise, or the improvement of manufacturing and operation management or technology selection, or the current equipment or products of an enterprise;
(3) stock breeding, livestock breeding (including marine product breeding), crop farming (including flower farming), fowl breeding, dog breeding, cat breeding and so forth;
(4) scientific research and development in connection with manufacturing technology; and
(5) providing storage and transportation services using self-owned transportation vehicles and storage facilities.

Thus, China granted foreign investors lower corporate tax rates relative to domestic investors in nearly all manufacturing sectors of the country.

Although the Two Free, Three Half program was removed from the new Enterprise Income Tax Law of China (EITL) that took effect on January 1, 2008, it will continue to be subject to USDOC's examination in the CVD investigations. The EITL provides the transition period for FIEs incorporated before March 16, 2007, and lasts for five years, until 2012.[56] In other words, the enterprises that previously enjoy the Two Free, Three Half program may, after the implementation of the EITL,

[55] See Notice of State Administration of Taxation on the Interpretation of Productive Foreign Investment Enterprises in Other Industries (No. 109 [1992] of State Administration of Taxation).

[56] See Notice of the State Council on the Implementation of the Transitional Preferential Policies in respect of Enterprise Income Tax (No. 39 [2007] of the State Council).

continue to enjoy the relevant preferential treatments and the time period prescribed in the prior laws and regulations until the expiration of the said time period.[57]

B. *USDOC's Position and an Evaluation*

In the Preliminary Determination, USDOC found that the Two Free, Three Half program is specific in law because it is only applicable to FIEs.[58] In this regard, the Government of China (GOC) argued that FIEs are a distinct business form and are taxed differently from other forms of businesses in the country. Moreover, 80% of FIEs that operated in a wide variety of industries were "productive FIEs" eligible for the Two Free, Three Half program.[59]

USDOC in the Final Determination disagreed with GOC's characterization of its finding. To USDOC, the determinative factor for this specificity test is not the corporate forms but the foreign ownership of FIEs. The restriction of the program to enterprises with foreign investments (at least 25% in the case of an equity venture) makes the subsidies specific as a matter of law under the U.S. law. Using the subsection (i) of 771 5(A)(D) of the 1930 Tariff Act as a basis for finding specificity,[60] the USDOC decided not to reach the issue of whether the programs are governed by well-established and transparent criteria (subsection (ii)), or whether the benefits are de facto specific (subsection (iii)).

The comment on the specificity test by the USDOC is far from detailed. USDOC found that the foreign ownership requirement was sufficient enough to constitute a de jure specificity, without providing any economic rationale or other legitimate policy considerations to justify its evaluation. Furthermore, USDOC's analysis has a technical problem: whether it is appropriate for USDOC to decide not to continue the analysis of determining whether the criteria of programs are well-established and transparent. This is related to the relationship between SCM Agreement Article 2.1(a) and Article 2.1(b).

The problem with Article 2.1(a) is, in what sense could enterprises or industries be characterized as a group and thus specific? The *Concise Oxford Dictionary* defines "group" as "a number of . . . things . . . classed together." To be classified as "a group," that group of enterprises or industries must share some common characteristics. Therefore, a group of enterprises or industries is always distinct from all the other enterprises or industries in an economy.

[57] If such an enterprise has not yet enjoyed the preferential treatments as a result of its failure to make profits, its preferential time period shall be calculated from 2008. Ibid.

[58] See *Preliminary Affirmative Countervailing Duty Determination: Coated Free Sheet Paper from the People's Republic of China*, 72 FR 17484 (April 9, 2007).

[59] USDOC, *Final Determination in the Countervailing Duty Investigation of Coated Free Sheet from the People's Republic of China*, 72 FR 60645 (October 17, 2007), p. 84.

[60] See Section 771(5)(A)(D)(i) of the Tariff Act of 1930 as amended by the Uruguay Round Agreements Act effective January 1, 1995.

According to Article 2.1(b), if "objective criteria or conditions" are governing the eligibility for a subsidy, the authorities have the obligation to examine whether the eligibility is "automatic" and whether such objective criteria or conditions both are strictly adhered to and are clearly spelled out in law, regulation, or other official document. Only if such objective criteria or conditions fail to meet these requirements could the authorities find a de jure specificity and complete the specificity test.

GOC contended that the "productive FIE" status in the Two Free, Three Half program is conferred and governed by well-established and transparent criteria.[61] In fact, whether an enterprise can benefit from the program depends on two conditions: "productive" and "foreign investment." However, USDOC determined the Two Free, Three Half program as a de jure specific industry solely on the basis of the level of foreign ownership. The refusal to examine whether the program is governed by well-established and transparent criteria creates an ambiguous legislative distinction between Article 2.1(a) and Article 2.1(b) of the SCM Agreement.

A more important problem with USDOC's analysis goes to the heart of the specificity test: what does "specific" mean? Can ownership-specific be characterized as meeting the specificity requirement provided by the WTO SCM Agreement?

IV. ARE OWNERSHIP-SPECIFIC SUBSIDIES COUNTERVAILABLE?

According to Article 2.1 of the SCM Agreement, specific subsidies are those available to an enterprise or industry or group of enterprises or industries. Article 2 does not define what constitutes an "industry" for the purpose of identifying domestic subsidies, nor does it provide any guidance about what constitutes a "group" of enterprises or industries for the specificity test.

WTO panels usually apply the Vienna Convention on the Law of Treaties (VCLT) to interpret WTO agreements.[62] According to Article 31(1) of VCLT, a treaty is to be interpreted "in good faith in accordance with the ordinary meaning to be given to the terms of the treaty in their context and in the light of its object and purpose." To answer the question of whether ownership-specific subsidies meet the specificity requirement provided by Article 2.1 of the SCM Agreement, we should begin by examining the ordinary meaning of key terms used in Article 2.1.

To identify the ordinary meaning, WTO Panels usually start with the dictionary definitions of the terms to be interpreted. In the CFS case, the key word that needs to be interpreted is the word "group" in Article 2.1. As noted in the previous part, the *Concise Oxford Dictionary* gives the meaning of "group" as "a number of . . . things . . . classed together." However, if we examine the wording in its context, especially taking account of the existence of Article 2.2(b), the meaning of "group"

[61] USDOC (2007), supra note 59, p. 85.

[62] See WTO Appellate Body Report, *United States – Standards for Reformulated and Conventional Gasoline*, WT/DS2/AB/R, adopted April 29, 1996, p. 23.

is not that simple. It echoes the Appellate Body's opinion in several cases that "dictionaries, alone, are not necessarily capable of resolving complex questions of interpretation."[63]

As we examined in the previous part, the existence of Article 2.2(b) suggests that a subsidy provided to a group of enterprises or industries according to objective criteria and conditions is not de jure specific. Footnote 2 to Article 2 defines such objective criteria or conditions as "criteria or conditions which are neutral, which do not favour certain enterprises over others, and which are economic in nature and *horizontal in application*, such as the number of employees or size of enterprise." It seems to suggest that the sector-targeting subsidies and sector-horizontally applied subsidies are discretely thus distinguishable.

Moreover, "supplementary means of interpretation, including the preparatory work of the treaty and the circumstances of its conclusion"[64] also confirm that the wording of "group" is to some extent related to certain sectors. The negotiating history of the SCM Agreement reflects the concern of the negotiators that "the existing international trade rules do not adequately address the trade damage that can result from industrial targeting programs."[65] The negotiators shared the common understanding that generally available subsidies are not countervailable because they are not the result of sector-specific government intervention and thus do not benefit particular industries.[66]

The examination of the negotiation history shows that the negotiators wanted to discipline sector-specific subsidies more stringently. Therefore, the level of foreign ownership alone cannot determine the specificity of a subsidy. USDOC's allegations that tax incentives granted to foreign investment enterprises are specific and thus countervailable cannot be justified by the context and the negotiating history of the SCM Agreement.

However, if we accept that the incentives given to foreign investment enterprises are countervailable, it will be inconsistent with the common practice adopted by the WTO system with respect to foreign investment policies. With such a multilateral trading system, the coverage of WTO agreements is not extended to all foreign investment policy issues. In fact, governments are unwilling to subject their investment policies to international rules at the creation of the GATT. They prefer to develop investment rules primarily at the bilateral level.[67]

[63] See Appellate Body Report, *United States – Softwood Lumber IV*, para. 59; Appellate Body Report, *Canada – Aircraft*, para. 153; and Appellate Body Report, *EC – Asbestos*, para. 92.

[64] See Article 32 of VCLT.

[65] See GATT, *Checklist for Issues for Negotiations*, MTN.GNG/NG10/W/9/Rev.2 (December 2, 1987), p. 8.

[66] Ibid., p. 10.

[67] See United Nations Development Programme, *Making Global Trade Work for the Poor* (New York: UNDP, 2002), p. 237.

Although no comprehensive international investment agreement currently exists, several WTO agreements deal with limited aspects of investment. The investment rules in the WTO system are far from complete and systematic. Different rules apply to different sectors. For example, the Agreement on Trade-Related Investment Measures relates to investment in the manufacturing sector, focusing on discriminatory investment measures such as certain performance requirements over imported and exported goods and local content requirements. The General Agreement on Trade in Services relates, inter alia, to investment in specific services sector through the establishment of certain rules governing market access and treatment of foreign investment. The Agreement on Trade-Related Aspects of Intellectual Property Rights has an investment dimension – but only indirectly – given that increasing shares of corporate investments are intangible assets such as brands, patents, and trademarks, whereas the SCM Agreement concerns subsidies but not other investment-related measures. This is mainly because the negotiations in the Uruguay Round were not intended to deal with the regulation of investment as such.[68] What the negotiators were concerned with was how to "elaborate, as appropriate, further provisions that may be necessary to avoid such adverse effects on trade."

Therefore, the WTO rules extend only to a relatively narrow range of investment measures that have a direct and immediately identifiable impact on trade. They also reflect a common understanding that what concerns the current WTO system is not the ownership of traders but the market structure in which traders operate.[69] The foreign-ownership-based specificity test, therefore, is a departure from the general position regarding foreign investment policies maintained by the WTO. Not only does it inappropriately add to the obligation of WTO Members provided in the covered agreements, it also constrains the policy autonomy developing countries can reserve on their investment policy-making power.

V. POLICY IMPLICATIONS FOR DEVELOPING COUNTRIES AND CONCLUSIONS

Foreign investment incentives exist in many countries. However, unlike many developed countries, some developing countries have adopted differential corporate

[68] The Punta del Este Ministerial Declaration, which launched the Uruguay Round, included the subject of trade-related investment measures as a subject for the new round through a carefully drafted compromise: "Following an examination of the operation of GATT Articles related to the trade-restrictive and trade-distorting effects of investment measures, negotiations should elaborate, as appropriate, further provisions that may be necessary to avoid such adverse effects on trade." See *Ministerial Declaration of the Uruguay Round*, GATT/1396 (September 25, 1986).

[69] See Aaditya Mattoo, "Dealing with Monopolies and State Enterprises: WTO Rules for Goods and Services," in T. Cottier and P. C. Mavroidis (eds.), *State Trading in the Twenty-First Century* (Ann Arbor: The University of Michigan Press, 1998).

income tax codes for domestic and foreign firms. The reason is not difficult to explain. Many factors in host countries influence the decision of foreign investors, such as infrastructure, transportation, financial services, and the existence of a transparent and stable legal infrastructure. However, it may be hard for developing countries to improve these factors without abundant capital. Thus, at the earlier stage of attracting foreign investment, general tax incentives available to foreign investment are perceived as a useful policy instrument to attract foreign investment.[70]

Take China as an example: separate and preferential tax treatment granted to FIEs did indeed significantly encourage the inflows of FDI in the early days of China's transition to a market economy. In the mid-1990s, China became the largest recipient of FDI in the developing world. By the end of 2004, China had attracted a total of USD 562.1 billion in FDI since its opening in the early 1980s.[71] In 2005, inflows reached a record high of USD 72 billion, corresponding to a 20% rise from 2004.[72]

Foreign capital has contributed to China's economic development by transferring technology, marketing skills, and management know-how. It is more striking that foreign capital, coupled with abundant and low-cost labor sources, has made China one of the biggest manufacturing countries. China's manufacturing not only meets the demand of the enormous local Chinese market but has also led China to become one of the biggest exporting countries for goods. Statistics show that China's trade is now 30 times what it was in 1980, and more than half of its trade is attributable to FIEs.[73] The trade surplus amounted to USD 285.8 billion in 2008.[74] China's trade surplus with the world increased more than 10% in the twelve-month period between January 2007[75] and January 2008. Commentators believe that FDI is a key contributor to China's record-high 9.5% average annual GDP growth rate during 1980–2004.[76]

The impact of FDI is not limited to China's economic growth. In 2003, FIEs in the industrial sector employed 126 million workers, accounting for 21.9% of the total employment in the industrial sector. Moreover, the manufacturing FIEs absorbed

70 See WTO Working Group on the Relationship between Trade and Investment, *Communication from ASEAN*, WT/WGTI/W/41 (July 3, 1998).

71 See *Foreign Capital Utilization in China: Prospects and Future Strategy*, World Bank Report (World Bank Beijing Office, 2007), p. 13.

72 See UNCTAD, *Investment Brief No. 2*(2007).

73 In 2004, these enterprises accounted for 57% of exports, 58% of imports, and 88% of processing trade. See World Bank Report (2007), supra note 72, p. 13.

74 See WTO, *International Trade Statistics 2009*, available at: http://www.wto.org/english/res_e/statis_e/its2009_e/its09_toc_e.htm.

75 See WTO, *International Trade Statistics 2008*, available at: http://www.wto.org/english/res_e/statis_e/its2008_e/its08_toc_e.htm.

76 See World Bank Report (2007), supra note 72, p. 44. A study shows that a 1% increase in FDI leads to a 0.049% rise in GDP in the short run, and a rise of 7.5% in the long run. See World Bank Report (2007), supra note 71, p. 34.

workers who were laid off from nonperforming State-Owned Enterprises and a large number of agriculture workers. This cushioned the impact of China's transition into a market economy.[77]

In addition to China, other Asian countries such as India and Vietnam have adopted similar differential corporate income tax codes for domestic and foreign firms. Without sufficient legal justification, USDOC's determination on the specificity of the Two Free, Three Half program will have a negative impact on developing countries' foreign investment policy making. It simply forces developing countries to abandon the differential tax codes for domestic and foreign enterprises and gives no consideration to any differences between developed countries and developing countries in the area of foreign investment.

USDOC's determination on China's Two Free, Three Half program exemplifies the growing concerns regarding the impact of economic globalization on state policy autonomy. How and to what extent should developing countries be allowed to utilize foreign capital for their benefit when making related policies? How should the trade rules be interpreted while recognizing the diversity of domestic institutions and policies among trading countries?

The specificity test raises the question of the extent the subsidy rules can override the ability of WTO Members to regulate their national economies on their own. It is thus a delicate task that requires reaching an acceptable balance between trade-distorting effects and the sound policy claims of member states. Any careless manipulation of the concept will inappropriately restrict the state autonomy of developing countries with respect to their investment-inducing policy making, in turn undermining the realization of the objectives of a multilateral trading system.

REFERENCES

General Agreement on Tariffs and Trade, *Basic Instrument and Selected Document*, 9S/84–85, 21/79, 38S/73 (1980).

______, *Checklist for Issues for Negotiations*, MTN.GNG/NG10/W/9/Rev.1 (October 22, 1987).

______, Non-Official Report, *The "Leutwiler Report," Trade Polices for a Better Future, the GATT and the Uruguay Round* (1987).

Horlick, Gary N., Judith H. Bello, and Michael K. Levine, *The Countervailability of Subsidies: Specificity*, 372 PLI/COMM (December 2, 1985).

Jackson, John H., *The World Trading System* (Cambridge, MA: MIT Press, 1995).

Jackson, John H., William J. Davey, and Alan O. Sykes Jr., *Legal Problems of International Economic Relations* (St. Paul, MN: Thomson West, 2002).

Madrid, Gustavo E., Luengo Hernandez de, *Regulation of Subsidies and State Aids in WTO and EC Law: Conflicts in International Trade Law* (Alphen aan den Rijn, the Netherlands: Kluwer Law International, 2007).

77 Ibid., p. 34.

Mattoo, Aaditya, "Dealing with Monopolies and State Enterprises: WTO Rules for Goods and Services," in T. Cottier and P. C. Mavroidis (eds.), *State Trading in the Twenty-First Century* (Ann Arbor: The University of Michigan Press, 1998).

Mavroidis, Petros C., Petrick A. Messerlin, and Jasper M. Wauters, *The Law and Economics of Contingent Protection in the WTO* (Cheltenham, England: Edward Elgar Publishing, 2008).

Southwick, James D., "The Lingering Problem with the Specificity Test in United States Countervailing Duty Law" (1988) 72 *Minnesota Law Review*.

Stewart, Terence P. (ed.), *The GATT Uruguay Round: A Negotiating History (1989–1992)* (The Hague: Kluwer Law International, 1993).

Trebilcock, M. J., and R. Howse, *The Regulation of International Trade* (New York: Routledge, 2005).

United Nations, United Nations Report of the High Commissioner for Human Rights, *Human Rights, Trade and Investment, UN*, E/CN.4/Sub.2/2003/9.

United Nations Conference on Trade and Development, *FDI from Developing and Transition Economies: Implications for Development*, World Investment Report (2006).

United Nations Development Programme, *Making Global Trade Work for the Poor* (2002).

U.S. Department of Commerce, *Preliminary Affirmative Countervailing Duty Determination: Coated Free Sheet Paper from the People's Republic of China*, 72 FR 17484 (April 9, 2007).

______, *Final Determination in the Countervailing Duty Investigation of Coated Free Sheet from the People's Republic of China*, 72 FR 60645 (October 17, 2007).

U.S. Government Accountability Office, *US–China Trade: Commerce Faces Practical and Legal Challenges in Applying Countervailing Duties*, GAO-050474, Report to Congressional Committees (Washington, DC, June 2005).

Wilcox, William K., "GATT-Based Protection and the Definition of a Subsidy" (1998) 16 *Boston University International Law Journal*.

World Bank, *Foreign Capital Utilization in China: Prospects and Future Strategy*, World Bank Report (World Bank Beijing Office, 2007).

World Trade Organization Appellate Body Report, *United States – Standards for Reformulated and Conventional Gasoline*, WT/DS2/AB/R, adopted April 29, 1996.

______, *United States – Final Countervailing Duty Determination with Respect to Certain Softwood Lumber from Canada*, WT/DS257/AB/R (January 19, 2004).

______, *United States – Final Countervailing Duty Determination with Respect to Certain Softwood Lumber from Canada Recourse by Canada to Article 21.5 of the DSU*, WT/DS257/AB/RW (December 5, 2005).

World Trade Organization Panel Report, *United States – Final Countervailing Duty Determination with Respect to Certain Softwood Lumber from Canada*, WT/DS257/R (August 29, 2003).

______, *United States – Subsidies on Upland Cotton*, WT/DS267/R (September 8, 2004).

______, *United States – Final Countervailing Duty Determination with Respect to Certain Softwood Lumber from Canada Recourse by Canada to Article 21.5 (DS257)*, WT/DS257/RW (August 1, 2005).

World Trade Organization Working Group on the Relationship between Trade and Investment, *Communication from ASEAN*, WT/WGTI/W/41 (July 3, 1998).

17

Nonconclusions

Gary N. Horlick

A book on international trade law and development may strike some as brave, or even foolhardy, because there is no consensus on what "development" is, how to measure it, what causes it, or what law has to do with it. This book does not resolve those great questions but discusses in considerable detail issues that have arisen, and are likely to continue to arise, in the connection between international trade law, especially but not limited to the World Trade Organization (WTO),[1] and development.

Trade is not an end in itself but a means to improve human welfare (as is development). Since the end of World War II, the global economic system has produced a better than 50% improvement in life expectancy in developing countries and a better than 90% reduction in maternal and infant mortality; 80% of the world's population now has access to clean drinking water, and billions of people have been lifted out of poverty. The work is far from done – roughly 30% of the world's population is still poor, but for the first time, there is at least reason to believe that most of those can reach a better level of welfare than they have now.

The global economic system that provided these benefits is, of course, not a system at all. Governments have a lot to do with managing (and sometimes mismanaging) the process, both through formal international organizations such as the WTO, International Monetary Fund, World Bank, and regional organizations, but also through fluid informal mechanisms such as G-7/8/20/xx coordination at head of government and ministerial levels. The much-derided United Nations helped prevent the destructive wars that marked the first half of the twentieth century, as did careful

[1] The WTO follows and builds on the failed International Trade Organization (ITO) of the postwar arrangements and the successful-beyond-anyone's-dreams General Agreement on Tariffs and Trade (GATT). The ITO negotiators had devoted considerable time to development issues. Even the pruned-down GATT, with "only" twenty-three members (which included leading developing countries such as Brazil and India, as well as a majority of the WTO's existing 154 members, because it included, whether they wanted it or not, the colonies of the colonial powers such as Britain and France, who were original members) had some special provisions for developing countries and added more within a few years.

management (to date, at least) of the nuclear standoff between the United States and the Soviet Union/Russia. A united Western Europe provided the longest period of internal peace since at least 843 CE. Governments also learned how to live with the "invisible hand" of literally tens of millions of private enterprises that provided much of the economic growth and welfare improvements. Furthermore, universities and private nonprofit groups provided much of the research and dissemination to make possible the productivity improvements that took the world out of the Malthusian trap that had kept almost every person in the world living at bare subsistence levels until the nineteenth century. (For example, the growth of the world's food supply since World War II is a complex interaction of increasingly well-educated farmers, university research, and international consortia including governments, universities, and the Rockefeller and Ford Foundations.)

Trade policy, and international trade law rules, played a major role in this achievement.[2] This book discusses many of those aspects. Although clear conclusions are difficult, some of the following issues are worth considering.

1. The classical international trade rules – tariff bindings, unconditional most-favored-nation treatment, and national treatment – seem to have held up reasonably well for developing countries. South Korea is a good example. It was perhaps one of the poorest countries in the world in 1960. The postwar GATT system provided South Korea two sets of benefits:
   - South Korea, once it joined the GATT, had "bound" access to developed-country markets, which South Korean policy makers used as an important part of an export-led development policy.
   - Probably the main benefit of the GATT system for South Korea was the prosperity it helped create among developed countries, which helped create a market for South Korea. Interestingly, South Korea, as a medium-sized developing country, could build an industrial base by gaining relatively small shares of developed-country markets (despite much talk about South Korean automobile exports, South Korea's share of the U.S. automobile market (split among several producers) never reached 10%, even in the unusual

[2] Trade alone does not lead to development. However, trade from early times provided necessities (such as salt), luxuries (Mediterranean archeological sites include amber from the Baltic), and high-tech weapons (such as the obsidian from the upper west of the United States found in Mexican sites). Most important for purposes of this book, trade permits specialization of labor. The first "trade" was probably families, or perhaps clans, leaving goods on river banks for another clan or family to trade. If the other party did not reciprocate, the "game" was over. A key point this early is that trade – and indeed all "foreign relations" – was inherently ambiguous: trade provided the necessities/luxuries/weapons/better choice/more wealth than otherwise possible, but any contact with "The Other" was inherently dangerous. Family A could not take its goods across the territory of Family B to trade with Family C without the likelihood of being killed, but Family A could trade with Family B, which could trade with Family C. The Silk Road was a very long version of that transfer, with goods moving farther than people, although people were surprisingly safe – sovereigns along the route had worked out that it was more prosperous to allow trade than simply to seize the goods for themselves and kill the traders.

circumstances of 2009). As many have noted, North Korea eschewed this path – and remains poor.

The full benefits of international trade rules are only available to WTO Members. Thus, the process of accession to the WTO becomes relevant. As explained in this book by Andrew D. Mitchell and Joanne Wallis through the cases of Tonga, Vanuatu, and Samoa, the process of accession to the WTO is lengthy and demanding, and the way the principle of special and differential treatment operates in practice in this context, transforms that principle into pure rhetoric. As explained by Mitchell and Wallis, the process of accession to the WTO needs to be reformed to better meet the needs of developing countries, and these reforms should be combined by reforms to special and differential treatment. This is demonstrated by the unprecedented choice of Tonga and Vanuatu to suspend their WTO accession processes.

2. Special and differential treatment (SDT) is more ambiguous in its outcomes. Certainly developing countries (now Organization for Economic Cooperation and Development members!) such as South Korea, Japan, Mexico, and others were able to use SDT status to close "strategic" product markets, for better or worse. However, SDT turned out to be a double-edged sword. Innovative research by Edward Gresser about U.S. tariff policy shows convincingly (at least to me) that SDT in practice hampered developing-country exports to the United States. The "headline" from Gresser's research is that Bangladesh pays more tariffs on its exports to the United States than does France, even though France exports roughly ten times as much as Bangladesh (and the same is true for many other country pairs). As Gresser points out, the underlying phenomenon is that SDT meant the developed-country negotiators in GATT rounds did not spend much effort negotiating on items of interest to developing countries, because the developed-country negotiators knew that they would not achieve reciprocal tariff cuts from the developing countries. So tariff negotiations focused on trade between developed countries, and tariffs on developing-country exports remained high. Thus, U.S. tariffs on luxury silk clothing from France range from 0 to low single digits, whereas tariffs on less expensive cotton clothing from Bangladesh range from 17 to 30 percent. Similarly, U.S. tariffs on stainless steel knives and forks run around 15 percent, whereas the tariffs on sterling silver knives and forks from developed countries are zero or close to it.
3. Tariff preferences for developing countries: the Generalized System of Preferences (GSP) was originated by Raul Prebisch, a brilliant Argentinean who was secretary-general of United Nations Conference on Trade and Development in the early 1960s. Prebisch had been one of the original developers of formal import substitution schemes, as a path for developing countries out of monocultural dependence on commodity exports, in a period when commodity

> prices appeared continually to trend downward, while final consumption products' prices continually rose. By the early 1960s, it was clear to Prebisch that for even medium-sized, advanced developing countries such as Argentina, the size of the internal market was too small to permit the economies of scale necessary for cost-effective manufacturing. GSP was intended to provide the additional markets so that developing-country industries could reach the necessary economies of scale. At that point, a "virtuous circle" would permit the developing country in question to be "graduated" from the preferences for that specific product (and eventually from the entire system), thus permitting a different developing country to benefit from the tariff preference for that product.

The data discussed in this book seem to show what has been increasingly argued: that GSP initially helped several industries in several more advanced developing countries but that the countries most in need of help received the least. This view is elaborated here by Caf Dowlah through an analysis of the United States' GSP through the least developing countries' eyes, concluding that the scheme is not beneficial to the latter and that therefore some reforms should be made to address the development needs of those poor countries. GSP was also marred by the (perhaps inevitable) politicization of developed-country implementation. Numerous products were excluded, often those most suitable for developing countries (such as apparel). In the United States, Democrats led the charge to exclude as much as possible, including products (watches!) where the U.S. industry more or less disappeared within ten years.

The United States and European Union both continually added more and more policy/political conditions (intellectual property rights, expropriation, narcotics controls) with the WTO Appellate Body providing arguable cover for the proposition that the developed country is the one best suited to determine the development needs of the developing country (perhaps the Appellate Body will find a way to clarify that in some future case). Disputes over product eligibility are often decided following highly political campaigns in which the express needs of developed-country multinationals are often important – another (if unconsciously) colonial overtone. Even the procedures for renewing preferences (in the United States, often done retroactively after the tariff preferences have lapsed) can prevent reliance on the tariff preferences to build significant manufacturing facilities.

All of these problems have surfaced in greater or lesser form in other preference schemes, such as the European Union's Everything-but-Arms and Economic Partnership Agreement (EPA) programs; the U.S. Caribbean Basin Initiative (CBI), Andean Trade Promotion and Drug Eradication Act (ATPDEA), and Africa Growth and Opportunity Act (AGOA); and similar programs. The programs remain important commercially for some industries and for the countries where those industries are located, but overall, they have hardly delivered their initial promise (if ever that was possible – by the early 1970s, Prebisch was sufficiently disillusioned with GSP to suggest that the only salvation for Latin America was to negotiate the elimination of new military purchases, at a time when many of the regimes in power were military).

One positive result of the preference systems has been to provide an area in which the interests of multinational corporations and developing countries align closely.

One legal aspect of interest is the role of the Enabling Clause as a tool for development. The Enabling Clause was signed in 1979 and further adopted by WTO Members in 1995 without any modification that would reflect the principles of the new trade era. The result is certain inconsistencies between the text of the Enabling Clause and the development principles embraced by the WTO. Perhaps the text of the Enabling Clause should be amended to reflect these principles and therefore allow developed countries to also use the clause to negotiate tariff reduction or elimination with developing and least developed countries, in the context of regional trade agreements (RTAs). As of today, this opportunity is only given to developing and least developed countries among each other.

1. RTAs have had similarly mixed results for developing countries. On their face, many, if not most, of the North–South RTA negotiations are embarrassingly one-sided, with high-tariff, developing countries eliminating tariffs and low-tariff developed countries keeping their panoply of nontariff barriers, particularly in the trade remedy field. (And the negotiating tactics famously may be even more high-handed than the results.) As developed countries enter into more and more North–South RTAs, the benefits for any one developing country are inevitably diluted. Yong-Shik Lee elaborates on this issue in this book through an analysis of the economic and geopolitical impact of the U.S.-Korea free trade agreement – in case of approval by the U.S. Congress. Moshe Hirsch also analyzes the flaws in current North–South RTAs and proposes some legal mechanisms to enhance the benefits accruing to developing countries under these RTAs. South–South RTAs have less history. The most important one to date, Southern Cone Common Market (MERCOSUR), has managed to hold together despite many challenges and indeed offers the occasional lesson to the WTO (i.e., dispute settlement proceedings are limited to three months from the date of the establishment of the panel). The real question is the one originally posed by Prebisch – does a South–South arrangement such as MERCOSUR spur development more than any North–South arrangement would have?

   Regionalism and multilateralism both seek trade liberalization, although they use different methodologies. As discussed by Mitsuo Matsushita and Yong-Shik Lee in this book, the former option has become a significant alternative to the latter because of a stalled multilateral system. However, the proliferation of RTAs also poses a challenge to the multilateral system because RTAs do not generally adopt some important multilateral protections provided under the WTO, such as special and differential treatment. However, as Matsushita and Lee propose, regional rules could be coordinated through, for example, the WTO Trade Policy Review Body, in order not only to seek convergence and harmonization of trade rules but to also promote the interest of developing countries.

2. The WTO, in short, looks better and better for developing countries. In addition to formal equality, the rules offer a lot of "policy space" for developing countries (although at the cost of nearly as much space for developed countries – in a context in which the largest markets often set the rules, although it should be recalled that the second largest market, China, is a developing country, with other developing countries also growing in size). Large developing countries visibly throw their weight around just as much as large developed countries – and (small and) medium-sized developing countries such as South Africa, South Korea, Chile, Malaysia, New Zealand, and others probably have an impact in the WTO (often by sending skilled officials to Geneva) disproportionately greater than their population would suggest. As this book points out, many of these developing countries played leading roles in the GATT as well. As Faizel Ismail explains in this book, developing countries have been active in the GATT era, as well as in the Uruguay and the Doha Rounds. According to Ismail, the role of developing countries has significantly increased along the road, up to the point at which, in the current Doha Round, these countries are shaping not only the content and the outcome of the negotiations but also the architecture and trajectory of the multilateral trading system.
3. A much-debated topic is the role of developing countries in the WTO dispute settlement system. Developing countries have had a strong representation on the Appellate Body over the years, and because the European Union and the United States insist in being parties in almost every case, developing countries provide a frequent majority of panel members. Developing-country students are strongly represented in "feeder programs" that lead to employment within the WTO system, such as the University of Berne's World Trade Institute and law school programs such as Georgetown, Columbia, and Cambridge.

As more and more countries become involved in dispute settlement, the process becomes more routine, but also poses real challenges internally. The decisions in the cases brought against China on auto parts, intellectual property rights, and trading rights all pose interesting problems internally for the Chinese trade regime, whereas the decision of the Appellate Body in the *U.S.-Softwood Lumber* countervailing duty case on "specificity" significantly narrows the policy space for governments seeking to use the system as a development instrument. Large countries, such as the United States and the European Union, have a structural advantage in WTO dispute resolution by being able to keep a large number of specialized litigators on staff (thus turning the marginal cost of hiring counsel into a fixed cost). However, Brazil has one of the best track records in WTO dispute resolution and a very strong institutional structure combining a medium-sized, highly skilled internal staff with outside counsel retained as necessary and typically paid for by the affected Brazilian industry. Some of the decisions coming out of the dispute settlement system are strikingly neocolonial programs (such as the EU GSP case mentioned earlier or the U.S. *Shrimp-Turtle* case). The *Shrimp-Turtle* decision may reflect a weighting of environmental concerns large enough to permit unilateral action by a developed country against developing countries, but it may also reflect an underweighting of human rights concerns. (Should the Appellate Body have balanced the environmental concerns of a developed country's citizens with the human rights of the impoverished fishers in the developing-country parties?)

As described by Katherine Fennell and me in this book, there is an imbalance in the access to the WTO dispute settlement system that should be addressed to increase the possibility of developing countries pursuing development under the existing multilateral trade scheme. As explained by Tomer Broude in his chapter, the international community could also start conceiving certain international economic disputes that involve the interpretation and application of development issues, as part of a new group of disputes – international development disputes – to reflect the idea that every dispute settlement mechanism in the international economic law arena should bear the responsibility of pursuing the development of developing and least developed countries.

Once access is obtained to the WTO dispute settlement system, developing countries could lose cases in the WTO forum, but those losses are also lessons for the future.

1. The role of human rights and human rights agreements has been broached within the international trading system. Much of the impetus has come from attempts by developed countries to impose their labor standards on competitive industries in developing countries (even where the developed countries in question do not formally accept those standards as binding). This issue has been explored by Anthony E. Cassimatis in this book.
2. Perhaps it is inevitable that the GATT and the WTO, as agreements between sovereign entities, do not really get at the heart of economic development in developing countries (and even some areas and sectors of developed countries). Greater difficulties are often encountered in those countries and sectors, especially by workers and small businesses, than would be the case for big enterprises in developed countries. The term in Brazil is *cousto Brasileiro,* and there have even been attempts to measure it. International trade rules generally do not reflect an understanding of how difficult it is to export from

developing countries and how many challenges must be overcome. Just as the "microfinance" movement has attempted to deal with this issue in the credit area, perhaps international trade rules need a "microtrade" framework reflecting the size of the obstacles posed by paperwork, border security measures, and the documentation needed to qualify for preferences for developing countries where documentation is difficult. Even the concept of access to an international dispute resolution system could be rethought. Indeed, as discussed by Yong-Shik Lee in this book, the "microtrade" option constitutes a potential means to reduce or eliminate poverty in LDCs, if implemented correctly.

3. Intellectual property is another area of trade that could be used to pursue the development of the developing world. One way of doing it, as discussed by Bryan Mercurio in his chapter, is by developing countries maximizing the flexibilities found in the Agreement on Trade-Related Aspects of Intellectual Property Rights. This could attract scrutiny from interested actors but, according to Mercurio, it is the only option for countries seeking to prevent the protection of intellectual property rights from becoming a completely one-sided proposition that benefits developed countries at great cost to the developing world.

The purpose of this book has been to explore some of the existing imbalances between developed and developing countries in the international trade arena – not with the purpose of undermining international trade as such but to improve it as a tool for development. As explained by Yong-Shik Lee, Young-Ok Kim, and Hye Seong Mun in their chapter, international trade is a key element for materializing development in developing countries such as North Korea. In his chapter, Colin B. Picker calls for taking into account the special development needs of "economically heterogeneous states" in the international trade arena, so that development is obtained at every state level as opposed to only some of them. Furthermore, through the application of the specificity test to China's foreign investment policies, Xiaojie Lu considers in this book that the use of international trade law rules should also reflect an acceptable balance between legitimate development objectives adopted domestically and the possible trade-distorting effects at the international level of specific governmental measures.

Epilogue

The concept of this book was born when a group of scholars from developing countries decided to publish a book on international trade law and economic development, subsequently titled *Economic Development through World Trade: A Developing Country Perspective* (The Hague: Kluwer Law International, 2008). As that book offered, probably for the first time, thirteen chapters of developing-country accounts and perspectives on international trade law, I thought that another book, written on international trade law from a developed-country perspective, would provide a necessary complement to the exercise. A couple of chapters overlap between the two books, but fourteen of the seventeen authors of this book are indeed academics and professionals from developed countries and offer developed-country perspectives.

It would no doubt be an inaccurate overstatement if one were to argue the existence of a uniform developing- or developed-country perspective. There are significant diversities and controversies among views of developing countries and developing-country scholars, as well as those between developed countries and developed-country scholars. Views from developed countries are not necessarily adversary to those from developing countries, and vice versa. Nonetheless, there is some unavoidable difference in interest between the countries that have already achieved economic development and those that have not, and the traditional North–South divide is still very much a reality and reflected in academic literature. We hope to see progression that bridges the gaps between developed and developing ones.

I note key contributions to this book made by prominent individuals and institutions. The Law and Development Institute (http://www.lawanddevelopment.net), an international academic network in law and development established in Sydney, Australia, has initiated and promoted it as its own project. Professor Won-Mog Choi, one of our editors, provided initial funding for a conference project leading to the book by donating a substantial amount from the Shimdang Academic Award he received in honor of Judge Sang-Hyun Song of the International Criminal Court.

I hope that both developed and developing countries, despite their inherent differences, will eventually reach some common understanding and consensus as to how international trade and its regulatory framework, such as WTO legal disciplines, can help economically developing countries. On the basis of this understanding and consensus, a better legal system of international trade, which will be beneficial for all, can become a reality.

Yong-Shik Lee, Chief Editor
Law and Development Perspective on International Trade Law
Yong-Shik Lee

Index